Practical Advocacy of Law

Professor (Dr.) SUNIL DESHTA

Dean Students Welfare
H.P. University Shimla
Ex-Director, UILS Shimla
Ex-Principal, SLS Dharamshala
Ex-Principal, GHG Inst. of Law Sidhwan, Ludhiana

and

Dr. Kiran Deshta

Author of : Uniform Civil Code; Privacy Law in India;
Fundamental Human Rights; Law & Manner of Child Labour

NEW ERA LAW PUBLICATION
FARIDABAD

Published by:
NEW ERA LAW PUBLICATION
Plot No. 33, 16/5, Karkhana Bagh,
Opp. D.P.S. School,
Mathura Road, Faridabad (Haryana)—121 002
Phone : (0129) 2295647, 2295768
Fax : 0129-4166099
e-mail : neweralawpublications@yahoo.co.in

ISBN : 978-93-80456-12-6

First Edition : 2006
Reprint : 2010
Second Edition : 2018

Price : ₹ 395 /-

Typeset at : **Neo Software Consultants,** Allahabad
Printed at : Compudata Services, New Delhi - 20

PRACTICAL ADVOCACY OF LAW INCLUDING

- Legal Profession and Ethics
- Contempt Law and Practice
- Accountancy for Lawyers
- Bench-Bar Relations
- Public Interest Lawyering
- Legal Aid and Para-Legal Services
- Moot Courts, Pre-Trial Preparations and Advocacy
- Social Responsibilities of Lawyers
- Law Office Management

Professor (Dr.) SUNIL DESHTA
Dr. Kiran Deshta

PREFACE TO THE SECOND EDITION

The second edition of the book is a humble attempt to weed out chaff from the grain of the most honourable profession which has done onerous services to the nation and to the litigant public from the day it has taken roots in the soil of India. The legal profession has no doubt produced titled gentry who not only made themselves the legal luminaries and attained great heights in the legal world but also had come out as the great champions of the cause of freedom and gave their lucrative practice when the nation demanded their services unstintedly. Lawyers are intermediaries between the public and the judiciary. Disputes are inevitable in any given society and the strength of any civilized society lies in the ability to resolve those disputes amicably and the assistance of lawyers has become increasingly necessary in every field of activity. Lawyers are expected to act as the pillars to safeguard justice, provide legal literacy and meet the highest standards of ethical responsibility. Respect for the Rule of Law and sensitivity to human rights should never be absent from the discharge of their professional duties.

After the previous edition of this book, several important decisions have been handed down by the Courts on ethical issues concerning the lawyer's right and duty. The authors have incorporated few additional chapters in this edition and these will certainly serve the needs of the students. Every work is said to be complete if it is done with sincerity, hardwork and dedication but it is also true that no target is accomplished without the help and support of all the associated persons. The authors are deeply indebted to Dr. Pankaj Musafir, Dr. Sujata Sirkeck, Mr. Abhishek Negi, Mr. Sandeep Nagta, Mrs. Sangeeta Verma and Dr. Bhupender Kumar for their help and encouragement in revising this work.

Professor (Dr.) SUNIL DESHTA
Dr. KIRAN DESHTA

PREFACE TO FIRST EDITION

Legal profession is one of the oldest profession and was practiced in one form or the other in the hoary past. There are two contradictory approaches with regard to legal profession in ancient India. The first approach denies existence of any such institution and is headed by P. Varadachariar and Professor Ludo Rocher. The other view supports the idea of the existence of legal profession in ancient India. K.P. Jayaswal is the main exponent of this approach. It also finds support from Julius Jolly and the Dean of Dharamsastra, Dr. P.V. Kane. H.H. Wilson, A.C. Ganguly and N.D. Basu who admit that there were people who functioned as lawyers during the Mughal period, though their functions and duties were not clearly defined as during the pre-Mughal and post-Mughal periods.

The modern legal profession has emerged from the constitution of courts and legislative enactments initiated by the British in India. In order to give effect to some recommendations of the Indian Bar Committee, 1923, the Indian Bar Council Act was enacted in 1926. The main purpose of the Act was to provide for the constitution and incorporation of Bar Council for certain courts, to conform powers and impose duties on such councils and also to consolidate and amend the law relating to legal practitioners of such courts. After independence, efforts were made to improve the efficiency of legal profession. In this process, in 1951, the All India Bar Committee was constituted under the Chairmanship of Justice S.R. Das. The committee considered at length questions of constitution and powers of the Bar Council and made detailed recommendations in 1953. These recommendations got strength by the endorsement and approval of its recommendation by the Law Commission of India which was constituted on 5th August, 1955. The Report of the Commission was submitted in 1958 and Bill with a view to give it effect was introduced in 1959 in the Parliament and this ushered in the promulgation of the Advocates Act of 1961. With the passage of this Act, it consolidated and amalgamated those various classes of legal practitioners into one class known as advocates and abolished other classes by repealing the Legal Practitioners Act, 1879; the Bombay Pleaders Act, 1920; the Indian Bar Council Act, 1926 and the Supreme Court Advocates' (Practice in High Courts) Act, 1951.

India has the second largest legal profession with more than 8,58,294 lawyers. The profession of law is a noble calling. It is one of the most brilliant, learned and attractive professions. The lawyers are looked upon as the protectors and defenders of life, liberty and property—of course at a price. They are expected to act in honest and upright manner because they have the privilege of discharging all those duties which those who are not the members of legal profession cannot do. It is said that a lawyer is an officer of the court and he is to assist in the administration of justice. But in actual practice, we find that he is a warrior who fights war for his client(s). Assuming that everything is fair in love and war, a litigant expects that his lawyer should give all assistance in winning his war. In this predicament, a lawyer is to keep a balance between the two. He is to repose confidence in the mind of his client that his interest, his welfare and his prosperity is foremost in his mind but he is also not to forget that he is a member of the noble profession and not a business man. He must not indulge in any activity which may lower the image of the profession. It is the primary duty of an advocate that he should uphold the Constitution and help in the maintenance of Rule of law. He should promote the advancement of justice and assist in the enforcement of fundamental rights of the people. Further, he has certain social obligations, e.g., to render "*pro bono*" service to the poor and unprivileged.

The legal profession in India is passing through a critical phase and the declining standards of the lawyers are the talk of the day. Every lawyer, at the entry into the profession itself, hopes to win a bundle. This sends out a perilous signal that the profession is not on the right path. The one who knows too little cares not for the one who knows much more. Judicial calmness is conspicuously absent. The lawyers are self-centred and are opposed to the changes which are likely to affect their personal interest and in that respect they exhibit trade unionists' spirit. A struggle to save the profession's soul is imperative. Touting has started to haemorrhage the profession. If the profession is to play its part in the service of the society, the lawyers must change and identify themselves more and more with current of modern thought of political, economic and social problems. In this age of ours, when science and technology have made real advances, complicated social and economic issues are crying for solutions, the lawyers will have to adapt themselves to new situations so as to ensure the greatest good to the largest number. In the social set up that is arising, the lawyers will have to come forward to use their skill or expert knowledge even at the sacrifice of their personal interest for the benefit of the community at large and thereby play a worthy part in the administration of justice.

To improve the standards of the profession, knowledge of various arts of advocacy is inevitable. Keeping this in mind, the Bar Council of India framed the training rules in 1995, to arrest the otherwise deteriorating condition of legal profession in India. The pre-enrolment rules did not find favour with the apex court on seminal grounds. The court in a sweeping judgment struck down the Bar Council of India Training Rules, 1995 as *ultra vires*. The Bar Council of India, the University Grants Commission, the Universities and the judiciary, etc. have made a concerted effort to revamp the syllabus of LL.B. throughout the country and the same has come into effect from 1998 onwards. The most appreciated aspect of this change in the syllabus has been in the form of introducing certain practical subjects like Professional Ethics, Public Interest Lawyering, Para-Legal Services, Moot Court, Pleading and Drafting. The study and practice of these subjects makes a law student well-equipped to fare better as an advocate when he enters the Bar. The present book has been divided into sixteen chapters.

We are deeply obliged to all those Indian and English authors whose study materials, such as, books, articles and legal reports, have been utilized by us.

To write this book, inspiration and encouragement have been received from many quarters especially the student community. We are greatly indebted and highly obliged to professor T. Bhattacharyya, Professor Veer Singh, Professor Chandra Pal Sheoran, Professor A.K. Koul, Professor Ranbir Singh, Professor A. Lakshminath, Professor J.L. Kaul, Professor Kashmir Singh, Professor R.K. Sabharwal, Professor Daljit Singh, Professor P.S. Jaswal, Professor S.M. Afzal Qadri, Professor D.C. Manooja, Professor Balraj Chauhan, Professor V.K. Aggarwal, Professor R.K. Gupta, Professor Versha Razdan, Professor Vinod K. Razdan, Professor Gurjeet Singh, Professor K.P.S. Mahalwar, Professor R.M. Dungawat, Professor Charanjit Singh, Professor B.R. Sharma, Professor Amar Singh, Professor Suresh Kapur and Professor P.L. Mehta, who have been constant source of inspiration for us during the course of this study.

We are indebted to Mr. S.S. Deshta (Advocate), H.P. High Court, Shimla, Mr. Sanjay Deshta (Asstt. Professor), Dr. Partap Singh, Commandant, C.R.P.F., New Delhi, Mr. Lalit Dadwal, Mr. Yashpal Singh, Mrs. Sanyogita Thakur (all Asstt. Professor) for their help and encouragement in accomplishing this work.

Over and above all, we owe, more than we could express our immense debt of gratitude to our parents and parents-in-laws for giving their love and understanding. We are also thankful to Deepika (daughter) and Arush (son) for their active co-operation while accomplishing this work.

Last but not the least, we are thankful to Mr. Dhiraj Narula for the quick and prompt execution of the printing.

We hope that the book will serve the needs of the students of law, Bar and Bench academicians and research scholars working on the subject of legal profession.

We solicit, with appreciation, constructive suggestions for the improvement of the book.

DESHTA NIWAS
SHIMLA
October 5; 2005 (2nd Navratras)

SUNIL DESHTA
KIRAN DESHTA

CONTENTS

1
LEGAL PROFESSION : ITS NATURE, EVOLUTION AND DEVELOPMENT

2
ADMISSION AND ENROLMENT OF ADVOCATES

3

BAR COUNCILS

6

PROFESSIONAL ETHICS AND ETIQUETTE OF LAWYERS

10
LEGALITY OF LAWYERS' STRIKE : AN EVALUATION IN THE RIGHT-DUTY DISCOURSE

11
SOCIAL RESPONSIBILITIES OF LAWYERS

12
CONTEMPT LAW AND PRACTICE

13
ACCOUNTANCY FOR LAWYERS

14
LAW OFFICE MANAGEMENT

17
PARA-LEGAL SERVICES AND PARA-LEGAL PERSONNEL

18
FUNCTIONING OF LOK ADALATS

19
MOOT COURTS, ADVOCACY AND PRE-TRIAL PREPARATIONS

21
IMPORTANT JUDGMENTS RELATING TO MISCONDUCT AND CONTEMPT OF COURT

APPENDICES

1

LEGAL PROFESSION : ITS NATURE, EVOLUTION AND DEVELOPMENT

I. Nature and Importance of Legal Profession

The term 'legal profession' if construed in its comprehensive form would include within itself all those categories of persons who use technical legal knowledge and skills in the course of performing their occupational roles and duties. These categories are many, viz., jurists, judges and magistrates, prosecutors, law officers and legal advisors attached to the government departments, legal technicians and legal practitioners. Technically, legal practitioners are not synonymous with lawyers. Lawyers are those who are licensed to practice law. They are also called attorneys, advocates and counsel. In England, there are two streams of lawyers : Barristers and Solicitors/Attorneys. In America, all are attorneys. India followed the English pattern. In India, all lawyers are not advocates, the majority do not appear in any court of law and are not even advocates.

Hence the term 'profession', is applied to a group of people pursuing a learned art as a common calling in the spirit of public service where economic conditions undoubtedly a necessary by-product. If legal profession is to remain an honourable profession, it will have to guard itself against its greatest enemy, viz., the spirit of commercialism. In trade, the rule is "business is business". The businessman's rule of conduct is to secure customers anyhow, and to get as much as he can in return for as little as possible, so long as, he does not lose the customer. Therefore, the object of all business is pursuit of wealth and all means are worthy so long as law is not transgressed. But this is not ideal for an advocate, who is a minister of justice and whose career is one of service and of great responsibilities not merely to the client who has paid him, but also to the court, the opposite party, the witnesses, the profession and the community. Previously to be an advocate was a mark of intellectual attainment and not an occupational description. To our utter dismay it has now been reduced to occupational description. It must not be forgotten at any time that the profession of law is a profession of experts.

Dean Roscoe Pound states that there is much more in a profession than a traditionally dignified calling. According to him, the term refers to a group of men pursuing a learned art as a common calling in the spirit of public service—no less a public service because it may incidentally be a means of livelihood. Gaining livelihood, Roscoe Pound says, is incidental. The three essentials involved in the legal profession, in the view of Roscoe Pound, are learning, organisation and spirit of public service.[1]

The technique of law is no less complicated than that of engineering or the medical profession, e.g., no one will hand over the running of a complicated machinery to a person unless he has thoroughly mastered the mechanism of it, and similarly, no one would entrust a brain surgery to a quack. But, techniques which enable one to expertise are not, however, learnt in a day. Firstly, there is a theory to be learnt. Without learning the theory of mechanics, a person can be a 'mistry', but not a mechanical engineer. Similarly, without knowing the theory of physiology and medicine, a person can be a quack, but not a doctor. Besides theory, practical training over long period is required. To be a good lawyer, one must of course be well acquainted with the theory of law. But a pure academical knowledge of law is not enough. Just as an engineer must go through a long course of apprenticeship, so a lawyer must go through a long course of training in actual handling of cases, before he can appear in courts and become a real practising lawyer. A lawyer must have a common sense and be analytic. He must be studious to find out the applicable law to the advantage of his client. He must strengthen his logic by delving into, if necessary, subjects other than law. It makes you work hard. It leads you to think. It helps you to analyse. It helps you to be persuasive. No other profession demands so much. A lawyer is primarily a seller. He has to perform and act as an excellent salesman for selling the case of his client to a person (i.e., Judge) who does not have any need to buy. And that is why legal profession is challenging and paying. Clients pay for your knowledge, skill and time.

Legal profession is and will remain the oldest enviable profession in the society. It is in the hands of the members of the legal profession to improve the quality of the service they render both to the litigant-public and to the courts, and to brighten their image in the society. Some members of the profession have been adopting a perceptibly casual approach to the practice of the profession as is evident from their absence when the matters are called out, the filing of incomplete and inaccurate pleadings—many times even illegible and without personal check and verification, the non-payment of court fees and process fees, the failure to remove office objections, the failure to take steps to serve the parties and so on. They do not realise the seriousness of these acts and omissions. They not only amount to the contempt of court but do positive disservice to the litigants and create embarrassing situation in the court leading to avoidable unpleasantness and delay in the disposal of matters. This augurs ill for the health of our judicial system.

The legal profession is a solemn and serious occupation. It is a noble

1. Quoted by Justice Padmanaban in his speech on Legal Profession on 9.12.1978 at the Kerala State Lawyers Conference held at Trivandrum. The speech is published in Supreme Court Weekly reporter in 1979, Vol. 1, pp. 1-10. For more details see Roscoe Pound, The Lawyer from Antiquity to Modern Times (1953), pp. 4-10.

calling and all those who belong to it are its honourable members. It is different from other professions in that what the lawyers do, affects not only an individual but also the administration of justice which is the foundation of any civilized society. It is not a vocation for private gain but is an institution created by the State for public good. Lawyer's profession has been regarded as an honourable or noble profession by the world for several centuries. It is a learned profession par excellence. No other profession touches human life at so many points than law. It has always been held in high esteem and its members have played an enviable role in public life. Canons of professional ethics are the most prestigious heritage of the Bar. The greatness and honour of the legal profession is due to the canons of conduct governing the relations of lawyers *inter se* and with others in their professional capacities.[1] The highest compliments paid to the legal profession is that "lawyers run our civilization for us." Summarizing as well as applauding the role of lawyers in our freedom movement, Kailash Nath Katju said, "The profession dominated the public life of our country and played prominent role in the national struggle for freedom. There was no movement in any sphere of public activity-educational, cultural, or humanitarian in which the lawyers were not in the forefront." The Canadian Code of Legal Ethics says that legal profession is branch of administration of justice and not a mere money-making occupation. Similarly, Canon 12 of the American Bar Association lays down that while fixing fees it should never be forgotten that the profession is a branch of administration of justice and not a money-making trade. Here, a question arises that what is the distinction between a profession and a business.[2] The essence of a profession lies in three things, viz. :

(i) Organization of its members for the performance of their function;

(ii) Maintenance of certain standards, intellectual and ethical, for the dignity of the profession; and

(iii) Subordination of pecuniary gains to efficient service.

Organization is the first thing. The profession of the lawyer is a profession, and not a business. Professions are often distinguished from occupations and businesses by the commitments they carry to certain basic values which every society upholds in the organization and delivery of public services. It is in this context that professions particularly earlier ones, were called "learned and noble". Sometimes professionals are also characterized as "conscience keepers" of the society.[3] The profession of law, as developed in England, was the profession of well-to-do persons who took the profession more as an act of public service than a means of earning livelihood. The persons who became Barristers were generally the sons of

1. G. Geethisha, Disciplining the Lawyers : Law and Professional Ethics, CULR, 2003, p. 153.
2. C.L. Anand, Professional Ethics of the Bar, (1987), pp. 15-16.
3. N.R. Madava Menon, Professional Ethics Education : The Law School Experience, *Lex ETJURIS*, January; 1989, p. 8.

well-to-do parents who did not have to worry about earning their livelihood and who traditionally looked down on all forms of trade and competitive spirit characteristics of such trade. The primary purpose was public; gaining livelihood was incidental. Therefore, the profession of law in India, being influenced by its counterparts in England, has naturally kept the same traditions and ideals before it. Hence, organization is not the distinguishing feature of a profession. The second normal characteristic of profession is the maintenance of certain standards, intellectual and ethical, on the part of the members, both for the dignity of the vocation and for better quality of service of the public. It assumes certain responsibilities for the competence of its members, and deliberately prohibits certain kinds of conduct on the ground that, though they may be profitable to the individual, they are calculated to bring into disrepute the organisation to which he belongs. The last characteristic which is the distinguishing feature of a profession is the subordination of pecuniary gains to efficient service. In business the only criterion of success is the financial return which it offers to its shareholders.

The essence of a profession is that though men enter it for the sake of livelihood, the measure of their success is the service which they perform to promote health, safety, and good of the society and not the gains which they amass. While in business any kind of conduct is allowable which increases the income, in a profession there are certain kinds of conduct which cannot be practised, however large the fee offered for them, because they are unprofessional. The practice of law is not a business but a profession is an important principle which forms the basis of some cardinal rules of legal ethics. For instance, not being business, an advocate must not solicit work or advertise himself. For that very reason accepting work from touts is to be totally shunned. Also he must not give or receive commission in connection with employment. The law being a profession and the lawyer being an officer of the Court, though the lawyer is an agent or representative of his client, he cannot afford to be a tool in the hands of the client. No member of the legal profession should accept such work which would make him disloyal to the court or place him in a compromising position. Hence, legal profession is associated with societal values such as "justice", "fair dealing", "integrity" and "probity". The lawyer is taken as a trusted advisor with whom the client can have a personal relationship on the basis of the former's professional competence, personal integrity and assured loyalty. The profession is today respected to the extent that it maintains high standards of legal skill and a reputation for integrity.

In legal profession, the two wings of administration of justice, namely, the Bench and the Bar have to work according to certain norms, which are collectively called legal ethics. Legal ethics mean usages and customs among members of legal profession, involving their moral and professional duties towards one another, towards clients and towards the courts; that branch of moral science which treats of duties which a member of the legal profession owes to the public, to the court, to his professional brethren, and to his client.

The legal profession is deemed to be a Royal profession but lawyers since time immemorial, have been subject-matter of criticism. One such criticism is that once a social reformist was asked to comment on a situation, the situation was, one hundred lawyers buried up to their neck in the sand. The social reformist innocently questioned "why didn't you get enough sand?"[1] Dean Swift, the famous English satirist described the bar as "a society fed up from their youth in the art of proving by words multiplied for the purpose that white is black and black is white, according to as they are paid."[2] Lord Macmillan in his address on 'The Ethics of Advocacy' has quoted a Latin couplet which is as follows :[3]

An advocate but not a thief,
A thinker well-nigh beyond belief.

Sir Walter Scott said that the clergy live by our sins, the medical faculty by our diseases and the law gentry by our misfortunes. It is also said that the banker handled other people's money, parson and priest other people's spiritual aspirations and a lawyer other people's troubles.[4] Shakespeare spoke through Dick the Butcher in Henry VI that : "The first thing we do let's kill all the lawyers."[5]

However, criticism of such kind is based on ignorance and misunderstanding of the true functions of law and the role that the lawyers play in the administration of law. On the other hand, great tributes have equally been paid to lawyers. D'Aquesseau, the great French Chancellor called the order of advocates "as old as the Magistracy—as noble as virtue".[6] The great Cardozo described the advocate in one of his opinions as a Minister of Justice.[7] Lord Langdale refers to those truly honourable and important services which counsel constantly perform as Minister of Justice in aid of the Judge before whom they practice.[8] In his lecture on "The Profession of Law", Justice Holmes said, "of course, the law is not the place for the artist or the poet. The law is the calling of thinkers." He added, "if your subject is law, the roads are plain to anthropology, the science of man, to political economy, the theory of legislation, ethics and thus by several paths to your final view of life." The lawyer as a 'social thinker' has to play a special role for the solidarity, unity, integrity, welfare and good of the society. As a 'social doctor', he has to cure the social ills of a democratic republic like India, where the majority of people sleep in the slum of illiteracy, superstition and poverty.[9] Thus, notwithstanding the criticism levelled against the legal profession, the profession has played

1. Hari Om Gupta and Inder Preet S. Josh, The Legal Profession : A Critique, Indian Journal of Contemporary Law, 1998, Vol. II, p. 101.
2. *Ibid*; at p. 102; see also supra note 1 at pp. 2-3.
3. Supra note 5 at pp. 101-102.
4. *Ibid*, at p. 102.
5. S. Prithvi Raj, Lawyers' Role in Upholding Democracy, The Cuttuck Law Times, 1987, Vol. 63, p. 21.
6. Supra note 1 at p. 3.
7. *Ibid*.
8. *Id*.
9. Speeches (1913), pp. 22-25.

and has to continue to play a great role in the administration of justice. The lawyers have proved themselves to be vital links in the chain of administration of justice between the litigants and the judge.

The profession of law is not a mere profession to keep the pot boiling but it is a noble great calling.[1] Though it is generally believed that lawyers are people who thrive in feuds, it cannot be said that the legal profession is anti-social. Legal profession is closely dovetailed with the ever constant changing society and the profession of lawyer can be elevated into a sublime vocation if he becomes the real saviour to ameliorate the suffering of the people. Times have changed at an increasing pace in the last few years. The globalisation of everything started to come in effect and it affected almost all walks of life directly or indirectly even though not slowly but steadily. No one can escape from its effect. It affected also our National Legal System. The professional in legal fields cannot sit tightly closing the door and windows of their Bar and Court rooms. Hence, the need of the hour is that the lawyers and the legal institutions have to create suitable roles to retain relevance in society. It has to be sensitive to the emerging social and economic trends which regulate affairs of the society. He should be a watchdog of the rights of every citizen. At the same time, it is his duty to impress on the citizen the necessity to adhere to the duties which go with the rights. Lord Eldon emphasized the need of hardwork for a lawyer. He states that "a lawyer must live like a hermit and work like a horse".[2] Law is known to be a jealous mistress. More attached to one is to such a mistress, better results are obtained in the cases argued before the courts. Lord Brougham has also observed that "a lawyer must know everything about something and something about everything".[3] Hence, the first equipment for a lawyer, is legal learning. He is required to have accurate learning, wide knowledge and the courage borne out of it. W.R. Riddle, an eminent American lawyer has said that the courage of an advocate, is not the courage of a prize fighter nor of the bully, but is the courage that will tackle all the problems or questions presented to investigate it, to find out the whys and wherefores, the ins and outs, the pleasing feature as well as those that are undisgraceful and then stand by your guns. In no profession it is more certain that "knowledge is power" and "cowardice is the result of ignorance".[4] Therefore, the advocate has a threefold obligation, viz., the obligation to his clients to be faithful to them; the obligation to the profession not to bring down its fair name or injure its credit by any act of his and an obligation to the court as a dependable arm of the machinery through which justice is administered. The core of the function of the profession is in its co-operating with the judiciary in the administration of justice according to law, and, in discharge of this function it gives its expert service to the public in general and to the

1. C. Rama Swamy Sarma, Lawyers' Role in Present Society, Andhra Law Times, 1987, Vol. II, p. 14.
2. Quoted by Sunil Deshta and Kiran Deshta, Dynamics of Legal Profession : Some Observations, CMLJ, Jan-March; 2002, Vol. 38, p. 45.
3. *Ibid.*
4. *Id.*

litigants in particular.[1]

II. Evolution and Development of Legal Profession

1. Prelude

"The profession of the Advocates is a permanent institution in the world's justice, coming down through the ages, and garnering traditions and wisdom from generation to generation for the edification of present and future ones. Clients and counsellor, advocate, jury and judge—their ways, their needs and their notions were known and studied in Athens, Rome, England and America. The world's business and its laws may change, but human nature's motives and foibles have formed a constant element. The psychology of a lawsuit is still the great problem for the lawyer and Quintilian, Scarlett and Choate come together on common ground."[2] The institution of lawyers is as old as the civilisation though it existed in different forms, in different times than we have in today's developed legal systems. It is the ancient Hindu texts and treatises, the authors find mention of representative suits but in the absence of adequate historical evidence, it cannot be said with certainty as to whether or not the representatives then did correspond to or were analogous to the advocates of the established legal system of today.[3] The authors do find clear historical evidence of establishment of legal profession in its institutionalised form in the Greek and Roman civilisations. In India, during Mughal times *vakils* were appointed to represent the government in courts of justice, along with *kazi*, and also act as legal advisor to the poor.[4] The modern legal profession as it exists today in India has emerged from the constitution of courts and legislative enactments initiated by the British rulers. It is not the outcome of the orderly growth of legal profession that existed prior to the coming of Britishers to this country. The legal system injected by the Britishers had no connection, whatsoever with the existing legal system earlier on the ground. So the legal profession today has the source of its origin in the legal system introduced by them. In other words, the common law of England found its way into the legal system of India.

There have been some traces of legal acumen in ancient Greece. There is reference of a great sophist Protagoras (c. 481-411 B.C.), who gave lesson to his public in art of argument on heavy charges of fees. In Rome, advocacy developed through persons who assisted another's case by giving advice. It took the form of patron-client relationship. With the complication of transaction there arose two new classes of persons who were conversant with law. They were known as jurists and agents. Juristsconsults used to give advice outside the court and agent were permitted to appear for parties in court. The service of juristconsult was gratuitous and service of agent

1. M. Natesan, The Legal Profession-Advertisement and Convassing, JBCI, February, 1973, p. 9.
2. Reed's Conduct of Law Suits (1st edn.).
3. Ludo Rocher, "Lawyers in Classical Hindu Law", Indian Bar Review, 1986, Vol. 13, pp. 353-370.
4. Philip B. Calkins, "A Note on Lawyers in Muslim India", Indian Bar Review, 1986 Vol. 13, pp. 373-376.

was for fees. Advocates developed forensic oratory after the second century B.C. In England, for centuries legal knowledge was a monopoly of the priest class who alone had the privilege of appearing before the court for the clients. It appears from the early writings that in the reign of Henry II certain persons of clerical training were appointed attorneys but their functions were not exactly defined. Edward I created order of sergeant who could appear in court for litigants.[1]

The pontifical control of legal profession continued till the twelfth century when the profession started acquiring secular characteristics. Particularly in France and England, the growth of a secular legal profession meant not only the replacement of the clergy by lawyers in the service of the State but also the successive weakening of monarchical power of the Church. The lawyers played the most crucial role in the vast process which led to the decline of Roman Catholic Church as a worldwide State. Also, it is from this period onwards that the impact of the legal profession can be clearly discerned on a variety of socio-political transformations in the European societies.[2]

Ever since human communities took form after the consolidation of the concept of 'family', an unwritten code of ethics prevailed for thousands of years. Gradually, as communities evolved into societies, ethnicity took root and fair and just interpretation of codes of ethics became an important aspect of social philosophy which is so inescapable and integral that its complexity in different times and different circumstances became a specialised branch of human thought and activity. Legal profession was thus born. This profession was not so sharply defined in olden times.

Keeping this in view, it is proposed to give a short history of legal profession in different countries, namely Greece, Rome, England, France, Germany, Italy, Australia, United States of America and India. Besides this an endeavour will be made to know the structure of legal profession and Bar in India.

2. Origin and Development of Legal Profession in Different Countries

(i) Profession of law in Ancient Greece

The profession of the Advocate is a permanent institution in the world's justice, coming down through ages, and governing traditions and wisdom from generation to generation for the edification of present and future ones. Client and counsellor, advocate, jury and judge—their notions, were known and studied in Athens, Rome, England and America.[3] In classical Greek thinking law in the lawyer's sense is not clearly differentiated from other agencies of social control. The Greek city was a politically organised society. It was very close to and in some respects in

1. V.S. Narsyant, Political Thoughts of Ancient Greece, pp. 72-73.
2. J.S. Gandhi, Lawyers and Touts : A Study in the Sociology of Legal Profession, 19-20 (1982).
3. P. Ramanatha Aiyar and N.S. Ranganatha Aiyer, Legal and Professional Ethics, 6 (2003).

transition from a king-oriented society. Much of its ethical custom and codified customary law spoke from an older tribal society. It was tending to but had not attained a stage of legal development which may be called the stage of strict law. In that stage social control through norms authoritatively established by politically organised society has been set off definitely from religion and ethical custom and is governed by ideas of certainty and uniformity in that ordering and of rule and form as the means thereto. Classical Greek law had not reached this stage. In consequence classical Greece did not develop lawyers, for law and lawyers grow up together. It is true that the germs of our institutions are to be found in Greece.

One may trace a continuous development of the advocate of today from those who represented or assisted others in litigation in Greek tribunals. In the beginnings of law the kin group rather than the individual was the legal unit. Hence, in politically organised societies still close to an older kin organisation dependents were represented before the tribunals by the head of the kin group. If one was not a dependent, he must represent himself. There was no advocacy. The kin group spoke though its head on behalf of dependents because their cause was its cause. The kinless man, the emancipated man, the man who was not a dependent, spoke for himself. The ordinary tribunal was a large body of citizens under oath to decide a particular cause and addressed not as jurors (*dikasts*) but as citizens. Those *dikasteries*, as they were called, could contain as few as two hundred and one or four hundred and one, or as many as fifteen hundred and one citizens. It was a difficult task for the ordinary man, even at Athens where citizens were accustomed to public speaking in the political assemblies, to present one's own case before so large a tribunal. The timid, the inexperienced, and ignorant were at a great disadvantage before such a court as compared with trial before a single Judge who by questioning can patiently and skillfully bring out what is to be said on both sides. In the Greek trial, each party made a speech in the course of which he adduced evidence, brought forward witnesses, and cross-examined his adversary in connection with his several points as he went along with his narrative. The speech was undifferentiated, or little differentiated, narrative, proofs, and argument. In case of any complexity, it called for a degree of skill beyond the everyday citizen. Hence, the average litigant employed a speech-writer or logograph who, for a fee, drew up a speech and turned it over to his client. The client learned it by heart and delivered it before the Tribunal.

Truly admitting that the speech-writer was not an advocate, yet the Roman orator, from whom the advocate of the day is derived, historically, took the Greek orator for his model. Indeed the successful speech-writer had to be something very like a lawyer. He had to be well versed in Athenian law and procedure. He might have to argue that the popular tribunal should steadfastly apply the law. He had to know the law which was to be applied or to be dispensed with. Also he had to know the psychology of Athenian Juries and be sensitive to their passions and prejudices. Above all he had to know how to adapt the speech which he wrote to the age, the condition, and the character of his clients and make it seem to flow naturally from the mouth of the speaker. All this is closely akin to the task of the advocate.

There was no clear differentiation of the function of the agent for litigation from that of the advocate. The word *syndic* (which came to mean agent) and *synegoros* (which denoted something very like an advocate) were often used as synonyms. Etymologically, *'syndic'* means one who intervenes in a legal proceeding. In the end it may be submitted that in ancient Greece we have the beginnings of lawyers rather than lawyers we as know them in developed legal systems.

(ii) Law and lawyers at Rome

In the Roman law of the later republic and especially in the classical Roman law of the early empire, the authors find law in the sense of the legal order—of a regime of social control adjusting relations and ordering conduct by the systematic and orderly application of the force of a politically organised society—well set off from other agencies of social control, and law in the sense of an authoritative body of materials for the guidance of judicial action well differentiated from ethical custom, religion, and public opinion. Also there is a well developed legal procedure, with a system of actions leading to defined remedies and grounded in defined legal duties, established by definite legal precepts, by which the judges considered themselves bound. In other words, the authors finds law in the lawyer's sense.[1]

In the fifth and sixth centuries great improvements took place which gave advocacy something very like its modern organisation. Indeed the modern continental organisation is simply a development of the Roman in this its final form. The advocates ceased to be merely orators. They were no longer trained merely in rhetoric. They had studied in one or another of the law schools which had grown up in the chief cities of the empire and attained the leading position once held by the *juriconsults.* A certain number of advocates was fixed for each of the courts in leading cities. Those attached to a court formed a sort of corporation. The law recognized fees and fixed the scale. Professional discipline was provided for. Thus, the main lines which exist today had become established.[2]

In the State of Rome, lawyers occupied the foremost place. As the complexity of the law increased, in course of time its interpretation rested largely with eminent non-official lawyers, whose opinions, called *Response Prudentium,* were generally adopted by the actual dispensers of justice. Besides them, there was also another class of lawyers known as *Juris Consulti* who were paid for their services and who might be compared to the modern chamber lawyer. The advocate who appeared before the Roman Tribunal often did not know much of the law himself, but coached himself in what was necessary for his particular task by seeking the help of these

1. Schulz, Roman Legal Science, 15-22, 111-122, 266-277 (1946).
2. Roscoe Pound, The Lawyer from Antiquity to Modern Times, 50-51 (1953).

juristic lawyers. The advocate was called an orator, and his profession was often the passport to high offices in the State, as it frequently is in modern England. The technical name applied to advocates was *patroni*, and these parties were known as their clients—that is the origin of modern word 'client'. At first the patron was who gratuitously threw his protection around his dependents and defended them before the public tribunals. But in course of time advocacy became the occupation and the acknowledged profession of many learned men. Those who wished to practise in the courts put themselves to a course of severe training for legal instruction under the *Juris Consulti*. As there was no limit to the number of counsel that might plead a litigant's cause a time-limit was fixed in Rome.

(iii) Growth of the Legal Profession in England

The institution of trained lawyers who might be engaged by the litigants to appear on their behalf in the law courts is of ancient origin in Europe as well as in the East. The emergence of common law in England roughly coincided with the common law profession.[1] In the middle ages, there were no professional Judges. The cases of the litigants were decided by a body of persons known as suitors. Of course there was a presiding officer, but he was not a Judge; the entire assembly, which may be called 'Folk Assembly' gave the decision.[2] In those days the litigant were required to appear in person and personally make 'the proof'. It is to be imagined that some suitors of the court on account of their age and ability be regarded as authorities to whose opinion on local custom great weight would attach, and that litigants would seek and perhaps pay for the advice of such men in the conduct of their suits, but the time of an organised legal profession had not yet come.[3]

English legal development stems from 1066 when William I of Normandy gained the Crown of England by right of battle. He introduced the institution of *Curia Regis*, whose original activities were for protecting the interest of the King—namely collection of revenue. The litigations continued to be tried in the old courts. But gradually *curia regis* entered in the arena of administration of justice and offered itself as a court where disputes among individuals could be judged. As the law and procedure of *curia regis* was better than those obtained in the old courts, people voluntarily submitted to the jurisdiction of *curia regis*, and eventually within about 200 years of the conquest, the Royal Courts became the normal forums for trial of cases in England.

It is also crystal clear from different studies that during the Angevin Rule (1154-1215) the administration of justice had undergone vast changes. During this period the disputes between the tenants-in-chief could be tried only by *curia regis*. A writ known as *praecipe* was issued to the Sheriff (*shire reeve*) directing him to order the defendant to yield up the disputed land or to appear before the Royal Court to explain as to why he had not done so. During the rule of Henry II (1154-1189) who was the Duke of

1. Manish Arora, Career in Law, 1 (2002).
2. J.H. Baker, Introduction to English Legal History, 132 (2nd edn.).
3. Radcliff and Cross, English Legal System, 379.

Normandy and Count of Anjoy, there was reorganization of *curia regis*. Some years later, in the reign of Edward I, was created the Order of Sergeants who could appear in courts to represent litigants.

By 1200 A.D. there was the practice of appointing as Judges the people of the clergy who served as clerks to the Judges of previous generation and thereby gained expertise. In the 13th century the profession of law passed from the hands of the clergy to non-clerical persons. The clergy was debarred by canon law from practicing in law courts except on behalf of the Church and the poor. In the middle ages, the litigants were required to appear in person in the court and to personally take steps. But when litigations increased, it became necessary to allow the parties to appear constructively through other person, who were called attorney. The attorneys were given power to act on behalf of litigants and default of the attorney was considered equivalent to default of the party. When the law became complicated, the attorneys were not well equipped with the skill to tell the case of the parties before the court. So a new class of people called 'narrators' or 'counters', who had the necessary skill in law appeared within the legal profession. The profession of Barristers originated in the 'narrators' or 'counters'. These narrators or counters organised themselves as a distinct class of persons practising law. In course of time within the body of narrators and counters two groups sprang up. The older and abler narrators or counters who became prominent in the profession organised themselves into a small fraternity or guild known as 'Sergeants-at-law', while the rest formed societies known Inns of Courts. This division took place in the fourteenth century. Sergeants-at-law were appointed by patents from the king. The first recorded call to the order of Sergeants was in 1338 A.D. By the time of Richard II (1377-1399) the admission to the order of Sergeants-at-law became like a degree ceremony. The Sergeants had to take oath to serve the King's people. They had a distinctive dress, the most prominent feature of which was a white silk of linen coif (cap) fastened under the chin, and this coif continued till the end of the nineteenth century, though in modified form. The members of this order had the exclusive right of audience in Courts of Common Pleas, which were then the jurist courts and as a result the Sergeants earned great fortunes. Their status could compete with knighthood. The prominent position of the Sergeants gradually declined due to various causes, and finally in 1846, by a statute the Courts of Common Pleas were opened to all practitioners, thus ending the monopoly of the Sergeants.

The other class, a very small in number became Sergeants-at-law. The narrators or counters other than the Sergeants came to be known as 'apprentices'. The term denotes they learnt at the feet of the Sergeants. These 'apprentices' were later on known as 'Barristers', perhaps from the middle of fifteenth century. The name 'Barrister' has a curious derivation. It relates to the 'Bar' not of the Court but to a bar in the Hall of the Inn. A 'Bar' was set in front of the Benchers who sat at the top of the hall during a moot, while the Barristers sat below the Bar. Those at the extremity were called 'outer' or 'utter' Barristers, while those at the centre were called 'inner' Barristers.[1]

In the reign of Edward I, Inns of Courts were established in proximity to courts for the training of apprentices in law. These were unincorporated societies of Lincoln's Inn, the Inner Temple, the Middle Temple and Gray's Inn.[2] In the fourteenth century the apprentices lived in certain inns or hostels near the city of London. In these inns the apprentices lived a semi-collegiate life, and were subject to a common system of education, discipline and Government. Besides this, there were originally more inns including Inns of Chancery and Sergeants' Inns, the latter being associations of sergeants ("Sergeants"-the king's servants) who were the most senior barristers, having the monopoly of audience in the Court of Common Pleas, and from whose ranks the judiciary were created. Even to this day no one can practice at the Bar unless he has been "called to the Bar" and become a member of an Inn.[3]

Originally, the Inns were like colleges, centres of legal learning and education, and by Shakespeare's time, fashionable training place for young men. Vestigially the remaining Inns still retain something of the atmosphere of colleges, with powers of control over their members, libraries and halls in which the members lunch and dine : and each Inn has its "Bench"of senior members and judges who are the "Masters" or "Benchers" of the Inn. But much of the central control of the profession has now passed to the Senate of the Inns of Court and Bar and the education of barristers under the ultimate surveillance of the Senate, is now a matter for the Council of Legal Education and the Inns of Court School of Law, situated in Gray's Inns.[4] Moreover, the General Council of the Bar ("Bar Council"), created in 1895, now represents the Bar as a profession. The General Council of the Bar is an elected body and has no disciplinary powers but as a matter of long accepted practice complaints are made to it which if necessary are referred by it to the Senate of Four Inns of Court. Matters such as maintenance of honour and independence of the Bar, defence of the Bar in relation with the judiciary and the executive encouragement of legal education, improvement of administration of justice, trial by jury, law reporting law reform, question of professional conduct, etc. are attended by it. In 1966, a Senate of Inns of Court was created to take over the functions previously exercised by each of the four Inns. The Senate deals generally with conditions for the admission of students, legal education and welfare; a Disciplinary Committee has been established.[5] When a barrister has acquired practical experience, skill and distinction in his profession, he may apply to the Lord Chancellor to 'take silk', i.e., become a Queen's Counsel. If the applicant's request is granted, letters patent are issued and he will then be called by his Inn of Court 'within the bar' thus relinquishing his former status of 'outer' or 'utter' barrister. Henceforth he wears a silk gown. By this new status the successful applicant will expect to attract more

1. J.H. Baker, *op cit. at 132.*
2. *Ibid.*
3. Philips S. James, Introduction to English Law, (1979), p. 56.
4. *Id.*
5. Colin F. Padfield, Law Made Simple, (1978), p. 90.

difficult cases and to command higher fees. He will not longer draft pleadings, conveyances, or similar documents. Thenceforward he will have the assistance of junior counsel who will be briefed with him and who will receive a proportion of his fee. A Queen's counsel is distinguished by the letters Q.C. after his name, and is referred to as a 'leader'.[1]

The English legal profession has traditionally been divided into barristers and solicitors and continues to remain so despite periodic attempt of fusion of the two branches. A practising barrister is defined as : (a) a barrister who is entitled to practise and who holds himself out as ready to do so, not being otherwise employed in the whole time occupation; or (b) a barrister whose regular occupation is that of editor or reporter of any series of law reports entirely written and edited by barristers for the use of the legal profession. A barrister is also known as a trial lawyer. The barrister's principal work lies in the oral presentation of cases, for the most part in the higher courts where barristers enjoy a practically exclusive right of audience, he is employed not directly by his client but almost always through the medium of a solicitor. A barrister may not normally see or advise a client or accept a brief to appear as an advocate on behalf of a client in any contentious business without the intervention of a solicitor. To act otherwise may result in disbarment. Many barristers take positions in industry, commerce, the universities, and the public services. A barrister intending to practise must choose in which part of the law he intends to specialize. A barrister is essentially an advocate whose task is to present his client's case effectively in court. To be successful he must possess certain personal and intellectual qualities and, above all, a capacity for hard work. A portion of his work includes the drafting of opinions on difficult points of law, the settling of pleadings and advice on evidence and procedural matters.

On the other hand, the solicitor may be colloquaially described as the 'front of house' man : the person who, like the general petitioner, deals directly with the client and, where litigation is involved, instructs the barrister. The origins of this side of the profession go back to the medieval 'attornatus' (attorney) who was—as the solicitor still is, but the barrister is not an officer of the court. The attorney's business was originally to help the client in the preparatory stages of cases. In the course of time a similar class of people practising in the Court of Chancery came to be called as 'solicitors'. By the close of the middle ages neither class was admitted to the Inns of Court, and the two sub-professions were merged. In the 16th century the position of the attorneys was downgraded. They were excluded from the membership of the Inns of Courts; and they became intermediaries between the Barristers and the clients. During this period some more courts such as Star Court, Admiralty Court and Chancery became popular and the litigants required the services similar to the services rendered by the attorneys in the Common Pleas Courts. The litigants chose some law agents to act on their behalf; and this new class of law agents came to be known as solicitors. The solicitors were admitted on the roll of chancery. The

1. Philip, S. James, op. cit, p. 57.

profession of solicitors, despite the fact that the title was of somewhat undignified nature, acquired a higher status in the seventeenth century. Side by side, in the Ecclesiastical and Admirately Courts a class of legal practitioners similar to attorney and solicitors grew and this new class was known as 'proctors'. Many proctors were 'Notaries Public'.[1]

In the eighteenth century all the three branches, viz., the attorney, the solicitors and proctors merged into one society under the name of the Society of Gentlemen Practitioners in the Court of Law and Equity. In the course of time the name of Proctors and Attorneys disappeared and they were known as solicitors. In 1831, a voluntary association—Law Society came into being and the Law Society had the custody of the Roll of Solicitors of Supreme Court. The Society controls the education of the article clerks and holds examination for qualifying for admission to the Roll of Solicitors. In other words,[2] it safeguarded the interests of its members and also regulated the profession. It took steps to uproot practitioners guilty of misconduct. It exercised great influence in those days. In 1832, the new and old societies existing in England were amalgamated and in 1837 took the name, "The Incorporated Law Society of the United Kingdom." By 1860, Attorneys, Proctors and Solicitors all became known as Solicitors and were placed on a roll kept by the Law Society. The law applicable to Solicitors is contained in Act of 1938 to 1941. It has wide powers under The Solicitors Acts : the latest of which is the Solicitors Act, 1974. The profession for all ordinary purposes in England now consists of two branches only "Barristers and Solicitors". A solicitor is an officer of the Court. He has no right of audience in open court or in the Crown Court. Many solicitors are active advocates in the lower courts, such as the Magistrates' Courts and Country Courts, in which (as opposed to the Superior Courts) they have right of audience. However, in High Court cases the solicitor must "instruct counsel", i.e., employee a barrister. But this does not mean that the solicitor takes no further interest in the case, for it is his function, acting upon the barrister's "advice on evidence" to prepare the witnesses and get the case ready for trial. When solicitors appear in the Magistrates Courts, they wear ordinary lounge suits or, for ladies dark coloured suits or dresses. Women are now permitted to wear trouser suits in court. When solicitors conduct cases in the higher courts they must 'appear robed'. Most solicitors are employed in private practices either alone or in a partnership firm. Others are employed in the public service industry and commerce.

Solicitors have direct contact with their clients. Barristers do not. Hence, the solicitor's relationship with a client is usually much more personal. In almost all cases, a client who needs the services of a barrister must go first to a solicitor, who will then instruct or brief the barrister. The relationship between them is based on professional confidence, and a solicitor cannot be compelled to disclose in court communications made in a professional relationship. Nor is a solicitor liable for defamation in respect of statements made in court during the course of trial. A solicitor is,

1. B.K. Goswami, Legal Profession & Its Ethics, (1995), pp. 13-14.
2. *Ibid*, at p. 14.

however, liable to be sued for damages for negligence in the conduct of his profession, e.g., where he has carelessly lost documents entrusted to him.

The work of a solicitor is too diverse to classify. Everyone knows that solicitors act as personal and family advisors to their clients that they affect conveyances of property, that they prepare wills, advise on matrimonial matters and handle the defences of accused people. The solicitors are governed by a professional body known as Law Society. The Law Society is responsible for the training of solicitors. In 1996, there were over 69,000 solicitors in the country who held practising certificates and were qualified to practise.[1] It is also the professional body which ensures that solicitors do their work properly and it has disciplinary powers. If a complaint against the solicitor is made by a client, it will be investigated and dealt with by an independent body, which may recommend that action be taken against the solicitor by the Law Society. The major aspect of legal work under the English system, namely, the prohibition against advertising by individual solicitors or firms has undergone significant changes in the recent years which culminated in new Practice Rules and Publicity Code published in 1987. Initially, the relaxations were in the area of collective advertising as opposed to advertising by individual solicitors or firms which continued to be prohibited under Solicitors' Practice Rules, 1936/72. Since the new Publicity Code is not merely an advertising code but a publicity code, it applies to all forms of publicity including advertising, professional stationery, name plates, media appearances and so on. On the whole, the new code stands for a considerable liberalisation of the rules governing solicitors' publicity subject to the overriding necessity to ensure that publicity is in conformity with the five guiding principles set out in Rule 1 of the Solicitors' Practice Rules, 1987, namely (i) the solicitors' independence or integrity, (ii) the client's freedom to instruct a solicitor of the client's choice, (iii) the solicitors' duty to act in the best interests of the clients, (iv) the good repute of the solicitor or of the solicitor's profession and (v) the solicitors' proper standard of work. While it was made clear that nothing must be done in the way of compromising or impairing these basic principles, it was equally imperative that the publicity must be "in goods taste".[2]

The difference between the two branches (Barristers and Solicitors) of the profession[3] may be summarized as follows :

(a) Solicitors have a right of audience in inferior courts and Crown Courts; barristers may appear in all courts.

(b) Solicitors are agents for their clients and can bind them by what they say; barristers cannot so bind their clients.

(c) Solicitors may make binding contracts with clients; barristers cannot make such contracts with clients.

(d) Solicitors deal with clients direct; barristers deal with clients only

1. G.B. Reddy, Practical Advocacy of Law (2002), pp. 58-59.
2. For more details see Ranu Basu, "Advertising by Solicitors", the Lawyers, May, 1987, p. 21.
3. Colin F. Padfield, op. cit, pp. 90-91.

through the medium of a solicitor, as a matter of professional etiquette.

(e) Solicitors are in close touch with the community and are to some extent businessmen; barristers are less so, and need a specialized knowledge of law and skill in forensic advocacy, i.e., in presenting a case in court.

(f) Solicitors are controlled by statute (Solicitors Act, 1839-1974); barristers are controlled by their Inns of Court and the established Senate, non-statutory bodies.

(g) Solicitors are liable for negligence in the conduct of a case, barristers are not so liable.

(iv) Growth of Legal Profession in United States of America

The second day of July, 1776, was the most memorable epoch in the history of America. This day the Continental Congress declared the United Colonies Free and Independent States. Of the fifty-six signers of the Declaration of Independence document that signaled the birth of a new America (Thomas Jefferson called them "that host of worthies"), twenty-five can be identified as lawyers. A few others were jurists without legal training. Some of the lawyers did not practice but were plantation owners who made their living from the land. Of the fifty-six signers, lawyers signers especially left their mark, becoming presidents, Supreme Court justices, members of Congress, governors, and attorneys general of the new states, giving today's legal profession a rich heritage. It was the lawyers delegates to the Continental Congress who had most to do with bringing about the Declaration of Independence.[1] On May 15, 1776, John Adams suggested that the Congress recommend that the colonies form new governments. On the same day in Williamburg, Virginia, the Virginia Assembly voted that delegates be instructed to propose that the United Colonies declare their freedom from the British Crown. Three weeks later, June 7, Richard Henry Lee of Virginia proposed the resolution. It was immediately seconded by John Adams, and a committee of five[2] (four of whom were lawyers) was appointed "to prepare a declaration to the effect of the said resolution." All but Livingston, became signatories of the final document. John Adams persuaded Thomas Jefferson to write the declaration, offering as good a legal amount as ever presented to a Jury :" Reason first-you are a Virginian, and a Virginiam ought to appear at the head of this business. Reason second - I am obnoxious, suspected and unpopular. You are very much otherwise. Reason third - you can write ten items better than I can."

The Committee's draft was presented to the Congress on June 28, and the stage was set for the debate. John Adams, who was the Chairman of twenty-five committee and a member of ninety, is sometimes called the political wheelhorse of the Congress and the Atlas of Independence. He

1. Journal of American Bar Association, January, 1976, p. 870.
2. The members were Benjamin Franklin and Lawyers Thomas Jefferson, John Adams, Roger Sherman and Robert R. Livingston.

piloted the resolution through to unanimous acceptance, but he had the help of fellow-lawyers professionals at legislative lobbying. Tom Mckean displayed his skill as a lobbyist. Overnight he persuaded two Pennsylvania opponents to stay away the next and also convinced James Wilson, a Pennsylvania lawyer to vote in favour of the resolution. Then he got commitment from Edward Rutledge, a lawyer from South Carolina who was the youngest delegate in the Congress. The lawyers who promoted, wrote, lobbied and piloted the Declaration of Independence from an idea to a document that eventually transformed crown provinces to indépendent colonies to United States were amazing, articulate, and brilliant patriots. They overcome almost overwhelming handicaps. They lived in a period when many lawyers were distrusted and lambasted as "Dirty pettifoggers". to use Ben Franklin's words. It was time of no law schools and few law books. The first American law school was not established until 1784 in Litchfield, Connecticut.[1]

The American Revolution had vastly affected the legal profession in that country in a variety of ways, both direct and indirect, namely, first the profession that a considerable number of its most prominent members 31 of the 55 members of the Constitutional Convention in Philadelphia and 10 of the 25 senators and 17 of the 65 representative in the First Congress were men who had been trained in the law but who were not necessarily practising law.[2] Secondly, a particularly bitter antipathy which had always existed among certain segments of the colonial population, soon made itself felt in many sections of the country; thirdly, a strong dislike of everything English, including the English common law, the English statutes, and the English way of administering justice, became widespread; and lastly, the lack of distinct body of American law as well as the absence of American Law Reports and law books for a while made the administration of justice, and concomitantly, the practice of law extremely difficult and haphazard.

Apart from the fact that many lawyers took an active part in the Revolution either as fighting men or as politicians who decided to stay in politics, the profession was sorely depleted by the loss of many of its prominent members who chose to remain loyal to the British Crown. These loyalist either left America or completely retired from practice, or were forcibly excluded from the profession by legislative acts or rulings of the court.[3]

The other statutes passed by other states like New York required "all attorneys, solicitors and counselors at law to produce certificates or residence of their attachment to the liberties and independence. These statutes required administration of loyalty oath, and forbidding all members of the legal profession who refused to take oath to pursue the practice of

1. Supra note 30 at pp. 871-872.
2. Boorstin, The Americans : The Colonial Experience, (1958), p. 205.
3. The State of Massachusetts passed an Act in 1778 to prevent the return of certain persons including lawyers who left the state or the U.S., and joined the enemies thereof. This Act was followed by another Act in 1779 to confiscate the Estates of certain notorious conspirators against the Government. Incidently the worst affected by these two statutes were lawyers.

law. In each of the other states, also, the legal profession was severally crippled by the loss of loyalists. It was estimated that 150 leading lawyers and another 200 lawyers of lesser standing left the country or retired from active practice.[1]

Judge Henry St. George Tucker asserted in 1841 that "from the formation of the republic, the most distinguished men in our councils have been of the legal profession, and it may not be indulging in too much *espirit de corps* to declare, that the ability, sagacity, public spirit, intrepidity and love of well regulated liberty, they have rarely found superiors in any other class of society." Having emerged from the colonial period when lawyers had directed their efforts almost exclusively towards establishing the profession as a viable agency in society, the bar in the years between the Revolution and the Civil War stood head and shoulders above all other professions in social status, potential political power, and economic ascendency. In this transitional period a firmly entrenched cadre of practitioners focused upon issues which never before had been faced by the bar.[2]

In January, 1878, the Connecticut Bar Association initiated steps for lawyer's meeting in Saratoga Springs, New York to consider the formation of a national Association. It was this meeting that gave birth to the American Bar Association. Seventy-five lawyers from twenty states and the District of Columbia heeded the call for a conference given by Simeon Baldwin of New Haven. The conference met in the courtroom of the town hall in Saratoga Springs on August 21, 1878. The founding of the American Bar Association also marked a turning point for the profession of law. By the next decade there were 176 Bar Associations in America.[3] Roscoe Pound characterized the final three decades of the nineteenth century as "progress in undoing the mischief wrought in the depersonalizing of the practice of law of America before and after the Civil War."[4] Over the years, the American Bar Association has been responsible for the further development of American jurisprudence, the establishment of formal education requirements for persons seeking to become attorneys, the formulation of ethical principles that govern the practice of law , and creation of the American Law Institute and the Conference of Commissioners on Uniform State Laws, which advance the fair administration of the justice through encouraging uniformity of states and judicial decisions whenever practicable. Today, after many struggles and re-organisation, the American Bar Association is a potent force in upholding and defending the Constitution and in promoting the public good. In 1950, there were approximately 1,76,000 lawyers and judges, in 1970, 2,60,000 and in 1987, an estimated 7,07,000. This computes to 11.6 lawyers and judges per 10,000

1. Supra note 30, at p. 29.
2. E. Lee Shepard, "Lawyers Look at Themselves, Professional Consciousness and the Virginia Bar, 1750-1850." The American Journal of Legal History, January, 1981, Vol. XXV, No, I, p. 1.
3. American Bar Association Journal, July, 1978, (Centennial Issue), pp. 994, 996 and 1018.
4. Roscoe Pound, The Lawyer from Antiquity to Modern Times (1953), p. 353.

in the population in 1950; 12.7 in 1970, and 29.0 in 1987—a dramatic increase.

W.M. Reece Smith, Jr., past President of American Bar Association once said : "many of the developments that we have experienced were seen first as grave threats to the traditions and welfare of the American legal profession. But rarely has that proved to be the case." He cited a few examples to make his point : "During the 1970s, both federal and State Government critically examined the regulatory structure of the American legal profession. As a result, lay members were added to governing and disciplinary boards of the bar in some jurisdictions. Many lawyers viewed lay involvement as an improper intrusion into professional concerns. Yet, generally speaking, the development has proved a satisfactory one. Our purposes and our problems have become better understood by others. Public confidence in the legal profession has improved. And often the lay representatives have come to be strong advocates and stout defenders of the profession. Moreover, after careful scrutiny both by legislative and administrative agencies, no significant structural changes were made in our regulatory scheme. Indeed our method of professional regulation has been vindicated. As a result, professional and public confidence in the system have been enhanced. Likewise, government has examined our so-called monopoly on the practice of law. Here there has been more telling change, particularly in the manner in which legal services are delivered Group and prepaid legal service programmes have developed and some work previously done only by lawyers has passed to laymen. Yet there has been no serious effect on lawyer's ethics or livelihood. Sheer growth within the profession itself is far more of a problem in each case."[1]

Similarly, the Supreme Court of United States has held that lawyers may advertise for legal business as an exercise of the American constitutional concept of free speech. Following these decisions, the code of ethics was amended. The American Bar Association has taken the lead in addressing the problems related to legal profession. Continuing legal education has become pervasive.

The cost of legal service is also receiving concerned attention. Legal fees a century ago varied as they do today. A minimum fee schedule adopted by the Bar Association of District of Columbia in 1873 suggested these fees : Arguing a cause in the Supreme Court of the District of Columbia \$50; Circuit Courts trials, \$25; Police Court, \$10; written contract or deed, \$10; printed contract, \$5; preparing a will, \$25; collection, 10 per cent up to \$5000, more than \$5000, 10 per cent on the first \$5000 and 5 per cent on the excess. When a prospective client consults a lawyer he should expect to pay him a fee for his advice.[2] The fees charged by lawyers are largely determined by the cost of doing business and by the competition. A lawyer's consultation fee may be \$10, \$25, or \$50 depending on the amount of time

1. W.M. Reece Smith, Jr., "The Profession's Response to the Challenge", Speech delivered in the 19th Biennial Conference of International Bar Association at New Delhi in 1982.
2. George Gordon Coughlin, Your Introduction to Law, (1975), p. 12.

spent with the client, the amount of research involved in obtaining the answer to the problem, the lawyer's experience and standing in the profession, and the size of the community in which he practices. It is sensible for the client to ask the lawyer in advance what the consultation fee will be.[1] There are several methods of paying a lawyer, if he is retained to handle a particular case. Probably, the two most widely used means for paying legal fees are (i) the contingent fee and (ii) the flat fee.

The Code of Professional Responsibility sets forth the following factors as guides for determining the reasonableness of lawyer's fees :

(i) The time and labour required, the novelty and difficulty of the questions involved, and the skill requisite to perform the legal service properly;

(ii) The likelihood, if apparent to the client, that the acceptance of the particular employment will preclude other employment by the lawyer;

(iii) The fee customarily charged in the locality for similar legal services;

(iv) The amount involved and the results obtained;

(v) The time limitations imposed by the client or by the circumstances;

(vi) The nature and length of the professional relationship with the client;

(vii) The experience, reputation, and ability of the lawyers performing the services;

(viii) Whether the fee is fixed or contingent.

(v) Growth of Legal Profession in France

The legal profession performed a national role and dominated the European political scene. This was especially the case for the Latin countries. The French Third republic was re-baptized 'the Republic of Lawyers', which was a not inaccurate definition if one considers that in 1881 some 41 per cent of French parliamentarians were jurists. In 1910, French jurists accounted for 37 per cent of all members of Parliament, but by 1919 their proportion had diminished to 28.5 per cent, yet despite this decrease, between 1898 and 1940 legal professionals still represented 26 per cent of French deputies. The legal professions formed the 'backbone' of governments. During the Third French Republic the presence of lawyers in the executive was far greater than the Chamber of Deputies, and it remained high even when the proportion in Parliament diminished. After the Second World War, the legal fields progressively lost their importance as the formative arenas of the national ruling classes. Their marginalization

1. Bar associations in more than 250 communities of the United States have lawyer reference plans so that a person who needs the advice of a lawyer may phone the local bar association, which will refer the prospective client to a local lawyer (knowledgeable in a particular field). The prospective client will be told in advance the lawyer's fee for the conference. The average fee is $10 for a half hour consultation.

was determined by the interweaving of various factors. The process formation of political class changed. The advent of mass political parties overwhelmed the old notability system and relegated jurists to below other social groups. At the same time, new higher institutes and schools, supplanted the faculties of law as the education agencies for future ruling classes. In 1986 only 5.2 per cent of the deputies in the *Assemblee Nationale* were lawyers; in 2002 the proportion rose, but only to 5.9 per cent.

The history of the French Bar well exemplifies the interweaving between conditioning by the public powers and the strength of the professional body's tradition. It was nourished by the 'political myth' of its origins. The 'classic bar' was born in the sixteenth century, when the bar first began to differentiate itself from the powers of the State, with which it was hitherto confused. Emancipated from the control of Parliament, the lawyers' *ordre* gradually conquered its autonomy. The *batonnier* (the head of the order) was selected from year to year on the criterion which combined eligibility, seniority and co-option. Until 1781, he nominated the members of the Council of the order, who thereafter were elected by the general assembly of lawyers.

Also, the acquisition of disciplinary power was a slow process. Only in the eighteenth century did Parliament (which at that time had jurisdictional functions) delegate albeit non-formally, all disciplinary power to the *ordre*, which could suspend or expel its members. The *ordre* finally formulated its code of conduct. From the early 1700s onwards, the *orders* sought to conjugate the improvement of legal culture with observance of ethical code. The reconstitution of the legal order came in 1810 with a derogation from the Le Chapelier Law that had abolished all guilds in 1791. The purpose was two-fold : on the one hand, it disciplined a profession whose 'factiousness' Napoleon deemed dangerous; on the other, it was tribute paid to the profession's tradition which enabled the advocates to 're-invent' the French Bar.

With the law of 1810, the State delegated governance of the profession to the *ordre*, although this was a self-governance restricted by the control exerted by the judiciary and by the Minister of Justice. The July Monarchy marked the beginning of the golden age of the French Bar when the legal orders acquired true self-governance. An Ordinance of 27 August, 1830 established the Disciplinary Council of the order and the *batonnier* were to be elected by all the lawyers enrolled at the Court of Appeal to which the order belonged. The decline of the orders began in the 1930s, when new associations arose in defense of the legal profession. The Association *Nationale des Avocats* campaigned to ensure that avocats maintained monopoly over defence, and for the stage to be given a more vocational structure. Whilst the association's first demand was not met immediately, the second was granted in 1930, when it became compulsory to spend one year of the stage in the Chambers of a lawyers, or notary, or at a court.

In the first half of the twentieth century, the French legal order was subject to rigorous regulation by the State and the French order did not have a national body of representation and coordination until 1990, when the *Conseil National des Barreaux* was founded. This was a public interest body which represented the Bar in dealings with the government and supervised the profession's rules and practices but it did not have disciplinary power. One wonders why the French legal profession was so belated in endowing itself with a national representative body. In this regard, it should be borne in mind that the order in Paris had since the 1800s performed the role of representing French advocacy in its entirety; and secondly, that the lawyers' trade unions continued the *Association Nationale des Avocats (ANA)* social protection of the profession after the Second World War, weakening the power of the orders and abating the need for a central representative body.[1]

On account of the progress in population, urbanisation, economic activity and social legislation the number of advocates in France has sizably increased. This expansion has brought into the profession, formerly dominated by the upper class, young people belonging to all strata of the society. But these developments did not undermine the image of the advocate in the society. He still commands respect from all quarters and enjoys high social status. The profession in France still attracts good talents. To become an advocate, the following conditions must be fulfilled, namely, one should be a French national subject to bilateral agreements of reciprocity; should hold the degree of Master of Laws, should not have been involved in any case in which honour, integrity, morality or solvency has been at stake; and should have obtained the certificate of aptitude for the profession of advocate.[2]

In France, there exists in each town, which is the seat of a court of appeal, a Centre of Professional Training. Its board consists in equal number of members of the Bar, members of the Bench and members of the Law Faculty, the Chairman being necessarily a member of the Bar. It is this centre which is responsible for preparing the advocates to the certificate of aptitude for the profession. The duration of the course is 12 months. The centre is also responsible for the training of advocates during the period of probation after enrolment. An advocate will be a probationer for a period of three years during which he should not absent himself for more than three months. He has to be present at the court sittings and has to actively practise as a junior under or an associate to an advocate. He is also authorised to practice in the office of the *Procure de la Republique* (Prosecution) or a Legal Consultant or a Chartered Accountant. He may also be authorised for a period of one year to practise in a foreign bar or to serve in the legal department of a private concern. Besides this, the probationer is entitled to perform all the acts of the profession. After the completion of three years' probation, the probationer gets himself enrolled as a full-fledged advocate in the bar of his choice.[3]

1. For more details see htpp//www.02—malatesta—2079—01.indd 26/09/2010; visited on 10.10.2012.
2. David Annoussamy, The Profession of Advocates in France, IBR, 1984, Vol. 11(2), pp 119-125.
3. *Ibid*; at p. 121.

Organisation of the Bar

In France, there exists a bar in each locality where there is a *Tribunal de Grande Instance* which is the principal civil court of original jurisdiction. The Bar consists of all the advocates enrolled including the probationers. Though several bars may form an association or some purposes there is no statutory link between them. Each bar is administered by a council elected by all the members. The chairman of the counsel is called "*Batonnier*". It is the council which decides on the enrolment of new advocate. It decides also on the deletion of the name of any advocate from the rolls on account of illness or infirmity, acceptance of activities incompatible with the profession, lack of honour, non-payment of the periodical contributions to the bar, non-exercise of the profession without valid reason. Such deletion is effected either *suo motu* or the request of the Procure4r General of the Court of Appeal or at the request of the concerned advocate. If any person feels aggrieved by enrolment or non-enrolment, the deletion or non-deletion he may file an appeal before the Court of Appeal.[1]

The Advocates in France have got two kinds of activities to perform. One is to represent the parties before the courts and tribunals. The second is to assist them before the courts and tribunals or give them legal advice. When an advocate represents a party he does not have to produce any vakalat. His statement of that effect before the court as to the advocate of the adverse party suffices. The advocate has got the monopoly of the representation of parties within the territorial jurisdiction of his bar and he cannot represent a party in a *Tribunal de Grad Instance* outside that jurisdiction. However, as far as the fact of representing the parties before the Court of Appeal is concerned, it is still reserved to solicitors.[2]

There is a special bar for the "*Cour de Cassation*" and "*Conseil d' etat*". It consists of 60 members having the monopoly of representation and assistance of the parties before those two courts. An advocate having three years' experience may be appointed in this category after successfully passing the competitive examination conducted by the Council of Administration of the Bar of the *Cour de Cassation* and *Counsel d' etat*. The Council of Administration of each Bar will act as the disciplinary authority in respect of the members of the bar as regards any misdeed of advocates in the performance of their duties. The Batonnier of each Bar who is given wide powers brings about settlement of the cases.[3]

(vi) Growth of Legal Profession in Germany

The experience of the legal profession in the *Third Reich* proved to be one of extreme frustration and abject humiliation. It saw its international and domestic reputation evaporate upon the altar of bizarre. Nazi legal/racial institutions; its ethics denigrated to fearful compliance with whimsical standards of justice, and its entire *raison d'etre* challenged by the emergence of an anti-legal, anti-rational, new philosophy of State

1. *Ibid*; at pp. 121-122.
2. *Ibid*; at p. 122.
3. *Id.*

power. It is explicitly clear from different texts and treatises that it never accorded a genuine position in the reorganisation of German society. The Nazis remained distrustful of German lawyers and consistently the 'mystique' of the law and its traditional servants as major obstacles to the realization of their ideologically oriented socio-political goals.[1]

The German Bar was established by the *Rechtsajnwaltsordnung* of July 1, 1878, which designated the practice of law one of the primary 'free professions'. As such the Bar was fundamentally free of State control and without a *numerus clausus* based on government dependence. It was organised on a regional basis under the limited supervision of the provincial justice ministries, but the officials and directors were elected solely by the constituent membership. The Bar was open to any attorney who met the necessary educational/professional qualifications and all members were competent to practice in any part of Germany.[2] A German lawyer was able to plead before any regular court with only minor restrictions placed upon the higher courts. Under the stipulations of the Bar statute an attorney could only be disbarred for conviction of a felony or a similarly serious offence against professional ethics, such cases being adjudicated in the special honor court of the Supreme Court (*Reichsgericht*).

Under these conditions of autonomy the Bar prospered in Imperial Germany and the early years of the Weimar Republic. One of the primary reasons for the continuing success of the legal profession was the large degree of professional stability found in the period. On the eve of World War I, the German Bar contained 12,297 practicing attorneys, and this was only slightly expanded so that in 1923 it had grown to 12,729.[3] On November 11, 1928 the 'Association for National Socialist German Jurists' was founded under Grank's leadership at the specific instructions of Hitler. Significantly, it was the first Nazi effort to enlist the support of a specific professional group amongst Germany's educated elite. Its stated purpose was to unite and cleanse the entire German legal profession in order to fulfil the promise of the party programme in returning Germany to a governance of indigenous racial law. While organised on a grandiose national scale, its initial appeal proved to be extremely limited.[4] Membership in a Nazi Legal Organisation was simply neither socially, nor economically beneficial to a legal class which enjoyed the respectability and prestige of its own long-standing organizations. Consequently, even as late as 1932 the Association for National Socialist German Jurists only had 1347 members with support coming characteristically from young jurists, law students, eastern emigres and the generally less successful elements of the profession.[5]

National socialism made good its promise to restructure the German Bar, though a bit more stringently than the legal profession may have

1. Kenneth C. 11. Willing, "The Bar in the Third Reich," The American Journal of Legal History, 1976, Vol. 20. p. 1.
2. *Ibid.*, at 2.
3. *Ibid.*
4. *Ibid.*, at 3.
5. *Ibid.*

desired. It cleansed the legal profession. Jews could no longer be admitted to the Bar and those already in practice were automatically disbarred with the exception of World War I veterans and legal practitioners pre-dating the establishment of the Weimar Republic. Even in this restricted group of 'privileged' Jews, the right to be a public defender, charity lawyer, tax-law advisor, liquidator, or sequester was denied. Not only Jews but communists and other politically unreliable elements were deemed ineligible to be attorneys. Since their numbers were not inordinately large, this brought little disruption to the profession.

The entire German Bar was reorganised and centralized twice during the Third Reich in 1934 and 1935. The National Lawyer's Chamber replaced its less official predecessor, the National Bar Association acted as a government licensing and disciplinary agency. The Bar which had previously been composed of regional, self-governing groups was transformed into a rigid system of chambers attached to each Supreme Regional Court. These Regional Chambers were under the complete supervision of the National Chamber and were responsible for the professional behaviour of their geographically assigned membership. The President and Directors of the National and Regional Chambers were appointed to office by the National Justice Ministry in consultation with the German 'Law-Leader'. Finally, in 1936 the old statute of 1878 was abrogated and in its place the Nazis promulgated a new National Lawyer's Code.[1] The new code was aimed at completely controlling the professional activities of the Bar and ensuring its adherence to National Socialist legal doctrines. Professional/educational qualifications were no longer deemed adequate for practicing law. Instead stress was laid on political awareness and the proper conduct for a 'Legal Guardian of the People'. Under the new provisions a candidate for the Bar after receiving his law degree had to spend a year probationary period in the courts, though not in the capacity of a practicing attorney. After the probation with the concurrence of Regional Director the Association for National Socialist German Jurists (BNSDJ) he was first licensed as an attorney-assessor[2] in which service he spent the next three years.[3] Thus, four years after leaving the University and only after having proved himself worthy of honour, that is, a firm National socialist, was he duly admitted into the German Bar. As part of his initiation into the legal profession he swore an oath of personal loyalty to Adolf Hitler which bound him in obedience to the *Fuehrer* till death.[4]

The new constitution of the German Bar declared in its preamble "the lawyer is a free servant of the law...an indispensable organ of the administration of justice, and as such a pillar of the German people..." The National Chamber dispensed instructions for the proper exercise of legal profession which included the demand that all attorneys join the NSDAP (never fully enforced) and actively participate in its programmes and

1. *Ibid.*, at 6.
2. *Ibid.*
3. Reduced in 1941 to one year.
4. Kenneth C. H. Willing, *op. cit.*, at 7.

affiliate organisations. For those members who refused to follow the new directions of the profession, disciplinary action was inevitable. The threat of disbarment was a serious one which carried the added possibility of future criminal proceedings. Under the Hitler regime, the grounds for disbarment were extended from three to seven. The majority of the cases brought before the legal Honour Court revealed the new attitude towards what was to be the norm of ethical and professional conduct. Some cases dealt with infractions of the lawyer's new responsibilities totally outside his former juridical functions. The lawyers were fined or suspended for failing to give the Hitler Salute, while common grounds for disbarment were not voting in elections or plebiscites. Another series of offences which warranted disbarment may be termed racial. Similarly, the changes taking place in courtroom procedure and actual legal dogma obviously had to have a tremendous bearing on the role of the German lawyer, diminishing his legal functions or removing them completely. Jews could not be represented by Aryan Counsel, except, ironically, if the accused (Jew) was brought before the People's Court (*Volksgerichtshot*), where an attorney of 'pure Aryan blood' was required to plead before the Bench.[1]

The most important characteristic of the German legal system is the fact, that all legal professions share the same professional education. Since the late 19th century law is studied at University and followed by two years' judicial traineeship (*Referendariat*) run by the State. The judicial trainees are the members of the civil services and are paid by the State. All legal professionals conduct trainings and work as judges at civil courts, State attorneys in criminal cases, in the public administration as well as lawyers in the courts room or legal consultant. These fully qualified lawyers (*volljurist*) have all the formal education to serve as Judge, State Attorney, Legal Advisor for public services or in the private sector or as lawyer (*Rechtsanwalt*). For those fully qualified lawyers admission to the Bar is just a formality. Unlike in the United States system, no further examination is needed. Furthermore, there is no distinction between legal services provided by a lawyer (*Rechtsanwalt*) in the German system today. Every legal professional, who has the joint chamber of lawyers, can practice all kind of legal services for their clients. The German system does not have any distinction as in the common law countries between Barrister, who is allowed to appear in court and to present the case and Solicitor, who prepares the statements and consults the client. Germany had also two similar categories of practising lawyers until the late 18th century : The so-called *'Prokurator'* appeared in court. The *'Advokat'* was a legal advisor paid by his clients similar to the common law model of today.[2]

Every practising lawyer has to be member of the Chamber of Lawyers. With the membership, the license to practice law is granted. This practice was established in 1713 in Prussia, when any *'Advokat'* had to be registered by the State authorities, which was intended to limit the freedom of

1. *Ibid.* at 7-8.
2. Volker Romermann and Wolfgang Hartung, *Anwaltliches Berusfrecht*—1 (2002) quoted by Lars Gerols, *The Legal Profession in Germany*, November 2008.

practicing the legal counselling. Today, the Regional Chambers grant the license and permission to practice law by admission of the lawyer to the Chamber.

By the end of 2007 there were 1,42,830 practicing lawyers in Germany. This number increased to 1,50,000 in 2009. By the end of 2007, Germany had a population of around 82 million people. 44,703 lawyers are female—around 30%. As a result there is one lawyer among 578 inhabitant. In other terms, 173 lawyers per 1,00,000 inhabitants. As Germany had 20,138 Judges (including part time Judges) in 2007 this cumulate to seven lawyers per Judge.

To reiterate, all practicing lawyers in Germany are members of Regional Chambers. Certain kinds of law firms with an own legal identity as well as their managing directors can be also members of the Chamber. The possibility to set-up such a law firm was just recently regulated. Thus, such types of law firms are very rare. Chambers are established in every higher regional court district. Additionally, all practicing lawyers at the Federal Court of Justice constitute their own Regional Chamber, Federal Chamber of Lawyers. The Chambers are public law corporations. The Federal Lawyer's Act, a parliamentary law, regulates the Chambers and the legal profession. The Chambers support and advise their members in matters related to their profession. They have to grant the right to practice to every qualified lawyer. If the right to practice law is granted to a lawyer, he automatically becomes member of the Chamber. The Chamber is fully funded by the fees of its members. The members elect the managing bodies of the Chambers. The Chambers are service providers for their members. They administrate the membership list and contact details to be shared among the lawyers. They distribute information which is relevant for the profession and run lawyer offices in every major courthouse with basic office equipment to assist lawyer to fulfil their duties. The Chambers run and observe continuing legal training to guarantee a high level of legal service provided by all members. Lawyer with a special focus, for example on criminal law, can run special courses and pass an examination to claim the title of a specialized criminal lawyer. A Commission of the Regional Chamber examines these candidates according to the charter on specialized lawyers as set by the Federal Chamber. The title of a specialized lawyer is not a further qualification, which grants any additional rights or duties, but is intended to serve as a sign of quality for the client in this particular area of law.

As the Chamber is a public institution regulating the profession and also a lobby group for the lawyers' profession, it conflicts from time to time those lawyers' associations, which have no public functions, but just consider themselves as a lobby group of the profession or at least parts of it. It is expected that the Chamber should stay neutral in political questions, but should speak out for its members' interests in public.

It is revealed from different study materials that several laws on the regulation of the lawyers' profession were launched by the legislature in the recent years in Germany. This was needed because the demands by the constitutional court to deregulate the profession and pull down old styled bans, for example, on advertisement, and to strengthen the right to practice law as a free profession. The European community also demands to harmonize the regulations in Germany in accordance with European standards. To open the market for legal services and to strengthen the competition within the market was the cross-cutting motivation for all changes in regulation in the recent years.

It may thus be summed up that in early nineteenth century Prussia, the profession of lawyers was characterized by a high degree of bureaucratization, and as such it has been classified by historians as a variant of the continental statist model. This anomaly with respect to the other European law professions had marked political overtones. Instituting a 'free Bar' in Germany, too, became one of the goals of German liberalism, and it had a significance which extended well beyond the mere issue of professionalism. One of the protagonists of this battle was legal associationism. Having arisen in the Germany of the *Vormartz* period, association of jurists performed a leading role in the organization of the legal profession. After 1878, in fact, representation of the German Bar assumed a binary public/private structure. The case of the legal profession under fascism, Nazism and the Vichy regime is a complex variant on this model. On the one hand, these regimes fuelled the professionalization of the Bar; on the other, they triggered a deprofessionalizing process which involved the collaboration of lawyers with the totalitarian regime. In the case of the German lawyers, deprofessionalization was manifest in total subordination to the Judge—*Führer*, before whom they even requested the death penalty for their clients, instead of acquittal or commutation of the sentence. The new federal system has increased the self-government of the Bar because disciplinary power has been restored to the courts of honour composed of three lawyers. As in other countries good practices from other legal systems are copied in Germany and the lawyers' profession tries to establish similar instruments also in Germany. This is done with the intention to provide suitable and effective solutions for the clients with legal certainty, and to provide high quality legal services.

(vii) Legal Profession in Italy

The law on the bar enacted in 1874 did not establish a precise boundary between the *avvocato* (lawyer) and the *procuratore* (attorney). The *procuratore* was the most important of the two figures and after 1874 formed the core of the law profession, whilst the *avvocato* had monopoly of defence : indeed, prosecutors who had been practising for six years could also defend in the Courts of Assize. The two professions were linked by propaedeuticity, and the 1933 professional law enacted during the facist period definitively established that qualification as *an avvocato* came after six years of exercising the profession of *procuratore*, or on passing a state examination after two years of practice.

The 1933 professional law remained in force until 1997, when two Italian legal professions were merged. Since then, qualification as an *avvocato* has required completion of a two-year postgraduate internship and success in a State examination. The unification of the two professions has removed the territorial constraints which impeded attorneys from exercising the profession outside the appeal court at which they were enrolled. The present position is that *an avvocato* can represent the parties at trial in all courts.

It may thus be summed up that the construction of the modern profession of lawyer came about in Italy within the space of about 60 years and so on the basis of a statist and centralized model. It moved through two main legislative stages : the first was the 1874 law on the profession of *procuratore (attorney) and avvocato* (lawyer) enacted in the post-unification period, and the second was the law of 1933 during the fascist regime. The 1874 law was one of the reforms undertaken to achieve national juridical unification. The new civil code came into effect in 1865, but it was not until nine years later that the traditions in force in the pre-unification States were amalgamated into a single professional law and the resistances of some regional professional groups were overcome. Practice at the Italian Bar after 1874 required possession of a degree in law, success in a theoretical-practical qualifying examination, and enrolment on the professional register. However, fascism did not undertake solely repressive action in regard to the professions, and particularly to the Bar. The law of 1933 was a response to demands for some time advanced by the lawyers. Enrolment on the professional register became compulsory for practice of the profession and to be able to use the title of *avvocato*; professional credentials were raised with the introduction of a more selective qualifying examination; and the numerous clauses were introduced for attorneys to defend the law market against the crisis of the 1930s. The 1933 professional law remained in force until 1997, when the two Italian legal professions were merged. The unification of the two professions has removed all the impediments existing in the profession.

(viii) Legal Profession in Australia

The law is an old and honourable profession, so old that the functions its member perform may be traced into the mists of pre-history where they became confused with the activities of the priests and priestesses and, before the priests, of the witch doctors and the medicine men of primitive tribes. Certainly, of the professions secular and civil and not responsible for religious matters nor directly concerned with the supernatural, the lawyers have a good claim to be the oldest to work with honour for civilised society. The lawyers' work is a necessary part of the administration of society's affairs. The work done by the legal profession is affected directly by the kind of society the profession serves. The legal profession in Australia is of independent nature. It must not be forgotten, however, that there is an increasing need for lawyers, or at least of men trained in lawyer's skill, in many parts of Australian society.

In Australia, many men trained in law are working on lawyers work, not as members of the independent profession, but as civil servants, as court officials, as officers of commercial and other corporations, as officers of important associations such as trade unions, as university teachers in law schools, and so on. Some of these maintain their membership in government, semi-government, or private undertakings and subject themselves to the requirements of the organisation they serve—whether it is the Attorney-General's Department of their Government, the State Saving Bank, the Broken Hill Proprietary Company Limited, the Australian Council of Trade Unions, or the University of Melbourne. These lawyers working as employees in such a way is a product of the increasing complexity of society and of the growing size and complexity of the organized group activities within the society. The number of lawyers so employed is likely to continue to increase. The work they do, however, is almost all matched by work done by lawyers who practise as members of the independent profession.[1]

The independence of the profession has more than one important facet. Its members can act, free of personal embarrassments, to challenge the exercise of governmental powers in a way officials could only rarely act. They can act in the interests of the individuals who are their clients freed from the influence of government or official policies or desires. Further, they can act detached from embarrassments or influence arising from their own interests or beliefs. Johnson puts his finger on one aspect of this independence when he said :

> "A lawyer has no business with the justice or injustice of the cause which be undertakes, unless his client asks his opinion, and then he is bound to give it honestly. The justice or injustice of the cause is to be decided by the judge...."[2]

The Organisation of the Profession in Australia

The history of the legal profession in Australia has been continuously influenced by the profession in England and for a comparatively short period by the development of the profession in the United States of America. Although there have been at times special branches of the profession in England, the structure of the profession for a very long time has been characterized by a broad division between what are not called barrister and solicitors.[3] In the beginning, admission to practice as a member of the legal profession in Australia was in the hands of the Judges appointed to the Supreme Court of New South Wales. Those judges came from the English or Irish professions and rather naturally they brought the traditions of the London or Dublin Bars with them. They carried the English division between barristers and solicitors into Australia.[4]

Barristers in Australia are divided into senior and juniors. The seniors are Queen's Counsel and their seniority has not necessarily anything to do with their age. The main difference between a senior counsel (Q.C.) and a junior are that the senior relinquishes a great deal of detailed work concerned with the preparation and drafting of court documents, which is

1. David Derham, F.K.H. Maher and Louis Waller, An Introduction to Law, (1966), p. 39.
2. Boswell, Tour to the Hebrides (15 August, 1773), p. 178.
3. Supra note 46, at p. 43.
4. *Ibid.*, at p. 44.

performed by the juniors, and the senior cannot be briefed to take charge of a case in court unless a junior is briefed to assist him. The junior is not in any sense a partnership with, nor he is engaged by the senior. On the contrary, the seniors accept the assistance of such junior as the instructing solicitor chooses to brief with him. Barristers who appear in courts other than courts of summary jurisdiction (e.g., Courts of Petty Sessions) appear in wigs and gowns. Queen's Counsel wear a specially designed silk gown, hence the term 'silk' to refer to a Queen's Counsel.[1]

Many of the Barristers-at-law became specialists on particular branches of law and spend as much time (or more) acting as advisors and consultants on difficult matters brought to them by solicitors, as they do arguing contested cases in court. In the superior courts only the Barristers have the right to be heard as representing clients. The solicitors, on the other hand, are those lawyers who take most of the responsibilities for the matters. However, they are not directly concerned with courts matters. They are also involved, of course, in all court matters because they instruct the barristers on behalf of the clients. They may practise alone, but many practise in partnerships with other solicitors.

In all States of Australia there are legal profession associations or societies. In Queensland, New South Wales, Victoria, and Western Australia, where the profession is divided either by law or by convention, there are two separate professional societies. These societies have cast upon them by the law a considerable degree of responsibility for the regulation and control of the professional conduct. The Law Council of Australia provides a national organisation through which all the professional societies carry on activities and pursue common aims at a national level.[2]

Legal Education in Australia

The legal profession in England, as early as the thirteenth century, began a long tradition of professionally organised legal education through the Inns of Court in London. The education provided was, to some extent, designed to protect the common law from continental influences. The Australian colonies adopted the English pattern of legal education as it was emerging in the second half of the nineteenth century. The University of Melbourne began law teaching in 1857 and the University of Sydney in 1858. It was not until the 1930's that any law school in Australia, other than that of the University of Sydney had more than one full-time teaching member. It is only after Second World War that University law schools have been able to develop so as to provide the kinds of academic assistance to students which have long been provided by other faculties.[3]

III. Evaluation and Development of Legal Profession in India

Legal profession is the oldest available profession in society. It is a great and noble calling. It plays an important role in the administration

1. *Ibid.*, at pp. 43-44.
2. *Ibid.*, at p. 45.
3. *Ibid.*, at pp. 49-52.

of justice. It is an excellent device to serve the public pursuit. In other words, public service is the primary aim of legal profession and gaining livelihood is incidental thereto. It aims broadly at understanding the proper functioning of law in the society. At present the legal profession in India is playing a vital role in the socio-economic terrain of the society and has earned a good reputation, even if not on the lines of the American Bar. In order to reach the present position, the legal profession in India had to struggle and was subject to many experiments over a period of time. In 1998 in India alone there were as many as 5 lakh lawyers. 50 Law Universities wherefrom about 25,000 law graduates are coming out every year. It is difficult to say how old is the legal profession in India. Hence, a historical account has to be taken to understand the present state of affairs relating to legal profession.

(i) Legal Profession in Ancient India

The profession of law has been recognised as profession of high calling and of the noblest order since time immemorial. In ancient India, law was understood as a branch of Dharma. However, it is difficult to draw a distinction between secular law and religious ordinances in ancient India. The Vedas were the original source of law, and the Smritis announced the message of the Vedas. *Sadachara, Custom, Nyaya* or *Yukti* were the base of legal processes in ancient India.[1] Dharmasastra (the science of righteousness) could not be modified by any ruler, or indeed any assembly but only by scholars with appropriate qualifications acting in the course of their functions. No king could abrogate *shastra* or render its provisions obsolete.[2] The *Dharmsastras* were written. The judicial advisors were required to give a ruling of *Shastra* on any point at issue. They were trained in the *shastra* by first studying the *Vedas*, later the science of interpretation and logic and finally the *Smriti* and their interpretation at the hands of leading jurists.[3] The institutions of men, learned in the law, who as private agents plead for others in courts is also of ancient origin in India.

There is a diverse opinion with regard to legal profession in ancient India. There are two contradictory approaches with regard to legal profession in India. The first denies the existence of legal profession in ancient India, whereas the other view supports the idea of the existence of legal profession. Those who deny the existence of any such institution are headed by P. Vardachariar, U.C. Sarkar and Ludo Rocher. The supporters are K.P. Jayaswal, P.V. Kane, Julius Jolly, Sir Ashutosh Mukherjee etc. K.P. Jayaswal observes that professional lawyers existed at least from the times of Manu Smriti and perhaps even earlier. It is revealed

1. K.L. Sharma, Sociology of Law and Legal Profession (A Study of Relations between Lawyers and their Clients) 1984, p. 43.
2. J. Duncan M. Derrett, Essays in Classical and Modern Hindu Law (1979), Vol. 2 pp. 64-65; see also Sir Henry Maine, Ancient Law (1972); P. V. Kane, History of Dharamshastra, 5 vols., 1930-1962, and Sunil Deshta, "Legal Profession in India : Retrospect and Prospect", Indian Bar Review, April-Sept., 2001, Vol. XXVIII, Nos. 2 & 3, p. 116.
3. J. Duncan, M. Derrett, op. cit. p. 140.

that legal practitioners existed at least from the time of *Mannava* code. Manu VIII, 169, shows that professional lawyers were already in existence in the time of *Mannava* code. The verse says that the people who suffer for the sake of others are witnesses, sureties and the judges, but that those who are benefited by legislation, are the King ("who gets court-fees"), the creditor ("who gets his decree"), the merchant ("the speculator who supplies money for defence to the defendant and acquires his property in return"), and the Brahmin....the Brahmin advised each party on law....The definition of *vidya-dhana*, with its history going back to the *Dharmasutras*, presupposes the existence of the profession much earlier.[1] The viewpoint of the Indian Dean of Dharamsastra, P.V. Kane is completely different. Concerning the legal profession in ancient times, P.V. Kane observes that no class of persons akin to the modern counsel, solicitors or legal practitioners who wee regulated by the State existed.[2] However, Kane too admits that "this does not preclude the idea that persons well versed in the law of *Smritis* and the procedure of the courts were appointed (*niyukta*) to represent a party and place his case before the Court." There appear to be three reasons to support P.V. Kane on this point. Firstly, he concludes from a story narrated in Asahaya's commentary on the Naradasmriti : "it appears that persons who had studied the *smritis* helped parties in return for a monetary consideration to raise the contention before the Court. Secondly, P.V. Kane's views are based on fee structure for lawyers given in *Sukranitisara.* It speaks as follows :

(i) The lawyer's fee is one-sixteenth of the interest involved, that is value defended or realized;

(ii) Or fees is one-twentieth or one-fortieth, or one-eightieths or one hundred and sixtieth portion, etc.;

(iii) Fees ought to be small in proportion as the amount of value or interest undertrial increases;

(iv) If there be many men who are appointed as pleaders in combination they are to be paid according to some other way;

(v) Only the men who know the *Dharma* should be appointed as pleader (Verses 112-115, *Sukranitisara*).

Dr. P.V. Kane has commented that "the rulers of *Sukra* made a clear approach to the modern institution of the Bar and the fees prescribed by Sukra are similar to those allowed by the Bombay Regulation II of 1827 and by Schedule II to the Bombay Pleader's Act (Bombay Act XVII of 1920).

Thirdly, the need of the lawyer's help is said to have been realized due to the technicalities involved in the court process. It is explicitly clear that "the procedure prescribed by Narada, Brihaspati and Katyayana reaches a very high level of technicalities and skilled help must often have been required in litigation."[3] An equally cautious opinion has been voiced by U.C. Sarkar : "There is no sufficient indication that at the time of the

1. K.P. Jayaswal, Manu and Yajnavalkya : A Comparison and A Contrast (A Treatise on the Basic Hindu Law) 1931, pp. 288-89.
2. P.V. Kane, History of Dharmasastra (1946), p. 288.
3. P.K. Kane, History of Dharmasastra, Vol. III, p. 290.

Smritis there was any legal profession in the modern sense of the term. Persons versed in the science of law could give their opinion for the consideration of the king and his councilors. The system was perhaps most analogous to the *Responsa Prudentium* of the early Romans. The opinions of the legal experts also were not binding on the king. They had no other part to play except giving their opinion."[1] P. Varadachariar observes that "it is not possible to say anything as to the existence of a legal profession in ancient India."[2] P. Vardachariar, the then Advocate General of Madras (1909) disputes K.P. Jayaswal's interpretation of *Vipra* used in Manu VIII, 169 was a "lawyer Brahmin". The other who joined this line of argument denying the existence of legal profession in ancient India is Ludo Rocher, a scholar from the University of Pennsylvania.

Ludo Rocher observes[3] that "the ancient Hindu Legal System was such that a legal profession not only did not exist, but that it was not called for and hardly could have existed." He gives three reasons in support of his argument : (i) that there was no uniform terminology for professional lawyers and no single Dharma texts pay special attention to professional lawyers; (ii) they were not allowed to practise in major criminal cases; and (iii) in Hindu law, there is no need for a class of professional representatives. Administration of justice was the concern of the king, it was a part of Rajadharama. There were no specialists on Dharamasastra, and a fortiori, no specialists or law that were part of it. However, in course of time, certain experts accumulated a very specialized knowledge of one aspect of *Dharma*: *Vivaha* and *Vyavahara*, that is law. At this stage, the nature of legal representation also underwent a certain change. The legal experts worked generally as personal friends for the aggrieved not as, formal pleaders. There is a reference in the texts for Vayavaharajna (a professional expert).

In Kautilya's Arthasastra, there are elaborate discussions about administration of justice; but according to R.P. Kangle[4] a commentator of Arthasastra there is no mention in the Arthasastra about the existence of legal profession. He said, "There is no reference in the text to the professional lawyers. Most probably, such a class did not exist." However, according to Sir Ashutosh Mukherjee, Judge, Calcutta High Court, legal profession existed in ancient India. He observed, "as regard Hindu Courts, it is clear that the legal profession existed in the seventh century of the Christian Era when Asahaya wrote his commentary on the Institutes of Narada.[5] To the same effect are the texts of Vrihaspati, Katayana, Sukra

1. U.C. Sarkar, Epochs in Hindu Legal History (1958), p. 37; Also see Ludo Rocher "Lawyers" in Classical Hindu Law, Indian Bar Review, Vol. 13 (3 & 4) : 1986, pp. 355-56.
2. S. Varadachariar, The Hindu Judicial System (1946), p. 156.
3. Ludo Rocher, "Lawyers in Classical Hindu Law", Law and Society Review, Vol. III Nos. 3 & 4, 1968-69, pp. 383-402.
4. R.P. Kangle, Kautilya's Arthasastra (1963), Part III, p. 220; also see B.K. Goswami, Legal Professions and Its Ethics (1995), p. 8.
5. Joly, Narada Smriti, Book-I, Verse 6, p. 47.

and Vyas quoted by Raghunandan in Vyavahara Tatwa.[1] It appears from their writings that before a person could plead and argue for another in court, he had to establish either that he was a relative or the appointed agent of the party. It was considered dishonourable for a person learned in law to charge fee for tendering legal advice or defending the cause of a litigant in Court. It is also fairly clear from the Buddhist books that the profession of lawyers existed in the first century before the Christian era; they were referred to as 'sellers of law' or 'traders of law'.[2] It may, therefore, be concluded that in ancient India there was a highly developed system of courts. The judges had the access of learned Brahmins but the legal profession as a whole was not developed as it is in modern times. In other words, it is difficult to find out whether in ancient India there existed any class of persons practising law similar to a class which is known as lawyers. Of course, representatives were appointed and had to establish either that he was a relative or the appointed agent of the party. This was simply linked by a personal tie of blood relationship.

(ii) Legal Profession During Medieval Era

Relatively little is known about the operation of legal systems during the period of Muslim political dominance primarily because most disputes were settled outside the courts that were maintained by the ruling powers.[3] The legal system in medieval India, as compared to the ancient period was less elaborate and confined mainly to the towns.[4] Philip B. Calkins, a scholar from University of Chicago observed that "most disputes were settled outside the courts."[5] The government was highly centralized, and the Mughal law enforcement seldom reached the village level. Only in cases where there had been a very considerable breach of peace, or where the revenue of the village had not been paid, were villagers likely to come into contact with Mughal law enforcement officials.[6] One reason why the Mughal legal system was relatively underdeveloped in the rural areas was that the Mughals possessed neither the manpower nor the means of communications that would enable them to staff and operate such a system of courts extensive enough to provide convenient access to the villagers.[7]

W.H. Mooreland observes that there was no group of professional lawyers during the Mughal period.[8] Other historians[9] admit that there were people who functioned as lawyers though their functions and duties were not as clearly defined as during the pre-Mughal and post-Mughal periods. The representatives of the litigants were known as 'Vakils'. However, Vakils

---

1. B.K. Goswami, op. cit., p. 8.
2. *Ibid.*, pp. 8-9.
3. Philip B Calkins, "A Note on Lawyers in Muslim India.", Indian Bar Review, Vol. 13 (3 & 4) : 1986, p. 373.
4. K.L. Sharma, op. cit, p. 45.
5. Supra n. 64 at p. 373.
6. Supra n. 54 at pp. 45-46.
7. Supra n. 66 at 373.
8. W.H. Moreland, India at the Death of Akbar (1962), p. 33.
9. H.H. Wilson, A., C. Gangully and N.D. Basu, A Glossary of Judicial and Revenue Terms (1940).

were rather representatives of parties involved in a deal than legal advisors. In fact, they were 'educated' intermediaries for a particular party or group who paid them some fee or .commission to effect a transaction. The court of the native administrations concerned determined who should be allowed to appear as Vakil in a Zila Court.[1] The Vakils acted more as agents for principals than the lawyers. Justice seldom prevailed because there were fewer laws, lawyers and legal procedures and bribery was a common feature.[2] Even though some authors[3] have sought to emphasize that a high standard was expected of Vakils in consonance of the dictum of Omar, the second Caliph of Islam, who said that the practice of law was to be in good faith, and to be pursued with sincerity, yet the overall picture of the actual working of the Vakils had little semblance with the legal profession of the day. Thus, there were both advantages and disadvantages, accruing from the legal system of medieval India, for the upper sections of the society as only they had recourse to the Mughal Courts, or could hire representatives to protect their interests. The job of the vakil was to negotiate with equals or superiors of his employer, in order to obtain a desired goal, such as trading privileges, a reduction of the revenue demand, a military alliance, or a favourable decision in a Civil or Criminal Court of law. In many cases, a vakil was a gatherer of information. Thus, most important nobles, landholders, and foreign trading companies employed vakils whose job was to attend the Court of the Governor of the Province in which they were situated (or perhaps even the emperor's court) in order to collect information that might be useful as well as to represent the interests of their employers when disputes between nobles arose, or when a favour from the Governor was needed.

There were, however, some vakils who were courtroom lawyers, although not as many as there were in contemporary Europe. French traveler, Francois Bernier remarked that "they have fewer lawyers and fewer law suits, and those few are more speedily decided".

(iii) Legal Profession During British Regime

The modern legal profession as it exists today has emerged from the constitution of courts and legislative enactments initiated by the British in India. However, it is notable that in early days of the British period the legal profession was not paid due attention and it was not well organised. Truly speaking, the East India Company was not interested in organizing the legal profession. There was no uniform judicial system in the early settlements of East India Company. It is said that the history of the legal profession in India begins with the establishment of first British Court in Bombay in 1672 by Governor Gerald Aungier. George Wilcox was appointed first Attorney General. Wilcox made rules for parties to be represented by

1. Per Courts Trotter, J. in *Namberumal Chetty* v. *M.P. Narasimhachari*, (1916) 37 IC 699.
2. Supra n. 54 at p. 46.
3. L.M. Singhvi,"The Legal Profession in India and its Social Responsibilities, IBR (1969), Vol. 9, p. 6. See also Mohamad Bashir Ahmad, The Administration of Justice (1st edn.) : p. 1.

attorneys. The term for a lawyer was Vakil. It was the term also used in Muslim India in the sense of an agent or ambassador who represented his principal for varied reasons.[1] Even a zamindar employed Vakil for clearing an arrears of revenue or other miscellaneous deeds. Thus, the term Vakil did not specify the class of legal practitioner. They were neither licensed nor trained for the practice of law though the British courts realized their importance for purposes of interpreting the local customs and assisting the litigants in a variety of para-legal functions. The character of the person and his competence in the English language were the only qualifications that the British Courts felt necessary to enable one to become a Vakil.[2] The Charter of 1726 introduced Royal Courts in India but did not make provision for the regulations of the legal practitioners. There was no provisions for the legal training. The legal profession was not organized. Many persons having no knowledge of law were practising. The establishment of the Supreme Court at Calcutta in 1773 can be considered as the beginning of modern legal profession in India. Clause II of the Charter of 1773 authorised the Supreme Court of Judicature to approve, admit and enrol such and so many advocates and attorneys at law as it deemed necessary to appear and plead and act for the suitors of the said court. The advocates and attorneys eligible for practice were only to be the British barristers and solicitors. As M. P. Jain[3] points out, the term 'Advocate' at that time extended only to the English and Irish barristers and the members of the faculty of advocates in Scotland. The expression 'attorney' then meant only the British attorneys or solicitors. The language of the courts was English. Indians were kept out of the profession. Clause 12 authorised the Supreme Court to settle a table of fees to be allowed to such sheriff, and all other officers, clerks and attornies for all and every part of the business to be done by them. The clause further directed that the table of fee shall be hung up on some conspicuous part of the hall, and shall be publicly holden. However, the position of the Company's Courts in Mofussil area was different. There the local Vakils who were working in the local courts before the company took over continued to work even after. But there was no proper organization cadre or code for these lawyers till Lord Cornwallis in 1793 by Regulation VII authorised the Sadar Diwani Adalat. A schedule for moderate fee to be charged by the pleaders was also provided beyond which the pleaders could not charge as their fee. The pleaders were entitled to a retainer fee of four annas and a fixed amount of remuneration, proportionate to the valuation of the suit. The litigants executed a Vakalatnama in favour of the pleader binding himself by all acts which the pleader might do on his behalf during the pendency of the suit. The Regulation prohibited them from demanding or accepting from their clients any sum of money or reward excepting the authorised fees for pleading their causes. The Vakils attached to one court were not allowed to plead in another court without the prior sanction of the Sadar Diwani

1. B.B. Misra, The Indian Middle Classes (1961), pp. 162-63.
2. *Ibid.*.
3. M.P. Jain, Outlines of Indian Legal History (1990), p. 669; see also C.L. Anand, Professional Ethics of Bar (1987), p. 3.

Adalat. For being absent without cause, pleaders could be fined and dismissed.[1]

Subsequent legislation concerning the profession followed the general pattern laid down in 1793. The rather lengthy and detailed Regulation of 1814 extended the provisions for licensing, discipline and removal of Vakils to the Provincial Courts. Rules concerning fees, practice, government leaders and malpractice were considerably more detailed than before. The strength of barristers was 9 in 1793 including the Attorney-General, and in 1861 it was 32 advocates and 60 attorneys/proctors or solicitors of whom only four were Indians. In Bombay by 1861 there were 13 advocates and 30 solicitors. The new sections of the 1814 Regulations indicate the kind of problems the courts were having with this rising profession. Section VIII stipulated that pleaders must take precaution to ascertain the real names of parties giving Vakalatnama and would be liable for dismissal if a Vakalatnama under fictitious name were accepted. Further, more, the pleader was warned to study plaints before they were filed and make sure that groundless, irrelevant points were not included, that useless witnesses were not summoned and that all exhibits were examined previous to being filed. If a Vakil continued, after warning to produce irrelevant exhibits or witnesses he was to be fined Rs. 20/- or made to forfeit his fee.[2]

The legal profession became distinct in 1833 when a Law Commission was appointed to ascertain and codify the laws of India. This was done to disassociate law and religion. Law was made a civil institution, not limited to a small priestly order but open to all interested persons regardless of caste or creed.[3] This was a significant and radical change in the early phase of the growth of legal profession in India. It was an attack on the monopoly of the traditional legal pundits. In 1835, the study of law was accepted as a separate faculty. Law education started first at Calcutta and then subsequently at Madras and Bombay. The next great step taken in the evolution of Indian Bar was the Legal Practitioners Act, 1846 which regulated the position not only of Vakils but also of barristers. It was an all India legislation for amending the law regarding the appointment and remuneration of pleaders in the Courts of East India Company. It liberalized payment of fees to pleaders by making a matter of settlement between clients and pleaders though the agreed amount was to be specified in the Vakalatnama. The Act also allowed for the first time attorneys and barristers to plead in any of the Sadar Courts of the East India Company. So far the Vakils were only allowed to practice civil suits, but in 1850 with the establishment of criminal courts they were also permitted to take up criminal matters.[4]

The next important statute was the Legal Practitioners Act of 1853

1. N.R. Madhva Menon, "Bar Council and Management of Legal Profession," Indian Bar Review, Vol. 13 (3 & 4), : 1980 pp. 419-20. Also see, Samuel Schmittheener, "A Sketch of the Development of the Legal Profession in India," Indian Bar Review, Vol. 13 (3 & 4) : 1986, pp. 318-19.
2. Samuel Schmittheener, op. cit., pp. 319-20.
3. B.B. Misra, op. cit., p. 172.
4. Supra n 54 at p. 48.

which provided that a pleader was not bound to attend the court except at the hearing of a case in which he was employed. While the barristers and attorneys could practice in the Supreme Courts in Presidency Towns and in Sadar Courts, the Indian Vakils and pleaders could not appear before the Supreme Court.

The end of the East India Company's rule and the setting up of a unified judiciary under the Indian High Courts Act of 1861 marked the beginning of a new phase in the development of legal profession in India. If the earlier phase only succeeded in creating a class of people to act as intermediaries between the courts and the litigants, the second phase laid the foundation for the evolution of an enlightened group of professionals assisting the courts in the delivery of justice. The passage of laws such as Civil Procedure Code, Criminal Procedure Code and Evidence Act as well as the establishment of law education in the Indian Universities during the period facilitated the process of the evolution of the organized Indian Bar. In 1865 an Act known as Pleaders *Mukhtars* and Revenue Agents Act was enacted to bring within its scope two categories of persons, namely, Mukhtars and Revenue Agents, who were practising law without any check or control. The *Mukhtars* were a class of people who acted as intermediaries between the client and the pleaders and for this they got payment either from the clients or the pleaders or sometimes from both. They were ignorant of law. Similarly, some people were practising in revenue courts as agents of the people who approached the Revenue Courts. It was found expedient not to allow these two classes of people to continue their activities without any check. So this Act was made. They were to get certificates from the Board of Revenue.

The next important Act was the Legal Practitioners Act, 1879, which brought all categories of legal practitioners in the High Court. The Act further empowered advocates, Vakils and attorneys of the High Courts to practise their profession in all the subordinate Courts to enrol lawyers for different courts and also make disciplinary proceedings against them. It authorised all High Courts other than the three Chartered High Courts to make rules, with the prior sanction of the respective provincial governments with respect to the qualifications and admissions of proper persons to be the advocates and Vakils in the Courts. Power to dismiss the advocates, after giving them an opportunity to defend was also given by these High Courts. An important provision of the Act which continues to exist even now was Section 36 which empowered the District Judges, Session Judges, District Magistrates, Collector and the Chief Judge of a Presidency small cause court to publish a list of touts who could be debarred from entering the premises of the courts and also be subjected to fine and imprisonment.[1]

Up to 1900, the legal profession was dominated by the Europeans. However, by the beginning of the century it became Indian in composition even in the highest ranks.[2] Among the prominent Vakils were Munshi Jawala Prashad, Pundit Moti Lal Nehru, Pandit Madan Mohan Malviya

1. Section 36 of the Legal Practitioners Act, 1879.
2. B.B. Mishra, op. cit., pp. 320-22.

and Sir T.B. Sapru, etc. Most of them were Hindus. Besides the advocates and Vakils, there were attorneys, solicitors, pleaders and Mukhtars. In 1923, the government of India set up the Indian Bar Committee under the Chairmanship of a retired Chief Justice Sir Edward Chamier of Patna High Court and so the committee was also known as Chamier Committee. This Committee was asked to report on : (i) the possibility of constituting an all India Bar, whether on an all India or provincial basis and its structure, etc; (ii) the possibility of removal of distinction between advocates or barristers and Vakils. On the first point, the Committee reported that the Constitution of an All India Bar was not possible, alternatively it recommended for establishment of a Bar Council for each High Court. On the second point the Committee could not make any specific recommendation because of sharp division among its members. The Chamier Committee submitted its report in 1924 and on its recommendation the Indian Bar Council Act, 1926 was passed with a view to consolidating and amending the law relating to legal practitioners. The Act introduced *inter alia* separate provisions for advocates and separate Bar Councils for every High Court. The purpose of the Act was to give effect to the recommendations of the Chamier Committee. However, no autonomous All India bar was formed. The Act, as amended in 1927, directs High Courts to prepare and maintain a roll of Advocates of the High Courts and prescribes the order of seniority recommended by the Chamier Committee. Attorneys were not included in this list. The amended Act authorises the Bar Council, with the prior permission of the High Court, to make rules to regulate the admission of persons to be advocates of the High Court without limiting the powers of the High Courts to refuse admission at its discretion. The High Court could reprimand, suspend, or remove from practice lawyers on being guilty of professional or other misconduct. The function of the Bar Council was of advisory nature and High Courts, in effect, had all the powers. The Britishers also passed in 1926 another important statute of legal practitioners, namely, the Legal Practitioners Fees Act. It conferred the right on a legal practitioner to sue for his fees under the agreement or if no fee had been settled, for a fee computed in accordance with the law in force as to the calculation of the costs. It also defined liability of legal practitioner to be sued in respect of negligence in the discharge of his professional duties.

In 1929, the distinction between the advocates was removed. Later the qualification of 10 years' experience to practice on the original side was also removed to abolish all distinctions among legal practitioners.

(iv) Legal Profession and Emerging Trends in Independent India

We witness a change in legal profession that Bar Council Act, 1926 and many other developments thereafter could not satisfy the aspiration of the legal profession and the demand for an "autonomous and unified" All India Bar was realised on the basis of a committee which was constituted in 1951 under the Chairmanship of Justice S.R. Das of the Supreme Court. The committee finalised and submitted its report in 1953. It recommended creation of an All India Bar with common roll of all advocates and also the Bar Councils for States with larger autonomy but it did not feel the need for a separate Bar Council for the Supreme Court.

In 1953, the total number of legal practitioners in India besides revenue agents and income-tax practitioners were 67,608 divided into following categories:

Sr. Advocates of the Supreme Court	316
Other Advocates of the Supreme Court	1,019
Agents enrolled in the Supreme Court	146
Advocates on the rolls of the High Courts	26,495
Vakils (in West Bengal, Saurashtra and Bhopal)	1,173
Pleaders	38,359
Mukhtars (in Bihar, Assam, Orissa, Punjab, U.P., West Bengal and Madhya Bharat)	6,330

Similarly, the Fifth Law Commission in its Fourteenth Report submitted in 1958, recommended for establishment of a United All India Bar. The Commission favoured the recommendation of the non-graduates pleaders or Mukhtars. It also recommended for the division of Bar into senior advocates and advocates. In 1959, the Legal Practitioner's Bill incorporating the recommendations was introduced in Parliament. To give effect to the recommendations of All India Bar Committee, the Parliament enacted the Advocates Act, 1961. The Act amended and codified the law relating to legal practitioners and provided for constitution of an All India Bar. The complete control and jurisdiction regarding enrolment of advocates and discipline of advocates, which had all along been with the High Courts, stood transferred to the Bar Council of India and the State Bar Councils. The Bar Councils have become completely autonomous bodies with elected representatives of advocates. Each State Bar Council sends a representative to the Bar Council of India.

The Act which extends to the whole of India provides a federal structure for legal profession with one category of lawyers known as advocates. It provides for a number of State Bar Councils and a Bar Council of India. An advocate is initially enrolled with the State Bar Council and a common roll of all the advocates in the country is maintained by the Bar Council of India. No advocate can get himself enrolled with more than one State Bar Council, though certainly he can get himself transferred from the State Bar Council to another and is also entitled to appear before any Court or Tribunal throughout the country. The State Bar Councils are named after their States though there are few Bar Councils common to two or more states. A State Bar Council consists of 15 to 25 members (depending upon the total number of advocates enrolled with that Bar Council) elected from amongst advocates on the electoral roll of that Bar Council. The Bar Councils are autonomous bodies. The All India Bar Councils known as the Bar Council of India consists of the Attorney General of India, the Solicitor General of India and one member elected by each State Bar Council from amongst its members. In 1976, during emergency, the Act was amended by Act 107 of 1976 to accommodate one representative of the Central Government in the Bar Council. But in 1977 by the Amendment Act 38 of 1977 the said provision was repealed. The Indian Bar is the second largest in the world with 1,82,000 advocates on the rolls as of 1st January, 1979. In absolute terms India has a very large profession second only to the United States of America comprising over 3,00,000 advocates on the rolls in 1988. In 1998, in India alone there were as many as 5 lakh lawyers, 50 Law Universities where from about 25,000 law graduates are coming out every year. As per the latest statistics made available by the Bar Council of India there are 8,58,294 advocates enrolled in India as on 31st December, 2004.

The Bar Council of India is a body corporate. The functions of the Council among others are : to lay down the standard of professional conduct and etiquette of the advocates; to lay down procedure to be followed by the Disciplinary Committee of the Bar Council of India and also the Disciplinary Committees of the State Bar Councils; to safeguard the rights, privileges and interest of the advocates; to promote legal education; to recognise degrees in law to qualify for enrolment of advocates, to recognise on reciprocal basis foreign qualifications in law for admission as advocate under the Advocates Act; to hold seminars, etc; to organise legal aid for the poor, etc.

Even though India has an organised Bar and disciplinary authorities to regulate the profession, we cannot run away from the reality that the reputation of the Bar is today at the lowest ebb. There are numerous reasons for the same. The main reason is the deviant behaviour from the accepted standards of professional ethics. But this deviant behaviour is mostly due to actual ignorance of ethical requirements. Further, there is practically no limit to the fees which a lawyer may charge to his client. If a litigant wants to engage one of the top most lawyers, he would have to pay exorbitant fees which may be demanded by the lawyer. This directly leads to inequality in the quality of legal representation as between the rich and the poor. Professional misbehaviour can be minimized through self-policing and legal education. The Bar Councils and Associations through its disciplinary committees have great responsibility in preserving the nobility and honour of the profession. Unless the lawyer observes the highest standards of professional ethics he cannot earn the respect of the community, nor do his peers in the profession accept him as an outstanding lawyer. The present declining standards of lawyers unless properly checked is likely to lead to a stage where the system will be found wrecked from within before it is wrecked from outside. Hence, the need of the hour is that the members of the profession examine and take corrective measures in time.

2

ADMISSION AND ENROLMENT OF ADVOCATES

I. Introduction

After independence, with the coming into force of the Constitution in 1950 and the establishment of a Supreme Court for India the need for an All India Bar was stressed by the legal fraternity. The Union Government accordingly set up an All India Bar Committee under the Chairmanship of Justice S.R. Das of the Supreme Court of India. The Committee considered at length the question of the constitution and powers of the State Bar Councils and the All India Bar Council and made detailed recommendations in 1953 including the following—

(A) Establishment of an All India Bar Council and a Common Roll of Advocates;

(B) Advocate on Common Roll to have a right to practice in any part of the country and in any court, including Supreme Court;

(C) Integration of Bar into a single class of legal practitioners known as advocates;

(D) Prescription of a uniform qualification for admission of persons as advocates;

(E) The division of advocates into seniors and other advocates based on merit, and

(F) The creation of autonomous Bar Council one for the whole of the India and the other for each State.

The Committee's recommendations got strength by the endorsement and approval of its recommendations by the Law Commission of India in 1953 which was presided over by the eminent jurist M.C. Setalvad, the then Attorney General of India. Further, the Law Commission of India in its Fourteenth Report on the Reform of Judicial Administration approved of the recommendations for the creation of a unified All India Bar as well as the establishment, composition and function of the State and All India Bar Councils. As a result of the recommendations, the Legal Practitioners Bill, 1959 was introduced in the Lok Sabha on November 19, 1959 with a view to implement the recommendations of the All India Bar Committee and of the Law Commission's 14th Report. When the Bill came to be passed, its name was changed from the Legal Practitioners Bill to the Advocates Act and was passed in the year 1961 by the Parliament. It received the assent of the President on 19th May, 1961 and came into force w.e.f. December 12, 1962 which gave statutory recognition to the long cherished necessity of the legal profession for its integration on all India basis. It has been enacted for the purpose of amending and consolidating the law relating to legal practitioners and also for providing the constitution of Bar Council and an All India Bar. The Act established an All India Bar and a common roll of Advocates. An Advocate on the common rolls has the right to practise in all Courts in India from the highest to the lowest. The Bar has been integrated into a single class of legal practitioners known as Advocates.

Section 1 of the Act provides that it extends to the whole of India. Section 2 of the Act provides definition of certain terms and it provides that, unless the context otherwise requires—

(a) "advocate" means an advocate entered in any rolls under the provisions of this Act;

(b) "appointed day" means the day on which certain provisions came into effect;

(c) ....[1]

(d) "Bar Council" means a Bar Council constituted under this Act;

(e) "Bar Council of India" means the Bar Council constituted under Section 4 for territories to which this Act extends;

(f) ......[2]

(g) "High Court" except in sub-section (a) and sub-section (1-A)[3] of Section 34 and in Sections 42 and 43 does not include a court of Judicial Commissioner, and in relation to a State Bar Council means—

(i) in the case of a Bar Council constituted for a State or for a State and one or more Union Territories, the High Court for the State;

(ii) in the case of the Bar Council constituted for Delhi, the High Court of Delhi;

(h) "Law graduate" means a person who has obtained a bachelor's degree in law from any University established by law in India;

(i) "Legal Practitioners" means an advocate or Vakil[4] of any High Court, a pleader, mukhtar or revenue agent;

(j) "Prescribed" means prescribed by rules made under this Act;

(k) "Roll" means a roll of advocates prepared and maintained under this Act;

(l) "State" does not include a Union Territory;

(m) "State Bar Council" means a Bar Council constituted under Section 3;

1. Omitted by Act 107 of 1976, Section 2 (w.e.f. 31.1.1974).
2. Omitted by Act 60 of 1973, Section 3 (w.e.f. 31.1.1974).
3. Inserted by Section 3 (w.e.f. 31.1.1974).
4. Substituted by Act 107 of 1976, Section 2(ii).

(n) "State Roll" means a roll of advocates prepared and maintained by a State Bar Council under Section 17.

Provisions have been made under Section 3 of the Advocates Act, 1961 for the establishment of a Bar Council in each State. Similarly, under Section 4 of the Act, it has been provided that there shall be a Bar Council for the territories to which this Act extends, to be known as Bar Council of India. Further, under Section 5, every Bar Council shall be body corporate having perpetual succession and a common seal, with power to acquire and hold property, both movable and immovable, and to contract, and may by the name by which it is known sue and be sued. Under Section 6, various functions of State Bar Councils, have been described, which includes to admit persons as advocates on its roll, to prepare and maintain such rolls, to entertain and determine cases of misconduct against advocates on its roll, to promote and support law reforms, to promote legal education in consultation with the Universities, and to provide legal aid to the poor in prescribed manner, etc. Under Section 7, functions of the Bar Council of India have been enumerated, which include, to lay down standards of professional conduct and etiquette for advocates, to lay down procedure to be followed by its Disciplinary Committee and Disciplinary Committee of each State Bar Council, to safeguard the rights, privileges and interests of advocates and promote and support law reforms, to exercise general supervision and control over State Bar Councils, to promote legal education and lay down standards of such education in consultation with the Universities whose degree in law shall be a qualification for enrolment of an advocate. Any advocate may, with his consent, be designated as a Senior Advocate if the Supreme Court or a High Court is of the opinion that by virtue of his ability, experience and standing at the Bar, he deserves such distinction.

The Advocates Act, 1961, has marked the beginning of a new era in the history of legal profession by vesting largely in the Bar Councils the power and the jurisdiction which the courts till then exercised, by fulfilling the aspirations of those who had been demanding an All India Bar and effecting a unification of the Bar in India, by the creation of a single class of practitioners with power to practise in all the Courts and bound by rules made and a code laid down by their own bodies to which the members could resort to for the protection of their rights, interests and privileges.

II. Admission and Enrolment of Advocates

Chapter III of the Advocates Act, 1961 makes provisions for the admission and enrolment of Advocates. This chapter consists of Sections 16 to 28 of the Act. An application for admission as an advocate shall be made to the State Bar Council within whose jurisdiction the applicant proposes to practise. A certificate of enrolment will be issued to every person whose name is entered in the roll of Advocates. But no person shall be admitted as an advocate—

(a) if he is convicted of an offence involving moral turpitude;

(b) if he is convicted of an offence under the provisions of the

Untouchability Offences Act, 1955 (Sec. 24-A).

(c) If he has been dismissed or removed from the employment or office under the State on any charge of moral turpitude.

(i) Senior and other Advocates

Section 16 provides for division of the Bar into senior advocates and other advocates.[1] According to this Section an advocate may, with his consent be designated as senior advocate, if the Supreme Court or a High Court is of the opinion that by virtue of his ability, standing at the Bar or special knowledge or experience in law, he is deserving of such distinction.[2] Hence, the status of a senior advocate will be conferred by Supreme Court or a High Court on merits only. A senior advocate is entitled to preference in audience and little more respect because of distinction. Designating Senior Advocate is therefore a rare privilege recognizing merits and standing of an advocate. By virtue of the pre-eminence which senior counsels enjoy in the profession, they not only carry greater responsibilities but also act as a model to junior members of the profession. A Senior Advocate will be prohibited from accepting certain kinds of minor legal works. Order IV, Rule 7 of the Supreme Court Rules, 1950 lays down that a senior advocate shall not draw pleadings, affidavits, advice on evidence, statement of cases or do any drafting work of an analogous kind in any court. This shall not, however, apply to settling any such matters in consultation with a junior. The classification of advocates under the Bar Council of Delhi Rules into those having more than ten years' standing and others is not inconsistent with classification under Section 16.

A senior advocate cannot appear without a junior in a case; he cannot act, he can only plead. A senior counsel more or less occupies a position akin to a Queen's Counsel in England next after the Attorney-General and the Solicitor-General.[3] It is an honour and privilege on advocates of standing and experience by the Supreme Court.[4] They, thus, become leading counsel, and take precedence on all counsels not having that rank. Rules under Section 16(3) and 49(1) (g) of the Advocates Act framed by the Bar Council of India regarding Senior Advocates provide that senior advocates shall, in the matter of their practise of the profession of law mentioned in Section 30 of the Act be subject to following restrictions—

(a) A senior advocate shall not file a vakalatnama or act in any court or tribunal or before any person or other authority mentioned in Section 30 of the Act or to do any act other than pleading required or authorised by law to be done by a party in such court, tribunal or before any person or other authority mentioned in the said Section either in person or by his recognised agent or by an advocate or any attorney on his behalf.

(b) (i) A Senior Advocate shall not appear without an Advocate on Record in the Supreme Court or without an Advocate in Part II

1. Advocates Act, 1961, Section 16(1).
2. *Ibid.*, Section 16(2).
3. Prafulla C. Pant, 'Sanjiva Row's the Advocates Act, 1961, (1995), p. 70.
4. *E.S. Reddi* v. *Chief Secretary, Govt of A.P.*, A.I.R. 1987 S.C. 1550.

of the State roll in any Court, or Tribunal, or before any person or other authorities mentioned in Section 30 of the Act. (ii) Where a Senior Advocate has been engaged prior to the coming into force of the rule in this chapter, he shall not continue thereafter unless an Advocate in Part II of the State Roll is engaged along with him: Provided that a Senior Advocate may continue to appear without an advocate in Part II of the State roll in cases in which he had been briefed to appear for the prosecution or the defence in a criminal case, if he was so briefed before he is designated as a Senior Advocate or before coming into operation of the rules in this chapter, as the case may be.

(c) He shall not accept instructions to draft pleadings or affidavits, advise on evidence or to do any drafting work of an analogous kind in any Court or Tribunal, or before any person or other authority mentioned in Section 30 of the Act or undertake conveyancing work of any kind whatsoever. This restriction, however, shall not be extended in settling any such matter as aforesaid in consultation with an Advocate in Part II of the State roll.

(d) A Senior Advocate shall, however, be free to make confession or give undertakings in the course of arguments on behalf of his client on instructions from the junior Advocate.

(e) He shall not accept directly from a client any brief or instructions to appear in any Court or Tribunal, or before any person or other authority in India.

(f) A Senior Advocate who had acted as an Advocate (Junior) in a case, shall not after he has been designated as a Senior Advocate advise on grounds of Appeal in a Court of Appeal or in the Supreme Court, except with an Advocate as aforesaid.

(g) A Senior Advocate may in recognition of the services rendered by an Advocate in Part II of the State roll appearing in any matter pay him a fee which he considers reasonable.

The rules also provide that a Senior Advocate who had acted as an Advocate (Junior) in a case cannot advise on grounds of appeal in a Court of Appeal or in a Supreme Court after he has been designated as a Senior Advocate, except with an advocate as aforesaid. It has also been provided that a Senior Advocate shall not accept directly from a client any brief or instructions to appear in any court or tribunal or before any person or other authority in India.

Section 24 of the Advocates Act, 1961 deals with the persons who may be admitted as Advocates on a State roll. It reads as under—

(1) Subject to the provisions of this Act, and the rules made thereunder, a person shall be qualified to be admitted as an Advocate on a State roll, if he fulfils the following conditions, namely—

(a) he is a citizen of India—

Provided that subject to the other provisions contained in

this Act, a national of any other country may be admitted as an advocate on a State roll, if citizens of India, duly qualified, are permitted to practice law in that other country—

(b) he has completed the age of 21 years;

(c) he has obtained a degree in law

(i) before the 12th day of March, 1967, from any University in the territory of India; or

(ii) before the 15th day of August, 1947, from any University in any area which was comprised before that date within India as defined by the Government of India Act, 1935; or

(iii) after 12th day of March, 1967, save as provided in sub-clause (iii) (a), after undergoing a three-year course of study in law from any reputed University in India which is recognized for the purposes of this Act by the Bar Council of India; or

(iii-a) after undergoing a course of study in law, the duration of which is not less than two academic years commencing from the academic year 1967-68, or any earlier academic from any University in India which is recognised for the purposes of this Act by the Bar Council of India; or

(iv) in any other case, from any University outside the territory of India, if the degree is recognised for the purposes of this Act by the Bar Council of India; or he is the barrister and is called to the Bar on or before the 31st day of December, 1967; or has passed the articles clerk's examination or any other examination specified by the High Court at Bombay or Calcutta for enrolment as an attorney of that High Court; or has obtained such other foreign qualification in law as is recognised by the Bar Council of India, for the purpose of admission as an advocate under this Act—

(d) (*********)

(e) he fulfils such other conditions as may be specified in the rules made by the State Bar Council under this chapter;

(f) he has paid, in respect of the enrolment, stamp duty, if any, chargeable under the Indian Stamp Act, 1899 (2 of 1899) and as enrolment fee payable to the State Bar Council (six hundred rupees and to the Bar Council of India, one hundred and fifty rupees by way of a bank draft drawn in favour of that council)—

Provided that where such person is a member of the Scheduled Castes and the Scheduled Tribes and enrolment fee payable by him to the State Bar Council shall be one hundred rupees and to the Bar Council of India, twenty five rupees.

Enrolment fee payable to the State Bar Council was Rs. 250/- in addition to Stamp Duty of any, under the Stamp Act, 1899. The Advocates (Amendment) Act, 1993 has raised the fee from Rs. 250/- to Rs. 750/- (Rs. 600/- payable to the State Bar Council and Rs. 150/- payable to the Bar Council of India). The fee to be paid to the Bar Council of India is Rs. 150/- in general category and Rs. 25/- in SC/ST candidates. Recently, the Himachal Pradesh State Bar Council has increased the fee to Rs. 2355/- in case of general category candidates and Rs. 1855/- in case of SC/ST candidates. This fee is exclusive to the fee paid to Bar Council of India. The fee by the Himachal Pradesh State Bar Council is taken in cash. The fee is charged as enrolment fee, Advocates Welfare Fund fee. cost of enrolment form, identity card and correspondents charges, etc.

Explanation.—For the purposes of this sub-section, a person shall be deemed to have obtained a degree in law from a University in India on the date on which the result of the examination for the degree are published by the University at its notice board or otherwise declaring him to have passed that examination.

(2) Notwithstanding anything contained in sub-section (1), a vakil or a pleader who is a law graduate may be admitted as an advocate on a State roll if he—

(a) makes an application for such enrolment in accordance with the provisions of this Act, not later than two years from the appointed days and

(b) fulfils the conditions specified in clauses (a), (b), (e) and (f) of sub-section (1).

(3) Notwithstanding anything contained in sub-section (1), a person who—

(a) (****) has, for at least three years, been vakil or a pleader or a mukhtar, or was entitled at any time to be enrolled under any law (***) as an advocate of a High Court (including a High Court of a former part B State) or of a court of a judicial Commissioner in any Union territory; or

(aa) before the 1st day of December, 1961, was entitled otherwise than as an advocate to practise the profession of law (whether by way of pleading or acting or both by virtue of the provisions of any law, or who would have been entitled had he not been in public service of the said date; or)

(b) (*****)

(c) Before the 1st day of April,1937, has been an advocate of any High Court in any area which was comprised within Burma as defined in the Government of India Act; or

(d) is entitled to be enrolled as an advocate under any rule made by the Bar Council of India in this behalf, may be admitted as an advocate on a State roll if he—

(i) makes an application for such enrolment in accordance with provisions of this Act; and

(ii) fulfils the conditions specified in clauses (a), (d), (e) and (f) of sub-section (1)

(4) (*****)

(ii) Rolls of Advocates

The legal profession in India is not open to every person. It is open only to those who get themselves enrolled as advocates in accordance with the provisions of the Advocates Act, 1961 and the Bar Council of India Rules. The law that governs the admission and enrolment is contained in the Advocates Act, 1961. Chapter III of the Act deals with "admission and enrolment of advocates" in Sections 16 to 28.

According to Section 17, every State Bar Council shall prepare and maintain a roll of advocates of all persons who were already entered as Advocates on the roll of any High Court under the Indian Bar Council Act, 1926, immediately before the appointed day (including all persons, being citizens of India, who before the 15th day of August, 1947, were enrolled as Advocates under the said Act in any area which before the said date was comprised within India as defined in Govt. of India Act, 1935, and who at any time) express an intention in the prescribed manner to practise within the jurisdiction of the Bar Council and all other persons who are admitted to be advocates on the roll of the State Bar Council under the Advocates Act, 1961 on or after the appointed day.

Each such roll of advocates shall consist of two parts, the first part containing the names and addresses of senior advocates and the second part, the names and addresses of other advocates in order of their seniority. Entries in each part of the roll of advocates shall be made in the order of seniority. The section lays down certain rules for determining such seniority. The seniority of an Advocate referred to in clause (a) of sub-section (1) shall be determined in accordance with his date of enrolment and the Bar Council Act, 1926, provided that the seniority of a vakil, pleader or an attorney who was enrolled as an Advocate after that day shall be determined in accordance with the date of his entry in the register of vakils, pleaders or attorneys. The seniority of any person who as a senior advocate of the Supreme Court immediately before the appointed day shall be determined in accordance with such principles as the Bar Council of India may specify. The seniority of any other person who is enrolled as a Senior Advocate or is admitted as an Advocate under this Act on or after the appointed day shall be determined to the date of such enrolment or admission, as the case may be. Section 17(4) makes it abundantly clear that no person shall be enrolled as an advocate in the roll of more than one State Bar Council. The seniority among attorneys shall be determined in accordance with the dates of enrolment as attorney. Subject to the provisions of the Advocates Act, and the rules made thereunder advocates shall be the only class of persons entitled to practice the profession of law. Thus, the Act provides for a unified Bar for the whole of India and the same has been done in response to a demand by the legal profession for unification of the Bar. However, it should be remembered that the existing vakils, pleaders, attorneys, mukhtars and agents can continue to practice law, as their right to practice law has been saved by Section 55 of the Act.

Section 18 of the Advocates Act, 1961 permits that an advocate on the roll of any State Bar Council may, by application in the prescribed form to the Bar Council of India, get a transfer of his name to the roll of any other Bar Council without loss of seniority. In **Rameshwar Dayal** v. **Union of India**,[1] it was held that the period of practice in Lahore High Court before partition can be counted in the required period of seven years for eligibility for appointment as District Judge. This section requires that that any advocate desirous of having his name transferred must make an application in the prescribed form to the Bar Council of India and on the receipt of such application the Bar Council of India shall direct that his name be removed from the roll from which it is sought to be removed and entered in the roll of the other State Bar Council where the advocate intends to practise. No fee is chargeable for the transfer of name from one State roll to another. In **re Mannava Venkata Rao**,[2] it was held that an advocate enrolled in Mysore High Court who after reorganization of State, applied for enrolment in Andhra Pradesh was entitled to exemption from payment of stamp duty. But the applications of advocates against whom any disciplinary proceeding is pending or which are not *bona fide* will be rejected.

Section 19 of the Advocates Act requires the State Bar Council to send the copies of rolls of advocates to the Bar Council of India. It requires that State Bar Councils must send to the Bar Council of India an authenticated copy of the roll of advocates prepared by them for the first time under this Act. Thereafter it is their duty to communicate the Bar Council of India all alterations in, and additions to, any such roll, as soon as the same have been made.

Hence, it is clear from the foregoing discussion that every advocate entered in the State roll will be entitled to practise in all Courts including the Supreme Court and before all authorities and persons throughout the territories to which the Act extends.

(iii) Special Provisions for enrolment of certain Supreme Court Advocates

Section 20(1) makes special provisions for enrolment of every advocate who was entitled to practice in the Supreme Court immediately before the appointed day and whose name is not entered in the roll of a State Bar Council may within the prescribed time, express his intention in the prescribed form to the Bar Council of India for the entry of his name in the roll of a State Bar Council and on receipt thereof, the Bar Council of India shall direct that the name of such advocate shall, without payment of any fee, be entered in the roll of that State Bar Council and the State Bar Council concerned shall comply with such direction.

Sub-section (2) of Section 20 lays down, that any entry in the State

1. A.I.R. 1961 S.C. 816.
2. A.I.R. 1957 Andh. Pra 350.

roll made in compliance with the direction of the Bar Council of India under sub-section (1) shall be made in the order of seniority determined in accordance with the provisions of sub-section (3) of Section 17.

Sub-section (3) of Section 20 provides that where an advocate referred to in sub-section (1) omits or fails to express his intention within the prescribed time, his name shall be entered in the roll of the State Bar Council of Delhi.

The Bar Council of India shall maintain a roll of advocates called the common roll of advocates. It will comprise of the entries made in the State rolls and include the names of Supreme Court advocates as are entitled to practise in that court prior to appointment day and whose name do not find place in the State roll shall also be in two parts of senior and other advocates.

(iv) Disputes regarding Seniority

Disputes regarding seniority of advocates can be settled by the device prescribed in Section 21 of the Act which reads as follows—

(1) Where the date of seniority of two or more persons is the same, the one senior in age shall be reckoned as senior to the other.

(2) Subject as aforesaid, if any dispute arises with respect to the seniority of any person, it shall be referred to the State Bar Council concerned for decision.

Hence, this section provides the manner in which disputes regarding seniority of Advocates, would be settled, albeit, such disputes are bound to arise occasionally.

(v) Certificate of Enrolment of Advocate

Section 22 of the Advocates Act, 1961 lays down provisions for the issue of certificate of enrolment in the prescribed form by the State Bar Council to every person whose name is entered in the roll of advocates, maintained by it. Sub-section (2) of this section provides that every person whose name is so entered in the State roll shall notify any change in the place of his permanent residence of the State Bar Council concerned within ninety days of such change.

Hence, Section 22 provides for issue of certificate of enrolment to every person whose name is entered in the Roll of Advocates whether a Senior Advocate or other Advocates. The certificate of enrolment would be issued by the concerned State Bar Council. In **Bar Council of U.P.** v. **State of U.P.**,[1] the Supreme Court observed that the stamps duty payable on the certificate or enrolment pertain to domain of taxation and imposition of stamp duty falls in pith and substance under Entry 44 of the List III. Hence the apex court upheld the levy of stamp duty on the certificates of enrolment of advocates under Section 22 of the Advocates Act, 1961, by U.P. Legislature, to be valid.

(vi) Right of Pre-audience

Right to pre-audience means the right of lawyer at Bar to be heard

1. A.I.R. 1973 S.C. 231.

before another. Section 23 of the Advocates Act governs the right of pre-audience in the following order—

> (1) Attorney General of India (2) Solicitor General of India (3) Additional Solicitor General of India (3A) The Second Additional Solicitor General of India (4) Advocate General (Among Advocate Generals *inter se*, the right is determined by their seniority) (5) Senior Advocates (6) other advocates. Among Senior Advocates *inter se*, and other advocates *inter se* the right of pre-audience shall be determined by their respective seniority *inter se*. Section 23 of the Act confers special right of pre-audience on those advocates occupying special position in the profession.[1] The Section does not impose any bar on a junior advocate in the matter of conducting the case when no other advocate is present on behalf of the client.[2]

(vii) Enrolment as Advocates

Section 24 of Advocates Act, 1961 provides for the qualification for admission as advocate on a State roll. Under this provision, a person shall be qualified to be admitted as an advocate on a State Roll, if he fulfils the following conditions, *viz*;

(a) he is a citizen of India;

(b) he has completed the age of 21 years;

(c) he has obtained a degree in law; or he is a barrister and is called to the Bar.

(a) He must be a citizen of India

The expression "citizen of India" is defined in Article 5 of the Constitution of India. A person who, at the commencement of Constitution (i.e., 26th day of January, 1950) had his domicile in the territory of India, and who was born in the territory of India {Article 5 (a)} or either of whose parents was born in India (irrespective of the nationality of his parents or place of birth of such person) {Article 5(b)} or who has been ordinarily been residing within the territory of India for not less than 5 years immediately preceding the commencement of the Constitution, {Article 5(c)} is a citizen of India.

A national of any country other than India also can be permitted and be enrolled as an advocate on a State roll, if citizens of India, duly qualified, are permitted, to practise law in his country. It is further subject to the other provisions contained in the Advocates Act. It may be noted in this context that the Indian lawyers have been agitating against the entry of foreign lawyers to practise in India, as the same facility is not given to Indian lawyers in other countries. However, sooner or later foreign advocates may have to be permitted to practise in India, as India has become a party to General Agreement of Trade in Services (GATS), one of the 28 agreements of WTO, and the provisions of the said agreement mandate India to provide access to foreign services including legal services.

1. *P.C. Jose* v. *Nanda Kumar*, A.I.R. 1997 Ker. 243.
2. *Tikka* v. *State of U.P.*, 1975 Cr. L.J. 337.

Since the reciprocity is insisted, the Indian law may not permit foreign lawyers to practise in India, if Indian lawyers are not allowed to practise in those foreign countries, which is the prevalent position now.

(b) He must have completed the age of twenty one years

There was no age bar under the Legal Practitioners Act but there is such a law under the Advocates Act, 1961 because under the Act a person cannot become an advocate unless he has attained the age of 21 years. Rule debarring persons who have completed 45 years of age from enrolment as advocates is *ultra vires* of the provisions of the Advocates Act. The rule violates the principle of equality enshrined in Article 14 of the Constitution of India. The rule is discriminatory arbitrary and unreasonable.[1]

(c) A degree in law as recognised by the Advocates Act

The Bar Council of India is conferred with unqualified power and discretion in respect of recognition of the degrees in law conferred by the Universities of India after 28th February, 1963 by Section 24(c) (iii) of the Act (before its amendment by Act 60 of 1973, by which the date is altered to 12th day of March, 1967). A person who has obtained a degree of law (i) either from any University in United India before 15th August, 1947, of (ii) from any Indian University before 12th March, 1967 or (iii) after 12th March 1967, from an Indian University offering 3-year law degree recognised by the Bar Council of India, of (iv) from any Indian University offering 2-year law course during the academic year 1967-68 or prior to that year, provided it was recognised by Bar Council of India. In any other case, from any University outside the territory of India, if the degree is recognised for the purposes of this Act by Bar Council of India, or he is a barrister and is called to the Bar on or before the 31st day of December, 1976; or has passed the article clerks examination or any other examination specified by the High Court at Bombay or Calcutta for enrolment as an attorney of that High Court or has obtained such other foreign qualification in law as is recognised by the Bar Council of India for the purpose of admission as an advocate under the Advocates Act, 1961.

(d) Other conditions

In addition to the above mentioned conditions laid down in Section 24, the person should also fulfil other conditions like payment of stamp duty chargeable under the Indian Stamp Act, 1899, and an enrolment fee of Rs. 600/- payable to the State Bar Council and one hundred and fifty rupees to the Bar Council of India, by way of Bank Draft drawn in favour of that council. The fee is enhanced to Rs. 2355/- in general and Rs. 1855/- in SC/ST categories whereas the fee to Bar Council of India is the same, i.e., Rs. 150/- and Rs. 25/- in general and SC/ST categories respectively :

Provided that where such person is a member of the scheduled castes or the scheduled tribes and produces a certificate to that effect from such authority as may be prescribed, the enrolment fee payable by him to the State Bar Council shall be Rs. 100/- and to the Bar Council of India Rs.

1. *Indian Council of Legal Aid and Advice* v. *Bar Council of India*, A.I.R. 1995 S.C. 691.

25/- only. No doubt he must fulfil the other conditions specified in the rules made by the State Bar Council [Section 24(i)(e)] Any person whose name is entered in the list of advocates has a right to practise in all courts including Supreme Court, before any tribunal or other authority. It is, therefore, within the exclusive domain of the State Bar Councils to admit persons as advocates on their rolls or to remove their names from the rolls. There is no provisions in Chapter III dealing with the admission and enrolment of advocates which restricts the entry of those who have completed 45 years as advocates. Nor has the State Bar Council made any rule under its rule making power. The Supreme Court declared the Bar Council of India rules debarring persons who have completed 45 years of age from getting enrolled as advocates invalid in **Indian Council of Legal Aid and Advice** v. **Bar Council of India**,[1] In **Satish Kumar Sharma** v. **Bar Council of Himachal Pradesh**,[2] a three Judge Bench of the Supreme Court through Justice Shivraj V. Patil held that a law graduate working as a full time salaried employee in any organisation cannot continue as an advocate on the rolls of a State Bar Council. The Court, in the instant case upheld the decision of the Bar Council of Himachal Pradesh withdrawing the enrolment of one Satish Kumar Sharma, who joined the Himachal Pradesh State Electricity Board as an Assistant (Legal) and who was later promoted as Deputy Secretary (Legal)-cum-Law Officer on *ad hoc* basis. The Court observed in para 10 of the case as under—

> *"The profession of law is called a noble profession. It does not remain noble merely by calling it as such unless there is a continued corresponding and expected performance of a noble profession. Its nobility has to be preserved, protected, and promoted. An institution cannot survive in its name or on its past glory alone. The glory and greatness of an institution depends on its continued and meaningful performance with grace and dignity. The profession of law being noble and honourable one, it has to continue its meaningful, useful and purposeful performance inspired by and keeping in view the high and rich traditions consistent with its grace, dignity, utility and prestige. Hence, the provisions of the Act and Rules made thereunder inter alia aimed at to achieve the same ought to be given effect to in their true spirit and letter to maintain clean and efficient Bar in the country to serve cause of justice which again is noble one."*

(viii) Disqualification for Enrolment

Even if a person fulfils the conditions laid down under Section 24 of the Advocates Act, 1961, he may not be enrolled if he incurs any disqualification under Section 24-A of the Act. No person shall be admitted as an advocate on a State roll :

(a) if he is convicted of an offence involving moral turpitude; or

(b) if he is convicted of an offence under the provisions of the Untouchability (Offences) Act, 1955;[3] or

---

1. A.I.R. 1995 S.C. 691.
2. A.I.R. 2001 S.C. 509.
3. Now Protection of Civil Rights Act, 1955.

(c) if he is dismissed or removed from employment or office under the State on any charge involving moral turpitude.[1]

These disqualifications are not permanent. These disqualifications for enrolment shall cease to have effect after a period of two years has lapsed since release of the person. Section 24-A of the Act indicates that the disqualification is only for a period of two years after release. This Section was inserted in the Act by the Advocates (Amendment) Act 60 of 1973 and became effective on January 31, 1976. The object of the provision is to disallow admission as an advocate on a State roll if a person has been convicted of an offence involving moral turpitude or under the provisions of Untouchability (Offences) Act 22 of 1955. Further, if a person is found guilty but dealt with under the provisions of the Probation of Offenders Act, 1958 shall not attract any disqualification for enrolment as an advocate.

In **J.N. Gupta v. I.G. Assam,**[2] it has been held that such admission would not be refused if two years have elapsed after the release and date of submission of application. A release on probation is not a release. However, a disqualification, is not permanent Further, for incurring disqualification, conviction means final conviction.

Rule 1(1) of the **Maharashtra and Goa Bar Council Rules** denied simultaneous practice of another profession along with practice of law. A medical practitioner obtaining a bachelor law degree in view of the above prohibition cannot be enrolled as an advocate if he wants to practise as an advocate over and above practising medicine. Such a prohibition has been challenged by a member of medical practitioner on various grounds in **Dr. H.L. Chulani v. Bar Council of Maharashtra and Goa.**,[3] The Supreme Court has rightly held that medical practitioner who acquires a law degree subsequently cannot be allowed to practise law simultaneously. The court has got the power to frame such a rule and the same is neither violative of Section 24 nor Section 24-A of the Act. In the instant case, the court observed that the legal profession requires full time attention and would not countenance an advocate riding two horses or more at a time. He has to be full time advocate or not at all

(ix) Authority to whom application for enrolment may be made

Section 25 of the Advocates Act, 1961 provides that an application for admission as an advocate shall be made in the prescribed form to the State Bear Council within whose jurisdiction the applicant proposes to practise. The form in which application for enrolment as an advocate may be made will be prescribed by a State Bar Council under Section 28(2)(c) of the Act.

Form of Application—Form of application for admission as an advocate prescribed by Bar Council of Uttar Pradesh is given below—

1. Under Section 24-A, as inserted by he Advocates (Amendment) Act (70 of 1993), which became operative with effect from 26th December, 1993.
2. A.I.R. 1959 Assam 134.
3. A.I.R. 1996 S.C. 1708.

Sl. No........ Issued to Sri......on receipt of Rs. 2

BAR COUNCIL OF UTTAR PRADESH

SEAL

APPLICATION NO..............OF 20.....

(Under Section 25, read with Section 24 of the Advocates Act, 1961)

In the matter of enrolment of Sri.. son/daughter/wife of...................................

To

The Chairman,
Bar Council of Uttar Pradesh
Allahabad

The humble petition of Sri.. son/daughter/wife of Sri.. r/o.. most respectfully showeth—

1. That your petitioner is a citizen of India and is above 21 years of age and prays for his/her admission as an advocate of the Bar Council of Uttar Pradesh.
2. That the necessary particulars are as follows—

   (i) Name...

   (ii) Father's name...

   (iii) Date of birth... (as shown in the High School Certificate)

   (iv) Date of having obtained a degree in law..........................

   (v) Name of the University...

   (vi) Certificate of having undergone a course of training in Law and passed an examination after such training as prescribed by the Bar Council of Uttar Pradesh...

   (vii) Exception to the provision of training and examination claimed on the ground of...

   (viii) Date of payment of Rs. 250 as Enrolment Fee..............
3. That your petitioner is a vakil, pleader or any attorney practising within the jurisdiction of the High Court of Judicature at Allahabad, and was enrolled as such on.......................................
4. That your petitioner is not a Law Graduate but was entitled to be enrolled as an Advocate of the High Court immediately before the appointed date by reasons of his practising as a pleader for a period of not less than 15 years with ability and repute as provided under proviso sixthly to Rule I framed under Section 9 of the Indian Bar Councils Act, XXXVIII of 1926, and is filing a certificate to the District Judge of...................................

Dated....... Signature of the Petitioner................

Address........

Enclosures—

(1) High School or equivalent examination's certificate showing date of birth or age.

(2) LL.B. Degree.

(3) Nationality certificate or declaration.

(4) Certificate as to character.

(5) Receipt of Rs. 250 paid to the Bar Council.

Declaration

I...son/daughter/wife of Sri...r/o.............................., an applicant to be enrolled as an advocate of the Bar Council of Uttar Pradesh do hereby declare as follows:

I solemnly affirm and say as follows—

(1) That I intend to practise ordinarily and regularly within the jurisdiction of the Bar Council of Uttar Pradesh.

(2) That I hold no appointment under Government or any other department.

(3) That I am not engaged in any trade or business.

(4) That I further declare in writing that I will truly and honestly and to the best of my knowledge and ability act and demean myself as an advocate and faithfully observe and obey all orders enforced or which shall hereafter be made by the High Court and all the rules made by the Bar Council for regulating the conduct of Advocates on the roll of Advocates of the Bar Council.

(5) That I am citizen of India.

Place.......... Signature of the applicant

Date..........

CERTIFICATE OF CHARACTER

(TO BE FURNISHED BY EVERY APPLICANT)

Certified that Sri...
Son/daughter/wife of Sri...
is personally known to me and he bears a good moral character and is a fit and proper person to be enrolled as an Advocate.

Date...... Signature

Designation

CERTIFICATE TO BE FURNISHED

BY PLEADERS ONLY

Certified that Sri...
son/daughter/wife of Sri...
was enrolled as pleader on..in the judgeship of..and is practising as such since them.

Data........

SEAL Signature of District Judge of............

CERTIFICATE TO BE FURNISHED BY A PLEADER OF OVER 15 YEARS PRACTICE BUT WHO IS NOT A GRADUATE IN LAW

Certified that Sri.. Son/daughter/wife of Sri..was enrolled pleader on...in the judgeship of.................... and is practising as such for more than 15 years with ability and repute.

His application to be enrolled as an Advocate is recommended by me. He is a fit and proper person to be enrolled as an Advocate.

Date.................... Signature of District Judge of............

SEAL

BAR COUNCIL OF UTTAR PRADESH
ORDER SHEET
Office Report

The applicant Sri.. Son/daughter/wife of Sri..is a graduate in law of the..University of the year......................and as such is entitled to be enrolled as an Advocate under proviso (i) to clause (d) to Section 24(1) of the Advocates Act 1961.

Or

The applicant Sri.. Son/daughter/wife of Sri...a pleader practising in the judgeship of..............................is a graduate in law and is entitled to be enrolled as an Advocate under Section 24(2) of the Advocates Act, 1961.

Or

The applicant Sri.. Son/daughter/wife of Sri.. is a pleader of over 15 years standing and has been recommended by the District Judge of..........................as a fit and proper person to be enrolled as an Advocate.

RECOMMENDATION

The applicant may be enrolled as an Advocate under Section 24 of the Advocates Act, 1961.

Date.......... Honorary Secretary

Order of Enrolment Committee

The applicant Sri.. Son/daughter/wife of Sri.. of... be enrolled as an Advocate under the provision of the Advocates Act, 1961.

(2) The applicant Sri.. Son/daughter/wife of Sri.. is not entitled to be enrolled for the reasons given separately.

Member Member Member
Enrolment on........
Enrolment No.
Date......... Honorary Secretary

(x) Disposal of applications for admission as an Advocate

Section 26 of the Advocates Act provides that an application for admission as an Advocate made to a State Bar Council shall be disposed of by the enrolment committee of the Bar Council. When an Enrolment Committee proposes to refuse an application for enrolment, it must consult the Bar Council of India stating ground of refusal. On receipt of the opinion, the Enrolment Committee of the State Bar Council, must dispose of the application in conformity with the opinion of the Bar Council of India. Where the Enrolment Committee of a State Bar Council has refused any application for admission as an Advocate, it shall intimate that fact stating the name, address, qualifications and grounds of refusal to all other State Bar Councils obviously to forewarn them against any attempt by such a person to seek his admission on the roll of other State Bar Council. Such application shall not be entertained by any other State Bar Council except with the previous written consent of the State Bar Council which refused the application, and of the Bar Council of India under Section 27 of the Act.

In **Joginder Singh v. Bar Council of India**,[1] the appellant got his name enrolled as an advocate in the U.P. State Bar Council in 1962 and was allowed by the Bar Council of India to transfer his name from U.P. to Delhi Bar. Later on, it was found that the appellant had been convicted in three cases under Sections 411 and 473, IPC and sentenced to imprisonment for one year in each case, to run concurrently. The Bar Council of India removed his name from the roll for being convicted in three cases. He challenged this order by filing a suit on the ground that the application form for enrolment contained no column wherein he was obliged to show his conviction. His suit failed as also his first appeal. The High Court in second appeal held that the proviso under Section 26(1), the Bar Council of India has power to strike off the name of any person from the roll if he got himself enrolled by fraud or misrepresentation, etc.

In **S.S. Mittal v. Bar Council of India**,[2] the order of removal passed by the Bar Council need not be communicated to the advocate concerned when the order was passed in his presence. It is not necessary to serve the copy of the order to concerned advocate in such a case to make the order effective.

(xi) Power to remove names from Roll

Section 26-A confers powers on the State Bar Council to remove from the State roll the name of any advocate who is dead or from whom a request has been received to that effect. This provision was inserted by the Advocates (Amendment) Act, 1973, and became operative with effect from

1. A.I.R. 1975 Del 192.
2. A.I.R. 1974 HP 32.

31st January, 1974. This is a simple provision which provides for the removal of advocates when he is dead or when he had made a request for removal of his name for any reason.

(xii) Power to make Rules

Section 28 empowers a State Bar Council to make rules for accomplishing the purposes of Chapter III. Under this Section a State Bar Council is empowered to make rules prescribing the term within which and the manner in which an intention to practise within the jurisdiction of the Bar Council shall be expressed, the form in which an application for enrolment as an advocate may be made, the conditions subject to which a person may be admitted as an advocate and the instalments in which the enrolment fee be paid. The rules will be effective only if they have been approved by the Bar Council of India.

Rule 1(1) of the **Maharashtra and Goa Bar Council Rules** prohibits persons engaged in any other profession such as medical profession, from being admitted as an advocate. Such rule has been challenged in **Dr. H.L. Chulani's case,**[1] on the ground of excessive delegation of legislative function and also *ultra vires* the rule making power. The Supreme Court has held that rule-making power conferred on the State Bar Council under Section 28 of the Act is certainly hedged with the obligation to frame only such rules regarding enrolment which would fructify the purpose of having efficient members of the Bar who can stand up to the expectation of the noble and learned profession to which they are to be given entry. When under clause (d) of sub-section (2) of Section 28, the State Bar Council has the power to lay down the conditions subject to which a person may be admitted as an advocate by any such rule, then Rule 1(1) falls within the parameters of the rule-making power as entrusted by the legislature to State Bar Councils as per Section 24(1)(c) and Section 28(2)(d) of the Act and it cannot be said that any disqualification laid down in Rule 1(1) of the Maharashtra and Goa Bar Council Rules could not be imposed by the State Bar Council. It is, therefore, held by the Supreme Court that Rule 1(1) is not *ultra vires* the rule-making power. The challenge to the said rule on the ground it contravenes Articles 14, 19(1)(g) and 21 of the Constitution has also been rejected by the Supreme Court.

---

1. A.I.R. 1976 S.C. 1708.

3

BAR COUNCILS

I. Introduction

After independence, with the coming into force of the Constitution of India in 1950 and the establishment of a Supreme Court of India, the lawyers' community wanted a unified autonomous Bar with no class distinction among lawyers. In view of their demand the Union Government accordingly set up a Committee known as the All India Bar Committee under the Chairmanship of Justice S.R. Das of the Supreme Court of India. The Committee considered at length questions of the constitution and powers of the State Bar Councils and the All India Bar Council and made detailed recommendations in 1953, viz., establishment of an All India Bar Council and a common roll of advocates; a right to practice in any part of the country and in any court, including the Supreme Court, etc. The Committee's recommendations got strength by the endorsement and approval of its recommendations by the Law Commission of India in 1953, which was presided over by the eminent jurist—M.C. Setalvad, the then Attorney General of India. The Law Commission of India in its 14th Report on the reform of Judicial Administration approved of the recommendations for creation of a unified All India Bar as well as the establishment, composition and function of the State and All India Bar Councils. Further, as a result of the recommendations, the Legal Practitioners Bill, 1959 was introduced in the Lok Sabha on November 19, 1959 with a view to implement the recommendations of the All India Bar Committee and the Law Commission 14th Report. When the Bill came to be passed, its name was changed from Legal Practitioners Bill to the Advocates Act and was passed in the year 1961 by the Parliament. It received the assent of the President of India on May 19, 1961. It extends to the whole of India. It came into force with effect from December 12, 1962. It provides a federal structure for legal profession with any category of lawyers known as advocates. An advocate may be designated as "Senior Advocate" if the Supreme Court or a High Court is of the opinion that by virtue of his ability he deserves such distinction. The Act broadly deals with the constitution and operation of Bar Councils, admission and enrolment of advocates, their right to practise, their conduct, along with some transitional provisions. The Advocates Act provides for the constitution of two types of Bar Councils—State Bar Councils and Bar Council of India. An advocate is initially enrolled with a State Bar Council and a common roll of all the advocates in the country is maintained by the Bar Council of India. No advocate can get himself enrolled with more than one State Bar Council, though certainly he can get himself transferred from one State Bar Council to another and is also entitled to appear before any court or tribunal throughout the country. In the following pages an earnest endeavour will be made discuss the organization, powers and functions of the Bar Councils.

II. State Bar Councils

(i) Constitution of a Bar Council

The original idea was to have separate State Bar Council for each State, however, the State Bar Councils are constituted High Court wise. Section 3 of the Advocates Act provides for the constitution of a Bar Council for each State and Union Territories being attached to the neighbouring States on the lines recommended by the All India Bar Committee. At present the following are the State Bar Councils—(1) State of Andhra Pradesh; (2) State of Bihar; (3) State of Gujarat; (4) State of Madhya Pradesh; (5) State of Karnataka; (6) State of Orissa; (7) State of Rajasthan; (8) State of Uttar Pradesh; (9) State of Himachal Pradesh; (10) Common Bar Council for the States of Assam, Manipur, Meghalaya, Mizoram, Arunachal, Nagaland and Tripura; (11) Common Bar Council of Tamil Nadu and the Union territory of Pondicherry; (12) Common Bar Council for State of Maharashtra and Goa and Union Territories of Dadra and Nagar Haveli and Daman & Diu; (13) Common Bar Council for States of Punjab and Haryana; (14) Common Bar Council for the State of Kerala and Union Territory of Laccadive, Minicoy and Aminidivi Island; (15) Common Bar Council for the State of West Bengal and Union Territory of Andaman and Nicobar Islands; (16) Union Territory (now State) of Delhi; (17) State of Chhatisgarh.

(ii) Members of the State Bar Council

A State Bar Council consists of the following members :

(A) Ex-officio Members

Advocate General of the State. (In case of the Bar Council of Delhi, the Additional Solicitor General of India is the Ex-officio member, in case of the Bar Council of Assam, Nagaland, etc. Advocates General of the State of Assam, Nagaland, Meghalaya, Manipur and Tripura are ex-officio members, in case of Punjab and Haryana, Advocates-General of Punjab and Haryana are ex-officio members).

(B) Elected Members

The Advocates who form the electorate, elect the members of the State Bar Council in accordance with the system of proportional representation by means of single transferable vote, from among the advocates on the electoral roll. The number of elected members vary, according to numerical strength of the electorate. A State Bar Council consists of fifteen to twenty-five members. In case of a council having electorate exceeding 5,000 the elected members are 15; in case of council having electorate exceeding 5000 but not exceeding 10,000 the elected members are 20; in case of council having electorate more than 10,000 the elected members are 25. The method of voting by secret ballot on the system of proportional representation by means of the single transferable vote is a desirable device adopted for the election of members to the State Bar Council. The object of introducing proportional representation is to give the voters, territory-wise or in other manner in which they choose to group themselves, an effective share of representation in the State Bar Council. The advantages claimed for the Single Transferable System, further, are :—

(i) All currents of opinion can be truly reflected under this system, and any group can elect one representative if it can muster sufficient votes to reach the 'quota'.

(ii) The power and interest of each vote is increased by giving him successive choices.

This objective could be achieved, if the voter "were permitted to indicate on his ballot his second and third choices, for whom his single vote should be counted, if it were not needed to elect his first choice, or if it were given for a candidate who could not be elected. This is the 'Single Transferable Vote', which, as its name would indicate, allows each elector to vote for one candidate, instead of the entire number to be elected, but permits him to indicate second and third choices. The total number of votes cast is therefore the same as the number of valid ballots, which divided by the number of members to be elected (or number of members plus one), give the unit or quota of representation necessary to elect a single representative. This quota is fixed thus—

$$\frac{\text{Total number of ballot papers}}{\text{Number of candidate to be elected} + 1}$$

Suppose the total number of ballot papers is 5001 and the number of candidates to be elected is 20, then the quota will be :

$$\frac{5001}{20+1} = 238$$

"Each voter marks his ballot with figures 1, 2, 3 etc., opposite the names of candidates in the order of his preference. In counting the ballots, at first only the first choices are counted, and as soon as a candidate his received a number of first choices equal to the quota, he is declared elected. After that no more votes are counted for him, but remaining ballots which give him first choice are counted for the candidates marked second choice, or if the second choice be declared elected, then for the third choice, and so on. After the ballots have been gone over once in this way, and it is found that the full number of members is not elected, as would usually be the case, then candidates whose total vote, either by way of first or secondary choices is less than a quota, are declared "out" in the inverse order of their vote, and their ballots are transferred to the successive choices indicated thereon, until the complete number of members is declared elected. One half of the elected members shall, as nearly as possible, be persons who have for at least ten years been advocates on a State roll. There is no provision for nomination of members by the High Court. Chairman and Vice-Chairman of each State Bar Council shall be elected by the Council in such manner as may be prescribed. In other words, the Bar Council of India may prescribe qualifications and conditions for the eligibility to vote, or for being chosen as a member, in the election of the members to the State Bar Councils. Subject to such rules that may be made, each State Bar Council shall prepare and revise the electoral roll from time to time. Some attempts were made in 1976 by the Government to curtail the autonomy of profession by making government officials as ex-officio Chairman or Vice-Chairman of the Councils and by inducting Government nominees into them. But the process was reversed in 1977 and status quo restored.

Section 8 of the Act fixed the term of office of an elected member of a State Bar Council as five years from the date of publication of the result of his or her election. Section 8 has been thoroughly revised by Advocates (Amendment) Act of 1993 and a specific provision has been made that, if the State Bar Council fails to provide for the election before the expiry of the said term, the Bar Council of India may, by order for reasons to be recorded in writing extend the said term for a period not exceeding six months. In such cases, the extension has to be granted before the expiry of the original term so as to maintain continuity of the term.[1] A new Section 8-A has also been incorporated by the said Amendment Act of 1993 under which the Bar Council of India has been authorised to constitute a Special Committee to perform the function for the State Bar Council if before the expiry of the term of five years or before the term as extended by the Bar Council of India no election was held. Such special Committee shall perform all the functions and duties of the State Bar Council and such special Committee has also been authorised to hold election to the election to the State Bar Council within a period of six months from the date of its constitution.

In **A. Mohammed Iqbal** v. **Bar Council of India, New Delhi**, A.I.R. 2000 Ker. 247. the High Court held that the Special Committee constituted under Section 8-A could also nominate a member of the Committee to the Bar Council of India since such Committee is statutorily permitted to discharge the functions of the State Bar Council until the Bar Council is constituted under the Act.

(iii) Functions of the State Bar Council

The State Bar Councils under the Advocates Act, 1961 have been entrusted with numerous functions under Section 6.

(1) The functions of a State Bar Council shall be :

(a) to admit persons as advocates on its roll;

(b) to prepare and maintain such roll;

(c) to entertain and determine cases of misconduct against advocates on its roll;

1. *Babu Varghese* v. *Bar Council of Kerala*, A.I.R. 1999 S.C. 1281.

(d) to safeguard the rights, privileges and interests of advocates on its roll;

(dd) to promote the growth of Bar Association for the purposes of effective implementation of the welfare schemes referred to in clause (a) sub-section (2) of this section and clause (a) of sub-section (2) of Section 7;[1]

(e) to promote and support law reform;

(ee) to conduct seminars and organise talks on legal topics by eminent jurists and publish journals and papers of legal interest;[2]

(eee) to organise legal aid to the poor in the prescribed manner;[3]

(f) to manage and invest the funds of the Bar Council;

(g) to provide for election of its members;

(gg) to visit and inspect Universities in accordance with the directions given under clause (i) of sub-section () of Section 7;[4]

(h) to perform all other functions conferred on it by or under this Act;

(i) to do all other things necessary for discharging the aforesaid functions.

(2) A State Bar Council may constitute one or more funds in prescribed manner for the purpose of—

(a) giving financial assistance to organise welfare schemes for the indigent, disabled or other advocates;

(b) giving financial assistance to organise welfare schemes for the indigent, disabled or other advocate;

(c) establishing law libraries.[5]

(3) A State Bar Council may receive any grant, donations, gifts or benefactions for all or any of the purposes specified in sub-section (2) which shall be credited to the appropriate fund or funds constituted under that sub-section.

This section prescribed the functions of a State Bar Council on the lines recommended by the All India Committee. A perusal of this section and those of Indian Bar Councils Act, 1926, clearly shows that changes have been effected in the power of the Bar Council.

(i) Under the Bar Councils Act, 1926, the High Court of a State had to admit persons as Advocates on its roll and not the State Bar Council as is the case under the Advocates Act, 1961.

(ii) Under the Bar Councils Act, 1926, the High Court of a State had to prepare and maintain the roll of Advocates. Under the Advocates Act, 1961, it is the State Bar Council that is to prepare

1. Inserted by Act No. 70 of 1993.
2. Inserted by Act No. 60 of 1973 and came into force with effect from 31st January, 1974.
3. *Ibid.*
4. Inserted by Act 70 of 1993.
5. *Ibid.*

and maintain such roll.

(iii) Formerly, though there was a tribunal of the Bar Councils, it could not finally decide the cases of professional or other misconduct against Advocates but could forward its finding to the High Court through the Bar Council. Under the present Act, all cases of misconduct have to be disposed of by the disciplinary committee of the State Bar Council. An appeal lies to the All India Bar Council from any order made by the disciplinary committee of the State Bar Council in any disciplinary proceedings. Section 38 of the Act provides remedy to the person aggrieved by the order passed by the disciplinary committee of the Bar Council of India. Under Section 38, appeal from the decision of the disciplinary committee of the Bar Council of India lies to the Supreme Court of India.

The Bar Council is a statutory body and has no jurisdiction to compel an Advocate to cease work. The functions of a State Bar Council are to safeguard the rights, privileges and interests of the Advocates on its roll and to promote and support law reform. In the name of safeguarding the rights, privileges and interests of the Advocates on its roll, the Bar Council cannot certainly do something which will take away, even though temporarily the statutory and the constitutional rights of an Advocate to practice. Resolution by the Bar Council calling upon Advocates to cease work in consequence of the failure of the State Government to shift Courts from dilapidated building to safer building is illegal and violative of Articles 19(1)(g) and 21 of the Constitution.[1]

The Bar Council are fairly large bodies. Their functions are numerous. Therefore, it is expedient and efficient if the work is done by the Standing Committees of the Bar Council. Section 9 of the Act provides for the constitution of the Disciplinary Committees, both by the State Bar Councils and the Bar Council of India. Further, Section 10 enables State Bar Councils to form an Executive Committee, Legal Education Committee, and an Enrolment Committee. The Bar Council of India has power to form a Legal Aid Committee and Executive Committee.

Every Bar Council is a body corporate having perpetual succession and common seal with power to acquire and hold property and to contract. It may by its name sue and be sued.[2] In **C.I.T. Bombay v. The Bar Council of Maharashtra,**[3] the Supreme Court observed that the dominant purpose of a State Bar Council as reflected by the various obligatory functions is to ensure quality service of competent lawyers to the litigating public, to spread legal literacy, promote law reforms and provide legal assistance to the poor while the benefit accruing to the lawyer-members is incidental. The court held that having regard to the preamble of the Advocates Act and the nature of the various obligatory functions, it is clear that the primary or dominant purpose of the State Bar Council is the advancement of the object of general public utility and as such the income

1. *Arunava Ghosh* v. *Bar Council of West Bengal*, A.I.R. 1996 Cal. 331.
2. See Section 5 of the Act.
3. A.I.R. 1981 S.C. 1462.

from securities held by the respondent Bar Council would be exempt from any tax liability.

(iv) Power of the State Bar Council

The State Bar Councils have certain powers under the Advocates Act, 1961, which are as follows :

(A) Power to make rules

The Bar Councils have got legislative functions. It is the rule-making power for the functioning and discharging the duties of the Committees. The State Bar Council has been given rule making powers. Section 28(i) provides that a State Bar Council may make rules to carry out the purposes of Chapter III (Sections 16 to 27) of the Act dealing with the admission and enrolment of the advocates. Section 28(2) provides that in particular and without prejudice to the generality of the foregoing power, such rules may provide for—

(a) the time in which and form in which an advocate shall express his intention for the entry of his name in the roll of a State Bar Council under Section 20;

(b) Clause (b) *omitted* w.e.f. 19.1.1974.

(c) the form in which an application shall be made to the Bar Council for admission as an advocate on its roll and the manner in which such application shall be disposed of by the Enrolment Committee of the Bar Council;

(d) the conditions subject to which a person may be admitted as an advocate on any such roll;

(e) the instalments in which the enrolment fee may be made;

(f) no rules made under this chapter shall have effect unless they have been approved by the Bar Council of India [Section 28(3)].

It is, therefore, crystal clear that under Section 28 of the Act, the State Bar Council is empowered to make rules prescribing the term within which and the manner in which, an intention to practise within the jurisdiction of the Bar Council shall be expressed, the form in which an application for enrolment as an advocate may be made, the conditions subject to which a person may be admitted as an advocate and the instalments in which the enrolment fee may be made. The matters on which the rules can be made are generally matters of procedure. However, rules made by the State Bar Council are subject to the approval by the Bar Council of India. The words 'carry out the purpose of the Act' used in sub-section 1 of Section 28 are wide enough to justify the exercise of rule-making power laying down substantive standard also. There is nothing in the language of the Section to justify the limiting of the rule making power to mean laying of procedure only. The rule-making power can take both substantive and procedural provisions.

In **Gummala Purshotam Reddy v. Bar Council of Andhra Pradesh,**[1] Rule 70 (AAA) framed by Bar Council of Andhra Pradesh

1. (1988) 1 A.P.L.J. 30.

permanently debarred from enrolment as advocate a person removed from service. The rule was struck down under Article 19 (6) of the Constitution of India.

(B) Power to punish advocates for misconduct

The Bar Council of States are vested with powers to look into the complaints of professional or other misconduct by Advocates, which power is exercised through their respective disciplinary committees. This power can be exercised either *suo motu* or an application made to the State Bar Council by any person interested.[1] Section 35 of the Advocates Act makes provisions for punishing advocates for their misconduct. Section 35 provides as follows :

(1) Where on receipt of a complaint or otherwise, a State Bar Council has reason to believe that any advocate on its roll has been guilty of professional or other misconduct, it shall refer the case for disposal to its disciplinary committee.

(1-A) The State Bar Council may, either of its own motion or on application made to it by any person interested, withdraw a proceedings pending before its disciplinary committee and direct the inquiry of that State Bar Council.

(2) The disciplinary committee of a State Bar Council, shall fix a date for the hearing of the case and shall cause a notice thereof to be given to the advocate concerned and the Advocate General of the State.

(3) The disciplinary committee of a State Bar Council after giving the advocate concerned and the Advocate General an opportunity of being heard, may make any of the following orders, namely :

- (a) dismiss the complaint or where the proceedings were initiated at the instance of the State Bar Council, direct that the proceedings be filed;
- (b) reprimand the advocate;
- (c) suspend the advocate from practice for such period as it may deem fit;
- (d) remove the name of the advocate from the State roll of advocates.

When an advocate is suspended under clause (c) above, during the period of such suspension, he is debarred from practising in any court or before any authority or person in India.

If the conduct of an advocate is such as to make the lawyer unworthy to remain a member of legal profession and unfit to be entrusted with the responsible duties that an advocate is required to perform, he will be held guilty of misconduct and may be punished thereafter. In such cases, following two tests have been laid down by court in a matter of an advocate :

(a) the misconduct is such that he must be regarded as unworthy

1. Under Section 35 of the Advocates Act, 1961.

to remain a member of the honourable profession; and

(b) the misconduct is such that he must be regarded as unfit to be entrusted with the responsible duties that an advocate is called upon to perform.

The fulfilment of any one of the said conditions would be sufficient to treat the conduct as misconduct.

Section 35 of the Advocates Act, 1961 prescribes punishment for an advocate who is guilty of "professional or other misconduct". The term other misconduct is not *ejusdem generis* with professional misconduct, and covers cases other than those of professional misconduct in the ordinary sense, as for instance, conviction for a crime involving dishonesty or moral turpitude, or gross and habitual contempt of court. However, the expression does not cover only moral turpitude; it is wide enough to cover any defect in the character of a legal practitioner which render him unfit to be a member of the honourable profession to which he belongs.

Even though Section 35 makes a provision for a State Bar Council to initiate appropriate enquiry against an advocate on receipt of a complaint or otherwise when it has reason to believe that any advocate on its roll has been guilty of professional or other misconduct to refer such complaint to disciplinary committee, yet the expression 'misconduct' has not been defined in the Act.

Section 35 uses the expression "misconduct, professional or otherwise." The word "misconduct" is a relative term. It has to be considered with reference to the subject-matter and the context wherein in such term occurrs. In literal sense, it means wrong conduct or improper conduct. The general meaning of the word 'misconduct' is improper and unacceptable behaviour, usually neglect of duties, by a professional or an employee. The Supreme Court of India in **State of Punjab v. Ram Singh**,[1] has categorically observed that the term 'misconduct' may involve moral turpitude, it must be improper or wrong behaviour, unlawful behaviour, a transgression of established and definite rule of action or code of conduct, but not mere error of judgment, carelessness or negligence in performance of duty. In **Noratanmal Chaurasia v. M.R. Murli**,[2] the Supreme Court held that misconduct has not been defined in the Advocates Act, 1961. Misconduct, *inter alia*, envisages breach of discipline, although it would not be possible to lay down exhaustively, as to what would constitute misconduct and indiscipline as it is wide enough to include wrongful omission or commission, whether done or omitted to be done intentionally or unintentionally. It means 'improper behaviour' 'intentional wrong doing or deliberate violation of a rule of standard of behaviour'. Professional misconduct may consist in betraying the confidence of a client, in attempting by any means to practise a fraud or impose on or deceive the court or the adverse party or his counsel, and in fact in any conduct which tends to bring reproach on the legal profession or to alienate the favourable

1. A.I.R. 1992 S.C. 2188.
2. A.I.R. 2004 SCW 2894.

opinion which the public should entertain concerning it.[1]

Both in law and in ordinary speech, the term "misconduct" usually implies an act done wilfully with a wrong intention. When this definition is applied to professional people, it includes unprofessional acts even though such acts are not inherently wrongful. Misconduct is a transgression of some established and definite rule of action, a forbidden act, a dereliction from duty, unlawful behaviour, wilful in character, improper or wrong behaviour, delinquency, impropriety, mismanagement, offence, but not negligence or carelessness. This definition cannot be accepted fully as a lawyer is liable for his negligence and carelessness also. Professional misconduct may consist in betraying the confidence of the client, in attempting to practice a fraud, or deceive the court or the adverse party or his counsel. In fact, any conduct which tends to bring reproach on the legal profession or to alienate the favourable opinions which the public should entertain concerning it may in wider sense constitute professional misconduct.

"Misconduct" itself is a sufficiently wide expression; it is not necessary, for instance, that it should involve moral turpitude. The court has a right to expect a higher standard of loyalty to the court under co-operation from those who practise profession of law. Any conduct which in any way renders a man unfit for exercise of his profession or is "likely to hamper or embarrass the administration of justice by the High Court or any of the courts subordinate thereto" may be considered to be misconduct calling for disciplinary action. What court has to consider in all these cases is the conduct of the Advocate (attorney) as it affects his position as an Advocate (attorney) and his relations to the court.[2] Justice V.R. Krishna Iyar said in **Bar Council of Maharashtra v. M.V. Dabholkar**,[3] that the vital role of the lawyer depends upon his probity and professional life-style. The central function of the legal profession is to promote the administration of justice. As monopoly to legal profession has been statutorily granted by notion, it obligates the lawyer to observe scrupulously those norms which make him worthy of confidence of community in him as a vehicle of social justice. "Law is not trade briefs—no merchandise." The test to determine professional misconduct within the meaning of Section 35(1) is whether the proved misconduct of the advocate is such that he must be regarded as unworthy to remain a member of the honourable profession to which he has been admitted and unfit to be entrusted with the responsible duties that an advocate is called upon to perform.[4] In **D. Saibaba v. Bar Council of India and Another**,[5] the wife of an advocate filed a complaint under Section 35 of the Advocates Act complaining of professonal misconduct committed by the appellant, alleging that in spite of his being a duly enrolled advocate, he was running a telephone booth allotted to him in the handicapped person's quota. After hearing, the State Bar Council directed

1. See Corpus Juris Secundum, Vol. 7, p. 740.
2. *In re, Tulsidas Amarlal Karnanmi*, A.I.R. 1941 Bom 228.
3. A.I.R. 1976 S.C. 242.
4. *O.P.D. Kandekar* v. *Bar Council of Maharashtra*, A.I.R. 1984 S.C. 100.
5. (2003) 6 S.C.C. 186 : A.I.R. 2003 S.C. 2502.

the complaint to be dropped as no case was made out. On appeal, the Bar Council of India directed the appellant to surrender the STD booth. The appellant sought some time for surrendering the licence of telephone booth becuase certain dues were to be realised from customers which would be difficult to do in the event of the business being suddenly discontinued. As the appellant failed to surrender the STD booth, the Bar Council of India passed an order advising the State Bar Council to delete the name of the appellant. After 26 days, the appellant surrendered the booth and sought for a review of the order of the Bar Council of India. The Council rejected the petition on the ground that the same was time barred. The appellant preferred an appeal by way of Special Leave Petition, the Supreme Court after due examination set aside the order of the Bar Council and restored the enrolment of the advocate.

A member of a legal profession is expected to maintain a standard of the professon in a dignified manner. The standard required to be maintained by the member of the legal profession must not hurt the nobility and honour of the profession. An advocate is obligated to observe the norms and ethics of legal profession. Some instances of misconduct are as follows :

(i) Offering bribes, giving bribes or taking money from client for giving bribe amounts to gross misconduct.[1]

(ii) An advocate stooping to bribe a judge to get an order in favour of his client is guilty of professional misconduct.[2]

(iii) A pleader who attempted to influence the judge through the judge's relative is guilty of misconduct.[3]

(iv) A suggestion by a Vakil that he can influence the judge is a serious misconduct.[4]

(v) A pleader appeared in court in a drunken state unable to conduct the case. He behaved in similar manner on two subsequent occasions. He was held to be guilty of misconduct and his name was struck off the roll.[5]

(vi) An advocate must uphold the dignity and decorum of the court and must not do anything to bring the court itself to disrepute. Advocate overstepped his limit when he made imputation of partiality and unfairness against the Munsif in open court. Scandalising the court in such manner is polluting the very fount of justice and the conduct of the advocate was held to be highly reprehensible.[6]

(vii) An advocate doing something regarded as disgraceful and dishonourable by professional brethren of good repute and competency is guilty of infamous conduct in professional respect.[7]

1. *Chandra Sekhar Soni* v. *Bar Council,* A.I.R. 1983 S.C. 1012.
2. *In the matter of U,* an Advocate, A.I.R. 1935 Rang 178.
3. *Emperor* v. *G, a Pleader,* A.I.R. 1936 Lah. 732.
4. *President, Vakil's Assam.* v. *A Vakil,* A.I.R. 1914 Mad. 635.
5. *In the matter of a Lower Grade Pleader,* A.I.R. 1934 Rang 156.
6. *Lalit Mohan* v. *Advocate General,* A.I.R. 1957 S.C. 250.
7. *In re, P, an advocate,* A.I.R. 1963 S.C. 1313.

(viii) The advocates positioned themselves at the entrance of the entrance of the Magistrate's Courts watchful of arrival of litigants. At sight they rush towards the clients in ugly scrimmage to snatch the briefs to lay claim to engagement even by physical fight, to undercut fees and by this unedifying exhibition sometimes carried even to the Bar Library solicited and secured work for themselves; such conducts are serious misconduct.[1]

(ix) An advocate was charged that in a trial for rape he attempted to put to the prosecutrix some indecent and unnecessary questions which were disallowed by the court. On appeal, the Supreme Court held that the advocate exceeded his privilege to some extent. The advocate was let off with a warning.[2]

(x) The failure of a pleader to appear to conduct the case before he has discharged himself in the manner prescribed by law unless such an act can be justified, renders him liable to disciplinary action. The advocate cannot justify his action of absence on the ground that his presence at the time of recording the statement of the accused was not necessary. This action is not mere negligence but dereliction of or deviation from duty. The absence of necessary remuneration does not absolve the legal adviser from his obligation unless the matter is brought to the notice of the client.[3]

(xi) An advocate filed a writ petition, knowingly suppressing the fact that earlier an identical writ petition was dismissed before another Bench. Conduct of the advocate deserves stern condemnation. The matter was referred to the State Bar Council for disciplinary action.[4]

(xii) Misappropriation of money paid to an advocate towards filing of a suit by the State Bank of India. The advocate raised the plea that the suit papers were misplaced/lost in the registry of the High Court. Suit papers were returned to the advocate by the High Court Registry for removing the objection. The advocate failed to refile the same for a long time. The advocate was guilty of misconduct.[5]

(xiii) An advocate who was engaged to file 2 suits, one for Rs. 15,000/- and another for Rs. 5,000/- filed the suit for Rs. 15,000/-. He did not file the other suit. The plaint for the suit for Rs. 15,000/- was returned; but it was not represented. The advocate falsely gave some dates of the suits and later told his client that the suits were decreed. He received the money from his client. On initiation of disciplinary proceeding, the advocate returned the money. The advocate was found guilty of misappropriation of client's money, false representation, fraud and deceit.[6]

---

1. *B.C. of Maharashtra* v. *M.V. Debholkar*, A.I.R. 1976 S.C. 242.
2. *Shiv Narayan Jafa* v. *Allahabad H.C.*, A.I.R. 1953 S.C. 368.
3. *In the matter of Maabat Ali Khan*, A.I.R. 1958 AP 116 (FB).
4. *Chandrika Prasad* v. *State of M.P.*, A.I.R. 1985 MP 254.
5. *D.S. Dalai* v. *State Bank of India*, A.I.R. 1993 S.C. 1608.
6. *V.C. Rangadurai* v. *D. Gopalan*, A.I.R. 1979 S.C. 281 (288).

(xiv) Advocate retaining client's money in spite of demands is guilty of misconduct.[1]

(xv) An advocate not returning the will which was entrusted to his custody by his client (the testatrix), despite demands from the testatrix, her new advocate and the legal representative, was held to be guilty of misconduct.[2]

(xvi) An advocate taking advantage of the client's illiteracy and ignorance demanded and received money on false representation that it was necessary for court purpose was held guilty of professional misconduct.[3]

(xvii) An advocate received full amount of court fee from his client. But filed the suit with deficit court fee and prayed for time before the court on the plea that he did not have entire court fee. The advocate was held guilty of misconduct.[4]

(xviii) An advocate received Rs. 50,397.00 on behalf of his client from the court receiver, but paid to the client only Rs. 18,000/-. He was found guilty of misconduct and his name was struck off the roll.[5]

(xix) An advocate entering into engagement with his client for sharing the decretal amount is guilty of misconduct, calling for disciplinary action.

(xx) An advocate who becomes a party to a forged document so as to facilitate commission of fraud is guilty of professional misconduct.[6]

In **Harish Chandra Tiwari v. Baiju,**[7] the advocate has withdrawn amount of compensation in land acquisition proceedings from court and not paid the same to the client. Amount of compensation was Rs. 8118/-. The Supreme Court dealt with an appeal from an advocate who was suspended from practice for three years for misappropriating the amount of compensation payable to client.

The Supreme Court held his removal from the rolls of advocates by observing as under :

"*Among the different types of misconduct envisaged for a legal practitioner, misappropriation of client's money must be regarded as one of the gravest.*"

The Court further held that "*by retaining such advocate on the roll of legal profession, it would be unsafe to the profession. The situation in this case thus warranted the punishment of removal of his name from the roll of advocates.*"

---

1. *In re, an advocate*, A.I.R. 1961 Ker 209 (FB) : *In the matter of P.J. Ratnam*, A.I.R. 1962 A.P. 201 (FB).
2. *John D'souza* v. *Edward Ani*, 1994 (2) S.C.C. 64.
3. *N.B. Mirzan* v. *D.C. Bar Council*, A.I.R. 1972 S.C. 46, 1972(4) S.C. 412.
4. *State* v. *Abani Kanta Roy*, A.I.R. 1959 Orissa 69 (SB).
5. *J.S. Jadhav* v. *Mustafa H. M. Yusuf*, A.I.R. 1993 S.C. 1335.
6. *M. Veerabhadra Rao* v. *Tek Chand*, A.I.R. 1985, S.C. 29.
7. A.I.R. 2002 S.C. 548.

In **Shamburan Yadav v. Hanuman Das Khatry,**[1] the advocate had written a letter to his client to send Rs. 10,000/- to bribe the judge. The Supreme Court took a serious view of the order of the disciplinary Committee in review proceedings and observed as under:

> *"The respondent was indeed guilty of a serious misconduct by writing to his client the letter. The name of the advocate be struck off from the roll of advocates, thus debarring him permanently from the practice."*

In **Sardool Singh v. Pritam Singh,**[2] a person enrolled himself as an advocate, by suppressing material facts about his earlier conviction by a criminal court. On detection thereof, he was suspended from practice, by the Bar Council of India for three years.

However, he continued to practise during the period of suspension and sought review of his suspension. The Supreme Court held that the misconduct on the part of the advocate was very grave and directed that a fresh order of prohibition of three years from practice should be issued by the Bar Council of Delhi.

In **R.D. Saxena v. Balaram Prasad Sharma,**[3] the main issue posed in an appeal before the Supreme Court was of sequential importance for members of the legal profession. The issue was whether the advocate has a lien for his fees on the client's papers.

The Court held that the refusal to return the files to the client when he demanded the same, amount to misconduct under Sec. 35 of the Advocates Act.

In **N.G. Dastane v. Srikant S. Shivde,**[4] The Supreme Court held that advocate abusing the process of court is guilty of misconduct. When witnesses are present in court for examination, the advocate concerned has a duty to see that their examination is conducted.

Seeking adjournments for postponing the examination of witnesses who are present in court even without making other arrangements for examining such witnesses is a dereliction of advocate's duty to the court as that would cause much harassment and hardship to the witnesses. Such dereliction, if repeated, would amount to misconduct of the advocate concerned.

In a matter, the Apex Court has held that an advocate may be punished not only when he is guilty of professional misconduct but also if he is guilty of other misconduct which may not be directly concerned with the professional activity as such, but it is of such a dishonourable or infamous character which would invite the punishment as grave as administered to a person guilty of professional misconduct.

Section 36-B of the Advocates Act, 1961, prescribes period for disposal of disciplinary proceedings. Sub-section (1) of this section provides that the

1. A.I.R. 2001 S.C. 2509.
2. A.I.R. 1999 S.C. 1704.
3. A.I.R. 2000 S.C. 2912.
4. A.I.R. 2001 S.C. 2028.

disciplinary committee of a State Bar Council shall dispose of the complaint received by it under Section 35, expeditiously and in each case the proceedings shall be concluded within a period of one year from the date of the receipt of the complaint or the date of initiation of the proceedings at the instance of the State Bar Council, as the case may be, failing which such proceedings shall stand transferred to the Bar Council of India which may dispose the same as if it were a proceeding withdrawn from inquiry under sub-section (2) of Section 36.

Sub-section (2) of this section provides that notwithstanding anything contained in sub-section (1) where on the commencement of the Advocates (Amendment) Act, 1973, (60 of 1973), any proceedings in respect of any disciplinary matter against an advocate is pending before the disciplinary committee of a State Bar Council it shall dispose of the same within a period of six months from the date of such commencement or within a period of one year from the date of receipt of the complaint, or, as the case may be, the date of initiation of the proceedings at the instance of the State Bar Council, whichever is later, failing which such proceedings shall stand transferred to the Bar Council of India for disposal under sub-section (1).

Section 37(1) provides in this context that any person aggrieved by an order of the disciplinary committee of a State Bar Council made under Section 35 of the Advocate General of the State may, within sixty days of the date of the communication of the order to him, prefer an appeal to the Bar Council of India.

According to sub-section (2) of the Section 37, every such appeal shall be heard by the disciplinary committee of the Bar Council of India which may pass such order including an order varying the punishment awarded by the disciplinary committee of the State Bar Council therein as it deems fit:

Provided that no order of the disciplinary committee of the State Bar Council shall be varied so as to prejudicially affect the person aggrieved without giving him reasonable opportunity of being heard. An advocate can be held guilty for misconduct if he betrays the court or his client. Section 49(1)(c) of the Advocates Act, 1961 empowers the Bar Council of India to make rules so as to prescribe the standards of professional conduct and etiquette to be observed by the Advocates. Chapter II of Part VI of the rules framed by the Bar Council of India deals with the Standards of Professional Conduct and Etiquette. The preamble of this code of conduct clarifies that the standards included in this are not exhaustive. The code does not, however, specify in explicit terms as to how far these rules are enforceable or as to how far they are directives without justiciability. This is so because some of the rules are in the nature of summons. Rule 46 describes the obligation to provide legal aid to the indigent and the oppressed, as the highest obligation of the advocates to the society. The rules as laid down in Chapter II of Part VI clearly specify the duties of an advocate to the court, client, opponent and colleagues etc. If an advocate deliberately neglects his duties towards court and client, which are laid down by Bar Council of India, he would be liable to be punished for misconduct.

Appeal to the Supreme Court

Any person aggrieved by an order made by the disciplinary committee of the Bar Council of India or the Attorney General of India or the Advocate General of the State concerned may prefer an appeal under Section 38 of the Act to the Supreme Court and the Supreme Court may pass such order as deemed fit by it on such an appeal. The limitation for filing an appeal is 60 days from the date of communication of the order appealed against. Generally, the Supreme Court does not interfere with the concurrent finding of fact of the disciplinary committee of Bar Council of India and also of the State Bar Council unless the finding is based on no evidence or it proceeds on mere conjectures and surmises.[1] The appeal to the Supreme Court under Section 38 is not a restricted appeal and not an appeal on the question of law alone, but also on fact. In appropriate circumstances the Supreme Court can review its previous order and set it aside.[2]

Review of Orders by Disciplinary Committee

Section 44 of the Advocates Act, 1961, is relevant to be mentioned provided for review of order by disciplinary committee. The word 'review' means 'reconsider' or 're-examine'. The matter and even subsequent conduct of advocate may be relevant for the porpoises of the review. This section empowers a disciplinary committee of a Bar Council to review its own motion or otherwise, review any order within sixty days of the date of that order passed by it :

Provided that no such order of review of the Disciplinary Committee of a State Bar Council shall have effect unless it has been approved by the Bar Council of India.

In **Sardul Singh v. Pritam Singh**,[3] the Bar Council held the first respondent guilty of professional misconduct and had suspended him from practice for three years, but the respondent continued to practice in a different name, thereby committing a fresh misconduct. At the time of enrolment, he also concealed the material fact of conviction by a criminal court. The Bar Council, in a review application reduced the punishment to admonition. Looking at the seriousness of the misconduct, the Supreme Court set aside the order of admonition and directed the Bar Council to pass fresh order of prohibition of practice for three years.

Bar Council of India has also framed rules for making review of orders. Chapter II of Part VII of the rules of Bar Council of India provides in this respect. Rule 1 provides that an application for review under Section 44 of the Advocates Act shall be in the form of a petition duly signed and supported by an affidavit accompanied by the prescribed fee and filed within 15 days from the date of order sought to be reviewed. Every such

1. *P.D. Khandekar* v. *Bar Council of Maharashtra*, A.I.R. 1984 S.C. 110; also see *Roshan Deen v. Preet Lal*, (2002) 1 S.C.C. 100.
2. *O.N. Mohindroo* v. *District Judge, Delhi*, A.I.R. 1971 S.C. 107.
3. A.I.R. 1999 S.C. 1704.

application shall be accompanied by the prescribed fee and filed within 15 days from the date of the order sought to be reviewed. Every such application shall be accompanied by a certified copy of the order complained of, five additional copies of the application, affidavit and the order and if there are more respondents than one, as many additional true copies as may be necessary. Every such application shall set out the grounds on which the review is sought and shall further state whether any proceedings in respect thereof was filed and is still pending or the result thereof, as the case may be. If a disciplinary committee of a Bar Council does not summarily reject the application under Section 44 of the Advocates Act, 1961 or wishes to exercise its power under Section 44 *suo moto*, the Secretary of the Bar Council shall issue as nearly as may in the form prescribed in this chapter, notice to the parties and to the Advocate General concerned or the Additional Solicitor General of India in the case of the Bar Council of Delhi. If, after such hearing, the disciplinary committee of the Bar Council of State does not dismiss the application and decides that the application for review shall be allowed, the copy of the order along with relevant record shall be sent to the Bar Council of India for approval.

(C) To Appoint Committees and Staff Members

Every Bar Council may appoint disciplinary and legal aid committees. Section 9 of the Advocates Act, 1961, provides that a Bar Council shall constitute one or more disciplinary committees, each of which shall consist of three persons of whom two shall be persons elected by the Council from amongst its members and the other shall be person co-opted by the council from amongst advocates who possess the qualifications specified in the proviso to sub-section (2) of Section 3 and who are not members of the Council, and the senior most advocate the members of a disciplinary committee shall be the Chairman thereof.

Besides this, sub-section (1) of Section 9-A of the Act provides that a Bar Council may constitute one or more legal aid committees each of which shall consist of such number of members, not exceeding nine but not less than five, as may be prescribed.

Sub-section (2) provides that the qualifications, the method of selection and the term of office of the members of a legal aid committee shall be such as may be prescribed.

Sub-section (1) of Section 10 of the Advocate Act provides that a State Bar Council shall constitute the following standing committees, namely—

(a) an executive committee consisting of five members elected by the Council from amongst its members;

(b) an enrolment committee consisting of three members elected by the Council from amongst its members.

Sub-section (3) of Section 10 provides that a State Bar Council and the Bar Council of India may constitute from amongst its members such other committees as it may deem necessary for the purpose of carrying out the provisions of this Act.

In addition to the appointment of above mentioned Committees, a Bar

Council may appoint staff of Bar Council. Sub-section (1) of Section 11 of the Advocates Act, provides that every Bar Council shall appoint a Secretary and may appoint an accountant and such number of other persons on its staff as it may deem necessary. According to sub-section (2), the Secretary and the accountant, if any, shall possess qualifications as may be prescribed.

(D) To Maintain Accounts and Conduct Audit

In this context Section 12 of the Advocates Act is quite relevant. Sub-section (1) of Section 11 provides that every Bar Council shall cause to be maintained such books of accounts and other books in such form and in such manner as may be prescribed.

Sub-section (2) provides that the accounts of a Bar Council shall be audited by auditors duly qualified to act as auditors of companies under the Companies Act, 1956 (1 of 1956), at such times and in such manner as may be prescribed.

Sub-section (3) provides that as soon as may be practicable at the end of each financial year but not later than the 31st day of December of the year next following, a State Bar Council shall send a copy of its accounts together with a copy of the report of the auditors thereon to the Bar Council of India and shall cause the same to be published in the Official Gazette.

III. Bar Council of India

(i) Introduction

The most significant achievement of the Advocates Act, 1961 was creation of a United National Bar in India called as Bar Council of India, with multifarious functions and extensive powers. The complete control and jurisdiction regarding enrolment of advocates and discipline of advocates, which had all along been with the High Courts, stood transferred to the Bar Council of India and the State Bar Councils. The Bar Councils are statutory bodies and have become complete autonomous bodies with elected representatives of advocates. Each State Bar Council sends a representative to the Bar Council of India.

(ii) Composition and Constitution of Bar Council of India

Bar Council of India is composed and constituted under Section 4 of the Advocates Act, 1961. The composition of Bar Council is not entirely on the lines recommended by the All India Bar Committee. The Bar Committee has suggested that each State Bar Council and where there are more than one thousand Advocates on the roll of State Bar Council, it should be entitled to one additional representative. The legislature accepted the provision for representation of State Bar Councils on the Bar Council of India by one member, but it felt that it was not desirable to make distinction between States in which a large number of persons had joined the legal profession and those in which a small number of person had joined the legal profession. There shall be a Bar Council of India for the territories to which this Act extends and shall consist of the following members :

(a) the Attorney-General of India, ex-offcio;

(b) the Solicitor-General of India, ex-officio; and

(c) one member elected by each State Bar Council from amongst its members.

There shall be a Chairman and Vice-Chairman of the Bar Council of India elected for a period of two years. Sub-section 1-A of Section 4 provides that no person shall be eligible for being elected as a member of the Bar Council of India unless he possesses qualifications specified in the proviso to sub-section (2) of Section 3. Every Bar Council is a body corporate having perpetual succession and a common seal with power to acquire freehold property, and to contract, and may by its own name sue and be sued. The advocates are emendable to the jurisdiction of the Bar Councils alone in case of professional actions.

(iii) Functions of the Bar Council of India

Section 7 of the Advocates Act, 1961 prescribes the functions of the All-India Bar Council. The chief functions of the Bar Council of India may be discussed under two heads, namely—

(A) General functions of the Bar Council of India; and

(B) Other functions of the Bar Council of India.

(A) General Functions of the Bar Council of India

(a) to prepare and maintain a common roll of advocates;

(b) to lay down standards of professional conduct and etiquette for advocates;

(c) to lay down the procedure to be followed by its disciplinary committee and the disciplinary committee of each State Bar Council;

(d) to safeguard the rights, privileges and interests of advocates;

(e) to promote and support law reforms;

(f) to exercise general supervision and control over State Bar Councils;

(g) to deal with the disposal of matters referred to it by the State Bar Council;

(h) to promote legal education and to lay down standards of such education in consultation with the Universities in India, imparting such education, and the State Bar Councils, to be observed by the Universities in India;

(i) to recognise Universities whose degrees in law shall be a qualification for enrolment as an advocate and for that purpose to visit and inspect the Universities;

(j) to conduct seminars and organise talks on legal topics by eminent jurists and publish journals and papers of legal interest;

(k) to organize legal aid to the poor in the prescribed manner;

(l) to recognise on a reciprocal basis foreign qualifications in law obtained outside India for the purpose of admission as an advocate under this Act;

(m) to manage and invest funds of the Bar Council;

(n) to provide for the election of its members;

(o) to perform all other functions conferred on it by or under this Act; and

(p) to do all other things necessary for discharging the aforesaid functions.

Under sub-section (2) of Section 7, it has been provided that the Bar Council of India may constitute one or more funds in the prescribed manner for the purpose of—

(a) giving financial assistance to organise welfare schemes for indigent, disabled brother advocates;

(b) giving legal aid or advice in accordance with the rules made in this behalf;

(c) establishing law libraries.

Section 7(3) provides that the Bar Council of India may receive any grants, donations, gifts or benefactions for all or any of the purposes specified in sub-section (2) which shall be credited to the appropriate fund or funds constituted under that sub-section.

Under Section 7(A), the Bar Council of India may become a member of international legal bodies such as the International Bar Association or the International Legal Aid Association, contribute such sums as it thinks fit to such bodies by way of subscription or otherwise and authorise expenditure on the participation of its representatives in any international legal conference or seminar.

(B) Functions of Bar Council of India

The other important functions of the Bar Council of India may be discussed as follows—

(a) Admission as Advocates—

Section 20 of the Advocates Act, 1961 provides that every advocate who was entitled as of right to practise in the Supreme Court immediately before the appointed day and whose name is not entered in any State roll may, within the prescribed time, express his intention in the prescribed form to the Bar Council of India for the entry of his name in the roll of a State Bar Council and on receipt thereof the Bar Council of India shall direct that the name of such advocate shall, without payment of any fee, be entered in the roll of that Bar Council and the State Bar Council concerned shall comply with such direction. The entry in the State roll made in the compliance with such direction shall be made in the order of seniority determined in accordance with the provisions of Section 17(3). Sub-section (3) provides that where an advocate omits or fails to express his intention within prescribed time his name shall be entered in the roll of the State Bar Council of Delhi.

Section 18 of the Act permits that an advocate on the roll of any State Bar Council may, by application in the prescribed form to the Bar Council of India, get, a transfer of his name to the roll of any other Bar Council. But the applications of advocates against whom any disciplinary proceeding is pending or which are not *bona fide* will be rejected. On transfer, the advocate shall retain the same seniority in the latter roll to which he was entitled in the former roll.

Section 19 of the Advocate Act makes it abundantly clear that every State Bar Council shall send to the Bar Council of India an authenticated copy of the roll of advocates prepared by it and shall also communicate all alterations in, and additions to, any such roll as soon as the same have been made.

(b) To appoint Committees and Staff Members

The Bar Council of India is fairly a large body and has been empowered by Section 9 to constitute one or more Disciplinary Committee or Committees consisting of three members each. Two members shall be persons elected by the Council from amongst its members and the other shall be person co-opted by the Council from amongst advocates who possess the qualifications specified in the proviso to sub-section (2) of Section 3 of the Act and who are not members of the Council and the senior most advocate shall be the Chairman thereof.

Section 9-A of the Advocates Act empowers the Bar Council of India to constitute one or more Legal Aid Committees. Each Committee shall consist of such number of members, not exceeding nine but not less than five, as may be prescribed. Besides this, Section 10(2) of the Advocates Act requires the Bar Council of India to constitute Standing Committees other than Disciplinary Committees. The Section reads as follows—

(a) an executive committee consisting of nine members, elected by the Council from amongst its members;

(b) a legal education committee consisting of ten members, of whom five shall be persons elected by the Council from amongst its members and five shall be persons co-opted by the Council who are not members thereof.

The Council may constitute one or more committees if so necessary for the purpose of carrying out the provisions of the Act.

Section 11 of the Advocates Act requires the Bar Council to appoint a Secretary. It also empowers the Bar Council to appoint an accountant and such number of other persons on its staff as the Council may deem necessary. Sub-section (2) of Section 11 provides that the Secretary and Accountant, if any, shall possess such qualifications as may be prescribed.

(c) To maintain accounts and conduct audit—

Section 12 of the Advocates Act enjoins the Bar Council to maintain books of accounts and other books in such form and in such manner as may be prescribed. The accounts are to be audited by auditors duly qualified to act as auditors of companies under the Companies Act, 1956 at such times and in such manner as may be prescribed. The State Bar Council shall send a copy of the accounts and audit report to the Bar Council of India. Copy of the accounts and audit report of the Bar Council of India, shall be sent to the Central Government and shall cause the same to be published in the Gazette of India.

(iv) Powers of Bar Council of India

Powers are given to Bar Council of India under Sections 15, 36, 36A, 36B, 37, 42A, 48AA and 49 of the Advocates Act. These powers may be discussed as follows—

(A) Power to make rules

The Bar Council of India may make rules under the provisions of Sections 15 and 49 of the Advocates Act, 1961. Section 15 confers rule making power on both the Bar Council of India and the State Bar Council. Sub-section (1) enables a Bar Council to make rules generally to carry out the purposes of Chapter II which deals with Bar Councils. Chapter II contains Sections 3 to 15. Sub-section (2) of Section 15 speaks of specific matters on which the State Bar Councils and the Council of India may make rules for all purposes specified in Sections 3 to 14. In order to avoid clash between rules framed by a State Bar Council and those framed by the Bar Council of India, sub-section (3) has specifically been provided under Section 15 that no rule framed by a State Bar Council shall be effective unless approved by the Bar Council of India.

Sub-section (1) of Section 49 provides that the Bar Council of India may make rules for discharging its functions under this Act and, in particular, such rules may prescribe—

(a) the conditions subject to which an advocate may be entitled to vote at an election to the State Bar Council including the qualifications or disqualifications of voters, and the manner in which an electoral roll of voters may be prepared and revised by a State Bar Council;

(ab) qualifications for membership of a Bar Council and the disqualification for such membership;

(ac) the time within which and the manner in which, effect may be given to the proviso to sub-section (2) of Section 3;

(ad) the manner in which the name of any advocate may be prevented from being entered in more than one state roll;

(ae) the manner in which the seniority among advocates may be determined;

(af) the minimum qualifications required for admission to a course of degree in law in any recognised University;

(ag) the class or category of persons entitled to be enrolled as advocates;

(ah) the conditions subject to which an advocate shall have the right to practise and the circumstances under which a person shall be deemed to practise as an advocate in a court;

(b) the form in which an application shall be made for the transfer of the name of an advocate from one state roll to another;

(c) the standard of professional conduct and etiquette to be observed by the advocates;

(d) the standards of legal education to be observed by the Universities in India and the inspection of Universities for that purpose;

(e) the foreign qualifications in law obtained by persons other than citizens of India which shall be recognised for the purpose of admission as an advocate under this Act;

(f) the procedure to be followed by the disciplinary committee of a State Bar Council and by its own disciplinary committee;

(g) the restrictions in the matter of practice to which senior advocates shall be subject;

(gg) the form of dresses or robes to be worn by advocates, having regard to the climatic conditions, appearing before any court or tribunal;

(h) the fees which may be levied in respect of any matter under this Act;

(i) general principles for guidance of State Bar Councils and the manner in which directions issued or orders made by the Bar Council of India may be enforced;

(j) any other matter which may be prescribed—

Provided that no rules made with reference to clause (c) or clause (gg) shall have effect unless they have been approved by the Chief Justice of India—

Provided further that no rules made with reference to clause (e) shall have effect unless they have been approved by the Central Government.

Hence, it is crystal clear that the standards of professional conduct and etiquette to be observed by the advocates and form of dresses or robes in regard to climatic conditions, appearing before any court or tribunal, shall have effect only when when they have been approved by the Chief Justice of India. Further, it has also been made abundantly clear that the rules made with reference to the foreign qualifications in law obtained by persons other than citizens of India, which shall be recognised for the purpose of admission as an advocate under this Act, shall have effect when they have been approved by the Central Government.

Sub-section (2) of Section 49 provides that notwithstanding anything contained in the first proviso to sub-section (1), any rules made with reference to clause (c) or clause (gg) of the said sub-section, and in force immediately before the commencement of the Advocates (Amendment) Act, 1973 (60 of 1973), shall continue in force until altered or repealed or amended in accordance with the provisions of this Act.

Under clause (ah) of Section 49(1), Bar Council of India can lay down the conditions subject to which an advocate shall have right to practice. On the strength of that provision the Bar Council cannot frame any rule which restricts entry of those who have completed 45 years as advocates.

In **Indian Council of Legal Aid and Advice v. Bar Council of India**,[1] the apex court has held that the rule debarring a person who has completed the age of forty-five years to be enrolled as an advocate is arbitrary, unreasonable and beyond the power of Bar Council of India. The rule violates the principle of equality enshrined in Article 14 of the Constitution of India and is hence void.

In **V. Sudeer v. Bar Council of India**,[2] the Supreme Court held that the Bar Council of India has no power to provide for pre-enrolment training as a pre-condition for enrolment.... Rules provided for pre-enrolment training and apprenticeship are *ultra vires* of the rule-making power of the Bar Council of India. Granting of admission to a person for being enrolled as an Advocate under the Act is a statutory function of the State Bar Council only. The Bar Council of India has no role to play on this aspect..... There is no such concept as "Trainee Advocates" under the scheme of the Act. Such a class of advocates cannot be created by the Bar Council of India, by exercising supposed rule-making power under Section 49(1).....All that the said provision enables the Bar Council of India to do is to frame rule under the said provision which may impose condition subject to which an enrolled advocate can carry on his full fledged practice as an advocate.

The Central Government has reserved to itself the power to make rules either for whole of India or for all or any of the Bar Councils for carrying out the purpose of the Advocates Act. It can make rules in respect to any matter for which the Bar Council of India or the State Bar Council has been authorised to make rules. The rules framed by the Central Government have to be published in the official Gazette. After the rules are framed by the Central Government under Section 49-A of the Advocates Act, the rules must be laid before each House of Parliament while it is in session for a total period of 30 days which may comprise in one session or two successive sessions. Before the expiry of the session in which it is so laid or the session immediately following, if both the Houses agree in making any modification in the rules or if both the Houses agree that the rules should not be made, the rules shall thereafter have effect only in such modified form or be of no effect, as the case may be. But the modification or annulment will not affect the validity of anything previously done. The text of Section 49-A is reproduced as under—

> **49-A. Power of Central Government to make rules**—(1) The Central Government may by notification in the official Gazette, make rules for carrying out the purposes of this Act including rules with respect to any matter for which the Bar Council of India or a State Bar Council has power to make rules.
>
> (2) In particular and without prejudice to the generality of the foregoing power, such rules may provide for—

1. A.I.R. 1995 S.C. 691.
2. A.I.R. 1995 S.C. 1167.

(a) qualifications of membership of a Bar Council and disqualifications for such membership;

(b) the manner in which the Bar Council of India may exercise supervision and control over State Bar Councils and the manner in which directions issued or orders made by the Bar Councils of India may be enforced;

(c) the class or category of persons entitled to be enrolled as Advocates under this Act;

(d) the category of persons who may be exempted from undergoing a course of training and passing an examination prescribed under clause (d) of sub-section (1) of section 24;

(e) the manner in which seniority among advocates may be determined;

(f) the procedure to be followed by a disciplinary committee of a Bar Council in hearing cases and the procedure to be followed by a disciplinary Committee of the Bar Council of India in hearing appeals;

(g) any other matter which may be prescribed.

(4) If any provisions of a rule made by a Bar Council is repugnant to any provisions of a rule made by the Central Government under this section, then, the rule under section, whether made before or after the rule made by the Bar Council shall, prevail and the rule made by the Bar Council shall, to the extent of the repugnance, be void;

(5) Every rule made under this section shall be laid, as soon as may be after it is made, before each House of Parliament, while it is in session, for a total period of thirty days which may be comprised in one session or in two or more successive sessions and if, before the expiry of the session immediately following the session or the successive sessions aforesaid, both Houses agree in making any modification in the rule or both Houses agree that the rule should not be made, the rule shall thereafter, have effect only in such modified form or be of no effect, as the case may be; so, however, that any such modification or annulment shall be without prejudice to the validity of anything previously done under that rule.

(B) Disciplinary Powers of the Bar Council of India

Like the State Bar Council, the Bar Council of India has the power to initiate the enquiry against an advocate when it has reason to believe that any advocate whose name is not entered on any State roll has been guilty of professional or other misconduct and in such a case it shall refer the case for disposal to its Disciplinary Authority. Under sub-section (2) of Section 36, the Bar Council of India on its motion or any report by any State Bar Council or on an application made to it by any person interested may withdraw for enquiry before itself any proceedings for disciplinary action against any advocate pending before the Disciplinary Committee of any State Bar Council and dispose of the same. It shall fix the date for hearing, and cause notice thereof to be given to the Advocate concerned and to the Attorney General of India.

Sub-section (3) lays down that the disciplinary committee of the Bar Council of India, in disposing of any case under this section, shall observe, so far as may be, the procedure laid down in Section 35, the reference to the Advocate-General in that section being construed as references to the Attorney General of India. It may, however, be noted that under sub-section (3) of Section 35 of the Advocates Act, 1961, it has been provided that the disciplinary committee of a State Bar Council after giving the advocate concerned and the Advocate General an opportunity of being heard, may make any of the following orders, namely—

(a) dismiss the complaint, or where the proceedings were initiated at the instance of the State Bar Council, direct that the proceedings be filed;

(b) reprimand the advocate;

(c) suspend the advocate from practice for such period as it may deem fit;

(d) remove the name of the advocate from the state roll of advocates.

In this context it has been provided in sub-section (4) of Section 36 that in disposing of any proceedings under this section, the disciplinary committee of the Bar Council of India, may make any order which the disciplinary committee of a State Bar Council can make under sub-section (3) of Section 35, and where any proceedings have been withdrawn for inquiry before the disciplinary committee of the Bar Council of India, the State Bar Council concerned shall give effect to any such order.

Section 36-A deals with the charges made in the constitution of Disciplinary Committee. If any proceedings were pending, the newly constituted Disciplinary Committee may continue the same from the stage at which they were left by its predecessor committee.

Section 3-B of the Act provides for expeditious disposal of complaints received under Section 35 and insists its completion within one year from the date of receipt or initiation *suo moto* failing which it shall stand transferred to the Bar Council of India which may dispose the same as if it was withdrawn from enquiry under Section 36(2). The period of one year prescribed is to be computed from the date of reference to the Disciplinary Committee and not from the date of complaint to the Bar Council.[1]

In **Mangu Sirhari v. Bar Council of Andhra Pradesh**,[2] it was observed that the allegations of misconduct against an advocate should be disposed of expeditiously within a period of one year so that either the cloud cast on the particular advocate is cleared at the earliest or the noble profession is kept clear of such members.

In **P.D. Gupta v. Ram Murti**,[3] the complaint was that the appellant, being the advocate, purchased property which is the subject-matter of the

1. *Karnataka State Bar Council* v. *Subramania Jois*, A.I.R. 1993 Kant 7.
2. A.I.R. 1983 AP 271.
3. A.I.R. 1998 S.C. 283.

suit, from his client at almost a throw away price by undue influence and especially when there was a doubt cast on his client's title to the property. He sold the property to a third person, made profits, and thus became a party to the litigation and created more complications in the pending suit, thereby raising serious questions about the fairness in the conduct of the trial touching professional conduct and bringing the process of administration of justice in disrepute. Since the Disciplinary Committee of the Bar Council of Delhi could not dispose of the complaint received by it within a period of one year, the proceedings were transferred to the Bar Council of India under Section 36-B of the Advocates Act. The Disciplinary Committee of the Bar Council of India found the advocate guilty of professional misconduct and suspended him from practice for a period of one year. On appeal, the Supreme Court confirmed the decision of the Bar Council of India.

(C) Appellate Power of the Bar Council of India

The appellate jurisdiction of the Bar Council of India is conferred under Section 37 of the Advocates Act. Any person aggrieved by the order of the Disciplinary Committee of the State Bar Council may prefer an appeal to the Bar Council of India and every such appeal shall be heard by the Disciplinary Committee of the Bar Council of India. Section 37 reads as below—

> 37(1) Any such person aggrieved by an order of the disciplinary committee of a State Bar Council made under Section 35 of the Advocate General of the State may, within sixty days of the date of the communication of the order to him, prefer an appeal to the Bar Council of India.
>
> (2) Every such appeal shall be heard by the Disciplinary Committee of the Bar Council of India which may pass such order including an order varying punishment awarded by the Disciplinary Committee of the State Bar Council thereon as it deems fit—
>
> Provided that no order of the Disciplinary Committee of the Bar Council of State be varied by the Disciplinary Committee of the Bar Council of India so as to prejudicially affect the person aggrieved without giving him reasonable opportunity of being heard.

Section 38 of the Act provides remedy to the person aggrieved by the order passed by the Disciplinary Committee of the Bar Council of India. It provides that any person aggrieved by an order made by the Disciplinary Committee of the Bar Council of India under Section 36 or Section 36-A of the Advocates Act or the Attorney General of India or Advocate General of the State concerned, as the case may be, may within 60 days of the date on which the order is communicated to him, prefer an appeal to the Supreme Court and the Supreme Court may pass such order including an order varying the punishment awarded by the disciplinary committee of the Bar Council of India thereon as it deems fit. The expression "as it deems fit" occurring in Section 37(2) confers a jurisdiction of widest amplitude on the Disciplinary Committee of the Bar Council of India hearing appeal under Section 37. But that does not mean that it can pass any order in total disregard of the statutory provisions under which it is created and is conferred jurisdiction to resolve disputes arising in the implementation of the statute. The Disciplinary Committee of the Bar Council of India is a creature of the Advocates Act, 1961 on whom the duty to lay down standards of professional conduct and etiquette for advocates is conferred and is further charged with the duty to safeguard the rights, privileges and interests of the advocates. Hence, when it is said that the Disciplinary Committee of Bar Council of India may decide the case "as it deems fit", the order has to be relevant to the functions of the Bar Council of India. The appellate body could exercise the State Bar Council even if the person aggrieved by mild punishment or Advocate General have not preferred an appeal. It can as well exercise this power in the appeal preferred by the delinquent advocate. This is what is meant when it is said that disciplinary proceedings against lawyer not only involves the particular lawyer but the profession as a whole.

Besides this, a comprehensive view of the legislation as a whole show that the Bar Council of India exercises general supervision and control over State Bar Councils and Disciplinary Committee of State Bar Council is a creature of State Bar Council. Hence, the question of jurisdiction has to be viewed in this broad perspective and not from any narrow or constricted view which one may take in a private dispute between two individuals. Further, a disciplinary proceeding against a member of a profession whose services are made available to society as a whole is to be viewed as between the profession and its erring member and not between the complainant and the delinquent advocate. This larger perspective must determine the jurisdiction of the bodies set up to carry out the purposes of the Act.[1]

Similarly, Section 38 of the Act deals with appeals to the Supreme Court against order passed by the Bar Council of India. The section reads—

> "Any person aggrieved by an order made by the Disciplinary Committee of the Bar Council of India under Section 36 or Section 37 or the Attorney General of India or the Advocate General of the state concerned, as the case may be, may, within sixty days of the date on which the order is communicated to him prefer an appeal to the Supreme Court and the Supreme Court may pass such order including an order, varying the punishment awarded by the Disciplinary Committee of the Bar Council of India thereon as it deems fit—
>
> Provided that no order of the Disciplinary Committee of the Bar Council of India shall be varied by the Supreme Court so as to prejudicially affect the person aggrieved without giving him a reasonable opportunity of being heard."

Appeal to the Supreme Court may be either against an order passed by the Disciplinary Committee of the Bar Council of India in its original jurisdiction, or against an order in its appellate jurisdiction. An appeal filed

1. *Narendra Singh* v. *Chhotey Singh*, A.I.R. 1983 S.C. 1990.

before the Supreme Court may be considered on both law and fact. The Supreme Court has also jurisdiction to review its decision and to pass such orders as it may deem fit and proper and even to set aside its order disbarring an Advocate if the case involves unusual circumstances. But no order of the Bar Council of India shall be varied by the Supreme Court so as to prejudicially affect the person aggrieved without giving him a reasonable opportunity of being heard.[1]

The disciplinary jurisdiction of the State Bar Council and the Bar Council of India to take action for professional misconduct is recognized by the Advocates Act, 1961. It is different from the jurisdiction of Courts to take action against Advocates for the contempt of Court. The court in **Supreme Court Bar Association v. Union of India,**[2] held that it cannot invest itself with the jurisdiction of the Disciplinary Committee of the Bar Council to punish Advocates for professional misconduct while dealing with a case of contempt of court.

In many cases it was held that the Supreme Court in appeal under Section 38 would not as a general rule, interfere with the concurrent finding of the fact by the Disciplinary Committee of the Bar Council of India and of the State Bar Council unless the finding is based on no evidence or it proceeds on mere conjecture and unwarranted inference....When a lawyer has been tried by his peers, there is no reason for the Supreme Court to interfere in appeal with the finding in such a domestic enquiry merely because on a re-appraisal of the evidence a different view is possible.[3]

If an appeal is dismissed for default of non-appearance, as no one appeared for the Advocate, his challenge in a subsequent suit that the decision of the Bar Council was illegal, loses its efficacy on dismissal of appeal.[4]

Section 40 of the Advocates Act enacts that an appeal to the Bar Council of India or to the Supreme Court shall not operate as a stay of the order appealed against, but the Disciplinary committee of the Bar Council of India, or the Supreme Court, as the case may be, and in cases where an application is filed for stay of the order before the expiration of the time for appealing, the concerned Disciplinary Committee may, for sufficient cause, direct the stay of such order on such terms and conditions as it may deem fit.

(D) Other powers and functions of the Bar Council of India

(a) According to Section 46-A inserted for the first time in the Advocates (Amendment) Act, (70 of 1973), the Bar Council of India may, if it is satisfied that the State Bar Council is in need of funds for the purpose

1. *O.N. Mohindroo* v. *The District Judge, Delhi and another*, A.I.R. 1971 S.C. 107.
2. A.I.R. 1988 S.C. 1895.
3. *V.C. Rangadurai* v. *D. Gopalan*, A.I.R. 1979 S.C. 281; *Chandra Sekhar Soni* v. *Bar Council of Rajasthan*, A.I.R. 1983 S.C. 1012; *P.D. Khandekar* v. *Bar Council of Maharashtra*, A.I.R. 1984 S.C. 110.
4. *Bar Council of India, New Delhi* v. *Manikant Tewari and others*, A.I.R. 1983 All 357.

of performing its functions under this Act, give such financial assistance as it deems fit to that Bar Council by way of grant or otherwise.

(ii) Section 47(1) of the Act provides that where any country, specified by the Central Government in this behalf by notification in the Official Gazette, prevents citizens of India from practising the profession of law or subjects them to unfair discrimination in that country, no subject of any such country shall be entitled to practise the profession of law in India. Subject to the provision of sub-section (1) of section 47 of the Act, the Bar Council of India, may prescribe the conditions, if any, subject to which foreign qualification in law obtained by person other than citizens of India shall be recognised for the purpose of admission as an advocate under this Act.

(iii) The Bar Council of India has been empowered under Section 48-A of the Act, with revisional power. Under Section 48-A(1), the Bar Council of India may, at any time, call for the record of any proceeding under this Act which has been disposed of by a State Bar Council or a committee therefor a member of a Bar Council or any committee thereof, and from which no appeal lies, for the purpose of satisfying itself as to the legality or propriety of such disposal and may pass such orders in relation thereto as it may fail. No order which prejudicially affects any person shall be passed under this section without giving him a reasonable opportunity of being heard.

(iv) Power to review is also provided to the Bar Council of India or any of its committees, other than its disciplinary committee, may of its motion or otherwise review any order, within sixty days of that order, passed by it under this Act.

(E) Power to give directions

According to Section 48-B(1), for the proper and efficient discharge of the functions of a State Bar Council of any committee thereof, the Bar Council of India may, in the exercise of its power of general supervision and control, give such directions to the State Bar Council or any Committee thereof as may appear to it to be necessary, and the State Bar Council or committee shall comply with such directions.

(2) Sub-section (2) further provides that where a State Bar Council is unable to perform its functions for any reason whatsoever, the Bar Council of India may, without prejudice to the generality of the foregoing power, give such directions to the ex-officio member thereof as may appear to it to be necessary and such directions shall have effect, notwithstanding anything contained in the rules made by the State Bar Council.

IV. Issues Related to Proposed Amendments in Advocates Act, 1961 and Recent Controversies

Presently the legal profession described as the second largest in the world, that is, next to the United States of America. The Advocates Act, 1961, in India which now governs the legal profession was enacted, giving effect, amongst others to recommendations of All India Bar Committee and the Report of the Law Commission of India (1958).

Proposals to Restructure Legal Profession

Proposals have been mooted in the past to restructure legal profession. On 3rd July, 1993, the then Chairman of the Bar Council of India in a letter to the Chairman of the Law Commission of India approved the recommendations made by the Committee on Subordinate Legislation of the 10th Lok Sabha for adequate funds to bring about qualitative improvements in the legal education; providing law course for five years' duration; renewal of registration of advocate once in every five years; making available for practising lawyers for refresher course after 3-4 years.

Subsequently, the Law Commission of India worked out proposals for restructuring the legal profession spelt out in a Working Paper on the Review of the Advocates Act, 1961, circulated by the Bar Council of India on 31st August, 1999, to the State Bar Councils. Views of the State Bar Councils were sought in view of the urgency of the matter. The Law Commission of India stated that the "strength of the Indian democracy lies in the legal system which has to respond to changes imaginatively." Further, that the legal profession is "beset with problems and challenges not entirely of its own making," the Advocates Act, 1961, which provides framework of the legal profession warrants "review in the light of perceived difficulties and anticipated challenges to enable it to meet the needs of the judicial administration and the cause of better services to the public."

The legal profession is graphically described as pyramidal structure, as those occupying the top have work, wealth and frame beyond limits, and those in the middle, have reasonable opportunities of making a living and prospects for joining the fortunate few at the top, but the vast majority constituting nearly 50% of the profession are left to struggle for work and survival. The irony of the situation is that there is a growing demand for legal services and large area of unmet legal needs in society, yet the surging number of advocates are unable to get employment unless they have godfathers in the profession or abundant political patronage.

In the changing scenario, the Advocates Act may need fresh look if judicial administration were to achieve expected results. The impending globalisation of legal services may also necessitate variety of changes to prepare the profession to face challenges ahead.

Substance of Proposed Changes

The proposed changes are of the nature that go to the very root of the legal profession. At the same time, the changes do not co-relate to the problems with which the legal profession is beset. The proposed changes as agreed to by the Bar Council of India vide its Chairman's letter dated 3rd July, 1993, ostensibly deal with the endeavour to improve 'qualitatively' the legal education and requiring all lawyers to attend 'refresher course after 3-4 years' and thereafter obtain renewal of 'registration once in every five years on payment of renewal fee.

The Working Paper on the Review of the Advocates Act, 1961, prepared by the Bar Council of India approves a number of amendments that transform the very nature and character of the legal profession and the autonomy accorded to it. Proposals of the Law Commission were by and large approved on 23rd October, 1999, in the Working Paper on "Amendments to the Advocates Act, 1961", by the Bar Council of India.

Substance of Proposals

An overview of the proposed amendments highlights the following broad areas which call for serious consideration :—

(a) There is a need to "qualitatively improve the legal education." Commanding position is given to the Legal Education Committee, prescribing five-year law course and setting up of State Law Academics, etc. Though a Committee of Bar Council, Legal Education Committee has been changed into a body comprising dominantly of outsiders, out of 15 members of the Legal Education Committee has only 5 members from the Bar Council. The very character of the Legal Education Committee is changed.

The proposed composition of the Legal Education Committee under Section 10 is as under :

(i) 5 members of the Bar Council;

(ii) 3 Judges sitting or retired, co-opted in consultation with the Chief Justice of India;

(iii) 3 Law Professors co-opted in consultation with the Chairman of the University Grants Commission;

(iv) Director, National Law School, Bangalore;

(v) Secretary, Government of India, Ministry of Law; and

(vi) Secretary, Bar Council of India.

The senior-most Judge in the Committee is to be its Chairman.

The professional legal education has been handed over to non-practising advocates, though still being under the 'aegis' of the Bar Council.

(b) The next area more directly deals with the nature and character of the legal profession. From a 'profession' it is transformed into a sort of 'commercialized venture'. For example, provision is inserted under Section 49 of the Act whereunder "non-lawyer professionals may be allowed to associate themselves in partnership with lawyers." This opens up the legal profession to multi-disciplinary partnerships. In the same strain, changes are proposed to be brought into Disciplinary Committee under Section 4 of the Act which would comprise as under :

(i) 2-3 members of the Bar Council of India;

(ii) 3 Judges, sitting or retired, nominated by the Chief Justice of India;

(iii) 2 nominees of the Union Law Minister;

(iv) President of the Supreme Court Bar Association;

(v) President of Bar Association of India (a non-statutory and non-registered body);

(vi) 2 Professors of Law;

(vii) A nominee of the Chairman of the Press Council of India.

Here again, the character of the Disciplinary Committee has been changed from a "Committee of Peers" to a Committee whose members are dominantly outsiders. Furthermore, it is not clear as to what disciplinary control such a Committee would exercise on "non-lawyer professionals".

(c) Another area to which serious exception must be taken is the proposed changes in completely diluting, rather destroying autonomy of the Bar. The character of the Bar Council has been changed under Section 3 and 4 of the Act by providing that State Bar Councils will comprise of one-half members elected as under :

(i) 30 members in case of electorate not exceeding 10,000;

(ii) 40 members in case of electorate not exceeding 20,000;

(iii) 50 members in case of electorate exceeding 20,000.

The other half of the members of the Bar Council will be filled up by nomination from amongst representatives of recognized Bar Associations in the State, Law Officers of the State Government; Judicial Officers, sitting or retired nominated by the Chief Justice of the High Court.

As for the Bar Council of India, it is to comprise as under :

(i) One member from amongst its members elected by the State Bar Councils not exceeding 10,000 electorate;

(ii) 2 members from amongst its members elected by the State Bar Councils exceeding 10,000 but not more than 20,000 electorate;

(iii) Three members from amongst its members by the State Bar Councils having more than 20,000 electorate.

Remaining members of the Council will be as under :

(1) 3 Judges, sitting or retired, nominated by the Chief Justice of India;

(2) 2 nominees of the Union Law Minister;

(3) President of the Supreme Court Bar Association;

(4) President of the Bar Association of India;

(5) Two Professors of Law in the Service of University teaching law to be nominated by the University Grants Commission;

(6) Nominee of the Chairman of the Press Council of India.

While destroying the autonomy of the Bar Council, wheel is turned to make the legal profession subservient to the dominance of judges, sitting or retired. The rampant practice to induct sitting and retired judges has already had deteriorative effect on the administration of justice. Numerous instances can be cited on Commissions, Tribunals, Arbitrators and a number of quasi-judicial and executive bodies in this regard. To place the legal profession again under the shadows of judiciary will perhaps be disastrous. The irony is that at a time when demand to make superior judiciary accountable is raised unequivocally, reins of the legal profession are sought to be put in the hands of judiciary, destroying the autonomy gained in 1961 after years of struggle.

(d) The next area deals with the entry of foreign lawyers. Proposals have been made to enturst the Bar Council with the power to prescribe rules for laying down conditions in respect of reciprocity and conditions upon which non-citizen foreign lawyers would be permitted to practise legal profession in India.

As has been pointed out, the three main areas to which exception is taken, deal with transforming the nature and character of the legal profession from 'profession' into a sort of 'commercialized venture' and destroying its autonomy. This changes the basic character that brings in its wake number of other consequences, such as permissibility of contingent fees and permitting members of the legal profession to participate in 'business ventures' and bidding good-bye to professional ethics and discipline.

The proposed amendments are such as would not be acceptable to members of the legal profession. The proposals sought to be introduced in the name of improving the standards of education and excellence of legal services provide sugar coating of the bitter pill.

Amendments Misconceived

The changes proposed do not emanate from problems proposed by the Law Commission itself, which has taken note of the fact that the legal profession is "beset with the problems and challenges not entirely of its own making" and also the prevalent conditions that the vast majority which "constitute nearly 50% of the professionals are left to work for survival, in the absence of having godfathers or abundant political patronage."

The proposed changes do not even superficially grapple with the state of legal profession that the Law Commission has graphically described. Rather than improving things, these will add to the misery of overwhelming majority of legal professionals and throw them at the mercy of unscrupulous tycoons and touts. Whatever semblance remains of ethics will be thrown to the winds.

The endeavour to "improve" legal services is an attempt to make them available for the globalised corporate entrants by the proposed amendments is a retrograde step that will destroy the character of legal profession and its autonomy.

Some other changes inconsequential in nature do not really change the nature of main amendments which are wholly unacceptable. The amendments by and large are retrograde an unacceptable. If things have to be improved, a dispassionate and thorough exercise must be taken up to identify the areas that are outmoded and solutions found to improve the nature of the legal profession, democratise its autonomous character and make its performance and services wholesome and useful to the administration of justice and the general public.

4

RIGHTS OF ADVOCATES

The members of legal profession, by virtue of law and usage, enjoy certain rights and privileges. Rights and privileges of advocates in India are not different from those of Barristers in England. There the advocate has the rights of audience as an Advocate in all the superior and most of the inferior courts. The advocate has the right to draw or prepare for or in expectation of fee or reward instruments relating to real or personal estate or any legal proceeding. Further, the advocate has the right to advise on question of law. The advocate has the right of authenticating by his name the report of case decided in court.

In India too, the authors find that the advocates have the following rights provided by law and usage.

(i) Right to Freedom of Speech and Expression

Article 19(1)(a) of the Constitution of India provides the right to freedom of speech and expression to all citizens. An advocate need not fear the police, bureaucrats, legislators and even the judiciary. But he should stick to the reasonable restrictions imposed on this right in the interest of the sovereignty and integrity of India, the security of the State, friendly relations with foreign states, public order, decency or morality, or in relation to contempt of court, defamation or incitement of an offence. He should not hurt the religious feelings of any sect. He should speak in decent language and should not use intemperate language.

(ii) Right to Practice and Audience

Prior to the enactment of the Advocate Act, 1961 there were different classes of Legal Practitioners viz., Barristers, Advocates, Vakils, Pleaders, Mukhtars, Agents etc. The Act of 1961 made several important changes and brought this profession into uniformity. Now there is only one class of legal practitioners, viz., Advocates. Chapter IV containing Sections 29 to 34 of the Advocates Act, 1961 explains the legal provisions about the right to practise. Section 29 of the Act imposes strict restriction that advocates are the only one class of persons to practice the profession of law. The right to practice is authorized only to the advocates, who have enrolled their names in the Roll of a State Bar Council. According to Section 30 of Act of 1961, every advocate, whose name is entered in the State roll is entitled as of right to practice throughout the territories to which this Act extends, subject to the provisions of this Act—

(a) In all courts including the Supreme Court;

(b) Before any tribunal or person legally authorized to take evidence; and

(c) Before any other authority or person before whom such advocate by or under any law for the time being in force entitled to practise. Only advocates have monopoly right to represent clients in courts.

The Advocates Act, 1961 virtually did not affect the position of the legal practitioners. In other words, the Advocates Act did not affect the right to practise the profession of law of the pleaders, mukhtars, vakils and revenue agents who were the legal practitioners prior to passing of the Act of 1961. Even though the Advocates Act prescribed certain qualifications and these legal practitioners are not qualified to be the advocates within the meaning of Section 2(1)(a) of the Advocates Act and they are entitled to continue their practice subject to the provision of law under which they enrolled. This protection is conferred by Section 55 of the Advocates Act, 1961. Section 55 of the Act makes it clear that the law prior to the passing of the Advocates Act shall be deemed to have not been repealed so far the existing legal practitioners as on the date of the enforcement of the provisions of the Advocates Act. Their rights are protected by those enactments and their conduct is regulated by actions as contemplated in them. At present an advocate must enroll himself under the Advocates Act only. The admission or enrolment as a pleader, mukhtar, vakil or revenue agent is done away with. Section 33 of the Advocates Act strictly prohibits any persons other than an advocate to practise law. The only exception to this rule is the provision laid down in Section 55 which preserves the rights of the legal practitioners in tact.

An advocate is entitled to sit in any Court, even though he has no work in that court. It is a right conferred by usage. It is called 'Right of Audience'.

(iii) Right for Welfare Fund

States have enacted Advocates Welfare Fund Act in 1987 and every advocate practicing in any court in the State becomes a member of the fund. As per Section 16 of the Act, a member of the fund shall, on cessation of practice, be entitled to receive from and out of the fund an amount at the rate specified in the schedule after five years of service at the rate of one thousand for a completed year.

(iv) Right of Fee

An advocate has right to his fee. This right is absolute and not conditional. It does not depend upon winning or losing of the case. The advocate can insist upon the payment of their fees in advance or rely on their lien on the clients papers and on the fruits of the litigation as well as on their right to sue for their fees. Rule 11 of Chapter II of Part VI of the Bar Council of India Rules provides that the advocate has a right for a fee consistent with his standing at the bar and the nature of the case. Sometimes, advocates do take up cases without any fees, then it will not be their right. An advocate is entitled to settle with his client his fee for any engagement having regard to the nature of assignment, extent of the professional skill required to be used in the case and also having regard to his standing in the Bar. But this always should be subject to the Advocate's Fees Rules. The fee allowed by the rules is generally known as scale fee as different scales are fixed by the rules. An advocate shall not accept a brief for an amount below the scale fee. It amounts to underselling, which is bad. The only exception to it is serving the cause of the poor, otherwise known as legal aid to the poor. It is, therefore, crystal clear that a highly skilled professional command fees that are commensurate with his eminence, expertise and experience. The methods of charging fees may be namely, fixed fee, hourly fee, per hearing fee, contingency fee, retainers fees, referred fees etc. The Legal Practitioners (Fees) Act, 1926 was limited in its application and did not provide for any Code of Conduct in regard to charging of fees. Section 50(5) of the Advocates Act, 1961 repealed the Legal Practitioners (Fees) Act, 1926. Till date, no statute has been enacted to regulate advocates' fees. The only regulation in India is found in the Bar Council of India's Standards of Professional Conduct and Etiquette. A lawyer has a right to settle his fees by private agreement with his client. But it should be borne in mind that a contract between a lawyer and his client is not as on a par with a common contract between two parties. A lawyer has always been regarded as a person who is in a position to dominate the will of his client. Section 16 of the Indian Contract Act, 1872 puts the burden on the person who is in a position to dominate the will of the other that the contract was not induced by undue influence, if the terms of contract are, on the face of it unconscionable. Needless to say that a contract for fee of an advocate must not be unconscionable. Legal Profession is a branch of the administration of justice and it can never be regarded as or equated with money earning trade. One who converts the profession to a trade degrades the profession. Therefore, an advocate while entering into an engagement with his client regarding the fee must bear this noble principle in mind. The nature of the profession is such that the fixation of fee of an advocate cannot be put in a straight jacket of a formula. It is not feasible to frame any rule laying down the precise standards for determination of fees of advocates.

(v) To Enter the Bar

An advocate has a right to sit in the seats provided for advocates, whether he is having a case or not and observe the proceedings of the court.

(vi) Advocate's Right to Refuse a Brief

According to Section 29 of the Advocates Act, 1961 the only one class of persons entitled to practice the profession of law, is namely advocates.

As per Rule 11 of Chapter II of Part Vi, an advocate is bound to accept any brief in the Courts or Tribunals or before any authority in or before which he professes to practice at a fee consistent with his standing at the bar and the nature of the case. Special circumstances may justify his refusal to accept a particular brief.

Defending a client known to be guilty neither involves violation of law nor ethics. No person is guilty unless otherwise proved. Any guilty person has the right to defend himself in court. A client approaches a particular advocate after satisfying that he has sufficient experience, knowledge and ability to safeguard his interests. No advocate refuses a brief. But in situation where he could not appear before court lawfully, then he has a right to refuse a brief and it is his duty also.

The following are the circumstances where an advocate should not plead in a Court and where he has to refuse a brief :

According to Rule 4 of Section 1 of Chapter II of Part VI of the Rules of the Bar Council of India, an advocate shall refuse to represent the client who persists in unfair practices and improper conduct.

According to Rule 6 of Chapter II of Part VI of the Bar Council of India rules, an advocate shall not enter appearance, act, plead or practice in any way before a court, tribunal or authority mentioned in Section 30 of the Act, if the sole or any member thereof is related to the advocate as father, grandfather, son, grandson, uncle, brother, nephew, first cousin, husband, wife, mother, daughter, sister, aunt, niece, father-in-law, mother-in-law, son-in-law, brother-in-law, daughter-in-law, or sister-in-law.

For the purposes of this rule, Court shall mean a Court, Bench or Tribunal in which above mentioned relation of the advocate is a Judge, Member or Presiding Officer.

Rule 8 of Chapter II of Part VI of the Bar Council of India Rules lays down that an advocate shall not appear in or before any Court or tribunal or any other authority for or against any organization or any institution, society or corporation, if he is a member of the Executive Committee of such organization or an institution, society of corporation, if he is a member of the Executive Committee of such organisation or institution or society or corporation. "Executive Committee" by whatever name it may be called, shall include any Committee or body of persons which, for the time being is vested with the general management of the affairs of the organisation or institution, society or corporation :

Provided that this rule shall not apply to such a member appearing as *'amicus curiae'* or without a fee on behalf of a Bar Council, Incorporated Law Society or a Bar Association.

Rule 9 of Chapter II of Part VI of the Bar Council of India Rules provides that an advocate should not act or plead in any matter in which he is himself pecuniary interested.

(i) He should not act in a bankruptcy petition when he himself is also a creditor of the bankrupt;

(ii) He should not accept a brief from a company of which he is a Director.

Rule 13 of Chapter II of Part VI of the Bar Council of India Rules lays down that an advocate should not accept a brief or appear in a case in which he has reason to believe that he will be a witness and if being engaged in a case, it becomes apparent that he is a witness of a material question of fact, he should not continue to appear as an advocate if he can retire without jeopardizing his client's interests.

While disposing the case, **Allahabad Bank Ltd. Fyzabad v. Thakur Bakhsh Singh**, the Privy Council held, "it is very important that men at the Bar should understand that they are members of a public profession. That is by their very calling engage and undertake to act for anybody who fulfills certain conditions. Therefore, if a client comes to them with proper instructions and prepared to pay a fair and proper fee and invites them to undertake a case of a kind which they are accustomed to do and they refuse, such refusal amounts to professional misconduct, and should be punished as such. That is to say, nor has a lawyer any right to reject a brief when offered to him on payment of fee agreed upon the ground of partnership for a party to the litigation."

No advocate should accept a fee less than the fee taxable under the rules when the client is able to pay the same. At the same time, Article 39-A of the Constitution of India provides that if the arrested person is poor, free legal aid and equal justice shall be provided to him. Hence no advocate has right to refuse a brief on the basis of fee.

If an advocate refuses to appear on the ground that the fee offered is not adequate enough for him, it is violation of professional ethics of a lawyer. An advocate should not bargain for higher fee and refuse a brief on that basis. Without any reasonable and honest excuse when a party offers fee and is ready to give instruction and the case is fair, refusal to accept a brief on some ground or other amounts to professional misconduct and the advocate is liable to be removed from the rolls. It was laid down in **Md. Inayat Khan v. Fazal-ul-Rahman**,[1] that a lawyer must, as a general rule, take up a case from any member of the public. Of course, he can decline to take up a brief for genuine reasons. But "to refuse to take up a case simply and solely on the ground that the advocate will not appear against a brother practitioner or to put forward untrue excuses when the reason is disinclination to appear is professional misconduct."

In India, there is no provision to refuse a brief legally. But it is the general opinion that defending a client known to be guilty neither involves violation of law nor ethics, and such client must be defended, irrespective of the personal opinion of the advocate. But, as the advocacy is a noble profession, an advocate should not counsel or maintain any suit or proceeding which is unjust and dishonest.

(vii) Right to Lien

Once a lawyer has filed a *vakalatnama* in a case it is his privilege that no one else can step in without his consent. Earlier the law was that a lawyer had a lien, for any unpaid fee, upon such papers of the client as were in hands. This lien was possessory. Even, courts could not grant leave

1. A.I.R. 1929 All 367.

to appear in the case if he remained unpaid when he had a right of lien upon the briefs and papers in his possession. Unless satisfactory arrangements for the payment of his fees has been made and the judge is satisfied on that account, even the judge cannot make an order to hand over the brief either to another advocate or to the client. In **New India Assurance Co. Ltd. v. A.K. Saxena,**[1] two Judge bench of the Supreme Court consisting of S.N. Variava and Dr. A.R. Lakshmanan, JJ. while considering the issue of returning of files by an advocate to his client between whom a dispute had arisen, took the position that the right of the litigant to have the files returned to him is a corresponding counterpart of the professional duty of the advocate and the dispute regarding fees is an issue to be decided in an appropriate proceedings. Whenever or not the fees were payable to the advocate, the court refused to consider that question and observed that the entitlement of the advocate to the fee would also be open for consideration in appropriate proceedings for recovery of his fees. The Court has curlty observed that in order to claim the unpaid remuneration from a client, advocates cannot retain the papers of their clients against his will. However, the advocates have the right to sue for unpaid fees. Earlier also the Supreme Court has in **R.D. Saxena v. Balram Prasad Sharma,**[2] held that advocates have no lien over the papers of their clients. It was held that at the most the advocate may resort to legal remedies for unpaid remuneration. The Court held that the litigant has the right to have the files returned to him and it is the corresponding professional duty of the advocate to return the same and if he refuses the same, he shall be held liable under Section 35 of the Advocates Act, 1961 for misconduct.

(viii) Right to have access to Judge

It is the right of a lawyer to have access to the judge in urgent judicial matter at any time during day or night, and the Judge cannot refuse to give audience to him.

Of course, when such urgent matters are taken after the working hours of the Court, the convenience of the judge has to be looked into. Though, it looks bitter and odd yet it is the right of the advocate to refuse to recognize and appear before a presiding officer/judge who is not in the prescribed robe of a judge in the Court. Similarly, a Judge can also refuse to give an audience to the lawyer who is not in the prescribed dress.

Besides these, the advocates have the right of audience, right to draw and prepare legal proceedings, right to advise on question of law, right to advise clients and to represent them, right to appear and argue for them in judicial proceedings, and liberty to address the court in regular course to combat and contest strongly any adverse views of the Judge or Judges expressed on the case during its argument, to object to and protest against any course which the Judge may take and which the advocate thinks irregular or detrimental to the interests of his client.

---

1. A.I.R. 2004 S.C. 311 : 2003 (9) SCALE 531.
2. A.I.R. 2000 S.C. 2912.

5

PRIVILEGES, DISABILITIES AND FUNCTIONS OF ADVOCATES

I. Rights and Privileges

The profession of law is a noble profession with serious responsibilities. The notability of it consists in this fact that the lawyers have to act as watchmen in order to protect the rights of the people. Hence, they are looked upon as the protectors and defenders of life, liberty and property—of course at a price. They are expected to act in honest and upright manner because they have the privilege of discharging all those duties which those who are not members, of the legal profession cannot do. Justice Mukherji in **Emperor v. Rajani Kanta Bose and others**,[1] has rightly observed that the practice of law is not a business open to all who wish to engage in it; it is a personal right or privilege...it is in the nature of a franchise from the state....' All rights attached to the office of advocate by virtue of law and usage are in a sense, his privileges. The lawyer is given an absolute privilege and this absolute privilege carries with it a special responsibility that should not be abused. It is true that no human society can exist or run unless it contains some privileged sections to function in their respective fields for public good, mass benefits and common man's interest. Officials supervising or safeguarding public interest should be protected with privileges or exemption from the burdens of legal consequences of their actions or omissions. You cannot penalise police or the military for any killings that might result in the normal course of their duties for maintenance of internal peace or defence against external aggression, King can do no wrong. Heads of the States, Ministers, Ambassadors, diplomats, Consuls and Envoys are entitled to immunities. However, these privileges and immunities are subject to restrictions. There is always a limit beyond which counsel should not go in attacking the opposite party or his witness. The counsel is a privileged person to espouse the cause of justice, for his client. By virtue of his status, the advocate belongs to the most noble and erudite segment of the society. He is an officer of the court. His rule in any justice system cannot be overemphasised. He is an inseparable wheel of the chariot of public cause for clean, speedy and fair justice. M. Duguit, the eminent French jurist and political theorist enunciates : "A man has only one right, viz; the right

1. I.L.R. 49 Cal. 804.

to do his duty." Therefore, the advocate is in urgent need of some privileges for his honest, sincere and diligent discharge of duties to uphold the law. To safeguard the interest of his clients he has to speak, write and otherwise expose many things against his client's opponent or to show the hollowness of other side's arguments, prove the character of the opponent and/or opponent's witnesses for rejection or ignoring their dispositions by the court. All these routine features of the law profession points out the serious necessity for privilege to be provided for protecting an advocate from the application of the general laws of the land if he acted as an ordinary person only, but not as an advocate.

A two day national seminar on "Privileges, Court Fees and Access to Justice" was held at Hyderabad on 11-12 December, 1982 under the joint auspices of the Bar Council of India Trust and the Bar Council of Ar dhra Pradesh. The seminar was attended by over 300 lawyers from District and Taluka Bars of Andhra Pradesh besides members of the Bar Council of India and representatives of State Bar Councils. It was inaugurated by the then Vice-President of India Hon'ble Mr. M. Hidayatullah. The speakers unanimously felt that the subject was of paramount importance. In his inaugural address, Mr. Hidayatullah stated that there was a duty owed by advocates to the court on the one hand, and their clientele on the other and pointed out that their privileges did not extend beyond the ends of justice.

On the occasion, Mr. Justice P. Rama Rao of the Andhra Pradesh High Court said that "brilliant advocates contributed to correct judgment. Advocates had unfettered right in the presentation of the cases. Arrest of advocates and employment of force against them by the executive are a sad situation." Learned Counsel F.S. Nariman said that "law is a profession and not a business. One has to be efficient and honest." He cautioned that mere honesty without efficiency was useless. He deprecated boycott of courts. He pointed out that "advocates" privileges are service oriented." The speakers unanimously felt that the advocates are the limbs of the administration of justice. Any attempt to interfere with the freedom of advocates constituted an act of contempt of court. There was near unanimity on all the following points : (i) Freedom of advocacy is the most important privilege and any attempt aimed to curb it will have to be deprecated; (ii) Among the Bench and the Bar there must be an element cf mutuality in the matter of extending respect and courtesy; and (iii) cases of professional misconduct have to be examined only by the statutory Bar Council and should not rest with the courts.

A difference of opinion surfaced at the seminar as to whether the privileges of advocates should or should not be codified. The question has been solved by the joint conference of Bar Council of India with the State Bar Council held at Bangalore on 25th and 26th February, 1984. "All the State Bar Councils were of the opinion that not only privileges but rights and interests of the Advocates shall be considered together according to sub-sections 6(1)(d) and 7(1)(d) of the Advocates Act, 1961. These State Bar Councils were of the opinion that the following privileges should be enjoyed by the advocates : (i) The freedom of advocacy in the courts so long that advocates think it necessary for pleading the case of his client; (ii) the judges should not interfere at the time of argument. If the judge interferes or asks the advocate to take his seat and if the advocate does not comply with the order of the judge for the best interest of his client and feels necessary to continue the argument and place the case of his client, then that will not amount to contempt; (iii) fair treatment from courts and the advocates should be strictly treated as officers of courts; (iv) immunity from penal action with regard to any communication made by an advocate on behalf of his clients on instructions; (v) immunity from arrest while going in courts for performing professional duties, returning from courts after performing professional duties, performing duties by orders of courts and practising the profession of law; (vi) immunity from arrest for custody of documents, paper, etc. of clients for the purpose of opinion and cases; (vii) taking full instructions from clients with regard to trial in camera; (viii) taking notes from records and/or documents, papers, etc. filed in courts and quasi-judicial authorities even if the same are prohibited by law; (ix) immunity from legal actions for expressions used at the time of argument on instructions from client; (x) communications between advocates and clients; (xi) immunity from proceedings for contempt and/or defamation for expressions used in courts during arguments under instructions from client."

As a member of legal profession, the lawyer enjoys certain exclusive privileges. These are as follows :

(i) The right to hold himself out as a lawyer.

(ii) The right to advise clients and to represent them.

(iii) The right to appear for them in judicial proceedings.

(1) Privilege to Claim Audience

In India, licensing of legal practitioners was till recently a judicial function and the judges had the power to debar them, but now by the Advocates Act, 1961, the power is vested in the Bar Council of India. In any court and in any proceeding the litigant has a right to appear in person but he does not choose to avail of that privilege and the law allows him to be represented by a counsel, then he must choose for his advocate someone from the ranks of the Bar. In India, there is no common law right of the litigants to be represented by Counsel. Under the Bar Council Act, the advocates' right of audience depended on Section 14 of the Act which run as follows. "As advocate shall be entitled as of right to practice—(a) Subject to the provisions of sub-section 4 of Section 9 of the High Court of which he is an advocate, and (b) save as otherwise provided by sub-section (2) or by or under any other law for the time being in force in any other court in British India and before any other tribunal or person legally authorised to take evidence."

The right of advocates to practise is now regulated by Section 30 of the Advocates Act, 1961. It lays down that subject to the provisions of the Act every advocate in common roll shall be entitled as of right to practice throughout the territories to which the Act extends : (i) in all courts including the Supreme Court; (ii) before any tribunal or person legally authorised to take evidence; and (iii) before any other authority or person before whom such advocate is by or under any law entitled to practice.

Although the advocates enrolled under the Advocates Act have been conferred an absolute right under Section 30 to practise before all courts and tribunals, but Section 30 has not yet been brought into force. Consequently, at present the right of an advocate brought on the rolls to practise is what is conferred by Section 14(1)(a), (b) and (c) of the Bar Council Act, 1926.

Advocates have the privilege of practising and pleading before the court and nobody else. In **Jaymal Thakore v. Gujarat State Charity Commissioner, Ahmedabad**,[1] Gujarat High Court ruled that the right of pleading and practising is monopolised by registered advocates. A chartered accountant holding power of attorney could only appear, file an application or act on behalf of the party in the proceedings as a recognised agent, but he could not plead or practise as a pleader or an advocate.

It is the privilege of a person who fulfills the prescribed qualification to become a member of the Bar; it is the privilege to represent his clients in the courts of law; it is his privilege to claim audience in courts so long he acts decorously; this is an exalted profession in which privilege is duty and duty is privilege. They both coincide. Words spoken by lawyer in his professional capacity in the course of a judicial inquiry or in the examination of witnesses are privileged. The advocate can insist on his right to be heard without any hindrance.

Bench and Bar are the two main limbs of judiciary and one without the other cannot function. It is, therefore, necessary that the harmony between the two must be maintained. Bench and Bar should give due respect to each other. In **T. Venkata v. The Hon'ble High Court of Mysore**,[2] the court held that when an advocate appears before the court as a litigant in person, he is not exercising any right under Section 30 of the Act. So, he cannot be permitted to argue with his robes on from the advocate's table.

(2) Privilege of Exemption from Arrest

Common law doctrine of absolute privilege does not apply to the criminal law of defamation in India. Privilege of the advocate is analogous to that of the clients. A lawyer while going to the court to attend a matter or while returning from the court is exempt from arrest under Section 135 of CPC. This privilege also does not appear to be his personal one because it is in furtherance of public interest and for the promotion of administration of justice. In other words, in civil process, other than process for contempt of court, while going to the court or attending the court for returning from court, a lawyer is exempted from arrest.

1. A.I.R. 2001 Guj. 279.
2. A.I.R. 1973 Mys. 127.

(3) Privilege of being offered judgeship and several other offices under the statute

It is the privilege of a lawyer that he is made eligible for holding several offices under the statutes, e.g., an advocate is eligible for appointment as a District Judge, Additional District Judge, Magistrate, Session Judge, Additional Sessions Judge, etc. An advocate of a High Court with 10 years' standing is eligible for appointment as Advocate General or a Judge of a High Court. He has also the privilege to become Munsif, Official Assignee, Official Receiver, PUblic Prosecutor, Government Pleader and Liquidator under administrative rules.

(4) Privilege of Public and Political Life

An advocate can enter public or political life without any fear, and play his part therein. He can be a member of Parliament or legislature. He enjoys overall privileged position in society at public places.

(5) Privilege of Independence

It is the privilege of an advocate that he is frank, fearless and independent. It is his privilege that he is subordinate to none except God, because he stands for justice and fights for justice alone and that makes him a leader of the society. It is the privilege of the advocate to exercise independent judgment in determining how he will conduct the case. So strong is the practice the etiquettes of the profession requires that counsel in this respect will not be guided even by the advice of the court. Thus, if the court tells him that the evidence already recorded was sufficient to support his client's case, that will not by itself justify the counsel not producing further evidence.

(6) Words Spoken in Professional Capacity are Privileged

The words spoken by an advocate in his professional capacity in the course of a judicial inquiry or examination of witnesses are privileged.

(7) It is an advocate's privilege to ensure that the forms and requirements of the law are strictly observed and carried out and to defend an accused person towards that end even though the advocate may have knowledge or reason to believe that he is guilty. In carrying out his duties the advocate enjoys broad powers and a blissful immunity from legal consequences for what he says. He has, as C.P. Harvey observed, a standing invitation 'to be clever at someone else's expense'.[1]

In order to 'encourage due freedom of speech in the lawful defence of their clients', advocates have a wide range of immunities. Counsel 'is at liberty to make strong, even calumnious observations against the party, the witnesses and the attorney in the cause'.[2] No action will lie against him for defamatory words spoken with reference to and in the course of a court hearing, even if they were spoken not with the object of furthering the cause of his client, but rather from personal ill will and without justification.

1. C.P. Harvey QC, The Advocate's Devil, 13 (1958).
2. *Flint* v. *Pike*, (1825) 4 B & C 473, 378 (Bayley J).

(8) It is also the advocate's privilege, resulting from the credit due to the honour and prestige of the profession, to make, on occasions, statements from your place in the Bar and without being sworn. For example, it appears sometimes in cases where advocate takes part in settling compromise of pending litigations, that disputes occur when the matter is brought before the Judge for being made an order of the court. The extent of advocate authority or any mistake he may have made or some other like question might be mooted. It is then advocate's privilege to make a statement from the Bar on matter that have transpired without making an affidavit. Lord Esher once said that they would never admit an affidavit in such cases but trusted to the honour of lawyer. In **Hickman v. Berens**, a dispute arose as to the extent of the authority given by the client to his advocate and the court accepted the statement of advocate made from his place in the Bar without requiring it to be made on oath. On the same principle, a barrister in England enjoys a peculiar privilege. He has the right to authenticate by his name the report of a case decided in court. As soon as the report is published of any case with the name of a barrister annexed to it, the report is accredited and may be cited as an authority before any tribunal. That marks the limit of the reliance placed on the integrity of the profession.

II. Disabilities

A lawyer should not only be well versed with his rights and privileges as an advocate, but also should be thorough with his ethical obligations, his responsibilities to abide by the legal ethics. An advocate should be able to distinguish between right and wrong in matters of professional conduct without difficulty or hesitation. He should not indulge in abusive and reckless charges of fraud, dishonesty and criminality. He is not allowed to take up a brief where his position makes him a party to the cause, and destroys his independence. He cannot appear, for instance, for or against a local authority of which he is a member. He should not accept brief on behalf of a society of whose executive he is a member. Further, he cannot accept brief for a company of which he is a Director. If he is instructed by a private person to prosecute in any court in a case of which the public prosecutor is in charge, the public prosecutor shall conduct the prosecution and he shall act therein, under the latter's direction. He must not divulge his client's communications. These disabilities are elaborated under the following heads :

(i) Advertising oneself and soliciting client

The duty of an advocate not to advertise or solicit is based, not only on history, but also on practical utility. Historically, the profession of law is developed more in the spirit of public service than as a means of earning livelihood. Hence, it is natural that the lawyer must impose on himself the duty of neither advertising nor soliciting. Even from the practical utilitarian point of view, advertising, solicitation or encroachment on the practice of others do not tend to benefit either the public or the lawyer. On the other hand, extensive advertising on the part of the lawyer might increase litigation which of course is definitely against public policy. Hence, advertising in any form by an advocate is highly objectionable. It is aimed at drawing attention of the public and is a device for obtaining public favour of notoriety. An advocate should not seek business by advertisement or otherwise. As advocacy is not a business, it can be said that the advocate is liable for misconduct if he advertises. It was held in **Kanepath Kaur v. Kasi Prasad Singh**,[1] that it is well recognised rule of etiquette in legal profession that no attempt should be made to advertise oneself directly or indirectly. Such conduct is unprofessional on the part of an advocate to solicit directly or indirectly to advertise through various methods—crude or subtle. Such a course of action tends to lower the dignity of the honourable profession and is akin to touting. An advocate should remember that attaining excellence in the profession and earning his reputation in the Bar and the Bench of being a devoted, diligent, hard working, learned and honest advocate is the most effective advertisement and he does not need inspired news item in the column of 'Law Court' in the newspapers displaying his name or sometimes his photographs.

It is an axiom of the profession that any form of self-advertisement by a practising member of the Bar is contrary to etiquette, and amount to seeking unfair advantage over other members of the Bar. In England, it is unprofessional for a barrister to do anything for touting directly or indirectly. Therefore, no barrister is allowed to write to solicitors or even to brother practitioners on circuit, extolling his services, experiences, ability or work. Advertisements of all forms are considered to be highly improper. The Canon 27 of the American Bar Association also states that "it is unprofessional to solicit professional employment by circulars, advertisements, through touters or by personal communications or interviews not warranted by personal relations." It may be noted that the rules framed by the Bar Council of India are also similarly worded. Section 49(1) of the Advocates Act, 1961 confers power on the Bar Council of India to make rules for discharging its functions. Rule 36 in Chapter II of the Standards of Professional Conduct and Etiquette of the Bar Council of India Rules, 1975 lays down that an advocate shall not solicit work or advertise either directly or indirectly, whether by circulars, advertisements, touts, personal communications, interviews not warranted by personal relations, furnishing or inspiring newspaper comments or procuring his photograph to be published in connection with cases in which he has been engaged or concerned. His signboard or name plate or stationery should not indicate that he is or has been President or member of a Bar Council or of any Association or that he has been associated with person or organisation or with any particular cause or matter or that he specialises in any particular type of work or that he has been a judge or an Advocate-General. **In re Thirteen Advocates of Allahabad**,[2] it was held that advertising in any form, by extolling of services, experience, ability or work in any branch of

1. A.I.R. 1934 All. 106.
2. A.I.R. 1934 All 1067; also see *C.D. Sekkizhar* v. *Secretary Bar Council*, A.I.R. 1967 Mad. 35.

law on the part of a lawyer is highly improper and amounts to a gross breach of professional etiquette.

An advocate should not seek business by advertisement or otherwise. As advocacy is not a business, it can be said that the advocate is liable for misconduct if he advertises. **In re A, an advocate**,[1] the Supreme Court held that the writing letters for a brief by advocate, stating his achievements and his knowledge in some specialised subjects amount to professional misconduct, makes him unfit to be a member of the Bar. In this case, an advocate on record of the Supreme Court wrote a letter to the Minister, Law, Maharashtra and in the letter, he wrote—"you might have got an advocate on record in this court but I would like to place my services at your disposal if you so wish and agree." The Supreme Court through Shah, J. held :[2]

> *"It was in utter disregard of truth. He has in this court, condemned himself as a liar and one who is either ignorant of the elementary rules of professional ethics or has no regard for them. In our opinion the Advocate has mischosen his profession. Apparently, he is a man of weak moral fibre. If he is ignorant of the elementary rules of professional ethics he had demonstrated the inadequacy of training and education befitting a member of the profession of law. If he knew that it was highly improper to solicit brief and even then he wrote the postcard in question, he is very unworthy member of the legal profession."*

The advocate was punished and was suspended from practice for five years.

In **Bar Council of Maharashtra v. M.V. Dabholkar**,[3] the allegations of misconduct against over a dozen advocates according to the testimony recorded by the State Disciplinary Committee were that the respondents positioned themselves at the entrance of the Magistrate's Courts, watchful of the arrival of potential litigants. They snatched away briefs from litigants, fought with each other and even tore clothes in grim competition, and in various ways showed grave misconducts in soliciting business. The matters were taken up in appeal before the Supreme Court and were considered together. V.R. Krishna Iyer, J., on behalf of himself and three other Judges (R.S. Sarkaria, A.C. Gupta and S. Murtaza Fazl Ali, JJ.) on the Bench observed "with deep sorrow" that a lawyer should scrupulously observe the norms of professional conduct and etiquette provided in Rule 36 of the Bar Council of India Rules made in this behalf and be worthy of the confidence of the community and not behave with doubtful scruples and strive to thrive on litigation. The court also regretted the low standard of enquiry conducted by the State Council prolonged for 8 years by clubbing together 16 cases and trying them together though the charges in each case were different and by misconstruing Rule 36 (which prohibits soliciting work by circulars, advertisements, touts, etc.) as rendering advocates

1. A.I.R. 1962 S.C. 1337.
2. *Ibid.*, at p. 1340.
3. A.I.R. 1976 S.C. 242.

amenable to disciplinary jurisdiction if they have : (i) solicited work; (ii) from a particular person; (iii) with respect to a case, and holding that "mere attempts to solicit is nothing". Considering fully well, the available evidence, circumstances, assurances, undertakings and unconditional regrets in each case separately, their Lordship took a lenient and sympathetic view against the respondents. Justice V.R. Krishna Iyer, in his characteristic style speaking about the profession of law said, "The canons of ethics and propriety for legal profession totally taboo conduct by way of soliciting, advertising, scrambling and other obnoxious practices, subtle or clumsy, for betterment of legal business. Law is no trade, briefs no merchandise and so the leaven of commercial competition or procurement should not vulgarise the legal profession." Canvassing for professional work in any manner is prohibited by Rule 34 of the Bar Council of India Rules. Even a signboard or a name plate should be of a moderate size.

In **P.D. Kandekar v. Bar Council of Maharashtra,**[1] the court held that touting or appointing touts is inconsistent with the rules framed under the Advocates Act, 1961 and such practice would be considered as professional misconduct. The underlying principle behind prohibiting advertising and touting is that lawyer's profession is entirely different from trade or business. It is well recognised rule of conduct that no attempt should be made to advertise oneself directly or indirectly. But in practice there are indirect advertising like publishing the name of the advocate who appeared in a case through the media, websites created by lawyers, taking part in radio-television programmes, engaging legal aid programmes, and engagement in public activities, etc.

Hence, the lawyers in India are averse to advertising their profession even if there is no restriction imposed by the Advocates Act. A lawyer thinks it below dignity, nobility and erudition and legal professional ethics. India is vehemently against lawyer advertising and seeks the protection of the International Bar Association to stop such advertisement and corrupt practices so that the image of the Bar of the world remains in highest esteem of entire humanity.

(ii) Restrictions on other employments

An advocate has a duty to stick on to the profession and elevate it. Rule 42 of the Bar Council of India provides that an advocate shall not engage himself in any business. Advocates shall not carry on any other profession or business or be active partners or salaried servants in connection with any business. But he may be sleeping partner in a firm doing business provided that, in the opinion of the Bar Council the nature of business is not inconsistent with the dignity of the profession. A lawyer may be a Director of a Company with or without any ordinary sitting fee, provided none of his duties are of an executive character but he should not be its Managing Director or Secretary. Further, an advocate who has inherited or succeeded by survivorship to a family business may continue it but may not personally participate in the management thereof. He may

1. A.I.R. 1984 S.C. 110.

continue to hold a share with others in any business which has descended on him by survivorship or inheritance or by will, provided he does not personally participate in the management. There is also a restriction that no lawyer shall be entitled to practise if in the opinion of the Bar Council he is suffering from such contagious disease as makes his practice of law a hazard to the health of others. This restriction shall last for such period as the Bar Council directs from time to time. Hence, restriction on other employment has been imposed with a view that the advocate should devote his whole time and entry to the learned profession of law which affords vast opportunities for service, and he should not join vocations in which the principles of conduct may be contrary to the rules of etiquette at the Bar and there is a possibility of ethical standards of the Bar getting lowered by the simultaneous pursuits of collateral occupations. The Supreme Court in **Hariraj L. Chulani v. Bar Council of Maharashtra and Goa**,[1] has observed that legal profession requires full time attention and would not countenance an advocate riding two horses or more at a time. The court further said that such a restriction is for ensuring the full time attention of law practitioners towards their profession and with a view to bringing out their best so that they can fulfil their role as an officer of the court and give their best in the administration of justice.

In **Satish Kumar Sharma v. Bar Council of H.P.**,[2] a three-judge Bench of the Supreme Court speaking through Justice Shivraj V. Patil held that a law graduate working as a full time salaried employee in any organization cannot continue as an advocate on the rolls of a State Bar Council. The court, in the instant case upheld the decision of the Bar Council of Himachal Pradesh withdrawing the enrolment of one Satish Kumar Sharma, who joined the H.P. State Electricity Board as an Assistant (Legal) and who was later promoted as Deputy Secretary (Legal)-cum-Law Officer on *ad hoc* basis. The court observed that the profession of law is called a noble profession and it does not remain, noble merely by calling it as such unless there is a continued, corresponding and expected performance of a noble profession. Its nobility has to be preserved, protected and promoted. An institution cannot survive in its name or on its past glory alone.

(iii) Restriction on taking up a brief where his position makes him a party to the cause and destroys his independence

An advocate cannot accept brief for a company of which he is a Director. He cannot appear for or against a local authority of which he is a member. He should not accept brief in which he has acted in a judicial or quasi-judicial character, e.g., as Commissioner or Arbitrator. He should not accept brief on behalf of a society, of whose executive he is a member. Further, a lawyer should not appear in a case in which he has to give testimony. This is not on account of conflict between interest and duty, but is based on a different principle, namely, "it might tend to throw suspicion on the lawyer's character which may entail loss of respect for the profession

1. (1996) 3 S.C.C. 342.
2. (2001) 2 S.C.C. 365 : A.I.R. 2001 S.C. 509.

as a whole and diminish public confidence in the purity of the administration of justice."

(iv) Advocate cannot buy or contract for any share of interest in an actionable claim

The duty of the counsel is to discourage dishonest or dubious litigation. Almost as a corollary to this duty not to stir up litigation, is is enjoined on a lawyer not to traffic in litigation. Section 136 of the Transfer of Property Act provides that no legal practitioner shall buy or traffic in or stipulate or agree to receive any share of, or interest in any actionable claim and no court of justice shall enforce, at his instance, of any person claiming by or through him, any actionable claim, so dealt with by him as aforesaid. It is not proper for a lawyer to contract for a share in the fruits of litigation. Detachment and objectivity are indeed the basis of the strength of the Bar and when a lawyer agrees to share in the profits of litigation, he can never retain due detachment and objectivity while advocating the cause.

(v) Advocate must not divulge client's communications

It is a duty of a lawyer to preserve his client's confidence. He should represent his client with fidelity and not divulge his secrets or confidences. Hence, the relation between the advocate and his client is of trust and confidence. Section 126 of the Indian Evidence Act lays down that an advocate is not permitted at any time, unless with his client's express consent, to disclose any communication made to him in the course and for the purpose of his employment by or on behalf of the client, or to state the contents of any document with which he has become acquainted in the course and for the purpose of his professional employment, or to disclose any advice given by him to his client in the course and for the purpose of such employment. Protection from disclosure, however, does not extend to : (a) any such communication made in furtherance of an illegal purpose; (b) any fact observed by an advocate in the course of his employment showing that any crime or fraud has been committed since the commencement of his employment.

The privilege extends to the documents of the client also which are entrusted to the advocate. The advocate shall not disclose the nature and condition of the documents entrusted to him by his clients as long as the client does not expressly permit. He is also debarred from disclosing the contents of the documents with him. He is the custodian of the documents of his clients. Further, a communication or document which is "once privileged is always privileged." The obligation continues after the employment in which the communication was made has ceased. It is not affected even if the party ceases to engage the same after the engagement and takes away the brief to some other counsel. Even if the relationship between the client and the counsel is changed, the obligation remains unaltered. The obligations continue even where the advocate ceases to be an advocate by virtue of his employment in some other manner or his suspension or removal from rolls. Even if the advocate becomes personally interested in the property of the title of which the communication relates, the obligation continues. Lastly, even the death of the party does not put an end to the obligation. It is, therefore, the reason why it is called "once privileged is always privileged."

The privilege is the privilege of the client, and not of the advocate or other professional advisors. It may be waived by the client, but never ceased unless waived by the client or his successors in title. Privilege is not waived by referring a document in a pleading, affidavit or list of documents, but it is waived when a document is disclosed to the other party in the course of litigation. Hence, the privilege can be claimed only in respect of a communication made to the advocate in his professional capacity. It cannot be claimed if the statement is not made to him in the course and for the purpose of his employment as a pleader. The reason for the rule is that if such communications are not privileged, the client might desist from fully disclosing his case, so as to be able to obtain proper professional aid. The rule protects both the advocate and the client.

Functions of an Advocate

Arthur T. Vanderbilt states the functions of a great advocate in the following terms :

(1) A truly great advocate is a wise counselor to all manner of men in the varied crises of their lives when they most need disinterested advice. Counselling calls for a wide and deep knowledge of human nature and of modern society and most difficult of all, truly great counseling calls for an ability to forecast the trends of the law.

(2) An able advocate is a skilled and trained one in the art of prosecuting and defending the legal rights of men both in the trial courts and on appeal. Advocacy is not a gift of God. It is trail as well as in its appellate aspects it involves several distinct arts, each of which must be studied and mastered. Unless an advocate has had experience, it is difficult to see how he can be a thoroughly competent counselor for he will not be able to evaluate his clients' cause in terms of the realities of the court room.

(3) An advocate is to do his part individually and a member of the organized Bar to improve his profession, the Court and the law.

(4) In a free-society every advocate has a responsibility that of acting as an intelligent, unselfish leader of public opinion.

(5) Every advocate must be prepared, not necessarily to seek public office but to answer the call for public service when it comes.

These five—(i) Counselling; (ii) advocacy; (iii) improving his profession, the courts and law; (iv) leadership in moulding public opinion; and (v) the unselfish holding of public office are the essential functions of the great advocate.

6

PROFESSIONAL ETHICS AND ETIQUETTE OF LAWYERS

I. Introduction

The profession of law is the only profession which is generally described as a learned and noble profession. It is called learned and noble because of its continuous quest for acquisition of further information and knowledge. Certainly by the standards that are available, the moment the person has obtained a degree in law and has satisfied certain requirements prescribed by the Bar Council, he is entitled to practise the profession of law. But, that alone will not make him either an effective or efficient or prominent lawyer. It is not enough if a lawyer is expert in law alone, he has to be an expert practically in every field and aspect of human life and knowledge. Many thinkers have put the legal professions even though having regard to life saving feature of the medical profession, that profession has been considered to be nobler than other professions. Hence, the members of the legal profession occupy a high status. It imposes a duty on legal practitioners to conduct themselves in a manner befitting the high position. A lawyer is equal to a person holding a public office. He has to infuse and generate compassion and he must endeavour to alleviate the element of injustice in the society. The lawyers while performing their professional duties not only earn their livelihood, but also influence the lives and conditions of life of many. A lawyer while lawyering, an advocate while doing advocacy is no doubt making his own fortune, but in addition to that his art of lawyering, his techniques of advocacy, his skills of argument, his scientific treatment to the law and the facts in hand cast definite shadows on the conditions in the society; lawyers make the most significant contribution to the final outcome of justice system, that is, the court verdicts and judgment which ultimately shape the future path of our society.

Professions are often distinguished from occupations and businesses by the commitment they carry to certain values which every society upholds in the organisation and delivery of public services. It is in this context that professions particularly earlier ones, were called "learned and noble". Sometimes professionals are characterized as the "conscience-keepers" of society. The legal profession is associated with societal values such as "justice", "fair dealing", "integrity" and "probity". The lawyer is taken as trusted advisor with whom the clients have a personal relationship on the basis of the former's professional competence, personal integrity and assured loyalty. The profession is today respected to the extent it maintains high standards of legal skill and a reputation for integrity. It is said that every lawyer must realise that "he is something more than the fuel in the engine of the law". Lawyers have a greater responsibility in the contemporary situation when people have to concentrate on public interest, legal aid to the poor, etc.

II. Meaning of Ethics

The word 'ethics' is derived from the Greek word **'ethos'** meaning custom or a habitual mode of conduct. The Latin term for morals or morality also is said to spring from the Greek word **'ethos'.** Ethics is essentially a moral science. It is that branch of philosophy which is only concerned with human character and conduct. Though generally 'ethics' is treated to be the same as moral philosophy, yet it is convenient to distinguish between 'ethics' which refers to systematic general science of right and wrong conduct, and morals or morality which refers to the actual patterns of conduct and direct working rules of moral action. Generally speaking, ethics can be said to be the study of human actions in respect of they being right or wrong actions of individuals and social groups supplying the subject-matter of ethics. The social group with which we are now concerned is the one belonging to the profession of law. Different people have evolved theories of what constitutes 'ethics'. In every one of them, the basic question has always been, what will be conducive to the welfare and good of all, in other words, the greatest common good, whether it is with reference to particular group, community or society as a whole. When the mind gets broadened and the notions of group get expanded, distinctions based on a particular social group, community or society disappear, and we are ultimately left with the test of what is good for the humanity as a whole.

In matters of ethics, several questions and aspects are involved. But the broad and the basic question with which all theories of ethics are concerned is "what ought men to aim at; and how ought they to live" as distinguished from what are men's aims and purposes. The answer to the question, what are men's actual aims and purposes, may not be complementary and flattering to many of us. But the answer to this question will always be enlightening and elevating. Unless we have our eyes fixed on "what ought men to aim at; and how they ought to live", progress will be impossible because we lose sight of the distinction between 'what is' and 'what ought to be'. 'What ought to be' has always been the noble aim of every person with reference to his or her activity, while 'what is' is the result of compromise, which a person has convinced himself to be inevitable in the practical humdrum world.[1]

Ethics is present in every human society. Ethics are born in human civilization since the beginning. Every religion preaches morals and ethics

1. Extracted from the address by Justice Ismail at the All India Law Seminar at Madurai on 9th April, 1978. Reported in *The Law Weekly*, 17th June, 1978, Vol. XCI (91), p. 77.

to every person, to that entire society. Ethics have no statutory force. It is something that maintains the moral integrity of a community. Ethics embodies a set of norms and principles which govern the moral conduct of a member of the community. They are essential because human nature tends to choose the easier path that often does not lead to good.[1] Ethical norms are, therefore, meant to chastise and reform a person and not to suppress desire. There is need to chastisement and straightening of the crooked will so as to enable it to cooperate with reason. Unlike other sciences which are more on the theoretical since, ethics is highly practical in its approach. It seeks to guide man's action by indicating which is good and which is bad or what is right and what is wrong. From this point of view, ethics is the noblest science. When we speak of ethics we are at once led to think of four key concept which are truly the cornerstones of ethical evaluation, they are 'good' and its opposite 'bad', 'right' and its opposite 'wrong'. If we are to remove these concept from dictionary of ethics, then we would have altogether destroyed ethics.

There is a need to examine what does the term 'good' imply. A thing is generally said to be good when it is valuable for some end.[2] Not to misunderstand this term, one should remember that there are three divisions of 'good', namely metaphysical good—the goodness of a thing or action in its very self; physical good—something that is related to conductiveness and suitability of a thing or the desirability of a thing; and lastly moral good—which applies only to acts of rational beings. One can term it as real good or apparent good.[3] Real good is that which is seen or judged as good for a thing and is really so. Apparent good is that which seems to be good but is actually not good for a being.

Similarly, the term 'right' which comes from the Latin root *rectus*, meaning straight or according to rule, 'right' applies only to conduct and not to things. The term 'right' has been generally accepted as a better term in determining the ethical nature of an action rather than the term 'good'. An action is right if it conforms to the norms of morality. For example, "I speak the truth", is a right action because it is in conformity with the ethical law which says "speak the truth".

These concepts of 'good' and 'bad', 'right' and 'wrong' are most universal concepts. They are present in every society and are inherent in every man. A person does not need to go to school to learn from them. These are termed as the voice of conscience which was endowed on human being by God. However, ethical evaluation of conduct varies from place to place. Certain types of conduct may be considered morally acceptable in one society while in other societies they may be morally prohibited.

Etymologically, the word 'ethics' denotes a location, a place where people lived together. With the passage of time, the word has acquired other meanings, including custom, temperament, character, and a way of

1. G. Spiller, Ethical Discipline in Encyclopedia of Religion and Ethics 405 (1937), Vol. V.
2. J. Mackenzie, A Manual of Ethics 2 (1980).
3. *Ibid.*

thinking. In ancient philosophy it possessed a terminological meaning denoting the nature or permanent character of a physical or social phenomenon.

The history of the word 'ethics' is similar in the Latin of Ancient Rome. The Latin word for *ethos* is, roughly, *mos*, which can be translated as mores, custom, character, behaviour; property inner nature; law, regulation, fashion, style of clothing. Relying on the Greek precedent and making a direct reference to Aristotle, Cicero formed the adjective *moralis* (that which pertains to character, customs), and later, in the 4th century A.D., Romans coined the term *moralitas*. Etymologically, the Greek *ethica*, and the Latin *moralitas* are the same; they did not evolve inside popular consciousness but are artificial terms coined to give a name to a certain field of research. The two terms, ethics and morality, gained currency throughout Europe, diverging in meaning as cultural development progressed. The term ethics has retained its original meaning and still denotes a scientific discipline, while morality is the phenomenon study by this discipline—i.e., its subject-matter.

Ethics is the discipline which studies morality. This definition outlines the field of research into morality but does not pinpoint its subject. The latter is liable to historical change; it conveys a certain interpretation of morality and registers a qualitative stage in cognition of its essence.

In a nutshell, ethics are morals. It is the science of morals and duties. There are the first stage in a society and are seen in every kind of human life. In other words, these are inherent in every man. Generally, these are found in religions. Ethics are bundle of habits and morals and are necessary to control and regulate every human being. If ethics are violated, there can be no punishment. There shall be no external enquiry, but only internal regret and confession. The person, who violates ethics, cannot be expelled from the society or profession. Ethics have their source from the tradition, culture and heritage. These guard the society at large and guide the person individually.

III. Nature of Ethics

Ethics is far from being purely a natural science which seeks only to explain things as they are, their nature and essence but it is a normative or critical science.[1] It is concerned not only with things and actions but our judgments upon them as well. Ethics deal with human acts. Human acts are done voluntarily with knowledge and free will.

Ethics is not a practical science unlike other sciences. Sciences of medicine and engineering perfect the practitioner. The student who studies them become an expert in those fields. On the other hand, the study of ethics does not necessarily perfect a person. The person who knows all about ethics need not be a saint. Knowledge of ethics does not make him or her a better person.[2] Even though ethics may not make better people

1. J.H. Muirhead, "Ethics" in Encyclopaedia of Religion and *Ethics* 414 (1974), Vol. 11.
2. Mackenzie, A Manual of Ethics 5 (1980).

yet we should not be forgetful of the valuable service it renders to humanity.

Ethics is essentially concerned with "right and wrong". How do we judge whether an action is right or wrong? This has been a perplexing question for mankind. Different groups of people have different approaches of criteria in judging the moral quality of an action. In general there seems to be three accepted tests for judging an action. These are :

(a) Judging by the consequence of an action for happiness

This is utilitarian approach to ethics. Utilitarianism judges the rightness of an action in terms of its utility of happiness as it is usually understood.[1] The universally accepted principle of utilitarianism is therefore "the greatest happiness of the greatest number." Thus, the adherents of utilitarianism hold that an action is morally right when it maximized utility or happiness and a morally good person is one who seeks to promote happiness in society.[2]

(b) Judging by the principles of universalization

This is based on the Kantian moral philosophy. According to this approach the principle for right and wrong is based on the golden rule of Christ "do unto others as you would like others do to you" or negatively it would be "do not do unto others what you would not have done to you." Therefore, the proponents of this principle of universal norm, hold that an action is morally right when it adheres to this universal norm.[3]

However, this principle cannot be applied to actions in any circumstances, for the same action in different circumstances does not produce the same consequence. This principle therefore can be effectively applied when one is able to judge the circumstances in which an action takes place.

(c) Treating persons as ends in themselves

This is another Kantian ethical proposition. As Kant himself opines this is not distinct from the second principle. This is reformulation of the previous principle. It is evident that when we want to universalize a principle of action, we need to respect and consider every person involved and grant them the basic dignity.[4] This principle of moral judgment says that an action is morally right and just if it contributes, directly or indirectly, to the realization of every person's well being and does not treat them as means to achieve some ends either for an individual or a group, however, noble that goal may be.

Ethics is of vital necessity to people. It regulates a person's life, his or her speech and conduct. It is our moral behaviour which makes us either acceptable to society or rejected by it. In our day to day life we perform many actions and it is necessary that we should be guided by sound ethical

1. M.J. Longford, The Good and the True : An Introduction to Christian Ethics 9 (1985).
2. *Ibid.*
3. *Ibid.*, at 12.
4. James F. Drane, Religion and Ethics 26 (1976).

norms.

(i) The Nature of Ethics—Ethics is a Normative Science

The fact that ethics is concerned with an end or ideal or standard serves at once to distinguish it from most of special sciences. Most of the sciences are concerned with certain uniformities of our experience with the ways in which certain classes of objects (such as rocks or plants) are found to exist, or with the ways in which certain classes of events (such as the phenomena of sound or electricity) are found to occur. Such sciences have no direct reference to any end that is to be achieved or to any ideal by reference to which the facts are judged. The knowledge which they communicate may, indeed, be useful for certain purposes.

The study of ethics is also distinguished from the natural sciences, inasmuch as it has a direct reference to an end that men desire to attain, or a type of which they wish to approximate. It is not by any means that only scientific study, however, which has such a reference. There are at least two other subjects, commonly recognized as scientific, that are in a similar position—viz. logic and esthetics. These are concerned, respectively, with the general conditions involved in the pursuit of truth and in the creation and appreciation of beauty, just as ethics is concerned with what is good and right in human purposes and actions. Such studies are sometimes said to be normative. They are concerned with standards of value, rather than with the simple apprehension and analysis of what exists or occurs. It may be pertinent to note that there appear to be three supreme values in our human experience—truth, beauty and goodness. They correspond somewhat closely to the three main aspects of our conscious life—knowing, feeling and acting. We learn by degrees to know what is true, to appreciate what is beautiful and to do what is right; and logic, esthetics and ethics deal, as thoroughly as they can with the general conditions that are involved in those three modes of experience.

(ii) The Nature of Ethics—Ethics is not a Practical Science

Ethics is concerned with action, it has sometimes been characterised as a practical science; but that is, on the whole, misleading. There are some scientific studies, that may rightly be characterized as practical, such as medicine, engineering or architecture. Such studies are directed onwards the realization of a definite result. The study of moral culture might be classed with these; but it would seem to be a part of the general study of education. Ethics, as a theoretical study, differs from this, just as logic and esthetics do. Logic deals with general conditions involved in the discovery and apprehension of truth; and esthetics deals with the general conditions involved in the rightness and goodness of conduct.

In all these cases it is true that reflection on the principles involved may be expected to help us in the application of them. One who has studied logic may be expected to think more accurately than he otherwise would. One who has studied esthetics may be expected to have a finer appreciation of beauty in nature and art than he would otherwise possess and to be more careful in artistic production. So also one who studies ethics ought to have a finer moral discernment and a more zealous and discriminating pursuit of what is right and good than he would otherwise have had.

(iii) The Nature of Ethics—Ethics is not the Art of Conduct

It is now generally recognized that truth, beauty and goodness are ultimate ends for human beings. It appears to be absurd to ask why we should want to know, to apprehend what is beautiful or to do what is right; but it is not immediately apparent what the exact nature of these great ends is, or what are the conditions that have to be observed for the attainment of them. The application of these conditions may be said to be an art; and in that sense we may say that there is an art of thinking and and art of conduct, just as there are arts of painting, music and poetry by which beautiful objects are created; but logic is not properly to be called the art of thinking, nor is the esthetic to be identified with any of the particular arts by which beautiful objects are called into being. In the same way, it does not appear to be right to describe ethics as the art of conduct. It is, on the whole, even somewhat misleading to describe it as a science, thought this is perhaps little more than a verbal question. In studying a science we are seeking to acquire knowledge about some particular mode of existence. In studying an art we are acquiring the power of dealing with some particular class of objects. The history of ethics is a history of views that are more or less erroneous; but the errors cannot be treated as due merely to human perversity. They are due rather to certain difficulties that are inherent in the nature of the subject; and it seems well to indicate at the outset the general nature of these difficulties.

IV. Meaning of Professional Ethics

The term 'professional ethics' which is otherwise termed as professional conduct refers to ideal good conduct and acts unworthy to be done. Professional ethics may be defined as that branch of moral science which treats of the duties which a professional owes to general public, to Court and his client in particular. It also refers to his duties to the profession and to himself. It covers the healthy traits of an advocate as a member of the Bar. Though there is not much difference basically and vitally between the ethics of one profession and another, or the ethics of one man and another the basic and vital factors which constitute what are ethics will ultimately turn out to be the same, viz., honesty, integrity, fair play, devotion, dedication and determination to be true to oneself, one's profession, one's cause, one's society and even to the State.

Ethics in relation to the profession of law is a code of conduct, written or unwritten, which prescribes the duties of legal practitioners and regulates their behaviour, in respect of such duties. Professional ethics is the most valuable subject which preserves the stream of justice 'pure and clean'. Lawyers, legal profession and the judiciary as a whole have, through the ages in all countries, been honoured as a pure foundation of justice, and have enjoyed esteem and respect in return of their high morality, considerable service of public utility and fearless trustworthiness of their client's causes.

Justice Ismail says "... ethics of a profession is the code by which it regulates actions and sets standards for its members; the professional code attempts to assure high standards of competence in a given field, strengthen the relationship among its members and promote the welfare of the whole community. A professional code does not automatically achieve these goals, but does serve to guide and remind the people; the code sometimes makes provisions for dealing with members who violate the professional ethics of the group."[1]

Justice Nageshwar Prasad of Patna High Court has defined professional ethics as a code of conduct written or unwritten for regulating the behaviour of a practising lawyer towards himself, his client, his adversary in law and towards the Court. A lawyer has no doubt adopted the calling of law for a living and thus he has to charge a fee. But the fee should not be exorbitant, it should not be extortionate. No doubt as the demand for his skill and attainments grow he has to make the price high by all rules of economics; but still there should be room for charity, for chivalry and for benevolence in the profession.[2] He should set apart some time for the poor and the indigent specially those whom he finds pitted against the rich and the powerful, whom he believes to be the victims of oppression at stinger hands. Justice Prasad further states that "this profession is forbidden by ethics to advertise its talents and draw clients. His best advertisement should be his reputation for industry, sincerity and legal and practical talents for bringing to his clients case thoroughness, reason and law. A lawyer should not try to secure clients through paid agents or through touts. Canons of professional ethics forbid his issuing circulars or seeking interviews for soliciting cases."[3]

To reiterate, professional ethics may be defined as a code of conduct written or unwritten for regulating the behaviour of a practicing lawyer towards himself, his client, his adversary in law and towards the Court. In other words, professional ethics is that code which lawyers have to observe primarily with themselves with public at large, with their clients and Courts during the period of their profession. Thus, ethics of legal profession means the body of rules and practice which determine the professional conduct of the members of Bar. The observance of the code of ethics for legal profession is necessary for stable growth of a clean and efficient Bar in the country. Every phase of morals and manners pertaining to two branches of the legal profession—Bench and the Bar—in their relation to administration of justice is embraced under legal ethics. A person by enrolling as an Advocate does not cease to be governed by general rules of law and morality, because "what is morally wrong cannot be professionally right, however, it may be sanctioned by time and custom." Though legal ethics is normally concerned with the conduct of lawyers in their professional capacity, members of the Bar are required to conform to

---

1. *Ibid.*
2. Nageshwar Prasad, "Professional Ethics", in B. Malik (ed.), The Art of a Lawyer (1969), p. 355.
3. *Ibid.*, p. 359.

high moral standards even outside the sphere of their professional activities. For instance, by reason of his criminal or dishonest conduct, an advocate becomes an unworthy member of the society, that may also justify forfeiting his right to remain in the profession as well.

V. Meaning of Etiquette

"Etiquette", on the other hand is slightly different. It generally connotes the pattern of behaviour and the mode in which a person is required to conduct himself. Though, 'etiquette' also springs from long habit and custom, ultimately it is a matter of prudence. An element of elegance, dignity and decency enter into the calculation of what constitutes 'etiquette'. Of course, at a particular stage of development of society, certain norms are prescribed as constituting 'etiquette'. These norms themselves have been the result of long and invariable practice, and ultimately they have attained the status of a standard to be observed and followed by others. Here again though every group of people have their own etiquette, still there are certain basic features common to all of them, such as decency, dignity, decorum, pleasantness, friendliness, etc. thus, the profession of law observes an etiquette which the members must respect as protecting the dignity of the profession and preventing injury to its members.

VI. Meaning of Legal Ethics

The expression 'legal ethics' is made up of noun 'ethics' qualified by the adjective 'legal'. Ethics is broadly a sense of duty. In other words, it is the sum of aggregate of the rules of right living. The term 'legal' means 'according to law'. 'Legal ethics' is that branch of moral science which lays down certain duties for observance which an advocate owes to the society; to the court; to the profession; to his opponent; to his clients and to himself. Legal ethics has their source from tradition. On regular practice after some generations, they become usages, from usages to customs, and from customs to statutory rules, i.e., etiquette. Dean John H. Wigmore, one of America's great legal writers, once said, "this living spirit of the profession, which limits it yet uplifts it as a livelihood, has been customarily known by the vague term 'legal ethics'...An apprentice must hope and expect to make full acquaintance with this body of traditions, as his manual of equipment, without which he cannot do his part to keep the law on the level of profession."[1] The term legal ethics has been defined as "that branch of moral science which treats of the duties which a member of the legal profession owes to the people, the court, his professional brethren and his client..."[2]

Generally, speaking, legal ethics denotes that body of principles by which the conduct of members of legal profession is controlled, more specifically and practically considered. More specifically and practically considered, legal ethics may be defined as that branch of moral science which treats of duties which an attorney-at-law owes to his clients, to the

1. Albert P. Blaustein, *et. al.*, The American Lawyers, 240 (1954).
2. Fransis Rawle, ed., Bouvier's Law Dictionary (1914).

courts, to the bar, and to the public.[1]

Legal ethics means the ethics of the legal profession. It is the body of rules and practices which determine the professional conduct of the members of the Bar and of the Bench. The phrase 'legal ethics' shows the existence of a set of professional norms for lawyers apart from the moral rules which regulate the conduct of men in general. Legal ethics means "usages and customs among members of the legal profession involving their moral and professional duties towards one another, towards clients and towards the courts; that branch of moral science which treats of the duties which a member of legal profession owes to the public, to the court, to his professional brethren, and to his client."[2]

VII. Object of Legal Ethics

The object of the ethics of legal profession is to maintain the dignity of the legal profession and friendly relations between the Bench and the Bar. The code of legal ethics is also necessary for the development of cordial relationship between all persons connected with the legal profession. A code is aimed at raising and upholding the basic standards of the legal profession. It is now recognised that "there can be no excellence in the law without excellence in lawyers." It is also said that the greatness and honour of the legal profession is mainly due to the code of its ethics which is a precious heritage of the profession which does not degenerate into trade or pursuit for livelihood of means for accumulation of wealth." Truly admitting, that the high character of the legal profession can be maintained only by means of an ethical code. The main object of Legal Ethics has been explained by Chief Justice Marshall of United States :

> "The fundamental aim of Legal Ethics is to maintain the honour and dignity of the Law profession, to secure a spirit of friendly co-operation between the Bench and the Bar in the promotion of highest standards of justice, to establish honourable and fair dealings of the counsel with his client, opponent and witnesses; to establish a spirit of brotherhood in the Bar itself; and to secure that lawyers discharge their responsibility to the community generally."[3]

Lawyers are expected to follow certain basic standards like decency and decorum. They should never bring disrepute to their profession. Hence, they have obligations to the clients, to the Court and to the profession. E.S. Venkataramaiah, J. has observed that a lawyer will be constantly confronted with conflicting loyalties which he may have to reconcile. He is answerable not only to the clients whose interest it is his primary duty to serve and promote but also to the Court of which he is an officer and further to his colleagues in the Bar and to tradition of profession.[4] Frankly

---

1. Henry Wynans Jessup, The Professional Ideals of Lawyer 4 (1986).
2. Henry Campbell (ed.), Black's Law Dictionary 894 (1990).
3. C.L. Anand, General Principles of Legal Ethics (1987), p. 63; also see A.S. Khan Afridi, "Legal Ethics : Traditions and Perspectives", IBR (1986), Vol. 13(1), p. 79.
4. Extracted from the Address by the Justice E.S. Venkataramaiah at the 22nd Annual Conference in Bihar State Lawyers' Association, A.I.R. 1983 Journal Section.

admitting, a profession demands from its members a conduct aimed at conciliation, love of truth and justice and enlightened regard for the weak and oppressed and gentlemanliness. Honesty, integrity, fair play, devotion to duty, dedication and determination to be true to oneself and to his own profession, society and State, are the important and basic factors which constitute professional ethics.

Legal Ethics are not exclusively rule based. The customs and cultures of lawyers, to the extent that they have some effect on the delivery of legal services, should also be included within an extended definition. Lawyers allegiance to these ethical values and canons of conduct have been shaped through ages. The ethics of the profession developed as the profession grew in the stature and assumed its dignified status as a strong arm of our judicial system. Such canon of conduct serve as a guide to understand the social as well as professional responsibilities of a lawyer.

The four interwoven ethics or conceptions of what a lawyer ought to do can be discovered in lawyers, ethical debates, treaties, and judicial pronouncements. They are :

(i) The ideal of devoted service to clients in a legal system where citizens need advice and representation to use the legal system (the advocacy ideal).

(ii) The ideal of fidelity to the law and justice if the system is not to be sabotaged by clients who will pay a lawyer to do anything (the social responsibility ideal).

(iii) The ideal of willingness to work for people and cause that are usually excluded from the legal system (the justice ideal).

(iv) The ideal of courtesy, collegiality, and mutual self-regulation against members of the profession (the ideal of collegiality).

These four basic ideals can be found in the U.S. Code of Legal Ethics. The American Bar Association's Model Rules of Professional Conduct, 1983 include : (1) Rules to ensure that lawyers zealously serve and represent their clients (the advocacy ideal), (2) Rules to ensure that they show candour to tribunals, fairness to opposing parties, and are allowed to reveal information to prevent a client committing a criminal act (the social responsibility ideal), (3) Rules regulating the way public service are given and encouraging lawyers to do *pro bono* work (the justice ideal), and (4) Rules governing relationship between lawyers within firms and upholding the integrity of the profession as a whole by reporting misconduct (the ideal of collegiality). In India, under Section 49(1)(C) of the Advocates Act, 1961 prescribe the Standards of Professional Conduct and Etiquette of Advocates.[1] The violation of these standards of conduct will affect the prestigious image of the profession and hence treated as professional misconduct. Section 35 of the Advocates Act, 1961 provides for punishment of advocates for professional or other misconduct. The relevant rules appear under Chapter II with the heading Standards of Professional Conduct and Etiquette under Part VI of the Bar Council of India Rules. The preamble

1. See S. 1 and Rule 1 to 10 under Section 49(C) of the Advocates Act, 1961.

of this Code of Conduct clarifies that the standard included in this are not exhaustive. The other canons of conduct which are equally imperative but not specifically mentioned are also deemed to be included in these rules. The Code does not, however, specify in explicit terms as to how far these rules are enforceable or as to how far they are directives without justiciability. This is because some of the rules are in nature of summons. Rule 46 describes the obligation to provide legal aid to the indigent and the oppressed, as the highest obligation of the advocates to the society. Professor Upendra Baxi, an eminent jurist compares such directives with the Directive Principles of the State Policy meaning thereby that the obligation is subject to 'economic condition' of the advocate himself hence not a binding rule, that is an unenforceable rule.[1] It is revealed from different studies that even the superstar lawyers, whose economic condition is unconsciously affluent, even refuse summarily to see an indigent person with urgent need for legal assistance. It is also seen that most senior lawyers stay away from legal aid programmes of the State.

An advocate enrolled under any State Bar Council has to strictly follow the Standards of Profession Conduct and Etiquette. As they are statutory rules, they are mandatory in nature and violation of any rule by any advocate attracts disciplinary enquiry by the State Bar Council which is competent to suspend him from practice for a period of some years and if the offence is very grave which renders him unfit to continue to practice law, then he can be permanently struck off from the roll as an advocate. Such power is exercised through the machinery of Disciplinary Committee of the State Bar Council. The legal ethics is normally concerned with the conduct of lawyers in their professional capacity, members of the Bar are required to conform to high moral standards even outside the sphere of their professional activities. If, for example, by reason of his criminal or dishonest conduct, an advocate becomes an unworthy member of the society, that may also justify forfeiting his right to remain in the profession as well. This provision is clearly deal in Section 35(1) of the Advocates Act, 1961.

Knowledge of legal ethics is an indispensable part of the intellectual equipment of every legal practitioner. A junior advocate, being a public functionary taking to practice at the bar should have the correct knowledge of privileges as well as the ethical obligations of the members of the profession. He should be able to distinguish between right and wrong in matters of professional conduct without difficulty or hesitation. This is important and necessary for the satisfaction of his own conscience, for the honour and good name of the profession, for the protection of the client and other concerned with litigation and for the welfare of general public.

A admittedly a lawyer is at times faced with considerable difficulty in determining what is right or wrong in matters of professional conduct. The researcher finds no settled traditions as yet, which may guide the younger entrants. There are so many temptations in the path to serve from

1. Upendra Baxi, "The Pathology of Indian Legal Profession", Indian Bar Review, 1986, Vol. 13, pp. 455-457.

the line of integrity in which so many delicate and difficult questions of duty are constantly arising. There are many pitfalls and mantraps at every step, and the younger lawyer at the outset of his career, needs often the prudence and self-denial, as well as moral courage which belong to riper years. Knowledge of legal ethics will inspire respect for its ideals. The rules framed by Bar Associations, statutory rules made by the courts and the rules made by the Bar Council of India lay down the standards of professional conduct and etiquette for advocates. Knowledge of high ideals of Bar will create in the young advocate satisfaction and pride in his calling. In India, the rules made by the Bar Council of India under Section 49(1) of the Advocates Act, 1961 prescribe the standards of professional conduct that affect the prestigious image of the profession and any deviation is treated as professional misconduct.

VIII. Necessity for an Ethical Code

In every profession, through practice and conventions some norms develop and such norms are also called professional ethics. Such norms, though not reduced in writing are handed down from generation to generation. No doubt, with the passage of time there may be changes of the norms, according to the demands of the time. Such norms in a profession are essentially matters of conscience or moral law. No profession can thrive by sacrificing its collective conscience or individual conscience of its members. Happily there is always a tendency among the people to adhere to moral laws, though they are not written down but have crystallised. However, there is no guarantee that all the members of the profession will strictly abide by such moral laws. In other words, law will not make a community virtuous nor will canons of professional ethics make dishonourable men honourable. However, in a democratic country good laws help to raise and strengthen the standard of professional honour.

All professions barring a few, such as the oldest profession in the world, are noble. The legal profession has always been regarded as a noble and honourable profession, throughout the world. The profession of lawyers ordains a high level of ethics as much as in the means as in the ends. Unfortunately, though the profession is held to be noble, the members of the profession are not always held in high esteem. Justice Sundara Ayyar of the Madras High Court said,

> *"while the profession of an Advocate has always been regarded as one of the noblest, lawyers themselves have been one of the most respected class of people."*[1]

The attitude of people towards lawyers has not always been flattering; it is mixed with respect from some section and disdain from some section.

While discussing the question of necessity of a code of legal ethics, two questions have primarily to be answered. Firstly, as to why a code of legal ethics is necessary, and, secondly, as to why this code of legal ethics cannot be reduced into legal enactment and to be made laws of conduct of a lawyer. The Committee or Bar Association of America, whilst answering

1. Quoted in B.K. Goswami, Legal Profession and Its Ethics (1995), p. 40.

these questions, has given the following reasons for the necessity of a code of legal ethics :

(i) As justice is the great interest of men on earth and the lawyer is the high priest at the shrine of justice, the quality of justice to a very great extent depends on the moral quality of the lawyer. It is on his integrity and fairness that the sanctity of the administration of justice depends.

(ii) With the growth of the complex nature of modern societies, the complexity of laws also will grow. With the growth of the complexity of laws, the opportunities and temptations for a lawyer to depart from the path of the right conduct, are many. There may be snares and traps which might lure him away from the path of right conduct. Hence, there must always be an ethical rule which vigilantly draws the attention of the members of the profession and prevents them from being distracted. On the other hand, if a lawyer lowers himself in his moral standard he might do great harm to the whole institution of law and justice.

(iii) This code of ethics will be particularly advisable for new entrants into the profession. It will pivot their attention on the standard of conduct expected of them and therefore, help them to form what may be called professional habits.

It might be asked, if the code of ethics of a lawyer is so important, why not reduce it in the form of a legislative enactment, and thus create certainty and predictability so far as the conduct of a lawyer is concerned. In India there was no written code of conduct for the lawyer prior to the framing of the rules by Bar Council of India in 1965. Of course, the Legal Practitioners Act, 1879 specified some misconduct of the legal practitioners. The provisions for punishing the Advocates for their misconduct was provided under Sections 13 and 14 of the Legal Practitioners Act, 1879. These Sections stand repealed since 1st September, 1963 when Chapter V of the Advocates Act, 1961, came into force. But this repeal is subject to the provisions of Section 55 of the Advocates Act, 1961, which keeps it alive in relation to pleaders and Mukhtars practising as such immediately before the date on which Chapter V of the Advocates Act, 1961 came into force, and who are not enrolled as Advocate under the provisions of the Act of 1961 for such pleaders and Mukhtars. Apart from the evolution, development and establishment of new canons of conscience depending upon the increasing responsibilities of the lawyers in the days ahead, there are certain settled and generally accepted ethical regulations to which the lawyers have to submit. The rules made by the Bar Council of India under Section 49(i)(c) of the Advocates Act, 1961 prescribe the standards of professional conduct and etiquette of Advocates. This Section has provided powers of Bar Council of India to make Rules prescribing standards for professional ethics and etiquette. The relevant rules appear under Chapter II with the heading Standards of Professional Conduct and Etiquettes under Part VI of the Bar Council of India Rules. The Preamble of this code of conduct clarifies that the standards included in this are not exhaustive.

According to the Preamble of the Standards of Professional Conduct and Etiquette published by the Bar Council of India, "An Advocate shall, at all times conduct himself in a manner befitting his status as an officer of the Court, a privileged member of the community, and a gentleman, bearing in mind that what may be lawful and moral for a person who is not a member of the Bar, or for a member of the Bar in his non-professional capacity may still be improper for an advocate. Without prejudice to the generality of the foregoing obligation, an Advocate shall fearlessly uphold the interests of his clients, and in his conduct conform to the rules hereinafter mentioned both in letter and in spirit. The rules hereinafter mentioned contain canons of conduct and etiquette adopted as general guides; yet the specific mention thereof shall not be construed as a denial of the existence of theories equally imperative though not specifically mentioned."

But the term "professional conduct" also covers the misconduct or acts which are unworthy of an Advocate and these have to be strongly deprecated as they tend to bring down the exalted status of lawyers in society and puts them to social obloquy and ostracism. A lawyer should be reliable, trustworthy and capable of vindicating the cause of his clients to the best of his knowledge and skills. K.V. Krishnaswami Iyer in his book on Professional Conduct and Advocacy has said that "every member of the Bar is a trustee for the honour and prestige of the profession as a whole." He advised the advocates :

(i) not to advertise themselves;

(ii) that their duty must prevail over their self-interest;

(iii) that the fee should not be their sole criterion;

(iv) that they should return unearned fees;

(v) that they should not postpone the settlement of fees with clients;

(vi) that they should not engage the relatives of the judges;

(vii) that they should speak loudly;

(viii) that they should cultivate passion for profession;

(ix) that they should cultivate the taste for study of literature;

(x) that they should cultivate self-reliance; and

(xi) that they should discourage dishonest litigation.

Codification of legal ethics has many advantages. Some of them are the following :

(1) The main reason for lawyer's deviant behaviour from the honourable and accepted standard of conduct is not intentional delinquencies. It is rather as a result of ignorance of the ethical requirement of the situation. The existence of a code of professional ethics will furnish an authoritative statement of ideals by which every lawyer, when in doubt, may be guided.

(2) Codification will tend to raise and strengthen the standard of professional honour. Any departure from the standards prescribed

by the organized Bar will lead to a loss of professional reputation and no lawyer in the ordinary circumstances is likely to risk it.

(3) Professional character cannot be built in a day. So in order to form a good character, it is necessary that a young lawyer should have correct standards of conduct held up before him. These rules should exist in a simple and readily accessible form, to influence his conduct from the commencement of his career.

(4) A code of this kind will be helpful to the Bar Councils and courts in judging and regulating acts of the lawyer.

(5) Existing of a code, based on ancient traditions, for the guidance of lawyers will be of great help in checking the growing tendency in the direction of commercialising the vocation of the Bar.[1]

The advantage of a disciplinary code is its ability to sanction delinquent lawyers while not intruding on the individual's moral space. It addresses the commonly expressed concern that we should not police what people think, but what they do. The idea is to provide clear rules with sanctions for unacceptable behaviour, but beyond that to leave lawyers free to do as they (or their clients) please. But to a large extent this turns ethics into merely a form of legal regulation where the rules are made by law societies. Even then, this makes it possible for the regulators to know the subject-matter and for those regulated to make a greater commitment to the standards of the profession.

One of the objections to a code is the danger of it being regarded as exhaustive and anything not coming within its express prohibition is allowable. It is not possible to formulate a code of legal ethics, which will provide the lawyer with a specific rule to be followed in all the varied relations of his professional life.[2] The maximum that can be done is to state with as much particularity as possible and with due regard to custom and tradition those general principles which experience has taught us to be observed, so that the profession occupies its high place in the social structure. This makes it possible to fulfil the important and responsible duties, which fall to its lot.

Unlike United States, India does not have a separate code of conduct to regulate the conduct of lawyers. The Bar Council of India Rules by virtue of Section 49(1)(e) of the Advocates Act, 1961 prescribes the canons of conduct and etiquette for advocates. But it seems that those rules are inadequate to meet the present situation. So far, no attempt has yet been made to codify the rules in an authoritative form. It is not disputable that codification of professional ethics is a difficult task. At the same time, it is not impracticable. This is evident from the successful attempts made by the American Bar Association and the Bar Association of other nations.

1. C.L. Anand, Professional Ethics of the Bar, (1987), p. 29.
2. *Bar Council of Maharashtra* v. *M.V. Dobholkar*, (1976) 2 S.C.C. 291 at p. 302, wherein Hon'ble Mr. Justice V.R. Krishna Iyer opined that "canons of conduct cannot be crystallized into rigid rules but felt by the collective conscience of the practitioner as right".

IX. Duties of Advocates

A lawyer, as a part of the profession, has many obligations and duties of a honourable nature. The first duty which an advocate owes to his brother at the Bar is professional courtesy. He should show equal consideration to all members of the profession. He should extend co-operation to fellow members. Senior members of the Bar should show sympathy and kindness to juniors. They should also help and encourage their junior brothers and juniors should always be respectful to their seniors. The rules framed by the Bar Council of India in exercise of the powers conferred by Section 49(c) of the Advocates Act, 1961, prescribed the duties of an advocate to the Court, client, opponent and colleague, etc. However, from the preamble it becomes clear that these rules contain canons of conduct and etiquette adopted as general guides and the specific mention thereof should not be construed as a denial of the existence of others equally imperative, though not specifically mentioned rules. A lawyer as a part of the profession has many obligations and duties of a honourable nature. The first duty which an advocate owes to his brother at the Bar is professional courtesy. It is his primary duty to render competent service to his clients, with utter fidelity, to their interest. At the same time it should be noted that when there arises a conflict between the duty to the Court and a duty to the client, the ultimate loyalty should be to the profession and to the cause of justice. The lawyer's duties can be elaborated as follows :

(1) Lawyer's Duties towards Court

A court, be that of a Magistrate or the Supreme Court is sacrosanct. The integrity or sanctity of an institution which has bestowed upon itself the responsibility of dispending justice ought to be maintained. All the functionaries, be it Advocates, Judges, and the rest of the staff ought to act in accordance with morals and ethics.[1] An advocate owes certain duties to the Court and to the presiding judge irrespective of his success or failure of the case. A lawyer's duty to the court is a fundamental obligation that defines a lawyer's role within the adversarial system. A lawyer's duty to the court relates to his or her status as a professional who serves, not only clients, but also public interest. It is a truism that dedication to serve the public good is not a matter of blind altruism, rather it is a foundation upon which lawyers earn the confidence of the community and, as a result, are able to play their essential role in the administration of justice. Further, a lawyer's duty to the court also relates to the profession's independence, that is the high degree of autonomy that lawyers experience from external controls other than those imposed by self-regulation.

(i) Duty to respect

The first and foremost duty of an advocate is to be always respectful to the Court. The advocate must be bold, fearless and independent in the Court and at the same time he must not be disrespectful to the Court and the judge. By this duty to be respectful to the Court, it is not expected of

1. *O.P. Sharma & Ors.* v. *High Court of Punjab & Haryana*, A.I.R. 2011 S.C. 2101.

a lawyer to be either meek or subordinate. It is his duty fearlessly to take exception of judicial corruption and incompetence. Lawyers must respect the court. Respect comes in all forms—preparedness and timeliness are one aspect of consideration. They must be familiar with the facts and law applicable to their cases. The lawyer should not abuse the court process. A lawyer should not unreasonably raise or defend an action for which there is no legal justification. Further, the lawyer should not waste time on irrelevancies, even if prompted to do so by the client and should not make frivolous and vexatious objections. In addition, requests for adjournments should not be taken lightly. Adjournments of cases can cause disruption to court sittings, inconvenience to judges and witnesses and also as a result of passage of time cause problems for a witness's memory. In essence, adjournments drain court resources.

On the other hand, the lawyers shall be courteous, civil and act in good faith with all persons with whom he or she deals with during the course of practice. This civil conduct extends to those in the legal profession and to those individuals who are integral to the legal process.

This is a delicate duty. He owes it to his client to protest against irregularities and illegality in the procedure and in the application of rules of evidence. He must maintain a respectful attitude towards the Court, even if he is convinced that a particular ruling given by a Court is erroneous or irregular. He must respectfully accept it and may invoke his remedy by appeal to a higher Court.

This duty also imposes an obligation on a lawyer not to publish any comments on a pending or anticipated litigation in such a way as to interfere with a fair trial in the courts or otherwise prejudice proper administration of justice.

(ii) Duty to attend the hearing

A legal practitioner should attend the hearing of the case throughout. He should not leave the Court without the permission of the court to do so. An advocate has to attend to a number of hearings in a day and has to run here and there. In this regard he knows well which one of his cases in the cause list of a particular day is of utmost importance requiring his personal attendance and so he should act accordingly.

(iii) Duty to receive judgment

It is the duty of an advocate to receive judgment but if an advocate cannot be present personally to receive the judgment when it is being pronounced, he must at least arrange his representation in the Court.

(iv) Duty to judge

A judge is the presiding deity in the temple of justice. He may be formed of stone or clay, but he is the image of justice installed to offer the much needed *'prasad'* to deserving votaries. He has to be maintained in dignity and strength so that the role assigned to him for the benefit of the people may be effectively discharged. An Advocates has to assist him with marshalling and exposition of facts and interpretation of law. In his judgment he is bound to agree with one side and to disagree with the other, but this is no ground for attributing motives. An independent Judge is the greatest need of democracy.

A Judge sleeps on no beds of roses. It may be all roses but no bed when a Session Judge has to pass a sentence of death or a Bench of High Court Judges has to confirm it. The following are the rules of conduct of an advocate towards the Judges :

(a) The conduct of the advocate towards the Judges should always be characterised by candour and fairness. He must be courteous and respectful in his attitude to the Court.

(b) He must be punctual in his attendance in the Court and avoid delaying tactics. He must inspire a sense of reciprocal honour and mutual confidence, so that the business of the Court can be carried on promptly and smoothly.

(c) The advocate must prosecute or defend his case vigorously and fearlessly on merits, but should never influence or attempt to influence the Judge for a verdict favourable to his client, and must not display temper if the ruling be adverse. He must not communicate or argue privately with Judge as to the merits of a pending case nor should he try to take any advantage of personal relations with him.

(d) If there is any proper ground for a serious complaint against a Judge or any judicial officer, it is the right and duty of the advocate to submit the grievance to the proper authorities in a proper manner.

(e) He should not advance before the Judge any cause known as "quickie divorces". Quickie divorces means the practice of advising both the parties, such as the husband and the wife on the question of successfully obtaining divorce without any legal hitch, which practice in its general application would mean collusive actions. In fact, an advocate is not supposed to deal or communicate with the adverse party.

(f) The advocate must equip himself properly for the case both on points of facts and law so that he may assist the Judge in the administration of justice.

(g) The advocate should avoid quarrels with the Judge as such an attitude is apt to put his practice in jeopardy. Judges sometimes have their own whims and vagaries. Even if the Judge's attitude be unfavourable or irritating or belittling, the advocate should avoid being harsh to him, though he may convey his feelings politely and in good humour.

(v) Duty not to adopt dilatory tactics

An advocate, being an officer of the Court must not unnecessary waste the time of the Court, and therefore, it is improper for him to obtain adjournment of a case for his own convenience without informing the Court about the fact of the matter.

(vi) Duty to assist the Court

An advocate must not forget that his main duty is to assist the court in the right direction and to assist it to come to a right finding. The institution of lawyer's profession has existed for this purpose only.

(vii) Duty not to exhibit friendship

It is very bad of a lawyer to say to his client that the Judge is his friend and/or familiar with him and he will weigh to his argument.

Even if the Judge happens to be fast friend of a lawyer, he owes the duty not to exhibit his familiarity with the Judge, and he must not take undue advantage of his personal relationship; such advocates do not enjoy the confidence of the Bar and much less eminence at the Bar.

Such facts not only bring discredit to the lawyer but impair the dignity and impartiality of the Judge. In other words, marked attention and unusual hospitality on the part of the lawyer to a Judge, which is likely to lead to misconstruction of motive, should be avoided. Testimonial dinner to Judges should be by one of the established Bar Associations, not by individual lawyers, nor by self-formed Committees. A loan by a lawyer to a Judge is improper. A lawyer should not communicate or argue privately with the Judges as to the merit of a pending case.

(viii) Duty to have good temper

A lawyer should never lose his temper in and outside the Court in restoration of an adverse ruling or a decision pronounced by the Judge.

(ix) Duty not to malign a judge

Never make a statement which may directly or indirectly malign the great office of a judge. Never be a part to an accusation against a judge, on the contrary, a lawyer should strongly put down such things which come to his notice. But, this does not mean that a bona fide complaint against a Judicial Officer, or judge should not be made.

(x) Duty not to mislead the court

A lawyer should win the confidence of the Court and be trusted by the Judge; for this purpose an Advocate should not cite a ruling which has been overruled or a statute already repealed and misguide to Court. A lawyer cannot knowingly offer or rely on false evidence or misstate evidence. Misleading the court includes actions such as knowingly misrepresenting or misstating the facts in argument, inducing a witness to state misleading and knowingly maintaining a false pretense. There are number of instances of a lawyer being sued or reprimanded for misleading the court on evidentiary issues. The lawyers are under a positive duty to make full disclosure of all the binding authorities relevant to a case. The element of the duty includes drawing a judge's attention to any legal errors which have been made so that they can be corrected.

(xi) Refuse to act in an illegal manner towards the opposition

An advocate should refuse to act in an illegal or improper manner towards the opposing counsel or the opposing parties. He shall also use his best efforts to restrain and prevent his client from acting in any illegal, improper manner or use unfair practices in any matter towards the judiciary, opposing counsel or the opposing parties.

(xii) Refuse to represent clients who insist on unfair means

It is the duty of an advocate not to represent any client who insists on using unfair or improper mean. The advocate should exercise his own judgment in such matters. He should not blindly follow the instructions of the client.

The Bar Council of India has laid down the duties of an Advocate to the Court in the shape of following ten rules :

(a) An advocate shall, during the presentation of his case and while otherwise acting before a Court, conduct himself with dignity and self-respect. He shall not be servile and whenever there is proper ground for serious complaint against a judicial officer, it shall be his right and duty to submit his grievance to proper authorities.

(b) An advocate shall maintain towards the Courts a respectful attitude, bearing in mind that the dignity of the judicial office is essential for the survival of a free community.

(c) An advocate shall not influence the decision of a Court by any illegal or improper means. Private communications with a Judge relating to a pending case are forbidden.

(d) An advocate shall use his best efforts to restrain and prevent his client from resorting to sharp or unfair practices or from doing anything in relation to the court, opposing counsel or parties, which the advocate himself would not do so. An advocate shall refuse to represent the client who persists in such improper conduct. He shall not consider himself a mere mouthpiece of the client, and shall exercise his own judgment in the case of restrained language in correspondence, avoiding scurrilous attacks in pleadings and using intemperate language during arguments in Court.

(e) An advocate shall appear in Court at all times only in prescribed dress, and his appearance shall always be presentable.

- All advocates must appear in robes, before the Supreme Court, in High Court and before Subordinate Courts unless the Presiding Judge is not in robes.
- It is not necessary to robe when appearing before a Judge in Chambers or before Administrative or Quasi-judicial tribunals.
- Where a non-practising Advocate is permitted to appear in Court as an officer of an authority or body by whom he is employed, he should not wear robes.
- An advocate shall not wear robes when appearing as a witness.

(f) An advocate shall not practise before a judge sitting alone or a Bench of Judges if the Judge or any member of the Bench is related to the Advocate as husband, father, grandfather, son, grandson, brother, father-in-law, son-in-law, brother-in-law, uncle, nephew, first cousin, wife, mother, daughter, sister, mother-in-law, sister-in-law, aunt or niece.

(g) An advocate shall not wear bands or gown in public places other than in Courts, except on such ceremonial occasions, and at such places as the Bar Council of India or the Court may prescribe.

(h) An advocate shall not appear in or before any Court or Tribunal or any other authority for or against an organisation or an institution, society or corporation, if he is a member of the Executive Committee of such organisation or institution or society or corporation.

(i) An advocate should not act or plead in any matter in which he is himself pecuniary interested. For example : (i) an advocate should not act in a bankruptcy petition when he himself is also a creditor of the bankrupt; and (ii) he should not accept a brief from a company of which he is a director.

(j) An advocate shall not stand as a surety, or certify the soundness of a surety, for his client required for the purpose of any legal proceedings.

C.L. Anand in his book "General Principles of Legal Ethics", has observed that the advocate owes respect and courtesy to the Court for the reasons stated below :

(a) An Advocate is like the Judge, himself, an officer of the Court and an integral part of the judicial machine. The legal profession consists of the Bar as well as the Bench and both have common aims and ideals.

(b) In theory it is the King or Sovereign who presides in the Court of justice and the Judge is merely the mouthpiece and representative of the sovereign. Respect shown to the Court, is therefore, respect shown to the sovereign whose representative the Judge is.

(c) Not only litigants and witnesses but the general public will get their inspiration in time respect from the example of advocates. It is necessary for the administration of justice that Judges should have esteem of the people. If judges are not respected it tends to impair public confidence in the administration of justice.

(d) It is good manners and advocates before anything else are "gentlemen of the Bar".

(e) Even from a purely practical standpoint, there is nothing to be gained but there is much to lose by antagonising the Court. Conflict with the Judge renders the trial disagreeable to all and has generally an injurious effect upon the interests of the client.

(f) The usual practice in modern times is to appoint Judges from among the members of the Bar and even where this rule is not strictly observed the Bench is fairly representative of the Bar.

(g) It is necessary for dignified and honourable administration of justice that the Court should be regarded with respect by the suitors and people. There is a perception that a lawyer's duty to the Court may conflict with a lawyer's other duties, such as the duties a lawyer owes to his or her client. Gavin Mackenzie in his article on "The Ethics of Advocacy" published in the Advocates' Society Journal in September 2008, states that a lawyer's duty to the client and duty to the court are given equal prominence. He emphatically writes that in the United States the duty to the client is generally seen as the lawyer's primary duty, while in Britain the duty to the Court is prominent. The Canadian rules give equal prominence to the client and the court. Australia and New Zealand follow in the footsteps of Britain. In India, too prominence is given to the court. While both a duty to the court and a duty to the client are recognized, the literature is clear that conflict is resolved in favour of the court. A lawyer's duty to the court touches upon nearly every aspect of his or her practice. The duties to the client are secondary to those owed to the court and the lawyer should be better prepared to address the varied circumstances and pressures faced by the profession and should be equipped with a fuller understanding of his duty to the Court.

(2) Duty to the Client

There is a general consensus amongst the vast majority of advocates that they have two primary duties : a duty to represent the client and a duty to the court.

The advocate wishes to promote his client's interests, and it is his duty to do so by all legitimate means.

The advocate also has an interest in the proper administration of justice, to which his profession is dedicated, and he owes a duty to the court to assist in ensuring that the same is achieved.

The duty owed by the advocate to his client is far from absolute.

The advocate owes a very substantial duty to the person who puts his life, liberty, finances, reputation, or general happiness into his hands. The client 'must rely on him at times for fortune and character and life.'

His obligation is to represent his client, any client, no matter how unmeritorious the case, 'no matter how great a rascal the man may be... no matter how undeserving or unpopular his cause'.

The advocate must 'make every honest endeavour to succeed...(and to) put such matters.... as in his discretion he thinks will be most to the advantage of his client'.

He has a professional duty 'to promote and protect fearlessly and by all proper and lawful means his client's best interests and do so without regard to his own interests or any consequences to himself or any other person (including his professional client or fellow members of the legal profession).

When counselling the client, a lawyer can and should express his opinions fully and frankly about all aspects of the case, legal and ethical. The client will insist on having clear and definite advice as to what is going to happen in court.

The advocate's duty to his client authorizes and obliges the advocate to say all that the client would say for himself (were he able to do so).

The advocate is entitled to take possible points, bad as well as good. He has no right 'to set himself up as a judge of client's case' and should not 'forsake (his) client on any mere suspicion of (his) own or any view (he) might take as to the client's chances of ultimate success'. Baron Bramwell has rightly explained in **Johnson v. Emerson and Sparrow**,[1] that 'a man's rights are to be determined by the court, not by his (solicitor) or counsel....A client is entitled to say to his counsel, I want your advocacy, not your judgment; I prefer that of the Court.'

The advocate has to clear his mind from all anxiety. A counsel's position is one of the utmost difficulty. He is not to speak of that which he knows; he is not called upon to consider whether the facts with which he is dealing are true or false. What he has to do, is to argue as best he can, without degrading himself, in order to maintain the proposition which will carry with it either the protection or the remedy which he desires for his client. Undoubtedly, the duty to the client is an important duty. As a matter of fact, the entire professional work commences with the acceptance of a brief from a client. In that capacity a lawyer undoubtedly has to discharge his duty to his client with all the earnestness and industry he is capable of, in view of the trust and confidence the client reposed in him, of which trust the confidence he must be worthy of. It is the duty of an advocate to welcome his client's presence in the Chamber. The client must not feel that his presence is unwanted. The advocate must give patient hearing to the client and where necessary must make inquiries. The relationship between an advocate and his client is dependent primarily on the principle of contract. The agreement between the counsel and his client bring them in a position of agent and principal. An Advocate has right to remuneration in lieu of services rendered in the court of law by him on behalf of his client.

Hoffman has stated that "to my client I will be faithful; and in their causes zealous and industrious."

Some of the rules regarding the conduct of lawyer towards his clients are as follows :

(i) Obtain full information and knowledge and give frank advice

The lawyer should obtain full information and knowledge of his client's cause and give frank advice on the merits and demerits of the client's cause. Rarely are all facts and law on the side of his client. He should, therefore, be cautious in giving bold assurance. It is his duty to tell the client frankly what the weak points in his case are. The lawyer has the duty to give patient hearing and examine all the papers of his client.

1. (1871) L.R. 6 Ex. 329, 367.

(ii) Duty to do his utmost for the client

A lawyer is under no obligation to accept every engagement that is offered to him, but once he accepts an engagement, he must do his utmost for the client. It is the duty of the lawyer to plead for his client with enthusiasm, vehemence and courage. The relationship between the counsel and the client is fiduciary, i.e., a relation of trustee and *cestui que* trust.

Being in a fiduciary position a lawyer should disclose to the client any interest he may have in the matter.

(iii) Duty not to represent conflicting interests

Often it happens that in a case, the interests of some defendants conflict with those of other defendants. An advocate, therefore, cannot represent all the defendants. He must represent one or the other, but he must not represent all of them.

In **R. v. Rajani**,[1] it was held that a lawyer appearing for the prosecution and who also prepared a draft of a written statement for the accused was guilty of having committed breach of the rule of professional conduct.

If the lawyer is satisfied that his client's case is hopeless and that a settlement would be better, it is the duty of lawyer to advice his client accordingly and encourage him to settle it.

(iv) Duty not to divulge confidential communication

A fundamental principle in the client lawyer relationship is that the lawyer maintains confidentiality of information relating to the representation. The client is thereby encouraged to communicate fully and frankly with the lawyer even as to embarrassing or legally damaging subject-matter. The observance of the ethical obligation of a lawyer to hold inviolate confidential information of the client not only facilitates the full development of facts essential to proper representation of the client but also encourages people to seek early legal assistance. The common law recognizes that the client's confidence must be protected from disclosure. Therefore, for rendering effectual legal assistance there needs to be full and unreserved disclosure of information. It should be ensured that the implementation of the draft rules does not hamper the free flow of information between a lawyer and his client. There needs to be a fine balance between what the draft rules prescribe and the historic and essential value of confidentiality between a lawyer and a client. The client has to reveal everything to his advocate and the advocate is under duty not to divulge his client's secrets or confidences to anybody else.

It is the duty of the lawyer to preserve his clients' confidence. This duty outlives the lawyer's employment. Besides, this being a rule of ethics, it is also enjoined on lawyers by Section 125 of the Indian Evidence Act, Section 126 of the said Act dealing with professional communications excepts a lawyer from this prohibition.

---

1. 37 C.L.J. 48.

(v) Duties regarding stipulation of fees

It is not proper for a lawyer to stipulate for a larger fee on the contingencies of a success in a litigation.

Similarly, it is also improper for a lawyer to agree to return the fee in case of failure in a litigation.

(vi) Duty to maintain scrupulous fidelity (loyalty; faithfulness; integrity)

The most scrupulous fidelity must be observed for ever on the part of the lawyer towards his client, so that he shall never betray or take advantage, either in word or deed, of anything that has come to his knowledge by means of any communication from his client or from papers or documents of the later put into his hands.

Therefore, a lawyer is never permitted to do anything that would tend to prejudice the interest of his client or cause a loss to him in reference to anything upon which he was consulted. It is the duty of an advocate fearlessly to uphold the interests of his client by all fair and honourable means.

(vii) Duty not to accept any compensation or other advantage from others

A lawyer should not accept any compensation, commission, rebate or other advantages from others without the knowledge or consent of his client after full disclosure.

(viii) Duty not to contract for a share in the fruits of the litigation

It is not proper for a lawyer to contract for a share in the fruits of the litigation. He should not enter into any champertuous agreement with his client and should never condescend to share the profits of the litigation.

(ix) Duty not to lend to the client

It is not proper for a lawyer to lend something to his client for the purpose of an action in which he is engaged. Such lending of money might effect the detachment and objectivity of a lawyer. However, the rule does not prevent a lawyer from accommodating his client temporarily in an emergency.

(x) To keep separate account of client's money

The advocate should keep a separate account of his client's money and should not mingle it with his own. Client's money is held by him in trust and should not be appropriated, except with his knowledge or consent. The unexpended money be returned to the client when the litigation ends.

(xi) Duty to return the brief of the client

When the litigation ends, the lawyer should return the brief to the client and he should not betray the confidence of the client even if he is not engaged in the appellate stage.

(xii) Duty to communicate results whether favourable or not

The advocate should not hesitate to communicate his client an unfavourable result and do it as promptly as he would have done a result to the contrary.

(xiii) Duty to give right and proper advice to client

It is the duty of an advocate to give proper advice to the client. Giving deliberately an improper advice to a client may bring an advocate within the clutches of law. Thus, it has been held that an advice by an agent or clerk to the client to absent himself so that the case might be dismissed for default and not on the merits is a gross professional misconduct.

(xiv) Bound to accept briefs

An advocate is bound to accept any brief in the courts or tribunals or before any other authority in or before which he proposes to practise. He should levy fees which is at par with the fees collected by his fellow advocates of his standing at the Bar and the nature of the case. Special circumstances may justify his refusal to accept a particular brief. For instance, when :—

(a) he is specialized in a particular branch of law and his training in such branch limits his usefulness;

(b) the client is not ready to pay or able to pay him his reasonable fee;

(c) the advocate has already been consulted by the adverse party;

(d) the advocate is likely to be called as a witness in the same case;

(e) he is physically disabled from appearing for the client;

(f) he may not be available to present the case in court;

(g) he confines his practice in some place and some court's only.

(xv) Not to suppress material or evidence

An advocate appearing for the prosecution of a criminal trial should conduct the proceedings in a manner that it does not lead to conviction of the innocent. An advocate shall by no means suppress any material or evidence, which shall prove the innocence of the accused.

(xvi) Not to adjust fees against personal liability

An advocate should not adjust fee payable to him by his client against his own personal liability to the client, which does not arise in the course of his employment as an advocate.

(xvii) Not to receive any share or interest in actionable claim

An advocate should not trade or agree to receive any share or interest in any actionable claim. Nothing in this rule shall apply to stock, shares and debentures of government securities, or to any instruments, which are, for the time being, by law or custom, negotiable to any mercantile document of title to goods.

In about 1668, an advocate was prosecuted for betraying his client's cause and taking fees from the other side in the case.[1]

Lord Eldon (Lord Chancellor at the beginning of nineteenth century) recalled that Sir Fletcher Norton 'was reputed to take fees on both sides and had acquired the nickname of Sir Bullface Doublefee'. In one case, Norton had accepted instructions from and been paid by, the plaintiff and the defendant in the same case. When it was suggested to him that he should return both briefs, and all the remuneration received, he declined. The parties, said Eldon, 'were forced to compromise, and he kept both fees'.[2]

Lord Justice Salmon has suggested that a "client can hardly be more dependent upon anyone than upon his counsel, nor can their relationship be closer."[3]

(3) Duty to opponent (counsel and client)

An advocate and his opponent, both of them are brothers in the profession, but representing the interests of different clients. Clients come and go, but advocates adhere to the Court. They meet frequently. They are the part and parcel of the administration of justice. They fight for justice. They struggle for the welfare and good of their clients. This does not mean that the advocate and opponent counsel are enemies with each other. There is a controversy and discrimination on the issue but not between them.

(i) Fair to opponent counsel and client

It is the duty of an advocate that he should be fair to his professional opponent counsel and to his client.

(ii) To give due respect

Give, always, due respect and importance to the opposite side's advocate.

(iii) Duty not to mislead

He should not mislead his opposing counsel by concealing or withholding the facts.

(iv) Duty not to interrupt amidst argument

Every advocate has a right to cross-examination, arguments, verification of documents, etc. while doing so, he shall not be interrupted unnecessarily.

Interruptions amidst argument should be avoided as far as possible. As one would not like to be interrupted, and so one should not interrupt his opposing counsel.

(v) Duty not to denigrate the performance of opposite counsel

Never denigrate the performance of the opposing counsel in the presence of the client. One should not laugh at argument of the opposing counsel. A lawyer should abstain from making disparaging personal

---

1. *R* v. *Walker*, (c. 1668), Tremaine's Pleas of the Crown, p. 261, cited in The English and Empire Digest (1978), Vol. 3, p. 787.
2. Lord Eldon's Anecdote Book (ed. Anthony Lincoln and Robert McEwen, 1960), p. 34.
3. *Rondel* v. *Worsley*, (1967) 1 QB 443, 522.

remarks or engaging in acrimonious speech or conduct toward opposing counsel or any participants in the legal process and shall treat everyone involved with fair consideration. A lawyer, when in the courtroom, should make all remarks only to the judge and never to opposing counsel. When in the courtroom a lawyer should refer to opposing counsel by surname preceded by the preferred title (Mr., Mrs., Ms. or Miss) or the professional title of attorney or counselor.

(vi) Duty not to communicate or negotiate with any party

An advocate shall not in any way communicate or negotiate upon the subject-matter of controversy with any party represented by an advocate except through that advocate.

(vii) Endeavour to fulfil all legitimate promises

An advocate shall do his best to carry out all legitimate promises made to the opposite party even though not reduced to writing or enforceable under the rules of the Court.

In addition to the obligation imposed on the members of the legal profession towards the Court and the clients, there have been a number of obligations which a member of the profession is expected to observe towards other members of the profession. Most of these obligations are the result of conventional understanding amongst the members of the profession. It is obligations such as these that distinguish the profession of law from business.

(i) Duty not to take away another's client

This profession of law, is expected to be free from the competitive elements which is the characteristic of a business. Therefore, it is one of the most incumbent obligations that lawyers must refrain from deliberately "stealing" one another's clients.

Efforts, direct or indirect, in any way to encroach upon the professional employment of another lawyer, are unworthy of those who should be brethren at the Bar. Therefore, a lawyer must not cause another's client to discontinue his service, so that they may be replaced. A lawyer must not make a competitive bid for professional service.

But quite often, a lawyer may be confronted with one delicate question. If one lawyer has been either unfaithful or negligent in the work of his client, and if such client approaches another lawyer, is such another lawyer justified in giving advice to the client? Would giving such advice amount to encroachment upon the professional employment of another?

Therefore, a lawyer must not try to mislead his opponent by concealing or withholding the position in his opening argument upon which he must rely for his side and never try to overreach him. He must not take advantage of a situation by forcing the opposite lawyer to trial when he is under affliction or bereavement.

In brief, a lawyer must shun most carefully the reputation of a sharp practitioner. He is to be liberal to the slips and foresights of his opponent, wherever he can do so. The client has no rights to require him to be wherever he can do so. The client has no rights to require him to be non-liberal.

(ii) Duty not to deal directly with the clients of other lawyers

A lawyer should not in any way communicate upon the subject of controversy with a party represented by counsel; much less should he undertake to negotiate or compromise a matter with him. He should deal only with his lawyer. The aim of his duty is to preserve the proper functioning of the legal profession as well as to prevent the adverse party from improper approaches.

(iii) Duty to avoid self-advertisement and solicitation of professional employment

As already observed, the absence of a competitive element is one of the most important characteristics of the profession of law. It is this which distinguishes the profession of law from a trade or business. This duty not to advertise or solicit is based, not only on history, but also on practical utility. Historically, the profession of law is developed more in the spirit of public service than as a means of earning livelihood. Therefore, it is natural that the lawyer must impose on himself the duty of neither advertising nor soliciting.

Even from the practical utilitarian point of view, advertising, solicitation or encroachment on the practice of others do not tend to benefit either the public or the lawyer. On the other hand, extensive advertising on the part of a lawyer might increase litigation which of course is definitely against public policy. Further, if the lawyer, being an officer of the Court, were to indulge in advertising and solicitation, it would lower the whole trend of the administration of justice.

This delicate question is answered by the Canons of Professional Ethics adopted by the American Bar Association. According to these Canons, it is the right of any lawyer without fear or favour, to give proper advice to those seeking relief against unfaithful or neglectful counsel, generally after communication with the lawyer against whom the complaint is made.

(iv) Duty to be candid, fair and courteous in his dealing with other lawyers

A lawyer must note that clients, not lawyers, are the litigants. Therefore, any ill-feeling existing between clients must not be allowed to influence the lawyers in their conduct and demeanour towards each other. All personality clashes between counsel be scrupulously avoided.

Shakespeare seems to have summed up the proper attitude between lawyers towards each other in his observation in 'Taming of the Shrew'. "Do as adversaries do in law; strike mightily, but eat and drink as friends."

As Chief Justice Hughes observes, "the highest reward that can come to a lawyer is the esteem of his professional brethren. That esteem is one in unique conditions and proceeds from an impartial judgment of professional rivals. It cannot be purchased. It cannot be artificially created....It is an esteem commended solely by integrity of character and by brains and skill in the honourable performance of a professional duty. No subservient 'Yesman' can win it, no mere manipulator or negotiator can secure it."

(4) Duty to Profession

A member of the legal profession owes an obligation to uplift his profession with dedication, honesty, integrity and commitment. Lawyers are privileged to enjoy an occupation that combines public avowals of high purpose with a dedication to service and selflessness. The public avowals of high purpose are embodied in the oath that lawyers take upon their admission to the Bar : to uphold the standards of the profession. The dedication to service and selflessness is a reflection of how lawyers engage their clients, their colleagues, the bar and the public.

Every lawyer owes duty to his professional brethren in particular and to the community of legal profession in general. Some of these duties are as follows :

(i) To keep best tradition of the Bar

A lawyer has to keep up the best traditions of the Bar. He should not be a party to the lowering of the standards maintained by the Bar.

(ii) Not to pursue profession in the spirit of competition and rivalry

It is bad of a lawyer to pursue the legal profession in a spirit of competition, vengeance, and rivalry with professional brethren.

(iii) Interest of the profession in higher

Bear in mind that the interest of the profession is higher than one's personal interest.

(iv) Respectful to seniors and kind to juniors

One should always be respectful to his seniors and seniors should show sympathy and kindness to juniors.

(v) Behave in manner befitting his status

An advocate should at all times behave himself in a manner befitting his status as an officer of the Court, a privileged member of the community, as Hon'ble member of an exalted profession and a fine gentleman.

(vi) Advocate should engrace the profession

The advocate should engrace the profession and must not disgrace it. He should fearlessly uphold the interests of his client. With the passage of time, the public's perception of the legal profession appears to be on the decline. The increasing complexity, delay and cost of legal services have caused the public to question its trust in lawyers. The need of the hour is for lawyers to renew their commitment to the legal profession so that legal profession continues to thrive and grow. Each individual lawyer must recognize and work to fulfil their duty to support and enhance the profession. The advocate must stick to the profession and try to elevate it. Lawyers must stay current on the law as the law is always changing. New statutes, changes to the law and rules of the profession are developments that all lawyers should follow. Building a strong profession involves not only helping oneself, but helping others in the profession. They must also help other lawyers to practice with integrity, honour and pride. Lawyers are expected to act courteously and with civility toward other members of the profession. Practicing civility and collegiality involves both developing one's own skills and helping to develop the skills of other lawyers.

Panchsheel of the Bar

As far as the legal profession is concerned, panchsheel of the Bar is based upon the following five qualities which Mr. Ram Keshav Ranade, former Distt. & Session Judge said in his presidential address in a Judicial Conference at Aurangabad on 25.4.1960 :

(i) Honesty

The first prerequisite of a lawyer is that he should be imbued with honesty. Honesty is the most important quality that an advocate should possess. He follows a noble profession, which is not in the nature of a trade. His thoughts, words and deeds should have sincere co-relation to each other with their origin from genuineness. He must be honest to the cause of his clients which he is espousing before the court. If he is not sincere enough in his effort, the result would be disastrous. But the honesty of purpose has a multi pronged facet. He must be honest to the cause of his clients. He must be sincere and honest to the Court before which he practices. Meaning thereby, he can't deliberately mislead the Court.

(ii) Industry

Industry denotes the quality of hard working. this quality is absolutely necessary on the part of an advocate. His knowledge of law should be up to date. Law changes according to the changing needs of the society. Changes of law are effected by amendments of existing laws, new legislations and precedents. An advocate should never be ignorant of the current law in force. He should get acquainted with the present law by systematic study. In the words of Edison, "Extraordinary talent is nothing but 2% inspiration and 98% perspiration." If one ignores the law, the law is also apt to ignore him. That is why it is said that "law is a jealous mistress". Lord Eldon emphasised the need of hard work for a lawyer. He stated that "a lawyer must live like a hermit and work like a horse." It requires regular, constant and systematic care and attention. Lawyers will do well to enshrine in their hearts the well-known maxim, "Industry is fortune's right-hand". Without industry the armoury of the advocate will lack weapons on the day of battle.

(iii) Justice

An advocate is an officer of the Court. He should help the judge in finding out the truth and arriving at the right decision. For this purpose, he shall point out and submit the proper position of law, facts and evidence in the case.

Truly speaking, he has to protect the interests of the client, but at the same time he must realise that he is not a mere mouthpiece of the client. He should be fair to his clients but at the same time he should be fair to the Court and his predominant business must be to advance the cause of justice. The most remarkable words of Lord Chief Justice Cockburn are that the arms which a lawyer wields are to be the arms of a warrior and not of the assassin, that his duty is to strive to accomplish the interest of his client.

(iv) Service

No profession can hope to exist in the world unless it serves the real needs of the society. Employment in any walk of life, if rightly understood, is a means to serve humanity and lawyers are to try their level best to carry on their profession in a spirit of service to society. Lawyers shall be willing to protect the defenceless and oppressed. They shall render their best legal services to such needy litigants. Law and legal profession are mainly concerned with the promotion of administration of justice and the establishment of a welfare society.

(v) Philosophy

It is suggested that lawyers should have some philosophical outlook. An advocate has to deal with a variety of human relations in their conduct, disputes, rights and duties in different causes and circumstances both favourable and unfavourable. As Plato has stated "All evils of the world would end when lawyers become philosophers and philosophers become lawyers."

It is, therefore, necessary that lawyers should be guided by some philosophical principles suitable to his life and profession.

(5) Duty to state

Lawyers in every country have played highly significant role in the progress of their nation and they have been in the vanguard in the struggle of freedom. None as a class or profession has done more; none has done as much to define, to develop and to defend the liberties of the country.[1] Lawyers are the servants of the society, officers of the Court of justice. They should be ready to give expert advice to those who propose progress and readjustment of the frontiers of justice. The lawyers have the duty to maintain the integrity of the State. In any society it is the elite which has to provide leadership. Undoubtedly the community of lawyer constitute a significant segment of the elitist society. The lawyers also have to face the dilemma which the nation has to face, i.e., the reconciliation of the individual liberty with socio-economic justice. On the one hand, the lawyer has to defend the client against the onslaught of the government, his liberty and freedom by the legislative and executive branches, and on the other hand he has to show his legal consciousness and political maturity in promoting and defending socially beneficial legislation by creating public opinion to implement the directive enshrined in the constitution for the establishment of the socialistic society. Further, the lawyers have to work

1. A.I.R. 1960 (Journal Section), p. 66.

a practical solution tentatively to reconcile the individual freedoms and the inevitable curtailment of the same in bringing socio-economic reforms by using laws as an instrument of social change.

The lawyers being the elite in the sense of the section of society possessing great consciousness of the dynamic and dimensions of life and familiar with all sections of society should provide effective leadership for the realisation of the goals and ideals enshrined in our Constitution, for the establishment of a new society free from exploitation, ignorance, illiteracy and securing liberty with economic justice. For this purpose there must be a strong and independent judiciary. Judiciary can be strong only if there is a strong Bar. It is the judiciary which analyses and interprets the laws made by the legislature in their proper application in the administration of justice which is the main function of a State. It is also a wrong belief that the lawyers promote disputes and differences in the society. The work of legal profession is not to create and promote difference, but settle the disputes whenever they arise. In fact, lawyers are harbingers of peace in the society.

(6) Duty to the Public

A duty which an advocate owes to the general public can be given utmost importance in the list of his duties which the professional ethics impose on him. It is to be remembered that lawyers in every country have played highly significant role essential to the establishment, existence and progress of the nation.

It is the primary duty of an advocate that he should uphold the Constitution and help in the maintenance of the rules of the law. He should promote the advancement of justice and assist in the enforcement of fundamental rights of the people. An advocate never hesitates to condemn tyranny or injustice. A lawyer stands for justice more than a Judge, as he pleads for it. It is the quality of a lawyer that he has capacity to analyse the facts and to penetrate into the innermost part of the human mind in order to discover the true motives of his actions, and to present them in an accurate and forceful form. There he has to perceive not only head but heart too. The welfare of the society demands protection of the law of the land. Lawyers are looked upon as protectors, preservers, saviours, and minister of justice aimed at the maintenance of a welfare society. Legal profession is a noble one where the lawyers have to deal with a variety of human relations. It is not merely a means to livelihood, which is only incidental thereto. The lawyer should gladly render his legal services to the really poor litigants without any fees. They should render their services to the public without any discrimination.

In all professional functions, an advocate should be diligent and his conduct should also be diligent and should conform of the requirements of the law by which an Advocate plays a vital role in the preservation of society and justice system. An advocate is under an obligation to uphold the rule of law and ensure that the public justice system is enabled to function at its full potential....An advocate being a member of the legal profession has a social duty to show the people a beacon of light by his conduct and actions rather than being adamant on an unwarranted and uncalled for issue.[1]

Lawyers have a duty to render their services to every cause whether small or big, simple or complex and shall not refuse to accept briefs except where special circumstances may justify the refusal to accept a particular brief. They must be ready and willing to render legal aid to the poor and the weak and also in matters involving public interest.

(7) Lawyers Duty to Colleagues

All advocates are part and parcel of the administration of justice. They are the officers of the court. Their primary aim must be the welfare of the people. An advocate should respect all his colleagues, that is members of Bar Association. He should not criticize any co-advocate. Section IV of the Bar Council of India Rules, describes the duties of an Advocate towards his colleagues. Under Rules 36, 37, 38 and 39, these duties of an Advocate, have been enumerated. The conduct of an advocate to his brothers in the profession must be characterised by candour and frankness. He must keep faith in his fellow members of the Bar. Even in provoking circumstances, their conduct and demeanour shall never be influenced by ill-feeling between the parties. He must fulfil all legitimate promises he has made, but must be careful not to give promises which cannot be fulfilled. He shall never snatch briefs of his colleagues. The advertisement or soliciting by a lawyer may affect the prospect of engagement of another lawyer and may encourage unhealthy competition for getting the clients. Advocate should not seek business by advertisement or otherwise. Lawyers should not intimate or defame their colleagues. They have a positive obligation to be courteous to each other and deal in a good faith and their communication with each other must maintain the proper tone of a communication; whatever stresses face lawyers in daily life cannot be allowed to interfere with these positive and important obligations. Civility is a foundation of a lawyer's duty to his colleagues.

> "No quarrels have we of our own, we manage other's broils; and though we fight all with our might; we have buttons on our foils; we scratch a brother lawyer's eyes until they are out, and then we go to dine with him that night and scratch them again."—3 Green Bag 152.

The following are the rules of conduct of advocates towards their colleagues :

(i) The advocate's conduct towards his fellow lawyers should be characterised by courtesy and good faith. The fact of ill feeling between the parties should not be allowed to influence the lawyers in their conduct and demeanour towards each other and the suitors in the case. All personalities between them should be avoided scrupulously.

Illustration

Benjamin H. Brewster, ex-Attorney General of the USA was once engaged as Chief counsel in a suit against the Pennsylvania Railway

1. *O.P. Sharma & Ors.* v. *High Court of Punjab & Haryana*, A.I.R. 2011 S.C. 2101.

Company. The proceedings were bitterly contested and Brewster seemed to get better of his opponent. During the argument, adverse counsel angrily exclaimed : "This grasping corporation is as dark, devious and scarified in its methods as is the face of its Chief Attorney and Henchman, Benjamin Brewster."

With this outburst of violent rage, the Court became breathlessly still and it seemed that Brewster would catch counsel by the throat and tear upon his guts. But he did nothing of the kind. Slowly he got up and said, "Your honour, in my chequered career I have never indulged in personalities and have never found myself called upon to explain my physical misfortune but I shall do so now. As a child my mother fondly called me a pretty boy. While playing around an open fire as a frolicking boy with a toddling sister. I found that my sister fell into the fire. I ran to her rescue and took her out before she was seriously injured, but in doing so I fell into the fire myself. When I was taken out, I found that my face was turned black—" and turning to the opposing Counsel completed, "as that man's heart."

The effect was electrical. Opposing counsel was publically condemned. His practice dwindled to such insignificance that he had to leave the city for a new field.

(ii) The advocate should as far as possible endeavour to suit the convenience of the opposing advocate if the interest of his client or the cause of justice is not thereby likely to be undermined.

(iii) He should not give an undertaking he cannot fulfil, and once it is given he should fulfil it.

(iv) He would not communicate upon the subject in controversy nor should compromise or attempt to compromise the matter directly with the parties represented by lawyer except such lawyers.

(v) The advocate should avoid all sharp practice and should by no means take advantage of any slip or technical error on the art of the adverse advocate. No client has a right to demand that his lawyer should be illiberal or that he should do anything repugnant to his own sense of honour and propriety.

(vi) He should remember that stratagem is a game which two can play at. He should also beware that "who so diggeth a pit may fall therein."

(vii) A lawyer should not lose self-control even under trying circumstance. There may be provoking circumstances, with witness, with opposing counsel and even with Judges; but a seasoned lawyer shall never lose mastery of himself.

Witticism is a favourite resource of the prevaricating witness, but it usually proves to be serious to the person in whose interest it is perpetrated.

It creates on the mind of the Court a strong impression that the witness is trying to keep something from the Court. No doubt it is a source of amusement in the Court, but it will be at the cost of the person whom the witness has come to support. Counsel should not, in cross-examination a prevaricating witness, find himself baffled at all.

Illustration I

Q. What are you?

The witness was silent.

Q. (Repeating) What are you?

Ans. A woman.

Q. What is your occupation?

Ans. I do my house work.

Q. And after your house work, what do you do?

Ans. I go to the park.

Q. And that is how you occupy your time?

Ans. No (burst of laughter in the Court).

Q. (Sternly) It is no laughing matter.

Ans. I should be sorry to laugh at you.

Q. How do you live? Do you do needle work?

Ans. Sometimes yes.

Q. Is that your answer?

Ans. Yes.

Q. How do you support yourself?

Ans. How do I support myself?

Q. Yes.

Ans. Do you mean, how do I live?

Q. (Judge interrupting), Yes, Yes.

Ans. (Slowing) I eat and drink.

Illustration II

I once heard a woman plaintiff in a default divorce case testify that her husband regularly came home drunk, beat her up, threw furniture out of the window, and created such a riotous disturbance that the police were regularly called. The parties lived in a lower duplex. Corroborating her testimony, her lawyer brought to the stand a man who had lived on the other floor of the duplex during that period.

Q. What sort of a man was the defendant?

Ans. He was a very orderly sort of man.

Q. (By the Judge). How can you say this defendant was very orderly sort of man? Didn't you hear testimony about his creating riotous situations?

Ans. Yes, your honour, I did.

Q. (By the Judge), Why then, did you say he was an orderly sort of a man?

Ans. Well, he was one of those guys who is always trying to order everybody around.

(vii) He should not attempt to steal the other's client.

Lawyers have always shown great consideration to the estimate regarding themselves of fellow members of the Bar. No one can be a great lawyer, and as a rule no one can prosper in the profession, who does not command the confidence of fellow members of the Bar. An advocate who is despaired by the profession cannot long retain confidence in his clients.

No one can form a better estimate of a lawyer's competency and character than his fellow members of the Bar.

Rules 36, 37, 48 and 39 framed by the Bar Council of India deal with the duties of an advocate to the colleagues. Rule 36 provides that an advocate shall not solicit work or advertise whether by circulars, advertisements, touts, personal communications, interview not warranted by personal relations, furnishing or inspiring newspaper comments or producing his photograph to be published in connection with cases in which he has been engaged or concerned.

His signboard or name plate or stationery should not indicate that he is or has been president or member of a Bar Council or of any association or that he has been associated with any person or organisation or with any particular cause or matter or that he specialises in any particular type of work or that he has been a Judge or an Advocate-General.

Rule 37 provides that an advocate shall not permit his name to be used in aid of, or to make possible, the unauthorised practice of law by any law agency.

Rule 38 makes it clear that an advocate shall not accept a fee less than the fee taxable under the rules when the client is able to pay the same.

According to Rule 39 an advocate shall not enter appearance in any case in which there is already a vakalatnama or memo of appearance filed by an advocate engaged for a party except with his consent; in case such consent is not produced, he shall apply to the Court stating reasons why the said consent could not be produced and he shall appear only after obtaining the permission of the Court.

(8) Lawyer's Duty to Self

Legal profession is a noble calling. It is a profession of learned people. The advocates are expected to observe the standards of the profession. They must observe and obey their multifarious duties as provided in the rules relating to professional etiquette and conduct. Violation of those rules will expose them to disciplinary proceedings under Section 35 of the Advocates Act, 1961.

An advocate must follow regular habits of systematic acquisition of knowledge of law. To be a good lawyer, one must of course be well acquainted with theory of law. But a pure academical knowledge of law is not enough for a lawyer. He must go through a long course of training in actual handling of cases, before he can appear in courts and become a real practising lawyer. There is no short cut to success so far as the career of law is concerned. It is best, that one takes the long and arduous path and receives a thorough training, which will help him ultimately to deliver the goods. A lawyer conducting a case must have numerous other qualifications. He must have the 'gift of the gab' as it is popularly called. He must have Himalayan patience and consummate skill in handling human beings. Further, a wide knowledge of human behaviour is necessary. It is also desirable that an advocate should acquire some special knowledge in certain branches of law.

A lawyer owes many obligations to the Court; and so also he owes duties to himself.

(i) The first duty he owes to himself is the duty of self-respect and independence which are by far the most important.

(ii) An advocate owes duty not to produce in the Court what he knows to be a false document or tender knowing a false witness.

(iii) He should not fight a cause which is false to his knowledge.

(iv) It is also advisable not to take up a case in which he is likely to be called as a witness.

(v) A lawyer should never make a difference between a small and a big case, equal attention and care should be given to the cases irrespective of their nature. This difference may be to the advocate and not the client.

Chief Justice Cockburn while emphasizing on the "fearlessness" as a quality of a lawyer in carrying out the interests of his client, has said that :

> "the arms which he wields are to be the arms of the warrior and not of the assassin."

(vi) Never burst into laughter in the Court, but give a gentle smile only whenever occasion demands. It is bad etiquette to burst into wide or noisy laughter in Court.

(vii) Never answer a question to the presiding Judge while sitting.

(viii) A lawyer should maintain a book of accounts.

(ix) Judges are entitled to be addressed as 'My Lord', 'Your Lordship', 'Your Honour or Your Worship', as the case may be, only when they act as Judges.

(x) Keep up regular habits of systematic study of law. Remember law is a jealous mistress.

(xi) Avoid the "easy-come, easy-go" method with your finances. Bank on no fee until received.

Law is nothing but "applied morality". It is truly said, "we are slaves of law, so that we may be free."

The following are generally accepted rules of duty of a lawyer to himself :

(i) In order to be a good lawyer one must first be a good man. He should develop a high sense of morality that would thwart him from doing anything he knows to be wrong. Cleanliness and purity of thought, words and deeds are as much necessary in the legal sphere as in other spheres.

(ii) The lawyers should stick to his profession and seek to elevate it. It is a profession and not a trade for making money.

(iii) It is a profession requiring for its mastery great and prolonged labour, intense study and concentration. It involves a profound and continued study of man. Law is not a fixed body of dogmatic rule; it is changing with the requirements of a progressive civilization. The lawyer should be alive to all the mutation or he will fail to meet the needs of his client.

(iv) Above all, the institution demands character.

(v) By his training the lawyer is better equipped than any other person to understand the proposed legislation, which casts on him the duty to share his responsibility in public affairs. Legal profession is the preparation of the ideal of unselfish public service.

Dr. Anajwala in his book, "Law Relating to Advocates", has stated some words of advice to a lawyer. The first advice is quoted from Abraham Lincoln's speech :

(i) Discourage Litigation. Persuade your neighbours to compromise whenever you can. Put out to them how the nominal winner is often the real loser in fees, expenses and waste of time. Never stir up litigation. A worse man can never be found than one who does this.

A French proverb says that a doctor never prescribes for himself; nor should a lawyer be foolish enough to go to law. There is nothing certain about a law-suit except the expense of it.

(ii) Social service, not personal profit, is the aim of your profession.

(iii) Exalt and loyalty magnify the prestige and power of the Court, so that the administration of law may be made efficient or the attainment of justice.

(iv) Other lawyers should be regarded as fellow soldiers in the common cause of justice and their honour as sacred to you as your own.

(v) Value your services to your client as above all price. Service is the right of the client; self is sold to none.

(vi) Follow the highest of the paths morally permissible; but as between two courses not so sanctioned, select none.

(vii) Cumulative character, no smartness, is your aid to success; instinct for truth is a sure guide. Self-interest cannot but mislead.

(9) Duty in Imparting Training

The Bench and the senior Advocates owe a duty to the juniors in the Bar. They should be given all encouragements. They are, in fact, a trust in the hands of the seniors. Senior lawyers have the duty to impart all necessary training to the junior members in the profession. The juniors can come up only with proper direction, training and help of the seniors. Further, the professional prestige hitherto enjoyed can be perpetuated only through the junior Bar. Hence, senior lawyers, in all age, have to discharge the duty of imparting training to the junior members of the profession. They are obligated under Rule 45 provided in Section V of the Standards of Professional Conduct and Etiquette as laid down by the Bar Council of India. The rule states : it is improper for an Advocate to demand or accept fee or any premium from any person as a consideration for imparting training in law under the rules prescribed by State Bar Council to enable such person to qualify for enrolment under the Advocates Act, 1961.

The High Court of Kerala has observed in **Ram Mohan v. Jayakrishnan**,[1] that "the Bench and the senior Advocates owe a duty to the juniors in the Bar. They should be given all encouragements. They are, in fact, a trust in the hands of the seniors. A junior is often elated when he filed a joint vakalat with the senior. He gets justifiable satisfaction when his name appears in the law reports with his senior. Encouragement to the juniors by allowing them to handle cases will, to a large extent, help courts to cut down the pendency of cases. Most of the juniors are competent and will prove their mettle if opportunities are given. That will help to mould their career and creation of an effective second line of offence and defence in the bar."

(10) Duty to Render Legal Aid

The lawyers are under obligation to render legal aid under Rule 46 in Section V of the Standards of Professional Conduct and Etiquette as provided by the Bar Council of India. This rule lays down that "every advocate shall in the practice of the profession of law bear in mind that anyone genuinely in need of a lawyer is entitled to legal assistance even though he cannot pay for it fully or adequately and that within the limits of an Advocate's economic condition, free legal assistance to the indigent and oppressed is one of the highest obligations an advocate owes to society.

---

1. 1981 KLT 745.

7

GENERAL RULES OF PROFESSIONAL CONDUCT

Legal profession is a noble profession, a profession of learned people. The profession which is performing a vital service to the society must also be expected to conduct itself to come upto the expectations of the society. His professional conduct must be above board. An advocate is bound to conduct himself in a manner befitting the high and honourable profession. The reiterate, the legal profession is a noble calling having high traditions. An advocate is expected to uphold those traditions. He is expected to follow strictly the rules of professional conduct as laid down by the Bar Council of India. All members of the legal profession are bound by the elaborate code of ethics codified in Part VI, Chapter II of the Rules promulgated by the Bar Council of Indian under Section 49 of the Advocates Act. Some general rules of professional conduct can be summarised as under :

Business

Law is a learned profession part excellence. It is not a profession for money. It is a career of service to the public utility. It is not a trade or business. It is a noble profession with serious responsibilities. An Advocate shall not carry on any other profession or business or be an active partner or salaried servant in connection with any business. However, an advocate may be a "sleeping partner" in a firm doing business provided the business "is not inconsistent with the dignity of the profession." An advocate may be a Director or Chairman of a company though not its Managing Director or a secretary. An advocate may inherit or succeed by survivorship to a family business provided he does not personally participate in its management. An advocate may accept part-time employment permitted by the Bar Council which "does not conflict with his professional work and is not inconsistent with the dignity of the profession." It is pertinent to compare business and legal profession. A business organization is formed with a motive of profit gaining and sharing. Their primary motto is profit and profit only. In business, the success is calculated only on the basis of money-returns. The legal profession, on the hand stands in a unique position. The profession is unlike business and is not for the gain. It is meant for public good and safety. It is a part of the administration of justice, and not a mere money-making occupation. It is a part and parcel of the judiciary. If law is to remain an honourable profession, it will have to guard itself against its greatest enemy, viz., the spirit of commercialism.

The object of all business is pursuit of wealth and all means are worthy so long as law is not transgressed. This is not ideal for an advocate, who is a Minister of Justice and whose career is one of service and of great responsibilities not merely to the client who has paid him, but also to the court, the opposite party, the witnesses, the profession, and the community. Of course, an advocate may take his fees for the services rendered to his client. But taking fee is subordinate to etiquette and ethics.

12th Canon of American Bar Association lays down that "in fixing fees it should never be forgotten that the profession is a branch of administration of justice and not a mere money-making trade." The success of an advocate cannot be calculated according to money, but it can be assessed by the good conduct, ability, presentation, attitude etc. He is not expected to do any acts which are harmful to the society. The legal profession is exclusively based on ethics and etiquettes, but not on money. The advocate's office is a public office, hence requires public trust.

Devilling

Devilling is strictly prohibited in the legal profession. Devilling connotes handing over a brief by one advocate to another without the consent of the client. But it does not mean that a counsel is precluded from seeking assistance of the juniors in the work of drafting, pleading etc. In such a case, the senior must hold himself responsible for the commitments of the juniors. The profession casts a duty on the counsel not to leave the work in the hands of unskilled persons. The work should be entrusted to the person who have consummate skill in handling the briefs. Besides theory, practical training over a long period in handling of cases before the courts are required from the legal professionals.

Sharing of Profits, Compensation and Rebate

A lawyer should not accept any commission, compensation, rebate and any advantages from others without the knowledge or consent of his client after full disclosure. Further, the lawyer should not give commission or presents to anyone introducing business. The Regulation VII of 1793 also prohibited the lawyers from demanding or accepting from their clients any sum of money or reward excepting the authorised fees for pleading their causes.

Champertous Agreements

Advocates are sometimes tempted to enter into agreements with their clients regarding the subject-matter of the litigation. They finance the clients in the litigation and agree that the expenses therefore would be reimbursed by the client later on. Champerty is an agreement to share the benefit of another's litigation. It is one sort of a bargain whereby a party is to assist another in recovering property and to share in the proceeds of the action. Under the English law such agreements are struck down as illegal and void. Champerty is not an indictable offence in India, yet it is unprofessional for a lawyer to stir up strifes and litigations. The legal profession demands that the lawyer should maintain detachment and must not get himself involved in the subject-matter of champertous agreement and should not share the profit of litigation. Rule 31 of the Bar Council of India Rules lays down that "an advocate shall not enter into arrangements whereby funds in his hands are converted into loans." Further, Rule 32 lays down that an advocate shall not lend money to his client for the purpose of any action or legal proceedings in which he is engaged by such client."

Soliciting Business

The advocate should not solicit business by different channels of advertisement which include radio, television, journals, newspapers, direct mail, bill board, yellow pages, transit space, posters, directories etc. The cardinal rule of professional etiquette is that attempts should not be made to advertise oneself to solicit work directly or indirectly. In India, lawyers do not have a right to solicit business and advertise themselves. Rule 36 of the Bar Council of India Rules on Standards of Professional Conduct and Etiquette provides that "an advocate shall not solicit work or advertise either directly or indirectly whether by circulars, advertisements, touts, personal communications, interviews not warranted by personal relations, furnishing or inspiring newspaper comments or procuring his photograph to be published in connection with cases in which he has been engaged or concerned." Hence, it is a well established rule of etiquette in the legal profession that no attempt should be made to solicit work and advertise oneself directly or indirectly. Such a course of action tends to lower the dignity of the honourable profession and is undoubtedly akin to touting.[1] It is for this reason that in England no barrister is allowed to write to solicitors or even to brother practitioners on circuit, extolling his services, experience, ability or work. Advertisements of all forms are considered to be highly improper.

Cross-examination

Cross-examination is acknowledged to be a powerful and effective weapon for the purpose of testing the veracity of a witness and the accuracy and completeness of his disposition. In other words, the examination of a witness by the adverse party shall be called his cross-examination. Witnesses shall be first examined-in-chief then cross-examined, later re-examined. The object of cross-examination is to discover the truth before the courts of justice. Therefore, the advocates must be very careful and responsible while cross-examining the adversary and the witnesses produced by him. Good cross-examination is an art which needs much preparation, deep thought, sound planning and powerful memory particularly when the case abounds in fact. While cross-examination, an advocate must not offend the personal feelings of the opposite party. In other words, an advocate has no right to disgrace and bully a witness by putting offensive questions. Questions, which affect the credibility of a witness by attacking his character should not be asked. Broadly speaking,

---

1. *In re Thirteen Advocates of Allahabad*, A.I.R. 1934 All 1967; *C.D. Sekkizhar* v. *Secy. Bar Council*, A.I.R. 1967 Mad. 35.

cross-examination of a witness may be either pleasant or savage. One has to adopt one's own style of cross-examination, generally on the lines of pleasant conversation, but if need be, in a severe and savage style. The pleasant style includes the pleasant, gentle, soft, humorous, sophisticated, persuasive and dramatic styles, whereas the savage style includes the bullying, severe, forceful, bold, quibbling and rapid methods. Therefore, cross-examination should be carefully done and to the extent when there is a reasonable chance that it will advance their client's theory of the case, or undermine some elements of the opponent's case or defence. The opponent counsel should not interrupt the cross-examining advocate. Cross-examination is the right of the advocate; but it should not be misused.

Advocate appearing as a witness

An advocate shall not act as a counsel and witness in the same case. He should not accept the brief or continue the same if he happened to be the witness in the case. It is a sound principle that a person who is appearing as counsel should not give evidence as witness. If in the course of proceedings it is discovered that he is in a position to give evidence and it is desirable that he should do so, his proper course is to retire from the case in his professional capacity. It is against the etiquette of the Bar that a member of the profession should give evidence in the case in which he is engaged as counsel and no self-respecting counsel would be prepared to conduct a case for the defence after having been called as a witness for the prosecution. If a lawyers knows, or has reason to believe, that he will be an important witness of fact in a case, he ought not to accept the brief. But the Court has no power to direct or deprive an advocate to appear in a case. There is no provision in law, which prohibits an Advocate to appear in such a case except the rules of the conduct framed under the Advocates Act. A Court has authority to direct a counsel to withdraw from a case if it comes to the conclusion that evidence, his material and his appearance in the court in the capacity of a lawyer would embarrass the trial of the suit to maintain the highest traditions of the profession and the Bar precludes the advocates from appearing for the opposite party as it gives rise to suspicion in the mind of the client about his advocate. An accused is entitled to be defended by a counsel of his own choice and the prosecution cannot fetter that choice merely by serving subpoena on the Advocate to appear as a witness. On the other hand, the court is bound to see that the due administration of justice is not, in any way, embarrassed. If, therefore, a court comes to the conclusion that the trial will be embarrassed by the appearance of an advocate who has been called as witness by the other side, and if, notwithstanding the court's expression of its opinion, the advocate refuses to withdraw, in such a case, the court has inherent jurisdiction to require the advocate to withdraw. Rule 13 of the Bar Council of India Rules clearly says that if a lawyer becomes a witness, he should not continue as a lawyer without jeopardising the interest of his client.

Dress

The legal costume in India is contributed by the English legal system. In England like Common Law and Equity, it evolved through customs, practices and traditions. It was through an adoption of the eccelesiastic and scholastic draperies. There is, however, no evidence to show that it evolved in England as a deliberately invented garb. It is revealed from different treatises that the present day gown originated from the pre-ceceronian Roman Civil dress called 'toga'. The toga was the common garment of all the respectable people during Anglo-Saxon period. During the Norman period and in the Middle Ages the clergy as well as the laity and 'common' lawyer wore long robe while appearing before courts. The long robe was not always black. The attorneys and sergeants of the Bar and the justices in the Bench used to wear scarlet, brown, blue or green robes with stripes in it. With the passing of the years the long robe gave way to tight tunic and surcoat. But amongst the common respectable people, the lawyers returned to their robe or gown. The long robe had a resemblance to the casock. But the gown was less lengthy free over wear. It had different forms. Further, it is evident from the literature that in early ages almost all the members of the Bar as well as the Bench were priests. Thus, the clergy lawyers and the academician lawyers already had priestly robes and gowns on their back. Similarly, one can trace it to the Indian traditions as evident in the terra-cota figure of the priest or pedagogics found in the Indus Valley excavations. In Middle Ages, one finds other things apart from the gown that is, the coif, the hood, the mitre, the bands etc. The origin of the coat and jacket is purely based on the fashions and popular choices of the elite British men. Formerly there were mere jackets, only then came tunics. The coat with lapels of different styles were followed. The uniform in black and white was developed by 17th century as a symbol of nobility. However, it is hard to find any mystic symbolism or myth behind the black and white. It is universally accepted as a simple dress. India, to some extent has adopted the colonial dress. Section 49(1)(gg) of Advocates Act, 1961 empowers the Bar Council of India to make rules prescribing the form of dresses or robes to be worn by advocates, having regard to the climate conditions, appearing before any Court or Tribunal. Order IV, Rule 3 of the Supreme Court Rules, 1966 provides that every advocate appearing before the Court shall wear such robes or costume as may from time to time be directed by the Court. In **Muraleedharan Nair v. N.J. Antony**,[1] the High Court of Kerala through Mr. Justice Bhaskaran Nambiar observed that "an Advocate's robe is steeped in tradition and has a class of distinction. It is worn when one practises as an advocate, not before he is borne in that profession or after he ceases to practise. It is not a casual wear. It is for serious occasion. Outside court, it has no place; it shall have none. Inside court, it represents cause; the cause of the client. When there is no counsel, there is no robe."

Advocates appearing in the Supreme Court, High Courts, Subordinate Courts, Tribunals or Authorities shall wear the following as part of their

1. 1985 KLT 1.

dress which shall be sober and dignified :

I. Advocates other than Lady Advocates

(i) A black buttoned-up coat, chapkan, achkan, black sherwani and white bands with Advocate's Gowns; or

(ii) A black open breast coat, white shirt, white collar, stiff or soft, white bands with Advocate's Gowns.

In either case long trousers (white, black stripped or grey) or Dhoti.

II. Lady Advocates

(i) Black and full or half sleeve jacket or blouse, white collar, stiff or soft, with white bands with advocate's Gowns;

(ii) Sarees, lady skirts (white or black) or flare :

Provided that the wearing of Advocate's Gown shall be optional except when appearing in the Supreme Court or in a High Court :

Provided further that in Courts other than the Supreme Court, High Court, District Court, Sessions Court or City Civil Court a black tie may be worn instead of bands.

Mr. Salman Khurshid, a noted Supreme Court lawyer and leader of Indian National Congress says that, "we lawyers, wear this black gown and band even in summer, which may otherwise look ridiculous, but this upholds the dignified image and values of the elite profession."

There is a general feeling that developed in the recent years that "advocates do not attend the courts in proper uniform. They wear coloured shirts and do not either fasten tie or do so of their own choice." The need of the hour is that advocates should attend the courts in proper uniform throughout in order to uphold the dignified image of the legal profession.

Fees

An advocate is entitled to settle with his client his fee for any engagement having regard to the nature of assignment, extent of the professional skill required to be used in the case and also having regard to his standing in the Bar. However, the rules do not lay down any standard for fee of advocates. Rule 11 of Bar Council of India Rules appear to lay down two factors which are relevant for the fee demanded by an advocate, namely, (i) the fee should be consistent with the standing of the advocate concerned in the Bar; and (ii) it should bear relation with the nature of the case. Rule 38 of the Bar Council of India Rules which speaks of a duty towards the colleagues states that an advocate shall not accept a fee less than the fee taxable under the rules, when the client is able to pay the same. The object of Rule 38 is to prevent unhealthy competition with the colleagues by undercutting his fees. In India, before the Legal Practitioners Act, 1846, the legal practitioners did not have any right to enter into an agreement with their client regarding the fee payable to them; the fee was prescribed by the Court. Later on, Legal Practitioners Acts gave freedom to the lawyers to enter into contract with their clients regarding fee. Section 3 of the Legal Practitioners (Fees) Act, 1926 provided that any legal practitioner who acts or agrees to act for any person may, by private agreement settle with such person the terms of his engagement and the fee to be paid for his professional services.

Rule 38 in Section IV of the Bar Council of India Rules in Chapter II emphasises that there should not be cut throat competition among lawyers to knock away an engagement by quoting less and less fees. It does not mean to say that if the client is poor, the lawyer should not accept from him fee less than the regulation fee, or when he cannot pay any fee at all to do the case for him without any fee. Although it is open to a lawyer to fix his own fee in any case or matter, it is well established that it should not be oppressive and should not vary with the wealth of his client. There is an instance wherein a promising barrister, who was then comparatively junior at the Bar approached Mr. B.E. O'Conor to engage him, on behalf of his client, for moving a stay application and told him "Sir, I have charged Rs. 5,00/- for drafting the stay application; the client is prepared to pay you a handsome fee for arguing the case." Mr. O'Conor in his inimitable style replied, "Youngman, my fee for a miscellaneous application is only Rs. 50/-. I cannot charge anything more."

The legal profession is not a business but profession and therefore in fixing the fees it should be kept in mind that the profession is a branch of administration of justice and not a mere money-making trade. The Canons of American Bar Association clearly demonstrate that the lawyer should avoid charges which over-estimate their advice and services as well as those which undervalue them. The fee allowed by the rules is generally known as scale of fee as different scales are fixed by the rules. An advocate shall not accept a brief for an amount below the scale of fee. It amounts to underselling, which is bad. The only exception to it is serving the cause of the poor otherwise known as legal aid to poor. The authors finds a number of types or modes of fee arrangements which are commonly known as methods of charging fees. These are :

(i) Fixed fee

This fee is also called as standard fee in some countries. The counsel may charge one fee upto admission and a further fee if the case goes for a final hearing or an additional fee if a case goes for longer than expected. Essentially however, these are lump-sum fee.

(ii) Hourly fee

Many lawyers charge by the hour. They record the number of hours spent on a particular case. In the advanced countries, hourly bill is very common. In our country, hourly billing is usually restricted to big firms carrying on transactional practice.

(iii) Per hearing fee

Such fees are normally charged by senior Advocates, Counsel and others who practise in the Superior Courts. Here there can be separate fee for 'effective' hearing and adjourned hearings.

(iv) Contingency fee

This is the most controversial aspect of lawyer's fee. Such fee depends upon the success of the suit or proceeding and is regarded as against the public policy. In other words, contingency fee is a system whereby a lawyer's fee is based on the outcome of the case. If the client loses, the lawyer does not get anything, but if the client succeeds, the lawyer gets a pre-determined percentage of the damages or compensation recovered.

(v) Retainer fee

Retainer fees are the fees which are paid in order to ensure the availability of lawyers and to ensure that they do not appear for opponents.

(vi) Referral fee

Such a fee is given as compensation for reference of a case. This is not permitted in most countries. It is touting, in sum and substance. Division of fee by lawyers and third parties amounts to misconduct. Division of fee between lawyers can only be made if the division is in proportion to the services performed by each lawyer, the client is advised and does not object, and the total fee is reasonable. We also find a prevalent practice in Tamil Nadu, where the senior advocate used to pay one-third of his fee to the briefing lawyer. The advantage of this practice is that the interests of junior advocates are protected. The Rules of Professional Conduct Part IV, Chapter I framed by the Bar Council of india explicitly states that "a senior advocate may in recognition of the services rendered by an advocate in Part II of the State roll appearing in any matter pay him a fee which he considers reasonable."

Legal Framework Relating to Fee Chargeable by Lawyers in India

Although it is open to a lawyer to fix his own fee in any case or matter, it is well established that it should not be oppressive and should not vary with the wealth of his client. The important statute relating to rights and liabilities of legal practitioners, namely, the Legal Practitioners Fees Act (XXI of 1926) was passed in 1926. It conferred the right under Section 4 on a legal practitioner to sue for his fee under the agreement or if no fee had been settled, for a fee computed in accordance with the law in force as to the calculation of the costs. The Fees Act, 1926 did not lay down guidelines about the extent or nature of fees which could be charged by lawyers. Section 3 of the Act clearly conferred the freedom on a lawyer who acted or agreed to act for any person, to settle with his clients the term of his engagement and the fee to be paid for his professional services by private agreement. Under Section 5, the legal practitioner was liable to be sued in case of any loss or injury to the client due to his negligence in the conduct of his professional duties. This Act gave the right to the legal practitioner to enter into private agreement with his client regarding the terms of his engagement and the fee to be paid for his professional services. The client had a right to sue his legal practitioner for damage on account of the loss or injury that may be caused to him due to the negligence of the lawyer in conducting his professional duties. This right of the client is specifically given by the Act. Though the Act gave freedom to contract to the legal practitioner and his client to enter into contract regarding engagement as regards the fees, it does not permit an advocate to stipulate for or receive a remuneration proportioned to the results of litigation or a claim whether in the form of a share in the subject-matter, a percentage or otherwise.[1]

The Legal Practitioners (Fees) Act, 1926, therefore, was limited in its application and did not provide for any code of conduct in regard to charging of fees. Section 50(5) of the Advocates Act, 1961 repealed the Legal Practitioners (Fees) Act, 1926. Till date, no statute has been enacted to regulate advocate's fees. The only regulation in India in regard to fee is found in the Bar Council of India's Standards of Professional Conduct and Etiquette, Part VI, Chapter II, Section II, Rules 11, 20, 23, 25, 26, 28, 29, 30, 38 and Section VI—Duty to Render Legal Aid.

The rules do not lay down any standard for fee of advocates. Rule 11 of the Bar Council of India Rules appear to lay down two factors which are relevant for the fee demanded by an advocate. They are :

—Firstly, the fee should be consistent with the standing of the advocate concerned in the Bar; and

—Secondly, it should bear relation with the nature of the case.

Third factor may be that the fee be stipulated at taxable limit.

Fee of the lawyer is basis of his movement. It provides initiative for his action. An advocate has to charge his fee appropriately and is not to charge a fee less than the fee taxable under the rules. But it is subject to the capacity of the client to pay. Rule 38 of the Bar Council of India Rules stipulates complete charging of fee so as to comply taxable liability. The object of Rules 38 is to prevent unhealthy competition with the colleagues by under cutting his fees. In other words, the rule emphasises that there should not be cut throat competition among lawyers to knock away an engagement by quoting less and less fees. It does not mean to say that if the client is poor, the lawyer should not accept from him fee less than the regulation fee, or when he cannot pay any fee at all to do the case for him without any fee. An advocate of some standing should not accept a brief if the party does not pay the proper fee. That will make way for the client to approach a junior member who will accept the brief at the fee the client is willing to pay.

The determination of proper fee requires consideration of interests of both client and lawyer. A lawyer should not charge more than a reasonable fee. An excessive charge of fee abuses the professional relationship between the lawyer and the client. The fees of a lawyer will depend upon the lawyer's experience, ability, reputation, the nature of the employment, the responsibility involved and results obtained.

The only regulation in India in regard to fee is found in the Bar Council of India's Standards of Professional Conduct and Etiquette. The regulations in the said Rules provide :

(a) An advocate is bound to accept any brief in the courts or tribunals or before any other authorities, in or before which he

1. *In the matter of 'G', Senior Advocate*, A.I.R. 1954 S.C. 557.

proposes to practice, at a fee consistent with his standing at the Bar and the nature of the case. Special circumstances may justify his refusal to accept a particular brief. [See Duties to Client—r 11].

(b) An advocate shall not stipulate for a fee contingent on the results of litigation or agree to share the proceeds thereof. [See Duties to Client—r 20].

(c) An advocate shall not adjust fee payable to him by his client against his own personal liability to the client, which liability does not arise in the course of his employment as an advocate. [See Duties to Client—r 23].

(d) An advocate should keep accounts of the client's money entrusted to him, and the accounts should show the amounts received from the client or on his behalf, the expenses incurred for him, and the debits made on account of fees with respective dates and all other necessary particulars. [See Duties to Client—r 25].

(e) Where moneys are received from or on account of a client, the entries in the accounts should contain a reference as to whether the amounts have been received for fees or expenses and during the course of the proceeding, no advocate shall, except with the consent in writing of the client concerned, be at liberty to divert any portion of the expenses towards fees. After the termination of the proceeding, the advocate shall be at liberty to appropriate towards the settled fee due to him, any sum remaining unexpended out of the amount paid or sent to him for expenses or any amount that has come into his hands in that proceeding. Where the fee has been left unsettled, the advocate shall be entitled to deduct, out of any moneys of the client remaining in his hands, at the termination of the proceeding for which he had been engaged, the fee payable under the rules of the court, in force for the time being, or by then settled and the balance, if any, shall be refunded to the client. [See Duties to Client—rr 26, 28 and 29].

(f) A copy of the client account shall be furnished to him on demand, provided the necessary copying charge is paid. [See Duties to Client—r 30].

(g) An advocate shall not accept a fee less than the fee taxable under rules when the client is able to pay the same. [See Duties to Colleagues—r 38].

(h) Every advocate shall in the practice of the profession of law bear in mind that anyone genuinely in need of a lawyer is entitled to legal assistance even though he cannot pay for it fully or adequately and that within the limits of an advocate's economic condition, free legal assistance to the indigent and oppressed is one of the highest obligations an advocate owes to society. However, where there is a government funded channel for legal aid the need for rigid implementation of this rule appears to be doubtful.

How to Determine Reasonableness of Fee

The lawyers have to charge a reasonable fee on the one hand and it should be sufficient on the other so as to earn livelihood and to cover the cost of operating their establishments, including rent, equipment, libraries, and employee payrolls and benefits. Taxes and insurance premium have to be paid. The code of conduct for lawyers of the European Community stipulates that the fee charged by a lawyer should be fair and reasonable. Most state laws in the United States also prescribe that lawyer's fee should be reasonable. Even in India, the Bar Council Rules provides that the fee of the lawyer should be reasonable. The moot question here is that how does one determine "reasonableness". The Model Rules for the American Bar Association sets out the factors which are vital to be considered in order to determine the reasonableness of fees :

1. Time and labour required, the novelty and difficulty of the questions involved, and the skill required to perform the legal service properly;
2. Likelihood, if apparent to the client, that the acceptance of the particular employment will preclude other employment by the lawyer;
3. The fee customarily charged in the locality for similar legal services;
4. The amount involved and the results obtained;
5. The time limitations imposed by the client or by the circumstances;
6. The nature and length of the professional relationship with the client;
7. The experience, reputation and ability of the lawyer or lawyers performing the services;
8. Whether the fee fixed is fixed or contingent.

In London (United Kingdom), there are separate rules as to counsel fees :

1. Counsel should charge separate fee for each case.
2. Fixed fee for advising over a period of time is not permitted.
3. Minimum rates of fee for Queen's Counsel and Junior Counsel are fixed.
4. Fee should be based on the length and difficulty of the case.
5. Once a fee is fixed it cannot be easily changed except in exceptional circumstances.
6. Fee is to be negotiated by the clerk.
7. A counsel is at liberty to say that he will not practice in a particular court without a special fee.

Despite these guidelines, it is very difficult in a given case to determine the reasonableness or otherwise of fees. While it may be easy to hold a fee unreasonable if on the face it is exorbitant, in most cases it is almost impossible to judge.

8

BAN ON ADVERTISEMENTS BY LAWYERS IN INDIA NEED TO RETHINK IN THE ERA OF GLOBALIZATION

I. Prelude

The lawyers in India are barred from advertising their profession considering the profession to be a noble one and such advertising to be derogatory to that profession.[1] The duty of an advocate not to advertise or solicit is based, not only on history, but also on practical utility. Historically, the profession of law is developed more in the spirit of public service than as a means of earning livelihood. The ethics of the legal profession forbid that an advocate should advertise his talents or his skill as a businessman advertises in order to secure customers. It is natural that the lawyer must impose on himself the duty of neither advertising nor soliciting. Even from the practical utilitarian point of view, advertising, solicitation or encroachment on the practice of others do not tend to benefit either the public or the lawyer. On the other hand, extensive advertising on the part of lawyer might increase litigation which of course is definitely against public policy. Advertising, therefore, is highly objectionable. Advertising is aimed at drawing attention of the public and it is a device for obtaining public favour of notoriety. It is a well recognised rule of etiquette in the legal profession that no attempt should be made to advertise oneself directly or indirectly.[2] An advocate should not seek business by advertisement or otherwise. The profession is firmly established on the strong winds of distorting commercialism. However, the winds of change that have been blown by the forces of consumerism and an emerging globalised commercial culture are strong enough to overcome even the strongest of oppositions. Lawyers as a class hold a special place in the society for the kind of job they do which is essentially subsumed in the canopy of public service. They are the part of a closed knit community and as a fraternity they follow the standards set by the bar. However, over the years a decline has been witnessed in the ideals of professionalism and the image of lawyers is said

1. *Indian Council of Legal Aid and Advice* v. *Bar Council of India*, A.I.R. 1995 S.C. 691; *Dr. Haniraj L. Chulani* v. *Bar Council of Maharashtra and Goa*, A.I.R. 1996 S.C. 1708.
2. C.L. Anand, Professional Ethics of the Bar 76 (1987); see also C. Rama Rao, Professional Ethics & Advocacy 133 (1987); Sunil Deshta and Kiran Deshta, Practical Advocacy of Law 101 (2006).

to have been falling in public estimation.[1] It has been said that the profession has become overcrowded and a lot of competition has created a kind of chaos in the system and the lawyers are indulging in self-aggrandizement. They are indulging in activities which were once being condemned by the fraternity as being against standards of professional conduct and etiquette. Advertising their services is one such activity that lawyers are resorting to in order to sustain themselves in the profession. The very important professional responsibility of each lawyer is that, every person in our society should have ready access to the professional services when really needed. Lawyers are expected to act as the pillars to safeguard justice, provide legal literacy and meet the highest standards of ethical responsibility. These are the things which are expected from a lawyer of integrity and competence. But the problem is that, how to identify a lawyer, who is specialist in any given subject of law, what is his experience in that field of knowledge? It is very much clear that public are deprived of this right to be informed of the details with respect to any lawyer as such. It is because lawyers in India are barred from advertising their profession, considering the profession to be a noble one and such advertising to be derogatory to that profession. In the last few decades, there has been an increased rethinking on the issue of advertisement by lawyers, which has resulted in the ban being withdrawn in a number of countries. Keeping in view this background, the authors propose to deal briefly with the aspects of laws banning the advertising for legal professionals in India and their implications, and the necessity to change the laws so as to adjust to the need of the day.

Concept of Advertising

Advertising is one of the most important and critical aspects of trade and business. It is a form of communication for promoting and marketing of products and services to the consumers. Once described as the life blood of free media, it has now become the life blood of competition in market. Generally, advertisements are initiated through different channels including radio, television, journals, newspapers, direct mail, billboards, yellow pages, transit space, poster directories etc. These media play a vital role in spreading communication, increasing data base and in expanding the customer retention. With rapid convergence of communication technology, the advertisers are evolving newer means of technologically advanced means of advertising. The advent of internet and mobile telecommunication has revolutionized the world. Advertising has broadened its horizons beyond comprehensions in the virtual world and cyber space is crammed with advertisements. Pop up ads, unsolicited commercial e-mail and other forms of spam are some examples how advertisers are using the virtual space to promote their products and services.

It is a truism that lawyer's professional service cannot be compared with any consumable goods. Strictly speaking, there is basic difference between the goods and merchandise and the lawyers, professional service.

1. Law Commission of India 131 Report on Role of Legal Profession in Administration of Justice, 1998.

Goods may be consumed as its utility is used up when its existence in some shape or form or use is ended. But a lawyer's service cannot be ended, wasted, decayed or used up in a strict sense. Service for his client means lawyer's efforts to vindicate the legal rights of that client. Irrespective of his success or failure in protection of such rights, the lawyer's services result in the court's interpretation on the points of facts and law placed by the lawyer which interpretation will be utilised by all the bar, bench, executive, legislature and future litigants until those interpretations are over-ruled or varied or modified by higher judiciary. A lawyer's service is not only to his client but to the entire community of litigants. It cannot be said that a service by lawyer to his client is consumed by that client. In India, lawyers are not allowed to advertise their profession. Bar Council of India Rules, 1975 restricted all sorts of advertisement by a lawyer.

II. The Law on Legal Advertising in India

After independence, it was felt that both the legal profession and the system of judicial administration required structural changes and a Committee under the Chairmanship of Justice S.R. Das was appointed in 1951 to suggest strategies for unification and standardization of legal practice in the country. The Committee recommended establishment of an integrated bar for the whole country and constitution of a single class of the legal practitioners (advocates) with uniform qualifications for admissions. Similarly, the Fifth Law Commission in its Fourteenth Report submitted in 1958, recommended for establishment of a United All India Bar. In 1959, the Legal Practitioner's Bill incorporating the recommendations was introduced in Parliament. To give effect to the recommendations of All India Bar Committee of 1951 and Law Commission, the Parliament enacted the Advocates Act, 1961. This Act under Section 4 forms a 'Bar Council of India (BCI)' to regulate all the legal professionals and legal education in India. Pursuant to the functions of the Bar Council of India under Section 7 and its power to make rules under Section 49 of the said Act, it has enacted the Bar Council of India Rules 1962 which are binding on all the legal professionals in India. Under Section 49(1)(c) of the Advocates Act, 1961 has framed Rules 36 of the Bar Council of India Rules under Section IV (Duty to Colleagues) of Chapter II (Standards of Professional Conduct and Etiquette) of Part IV (Rules Governing Advocates). Rule 36 reads as under :

> "An Advocate shall not solicit work or advertise, either directly or indirectly, whether by circulars, advertisements, touts, personal communications, interviews not warranted by personal relations, furnishing or inspiring newspaper comments or producing his photographs to be published in connection with cases in which he has been engaged or concerned. His sign-board or name-plate should be of a reasonable size. The sign-board or name-plate or stationery should not indicate that he is or has been President or Member of a Bar Council or of any Association or that he has been associated with any person or organisation or with any particular cause or matter or that

he specialises in any particular type of work or that he has been a judge or Advocate General."

Thus, it is against an advocate's code of ethics to solicit or advertise work and amounts to misconduct on the part of the advocate. Both direct and indirect advertising is prohibited. An advocate may not advertise his services through circulars, advertisements, touts, personal communication or interviews not warranted by personal relations. Similarly, the following forms of indirect-advertising are prohibited :

(i) issuing circulars or election manifestoes by a lawyer with his name, profession and address printed on the manifestoes, thereby appealing to the members of the profession practicing in the lower courts who are in a position to recommend clients to counsel practicing in the High Court;

(ii) canvassing for votes by touring in the province or sending out his clerk or agents to the various districts, which must necessarily mean directly approaching advocates practicing in subordinate courts.

Further, the signboard or name-plate displayed by an advocate should be of reasonable size. His signboard or name-plate or stationery should not indicate that he is or has been President or member of a Bar Council or of any Association or that he has been associated with person or organisation or with any particular cause or matter or that he specialises in any particular type of work or that he has been a judge or an Advocate General.

Further, advertising on internet is also prohibited. The Bar Council of India, in a notice dated 21st October, 1991,[1] reaffirmed that such 'advertisements' on internet are considered an offence. It ordered all the legal websites to be withdrawn immediately, under threat of legal action ranging from temporary suspension to permanent debarring of the lawyer from practice. Also publishing in on-line directories is a bar for advocates. But a change has been made on 30th April, 2008 which initiates a liberal view regarding advertisements by advocates. A resolution was passed by the Bar Council of India which says :

"Resolved that the following amendment of Rule 36 in Section IV, Chapter II, Part VI of the Bar Council of India Rules by incorporating a proviso in terms of resolution passed by the Joint Consultative Conference and approved that this rule shall not stand in the way of advocates furnishing website information as prescribed in the schedule, under intimation to and as approved by the Bar Council of India. Any additional other input in the particulars than approved by the Bar Council of India, will be deemed to be violation of Rule 36 and such advocates are liable to be proceeded with misconduct under Section 35 of the Advocates Act, 1961.[2]

Recently, the Bar Council of India has proposed a new draft code of

1. http://www.barcouncilofindia.org/about/legislative—research/visited on 13.09.2014.
2. http://www.scribed.com/doc/3935967/Advertising-by-Advocates-in-India, visited on 13.09.2014.

ethics which is being circulated in the legal fraternity for a discussion.[1] While analyzing the proposed rule, certain things are visibly deduced. One, that a lawyer or a law firm can provide only their basic information and details about areas of practice on a website and secondly, whatever was prohibited for him under the earlier rule is still prohibited for him, just that he is explicitly deterred from giving any comments with pictures of him published in newspapers alongwith case details. Now this makes the existing rule more absurd than earlier and out of the sync with modern times.

Justifications for Baring Advertisements for Legal Professionals

To reiterate, the profession of law in India is developed more in the spirit of public service than as a means of earning livelihood. Advertising is considered unethical and contrary to the service orientation of the legal profession. The advocate should not seek business by advertisement or otherwise. Advertising was always condemned in India as much as it was loathed in the country of origin. The first reported case wherein the court condemned the practice of advertising in a very plain and simple manner is **Government Pleader v. S, a Pleader.**[2] The facts of the case were that one Mr. *S*, a district Pleader holding a sanad for the Surat District, sent various circular post cards to the public with reference to the examination of the accounts of wakf properties. The post cards were signed by him as High Court Pleader. The Court held that it was improper conduct on his part to issue these post cards and to canvas for this particular work in the way that he did would result in getting an improper advantage in legal work over his fellow pleaders, who did not descend to such devices. As advocacy is not a business, it can be said that the advocate is liable for misconduct if he advertises. In another case,[3] it was held that it is a well recognised rule of etiquette in legal profession that no attempt should be made to advertise oneself directly or indirectly. Such conduct is unprofessional on the part of an advocate to solicit directly or indirectly to advertise through various methods—crude or subtle. Such a course of action tends to lower the dignity of the honourable profession and is akin to touting. An advocate should remember that attaining excellence in the profession and earning his reputation in the Bar and the Bench of being a devoted, diligent, hardworking, learned and honest advocate is the most effective advertisement and he does not need inspired news item in the column of 'Law Court' in the newspapers displaying his name or sometimes his photographs.

In **re thirteen Advocates of Allahabad,**[4] it was held that advertising in any form, by extolling of services, experience and ability or work in any branch of law on the part of a lawyer is highly improper and amounts to a gross breach of professional etiquette. The court unambiguously declared

1. http://www.barcouncil of india.org, visited on 13.09.2014.
2. A.I.R. 1929 Bom. 335.
3. *Kanepat Kaur* v. *Kasi Prasad Singh*, A.I.R. 1934 All 106.
4. A.I.R. 1934 All. 1067; also see *C.D. Sekkizhar* v. *Secy. Bar Council*, A.I.R. 1967 Mad. 35.

that it is a well recognized rule of etiquette in the legal profession that no attempt should be made to advertise oneself directly, or indirectly. Such a course of action tends to lower the dignity of the honourable profession and is undoubtedly akin to touting. In **re A, and an Advocate**,[1] the Supreme Court held that the writing letters for a brief by advocate, stating his achievements and his knowledge in some specialized subjects amount to professional misconduct, and makes him unfit to be the member of the bar. In the instant case, an advocate-on-record of the Supreme Court wrote a letter to the Minister, Law, Maharashtra and in the letter, he wrote—"you might have got an advocate-on-Record in this Court but I would like to place my services at your disposal if you so wish and agree." The Supreme Court through Justice Shah held that the advocate is either ignorant of the elementary rules of professional ethics or has no regard for them. The court held that the advocate has mischosen his profession. Apparently, he is a man of weak moral fibre. If he is ignorant of the elementary rules of professional ethics, he had demonstrated the inadequacy of training and education befitting a member of the profession of law. If he knew that it was highly improper to solicit brief and even then he wrote postcard in question, he is very unworthy member of the legal profession. The advocate was punished and was suspended from practice for five years.

The most important case on soliciting/advertisement happens to be **Bar Council of Maharashtra v. M.V. Dabholkar and Ors.**,[2] wherein the Supreme Court while condemning soliciting work by advocates with strong valor has set high ideals for the professionals. The Court categorically said that lest there should be lingering doubts, we hold that the canons of ethics and propriety for the legal profession totally taboo conduct by way of soliciting, advertising, scrambling and other obnoxious practices, subtle or clumsy, for betterment of legal business. Law is no trade, briefs no merchandise and so the leaven of commercial competition or procurement should not vulgarise the legal profession. The instant matter was taken up in appeal before the Supreme Court and was considered by Justice V.R. Krishna Iyer and three other judges R.S. Sarkaria, A.C. Gupta and S. Murtaza Fazl on the Bench observed "with deep sorrow" that a lawyer should scrupulously observe the norms of professional conduct and etiquette provided in Rule 36 of the Bar Council of india Rules made in this behalf.

Hence, letting advocates advertising, would lead to several ill effects which may be as under :

(i) Advocacy is a noble and honourable profession, the commercialization of this would degrade it. Because, the words of Section IV of Chapter II of Part IV of the Bar Council of India Rules are crystal clear, that is, "Duty to Colleagues". This means that the reason behind enactment of such a norm is to prevent the advocates, law firms, etc. from enticing the clients of their adversary and not to

1. A.I.R. 1962 S.C. 1337.
2. A.I.R. 1976 S.C. 242.

snatch away the business of their adversary.[1] The legal profession is a service oriented profession. Permitting advertising would affect the service orientation of the profession. It would cause a proliferation of unethical and mercenary practices among lawyers.

(ii) The law is made in order to help the small and unknown advocates and firms to rise in market and do business. The purpose behind it is to prevent a set of lawyers from taking unreasonable advantage, otherwise, the same names would appear time and again.[2]

(iii) Advertising often leads to unhealthy competition among competitors. The quality of the legal services will deteriorate. Lawyers will resort to practices such as price undercutting, bargain deals etc. in an effort to draw the consumers, and then will be forced to cut corners so as to fit within the promised budget.

(iv) It is also argued that permitting advertising will result in an increase in costs. The costs incurred on advertising would ultimately be transferred to the clients. Advertising is generally expensive; this burden will fall squarely upon the client. Further, the advertisements by lawyers are essentially misleading. The clients will not be able to differentiate between puffery and the true qualifications of a lawyer. Misleading advertisements, increase in the costs and legal fees result in unhealthy competition amongst lawyers and encourage litigation. The courts will get clogged with cases on frivolous or baseless causes of action.

Lawyers in India, are therefore, averse to advertising their profession even if there is no restriction imposed by the Advocate Act. They think it below dignity, nobility and erudition and legal professional ethics.

Justifications for Providing Advertisements for Legal Professionals

In the socio-economic changes of the present times all professions and all jobs have become dignified and it is unjustifiable to restrict the lawyers alone in this regard, keeping them away in a watertight compartment under the mask of superior dignity and nobility. The view that lawyers are superior to other professionals has become an anachronism. The proponents of advertising by lawyers raise a number of arguments to justify their stand. They content that advertising will serve the fundamental purpose of providing information to the public. It would help the lawyers, reaching out and serving the community by providing public with important information about the availability of legal services.

In **Tata Press Ltd. v. Mahanagar Telephone Nigam,**[3] the apex Court, in a three judge bench, held that, "Advertising as a 'commercial

1. Trushil Vora, A Bar on Advertising for Advocates in India under Advocates Act, 1961 at http//jurisonlinein/2008/02/% E 2%/80% 9 Ca-bar-on-advertising-for-advocates-in-India-under-advocates-act, 1961; visited on 12.10.2014.
2. Lawyer can't be blamed if his name appears in print, says Punjab A.G., May 25, 1999, at http://www.indian express.com/res/web/ple/i.e./daily/19990525/ige 25114 html (last visited on 12.10.2014).
3. A.I.R. 1995 S.C. 2438.

speech' has two facets. Advertising which is no more than a commercial transaction is nonetheless dissemination of information regarding the product-advertised. Public at large is benefited by the information made available through the advertisement. In a democratic economy, free flow of commercial information is indispensable. There cannot be honest and economical marketing by the public at large without being educated by the information disseminated through advertisements. The economic system in a democracy would be handicapped without there being freedom of "commercial speech". Examined from another angle, the public at large has a right to receive the "Commercial Speech." Article 19(1)(a) not only guarantees freedom of speech and expression, it also protects the rights of an individual to listen, read and receive the said speech. So far as the economic needs of a citizen are concerned, their fulfilment has to be guided by the information disseminated through the advertisements. The protection of Article 19(1)(a) is available to the speaker as well as to the recipient of the speech."

It is argued that advertising provides the public with information about fees and services and reaches out to people who may not have the contacts and would lead them to a competent lawyer. It is suggested that the increased public access to the courts would help redress wrongs committed on the ignorant and oppressed classes to enable people to vindicate their legal rights. It is also suggested that regulatory control can check advertising that might be misleading, but prohibition cannot be sustained as it restricts availability of legal services to the persons who may be in need of the same.

It is also suggested that Rule 36 of the Bar Council of India Rules violates Article 19(1)(a) of the Constitution. Apart from commercial free speech being part of the freedom of speech, there are other constitutional perspectives, which must be borne in mind. The right to information has been read into Article 19(1)(a). Surely, the client has a right to be informed about legal services available. If the right to free legal aid is part of the fundamental right to life and personal liberty under Article 21, so must be the right to paid legal services. Furthermore, under Article 32 of the Constitution of India, the right to move the Supreme Court for the enforcement of a fundamental right is itself a fundamental right. These rights would be meaningful only if a person can make an informed choice in the matter of legal services, and ultimately, the value of advertising lies in enabling him to make such a choice.[1] The most important development that ignited the debate throughout the country over the lawyers advertising was a writ petition filed by V.B. Joshi in the year 2000 challenging the constitutional validity of Rule 36 of Bar Council of India Rules.[2] The petitioner claimed the rule to be violative of Article 19(1)(a), 19(1)(g), 21 and 22. The petitioner made a very persuasive argument with respect to Article 22 when he says, "if one has to choose an advocate or a lawyer he

---

1. Raju Ramchandran, Professional Ethics for lawyers : Changing Profession, Changing Ethics 126 (2014).
2. *V.B. Joshi* v. *Union of India*, W.P. Civil 538 of 2000.

must have the information of list of lawyers and their standing, knowledge of law, experience and expertise in particular branch of law which cannot be made available to a person in jail if Rules 36 does not permit to give such information."

To be honest we find that advertising will provide clients with inexpensive information about the attributes of professionals. Presently, people are forced to rely on the personal recommendations of their colleagues and acquaintances who have used lawyers in the past. Such personal information may depart significantly from the optimum decision. Consider, for example, the case of a person who recommends a lawyer who he used in a criminal matter, to a friend desirous of employing a lawyer to handle his divorce proceedings. Lawyers have different areas of expertise. No doubt all lawyers would meet the minimum requirements to practice at the bar, they will vary in their knowledge, experience and ability. Removal of the ban on professional advertising will help the public to choose the correct lawyer.

We also find that some Indian law firms are working around the legal advertising ban by emulating the alternative methods used by their international counterparts. They resort to surrogate advertising. For instance, some big firms in terms of number of partners and associates, have an in-house strategic communication department to build a brand presence. Few firms present the press and prospective clients' information about the latest developments of the firm, such as awards and accrediations received by its partners, and data on merits to show their growth. many advocates think that advertising in print or on television could confuse or mislead the common man and opt for some alternative methods, such as awareness programmes on legal and through non-profit groups and redressal forums.

Further, the proponents of advertising argue that advertising will produce better quality professional services, lower prices, productive competition, and more efficient exploitation of resources. Professionals will engage in productive competition in order to draw clients and provide the services desired by their clients. New firms and lawyers will find it easier to enter the market. This will definitely reduce the monopoly or domination of the large and old law firms. Further, established lawyers and law-firms will no longer be in position to charge excessive prices. This will also result in the removal of the providers of inferior services in the market.

The courts in India have recognized 'Legal Service' as a 'service' rendered to the consumers and have held that lawyers are accountable to the clients in case of any deficiency in their legal services.[1] After Globalization and India's joining to WTO, it has become indispensable to let lawyers advertise to compete in the global market. India being a signatory to the GATTS which is an organ of WTO is under an obligation to open up the service sector to Member Nations. 'Services' would include

1. *Srinath* v. *Union of India*, A.I.R. 1996 Mad. 427.

any service in any sector except services supplied in the exercise of governmental authorities as defined in GATTS.[1] Legal profession is also taken to be one of the services which is included in GATTS. This has led to the idea of entry of foreign legal consultants and liberalization of legal practices in India, keeping in view the guidelines evolved by the International Bar Association (IBA) and the GATTS. Many western nations allow their lawyers to advertise, whereas in India the lawyers are not allowed to do so. If this idea is to be put into practice, the Advocates Act, 1961 which governs legal practice in India needs to be amended.

The proponents also argue that advertising by lawyers will also achieve the salutary goal of educating the public of their service needs. Many legal problems requiring the services of lawyers go unnoticed by the public. To an extent education of public is achieved by the legal literacy programmes and workshops organized by the Bar Councils. In addition to legal workshops, advertising by advocates will serve the important goal of educating the public at large.

The Bar Council of India has proposed a new draft code of ethics which is being circulated in the legal fraternity for a discussion. The authors find that "soliciting work or advertising" used in the draft code would not mean and include setting up of a website by an advocate or a law firm giving only basic information about the names and number of lawyers in a law firm, the contact details and areas of practice. This would also apply to lawyers' brochures and directories. At present the lawyers are allowed to furnish websites information as prescribed and as approved by the Bar Council of India. Any additional other input in the particulars than approved by the Bar Council of India, will be deemed to be violation of Rule 36 and such advocates are liable to be proceeded with and punished for 'misconduct' under Section 35 of the Advocates Act, 1961.

The then Bar Council of India Chairman in the vision statement for the year 2010/12 has resolved to aim at creating a database of lawyers, law schools, academia and law students across the country so that the resources can be efficiently deployed and common platforms can be created. If this vision statements becomes a reality, information about all lawyers, law firms and law students can simultaneously be linked to Bar Councils' website. This will definitely go a long way in reducing the information asymmetry. The website of the Bar Council of India is a public website and which can be accessed without much of hastle by the public in ascertaining any information about lawyers practising in any court in any part of the country. The need of the hour is to create enough infrastructure and develop a mechanism for checking defaults in the internet related advertising norms. The Bar Council of India is also planning to introduce Uniform Identification Number (UIN) for all the lawyers to keep in track

1. http://www.parlavidayjusticia.com/tag/world-trade-organisation visited on 13-09-2014.

of the Bar members whereabouts.[1] Currently as per Bar Council of India Rules on Standards of Legal Education and Recognition of Degrees in Law for the purpose of enrolment as advocates and inspection of universities for recognizing its degrees in law, Chapter VI, Rule 41 requires each university and approved institutions to send particulars as prescribed in the schedule for the purpose of building up of uniform date of the faculty and the students of law for issuance of UIN of students and faculty against a fee prescribed by the Bar Council of India from time to time.

Sum Up

The foregoing study reveals that there are two schools of thought, one in favour of permitting advertisement and other against it. Those in favour state that Rule 36 of the Bar Council of India Rules on Standards of Professional Conduct and Etiquette is unconstitutional, and there is an urgent need to review the policy on advertising by lawyers. It is argued that the ban serves no contemporary purpose, and should be removed. To be true, the practice of law is a public utility of great implications; it obligates the lawyer to observe scrupulously those norms which makes him worthy of the confidence of the community in him as a vehicle of justice—social justice. But restrictions on advertising by lawyers in India have resulted in a situation where consumers cannot make an informed choice from the competitive market since the information relating to service is not available to them. Advertising for advocates may provide information about fees, indicating advocates area of specialization, better professional services and achieve the salutary goal of educating the public. Further, the clients would get more information about small competent firms with low-cost options. The need of the hour is to lift the ban on advertising by advocates but not to completely let it free. Advertising should be informative advertising, but not competitive or comparative advertising. It should not be like soliciting clients but informing clients about their cases, capabilities, fees, and success. Further, the need is to regulate advertising. Besides, this advertising needs to be monitored. There should not be malpractices or misrepresentation, deceptiveness and false advertisements which would affect the society and degrade the nobility of this learned profession. All existing laws to regulate the advertising can be used to control inflow of advertising. Self regulation is the best regulation. Advocates and legal firms may regulate themselves and advertise moderately; otherwise it will be the task of the Bar Council of India to charge them for 'professional misconduct' under Section 35(1) of the Advocates Act, 1961.

---

1. In an interview Gopal Subramaniam, Attorney-General has said that "the Bar Council will also be collaborating with various courts, through a UIN scheme for lawyers, to ensure that only those graduates who have passed the AIBE have the right to practice. The UIN scheme, apart from ensuring that every fresh graduate passes the exam proposes to provide a unique identity to every advocate in the country today, making him eligible for a variety of services such as insurance and counseling. At the meeting Bar Council of India also proposed to establish a knowledge web with access to some of the largest databases of information at subsidized rates." Available at htpp://barandbench.com/brief/2/936/bci-meets-to discuss-foreign-law-and legal-education-foreign-law-firms last visited on 23.9.2015.

9

BAR-BENCH RELATIONS

I. Introduction

Legal profession is a noble calling which is to be carried out with utmost care and co-operation. As it is a noble profession, professional ethics concept though nebulous, is essential for smooth functioning of judicial system and administration of justice in the country. Courts are meant for dispensing justice and Bar is not to create a bar or an obstacle in access to justice. It is the duty of the Bar to remove all stumbling blocks and obstacles from the path of those desiring justice. Administration of justice, which is a task of the judiciary, involves judges, lawyers, litigants and even general public as well. Independent and fearless judiciary is a *sine qua non* for the administration of justice. The real strength of the judiciary lies in its lawyers. Without good lawyers it is almost impossible to discharge the functions of an able and independent judiciary. It is gratifying that the Bar of India provides in abundant measure the high qualities of head and heart which are necessary for carrying on the profession of law with ability in a fearless manner. Today, professionalism, which had made lawyers self-centred, should be shed and should make themselves service and society oriented.

The Bench and the Bar are complementary to each other. The lawyers and judges have got to share responsibility for the prevailing situation in courts. The Bar and the Bench are the joint guardians of the rule of the law. It is their joint duty to create an atmosphere which will enable the citizens of the Republic to enjoy that freedom from fear which can only come from an assurance that the two guardians of freedom are always on the look-out for any temptation for arbitrary action which may be lurking in the darker recesses of all-too human executive mind, and from a feeling of confidence that whenever and wherever in the Republic any act of coercion takes place, the long arm of law will reach forth and crush it.

No discussion on the judicial system is ever complete without studying the significance of the relationship between the Bench and the Bar. This is so because the judicial system gets complete not with Bench alone or with the Bar alone, but it acquires fullness only with both the Bench and the Bar. Sir Cecil Walsh rightly remarked that nothing is more calculated to promote the smooth and satisfactory administration of justice than complete confidence and sympathy between the Bench and the Bar.[1] Hence, it is inevitable that where the judicial system comes to be discussed the relationship between the Bench and Bar figures as an important subject. This happens because of the realization that if the judicial system has to remain healthy, that will be possible only when the relationship between the Bench and Bar does not get derailed. The subject of the Bench and the Bar has continued, for long years to be an important theme at various law seminars and conferences. It is suffice to say that the professionals are expected to represent cases within the permissible limits and not beyond the permissible limits. At certain times it is really unfortunate that the professionals transgress the limits resulting in some confrontation with the Judges. Equally the Judges should be more careful and cautious since it is the amity between the Bar and the Bench which is more essential for the smooth functioning of the judicial system and not the arrogance and the superiority.

There are however, some basic parameters upon which, depend a happy and healthy relationship between two individuals or two institutions. Firstly, it depends on the spirit of give and take and if one only believes in taking from the other and not giving him anything in return, no relationship can survive for long on a healthy level. Meaning thereby, the principle of mutuality plays the key role in sustaining and developing a relationship, and this truly applies to the relationship between the Bench and the Bar too. Secondly, there are certain basic values which two sides are expected to follow in their mutual relationship. If either of the two commit a breach of the principles of good behaviour and positive attitudes towards the other, mutual relationship between the two develops serious cracks.

The Bar and the Bench constitute the two integral parts of the judiciary. There can be no courts without lawyers and there can be no lawyers without courts. One cannot exist without the other. Administration of justice, even though is the duty of the Court, should be treated as the joint responsibility of both the Bar and the Bench. The duty is to be discharged with the mutual co-operation with each other. Judicial office is essentially a public trust. Judges hold a unique position in society because society values justice more than anything else and a Judge who has acquired the virtue of a truly judicial mind is given highest respect in society. Society is, therefore, entitled to expect that a Judge must be a man of high integrity, honesty and required to have moral vigour, ad ethical influences. He is required to keep most exacting standards of propriety in judicial conduct. Any conduct which tends to undermine public confidence in the integrity and impartiality of the court would be deleterious to the efficacy of judicial process. Hence, it is a basic requirement that a Judge's official and personal conduct be free from impropriety, the same must be in tune with the highest standards of propriety and probity. The relationship between the judge and the lawyer is unique. This is fraught

1. The Advocate, 1926, p. 1; also see Anirudh Prasad, Principles of the Ethics of Legal Profession in India, (2004), p. 88.

with the hazards of tempers that sometime seethe in the stormy billows of the courtroom and of antagonisms that occasionally arise from the loss that must, inevitably, be sustained by one side as every legal battle ends. The desirable future of the nation may well depend upon the proper balancing of such relationship and upon an understanding by the lawyer and the judge that without mutual assistance and respect of each toward the other neither can carry out his assigned role, despite great learning and dedication to duty. Justice has been pictured in Roman mythology as a Goddess wearing a blindfold and holding scales. The scale connote the weighing and balancing of rights and privileges—a process that led to Shakespeare's phrase : "even handed justice". The judge and the lawyer should remember, first and foremost, that in weighing and balancing rights and privileges, they are building together a monument in the Temple of Justice that is, as Daniel Webster once put it, "the greatest interest of man on earth". The building process of the justice is never finished. It reproduces itself generation after generation in ever-changing forms. In this perspective, the lawyer and the judges are, together, fashioning for tomorrow's chronicle yesterday's experiences in the law; and their daily labours, though seeming at times tedious, uninteresting, and unimportant, will ultimately play a part in the vast reaches of the future of all mankind. It is only by working harmoniously together for the advancement of this justice that the lawyer and the judge, as guardians of our constitutional government, can stretch our horizons to meet and match the stupendous dimensions of the fundamentals of our Constitution. The only one rule for covering all the varying facets of the ideal relationship between the lawyer and the judge would be that each would do to the other as he would have the other do to him. The Canons of Ethics of the American Bar Association lays down that "it is the duty of the lawyer to maintain toward the Courts a respectful attitude, not for the sake of the contemporary incumbent of the judicial office, but for the maintenance of its supreme importance. Judges, not being wholly free to defend themselves, are peculiarly entitled to receive the support of the Bar against unjust criticism and clamor. Whenever there is proper ground for serious complaint of a judicial officer, it is the right and duty of the lawyer to submit his grievances to the proper authorities. In such cases, but not otherwise, such charges should be encouraged and the person making them should be protected."

On the other hand, an Advocate is an officer of the court, and more, a friend of the court. Lawyers have been treated, from the very beginning, as professionals with a social purpose. They owe a duty to their clients requiring high degree of honesty and integrity. Besides, they also owe a duty to the court to facilitate 'justice' and for this purpose to maintain decency and decorum. With the passage of time, they have come to be accepted as "messengers of justice" and enjoy a high respectable status in the society. They, therefore, owe a public duty to maintain people's faith in the system of administration of justice. A lawyer is more than a mere agent or servant of his client. He is also an officer of the court and as such he owes the duty of good faith and honourable dealing to the Court before which he practices his profession; his vocation is to inform the Court as to the law and facts of the case and to aid it to do justice by arriving at correct conclusions. The practice of the law is not a business open to all who wish to engage in it; it is a personal right or privilege limited to select persons of good character and special qualifications duly ascertained and certified; it is in the nature of a franchise from the State conferred only for merit.

Lawyers being officers of the court must act with integrity and professionalism while maintaining their overarching responsibility to ensure civil conduct. They are to avoid sharp practice, which includes taking advantage or acting without fair warning upon slips, irregularities, or mistakes on the part of other lawyers. The lawyer should not take advantage of slip ups which refers to lawyer's duty to the court and requires that lawyers to refrain from influencing the decisions or actions of courts or tribunals by anything other than open persuasion. This rule applies both inside and outside the courtroom. Lawyers should not make allegations of dishonesty unless they have evidence to support such allegations and shall not interfere with the administration of justice.

More helpful would be a continuing self-reminder that the fundamental basis for the respect the lawyer owes the judge is that he is an officer of the court over which the judge presides, the judge there acting under the authority and the power of the State. By taking his oath as an officer of that court, the lawyer has become bound jointly with the judge to uphold the due and orderly administration of justice. This definitely obligates him also to show to and promote in others respect for the dignity of the judicial office. By his proper attitude and actions toward the individual judge, the lawyer encourages such respect in the minds of the litigants and the general public, for habitual conduct is and always has been more the product of example than of concept. The lawyer should on all occasions and everywhere be as jealous of the honour and repute of the court as he is of his own, because by lowering the court's dignity he degrades the legal profession of which he is a member. He not only owes duty to his client but also to the court, to assist the court to the best of his ability in the administration of justice. It is the duty of the Advocate to maintain the honour and dignity of the court. He should not do anything which would lower public confidence in the administration of justice.

The Judge must be supported in this independence and an Advocate should not do anything which is calculated to obstruct the Judge in the discharge of his duties. The Judges and advocates may be described as the two wheels of the chariot of justice. Judges are the priests in the temple of justice as observed by Ronald Dworkin. Whereas we would say lawyers are worshippers of Goddess of Justice in the temple. Worshippers through the medium of priests have to reach to the Goddess of Justice. For the same, both are necessary and in the absence of one, another is incomplete. Both are equal and none of them is superior or inferior. Both share equal responsibility in settling down the controversies before the court in accordance with law. The equal position and co-operation in administration of justice of the both is reinforced through certain practices of the courts itself. In early days in England, Sergeants-at-law were addressed by Judges as brothers. It shows that honourable justices and lawyers enjoyed equal status and respect.[1] Hence, lawyers and Judges have to co-ordinate, co-operate and collectively work towards the delivery of justice. Bench and Bar need to harmonise and balance their functioning to achieve the sacred goal, that is, justice. The judge shall have the quality to command the confidence and the goodwill of the Bar. The Judges are paid to listen while counsel are paid to talk, and it is best that they should perform their respective duties.

Both the Bench and the Bar are inseparable parts of the judicial system and if one gets separated from the other, the system cannot work. This must be clearly realised by both. The Bench and the Bar are complementary to each other. But both must observe their respective value systems in their conduct and behaviour towards each other. Once, there is any deviation from this, either from the side of the Bench or from the side of the Bar, tensions build up between the two and the very working of the judicial system gets affected. We see this happening in the courts when a situation develops, making the Bench and the Bar confront each other. The legal system now suffers from several problems which includes long delays, mounting arrears, great expense, etc. The remedial measures to avoid or solve these problems depend upon the joint efforts of both the Bar and Bench. Here comes the relevance of the subject "Bar-Bench Relations." The Bench and the Bar must co-ordinate and co-operate with each other. Unless the Bar extends its helping hand, the Bench cannot achieve anything single-handed but together they can meet every challenge including threat to its independence from within.

Justice A.S. Anand in his address reminded of a story in Mahabharat. Duryodhana was arrested by Gandharvas and was being taken away. Yudhisthra told his two brothers, Bhima and Arjuna, to fight against the Gandharvas and get Duryodhana released. When they expressed their unwillingness to do so, Yudhisthra pointed out that differences and quarrels among Kauravas on the one hand and Pandavas on the other were differences among the members of the same family and as regards such differences and quarrels, they were 100 versus 5, but, if a stranger intervenes, as against him, they were 100 plus 5. We shall not allow anyone to overcome any one of us, whether Pandava or Kauravas. It is in this spirit that the Bench and the Bar have to remain together to protect the independence of the judiciary.[2] Hence, a vigilant Bar is a great asset of the judiciary. Every lawyer must be prepared to meet the new challenges in the 21st century particularly those arising out of globalised economic structure.

II. Relation of the Bar Towards the Bench

In the adversary system of administration of justice that we have in

1. Anirudh Prasad, *op. cit.*, at p. 89.
2. Nyaya Deep, July-September, 1999, p. 15.

this country, an advocate, as a member of the Bar, is treated as an officer of the court and is expected to aid and assist judicial decision-making in accordance with law. As an officer of justice and friend of the court, he owes a duty to uphold the dignity and decorum, reflect wisdom and knowledge and refrain from doing anything that may bring either the court or the system of justice into disrepute. Advocates with their past meritorious record of service, are generally considered indispensable and their absence, by itself and under certain circumstances, is considered sufficient to infer denial of justice. The relationship between the Bar and the Bench, developed for a noble cause during the course of time. This relationship is of mutual trust, confidence and respect, leading to a partnership for justice. Both sides of the Bar i.e., Judges and advocates, have zealously guarded this relationship through their acts, utterances and conduct and have promoted a common interest of justice. An advocate has many duties. there are duties to the courts, to the client, to the opponent, to the colleagues, duty in imparting training to the juniors, duties in respect of restrictions on other employments, duty to State, to the public, to law, to the profession, duty to self and duty to the Judge. In order to maintain the Bar-Bench relations, an Advocate should always bear in mind and follow his duties towards the court and the Judge. These duties are as follows :

(i) Duty to the court

Being officer of the court, the lawyer owes the duty to maintain respectful attitude towards the court. He must be bold, fearless and independent in the court and at the same time he must not be disrespectful to the court. This is a delicate duty. The lawyers have to assist the court in the administration of justice for which they have to collect the case-law and thereby help the court to arrive at proper decision of the case. During presentation of the case as well as on arguing the case before the court, they are required to behave with dignity and self-respect. The lawyer must maintain a respectful attitude towards the court, even if he is convinced that a particular ruling given by the court is erroneous or irregular. He must respectfully accept it and may invoke his remedy by appeal to a higher court. He should not influence the decision of the court by any illegal or improper means. This duty imposes an obligation on a lawyer not to publish any comments on a pending or anticipated litigation in such a way as to interfere with a fair trial in the courts or otherwise prejudice the proper administration of justice. By the duty to be respectful to the Court, it is not expected of a lawyer to be either meek or subordinate. It is his duty fearlessly to take exception to judicial corruption and incompetence. The advocate should never try either to misstate facts or mislead the court. His argument should be pointed, clear, precise and concise. He should try to win the confidence of the Court. He should not consider himself mere mouthpiece of the client and should exercise his own judgment in the use of restrained language in dealing with the Court. He should not use intemperate language during arguments in the court. He should avoid scurrilous attacks in pleading. Further, an advocate being an officer of the court, must not necessarily waste the time of the court, and therefore, it is improper for him to obtain an adjournment of a case for his own convenience without informing the court about the fact of the matter. Another duty of a lawyer towards the court is that he must equip himself properly for the profession, so that he might be of assistance to the court in administering justice. The rules of good behaviour and etiquette, expected of a lawyer, must be strictly observed by him, and if he does not do so or appears to be doing a poor job while preparing his client's case, he should have no grudge but try to learn when he gets the court's adverse comments. The lawyer functions in the court not to serve his personal ego or emotions but safeguard and promote the cause of justice for which litigants, at enormous cost and sufferings come to the court everyday. A lawyer should be true to the ethics, requirements and parameters of his legal profession and this must get reflected through his conduct towards the Bench. He must know what are his limits which he cannot cross. While in court he represents the causes of his clients and, therefore, by his conduct and thorough preparation of the cases and his presentation before courts in a systematic manner, he must demonstrate that he is in the court to safeguard the legal interest of his litigant clients. The function of advocate is not to act as a Judge. His business is to present the case of his client vigorously, attractively and independently. In doing so he is performing a duty to the court and to his client. However, there are many misconceptions in the mind of an average man in regard to the profession of lawyer. He is apt to regard a lawyer as a person whose one function is to throw dust in the eyes of courts and to win cases for his clients. Most people think that he indulges in truths, half-truths and untruths. The feeling uppermost in their mind is that the lawyer is a parasite who trades in the weaknesses and failing of fellow men.

(ii) Duty to judge

A judge is the presiding deity in the temple of justice. He may be formed of stone or clay, but he is the image of justice installed to offer the much needed *'prasad'* to the deserving votaries. He has to be maintained in dignity and strength so that the role assigned to him for the benefit of the people may be effectively discharged. A Judge has to discharge his functions with the assistance and co-operation of advocates. Very often Judges may find themselves into difficulties, perplexities, suspicions and vacillations and get into a dilemma to make up their mind as to what is right and what is wrong. These weaknesses result in overruling and reversing of the judgments. Without the assistance of lawyer it would be a superhuman task for the Judge to separate the wheat from the chaff and arrive at satisfactory judgment. It is the duty of the Advocate to assist the Judge with his marshalling and exposition of facts and interpretation of law. He should never conceal any fact or law or piece of evidence. He should give the best interpretation to help the Judge in finding out the truth and arriving at the decision. In this judgment he is bound to agree with one side and to disagree with the other; but this is no ground for attributing motives. An independent Judge is the need of democracy. It is the duty of the Bar to support Judges in their independence. The advocate should not do anything which is calculated to obstruct, divert or corrupt the stream of justice.

Dr. K.N. Katju in his address to the Allahabad University Law College Society, on the subject "Law and Lawyers" said : I regard the Judge as really an extremely unfortunate individual. That is my approach to him always for the last 32 years, a person who is entitled to my utmost sympathy because it is really a misfortune to decide controversies and definitely to come to a decision amongst a mass of false evidence, or perjuries, forgeries, fabricated documents and all that."[1]

An advocate must be courteous, respectful and fair in his attitude and conduct towards the Judge. It is because of the relationship of trust and confidence between the Bench and the Bar as a partnership for justice, that is realized that the majesty of law and dignity of courts cannot be maintained unless there is mutual respect between the Bench and the Bar and the counsel act in full realisation of their duty to the court alongside their duty to clients and have the grace to reconcile themselves when their pleas and arguments do not find acceptance with the court.

There is also the exhortation that an advocate should not indulge in abusive and reckless charges of fraud, dishonesty and criminality against a Judge. Imputations of partiality and unfairness against Judge are serious instances of misconduct. Even if the attitude of the Judge is irritating, the advocate shall never quarrel with him but may convey his feelings only politely and with good humour. An advocate shall not advance any collusive actions. He shall give the best interpretation to help the Judge in finding out the truth and arriving at the decision. It is bad of a lawyer to say to his client that the Judge is his friend or familiar with him, and he will lend weight to his argument. Even if the Judge happens to be the fast friend of the lawyer, he owes a duty not to exhibit his familiarity with the Judge and must not take undue advantage of his personal relationship.

III. Relation of the Bench towards the Bar

The Judges hold a unique position in society because society values justice more than anything else and a Judge who has acquired the virtue of a truly judicial mind is given the highest respect in society. The relationship between the Bench and Bar, developed for a noble cause during the course of time. Bench and Bar are just like two wheels of a democratic chariot wherein sits the Goddess of Justice, and if one wheel goes amiss, the chariot declines to go smoothly. Their relationship is of mutual trust, confidence and respect, leading to a partnership for justice. Both sides of the Bar, that is, Judges and advocates, have zealously guarded their relationship through their acts, utterances and conduct and have promoted the common interest of justice. There cannot be a good judiciary unless there are good Bars.

A Judge should behave or deal with the advocates appearing before him as his younger or elder brother or even as father or mother, as the

1. B. Malik, The Art of a Lawyer (1969), p. 365.

case may be, being junior or senior advocates. He should display his highest learning of the law relating to the subject-matter of the dispute before him. He should display an extraordinary sense beyond common sense but never losing common sense in any circumstances and display idiocy or prejudice. The Judge should be a mental umpire for the performance of lawyers appearing for different sides. Judges have to decide cases correctly, honestly and expeditiously as possible. A Judge must never forget his limits, he must not forget that while sitting on the Bench, he is representing the sacred cause of justice, and he must give expression not to his personal whims or ego, but to his judicious sense while hearing and deciding cases. Judges are the priests in the temple of justice, whereas lawyers are the worshippers of Goddess of justice. For the same, both are necessary and in absence of the one, another is incomplete. Hence, Judges and lawyers have to co-ordinate, co-operate and collectively work towards the delivery of justice. Bench and the Bar need to harmonise and balance their functioning to achieve the sacred goal, i.e., justice. Proper discharge of the function of administration of justice depends upon the following two important aspects :

(i) Effective control over the proceedings;

(ii) Personal qualities of the Judges.

(i) Effective Control over the Proceedings

Effective control over the proceedings of the court may be made possible by the observance of certain essentials, viz., patient hearing, judicial restraint, proper interpretation, avoidance of interruptions and unreasonable adjournments and expeditious disposal. Lack of effective control over the proceedings may cause mounting arrears of cases.

1. Opportunity to present case/patient hearing

It is the duty of the Judge to give fullest opportunity to the counsel to present his client's case. For this purpose the Judge should sit in the court with a receptive mind. Otherwise all argument on the part of advocate becomes useless. A Judge should never be rash or haughty before the advocates appearing for clients before him or even to the clients, but always be calm, sober, dignified, peaceful and rather cold. In every case, a Judge's conduct should be above reproach. He should be conscientious, studious, thorough, courteous, patient, punctual, just, impartial, fearless of public clamour, regardless of public praise and indifferent to private, political or partisan influences. The Judge should always bear in mind the statement of George Sharwood that where passion is allowed to prevail, the judgment is dethroned. He should have patience and gravity of hearing. A good Judge is invariably a good listener. The Judges are paid to listen while counsel are paid to talk, and it is the best that they should perform their respective duties.

2. Judicial restraints

The expression 'Judicial Restraint' is often termed as Judicial Discipline'. Sometimes it is also used to denote 'judicial respect' in the sense that judicial restraint is necessary to command judicial respect. It is the respect by the judiciary to the independence of the judiciary, to brethren Judges, to those who come before the court, advocates, clients, witnesses and also other organs of the State, namely, the executive and the legislature.

The Supreme Court, in the case of **State of Rajasthan v. Prakash Chand,**[1] quoted the observations made in the decision of **A.M. Mathur v. Pramod Kumar Gupta,**[2] which reads as under :—

> "Judicial restraint and discipline are as necessary to the orderly administration of justice as they are to the effectiveness of the army. The duty of restraint, this humility of function should be constant theme of our Judges. The quality in decision making is as much necessary for Judges to command respect as to protect the independence of the judiciary. Respect to those who come before the court as well as other co-ordinate branches of the State, the executive and the legislature. There must be mutual respect when these qualities fail, or when litigant and public believe that the Judge has failed in these qualities, it will be neither good for the Judge nor for the judicial process."

The Court further said :

> "The Judges Bench is a seat of power. Not only do Judges have the power to make binding decision, their decisions legitimate the use of power by other officials. The Judges have the absolute and unchallengeable control of the court domain. But they cannot misuse their authority by intemperate comments, undignified banter or scathing criticism of counsel, parties or witnesses. We concede that the court has inherent powers to act freely upon its own conviction on any matter coming before it for adjudication, but it is a general principle of the highest importance to the proper administration of justice that derogatory remarks ought not to be made against persons or authorities whose conduct comes into consideration unless it is absolutely necessary for the decision of the case."

3. Proper interpretation

During the process of administration of justice, the courts often have to interpret the law in order to ascertain the actual meaning of the provisions or to remove ambiguity or inconsistency or to supply omissions. Interpretation is not limited to statutes alone. It also extends to rules, orders, notifications and all other documents and deeds which are necessary for the decision of cases. The object of interpretation must be rendering complete justice to the parties. While interpreting the law, courts have to follow the well established principles of interpretation. It is the duty of the court either to enlarge the scope of the legislation or the intention of the legislature when the language of the provision is plain and unambiguous. The court cannot rewrite, recast or reframe the legislation, for the very

1. A.I.R. 1998 S.C. 1344 (Paras 34, 35 & 36).
2. A.I.R. 1990 S.C. 1737.

good reason that it has no power to legislate. The courts shall decide what the law is and not what it should be.

4. Avoidance of interruptions

The duty of the Judge is to avoid interruption of the counsel in their argument and in the examination of witnesses. There should be no interruption of the counsel except to prevent repetition or irrelevancy or to clear up some obscurity in counsel's line of argument or representation of facts or to indicate to the advocate the courts view regarding facts or law in the case.[1] Advocate must have the freedom and opportunity to present the case satisfactorily. Unwarranted interferences and adverse comments by the Judges may upset the counsel. If the Advocate becomes upset, he may not be ale to present his case properly. This may cause the failure of justice. On the other hand, this will cause waste of time and delay in the proceedings.

5. Avoidance of unreasonable adjournments

Since the time of Shakespeare, Law's delays have become notorious and the urgent need of the hour is to bear in mind that justice delayed is justice denied. The main reason for mounting arrears of cases is said to unreasonable adjournments. Adjournments are provided mainly to afford reasonable opportunity to prevent miscarriage of justice. Hence, it must be limited only to those circumstances where serious injustice will otherwise be caused. Adjournments on the grounds of personal inconvenience may, as far as possible, be avoided. The grant of frequent and long adjournments are certainly to be checked and regulated. It can be checked only if Judges and lawyers are honest and sincere in the administration of justice, it behoves them to raise a crusade against delays in litigation. Chief Justice Arthur Vendarbilt of America always said that problems of delays could be easily solved if the Judges and lawyers seriously endeavoured to put an end to 'law's delays'. This does not mean that there should be undue haste. Just as justice delayed is justice denied, similarly justice hustled is also justice denied. Hence, cases shall not be adjourned without reasonable and sufficient grounds.

6. Expeditious disposal

"Justice delayed is justice denied". Because of the fear of delay in disposal of cases, people may try to avoid approaching courts. It is a fact that courts are burdened with heavy work-load. It is the duty of the State to establish sufficient number of courts and thus balance the work-load for the effective administration of justice. It is the paramount duty of the court to see that justice is delivered to the people as expeditiously as possible.

(ii) Personal Qualities of the Judges

The efficacy of administration of justice depends upon the character and integrity of the persons presiding over the courts. The strength and stability of a modern democratic State pivots upon the vision and wisdom of the legislature, the efficiency and incorruptibility of the executive and

1. C.L. Anand, General Principles of Legal Ethics, p. 226.

the integrity of the judiciary. Hence, Judges should have certain important qualities in terms of personality viz., knowledge, impartiality, independence, integrity, industriousness, courtesy, frankness, dignity, respect to the Bar, decisiveness quality of social consciousness, patience and courage.

(1) Knowledge

Judges should have profound knowledge of all branches of law. They should be able to apply the correct law, to the fact of the case. They are not merely to hear the advocates and decide the case on the basis of what the advocates submitted and presented. It is true that a Judge should cultivate an objectivity of mind and as far as possible he is not to enter the arena of conflict.

(2) Impartiality

It is a trite saying that the visible symbol of a sovereign democratic State is an impartial judiciary and the disappearance of that symbol marks the end of the Rule of Law. It is the first and foremost duty of the Judge to see that his court is surcharged with an atmosphere of impartiality. No Judge worthy of his office would knowingly permit any cloud of prejudice to darken his understanding or to influence his decision. A Judge is horrified to have his impartiality questioned. Impartiality implies an appreciation and understanding of differing attitudes and viewpoints of those involved in a controversy. A great jurist once said that impartiality is difficult to attain in any system. A judge has acquired habits; has mixed with a certain class of people, has developed certain ideas so that when you are required to deal with other ideas you do not give as sound and accurate judgment as you would wish. For the Judge to detach himself from his whole personality is a difficult if not an impossible task. It is easy for a person to rationalize his behaviour; he cannot find excellent reasons for doing what he wants to do. The conscientious Judge does everything in his power to safeguard his impartiality against evasion by wishful thinking. He should be above caste, creed or religion and he should administer justice in a perfectly impartial spirit.

(3) Independence

The independence of the Judge is the chief of all cardinal judicial virtues. Without independence the Judge would cease to be a Judge and hence Vendarbilt has said that in a representative democratic Government the power of judiciary depends largely on its reputation for independence. An independent judiciary is certainly the repository of the confidence of the people. The Judge should have a very high conception of independence of the judiciary and strove to maintain and uphold its integrity. The Judge must be entirely free from all external influence and subservient only to his own conscience. For the purpose of ensuring the independence of the judiciary, Judges are given constitutional guarantees of security of service and service conditions. They have the immunity from personal criticism in respect of their judicial acts. They have absolute freedom from subordination to any other authority. In **C. Ravichandran Iyer v. Justice**

A.M. Bhattacharjee,[1] the Supreme Court observed that the independence of judiciary is an essential attribute of rule of law which is a basic feature of the Constitution and so that judiciary must be free from not only executive pressure, but also from other pressures. The head of judicial independence is judicial individualism.

(4) Integrity

Integrity is the quality of being honest and morally upright. A Judge should be above suspicion and the people must feel that his integrity is incarnate. A Judge is asked to wear black gown and white bands and that means that in an otherwise black side of the life coming before him as represented by black gown, justice should be white and that is a silver lining of hope. The white bands refer to the purity and unadulterated integrity of justice. A Judge should have personal, judicial and intellectual integrity. His identity and individuality should be commendable. His character and conduct should be worthy of general acceptance so that both lawyers and laymen should have confidence in him. He must give equal treatment and consideration to all lawyers. The pillar of the power and prestige of the judiciary is the public confidence that it enjoys. This depends, along with the other qualities of the Judge, upon his integrity.

(5) Industriousness

It is also important that a Judge should be extremely industrious and he should remember that it is not sufficient that justice is done but it must predominantly appear that justice is being done. Judge's knowledge of law should be up to date. Some Judges do not work hard and adopt hocus-pocus tactics to get at the requisite number of disposals. It is better for a Judge to be honest and, industrious, for them it happens that instead of Judges being after disposals, disposals are after them. The Judges should get acquainted with the recent law by systematic study and work and if they ignore the law, law is also apt to ignore them. Law is a jealous mistress. It requires regular, constant and systematic care and attention. Further, hard work on the part of the Judges are also required for expeditious disposal of cases. Hence, Judges should possess the quality of industriousness and maintain the same for the effective administration of justice.

(6) Courtesy

Of all cardinal qualities courtesy belongs in the front rank. Courtesy denotes good manners and behaviour. It is very essential quality required for Judges. Men come into court for the redress of grievances. Both sides to a controversy cannot win. It rarely happens that both sides are satisfied with the decision. There is no reason, however, why each should not leave the judgment seat convinced that the case has been fairly tried. The conduct of the Judge towards the Bar, the litigants and the witnesses is, therefore, a matter of great concern. They are entitled to be treated with courtesy. Severe attitude towards the Bar, clients and the witnesses should be avoided. A Judge should never be rash of haughty before the Advocates

1. A.I.R. 1995 SCW 3768.

appearing for clients before him or even to the clients, but always be calm, sober, dignified, peaceful and rather cold. Hence, the Judges must be courteous in their approach and behaviour towards all those who come before courts. They must try to advance, promote and protect the high standards and traditions of the legal profession.

(7) Open-Mindedness

Open-mindedness is frankness. The ability to receive impressions, but to keep the mind open and flexible, and emancipated from over-certainty, is one of the great judicial qualities. It is the quality of showing thoughts and feelings openly. He should be honest and true to his attitude, approach, behaviour and acts. He should be willing to consider new ideas. Judges must be free and frank in respect of their judicial acts. They should maintain transparency in the judicial process. But the quality of open-mindedness, consists not only in actually keeping the mind open and receptive, but in saying or doing nothing to suggest the contrary. The Judge ought to be wise enough to know that he is fallible and, therefore, ever ready to learn; great and honest enough to discard all mere pride of opinion, and follow truth wherever it may lead; and courageous enough to acknowledge his errors.[1]

(8) Dignity

Dignity is the quality that deserves, brings, and earns respect. It also signifies high or honourable rank or position. The position of a Judge is honourable and the power of the Judge cannot be equated with that of any other functioning. The possession of all the qualities such as knowledge, independence, impartiality, open-mindedness, integrity, industriousness, courtesy, etc. certainly aid to add and strengthen dignity of the Judges. A law suit is an important event for those involved in it either directly or indirectly. It is essential, therefore, that it be conducted with a dignity and a decorum befitting the occasion, seriously, not lightly or frivolously. Of course this, too, can be carried to an extreme. Dignity, however, is by no means synonymous with pompousness or arrogance. There are two kinds of men who come to the Bench—those who swell or those who grow.

(9) Respect to the bar

Legal profession is a noble, honourable and honoured profession. Lawyers assist the Judges in analysing facts, locating the law and arriving at the right decision in the process of administration of justice. The labour and skill of the lawyers deserve sincere admiration from the Bench. Judges must be fair in their attitude and conduct towards the advocates. They must have high regards, great admiration, sincere consideration and deep respect towards the advocates.

(10) Decisiveness

Decisiveness is the important judicial virtue of having the power, capacity and ability in arriving at a clear and proper conclusion and quick decision. There are two kinds of Judges. First is the quick Judge who is

1. David H. Jacobs, "The Personality of the Judge", Lawyer, Vol. 17, p. 31

troubled by any great legal learning. Experience has taught him that if he deliberates, he is lost. He relies mainly on his native shrewdness and sagacity. Another is the type of mind which is tortured by anxiety of making decisions. It is a mind tormented by doubt and painful indecision. Between those two extremes—the quick Judge and the Judge of indecision we find the judicial mind that proceeds with all deliberate speed, a mind in which thought is excited, rather than confused. Hence, Judges must be prepared to meet any point that may be raised by the counsels and they should have adequate presence of mind so as to enable them to cope with any situation that might arise in the case.

(11) Quality of social consciousness

The duty of a Judge may be to objectify in law, not his own aspirations and convictions and philosophies, but the aspirations and convictions and philosophies of the men and women of his time. There is a kind of Judge who spurns social consciousness. For that type of Judge the law moves in stately isolation untouched by the other social sciences, unrelated to and unaffected by alterations in economic, political and social conditions. His mind lives in the past, immutable, constant and fixed. Hence, a Judge must sense the rising social forces, he must give direction and impetus to future convictions and aspirations.

(12) Patience

Patience of the Judge is a cardinal judicial virtues. The conduct of the Judge towards the Bar, the litigants and the witnesses is, therefore, a matter of great concern. They are entitled to be treated with courtesy, with patience and with consideration. Judges must be polite to the lawyers. A Judge has to deal with a number of cases everyday. The cases might be of different nature, on different facts and causes of action for different reliefs and have reached at different stages of the proceedings. The duty of the Judge is to give patient and considerable hearing to the counsels.

(13) Courage

Courage in context of personal virtues of the Judges signifies the ability to pass orders and judgments without fear or favour, affection or ill will. A Judge shall be free from all sorts of pressures and influences of any kind or from any source whatsoever. In the matter of administration of justice, he shall be guided by the well established principles of law and justice only.

IV. Conclusion

The fact that the personality of the Judge plays an important part in the administration of justice cannot be denied. On the other hand, advocates also play pertinent role in the administration of justice. Hence, the Bar and the Bench constitute the two integral parts of the judiciary. Administration of justice, even though is the duty of the Court, should be treated as joint responsibility of both the Bar and the Bench. The duty is to be discharged with the mutual co-operation with each other. The need of the hour is that the Bar-Bench relations as mentioned in the foregoing study be preserved, maintained and promoted. This should be the main concern of the Bar and the Bench. For this, an intra-professional culture is required to be developed and strengthened between the Bar and the Bench. We witness that the Bench and the Bar have failed to maintain the graceful partnership and co-operation in administration of justice. Hon'ble Mr. Justice V.R. Krishna Iyer very aptly remarked during the Third International Conference of Appellate Judges, New Delhi, 1984, when he said, "Today, unfortunately, there is an 'iron curtain[1] between the Bench and the Bar. The Bar goes on with its criticism of the Bench." Why is it so? The Bench and the Bar both are becoming intolerant, lacking in traditions and losing decorum. Gone are the days when an alert presence of mind, spontaneous wit, felicity of language and a natural aptitude for a *bon mot*, an unfailing sense of humour and above all an unflappable temperament and persuasiveness worked well.[2] The reasons for deterioration of relationship between the Bench and the Bar appears to be lack of a common forum, where these things could be discussed between the Bench and the Bar frankly without inhibition, so that they may recognise the fact that the gown and the robe together have one mission and the constituency that is recognized for the Bench and the Bar is the community at large.[3] Hence, a common forum should be constituted for redressal of grievances of the Bench and the Bar. Besides this, a code of ethics for higher judiciary is the need of the hour. Superior courts justices should avoid taking membership of various societies, chamber sitting, investment, lending or borrowing, attending private parties, attending private functions, accepting priorities/privileges and post-retirement engagements.[4]

---

1. Anirudh Prasad, *op cit.* at p. 102.
2. Anirudh Prasad, *op cit.* at p. 102.
3. Speeh delivered by Hon'ble Mr. Justice V.R. Krishna Iyer in Third International Conference of Appellate Judges, 1984 at p. 313.
4. K. Chandru, A Code of Ethics for Higher Judiciary, Indian Bar Review, 1988, Vol. XV, pp. 158-165.

10

LEGALITY OF LAWYERS' STRIKE : AN EVALUATION IN THE RIGHT-DUTY DISCOURSE

I. Introduction

Professions are service oriented callings which require learning and intellectual equipments. Success in a profession is not measured in monetary terms. Professions also enjoy autonomy. Some of them like law and medicine have self-governing statutory bodies. Every profession has its own ethics and customary code of conduct. The legal profession is one of the oldest professions. It has its traditions of love and service to the country. Its contribution to national leadership and the freedom struggle has been significant. People have high hopes from legal profession. Lawyers are expected to be not only learned people but a highly responsible, upright and dignified section of the society. Today, however, the situation is otherwise. Not a single day passes without a strike by professionals in some part of the country or the other. Very often it is by the lawyers. Lawyers boycotting the courts on one ground or the other has become a common phenomenon. Lawyers' boycott of the courts is popularly known as the lawyers' strike. It is a very serious and drastic weapon in the hands of the legal profession to get its grievances publicly known and registered or demands fulfilled. However, such an act not only causes a lot of hardship and inconvenience to the litigants but also impedes the process of administration of justice. The right of the lawyers to strike has to be judged in the light of their corresponding duties towards their clients as well as towards the courts. The present chapter seeks to examine the various issues involved in this regard.

II. Historical Background of Lawyers' Strike

Resort to strike by lawyers is not a new phenomenon. The practice of boycott in Indian context had its origin in *Satyagraha* philosophy. During the struggle for independence Gandhiji gave a call to boycott the British rule and many lawyers responded by giving up their lucrative practice and joined the freedom movement. Amongst the titled gentry in India, a good number came from the legal profession such as, Mahatma Gandhi, Moti Lal Nehru, C.R. Das, Rajendra Prasad, Pt. Jawaharlal Nehru, Sardar Patel, Lala Laj Pat Rai, Sir Pherozshah Mehta, Madan Mohan Malviya and soon. They resorted to strikes a number of times, sometimes on the arrest of senior national leaders, sometimes on other popular causes and thereby contributed their might to the national cause. The legal profession and individual members participating in such strikes did earn a series of adverse court judgments in a number of cases[1] that came before different High courts during the British Raj. They were convicted of professional misconduct in almost all the cases. But at the same time the legal profession, which did not enjoy a very high respect and esteem in the Indian society started becoming dear to the masses. Its honour, respect, esteem and status touched new heights in the eyes of public with their openly coming out to join the national freedom struggle. The lawyers had then, used the strongest weapon in their armoury, that is, the boycott of courts. They used this weapon for a strong cause—the cause of independence of the country which was so dear to the community at large. So, the overall gains for the legal profession were more than what they had lost by resorting to this strongest measure in those peculiar circumstances. Hence, the cause for which the strikes were resorted to by the legal professionals was a very important and a vital factor so far as the justification of lawyers' strike in the eyes of the community is concerned. At the same time we should not lose sight of the fact that legally these strikes were held to be illegal by different High Courts of the country.[2]

Apart from the calls given during the freedom struggle to boycott all institutions of the British, including, courts, boycott of courts were unheard of. In 1973, Mrs. Indira Gandhi's Government superseded three senior Judges of the Supreme Court and appointed Justice Ray as Chief Justice. In most parts of India the bar abstained from work for one day.[3] No doubt protest is essential to a democracy, like other forms of protest, the right to strike places pressure on those in power to recognise dissent and respond to just demands. It is difficult to concede a right to boycott courts to the lawyers on the analogy of conceding right to strike of employees. Moreover, the right to strike work in India is admittedly not absolute. But, even if there is no fundamental right to strike, a strike is not *per se* illegal. Since then there have been frequent cases of such boycotts.

III. Causes and Instances of Lawyers' Strike

There are many instances where lawyers have adopted a very strange and unjustified attitude of boycotting the court work and that also for indefinite periods irrespective of the seriousness or the nature of their grievances. Even for small matters, which do not warrant resorting to this strongest weapon, they go for boycotting the courts for months together with the result that the purpose of boycott loses its importance and value. In the year 1986, the lawyers of Allahabad High Court went on a long

1. *In re, Jivan Lal Desai*, A.I.R. 1920 Bom 168; *In the matter of a Second Grade Pleader of Ramachandra Nagar*, A.I.R. 1924 Mad. 129; *Emperor* v. *Rajani Kanta Bose*, A.I.R. 1922 Cal. 515 and *Emperor* v. *Kishori Mal*, A.I.R. 1923 Cal. 853.
2. *Ibid.*
3. Atul Setalvad, 'Courts Boycotts : Are they Proper'? Lex Et Juris, April, 1987, p. 13, also see R.K. Mahajan, 'Boycott by Lawyers' Legitimacy and Alternatives, SCJ, 1989, Vol. 1, p. 2.

strike for about 50 days because of differences within the Bar as to whether a Bench of the High Court should be established in Western Uttar Pradesh, and if so, where. No one was allowed to enter the court premises. The court offices remained closed throughout the strike period. Litigants who wanted to approach and Judges at their residence seeking urgent relief were prevented from doing so.[1] The largest, so far, was the strike by Delhi lawyers in the case, which is popularly known as Kiran Bedi's case. Throughout this agitation of about 99 days the issue remained personalised one. By this strike the backing of arrears of pending cases in Delhi Courts increased by over 10,202 cases.

The causes of the lawyers' strike have been quite varied. The supersession of Justice Shelat, and other two Judges for political reasons aroused justified indignation. The failure to confirm Chief Justice T.P.S. Chawla (which closed the Delhi High Court for some weeks) was outrageous. Other causes have been of a more questionable nature. The reason why the Bar in Uttar Pradesh was agitated about the establishment of a Bench in Western Uttar Pradesh—with the consequent curtailment of the territorial jurisdiction of the main Bench at Allahabad raised few (if any) issues of principle. The Bar at Allahabad was afraid of losing work. The Bar at various towns, Meerut, Agra etc., where the proposed Bench was to be located wanted more work. The cause of agitation which caused untold harm to the litigating public were merely the parochial pecuniary interests of the members of the Bar. Further, no pettier cause for a boycott can be imagined than the fact that the holidays of a subordinate court did not coincide with the holidays of the higher courts. In Delhi, the cause of the strike was that an advocate was arrested and handcuffed by Delhi Police on January 15, 1988. The outcome of 99 days old strike was the suspension of Mrs. Kiran Bedi, Deputy Commissioner of Police, Delhi.

The boycott of the courts also took place over the indiscriminate killings of innocent people in Punjab, introduction of the Defamation Bill, proposal of repealing the anticipatory bail provisions, arrest of lawyers by the police, misbehaviour of the police with the lawyers, etc. The boycott of the courts has been sometimes on petty matters devoid of any social significance, e.g., introduction of five day week in the subordinate courts. There has also been boycott for creation of Benches in different States. The boycott is sometimes done to show the solidarity for independence of judiciary, freedom of press but on some occasions it is otherwise.

The boycott of courts has sometimes been resorted to exhibit their displeasure or protest against transfer of judges, shifting of the venue of the courts, wrongful conduct against an advocate, ill-treatment of a member of the profession by the executive, irregular appointment of judges and so on. The cases have happened where the boycott have been resorted to for some days if the judicial officer is not liberal in giving adjournments or is strict and does not wait for them.

The friction stems for the lawyers repeatedly stopping work and

1. P.P. Rao, 'Boycott of Courts by Lawyers' in K. Gururaja Chari, Advocacy and Professional Ethics (2000), p. 699.

consequently all proceedings in court. While Calcutta has had its fair share of stoppage of work in court, Allahabad had earned notoriety when the President of its Bar Association allegedly threatened a sitting Judge to have him transferred to a remote part of the country. The Judge took cognizance of this statement and the Bar Association reacted by calling a strike in the High Court and threatened to stop all proceedings. The Judge not being on strike, attended work, sat in court and even heard matters without the assistance of lawyers. Some advocates had not heeded the Bar Association's high-handed directives and were attending court. A group of advocates supported by police and members of ruling party stormed the court room of Justice B.M. Lal, drove out litigants and advocates, assaulted the Judge and even threatened to kill him. Contempt charges were drawn up and five lawyers were sentenced to a month's imprisonment and a fine of Rs. 1000/- each. The lawyers filed review petitions with the same Bench and also prayed for leave to appeal to the Supreme Court in case their sentence was not revoked. Simultaneously, Common Cause, a voluntary organization filed a Public Interest Litigation in the Supreme Court on this issue to draw national attention. The apex court accepted the petition and issued instructions for collection of views of lawyers from 150 Bar Associations throughout the country. The lawyers also held a peaceful march to Parliament on 24th February, 2000 in order to lodge a protest against the proposed changes in the Code of Civil Procedure. It was met with brutal lathi-charge by the police. The lawyers were seriously and grievously injured. This led to the boycott of courts by the lawyers and it continued for more than one month demanding an enquiry into the whole incident and the immediate suspension of the police officials responsible for the lathi-charge.[1]

The District Bar Associations in Punjab boycotted courts in protest against the alleged involvement of certain High Court Judges in the Punjab Public Service Commission recruitment scam. These Associations supported the resolutions passed by the Bar Association of Punjab and Haryana High Court, Chandigarh with regard to involvement of judicial officers of the High Court in the alleged recruitment scam. The advocates asserted that the Judges, allegedly involved in the scam, should themselves submit their resignation or else the President should be asked to intervene. They also argued that their confidence in the justice delivery system had been eroded.[2] Mr. Dipankar, the learned *Amiscs Curiae*, in Supreme Court submitted that the reasons why strikes have been called by the Bar Associations and/or Bar Councils are : (a) confrontation with the police and/or the legal administration; (b) grievances against the Presiding Officer, (c) grievances against judgments of courts; (d) clash of interest between groups of lawyers; and (e) grievances against the legislature or a legislation.

Besides this, the extracts of the joint meeting of the Chairpersons of

1. K. Mony and K. Usha, 'Legal Drafting, Conveyancing, Professional Ethics and Advocacy' (2001), pp. 477-78.
2. The Tribune, 9th and 10th May, 2002.

various State Bar Councils and members of the Bar Council of India, held on 28th and 29th September, 2002 have set out some of the causes which results in lawyers abstaining from work as follows :

(A) Local issues

(i) Disputes between lawyer/lawyers and the police and other authorities;

(ii) Issues regarding corruption, misbehaviour of judicial officers and other authorities;

(iii) Non-filling of vacancies arising in Courts or non-appointment of judicial officers for a long period;

(iv) Absence of infrastructure in courts.

(B) Issue relating to one section of the Bar and another section :

(i) Withdrawal of jurisdiction and conferring it to other courts (both pecuniary and territorial);

(ii) Constitution of Benches of High Courts. Disputes between the competing District and other Bar Associations.

(C) Issues involving dignity, integrity, independence of the Bar and Judiciary

(D) Legislation without consultation with the Bar Councils

(E) National issues and regional issues affecting the public at large.

On July 25, 2003, thousands of litigants had to return home without their cases being heard at Delhi High Court as their lawyers abstained from Courts in protest against enhancement of the pecuniary jurisdiction of High Court from Rs. 5 lakhs to Rs. 20 lakhs. The call for abstaining from the courts was given by the Delhi High Court Bar Association in protest against the Union Government's July 16 notification enhancing the pecuniary jurisdiction of the High Court. Following the increase in the pecuniary jurisdiction, thousands of civil cases of the value of up to Rs. 20 lakhs will now have to be transferred to three lower courts—Tis Hazari, Patiala House and Karkardooma.[1] The lawyers protested against the Delhi Government's move of setting up four Permanent Lok Adalats in the capital, the Bar Associations at Patiala House, and Tis Hazari announced one day strike.[2] The Vice-President (Civil), Delhi Bar Association has said that the provision of the Lok Adalats are being grossly misused by Magistrate to get an extra unit. The fact is that the cases that go to the Lok Adalat can be compounded and decided by the Magistrate Courts themselves. The government is not trying to strengthen the system that is best suited in the country. An impression is being given that cases are being sent to Lok Adalats as the present system delays dispensation of justice.[3]

In the chart below the authors have tried to collate the information under different heads pertaining to lawyers' strike during the period

1. Hindu, July 26, 2003 at p. 4.
2. Hindustan Times, August 6, 2003 (New Delhi ed.).
3. *Ibid.*

Chart of Lawyers' Strike 1984-2015

Source of Information	Details of Strike	Time and Duration	Cause of the Strike	Demands	Outcome	Remarks
Hindustan Times 7.5.90	Shahdara Lawyers resorted to strike	w.e.f. 23 Feb., 1984 six months	Recommendation of the Delhi High Court for creation of five judicial districts in Delhi	Implementation of the High Court recommendations (as per col. 55)	Demand not yet fulfilled	It cost 6480 man hours of six criminal courts
Hindustan Times dated 7.5.90	New Delhi lawyers go on strike	1984 for 65 days	—do—	Same issue as above	—do—	—
Indian Express 24.4.86	Lawyers of Agra boycott the Courts	April, 1986	—	To pressurize Union Law Minister for establishment of a High Court Bench at Agra	—	—
Hindustan Times dated 21.4.86	Lawyers of Tamil Nadu and Pondicherry go on strike	w.e.f. 23.4.86	Regularisation of district, judicial officers of T.N. Government who were temporarily appointed from amongst the different departments	The District judicial officers must be appointed from the lawyers. The regularisation should be revoked		
Indian Express dated 5.5.86	Allahabad lawyers strike	Completed 42 days on 5.5.86 (lasted for 50 days)	—	Demand against establishment of a separate Bench of the High Court in Western U.P.	Status quo continues	During this strike the gates of the court were picketed, litigants not allowed to enter, the residences of the judges kept under watch lest some litigants may seek relief, not even a single petition could be made by public during this period

Hindustan Times dated 22.7.86	Lawyers from Western U.P. hold a rally at the Boat Club in New Delhi, the democracy ground of India	One day	—	Demanding a separate bench of Allahabad High Court in Western U.P.	Demand yet to be fulfilled	—
Hindustan Times dated 29.7.86	Supreme Court lawyers go on token strike	28.8.86 one day token strike	—	To protest against the Centre's failure to regularize the appointment of T.P.S. Chawla as the Chief Justice of Delhi High Court	—	—
Indian Express Lucknow dated 27.8.86	60 leading lawyers of Western and Hill district of U.P. sit on Dharna	26.8.86 A day's Dharna in front of Vidhan Sabha	—	To support demand of establishment of a bench of Allahabad High Court in Eastern U.P.	—	—
Hindu dated 11.9.86	Delhi lawyers strike	August/Sept., 86	—	Demanding appointment of T.P.S. Chawla as Chief Justice of Delhi High Court	T.P.S. Chawla appointed as Chief Justice of Delhi High Court	Strike ended after, the P.M.'s appeal on 10.9.86
Indian Express Baroda, dated 6.10.86	Baroda lawyers decide to continue their 12 day old strike	Strike completed 12 days	—	To protest against the alleged high handedness of police	—	—
Hindustan Times, New Delhi dated 20.10.87	Lawyers of lower courts of Delhi went on a day's token strike	19.10.87 a day's token strike	—	To support their demands for allowing lower courts to take up cases involving sums above Rs. 1 lakh	—	—

Statesman dated 13.11.87	Lawyers of New Delhi Court to Boycott Courts	w.e.f. 13.11.87	—	In protest of the non-implementation of the decision to bifurcate Delhi Courts into five districts	—	—
Indian Express dated 20.1.88	The Hazari (Delhi) lawyers struck work	w.e.f. 21.1.88 lasted 99 days	Arrest and handcuffing of an advocate by Delhi Police on 15.1.88	To protest against the manhandling and handcuffing of the advocate	Suspension of Mrs. Kiran Bedi DCP Delhi	Backlog of cases in Delhi Court increased by 10,202 during lawyers' strike (Hindustan Times dated 5.4.89)
Hindustan Times dated 7.5.90	Jammu lawyers strike	57 days strike ended in Jan., 1989	On the question of alleged assault on a Jammu Session Judge by hooligans	—	—	—
Hindustan Times dated 7.5.90	Gujarat lawyers	2.9.89 to 18.10.89	—	To protest against the arrest of CJM by men in uniform	—	—
Hindustan Times, New Delhi 19.2.88	Supreme Court lawyers go on indefinite strike	w.e.f. 19.2.88 (18 days)	To protest against the attack of hoodlums allegedly with the help of police and Union Govt. on lawyers at Tis Hazari Courts on 17.2.88	—	—	—
Hindustan Times, New Delhi 8.7.89	Lawyers of Delhi High Court and three District Courts struck work for the day	One day (7.7.89)	To express sympathy with striking J & K advocates who were on indefinite strike against alleged police lathi-charge on their colleagues in Court premises at Jammu	—	—	—
Indian Post, Bombay, 28.6.89	Maharashtra lawyers call for a day's boycott of courts	29.6.89	Increase in professional tax	To protest against the increase in professional tax	—	—

Hindustan Times, 11.9.89	Delhi Bar Association decided to observe a day's strike	12.9.89	E.S. Venkataramaiah C.J. declared that "Lawyers commit suicide when they go on strike : (Hindustan Times, dated 8.9.89)	The protest against these remarks by the C.J.	—	—
Hindu 21.10.89	Madras High Court Advocates Association decide to continue the court boycott	20.10.89	—	The police official involved in the arrest and ill treatment of the advocate be arrested and prosecuted	—	—
The Tribune, 1989	Lawyers of Haryana went on strike	1989 and lasted for several weeks	An advocate was assaulted by police officer	Supersession or transfer of the official	The government did not yield	Initially it was limited to the district bar but subsequently it paralysed work in all courts in the state
Hindu 22.10.89	Jammu lawyers continue their indefinite strike	w.e.f. 21.10.89	To protest against the alleged police raid and search of the house of a lawyer	—	—	—
Indian Express, New Delhi 10.3.90	The lawyers of Delhi High Court and Supreme Court struck work	—	Token strike to protest against the alleged misbehaviour of a police officer with an Additional District Judge	—	—	—
Indian Express, New Delhi dated 10.4.90	The lawyers of Tis Hazari Court in Delhi go on indefinite strike w.e.f. 10.4.90	w.e.f. 10.4.90	—	The protest against the decentralization of the civil courts into five districts	—	The lower courts have been already on long strike on this issue but taking the opposite stand
Patriot dated 19.4.90	Delhi Bar Association launches an indefinite strike	w.e.f. 5.4.90 decided to continue further	—	Against the proposed bifurcation of subordinate courts	—	—

Patriot dated 17.9.90	The Supreme Court Bar Association protested against Government decision to implement the Mandal Commission Report	17.9.90 Abstained from work for one day	Protest against Govt's decision to implement the Mandal Commission Report	—	—	Pursuant to the resolution the entire Bar, barring a very few, abstained from work
Calcutta Weekly Notes 26.9.994	Calcutta High Court Lawyers observed a two week cease work	Two weeks	Court did not announce a holiday to condole the death of one of their colleagues	One day holiday to condole the death	—	—
Calcutta Weekly Notes 26.9.1994	A Magistrate was apprehended without ticket on a State Transport Bus (Calcutta)	One day	A Magistrate is conveniently taken by the Bar to above the law	Cease of work to extract an apology from the offending party	Apology tendered	His reported defence that he was a Magistrate on way to attend court and he was being prevented from attending to his duties which constituted contempt
Calcutta Weekly Notes 26.9.1994	Advocates of Calcutta High Court again struck work for a week more	Late July & August 1994	Not enough Judges in Court	—	—	—
Calcutta Weekly Notes 26.9.1994	Chief Justice B.M. Lal of Allahabad High Court was threatened and his court ransacked by a bunch of lawyers	Last week of Sept., 1994	The President of the Bar Association allegedly threatened a sitting Judge to have him transferred to a remote part of the country	The Judge took the cognisance of this statement and the Bar Association reacted by calling a strike	Contempt charges were drawn up and five lawyers were sentenced to a month imprisonment and a fine of Rs. 1000/- each	The lawyers filed review petition with the same Bench and also prayed for leave to appeal to Supreme Court in case their sentence is not revoked

(1995) 5 S.C.C. at page 716	Strike by lawyers effect on rule of law	In Ref (1995) 3 S.C.C. 619	—	—	—	See Contempt of Courts Act, 1971 Section 2(c)
Indian Express 11.3.2002 (Delhi)	Against the hike in court fee in West Bengal	Entered for 35th Day	Hike in Court fee	To withdraw the hike in court fee	—	—
Indian Express Chandigarh 23.5.2002	Against the alleged corruption in judiciary	One day on 24.5.2002	Corruption in higher judiciary	To initiate inquiry against three judges of Punjab and Haryana High court	—	—
Times of India 18.10.2002	Against the police decision to register a case against three advocates who were allegedly beaten up by Delhi police constable	One day on 17.10.02	Dispute regarding quarrel between police and lawyers in New Delhi	To withdraw the case against the lawyers registered by the police	Called off their strike following reassurance by Senior Police Officer to conduct fair investi-gations into the incident	Patiala House, Karkar dooma and Tis Hazari Courts bore a deserted look as 20,,000 advocates stayed home
Hindustan Times 9.11.2002	Against the amendment in Legal Services Authorities Act which provided for setting up of Permanent Lok Adalats in all public utility services for resolving disputes	One day strike on 8.11.2002	Against setting up of Permanent Lok Adalats	Not to set Permanent Lok Adalats	—	Work remained suspended in the Delhi High Court and other city courts with 35,,000 lawyers participating in the strike

Hindustan Times 17.12.2002	The controversial Judges Amarbir Singh Gill and Gopala Gowda were transferred to the Gauhati High Court	One day strike on 1.12.02	Transfer of tainted Judges from Punjab and Haryana High Court and Karnataka High Court to Gauhati High Court	Withdrawal of transfer orders	Transfer order withdrawn	Justice Amarbir Gill was transferred to the P & H High Court for his alleged role in the Punjab Public Service Commission scam, whereas Gowda has been shifted from Karnataka High Court because of his alleged involvement in sex scandal
2002 (9) SCALE *Ex-Capt. Harish Uppal* v. *Union of India and Others*	Non-incorporation of Clauses (1), (2), (3) and (4) in the Bar Council of India (Conduct and Disciplinary) Rules as reported in 1995 (1) SCALE 6	—	—	—	It is directed by the Supreme Court that the Bar Associations in the country shall implement the resolutions dated 29th September 2002 passed by the Bar Council of India	A five judge Constitution Bench held that the courts must not be privy to strikes. The Bench noted that repeated strikes had shaken the confidence of the public in the legal profession and affected administration of justice
Hindu 26.7.2003	Against the enhancement of the pecuniary jurisdiction of High Court from Rs. 5 lakhs to Rs. 20 lakhs	One day on 25.7.2003	Notification of Union Government regarding enhancement of pecuniary jurisdiction	To withdraw the notification regarding enhancement of pecuniary jurisdiction	Yet to come	—

Hindustan Times 6, 7.8.2002	Against the move of setting up four Permanent Lok Adalats in the capital at (Patiala House, New Delhi)	One day strike on 6.8.2002	Setting up four permanent Lok Adalats in the capital	Not to set up Lok Adalats in the present form	Yet to come	—
Hindustan Times 26.8.2003	Against the creation of 21 Civil Courts in Karkardooma	Two days strike on 25th and 26 August, 2003	Creation of 21 Courts in Karkardooma	Not to create 21 Civil Courts	Yet to come	—
22.4.15	Against the enhancement of pecuniary jurisdiction of trial from 20 lakhs to Rs. 2 crore (Delhi)	One day strike on 22 April, 15	Enhancing of pecuniary jurisdiction	—	Protesting against the delay in passing an amended Bill to enhance pecuniary jurisdiction of trial court	Lawyers of Six District Courts in Delhi have been on strike
10.2.15	Clearing of backlog of arrears of cases (Madhya Pradesh)	One day strike on 10 Feb., 15	Orders issued by Chief Justice A.M. Khanwilkar fixing deadline for clearing backlog	—	More than one lakh lawyers from High Court and lower courts in Madhya Pradesh abstained on 10 Feb., 15 to protest the radical changes made by Chief Justice	Advocates from 51 districts of the state decided to boycott court and demanded his immediate transfer

14.2.15	District Bar Association Jalandhar decided to boycott the National Lok Adalat	Scheduled on 14.2.15	Lok Adalat organized on Second Saturday which was usually a holiday	Boycott of National Lok Adalat	Announced to hold 'no work day' on Friday in the backdrop of the fact that it was being organized on Second Saturday	
Times of India 14.2.15	Lawyers of Kanpur Dehat observed strike on Friday to lodge protest against the decision of District Judge to vacate the court premises	Kanpur on 14.2.15	Removal of temporary chambers	Boycotted the judicial proceedings and also locked the main gate	—	—
11.3.15	A lawyer was shot in Allahabad by Sub-Inspector	Allahabad on 11.3.15	A lawyer named Nabi Ahmed was shot in Allahabad by Sub-Inspector Shailender Singh	Protest by lawyers in whole U.P.	Angry lawyers torched vehicles, resorted to violence at Allahabad District Court and blocked traffic on the highway	Ten people were injured when police resorted to use of batons to disperse the enraged crowd
11.3.15	As many as 400 lawyers of Maharashtra protested in Mumbai	Bombay High Court on 11.3.15	Demanded a separate Bench of Bombay High Court	Protest at Azad Maidan in Mumbai	Separate Bench of High Court	—

11.3.15	Boycott of National Lok Adalat	Mumbai on 11.3.15	About 16000 lawyers from six districts including 3500 from Kolhapur district boycott the Maha Lok Adalat	Abstained from proceedings	—	—
16.3.15	South Goa Advocates Association strongly condemned the ghastly and brutal murder of an advocate on 11.3.15	Goa on 16.3.15	Murder by Sub-Inspector, Shailender Singh inside the District Court campus in Allahabad on 11.3.15	The members of the Association unanimously resolved to abstain from work on 16.3.15 as mark of protest	—	Similar boycotts were made in other courts of the country as well
The Times of India 29.4.15	Litigants in Delhi faced a tough time as lawyers resort to strike for 4 days	Delhi from 29.4.15 to 2.5.15	Lawyers in all district courts in Delhi resorted to strike	—	—	—
The Time of India 5.5.15	Lawyers strike entered second week in Delhi	29.4.15 to 5.5.15	District Courts in Delhi wore a deserted look as lawyers entered 2nd week on Monday causing inconvenience to the litigants	Protesting against the delay in passing of an amended Bill to enhance pecuniary jurisdiction of the trial courts	—	—
Indian Express 8.5.15	Delhi High Court Bar Association issued a notice to all High Courts lawyers to abstain from work on Friday and Monday	8.5.15 and 11.5.15	Protest against the Bill	The Rajya Sabha on Wednesday had passed the Delhi High Court Act (Amendment) Bill which enhances the pecuniary jurisdiction of the District Courts to cases upto Rs. 2 crores		

1984-2015.

IV. Chart Analysis and Public Reactions

An analysis of the above chart reveals that the causes of lawyers' strike have been varied and with few exceptions these strikes have been made not with the view to serve the public cause but for agitating against any action and any governmental agency or officer allegedly affecting them personally or in their profession. It has also been noticed that the decisions to go on strike or to prolong strike have not been the outcome of cool, deliberate, calm and composed mind. In most of the cases these strikes appear to have been undertaken in excited moods in the emotionally charged atmosphere even without considering other strategies for the resolution of matters. Such extreme decisions are taken in undemocratic manner without following any voting procedure. Reports also indicate that the rowdy elements have also crept into the legal profession. We are well aware of the incident of snatching the ballot boxes in the Supreme Court when voters in favour or against were being polled.[1] The President of the Supreme Court Bar Association was manhandled during the strike in front of Chief Justice Court. The agitated lawyers heckled and roughed up some of their colleagues including senior counsels who attempted to get inside the court room to argue their cases. These included senior advocates K.K. Venugopal, Ram Jethmalani, O.P. Sharma and Murli Bhandari.[2] Such an uncalled for behaviour of the lawyers has been strongly decried by the media.[3]

There have been mixed reactions about lawyers' strike. Soli J. Sorabjee has observed that lawyers resorting to indefinite strike are striking at the heart of the Constitution. He has pointed out that lawyers may adopt any other remedy, judicial or extra-judicial, for remedying their grievances, if any, but they should not go on indefinite strike. It is not the right method to adopt because the public has become ultimate target.[4] H.M. Seervai has also forcefully criticised lawyers for participating in strike. In Kiran Bedi's case he stated that the Supreme Court and the Delhi High Court must indicate that they will not tolerate interference with the day to day administration of justice, no matter from what quarter that interference comes. He further stated that if it is conceded that lawyers are above the law and the law courts, there can be no limit to lawyers taking the law into their hands and paralyse the working of the Court.[5] Ram Jethmalani supported it in the famous handcuffing case. However, he condemned the lawyers' strike on the proposed amendments in the Civil Procedure Code to effect the radical changes in the procedural hindrance which cause delay of justice in civil litigation, when he was the Union Minister of Law.

The idea is not to blame the whole legal profession. This was an

1. Hindustan Times, March 9, 1988, also See Times of India, March 8, 1988.
2. Times of India, March 8, 1988.
3. *Ibid.*
4. Abha S. Joshi, 'Lawyers Strike—Abortive Quest for Dignity', 3 Lex Et Juris 30 (1988).
5. Supra note 4 at p. 548.

activity of a limited section of lawyers only, which shocked not only the public in general but also the majority of legal professionals themselves. They also do feel anguish and betrayed by such incidents. Number of good lawyers within the legal profession is not small. But the only thing is that their viewpoints seldom surface because they rarely take public positions on issues concerning the legal profession.[1] But when the blame comes, the entire legal profession is put to public scrutiny. The role which the legal profession is supposed to perform is to help in the administration of justice, maintenance of rule of law and assist in the enforcement of fundamental rights of the people. So any deviance in their conduct in the performance of their duties is soon noticed with the scrutinising eyes of the society. Hence, litigants are not the only sufferers. The non-affluent sections of the Bar too suffer silently. The judges are handicapped in disposing the cases without the assistance of layers. It involves tremendous loss on the clients, wastage of time of the courts and their energy. Therefore, lawyers are an integral part of the machinery of administration of justice, when they go on strike, the whole process of administration of justice gets paralysed. They exist essentially to serve the interests of their clients. If a boycott prevents the making of urgent applications so that a man remains in jail, or his property is demolished, the harm to the client is incalculable. There are others also who suffer by the lawyers' strike. There are the public interest, the people's faith or confidence in the administration and last but not the least the legal profession itself, due to its fallen esteem, which is also ultimately a loss to the society.

The present discussion would be incomplete if we do not take note of the viewpoints of lawyers and others in favour of lawyers' strike. Unfortunately, the material on this front is very little published in the legal periodicals and journals. S.P. Jain mentions thus[2] :

> "*Not all strikes by the professionals, however, can be tarnished with the same brush. Some of these involve the basic features of human dignity in a democratic society, such as the freedom of press, the independence of judiciary, the larger interests of the people, the nation, the profession itself and so on. Striking work in such situations not merely carries justification : it may be in the nature of a compelling duty.*"

Justice R.K. Mahajan has suggested that if the lawyers want to redress their grievances, they can do so possibly after the court work is over for limited time.[3] They can make their voice heard by organising peaceful procession or other non-violent methods as permissible under Article 19 of the Constitution of India. Atul Setalvad has stated that the mode of organising protests which the bar should adopt must be consistent with its position in society and duties to the litigating public. He further

1. Upendra Baxi, 'Professional Terrorism : Lawyers Strike' Lex Et Juris, August, 1986, pp. 10.11.
2. S.P. Jain, "Strikes by Professionals : Just and Unjust Causes", Times of India, Dec. 15, 1986.
3. R.K. Mahajan, op. cit; p. 3.

stated that there can be resolutions; there can be silent and dignified processions outside court hours; there can be symbolic gestures such as wearing protest arm bands.[1]

Dipankar Gupta points out that the Supreme Court has declared the strikes illegal and he submitted that even a call for strike is bad. He further submitted that it is time that the Bar Council of India as well as various State Bar Councils to monitor strikes within their jurisdiction and ensure that there are no call for strikes and/or boycotts. Prashant Bhushan, Senior Advocate submitted that the Court should also declare that lawyers who do not want to participate in a strike should not be coerced by other lawyers or committee members. He submitted that such coercion amounts to interference with the administration of justice and is, therefore, clearly contempt of Court.

Hence, one can think of many methods which are dignified and consistent with our duty to the courts and our clients. Such orderly methods may be less dramatic and, perhaps less effective. Even so, what, is wrong remains wrong. And the Bar, which lives in and for the law, cannot as a body, flout the rules of an orderly society to achieve an end, however, desirable the end may be. We never had lawyers' strike for bringing out any reform in the law or legal reforms in general; in repealing the ambiguous, unjust or the undemocratic laws; we have never seen lawyers agitating for better services or speedy trials to the clients and litigants. Lawyers never resorted to strike, demanding simplification of the so-called complex laws. Had it been so it would have really been a very positive development in our system of administration of justice. It must be remembered that an advocate is an officer of the court and enjoys special status in society. Advocates have obligations and duties to ensure smooth functioning of the court. They owe a duty to their clients. Strikes interfere with administration of justice. Hence, they cannot disrupt court proceedings and put interest of their client in jeopardy. It is no doubt true that the Bar should be strong, fearless and independent and should be in a position to lead the society.

V. Legal Position

The lawyers are part and parcel of the court and they are designated as officers of the court. Administration of justice cannot be carried out without their active participation. The lawyers are considered to be the exploiters by some eminent philosophers and jurists. On the other hand, some eminent men treat the legal profession as a noble one. Lawyers are looked upon as protectors and defenders of life, liberty and property of course at a price. They are also called friends of the court when their services are engaged as *amicus curiae* at the request of the court. Now the point for discussion is that how to view the legality of the lawyers' strike in the context of the statutory provisions. In 1961, the control of the High Court over the lawyers' discipline was taken away and in independent body was created under the Advocates Act, 1961, i.e., Bar Council at the State

1. Atul Setalvad, op. cit.; p. 13.

level. The Bar Council of India Rules, 1975 are also framed under this Act. Therefore, the statute which governs the advocates are the Advocates Act, 1961 and the Bar Council of India Rules, 1975. Section II of the Chapter VI of these rules lays down the standards of professional conduct and etiquettes. The Bar Council of India and the Bar Council of the States are the authorities to see observance of these rules and impose sanctions in case of deviance. It is surprising to see that the members of the Bar Council of India have been party to agitations and have itself adopted resolution in support of some strikes.

Neither in the Advocates Act, 1961 nor in the Bar Council of India Rules, there is any specific provision or rule which imposes a restriction on boycotting the courts by advocates. But the absence of any specific rule precluding an advocate from boycotting the court does not simply mean permission to do so. The codes of conduct are not meant to be rigid rules. These are not exhaustive also. No mention of any rule, which is equally imperative does not mean, that it is not applicable to advocates. The preamble of the chapter on Standards of Professional Conduct and Etiquette clearly mentions thus :

> "*An Advocate shall, at all times, conduct himself in a manner befitting his status as an officer of the court, a privileged member of the community, and a gentleman, bearing in mind that what may be lawful and moral for a person who is not a member of the Bar, or for a member of the Bar in his non-professional capacity may still be improper for an Advocate.*"

Without prejudice to the generality of the foregoing obligation, a lawyer owes duty to his client to defend his case fearlessly in the court and simultaneously, he must bear in mind that the dignity of the judicial office is essential for the survival of a free community. In India, the counsel's relations with his client are primarily a matter of contract. The relation is in nature of agent and principal. In other words, the advocate enters into a contract with a client on payment of fees to defend his client's case. An advocate occupies a position of trust in relation to his client. He is to protect the interest of his client. The relation between them is highly fiduciary in its nature, and of a very delicate, exacting and confidential character requiring a high degree of fidelity and good faith. An advocate is not permitted to withdraw from an engagement once he has accepted it, without sufficient notice is given to the client. Absence of Advocate from the court without informing the client, on the ground that members of the Bar decided to stay away from appearing in court, amounts to negligence to duty towards the client. There is no legal sanctity behind the resolution passed by the Bar Association calling upon the lawyers to abstain from appearing in court. Lawyers have been granted right of audience in courts under the Advocates Act and to conduct cases of their clients on getting remuneration for the same. If they consciously, intentionally and deliberately abstain from conducting the cases in the courts on behalf of the clients, they would be committing a breach of contract and subjecting themselves to the consequences flowing from such a breach.

VI. Judicial Response to Lawyers' Strike

Right from more than half a century lawyers' strike is being disapproved and reprehended by the Supreme Court and various High Courts. In 1923, the full Bench of Calcutta High Court in **Tarini Mohan Barari's case**,[1] deprecated the pleaders act of boycotting the court and abstaining from attending the court deliberately. Similarly, the Division Bench of Rangoon High Court in case of **re : Pleader**,[2] held the abstaining of pleader from court without client's consent and leaving him undefended amounted to professional misconduct. Further, in **Bar Council of Maharashtra v. M.V. Dabholkar**,[3] their Lordships of the Supreme Court observed that the central function of the legal profession is to promote the administration of justice and the Bar cannot behave with doubtful scruples or strive to thrive on litigation. Canons of conduct cannot be crystallised into right rules but felt by collective conscience of the practitioners as right.

In **Pandurang Dattaraya v. Bar Council of Maharashtra**,[4] the court observed that the Advocates are expected to follow norms of professional ethics and try to protect the interest of their clients. Thus, it would be against professional ethics for a lawyer to abstain from the court when the cause of his client is called for hearing.

Further, the Supreme Court reminded in a case[5] that a lawyer is under obligation to do nothing that shall detract from the dignity of the court, of which he is himself a sworn officer and assistant. He should all times pay differential respect to the Judge, and scrupulously observe the decorum of the court room. The court further observed that having accepted the brief, if the advocate abstains from attending the court then he will be committing a breach of his professional duty.

The Punjab and Haryana High Court in the case of **Maharaj Singh v. Smt. Charan Kaur**,[6] relied on **Karan Singh v. State of Punjab**,[7] where it ruled that the profession of law enjoys a high and respected status and reputation in our Republic, but this status also carries with it a corresponding necessary obligation which to an extent partakes of fiduciary character. The client places in his lawyer full and implicit faith for representing the former and looking after and protecting his interest in the litigation in the court. The court added that the counsel abstaining from appearing in court cannot, therefore, but be construed as being contrary to the manner and norms of this great and noble profession as Justice Holmes has aptly put it as "a calling of thinkers".

In **State of Haryana v. Rai Sahib**,[8] the court taking a strict view held that only due to advocate's abstaining from court work, courts should not strike their responsibility by not deciding cases in accordance with law.

1. A.I.R. 1923 Cal. 212.
2. A.I.R. 1924 Rangoon 320.
3. A.I.R. 1976 S.C. 242.
4. A.I.R. 1984 S.C. 110.
5. *S.J. Chaudhary* v. *State (Delhi Administration)*, *A.I.R. 1984 S.C. 618.*
6. 1984 S.C. 618.
7. A.I.R. 1987 P & H 213.
8. I.L.R. (1966) 2 Punjab 609.

Similarly, in **Rajendra Singh v. Union of India**,[1] the court held that in case of lawyers' strike, judges can dispose of cases themselves even when unaided by lawyers. Further, in **Common Causes, A Society v. Union of India**,[2] the Supreme Court held that the cases must proceed when they appear on board and should not originally be adjourned on account of the absence of lawyers unless there are reasons to do so. In **Mahabir Prasad v. Jack Aviation**,[3] the Supreme Court considered various aspects on the matter. The court has severely criticized the Delhi High Court for failing to protect the lower judiciary from pressure tactics of advocates who had boycotted the court of an Additional District Judge. The Division Bench comprising of S. Saghir Ahmad and K.T. Thomas JJ. has held that if any counsel does not want to appear in a particular court, that too for justifiable reasons, professional decorum and etiquette require him to give up his engagement in that court so that the party can engage another counsel. But retaining the brief of his client and at the same time abstaining from appearing in that court, that too not on any particular day on account of some personal inconvenience of the counsel, but as permanent feature, is unprofessional as also unbecoming of the status of an Advocate. No court is obliged to adjourn a case because of the strike call given by any association of Advocates or a decision to boycott the court either in general or any particular court. It is the solemn duty of every court to proceed with the judicial business during court hours. The court further observed that judicial function cannot and should not be stonewalled by browbeating or bullying methodology, whether it is by the litigants or by counsel. Judicial process must run its even course unbridled by any boycott call of the Bar, or tactics adopted by any member.

In **B.L. Wadehra v. State (N.C.T. of Delhi)**,[4] the Delhi High Court held that strike by lawyers is illegal, unethical and amounts to professional misconduct. It is a breach of contract, breach of trust, and breach of professional duty. The court further held that preventing a lawyer from discharging his duty is a criminal offence. It is interference with the administration of justice and hence amounts to contempt of court. The Supreme Court held in **Roman Services Pvt. Ltd. v. Subhash Kapoor**,[5] that when a court passed ex-parte decree due to the absence of an Advocate in pursuance of strike, and subsequently when the ex-parte decree is set aside on conditions of payment of cost, the party is entitled to realise the amount of the cost from the Advocate concerned. The court added that the litigant who suffers entirely on account of his Advocate's non-appearance in court, he has also the remedy to sue the Advocate for damages.

This judgment of the Supreme Court is a milestone and clear mandate in the matter and the subordinate judiciary in case of lawyers strike has now no option but to proceed with the case unless there are some cogent

1. 1993 Cr. L.J. 1968.
2. (1994) 5 S.C.C. 557; Also see *K. John Koshy* v. *Tarakeshwar Prasad*, (1998) 8 S.C.C. 624.
3. A.I.R. 1999 S.C. 287.
4. A.I.R. 2000 Delhi 266.
5. A.I.R. 2001 S.C. 207.

and justiciable reasons to adjourn the case.

In **Ex-Capt. Harish Uppal** v. **Union of India**,[1] the facts of the case were that a number of writ petitions were placed before five member Constitution Bench headed by the then Chief Justice of India, Mr. Justice G.B.Pattanaik in which the questions raised were : whether lawyers have a right to strike and/or give a call for boycott of courts. In all these petitions a declaration is sought that such strikes and/or calls for boycott are illegal. As the questions vitally concerned the legal profession, public notices were issued to the Bar Associations and Bar Councils all over the country. The Bar Associations had proceeded on strike on several occasions in the past, at times, statewide or nationwide, and 'while the profession does not like it as members of the profession are themselves the losers in the process' and while it is not necessary to sit in judgment over the wider question whether the members of profession can at all go on strike or boycott of courts, it was felt that even if it is assumed that such a right ensures to the members of the profession, the circumstances in which such a step should be resorted to should be clearly indicated. It was stated that the Bar Council of India had made its position clear to the effect '(a) the Bar Council of India is against resorting to strike excepting in rarest of rare cases involving the dignity and independence of the judiciary as well as of the Bar; and (b) whenever strikes become inevitable, efforts shall be made to keep it short and peaceful to avoid causing hardship to the litigant public.[2]

It was in response to the above that a consensus was reached at the Bar at the hearing of the matter that instead of the Court going into wider question whether or not the member of the legal profession can resort to strike or abstain from appearing in cases in court in which they are engaged, the court may see the working of the interim arrangement, and if that is found to be satisfactory, it may perhaps not be required to go into the wider question at this stage. The learned counsel has suggested that to begin with, the following interim measures may be adequate for the present :

(i) In the rare instance where any association of lawyers including statutory Bar Councils considers it imperative to call upon and/or advise members of the legal profession to abstain from appearing in courts on any occasion, it must be left to any individual member/members of the association to be free to appear without fear or hindrance or any other coercive steps.

(ii) No such member who appears in court or otherwise practises his legal profession, shall be visited with any adverse or penal consequences whatever, by any association of lawyers, and shall not suffer any expulsion or threat of expulsion therefrom.

(iii) The above will not preclude other forms of protest by practising lawyers in court such as, for instance, wearing of armbands and other forms of protest which in no way interrupt or disrupt the

1. (2003) 2 S.C.C. 45.
2. *Common Cause. A Regd. Society* v. *Union of India*. (1995) 1 SCALE 6.

court proceedings or adversely affect the interest of the litigant. Any such form of protest shall not however be derogatory to the court or to the profession.

In spite of the interim directions, the Bar Council of India has not incorporated these clauses in the Bar Council of India (Conduct and Disciplinary) Rules. The phenomenon of going on strike at the slightest provocation is on the increase. Strikes and calls for boycott have paralysed the functioning of the Courts for a number of days. The Bar Council of India has since filed an affidavit wherein extract of a Joint Meeting of the Chairmen of various State Bar Councils and members of Bar Council of India have been annexed. The minutes set out that some of the causes which result in lawyers abstaining from work are :

I. Local Issues :

(1) Disputes between lawyer/lawyers and the police and other authorities;

(2) Issues regarding corruption/misbehaviour of judicial officers and other authorities;

(3) Non-filling of vacancies arising in courts or non-appointment of judicial officers for a long period;

(4) Absence of infrastructure in courts.

II. Issues relating to one section of the Bar and another section :

(1) Withdrawal of jurisdiction and conferring it to other courts (both pecuniary and territorial);

(2) Constitution of Benches of High Courts. Disputes between the competing District and other Bar Associations.

III. Issues involving dignity, integrity, independence of the Bar and Judiciary.

IV. Legislation without consultation with the Bar Council.

V. National issues and regional issues affecting the public at large/the insensitivity of all concerned.

It was also resolved in the meeting that Grievance Redressal Committees at the taluk/sub-division or tehsil level, at the district level, High Courts and Supreme Court levels be constituted. It was also resolved that in case the Bar Associations deviate from the resolutions and proceed on cessation of work in spite or without the decision of the Grievance Redressal Committee concerned, except in the case of emergency, the Bar Council of the State will take such action as it may deem fit and proper, the discretion being left to the Bar Council of the State concerned as to enforcement of such decisions and in the case of an emergency the Bar Association concerned will inform the State Bar Council.

The Court has appreciated the efforts made, in view of the endemic situation prevailing in the country, but on the other hand stated that these resolutions are not enough. It was expected that the Bar Council of India would have incorporated clauses as those suggested in the interim order of this court in their Disciplinary Rules. This they have failed to do even now. What is at stake is the administration of justice and the reputation of the legal profession. It is the duty and obligation of the Bar Council of India to now incorporate clauses as suggested in the interim order. When there is an apparent threat to the administration of justice and fundamental rights of citizens, that is, the litigating public, courts will always have authority to compel or enforce the exercise of the power by statutory authority.

A five-member Constitution Bench of the Supreme Court in **Ex Capt. Harish Uppal v. Union of India**,[1] has expressed serious concern and anguish over lawyers going on strike in different parts of the country and held that strikes by lawyers are illegal and they have no right to go on strike or give a call for boycott, not even on a token strike. The protest, if any is required, can only be by giving press statements, T.V. interviews, carrying out on court premises banners and/or placards, wearing-black or white or any colour arm bands, peaceful protest marches outside and away from court premises, going on *dharna* on relay, fasts, etc. It is held that lawyers holding Vakalats on behalf of their clients cannot attend courts in pursuance to a call for strike or boycott. All lawyers must boldly refuse to abide by any call for strike or boycott. No lawyers can be visited with any adverse consequences by the Association or the Council and no threat or coercion of any nature including that of expulsion can be held out. It is held that no Bar Council or Bar Association can permit calling of a meeting for purpose of considering a call for strike or boycott and requisition, if any, for such meeting must be ignored. But this prohibition is not absolute. In the rarest of rare cases where the dignity, integrity and independence of the Bar or the Bench are at stake, courts may ignore (turn blind eye) to a protest abstention from work for not more than one day is permissible. In such cases the President of the Bar must consult the Chief Justice or the District Judge before Advocates decide to absent themselves from court. The decision of the Chief Justice or the District Judge would be final and have to be abided by the Bar. It is held that courts are under no obligation to adjourn matters because lawyers are on strike. On the contrary, it is the duty of all courts to go on with matters on their boards even in the absence of lawyers. In other words, courts must not be privy to strikes or call for boycotts. The court further held that if a lawyer , holding a Vakalat of a client, abstains from attending court due to a strike call, he shall be personally liable to pay costs which shall be in addition to damages which he might have to pay to his client for loss suffered by him. The underlying rationale of the judgment is that members of the legal profession are officers of the court. They are obliged by the very nature of their calling to assist in the dispensation to justice. Strikes impair the administration of justice and are thus inconsistent with their calling as lawyers. Lawyers more than others should grasp this essential fact. It behoves them to abide by the law laid down by the apex court if their commitment to the rule

1. 2002(9) SCALE 357 (The five member Constitution Bench comprised of Justice G.B. Pattanaik, Justice M.B. Sood, Justice Doraiswamy Raju, Justice S.N. Variava and Justice D.M. Dharmadhikari).

of law is genuine.

On 2nd November, 2014 in a stern warning to lawyers, the Bombay High Court, while hearing a Public Interest Litigation filed by Manoj Laxman Shhirsatthe, a lawyer registered with the Bar Council of Maharashtra, said that those who partake in any sort of strike or other disruptive activities that affect the judiciary's day-to-day affairs are likely to face contempt charges. The Chief Justice Mohit Shah lead High Court bench hearing the case also said that the Bar Council of Maharashtra with whom the advocates are registered, may also choose to take action against such lawyers. In the PIL, the complainant alleged that the strike observed on appeals by the District Bar Association on August 29, 2013 and by the Bar Council of India on March 11, 2013 were totally illegal.

In **Akash Pratap Singh @ Sunny v. The State of Madhya Pradesh,**[1] petition was listed under caption "Top of the List" in terms of order dated 21.04.2015, however, none appeared for the petitioner when the matter was called out. Presumably, the Advocates on record have chosen not to appear because of the call given by the Madhya Pradesh High Court Bar Association in its meeting dated 24th April, 2015 to boycott Court work. The Supreme Court observed that, "we, *prima facie*, find that the Advocates have chosen not to appear on account of illegal call given by the Bar Association, have committed professional misconduct, for which, they must be noticed and called upon to explain as to why appropriate action should not be taken including to impose cost." The case is finally to be decided by the Hon'ble Supreme Court.

In **Anand Trust v. The Bar Council of India,**[2] was listed before the Supreme Court on 27th April, 2015 an application has been filed by the petitioners bringing to the notice of the Supreme Court the resolutions of the High Court Bar Association, Jabalpur and the District Bar Association, Jabalpur in the matter of calling for a one day token strike and boycott of the Courts. Petitioners submitted that the grievances of the District Bar Association in the matter does not fall in the exception to the general rule as indicated by the Supreme Court in the case of **Ex-Capt. Harish Uppal v Union of India and others.**[3] The action is contrary to the dictum of the Supreme Court as indicated in para 35 of the judgment in the case of Ex-Capt. Harish Uppal (supra). Petitioner also points out that the Court has already taken cognizance of the original prayer made in this writ petition and in spite of notice again a call for strike is given. The Supreme Court observed that, "the action of the Bar Associations being in violation to the law laid down by the Supreme Court, the same *prima facie* amounts to contempt of court, violation of Supreme Court mandate and a case for taking action against the office bearers. Not only they are rendered themselves liable to be proceeded against for contempt but also to pay the cost and damages to the litigants, who have suffered because of non hearing of their cases today. However, the principles of natural

1. W.P. NO. 3965 of 2015.
2. W.P. No. 3809 of 2015.
3. 2003 (2) S.C.C. 45.

justice and process of law requires that before taking any action as indicated by us herein above, the law mandates us to issue notice to all concerned and thereafter proceed in accordance with law. Accordingly, we direct the office to issue notice to all the office bearers of M.P. High Court Bar Association and the District Bar Association, along with a copy of this order directing them to show cause as to why action as contemplated by the Supreme Court in the case of Ex-Capt. Harish Uppal should not be taken against them. That apart, a copy of the order be also forwarded to the Chairman of M.P. State Bar Council and the Chairman of Bar Council of India asking to show cause on the next date and to indicate as to why further action should not be taken as prayed for by the petitioners in the matter of frequent call for boycott being given by the Bar Association in the State of M.P. and any action to be taken for restraining them and prohibiting them from doing so. The case is yet to be decided by the Hon'ble Supreme Court.

Constitutional Protection

The Constitution of India recognises the importance of advocates in protecting the life and liberties of individuals. The fundamental right to be defended by a legal practitioner is one's choice guaranteed under Article 22(1) is a clear testimony to this. But the important point is that whether the Constitution provides any safeguards to an accused person, so far as criminal jurisprudence is concerned. When a lawyer is engaged by an accused person, in concert with others, boycotts the court and adds to his misery by his increased incarceration. The Constitution of India appears to be silent on this. But the Constitution as prescribed and interpreted by the apex court of the land does show some hope. There is no fundamental right, either under Article 19 or under Article 21 of the Constitution, which permits or authorises a lawyer to abstain from appearing in court in a case in which he holds the Vakalat for a party in that case. On the other hand, a litigant has a fundamental right of speedy trial of his case, because, speedy trial, as held by the Supreme Court in **Hussainara Khatoon v. Home Secretary, State of Bihar**,[1] is an integral part of the fundamental right to life and liberty enshrined in Article 21 of the Constitution. Strike by lawyers will infringe the above mentioned fundamental right of the litigants and such infringement cannot be permitted. Assuming that the lawyers are trying to convey their feelings of sentiments and ideas through the strike in exercise of their fundamental right to freedom of speech and expression guaranteed by Article 19(1)(a) of the Constitution, it is crystal clear that the exercise of the right under Article 19(1)(a) will come to an end when such exercise threatens to infringe the fundamental right of another. Such a limitation is inherent in the exercise of the right under Article 19(1)(a). Hence, the lawyers cannot go on strike infringing the fundamental right of the litigants for speedy trial. The right to practice any profession or to carry on any occupation guaranteed by Article 19(1)(g) may include the right to discontinue such profession or occupation but it will not include any right to abstain from appearing in court while holding

1. A.I.R. 1979 S.C. 1360.

a Vakalat in the case. Similarly, the exercise of the right to protest by the lawyers cannot be allowed to infract the litigant's fundamental right for speedy trial or to interfere with the administration of justice.

There is no doubt that the legal profession is an independent and serious profession, it is not under the subjugation of the State. State cannot be asked to direct the lawyers concerned in a given case not to come in the way of speedy trial as a result of the strike. But we should not forget that the Bar Councils, which are the disciplining authorities with respect to lawyers, are 'State' within the meaning of Article 12 of the Constitution. As such Bar Councils of the State and the Bar Council of India, 'as State' are under a constitutional mandate to ensure that the speedy trial in criminal justice is ensured, it is not allowed to be hampered by the strikes of the lawyers, which is a breach of duty to the client, and hence actionable under Bar Council of India Rules, 1975. The court has recognised 'the right to protest' of lawyers in Ex-Captain Harish Uppal's case but at the same time said that they do not have a right to strike or boycott. The right to protest should not be curtailed. Further, as our constitutional system becomes more majoritarian, role of protest has increased. Wearing armbands are not effective of protest. Hence, protest must be resorted to on a non-coercive basis as a last resort for a limited duration bearing in mind the work-load of the courts and the effects of protest on the administration of justice. Indeed, it is the Bar that should come to the rescue of the Bench when the judicial power is under threat and judges pressurized. Browbeating lawyers may undermine judicial independence. It is, therefore, submitted that the Bar Association should seriously discuss the issues involved in boycotting the courts, for the purpose of protecting the rights of the litigants and to carry out the objects underlying Articles 22 and 39-A of the Constitution of India and evolve other appropriate legal measures as an alternate to strike to seek redressal of grievances.

VII. Conclusion

The foregoing study clearly indicates that frequent and prolonged strikes by lawyers directly hit the public interest, the people's faith or confidence in the administration and last but not the least, the legal profession itself. The abstention of courts should be desperate step of last resort, even if justified. The legal implications of abstention of lawyers is that it is reprehensible for an advocate as an officer of the court, who is to assist the administration of justice, boycott courts of law and thereby impede, obstruct or prevent administration of law. Such conduct of the lawyer constitutes ground for disbarment or suspension. Therefore, he must be honest in espousing the cause of clients before the court. If he is not sincere enough in his effort, the result would be disastrous. Hence, before going on strike the lawyers should ask themselves the following questions[1] :

(a) Is the strike in public interest?

(b) Does the cause deserve so much sacrifice on the part of the Bar and so much suffering to the clients?

1. Supra note 4 at p. 702.

(c) Is it conducive to administration of justice?

(d) Is it going to add to the credibility of the profession and improve its image?

(e) Is it unavoidable?

The conflict or tug of war between the Bench and the Bar should be minimized. Even if there is a dispute between them or where there is a genuine allegation about the conduct of a Judge, the Bar may complain to the appropriate forum. The members of the Bar Association have no right to boycott courts in view of the duties, which they are required to discharge. It is true that under the Constitution of India, freedom of association is guaranteed as a fundamental right, but this right is subject to reasonable restrictions in the interest of public order or morality. The prohibition against strike by lawyers is inbuilt in the Advocates Act, 1961. The duties to the court and duties to the clients prescribed by the Bar Council of India go to provide that strike or boycotting of courts is antithesis to practice in the court, and is a professional misconduct. An advocate being an officer of the court is bound to submit to its authority and cannot join in an action to boycott the court. At the same time, lawyer's right to protest should not be curtailed. Hence, the need is to constitute an appropriate forum to redress the grievances of the advocates.

11

SOCIAL RESPONSIBILITIES OF LAWYERS

I. Prelude

The profession of law is a great profession with serious responsibilities, which no person carrying on any other profession has to shoulder. The lawyers perform different types of work in today's competitive world. Legal professionals are always free from political colour and pressure. They are also not subordinate to the functioning of the Legislatures, Executives and Judiciary. There is no protocol of the legal profession in the society, they are simple and neutral like pure water and they are always adjustable to all the members of the society. They are free to mix with the members of different communities without any rank and file in the society. In other words, the legal professionals are having free access to every section of the society so as to seek the truth for assisting the court in justice delivery system subject to the professional ethics.

At present, the society is moving very fast. Law, lawyers and judiciary are not in a position to keep pace with fast moving society. The legal profession has to be sensitive to the emerging social and economic trends which regulate affairs of the society. It has to be alive to the challenges posed by liberalization and globalization. It may be clearly stated that the social responsibility here does not imply the traditional and routine legal services rendered by the lawyers, it means something more than that. It envisages the duty to help and protect the society in overcoming the major problems which cannot be solved by the state and its agencies alone and which need the participative co-operation of different sections of the society including the lawyers for their solution. While discharging his functions, a lawyer may be responsible to numerous actors.

The lawyers owe responsibilities to clients, profession, the public and the courts. Lawyers play a vital role in the preservation of society. The members of the legal profession individually and collectively respond to the call towards social responsibilities to help in solving numerous serious problems facing the community concerning law, lawyers and justice. These responsibilities generally relate to the obligations one has to the society, to the conscience, to the morality and to the feeling of being one with the society. These obligations are generally in the interest of the overall legal health of the community. On the other hand, continued neglect of the social responsibilities is bound to bring strong adverse public opinion. This may not only shake the confidence of the public in the system of administration of justice, but it may also result in revolting situations. The legal profession has a special role to perform to defend the rights of the weaker, unprivileged and disadvantaged sections of the society. There is a need to go to the people, educate them and organize them to be involved in nation's reconstruction programme. Lawyers may be the perfect persons to go to the people both in town and country, awaken and organize the people to build up a conscious constructive movement for achieving the goals as enshrined in the Constitution of India. To resolve such conflicts, only the lawyers can help. Lawyers have a significant role to play in reaching the goal of social justice. They precisely know what the law is, what the citizen's rights are, what the claims of the society are in tune with our constitutional goals and philosophy, can act as a catalyst to make our constitutional declarations to turn into reality. Hence, the importance of the legal profession cannot be underestimated in this gigantic task, the contours of which have been laid down by the Constitution-makers.

II. Legal Profession Responded to the Call for Social Responsibilities

The legal profession is a profession of service—service to the community. The most important duty of the profession is to act as the interpreter, guide and faithful servant of the community. The role of lawyers in a developing society is linked with the question of the contribution which law can make for the development of society. Used as instrument of social engineering, law can introduce smoothness in the act of change, prevent upheavals and eliminate jolts in the onward march of society. There is no doubt that the legal profession in India has responded to the call for social responsibilities by espousing the cause of public interest, social interests and community interest. Legal profession has raised an effective voice through the famous Judges case, that is **S.P. Gupta v. Union of India,**[1] which helped in expanding the whole concept of *locus standi* and gave birth to the chapter of public interest litigation. The lawyers have come to the service of the underprivileged and disadvantaged classes of people through the famous cases of construction workers, bonded labour, slum dwellers, undertrials and so on. It is an established fact that the politician, the clergy or the merchant man cannot deliver the goods to the poor and downtrodden of our vast country. Only the lawyers, by strict adherence of truth, honesty and justice can do real help to weaker section. The need of the hour is that the lawyers must evaluate their role within legal profession and in the broader community at a time of rapid social change. The imminent need is to break from the traditional *laissez faire* norms of society. "Beaten path is the safe path", no longer holds good. The lawyer must respond to the changing needs of the society. The lawyer as a social thinker has to play a special role for the solidarity, unity, integrity, welfare and good of the society. The legal profession, individually and collectively, has to respond to the call towards social responsibilities to help in serious numerous problems, facing the community, concerning law, lawyers and justice.

1. A.I.R. 1981 (Sup) S.C. 87.

III. No Specific Provision in the Advocates Act which Fixes Social Responsibilities

There is no specific set of provisions in the Advocates Act, 1961 and the Bar Council of India Rules, 1975 fixing and enlisting social responsibilities of the legal profession. But that does not mean that the statute is totally silent on this aspect. A careful scrutiny of the relevant law would lead us to conclude that there are numerous indicators which recognize the importance of this vital aspect. The words "obligations an Advocate owes to society" do find a specific mention, while laying down the Code of Legal Ethics for the Advocates in the last line of Rule 46 of the "Standards of Professional Conduct and Etiquette". It clearly states that rendering legal aid to the poor is one of the highest obligations a lawyer owes to the society. This is not the only obligation of an advocate which he owes to society. The lawyers have a number of other obligations to the society or to the community for instance, they are to help in maintenance of Rule of Law, duty to maintain the dignity of the State, they should uphold the Constitution, promote the advancement of justice and assist in the enforcement of fundamental rights of the people and so on.

The lawyers' responsibilities are beyond the bread and butter activities. They must, not only add their contribution to the improvement of law, the courts and profession, but they must assume the obligation to intelligently and carefully mould public opinion in spheres and areas where their training and experience give them a peculiar competence and they must be prepared to perform public service when duty dictates.

There are some provisions in the Advocates Act, 1961, which point towards the aspect of social responsibility of the legal profession. Sections 6 and 7 of the Act enumerate the functions of the State Bar Council and Bar Council of India respectively. Clause (eee) of sub-section (1) of section 6 says that it is one of the functions of the Bar Council to organise legal aid to the poor in prescribed manner. Section 6(2) further empowers the Bar Council to constitute funds for this very purpose. Further, Section 15(2) empowers the Bar Councils to make rules for organizing legal aid and advice to the poor. On the similar analogy, Section 7(i)(b) empowers the Bar Council of India to organize and render legal aid and advice to the poor. Further, Section 7(2) empowers to constitute funds for giving legal aid and advice to the poor in prescribed manner. Similarly, Rule 46 of the Standards of Professional Conduct and Etiquette under Chapter VI of the Bar Council of India Rules, 1975 casts a duty on the advocates to render free legal assistance to the poor as one of the highest obligations an advocate owes to the society. Further, Rule 15 under Chapter IX of the Bar Council of India Rules, 1975, deals with conditions for enrolment as an advocate, in addition to the provisions of Section 24 of the Advocates Act.

Sub-rule (2) of this Rule is relevant for the purpose which reads as under :

"Enrolment (1) ......

(2) Every candidate seeking enrolment as an advocate shall be

required to affirm and subscribe to the following declarations :

(a) "I shall uphold the Constitution and the laws."

(b) "I shall faithfully discharge every obligation cast on me by the Act and the Rules framed thereunder."

This rule is of paramount importance. This not only binds an advocate to abide by the Constitution, as amended and interpreted by the judiciary of the land, and the laws of the land, but also to faithfully discharge every obligation cast on him as emanating from the Act and Rules framed thereunder. Hence, an advocate like any other citizen, or rather than an ordinary citizen, is bound by the law and Constitution of the land. Therefore, it is explicitly clear that the advocate is not above law.

IV. Judicial Response Towards Legal Profession

There is no doubt that the legal profession has responded to the call for social responsibilities by espousing the cause of public interests, social interests and community interest. It is a truism that in a system governed by rule of law judiciary is the final interpreter of the provisions of law. The judiciary has responded with warmth and enthusiasm in showing and laying down the highway path of social responsibilities of the legal profession. Recognizing the importance of the role of the lawyers in general in creating an environment of free community, Justice Dhawan of Allahabad High Court observed in the case of **Harbans Lal Arora v. Divisional Supdt. Central Railways,**[1] as early as 1960, that the Bar and Bench are the joint guardians of the rule of law. It is their joint duty to create an atmosphere which will enable the citizens of the Republic to enjoy that freedom from fear which can only come from the assurance that the two guardians of freedom are always on the look out for any temptation for arbitrary action which may be lurking in the dark recesses of the all too human executive mind, and from a feeling of confidence that whenever and wherever in the Republic any act of *zabardasti* (coercive force) or *zulum* (cruelty) takes place, the long arm of the law will reach forth and crush it.

In another important case,[2] the Punjab and Haryana High Court has observed that to preserve the administration of justice under the law is the special responsibility of the professional lawyer in Indian Republic since in addition to his being the pleader of his client and defender of his right, he is an officer of the court. It is, therefore, abundantly clear that when a lawyer is looked as an officer of the Court, he has dual responsibilities. On the one hand, he has to protect the interests of his client, and on the other hand he has to assist the court so that the court reaches at its final decision. He must be loyal to the Constitution and the laws of the Republic of India, which taken as a whole are committed to social justice, equality, liberty and fraternity which are sufficient indicators towards the goal of social responsibilities. Similarly, the Supreme Court of India has made a

1. A.I.R. 1960 All. 164.
2. *Dr. Hardit Singh* v. *Bhagat*, A.I.R. 1964 Punj. 277.

pointed reference to this aspect in **Bar Council of Maharashtra v. M.V. Dabholkar.**[1] Justice V.R. Krishna Iyer observed that the vital role of lawyer depends upon his probity and professional life style. He further observed that the central function of the legal profession is to promote the administration of justice. As monopoly to the legal profession has been statutorily granted by the nation, it obligates the lawyer to observe scrupulously those norms which make him worthy of the confidence of community in him as a vehicle of social justice. The Court has categorically stated that in addition to the normal bread and butter activities, the legal profession is also entrusted with the tasks, outside his routine job to the tasks of ensuring social justice, a clear pointer to the realization of social responsibilities. The advocate has important responsibilities to the court as well as to his client. They are criticized as the "hired gun". The advocate is more than a mouthpiece. An advocate is a privileged member and watchdog of society.

In **R.D. Saxena v. Balram Prasad Sharma**,[2] the Supreme Court has rightly observed that "it is high time for the legal profession to join hands and evolve a code for themselves in addition to Advocates Act and Rules made thereunder and the Rules made by the High Courts and Supreme Court, for strengthening the belief of the common man in the institution of judiciary in general and their profession in particular. Creation of such faith and confidence would not only strengthen the rule of law but also result in reaching excellence in the profession."

The gist of these cited opinions with regard to social responsibilities of the legal profession may appear to be too heavily dosed ideals and respect to the courts is directed to be maintained because it is essential for the survival of free community. Social responsibilities fall under the category of all those duties which are essential to preserve our democratic fabric, rule of law, social justice, independence of judiciary and the Bar and so on : Anything which hampers the conditions of justice for the masses, that subverts the democratic fabric of our system, interfere in the independence of judiciary and Bar would call for participative action from the legal profession and call them upon for social responsibilities. As a matter of fact, majority of the social responsibilities can be anchored to this single pillar of survival of free community.

V. Existing Position on Social Responsibilities

So far as the actual working of legal professionals in regard to the understanding of their social responsibilities, a good number of empirical research projects have been undertaken by the scholars, institutions, sociologists and academicians in the field of law. The first study on 140 lawyers of Jaipur in Rajasthan was conducted by K.L. Sharma which reveals that the lawyers were organised only to the limited extent and were not found united for social service. The autonomy enjoyed by the legal profession had not been used to promote the interests of the poor. Due to

1. A.I.R. 1976 S.C. 242.
2. (2000) 7 S.C.C. 264 at 280.

lack of self-reliance, advocates behaved only as a formal functionary and the concern for any sort of social engineering for the problems of the people and society was missing. Another study was conducted on about 243 lawyers of Pune in Maharashtra and reveals that participation by them in social activity was very rare. The thrust for using law as an instrument of social change was found to be almost missing among the lawyers in general.

The study conducted by J.S. Gandhi on District Court lawyers of Punjab reveals that it is very difficult for the lawyers at the district bar to switch over to the task of social change. The study concluded that any programme, which seeks to involve legal profession in the process of social change in the Indian society would succeed only to the extent to which it is informed by some of its fundamental shortcomings. Further, a survey conducted on a sample of nearly 1151 advocates belonging to Tamil Nadu Bar revealed that lawyers as a class lack social awareness. It is revealed from the study that only 23% of the lawyers were doing legal aid work and that too, as little as less than five cases a year. An empirical study of Shimla town was conducted by Dr. Pankaj Musafir in 2015. The researcher served questionnaire to 200 lawyers of District Court, Shimla and High Court of Himachal Pradesh. On the question whether there is a gap between courts and the lawyers on the matter, specifically social responsibilities connected with the legal profession, it is revealed from the responses that there is a need to create better awareness and dedication among the lawyers. One should not forget that the output in terms of respect, esteem, honour and nobility conferred on legal profession by the society is directly proportional to the level of input of response towards social responsibilities by the legal profession. The study clearly reveals that the path of social responsibility is not a bed of roses. It is hazardous path. It is a path of service, sacrifice, devotion and dedication. It is a path where duties are performed not with an eye on the returns or the rewards. The greatest reward is the satisfaction that one has done his duty, and one is regarded so in the eyes of others.

When a lawyer is lawyering, it is wrong to say that there are only two parties. The society is standing as client of the legal profession. Social problems are there crying out to be solved. It is for the profession to answer the challenge. The lawyer has not to wait for the problem to arrive at his door-step. He should be able to fore-stall it by taking his professional skill to the people. The social responsibilities entrusted to the legal profession direct it to turn and synchronise its efforts and activities to meet the aspirations and expectations of the society and community from which it draws its sustenance. Many of the lawyer never visualize as what the society expects of the legal profession. For them responsibilities begin and end with serving their client and for them law is only a set of mechanical roles which they attempt to manipulate for the interest of the clients. A lawyer with such an outlook on his profession is not likely either to attract his clients or to serve them well, nor will he enjoy the solid and durable satisfaction that comes from a well rounded complete life in law.

The views of some leading scholars and jurists are also of great relevance here. Professor Upendra Baxi, commenting on the role of Indian lawyers has concluded that : "The Indian lawyer is a role specific in all contexts and levels, that is, he largely confines his occupational role playing to that of dispute processing in the court-setting. He hardly takes on or creates conditions so that he be given role such as planner, negotiator, law reformer, etc."[1]

Professor N.R. Madhava Menon in his article "Restructuring the Legal Profession for Strengthening Administration of Justice" has arrived at the conclusion that the profession has fallen in the estimate of the society.[2] It appears to be living in its cherished complacency closing its eyes to regrettable realities. There is a discernible maladjustment of the profession to the legal needs of the people. The legal profession continues to project the image of a spokesman of the rich and powerful sections of Indian society.[3] T.K. Oommen clearly point out that the Indian lawyer invariably prompts him to prolong and perpetuate dispute processing. This is so because they lack the classification of their roles to other fields like those of negotiator, advisor, reconcilor or the law reformer. The consequence of such trend are disastrous for the legal profession as a whole.[4]

Hence, it is, therefore, crystal clear that the commitment to public service has declined and the profession at times has tended to become a trade or business run on capitalist market models of demand and supply. Boycott of courts on flimsy grounds has become a common phenomenon. Lawyers as a class show no obligation to assist the process of law reforms.

VI. Areas of Social Responsibilities

In spite of lot of criticism leveled against the legal profession, the profession has played and has to continue to play a great role in administration of justice. The lawyers are the only vital link in the administration of justice between the litigant and the judge. For a layman, the lawyer's functions are nothing more than advocacy and lawyering in the courtroom. But the society has great expectations from the legal professionals. They are expected to perform many functions beyond their bread and butter activities. The professionals are required to answer crying social problems and to synchronise their efforts and expectations of the society and perform the role of a planner and law reformer. Arthur T. Vanderbilt has stated five functions of great lawyers, namely : (i) counseling; (ii) advocacy; (iii) improving the profession, the courts and the law, (iv) leadership in moulding public opinion; and (v) public service. Keeping these in view, the authors would proceed to earmark the areas which call upon the legal profession of social responsibilities.

1. Crisis in Indian Legal System (1982).
2. 1988 (15) I BR 82 at 92.
3. V.K. Theru Venkatachari, Lawyer and Social Change (1972 (2) J.I.L.J. 114 at 115 and 93.
4. The Legal Profession in Independent India : A Sociological Overview, 1986 (13) I BR 377 at 403.

(A) Improvement in Law

Arthur D. Vanderbilt, the then Chief Justice of New Jersey State in United States of America has very rightly elaborated this duty to improve the profession, the court and the law. He has curtly stated that with the advancement of science and technology, the law as a social science may face great danger of being extinguished if it lags behind and does not awaken from lethargy. Hence, the need of the time is to adjust and synchronise the law with the changing needs of the society. The legal profession must set up adequate machinery for a continuous study and analysis of legislation and judicial pronouncements and it should make its views available to the legislatures as well as to the public at large. The legal profession should give a new orientation to the instruction of law and justice so that these function in response to the zeitgeist of time. The lawyer as a social thinker has to play a special role for the solidarity, unity, integrity and welfare of the society. The need of the hour for the legal professionals is to respond individually and collectively to the call for social responsibilities, to help in serious problems facing community, concerning law, lawyers and justice.

(B) Moulding Public Opinion

The other important function of a lawyer is to be alive to the social responsibilities and to mould public opinion. They are to act intelligently in moulding public opinion. The legal professionals did a praiseworthy role during the last days of British rule in India, when they became the first to imbibe the spirit of resistance to the foreign rule at the call of Mahatma Gandhi, who himself was a lawyer of undisputable eminence. The need of the hour for the legal profession is to come forward in remoulding our social system and help in achieving the goals enshrined in our Constitution which envisages the setting up of a secular, democratic, socialist system free from exploitation of any kind of any person. The so far unsatisfactory response of the legal profession to this arena is a big challenge to it.

(C) Public Service

Public service, to which every great lawyer must be prepared is next among the important functions of the lawyers, who bow before the altor of social responsibilities. Public service here connote answering the call for the service to society, *pro bono* service, as and when the call comes. The lawyers must be ready to respond to the duty of public service which has a vast area and includes understanding the problems of the society and extending co-operative participation in finding out their solutions. The socio-legal evils of the society will expect the members of the profession, learned in law, to respond to social responsibilities. Dowry deaths, bonded labour, undertrial prisoners, corruption in administration, exploitation of downtrodden sections of the society, oppression against women, violation of human rights etc. cannot be tackled by the State alone. The legal professionals should intelligently provide possible solution to these problems.

(D) Avoiding Law Delays

Justice delayed is justice denied, and on the other hand justice hurried is justice buried. Denial of justice to the masses of a certain section of people all the time hit at the very confidence of the people in the system of administration of justice. It breeds contempt for the whole system, law and the courts. The lawyers may perform a greater role in avoiding law delays, particularly those law delays which are avoidable and which if not avoided, will breed injustice to the people and to the society. Broadly speaking, 50% of the law delays can be averted without much difficulty and without bringing in any increase in the number of Judges. In 2012, there were 61,876 cases pending in the Supreme Court. According to the latest statistics available, there are 42,17,903 cases awaiting disposal in country's 21 High Courts. At subordinate level, the pendency stood at 2,79,53,070 cases. The main reason for this is the vacant posts of Judges, adjournments, delay in investigation, delay in service of summons etc. According to the latest data compiled by the Law Ministry, of the approved strength of 1044 Judges in the 24 High Courts, there are 443 vacancies. In other words, the High Courts are functioning with 601 Judges as on January 1, 2016.[1] With an approved strength of 31 Judges, the Supreme court has five vacancies.[2]

(E) Disputes Resolving

Disputes resolving refers to the non-formalistic, out of court settlements of disputes through negotiation, mediation and reconciliation. The 114th Report of the Law Commission of India has recommended structural and institutional reforms in the administration of justice system. The informal dispute resolution mechanisms outside the court system, namely Lok Adalats, Nyaya Panchayats, Tribunal Councils, Arbitration Councils, Special Tribunals, Professional Committees were certainly better and preferable in many cases. The lawyers can and should try to arrive at dispute resolution out of the court in a large number of cases and thus reduce the pressure on the already overburdened courts. The words of Abraham Lincoln addressed to lawyers need a specific mention here : "Discourage litigation, persuade your neighbours to compromise whenever you can. Point out to them how the nominal winner is often a real loser in fees, expenses and waste of time."

(F) Strengthening the Legal Profession

A large number of duties are cast upon the legal profession in the social responsibilities arena which tries to strengthen the legal profession itself for being better equipped to meet the expectations of the society and to continuously deserve high esteem and respect of the society. The need of the hour is provide legal education which inculcate the spirit of competence and responsibility. They should have the sense of belongingness to the profession. The newcomers or the beginners in the profession of law

---

1. PTI, High Courts need 443 Judges, S.C. 5 quoted by the Tribune, 19th January, 2016 at p. 10.
2. *Ibid.*

are the tiny plants of the future. A tender care and upbringing of the new entrants to the profession, therefore, becomes the responsibility of the legal profession.

(G) Legal Aid

The equal and even handed justice has been the cherished ideal of the administration of justice since the dawn of civilization. In the wake of changing socio-economic and political conditions in the modern world, the social scientists, jurists, scholars and politicians gave their thoughts to the philosophy of legal aid and they made the State responsible for eliminating social and economic wrongs, as also ensuring just and decent human living to the people at large. Providing free legal aid to the poor is one of the most essential duties and obligations of the lawyers to the society. Rule 46 of the Standard of Professional Conduct and Etiquettes ordains the legal profession to extend free legal aid to the poor. This is a mere directive and subject to the economic condition of the lawyer himself. Article 39-A of the Constitution of India has promised socio-economic quality by providing free legal services to the weaker sections of the community. It is clearly stated that socio-economic equality will become a living reality only if free legal services to the weaker sections of the community are guaranteed as a State responsibility. In spite of all the clear directives, somehow or other, the responsibility of free legal aid to the poor has not been discharged with any degree of satisfaction to the society by the legal profession and as well as to the underprivileged and disadvantages masses. There appears to be some inherent inertia and indifference within the legal profession. No doubt the society has also to contribute in achieving this goal, but it is also indisputable that the main initiative and thrust has to come from the legal profession itself. The need of the hour is that the lawyers should perform the duty more effectively in a collective manner.

VII. Sum Up

It may, therefore, be summed up that the challenge before the legal profession today is to resolve the basic paradoxes, which it faces, to adapt to the changing social values and revolutionary technology, to recognize itself in such a way as to provide more effective, real and affordable access to legal advice and representation by ordinary citizens, to preserve and where necessary, to defend the best of old rules requiring honesty, fidelity, loyalty, diligence, competence and dispassion in the service of clients and to adapt to the growth and changing composition of our society and of its legal profession. There is a need to mould the legal profession to the fast changing content and complexity of substantive and procedural law. Lawyers should not be averse to acknowledging that many changes which change to some extent the character and activities of the legal profession. Clinging to old dogmas, just because they are old, is not very rational, least of all in a profession, which boasts of being 'learned'. Thus, old dogmas have to give way. The lawyers in general cannot afford to run away from their social responsibilities. The social interest, the public interest, the interest of social justice, the interest of preservance of the fabric of our democratic republic and survival of free community, and last but not the least, the interest of the legal profession in its status of independence and monopoly, all in one voice, demand of responsible lawyers, the great lawyers to respond to the call towards social responsibilities. A rejection to this call will hit the legal profession the most, besides hitting considerably the other interests also. The path of social responsibilities is not bed of roses, it is a hazardous path. It is a path of sacrifice, service, devotion and dedication. The role of lawyers as social engineers and thinkers can come up as instruments of social change to meet the multi-dimensional challenges facing the country in particular and the globe in general. The lawyers are looked upon as protectors, preservers, saviours and ministers of justice aimed at the maintenance of a welfare society. It may, therefore, be concluded that 'Be good, see good, do good', is the oxygen, the lawyers have to breathe if they want to see the survival of the Rule of Law in our Democratic Republic.

12

CONTEMPT LAW AND PRACTICE

I. Background of Law of Contempt

Ever since the dawn of civilization, the Courts of justice have been surrounded by a halo of solemnity. Law Courts have, from time immemorial, been considered as sacred temples where justice is dispensed by their high priests, the Judges.[1] Most of the disputes were settled by the Courts on the basis of guidelines, given by the King. Still the King retained his right to hear any dispute himself. In this way, the decisions given by the Courts were the decisions of the King in law. If the Kings' authority could not be questioned, then authority of the courts could not be questioned, too. If the King could not be abused or scandalized, so also the Courts could not be abused or scandalized. Just as the proceedings before the King could not be prejudiced, or obstructed; similarly, the proceedings before the Court could not be prejudiced or obstructed. If anyone interfered in the administration of justice, he was liable to be punished. It is the genesis of the law of contempt of Courts. King's word was law. He could not be disobeyed. If a person was asked to stay, he had to stay. If he was asked to depart, he had to depart. Anyone, howsoever high he may be, could be punished for disobedience. The punishment had no limits. The condemned man could lose his property, liberty, limbs or even his life. Since the king had the right to punish, he also had the right to pardon. A sincere apology for any lapse, could save the man from the wrath of the King.[2]

The authority of the King travelled down to the superior Courts, their word was also final, in the ladder of various stages of litigation. No one could question the authority of the Courts. No one could humiliate the Courts or scandalize them. No one could prejudice or obstruct the course of justice. Anyone who did all this, was punished.[3] In ancient India, there was a developed judicial system. Maintenance of the sanctity of administration of justice was considered of prime importance. However, the existing law relating to contempt of court is based on the English law and, therefore, the study of the contempt law as prevalent in ancient times in

1. Tek Chand, The Law of Contempt of Court and of Legislature (1949), p. 1.
2. S.K. Mookerji, Iyer's Law of Contempt of Court, (1999), p. 19.
3. *Ibid.*, at p. 20.

India is not of much use.[1] In England from the earliest times of legal history, the courts have assumed the power to coerce all those persons who obstruct the administration of justice. It is revealed from the writings of the authors of later part of the twelfth century that on various occasions a party to a suit, who failed to appear before the Court, had been punished for contempt of the Court.

In India, the first attempt for comprehensive legislation of law relating to Contempt of Court, was made in 1926. The Contempt of Courts Act, 1926, introduced the salutary concept of limiting the punishment which was to be awarded in the cases of Contempt of Court. But this Act was not successful as the Act did not contain any provision for punishment with regard to contempt of Courts subordinate to the High Courts, that is, the Courts subordinate to Chief Court and the Judicial Commissioner's Court also. The Act was replaced by the Act of 1952. In both these Acts, the object was mentioned as, "An Act to define and limit the powers of certain Courts in punishing Contempts of Court." Similarly, the Contempt of Courts Act, 1952, could not prove to be a successful Act. While its provisions were capable of being retained but its scope required to be widened. On April 1st, 1960, a Bill was introduced in Lok Sabha by Bibhuti Bhushan Das Gupta to consolidate and amend the law relating to Contempt of Courts. On an examination of this Bill, the Government of India constituted a special committee to scrutinize the entire law of contempt. Shri H.N. Sanyal, the Additional Solicitor-General of India, was appointed the Chairman of the Special Committee on 29th July, 1961. The Committee scrunitized the existing law of contempt and submitted its report on 28th February, 1963. The Bill was thereafter referred to the Joint Select Committee of the Parliament, headed by Shri M.P. Bhargava, Member of Lok Sabha, which submitted its report on 20th February, 1970. Ultimately according to the report of Joint Selection Committee, the Contempt of Courts Act, 1971, was enacted by the Parliament. The Act extends to the whole of India, provided that it shall not apply to the State of Jammu and Kashmir, except to the extent to which the provisions of this Act relate to contempt of Supreme Court.

II. Contempt of Court—Its Meaning and Nature

The law of contempt is said to be of ancient origin and yet of fundamental contemporary importance.[2] Prior to the Contempt of Courts Act, 1971, there was no statutory definition of the concept, 'Contempt of Court'. Even the definition given in the Contempt of Courts Act, 1971, is not a definition in real sense, but only the classification or categories of contempt of Courts. The Sanyal Committee has also concluded in Chapter XII of its report that the concept of 'contempt of Court' cannot be defined except by enumerating the heads under which it may be classified—heads

1. In John Fox, The History of Contempt of Court, (1927) at p. 1, it is said that Contempt of Court has been recognised in English law from 12th century to the present time; also see Arlidge, Eady & Smith on Contempt (1999), p. 1.
2. Anirudh Prasad, Principles of The Ethics of Legal Profession in India, (2004), p. 107.

which can never be exhaustive. The Shawcross Committee as quoted in Sanyal Committee Report has also expressed the view that there is no authoritative definition of the concept, 'Contempt of Court'.

Oswald has observed,[1] "contempt in the legal acceptance of the term, primarily signifies disrespect to that which is entitled to legal regard; but as a wrong purely moral or affecting an object not possessing a legal status, it has in the eye of the law no existence." In his opinion contempt of Court may be said to be constituted by any conduct that tends to bring the authority and administration of law into disrespect or disregard or to interfere with or prejudices parties, litigation or their witnesses during the litigation.

According to *Corpus Juris Secondum*, the contempt of Court is disobedience to the Court by acting in opposition to the authority, justice and dignity thereof. It also signifies a wilful disregard or disobedience of the Court's order.

Halsbury has defined it as, "Any act done or writing published which is calculated to bring a Court or Judge into disrepute or to lower his authority or to interfere with the due course of justice or the lawful process of the Court is contempt of Court."

As per Section 2(a) of the Contempt of Courts Act, 1971, "Contempt of Court" means civil contempt or criminal contempt. Section 2(b) of the Act provides that 'civil contempt' means wilful disobedience to any judgment, decree, direction, order, writ or other process of a Court or wilful breach of an undertaking given to a Court. In **Algeria Municipal Board v. Ekka Tanga Mazdoor Union**,[2] the Supreme Court of India pointed out that civil contempt serves dual purpose of : (i) vindication of the public interest by punishment of contemptuous conduct; and (ii) coercion to compel the contemner to do what the Court requires of him.

In civil contempt two things are to be proved :

(i) There is disobedience of the order, decree, act of the Court of breach of undertaking given to the Court; and

(ii) The disobedience or breach is wilful. Thus there will be no civil contempt : (i) where disobedience or breach is not wilful, or (ii) the order the Court is passed without jurisdiction, or (iii) order passed by the Court is vague; or (iv) order is open to more than one reasonable interpretation; or (v) compliance of order is impossible; or (vi) alleged contemner has no knowledge of the order. A civil contempt proceeding may also be avoided by substantial compliance with the order of the Court.

Section 2(c) of the Act provides that 'criminal contempt' means the publication (whether by words, spoken or written or by signs or by visible representation or otherwise) of any matter or the doing of any other act whatsoever which :—

(i) scandalizes or tends to scandalize or lowers or tends to lower,

1. Oswald on Contempt of Court, 3rd ed., p. 1.
2. A.I.R. 1970 S.C. 1767.

the authority of, any Court; or

(ii) prejudices or interferes or tends to interfere with, the due course or any judicial proceeding; or

(iii) interferes or tends to interfere with or obstruct or tends to obstruct, the administration of justice in any other manner.

The above definition is not exhaustive but classifies the contempt into civil and criminal contempts. One of the major differences between the civil and criminal contempt is that in the former intention plays the vital role, whereas in the latter it plays no role. Thus, criminal contempt provides for strict liability. Hence, it is better to leave it to the Court to decide each case as it comes and the provisions of appeal will solve the defects in the application of contempt law.

The main forms of contempt of Courts are insult to Judges, attacks upon them, comment on pending proceedings with a tendency to prejudice fair trial, obstruction to officers of the Court, witnesses or the parties, abusing the process of the Court, breach of duty by officers connected with the Court and scandalizing the Judges or the Courts.

The contempt proceedings are always with reference to the administration of justice. In determining whether or not the act or omission complained amounts to contempt of Court, the test which is applied and should be applied whether in the circumstances, it is calculated to obstruct or interfere or tends to obstruct or interfere with the administration of justice. With this, the contempt of Court means "an act or omission which interferes or tends to interfere with the administration of justice" :

Provided that if the interference with the administration of justice is in the form of disobedience to the order of the Court or breach of undertaking given to the Court, it will amount to Contempt of Court only when the disobedience or breach is wilful.

Here, the 'administration of justice' includes all the functions of a Judge, whether administrative, adjudicatory or any other necessary for the administration of justice.

Interference with the function of any officer of the Court amounts to contempt of Court. Casting aspersions and attributing motives to the Judges amounts to contempt of Court. For example, abusing, assaulting or obstructing a process-server in the execution of his duties pursuant to the Court's order amounts to contempt of Court. Similarly, interference with the Receiver appointed by the Court, casting aspersions on counsel which tends to deter him from discharging his duties amounts to contempt of Court.

Interference with parties to a suit also amounts to interference with the administration of justice. Every person is entitled to the redress of his grievance through the Court and therefore any act which prevents or tends to prevent a party to obtain the remedy through Court amounts to interference with the administration of justice and consequently it can be taken as contempt of Court.

Interference with witnesses is also taken as contempt of Court as it amounts to interference with the administration of justice as the witnesses are integral part of the judicial process.

Abuse of process of Court is also considered a serious interference with the administration of justice and consequently it is taken as contempt of Court.

To constitute contempt, it is not necessary to find that there has been actual interference with the administration of justice. If the act complained of is calculated to or tends to cause such interference, it may be taken as contempt of Court.

Contempt of Courts Act, 1971 has not defined the word 'Court'.

'Court' must have three constituent parts :

(i) the plaintiff (the actor) who complains of an injury done;

(ii) the defendant (the reus) who is called upon to make satisfaction for it; and

(iii) the judicial power (judex) which is to examine the truth of fact and to determine the law arising upon that fact and if any injury appears to have been done, to ascertain and by its officers to apply, the remedy.

To constitute a Court, an authority or a body or tribunal must exercise the judicial power of the State to decide disputes in judicial manner and declare the rights of parties in a definite judgment which has finality and authoritativeness and must have this power from the State.

The Court as employed by the Contempt of Courts Act should consist of :

(1) The power entrusted to the authority must be judicial power of the State.
(2) The source of the power must emanate from the statute and must not be based merely on agreement between the parties.
(3) The manner of exercise of power must partake of essential attributes of Court.
(4) The decision of the authority must result in a binding decision between the parties.

The following are also Courts which come under Contempt of Court :

(i) Arbitrator appointed, by the Court under the Arbitration Act;

(ii) Election Tribunals constituted under the Representation of People Act, 1951;

(iii) Bar Council of India or of State and their Disciplinary Committee constituted under the Advocates Act, 1961.

Supreme Court and High Courts have inherent powers to punish for contempt of subordinate Courts under Articles 129 and 215 of the Constitution of India. However, the Commission of Inquiry constituted under the Commission of Inquiry Act is not Court. The word 'Court' cannot be interpreted to include all Tribunals. However, a Tribunal in which justice is judicially administered and which is empowered to arrive at an independent judicial decision on legal evidence is a Court.

The provisions of the Contempt of Courts Act, 1971, do not apply in relation to contempt of Nyaya Panchayat or other Village Courts, for the administration of justice established under the law as per Section 21 of the Act.

Object of Law of Contempt

The object of the contempt jurisdiction is to uphold the majesty and dignity of the courts. Action for contempt is not for the purpose of placing judges in a position of immunity from criticism but is aimed at protection of the freedom of individuals and the orderly and equal administration of laws.[1] The object of proceedings in contempt of court is to ensure proper administration of justice and to maintain the confidence of the public in the fair and impartial administration of justice by the Court of law. If anybody wrongly attacks the reputation of judicial system by falsely alleging that court has been unfair or partial in administration of justice, he pollutes the judicial system and has to be punished.

The object of the law of contempt is not to protect the prestige or position of a Presiding Officer of a Court, but to maintain the fair and impartial administration of justice. The object of the law is not to provide a cloak for judicial authorities to cover up their inefficiency and corruption, or to stifle criticism made in good faith against such officers.[2] Further, the law of contempt is intended to be a protection to the public whose interest would be very much affected, if by the act or the conduct of any party the authority of the court is lowered and the sense of confidence which people have in the administration of justice by it is weakened.[3]

It is a truism that the contempt law empowers the Judges to punish contempt to keep the course of justice free from any obstruction. A Court of justice without power to vindicate its own dignity, to enforce obedience to its mandates, to protect its officers or to shield those who are entrusted to its care, would be a deviation in course of administration of justice. Without such protection Courts of justice would soon lose their hold upon the public respect and maintenance of law and order would be rendered impossible. Hence, it is that the summary power of punishing the contempt has been given to the Court to ensure that public respect the orders and procedure of court. This would ensure an ordered life in society. The object of punishing contempt is not to safeguard or protect the dignity of the Judge or the Magistrate. Its serious concern is to preserve the authority of court to ensure an ordered life in society.

In a nutshell, the object of contempt law is to empower the court to punish contempt so as to prevent any interference with the due administration of justice. The interference with the administration of justice may be in the form of disobedience, of the Court's order or in the form of scandalising the Court or lowering the authority of the Court in the eyes of the public or interfering with the course of any judicial proceeding, etc.

1. *Omesh Saigal and Anr.* v. *R.K. Dalmia*, A.I.R. 1969 Del. 214.
2. *Ram Surat Singh* v. *Shiv Kumar Pandey*, A.I.R. 1971 All. 170.
3. *Brahm Prakash Sharma and Others* v. *The State of Uttar Pradesh*, A.I.R. 1954 S.C. 10.

The contempt power has been given to the Court for preventing any kind of such interference with the administration of justice. The contempt jurisdiction should be exercised only when there is real prejudice which can be regarded as substantial interference with the due course of justice.

III. Classification of Contempt of Courts as Civil and Criminal

(Kinds or Categories of Contempt of Courts)

Section 2(a) of the Contempt of Courts Act, 1971, provides that contempt of Courts means civil contempt or criminal contempt. The wilful disobedience to the order of Court is considered civil contempt, while the scandalizing or lowering the authority of the Court in the public eye is considered criminal contempt. The classification or categorization of contempt of Court into civil and criminal are not closed. There are several contempts which do not fall in any of them. For example, undue delay in pronouncing the order by a Judge or Judge coming late to the Court may amount to contempt of Court, but they are not covered exactly by the definition or classification of contempt in the Act.

(i) Civil Contempt

To reiterate, according to Section 2(b) of the Contempt of Courts Act, 1971, 'civil contempt' means "wilful disobedience to any judgment, decree, direction, order, writ or other process of a court or wilful breach of an undertaking given to a Court." The primary dimension of civil contempt is private right protection. It plays an important role within a legal system as it assists the enforcement of Court's orders. Civil contempt of Court provides the ultimate sanction against one who refuses to comply with the order of a properly constituted Court.

Civil contempt involves only the wilful disobedience of the Court's order or breach of undertaking given to the Court. The purpose of the proceeding for civil contempt is not only to punish the contemner but also to exercise enforcement and obedience to the order of the Court.

Civil contempt serves two purposes—

(i) vindication of the public interest by punishment of contemptuous conduct; and

(ii) coercion to compel the contemner to do what the Court requires of him.

To constitute 'civil contempt' the following are required to be proved :

(i) There is disobedience of the order, decree, etc. of the Court or breach of undertaking given to the Court; and

(ii) The disobedience or breach is wilful.

For civil contempt it is necessary that order which has been disobeyed must have been passed by the Court having jurisdiction to pass such order. If the order has been passed without jurisdiction, it is not binding on the party against which it has been passed and therefore, the disobedience of such order will not amount to contempt of Court. The burden to prove that the Court has no jurisdiction to pass the order lies on the person who alleges it.

When the Court orders a person to do something or not to do something, it is incumbent on that party to comply with that order forthwith. The person disobeying the order of the Court will alone be responsible for the consequence and he cannot be heard to say that he referred the matter to his higher officer.

The breach of undertaking given to the Court is also taken as contempt, if it is wilful. The basis for taking the breach of undertaking as contempt of Court is that the contemner by making a false representation to the Court obtains a benefit for himself and if he fails to honour the undertaking, he plays a serious fraud on the Court itself and thereby obstructs the course of justice and brings disrepute to the judicial institution. But the breach of undertaking recorded or forming part of compromise decree, would not amount to contempt of Court.

For civil contempt, the disobedience of the order, decree, etc. of the Court or breach of undertaking given to the Court must be wilful. Wilful means the action or state for which compulsion of ignorance or accident cannot be pleaded as excuse, intentional, deliberate, due to perversity or self-will. To establish that the disobedience is wilful, it is not necessary to show that it is contumacious in the sense that there is a direct intention to disobey the order, it is sufficient to show that effective administration of justice requires some penalty for disobedience to the order of the Court, if it is more than casual, accidental or unintentional.

The essence of the civil contempt is wilful disobedience to any judgment, decree, direction, order or writ of a Court, and not mere inaction to give effect to it. The conduct of the alleged contemner must be wilful showing deliberate and conscious disregard of the Court's order, or a despising or disdainful attitude towards the verdict of the Court.

If a party who has full knowledge of the order of the Court or is conscious and aware of the consequences and implications of the Court's order, ignores it or acts in violation of the Court's order, it must be held that disobedience is wilful. Whether the disobedience has been wilful or not is an issue to be decided by the Court, taking into account the facts, the circumstances of the case.

(ii) Criminal Contempt

Section 2(c) of the Contempt of Courts Act, 1971 explains criminal contempt. It says, "Criminal Contempt" means the publication (whether by words, spoken or written, or by signs, or by visible representations, or otherwise of any matter or the doing of any other act whatsoever which :—

(i) scandalizes or tends to scandalize, or lowers or tends to lower, the authority of any Court; or

(ii) prejudices, or interferes or tends to interfere with, the due course of any judicial proceeding; or

(iii) interferes or tends to interfere with, or obstructs, or tends to obstruct, the administration of justice in any other manner.

The essence of offence of criminal contempt lives in the tendency to interfere with the administration of justice. It may be done by publication or otherwise. Criminal contempt is a conduct directed against the power and dignity of Court. The definition of criminal contempt is wide enough to include any act of a person which would tend to interfere with the administration of justice or which would lower the authority of the Court.

To constitute the criminal contempt it is not necessary that the publication or other act should have actually resulted in scandalizing or lowering the authority of the Court but it is enough that the act is likely to result in scandalizing. Thus, the offence of contempt is complete by mere attempt and does not depend on actual deflection of justice.

'Scandalize' connotes to speak falsely or maliciously, to bring into reproach, dishonour, disgrace, to offend the feelings, conscience or propriety of an action. 'Scandalize' also means to offend moral feelings, and to make a public scandal of, to utter false or malicious reports of a person's conduct, slander, or to bring some discredit or to disgrace. Hence, the word 'scandalize' means the defamatory, derogatory, false, malicious, disgraceful statement regarding the persons as Judges.

It is for the Court to decide whether or not the publication or act is likely to scandalize or lower the authority of the Court or interfere with due course of any judicial proceedings or administration of justice.

The publication act will be taken as criminal contempt, if it has resulted in scandalizing the authority of Court or interference with the due course of judicial proceedings or interfering with the administration of justice in any matter.

The word 'publication' was given very wide meaning. The publication may be by words (written or spoken) by signs or by visible representations or otherwise of any matter. But, in the Act, it is not clear as to whether the publication would be taken to mean publication to the general public or any kind of publication.

Scandalizing the Court means any hostile criticism of the Judge; any personal attack on him, unconnected with the office he holds, is dealt with under the ordinary rules of slander and libel. The criticism can form the basis for committal of contempt of Court only if it is made against the Judge in the exercise of judicial function.

The publication which prejudices or interferes or tends to interfere with, the due course of any judicial proceeding is taken as contempt of Court. Whenever the publication or any other act unduly influences the result of a litigation, it is treated as criminal contempt of Court and is punished therefor. If the parties to a pending proceeding are abused and vilified and the words are likely to cause prejudice to the case, it will amount to contempt of Court.

The publication or doing of any other act which interferes or tends to interfere with or obstructs or tends to obstruct the administration of justice in any other manner is also taken as contempt of Court.

An advocate is an officer of the Court and hence undue interference with the advocate in the discharge of his professional functions amounts to contempt of Court.

Any conduct by which course of justice is prevented either by a party or a stranger is a contempt of Court. Any person who interferes or prevents other person from coming to the stream of justice is held liable for contempt of Court. The Court must be very careful in analyzing the facts and circumstances of the case for determining whether or not the action taken by a person amounts to interference with the course of justice.

Witnesses are also integral part of the judicial process and they must have freedom to perform their duties and so interference with the performance of their duties is taken as contempt of Court.

Abuse of the process of Court calculated to hamper the due course of a judicial proceedings or the administration of justice amounts to contempt of Court.

IV. Defences Available to the Contemner

(i) Defences in Criminal Contempt

Sections 3 to 7 of the Contempt of Courts Act, 1971 provide the following provisions for providing defences to the persons charged with criminal contempt :

(A) Innocent publication and distribution of matter not contempt (Sec. 3)

(1) A person shall not be guilty of contempt of Court on the ground that he has published (whether by words spoken or written, or by signs or by visible representation, or otherwise) any matter which interferes or tends to interfere with, or obstructs or tends to obstruct, the course of justice in connection with any civil or criminal proceedings pending at the time of publication, if at the time he had no reasonable grounds for believing that the proceeding was pending.

(2) Notwithstanding anything to the contrary contained in this Act or any other law for the time being in force, the publication of any such matter as is mentioned in sub-section (1) in connection with any civil or criminal proceeding which is not pending at the time of publication shall not be deemed to constitute contempt of Court.

(3) A person shall not be guilty of contempt of Court on the ground that he has distributed a publication containing any such matter as is mentioned in sub-section (1), if at the time of distribution he had no reasonable grounds for believing that it contained or was likely to contain any such matter as aforesaid :

Provided that this sub-section shall not apply in respect of the distribution of :—

(i) any publication which is a book or paper printed or published otherwise than in conformity with the rules contained in Section 3 of the Press and Registration of Books Act, 1867 (25 of 1867);

(ii) any publication which is a newspaper published otherwise than in conformity with the rules contained in Section 5 of the said

Act.

Explanation.—For the purposes of this section, a judicial proceedings :—

(a) is said to be pending—

(A) in the case of a civil proceedings, when it is instituted by the filing of a plaint or otherwise;

(B) in the case of a criminal proceeding under the Code of Criminal Procedure, 1898 (5 of 1898), or any other law—

(i) where it relates to the commission of an offence, when the charge-sheet or challan is filed or when the Court issues summons or warrant, as the case may be, against the accused, and

(ii) in any other case, when the Court takes cognizance of the matter to which the proceedings relates, and in the case of a civil or criminal proceeding, shall be deemed to continue to be pending until it is heard and finally decided, that is to say, in a case where an appeal or revision is competent, until the appeal or revision is heard and finally decided or, where no appeal or revision is preferred, until the period of limitation prescribed for such appeal or revision has expired;

(iii) which has been heard and finally decided shall not be deemed to be pending merely by reason of the fact that proceedings for the execution of the decree order or sentence passed therein are pending.

(B) Fair and accurate report of judicial proceeding not contempt (Sec. 4)

Subject to the provisions contained in Section 7, a person shall not be guilty of contempt of Court for publishing a fair and accurate report of a judicial proceeding at any stage thereof.

(C) Fair criticism of judicial act not contempt (Sec. 5)

A person shall not be guilty of contempt of Court for publishing any fair comment on the merits of any case which has been heard and finally decided.

Section 5 of the Contempt of Courts Act, 1971 makes fair comment a good defence provided the comment is on the merits of the case and the case has been heard and finally decided. In order that a comment may be fair, the following conditions must be satisfied :

(1) It must be based on facts truly stated. No comment is fair if it is based on a mistake of facts.

(2) It must not contain imputation of corrupt or dishonourable motives on the person whose conduct or work is criticised, save in so far as, such imputations are warranted by the facts.

(3) It must be honest expression of the writer's real opinion.

(D) Bona fide complaint against Presiding Officers of Subordinate Courts not contempt (Sec. 6)

A person shall not be guilty of contempt in respect of any statement made by him in good faith concerning the Presiding Officer of any Subordinate Court to :—

(a) any other Subordinate Court; or

(b) the High Court, to which it is subordinate.

Explanation.—In this section, 'Subordinate Court' means the Court subordinate to a High Court.

Under Section 6 of the Contempt of Courts Act, 1971, it is open to a litigant, if not satisfied by the orders of the subordinate court to submit a petition to the High Court. However, it is submitted that the courts or the authorities to whom complaints are made have to be very careful in entertaining such complaints. Most of the complaints are made by disgruntled lawyers on litigants or politicians with oblique purposes and to embarrass their opponents. The real problem before the court is in discovering whether such letters or petitions are bonafide criticism and made in good faith.[1]

(E) Publication of information relating to proceedings in Chambers or 'in Camera' not contempt except in certain cases (Sec. 7)

(1) Notwithstanding anything contained in this Act, a person shall not be guilty of contempt of Court for publishing a fair and accurate report of a judicial proceedings before any Court sitting in Chambers or 'in camera' except in the following cases, that is to say :—

(a) where the publication is contrary to the provisions of any enactment for the time being in force;

(b) where the Court on grounds of public policy or in exercise of any power vested in it, expressly prohibits the publication of all information relating to the proceeding or of information of the description which is published;

(b) where the Court sits in chambers or 'in camera' for reasons connected with public order or the security of the State, the publication of information relating to those proceedings;

(d) where the information relates to a secret process, discovery or invention which is an issue in the proceedings.

(2) Without prejudice to the provisions contained in sub-section (1) a person shall not be guilty of contempt of Court for publishing the text or a fair and accurate summary of the whole, or any part, or an order made by a Court sitting in chamber or 'in camera' unless the Court had expressly prohibited the publication thereof on grounds of public policy, or for reasons connected with public order or the security of the State, or on ground that it contains information relating to a secret process, discovery or invention, or in exercise of any power vested in it.

1. *B.K. Mishra* v. *Registrar, Orissa High Court*, A.I.R. 1974 S.C. 710.

(F) Contempts not publishable in certain cases (Sec. 13)

Notwithstanding anything contained in any law for the time being in force, no Court shall impose a sentence under this Act for a contempt of court unless it is satisfied that the contempt is of such a nature that it substantially interferes, or tends substantially to interfere with the due course of justice.

The contempt jurisdiction is a special jurisdiction and, therefore, it has to be exercised in the exceptional cases. To initiate the contempt proceedings, it is not sufficient that there is a technical contempt of courts. Even though the person has technically committed contempt, the Court should not punish the contemner, unless there is a substantial interference with the due course of justice. Section 13 of the Act is based on the principle that the law does not take account of trivialities. If the publication or other act is merely a defamatory attack on the Judge and is not calculated to interfere with the due administration of justice, it will not be taken as contempt of Court but the Judge can claim under the ordinary remedies for defamation.

In order to constitute criminal contempt, it is not necessary that there should be an actual interference with the administration of justice, but it is sufficient if the publication or act complained of is likely to interfere with the administration of justice. The offence of contempt is taken as complete by the attempt and does not depend on actual deflection of justice and purity of the motive of the contemner.

(ii) Defences in Civil Contempt

The following are the valuable defences available to a contemner in civil contempt.

(A) Disobedience or breach was not wilful

For civil contempt the disobedience of the order, decree, etc. of the Court or breach of undertaking given to the Court must be wilful. Hence, it would be a defence in the contempt proceedings that the disobedience or breach has not been wilful.

(B) The order has been passed without jurisdiction

If the order disobeyed is proved to have been passed by the Court without jurisdiction or the undertaking violated is proved to have been given in a proceeding which was without jurisdiction, the disobedience or violation would not amount to contempt of Court. Actually order passed without jurisdiction is void and a void order binds nobody.

The jurisdiction of the Court may be taken to mean the authority which a Court has to decide matters that are litigated before it or to take cognizance of matter represented in a formal way for its decision. The limit of the authority is imposed by the Statute, charter or commission under which the Court is constituted. If no restriction or limit is imposed, the jurisdiction is said to be unlimited.

The decree or order passed by the Court will be a nullity if it has no jurisdiction with the subject-matter of the proceedings or if the organization of the Court is illegal.

(C) Order disobeyed is vague or ambiguous

Vague and ambiguous orders are the defence in the contempt orders which are not specific and complete are considered as vague orders. In a contempt proceedings, a person may take the plea that the terms of the order of injunction are ambiguous. If the direction in the order of the Court depends on certain other facts and such facts are left undefined by the order, the order will be taken as ambiguous order and its violation will not amount to the contempt of Court.

(D) No knowledge of order

A person cannot be held guilty of contempt in infringing an order of the Court of which he knows nothing. Where an order of status quo is passed by the Court but the party continues to work prior to receiving the order and also he has no actual knowledge of the order, he will not be liable for contempt of Court.

(E) Compliance with the order is impossible

In civil contempt of Court, it would be a valid defence to say that compliance with order of the Court was impossible. Actually impossibility plea is tested on a case by case basis and if it is found that the implementation of the order was not practically possible and it is proved by the contemner, it is allowed as a defence.

(F) Order involves more than one reasonable interpretation

If the court's order involves more than one reasonable and rational interpretation and the respondent adopts one of them and acts accordingly, he cannot be held liable for contempt of Court. If there is no doubt and a doubt is sought to be created, his defence will not be allowed.

(G) Other defences not affected (Sec. 8)

Nothing contained in this Act shall be construed as implying that any defence which would have been a valid defence in any proceedings for contempt of Court has ceased to be available merely by reason of the provisions of this Act.

(H) Act not to imply enlargement of scope of contempt (Sec. 9)

Nothing contained in this Act shall be construed as implying that any disobedience, breach, publication or other act is punishable as contempt of Court which would not be so punishable apart from this Act.

V. Contempt Jurisdiction of the High Court and the Supreme Court

The contempt law in India has been developed mainly on the basis of English contempt law. In England a superior Court of Record has been exercising the power to indict a person for its contempt in a summary manner. This power is taken as a necessary attribute of a superior Court of Record. In India also, this practice has been followed. It is now settled that the Constitution of india declares the Supreme Court in Article 129 and High Court in Article 215 as the Courts of Record and that they have all the powers including the power to punish for contempt of themselves.

A Court of Record has been defined in *Corpus Juris Secondum* as a Court, where the acts and judicial proceedings are enrolled in parchment for a perpetual memorial and testimony, and which has power to fine and imprison for contempt of its authority; a Court which is bound to keep a record of its proceedings are enrolled in parchment for a perpetual memorial or testimony, which rolls are called records of the Court, and are of such high and super imminent authority that their truth is not to be called in question; a judicial organized tribunal having attributes and exercising function independently of the person of the Magistrate designated generally to hold it and proceeding according to the course of common law; and a Court having a seal.

Thus, the Supreme Court and High Court as Courts of Record have inherent power to punish for contempt. Even in U.S.A., a Court of Record has inherent power to punish for the contempt of Court.

In addition that, the Contempt of Courts Act, 1971 provides the contempt jurisdiction of High Court and the Supreme Court.

According to Section 11 of the Act, a High Court shall have jurisdiction to inquire into or try a contempt of itself or of any Court subordinate to it, whether the contempt is alleged to have been committed within or outside the local limits of its jurisdiction, and whether the person alleged to be guilty of contempt is within or outside such limits.

The proviso to Section states that no High Court shall take cognizance of a contempt alleged to have been committed in respect of a Court subordinate to it where such contempt is an offence punishable under the Indian Penal Code, 1860. This proviso excludes the jurisdiction of the High Court only when the acts come under the Indian Penal Code, 1860. According to Section 10, every High Court shall have and exercise the same jurisdiction, powers and authority in accordance with the same procedure and practice, in respect of contempts of Courts subordinate to it as it has and exercise in respect of contempts of itself.

According to Section 14, when it is alleged, or appears to the Supreme Court or the High Court upon its own view, that a person has been guilty of contempt committed in its presence or hearing the Court may cause such person to be punished.

Appellate Jurisdiction (Sec. 9)

An appeal shall lie as of right from any order or decision of High Court in the exercise of its jurisdiction to punish for contempt :—

(a) where the order or decision is that of a single Judge, to a Bench of not less than two Judges of the Court;

(b) where the order or decision is that of a Bench, to the Supreme Court.

Powers of Supreme Court and High Court to make rules

According to Section 23 of the Act, the Supreme Court, as the case may be, any High Court, may make rules, not inconsistent with the provisions of this Act, providing for any matter relating to its procedure.

The question whether a Judge of a Supreme Court or a High Court can be held liable for committing contempt of Court by same undignified act or conduct, has not yet been authoritatively settled. But preponderance of judicial opinion appears to favour the exclusion of superior Courts judges from the contempt of Court liability. **Harish Chandra Mishra v. The Hon'ble Mr. Justice S. Ali Ahmed,**[1] is a leading case on this point. This case was heard by the Full Bench consisting of five judges. In this case, three advocates of Patna High Court filed an application alleging that a judge of that Court had committed contempt of Court by making insulting and uncharitable remarks on advocate Dr. Sadananda Jha while hearing a civil revision application for admission. The majority (4 : 1) held that the Judge of the Supreme Court and High Court are not subject to contempt of Court proceeding. However, Birendra Prasad Sinha, J. did not agree with the proposition that the Judges of the High Court and the Supreme Court are immune from the contempt of Court's proceeding. On the other hand, P.S. Sahay, J. differed from majority view on the issue of impeachment. He said that impeachment of a Judge is an extreme step to be resorted to only in extraordinary situation and it will not be for the purpose of punishing a Judge for committing contempt of his own Court.

VI. Summary Procedure in Contempt Proceedings

The summary procedure has very ancient origin. The instances of the exercise of the contempt power following the summary procedure are found even in the 13th century. Thus, the common law Courts did have powers to deal summarily with contempt committed in their presence. However, in the early days a distinction was made between the acts in and out of presence of the Judges. The summary procedure was adopted in case of the contempts committed in the presence of the Court and not in case of the contempts committed outside the Court except the contempts by the officers of the Court. In India also the Courts of record can deal summarily with all types of contempts.

The contempt proceedings are neither civil proceedings nor criminal proceedings. They are *sui generis.* The power of the Supreme Court and of the High Court to institute proceedings for contempt and punish therefor is a special jurisdiction which is inherent in all Courts of Records. The power of the Court of Record under Article 215 of the Indian Constitution is not limited to imposing punishment upon the contemner but the main purpose of this power of the Court is to see that the order of the Court is given effect to. Contempt proceedings are not criminal proceedings, but are summary proceedings and the Court can evolve its own procedure.

(i) Procedure where contempt is in the face of the Supreme Court or a High Court (Sec. 14)

(1) When it is alleged, or appears to the Supreme Court or the High Court upon its own view, that a person has been guilty of contempt

1. A.I.R. 1986 Pat. 65.

committed in its presence or hearing, the Court may cause such person to be detained in custody, and, at the time before the rising of the Court, on the same day, or as early as possible thereafter, shall :—

(a) cause him to be informed in writing of the contempt with which he is charged;

(b) afford him an opportunity to make his defence to the charge;

(c) after taking such evidence as may be necessary or as may be offered by such person and after hearing him, proceed, either forthwith or after adjournment, to determine the matter of the charge; and

(d) make such order for the punishment or discharge of such person as may be just.

(2) Notwithstanding anything contained in sub-section (1), where a person charged with contempt under that sub-section applies, whether orally or in writing, to have the charge against him tried by some Judges other than the Judge or Judges in whose presence or hearing the offence is alleged to have been committed and the Court is of opinion that it is practicable to do so and that in the interests of proper administration of justice the application should be allowed, it shall cause the matter to be placed, together with a statement of the facts of the case, before the Chief Justice for such directions as he may think fit to issue as respects of trial thereof.

(3) Notwithstanding anything contained in any other law, in any trial of a person charged with contempt under sub-section (1) which is held, in pursuance of a direction given under sub-section (2), by a Judge other than the Judge or Judges in whose presence or hearing the offence is alleged to have been committed, it shall not be necessary for the Judge or Judges in whose presence or hearing the offence is alleged to have been committed to appear as a witness and that statement placed before the Chief Justice under sub-section (2) shall be treated as evidence in the case.

(4) Pending the determination of the charge, the Court may direct that a person charged with contempt under this section shall be detained in such custody as it may specify :

Provided that he shall be released on bail, if a bond for such sum of money as the Court thinks sufficient is executed with or without sureties on condition that the person charged shall attend at the time and place mentioned in the bond and shall continue to so attend until otherwise directed by the Court :

Provided further that the Court may, if it thinks fit, instead of taking bail from such person, discharge him on his executing a bond without sureties for his attendance as aforesaid.

(ii) Cognizance of criminal contempt in other cases (Sec. 15)

(1) In the case of a criminal contempt, other than a contempt referred to in Section 14, the Supreme Court or the High Court may take action on its own motion or on a motion made by :—

(a) the Advocate-General, or

(b) any other person, with the consent in writing of the Advocate-General, or

(c) in relation to the High Court for the Union Territory of Delhi, such Law Officers as the Central Government may, by notification in the Official Gazette, specify in this behalf, or any other person, with the consent in writing of such Law Officer.

(2) In the case of any criminal contempt of a subordinate Court, the High Court may take action on a reference made to it by the subordinate Court or on a motion made by the Advocate-General or, in relation to a Union Territory, by such Law Officer as the Central Government may, by notification in the Official Gazette, specify in this behalf.

(3) Every motion or reference made under this section shall specify the contempt of which the person charged is alleged to be guilty.

Explanation.—In this section, the expression 'Advocate-General' means :—

(a) in relation to the Supreme Court, the Attorney-General or the Solicitor-General;

(b) in relation to the High Court, the Advocate-General of the State or any of the States for which the Court has been established;

(c) in relation to the Court of a Judicial Commissioner, such Law Officer as the Central Government may, by notification in the Official Gazette, specify in this behalf.

(iii) Contempt by Judge, Magistrate or other person acting judicially : (Sec. 16)

(1) Subject to the provisions of any law for the time being in force, a Judge, Magistrate or other person acting judicially shall also be liable for contempt of his own Court or of any other Court in the same manner as any other individual is liable and the provisions of this Act shall so far as may be, apply accordingly.

(2) Nothing in this section shall apply to any observations or remarks made by a Judge, Magistrate or other person acting judicially, regarding a subordinate Court in an appeal or revision pending before such Judge, Magistrate or other person against the order or judgment of the subordinate Court.

The Judge or Presiding Officer of a Court is only a part of the Court. Like any other person it is his duty too to maintain the dignity and decorum of the Court. He too should do nothing which may obstruct or interfere with the administration of justice. If he does so, he is liable to contempt of Court. For the purpose of the contempt of court by Judges a clear distinction is drawn between Judges, that is, presiding officers of the subordinate or inferior Courts and Justices, i.e., Hon'ble Justices of the Supreme Courts like the Supreme Court and the High Courts of the States. The former commit contempt of their own courts as well as superior Courts. But the latter do not commit contempt of Court.

In **re Abdul**,[1] acceptance of illegal gratification by a Judge or Magistrate was held to be contempt of Court. In **State v. P.C. Mall**,[2] a Magistrate was held guilty of the contempt of his own Court for delivering a reserved judgment after eight months without any reasonable cause. A Judge has to maintain dignity and decorum of the Court and if his act amounts to interference in administration of justice he may be guilty of contempt of his own Court. In **Bar Association, Moradabad v. Kothari S.D.M.**,[3] it was held by the High Court that the order of a Judge to leave the Court given to a counsel without any reason would amount to contempt of Court by the Magistrate of his own Court.

The subordinate Court judges may commit contempt of superior Courts in a number of ways, for example, by wilfully disobeying the order of the superior court or disobeying the law laid down by the superior Court or by labelling scurrilous allegations against the superior Courts.

(iv) Procedure after Cognizance (Sec. 17)

(1) Notice of every proceeding under Section 15 shall be served personally on the person charged unless the Court for reasons to be recorded directs otherwise.

(2) The notice shall be accompanied :—

(a) in the case of proceedings commenced on a motion, by a copy of motion as also copies of the affidavits, if any, on which such motion is founded; and

(b) in the case of proceedings commenced on a reference by a subordinate Court, by a copy of the reference.

(3) The Court may, if it is satisfied that a person charged under Section 15 is likely to abscond or keep out of the way to avoid service of the notice, order the attachment of his property of such value or amount as it may deem reasonable.

(4) Every attachment under sub-section (3) shall be effected in the manner provided in the Code of Civil Procedure, 1908 (5 of 1908), for the attachment of property in execution of a decree for payment of money, and if, after such attachment, the person charged appears and shows to the satisfaction of the Court that he did not abscond or keep out of the way to avoid service of the notice, the Court shall order the release of his property from attachment upon such terms as to costs or otherwise as it may think fit.

(5) Any person charged with contempt under Section 15 may file an affidavit in support of his defence, and the Court may determine the matter of the charge either on the affidavits filed or after taking such further evidence as may be necessary, and pass such order as the justice of the case requires.

---

1. 8 W.R. Cr. 32.
2. (1973) 39 Cut. L.R. 358.
3. 1966 All WRCHC 197.

(v) Hearing of cases of criminal contempt to be by Benches (Sec. 18)

(1) Every case of criminal contempt under Section 15 shall be heard and determined by a Bench of not less than two judges.

(2) Sub-section (1) shall not apply to the Court of a Judicial Commissioner.

VII. Rules to Regulate Proceedings for Contempt of the Supreme Court

In exercise of the powers under Section 23 of the Contempt of Courts Act, 1971, the Supreme Court made with the approval of the President, "The Rules to Regulate Proceedings for Contempt of the Supreme Court, 1975."

Rule 2.—(1) Where contempt is committed in view or presence or hearing of the Court, the contemner may be punished by the Court before which it is committed either forthwith or on such date as may be appointed by the Court in that behalf.

(2) Pending the determination of the charge, the Court may direct that the contemner shall be determined in such custody as it may specify :

Provided that the contemner may be released on bail on such terms as the Court may direct.

Rule 3.—In case of contempt other than the contempt referred to in Rule 2, the Court may take action :—

(a) *suo motu*; or

(b) on a petition made by Attorney-General, or Solicitor-General, or

(c) on a petition made by any person, and in the case of a criminal contempt with the consent in writing of the Attorney-General or the Solicitor-General.

Rule 4.—Every petition under Rule 3(b) or (c) shall contain :

(i) the name, description and place of residence of the petitioner or petitioners and of the person charged;

(ii) nature of the contempt alleged and such material facts, including the date or dates of commission of the alleged contempt, as may be necessary for the proper determination of the case;

(iii) if a petition has previously been made by him on the same facts, the petitioner shall give the details of the petition previously made and shall also indicate the result thereof.

(b) The petition shall be supported by an affidavit.

(c) Where the petitioner relies upon a document or documents in his possession or power, he shall file such document or documents or true copies thereof with the petition.

(d) No Court-fee shall be payable on the petition and on any documents filed in the proceedings.

Rule 5.—Every petition under Rule 3(b) and (c) shall be posted before the Court for preliminary hearing and for orders as to issue of notice. Upon such hearing the Court, if satisfied that no prima facie case has been made out for issue of notice, may dismiss the petition, and, if not so satisfied, direct that notice of the petition be issued to the contemner.

Rule 6.—(1) Notice to the person charged shall be in Form I. The person charged shall, unless otherwise ordered, appear in person before the Court as directed on the date fixed for hearing of the proceeding and shall continue to remain present during hearing till the proceeding is finally disposed of by order of the Court.

(2) When action is instituted on a petition, a copy of the petition along with the annexures and affidavits shall be served upon the person charged.

Rule 7.—The person charged may file his reply duly supported by an affidavit or affidavits.

Rule 8.—No further affidavit or document shall be filed except with the leave of the Court.

Rule 9.—Unless otherwise ordered by the Court, seven copies of the paper book shall be prepared in the Registry, one for the petitioner, one for the opposite party and the remaining for the use of the Court. The Paper Book in the case shall be prepared at the expense of the Central Government and shall consist of the following documents :

(i) Petition and affidavit filed by the petitioner;

(ii) A copy of, or a statement relating to, the objectionable matter constituting the alleged contempt;

(iii) Reply and affidavits of the opposite party;

(iv) Documents filed by the parties;

(v) Any other documents which the Registrar may deem fit to include.

Rule 10.—The Court may direct the Attorney-General or Solicitor-General to appear and assist the Court.

Rule 11.—(1) The Court may, if it has reason to believe, that the person charged is absconding or is otherwise evading service of notice, or if he fails to appear in person or to continue to remain present in person in presence of the notice, direct a warrant bailable or non-bailable for his arrest, addressed to one or more police officers or may order attachment of property. The warrant shall be issued under the signature of the Registrar. The warrant shall be in Form II and shall be executed, as far as may be in the manner provided for execution of warrants under the Code of Criminal Procedure.

(2) The warrant shall be executed by the officer or officers to whom it is directed, and may also be executed by any other police officer whose name is endorsed upon the warrant by the officer to whom it is directed or endorsed.

(3) Where a warrant is to be executed outside the Union Territory of Delhi, the Court may instead of directing such warrant to police officer

forward it to the Magistrate of the District or the Superintendent of Police Commissioner of Police of the District within which the person charged is believed to be residing. The Magistrate or the police officer to whom the warrant is forwarded shall endorse his name thereon, and cause it to be executed.

(4) Every person who is arrested and detained shall be produced before the nearest magistrate within a period of twenty-four hours of such arrest excluding the time necessary for the journey from the place of arrest to the Court of the Magistrate, and no such person shall be detained in custody beyond the said period without the authority of a Magistrate.

Rule 12.—The Court may, either *suo motu* or on motion made for that purpose, order the attendance for cross-examination, of a person whose affidavit has been filed in the matter.

Rule 13.—The Court may make orders for the purpose of securing the attendance of any person to be examined as a witness and for discovery or production of any document.

Rule 14.—The Court may pass such orders as it thinks fit including orders as to costs which may be recovered as if the order were a decree of the Court.

Rule 15.—Save as otherwise provided by the Rules contained herein the provisions of the Supreme Court Rules, 1966, shall, so far as may be, apply to proceedings in relation to proceedings in contempt under this Part.

Rule 16.—Where a person charged with contempt is adjudged guilty and is sentenced to suffer imprisonment, a warrant of commitment and detention shall be made out in Form IV under the signature of the Registrar. Every such warrant shall remain in force until it is cancelled by order of the Court or until it is executed. The Superintendent of the Jail shall in pursuance of the order receive the person so adjudged and detain him in custody for the period specified therein, or until further orders.

VIII. Punishment for Contempt of Court

According to Section 12 of the Contempt of Courts Act, 1971, the following are the punishments for the contempt of Court :

> (1) Save as otherwise expressly provided in this Act or in any other law, a contempt of Court may be punished with simple imprisonment for a term which may extend to six months, or with fine which may extend to two thousand rupees or with both :
>
> Provided that the accused may be discharged or the punishment awarded may be remitted on apology being made to the satisfaction of the Court.
>
> *Explanation.*—An apology shall not be rejected merely on the ground that it is qualified or conditional if the accused makes it bona fide.
>
> (2) Notwithstanding anything contained in any law for the time being in force, no Court shall impose a sentence in excess of that

specified in sub-section (1) for the contempt either in respect of itself or of a Court subordinate to it.

(3) Notwithstanding anything contained in this section, where a person is found guilty of a civil contempt, the Court, if it considers that a fine will not meet the ends of justice and that a sentence of imprisonment is necessary shall, instead of sentencing him to simple imprisonment, direct that he be detained in a civil prison for such period not exceeding six months as it may think fit.

(4) Where the person found guilty of contempt of Court in respect of any undertaking given to a Court is a company, every person who, at the time the contempt was committed was in charge of, and was responsible to, the company for the conduct of the business of the company, as well as the company, shall be deemed to be guilty of the contempt and the punishment may be enforced, with the leave of the Court, by the detention in civil prison of each such person :

Provided that nothing contained in this sub-section shall render any such person liable to such punishment, if he proves that the contempt was committed without his knowledge or that he exercised all due diligence to prevent its commission.

(5) Notwithstanding anything contained in sub-section (4), where the contempt of Court referred to therein has been committed by a company and it is proved that the contempt has been committed with the consent or connivance of, or if attributable to any neglect on the part of, any director, manager, secretary or other officer of the company, such director, manager, secretary or other officer shall also be deemed to be guilty of the contempt and the punishment may be enforced, with the leave of the Court, by the detention in civil prison of such director, manager, secretary or other officer.

Explanation.—For the purpose of sub-sections (4) and (5) :—

(a) *'Company'* means any body corporate and includes a firm or other association of individuals; and

(b) *'Director'*, in relation to a firm, means a partner in the firm.

Contempt not punishable in certain cases

According to Section 13 of the Contempt of Courts Act, 1971, notwithstanding anything contained in any law for the time being in force, no Court shall impose a sentence under this Act for a contempt of Court unless it is satisfied that the contempt is of such a nature that it substantially interferes, or tends substantially to interfere with the due course of justice.

Limitation for action for contempt

Section 20 lays down that no Court shall initiate any proceedings for contempt either on its own motion or otherwise, after the expiry of a period of one year from the date on which the contempt is alleged to have been committed. However, there was no provision like Section 20 in the old

Contempts of Courts Act. Even the Sanyal Committee did not recommend that any period of limitation should be provided in the Statute. It was by the Joint Select Committee of Parliament on Contempt of Court (Bhargava Committee) that a period of limitation has been included in the Act. In **Om Prakash Jaiswal v. D.K. Mittal,**[1] the Supreme Court of India asserted that Section 5 of Limitation Act does not apply to contempt proceedings and therefore any type of lapse or delay is not condonable.

IX. Remedies Against the Punishment for the Contempt of Court

It is noteworthy that according to Section 12 of the Contempt of Courts Act, 1971, in case of civil contempt, the sentence of fine alone may be imposed on the contemner. But where only imposing of fine does not meet the ends of justice, a sentence of imprisonment may be necessary by detaining the contemner in a civil prison for a period not exceeding six months. The civil contempt is considered less serious than the criminal contempt. Consequently in the case of civil contempt the general rule is to impose a fine and imprisonment is an exception.

The remedies available to the contemner against the punishment are as follows :

(i) Apology

According to provision under Section 12(1) of the Contempt of Courts Act, 1971, the accused may be discharged or the punishment awarded may be remitted on apology being made to the satisfaction of the Court. The Court is not bound to accept the apology, unless there is real feeling of repentance in the contemner. The contemner cannot be allowed to get away by simply feeling sorry by way of apology as the easiest way. The apology should not be tendered with the object to avoid punishment, but it should be sincere and made in good faith with the real feeling of repentance.

Acceptance of apology depends on factors like attitude of the contemner, gravity of contumacious conduct, his past record, etc. Generally, apology is not accepted from those who are found to have indulged in repeated disobedience or from those who persist in justifying the action rather than express the genuine regret or from those who do not have real feeling of repentance and blame the circumstances which led to the contempt.

The Court, when it considers that the apology tendered in the Court is not sufficient, may say that the apology will be accepted only when it is made to the Court before the public.

The Explanation to sub-section (1) of Section 12 of the Act makes it clear that an apology shall not be rejected merely on the ground that it is qualified or conditional, if the accused makes it bona fide.

While reading the proviso and explanation of Section 12 of Contempt of Courts Act, 1971 certain conclusions emerge. Firstly, the apology may be qualified or conditional; Secondly, the apology has to be made to the

1. A.I.R. 2000 S.C. 1136.

satisfaction of the Court; Thirdly, the apology should not be tendered with the object to avoid punishment, but it should be sincere and made in good faith with real feeling of repentance. Hence, apology must be bona fide, and lastly, the effect of apology may be discharge of guilt or remittance of punishment.

In **Pritam Pal v. High Court of M.P.**,[1] the Supreme Court observed that to punish an advocate for contempt of Court, no doubt must be regarded as an extreme measure, but to preserve the proceedings of the Courts from being deflected or interfered with, and to keep the streams of justice pure, serene and undefiled it becomes the duty of the Court, though painful, to punish the contemner in order to preserve its dignity.

In **M.B. Sanghi v. High Court of Punjab and Haryana**,[2] the practicing lawyer had made disparaging and derogatory remarks against the Judge. The contempt proceedings had been initiated against the said lawyer not for the first time but on an earlier occasion too in which he had been discharged on tendering unconditional apology before the High Court. In earlier proceeding also the charge against him was to have made disparaging remarks against the Judge. This time High Court was of the view that the appellant could not be allowed to get away by simply feeling sorry by way of apology as the easiest way and was sentenced to Rs. 1000/- as fine and in case of default in payment of fine, to undergo simple imprisonment for seven days. The Supreme Court agreed with the High Court and said taking into consideration the facts and circumstances of the case and the fact that the appellant, a fairly senior advocate, is prone to use disparaging and contemptuous remarks against Judges, this is not a case in which the apology tendered by the appellant may be accepted. The Supreme Court observed that it is well settled that an apology is not a weapon of defence to purge the guilty of his offence, nor it is intended to operate as an universal panacea, but it is intended to be evidence of real contriteness.

In **re Nand Lal Balwani**, the Supreme Court held that the advocate shouted slogans in open Court and hurled his shoe towards Court. His action intimidated the Court and caused interference with judicial proceedings. The advocate was found guilty of gross criminal contempt. The Court held that law does not give a lawyer, unsatisfied with the result of the litigation, licence to permit himself the liberty of causing disrespect to the Court or attempting, in any manner to lower the dignity of the Court. A lawyer does not enjoy any special immunity under the Contempt of Courts Act, where he is found to have committed a gross contempt of Court. The Courts cannot be intimidated to seek favourable orders. The action of the contemner advocate in the instant case is most reprehensible and has the tendency to interfere with the administration of justice and undermine the dignity of the Court and the majesty of law. The contemner advocate has tendered unqualified apology but the same cannot be accepted as it does not appear to be at all bona fide and genuine in view of his attitude

1. A.I.R. 1992 S.C. 904.
2. A.I.R. 1991 S.C. 1834.

exhibited in the Court during his questioning and seems to have been made only to escape punishment. Keeping in view the seriousness of the offence committed by the contemner, deterrent punishment is imposed on him so that it serves as an example to others and no one indulges in repetition of such acts. The Court sentenced him to suffer simple imprisonment for four months and to pay a fine of Rs. 2000/- and in default of payment of fine, to further undergo simple imprisonment for two months.

(ii) Appeal

According to Section 19 of the Contempt of Courts Act, 1971, the contemner has the right of appeal.

(1) An appeal shall lie as on right from any order or decision of High Court in the exercise of its jurisdiction to punish for contempt :—

(a) where the order or decision is that of a single Judge, to a Bench of not less than two Judges of the Court;

(b) where the order or decision is that of a Bench, to the Supreme Court :

Provided that where the order or decision is that of the Court of the Judicial Commissioner in any Union Territory, such appeal shall lie to the Supreme Court.

(2) Pending any appeal, the Appellate Court may order that :—

(a) the execution of the punishment, or other appealed against the suspended;

(b) if the appellant is in confinement, he be released on bail; and

(c) the appeal be heard notwithstanding that the appellant is not purged of his contempt.

(3) Where any person aggrieved by any order against which an appeal may be filed, satisfies the High Court that he intends to prefer an appeal, the High Court may also exercise all or any of the powers conferred by subsection (2).

(4) An appeal under subsection (1) shall be filed :—

(a) in the case of an appeal to a Bench of the High Court, within thirty days;

(b) in the case of an appeal to the Supreme Court, within sixty days, from the date of the order appealed against.

Thus, Section 19 of the Act provides right of only one appeal.

Where an appeal is filed against the order of the learned single Judge to a Division Bench, the statutory right of appeal gets exhausted and there is no further right of appeal to the Supreme Court under the Contempt of Courts Act. However, the remedy by way of special leave petition under Article 13 of Indian Constitution is still available.

(iii) Review

The Contempt of Courts Act, 1971 does not provide any provision to the Court for review. The order of punishment is amenable to correction only in appeal under Section 19 of the Act. Proviso to Section 12(1) provides that the accused may be discharged or the punishment awarded may be remitted on apology being made to the satisfaction of the Court.

X. Contempt of Courts by Advocates, Judges, State and Corporate Bodies

It is common knowledge that the administration of justice is a cooperative effort. It is an effort in which the Judge and the lawyer act in concert with each other. Frankly, the administration of justice is made possible not only by a fair and impartial judge, but also by a courageous and upright advocate. The role of an advocate is very delicate. He has to protect the client's interest to the best of his capabilities and sincerity. He enjoys certain privileged position. At the same time he owes certain duties to the Court in particular and to administration of justice in general. An advocate is always expected to respect the court and to maintain its dignity and decorum. His conduct should always be characterised by candour and fairness and should not be of picking of cudgels with the presiding officers, even when judges have their own whims and fancies and their attitude be unfavourable, or belitting.

Advocates are known as gentlemen of the Bar and officers of the Court. On account of the nature of duties in Court sometimes the advocates and Judges may get into heated dialogue which may result in contempt of Court. The following instances are considered as commitment of contempt.

(1) Advocates using intemperate language and casting unwarranted aspersions on various judicial officers and attributing motives to them while discharging their judicial functions would be held guilty of gross contempt of Court.[1]

(2) Communication with the Judge by advocate amounts to contempt of Court only when it interferes with the administration of justice.[2]

(3) Comment by an advocate stating that a common man on the street has lost confidence in the judiciary amount to contempt of Court.

(4) A private communication of a letter thanking the Judge amounts to contempt of Court.

(5) Publication of pamphlet by an advocate seeking election to Bar Council making derogatory remarks about the Court amounts to contempt.

(6) Criticizing the methods adopted by a Judge amounts to contempt of Court.

(7) Making a false endorsement by an advocate is contempt of Court.[3]

---

1. *K.A. Mohd. Ali* v. *C.N. Prasaman*, 1994 Supp. (3) S.C.C. 509; *In re, Ajay Kumar Pandey*, A.I.R. 1998 S.C. 3299; *Re, V.C. Mishra*, A.I.R. 1995 S.C. 2348.
2. *Re, Brahma Islands*, (1893) AC 138 (P.C.).
3. *U.P. Resi. Emp. Co-op. House B. Society* v. *New Okhla Indus. Dev. Authority*, A.I.R. 2003 S.C. 2732.

(8) The advocates who sign application or pleading containing matter scandalizing the Court are themselves guilty of contempt of Court.

(9) Circulating a letter to various dignitaries in order to undervalue the confidence in Judicial Authority amounts to contempt.

(10) Hurling shoe at the Judge amounts to contempt of Court.[1]

(11) Scurrilous attack upon a Judge by an advocate amounts to contempt of Court.

(12) Storming of Court and disruption of judicial proceedings are considered as the acts of contempt of Court.

(13) Criticism of Court in pleadings amounts to contempt of Court.[2]

(14) Protest against the Court may amount to contempt of Court.

(15) Contemptuous allegation against the presiding Judge in a Court amounts to contempt.[3]

(16) Sending notice to party to withdraw plea taken in written statement by an advocate is also an act of contempt.

(17) To allege that the Judge has acted with prejudice, bias and malice in the course of his judicial duties amounts to professional contempt of Court.[4]

(18) A counsel who advises his client to disobey the order of the Court is also held liable for contempt of Court.

(19) If a counsel refuses to answer the questions of the Court he is liable for contempt of Court.[5]

(20) Boycott of Court or strike by advocates amounts to contempt of Court as the advocates violate their duties not only towards the clients but also towards the Court.[6]

(21) Unfounded allegations of corruption of Judge by an advocate amounts to contempt of Court.[7]

(22) Allegation that 'justice is sold' or 'justice is auctioned'.[8]

(23) To say that a Judge is a prejudiced Judge.[9]

(24) Scandalous allegations against Supreme Court Judges in affidavit without basis.[10]

(25) Speech published in newspaper alleging *inter alia* that the

---

1. *R.K. Garg* v. *State of Himachal Pradesh*, A.I.R. 1981 S.C. 1382; *Municipal Corporation of Greater Bombay* v. *Smt. Annattee Remond Uttanwala*, 1987 Cr. L.J. 1038; *In re, Nand Lal Balwani*, 26th Feb. 1999.
2. *M.Y. Shareef* v. *The Hon'ble Judge of High Court of Nagpur*, A.I.R. 1995 S.C. 19; *In re, D.C. Saxena*, A.I.R. 1996 S.C. 248.
3. *M.B. Sanghi* v. *High Court of Punjab and Haryana*, A.I.R. 1991 S.C. 1834.
4. *Mohd. Vamin* v. *Om Prakash*, 1982 Cr. L.J. 322 Raj.
5. *Re, Vinay Chandra Mishra*, A.I.R. 1995 S.C. 2348.
6. *Captain Harish Uppal* v. *Union of India*, A.I.R. 2003 S.C. 739; *Tarini Mohan* v. *Pleaders*, A.I.R. 1923 Cal. 212.
7. *L.D. Jaikwal* v. *State of U.P.*, A.I.R. 1984 S.C. 1374.
8. *Umed* v. *Bahadur Singh*, 1981 Cr. L.J. 85 Raj.
9. *B.K. Lala* v. *R.C. Dutt*, A.I.R. 1967 Cal. 153.
10. *Amrik Singh* v. *state*, 1971 3 S.C.C. 215.

Judges do not mete out justice, they deliver judgments at the court with an eye towards their self-interests; brief cases full with currency notes find their ways to the Judge's house, etc.[1]

Instances in which no contempt of Court was committed

(1) Application mentioning that the order passed by the Court was against rules does not make out a case of contempt of Court.

(2) High flown language used by an advocate to persuade a Court to a particular view would not amount to contempt.

(3) Statement of advocate though wrong does not amount to contempt.

(4) An advocate in the course of arguments oversteps the limits of decency, facts have to be examined whether contempt is committed.

(5) Merely stating on a transfer application that the Presiding Officer of a Court is friendly with an advocate is not contempt of Court unless it has a tendency to create distrust in the public mind about the impartiality of the Court.

(6) An advocate appearing drunk in the Court may not have committed contempt of Court though he shows disrespect to the Court.

(7) An advocate with zeal and enthusiasm may annoy a particular Court and this annoyance to the Judge is no contempt.

Contempt by Judges, Magistrates or other persons acting judicially

The other controversial issue is that whether a presiding judge himself be liable for committing contempt of his own court. According to Section 16 of the Contempt of Courts Act, 1971, a Judge, Magistrate or other person acting judicially shall also be liable for contempt of his own court or of any other court in the same manner as any other person is liable and the provisions of this Act shall, so far as may be, apply accordingly.

(1) If the Judge uses indecorous words and indulges in unseemly and indecent language, then the impersonal concept of the seat of justice is attended against even by its occupant in bringing into disrepute the administration of justice and he may be held liable for contempt of Court.

(2) If the inferior or Subordinate Court does not follow the law laid down by the Supreme Court, it will amount to contempt of Court.[2]

(3) A Judge of the Subordinate Court is held liable in contempt for disobeying the order of the High Court only when the disobedience is deliberate and wilful.[3]

(4) A Judge may be held liable for criminal contempt, if his act or conduct amount to scandalizing or lowering the authority of the

1. *In Re, Biman Bose*, (1994) 2 Cal HN 299 (SB).
2. *Session Judge, Meerut* v. *F.S. Fanthome*, A.I.R. 1955 All 161; *Barad Kant Mishra* v. *Bhim Sen Dixit*, (1973) 1 S.C.C. 446.
3. *Harkusum Singh* v. *Chhottan Mahton & Others*, A.I.R. 1951 Pat. 494; *B.K. Kar* v. *Chief Justice of Orissa*, A.I.R. 1961 S.C. 1367.

Court or interference with the due course of any judicial proceeding or interference with administration of justice in any other manner.

(5) If a Judge or Magistrate accepts illegal gratification, it is considered contempt of Court.[1]

Committing contempt of his own Court was involved in **Board of Revenue v. Vinay Chandra.**[2] It was alleged that the Member, Board of Revenue, has said in respect of a lawyer appearing before him—"*Nalayak Gadhe Saale ko Jail Bhijwa dunga, Kis Idiot Ne Advocate Bana Diya Hai.*" The Advocate prayed to the High Court for taking cognizance *suo motu* and High Court issued notice. A preliminary objection was overruled by the High Court. The Supreme Court agreed with the High Court for deciding the case on merit. These instances clearly demonstrate a titanic clash between two sides of the judicial proceedings, wherein the interest, dignity and honour of both sides need to be maintained.

But Section 16 of the Contempt of Courts Act, 1971 does not apply to the Judges of the Court of Record, but only to the subordinate judiciary. The High Court and Supreme Court are the Courts of Record and therefore, the contempt proceedings are not maintainable against the Judges of the Supreme Court and High Courts.

Contempt Liability of State, Corporate Bodies and their Officers

At present, in India, the State is not immune from the contempt liability and therefore, it may be held liable for contempt of Court.

(1) If the injunction or order is passed against the State or corporate body and it is found that there has been wilful disobedience thereof apart from the State or the corporate body, the officer responsible for its implementation will also be liable for contempt, if it is established that he was the person in charge of the subject-matter to which the injunction or order alleged to have been disobeyed related and had knowledge of the order.[3]

(2) Where an order is passed against an officer, his successor is also bound to obey the order and in the case of wilful disobedience he may be held liable for contempt of Court.[4]

(3) As regards the liability of the minister, it may be pointed out that, he may be liable for contempt in his personal capacity when he violates the law resulting in contempt of Court. In his official capacity, Minister or Chief Minister are held liable when they are party to the case for any wilful disobedience of the orders of the Court.

(4) In the case of Corporation, apart from the Corporation, the officer or agent when acts for Corporation and knowingly disobeys the

1. *In re, Abdul*, 8 W.R. Cr. 32.
2. A.I.R. 1973 S.C. 723.
3. *Trafutallah* v. *S.N. Maitra*, A.I.R. 1952 Cal. 919.
4. *T.R. Dhananjaya* v. *J. Vasudevan*, A.I.R. 1996 S.C. 302 at 305.

order of the Court against the Corporation, will be held liable for contempt even though the officer is not a party to suit.[1]

(5) In the case of a company, apart from the company, the directors and other officers may also be held liable for contempt even if the order is made against the company as per the sub-section (4) and (5) of Section 12 of the Contempt of courts Act, 1971.[2]

XI. Constitutional Validity of the Contempt of Courts Act, 1971

Article 129 of the Constitution of India lays down that the Supreme Court shall be a Court of Record and shall have all the powers of such a Court including the power to punish for contempt of itself. Similarly, Article 215 of the Constitution of India states that, every High Court shall be a Court of Record and shall have all the powers of such a Court including the power to punish for contempt of itself.

Parliament and State Legislature both have power to make laws with respect to any of the subject enumerated in List III (Concurrent List) of the Seventh Schedule of the Constitution. The Parliament has exclusive power to make laws with respect to any of the matters or subjects enumerated in List I (Union List) of the Seventh Schedule of the Constitution. The State Legislature has exclusive powers with respect to any of the matters or subjects enumerated in List II (State List) of the Seventh Schedule of the Constitution.

Entry 77 of List I is as follows : "Constitution, Organization, Jurisdiction and Powers of the Supreme Court (including contempt of such Court) and the fees taken therein; persons entitled to practice before the Supreme Court."

Entry 15 of the List II is as follows : "Contempt of Court but not including contempt of Supreme Court."

The Legislature is fully competent to legislate with respect to contempt of Court subject only to the qualification that the legislature cannot take away the power of the Supreme Court or the High Court to punish for contempt or vest that power in some other Court.

Article 142(2) of Constitution of India states that the Supreme Court shall have all and every power to make any order for the purpose of securing the attendance of any person, the discovery or production of any document, or the investigation or punishment of any contempt of itself.

According to Article 372 of Constitution of India, all the laws in force in the territory of India immediately before the commencement of this Constitution shall continue in force therein until altered or repealed or amended by a competent Legislature or other competent authority. That is why, Section 22 of the Contempt of Courts Act, 1971, makes it clear that the provisions of the Act shall be in addition to and not in derogation of the provisions of any other law relating to contempt of Courts.

---

1. *Narain Singh* v. *Hardayal Singh*, A.I.R. 1958 Punj. 180; *S.N. Banerjee* v. *Kuchwar Lime Stone Co. Ltd.*, A.I.R. 1938 PC 295.
2. *Rex* v. *J.G. Hammond & Co. Ltd.*, (19140 2 KB 866.

The Contempt of Courts Act is not the violation of guarantee of equality under Article 14 as the classification is founded on an intelligible differential which distinguishes persons or things that are grouped together from others left out of the group and the differential has a rational relation to the object sought to be achieved by the Statute in question is reasonable.

As the existing law relating to contempt of Court imposes reasonable restriction within the meaning of Article 19(2) and, therefore, it is not violative of the Fundamental Right to freedom of speech and expression guaranteed by Article 19(1)(2) of the Constitution.

According to clause (10) of Article 366, the existing law means any law, ordinance, order, by-law, rule or regulation passed or made before the commencement of this Constitution by a legislature, authority or person having power to make such a law, ordinance, by-law, rule or regulation.

The contempt law is not violative of Article 21 which provides that no person shall be deprived of his life or personal liberty except according to the procedure established by law as the existing procedure for contempt proceedings have statutory sanction. Section 10 of the Contempt of Courts Act, 1971, makes it clear that every High Court shall have and exercise the same jurisdiction, powers and authority in accordance with the same procedure and practice in respect of contempt of Courts subordinate to it as it has and exercises in respect of contempt of itself. Besides this, Article 225 of the Constitution of India makes provision for its continuity.

Hence, it is abundantly clear from the foregoing study that the Contempt of Courts Act, 1971 is not violative of any of the provisions of the Constitution and it is constitutionally valid.

13

ACCOUNTANCY FOR LAWYERS

Lawyer-client relationship is fiduciary, contractual and trustworthy. Lawyers practice law for fee and earn income. Though it is contractual, the bargaining partners are not equal and there is always a chance of dominance and undue influence exercised by better placed lawyers. Therefore, an advocate must deal honestly and carefully with money or other property held by him on behalf of his client. He must act according to the instructions of his client. He must keep books of accounts. Separate account for the money of each client should be opened. An advocate may receive instructions from his client or his recognized agent, servant, relation or friend who is authorised by his client to give instructions. An advocate who does not take care to ascertain whether that person instructing him has got authorization or not, his conduct is improper and is exposed to severe punishment. Hence, every person carrying on legal profession whether on the civil side, or criminal side or otherwise and wherever practicing would be required to compulsorily maintain certain books of accounts and other documents. The books of accounts and other documents which would be maintained by every lawyer are the following :

> (i) a daily cash book; (ii) a journal, if the accounts are maintained according to the mercantile system of accounting; (iii) a ledger; (iv) duplicate copies of machine numbered bills and receipts issued by the person; (v) original bills and receipts in respect of expenditure incurred by the person, or where such bills and receipts are not issued and the expenditure incurred does not exceed twenty five rupees, payment vouchers prepared and signed by the person.

The books of account and other documents have to be kept and maintained by the lawyers at the place where he is carrying on the profession. Where the lawyer does not compulsorily maintain the books of account and documents as required by Section 44-AA, then it has been under Section 271A of the Income Tax Act that such a person would be liable to pay by way of penalty, a sum of which shall not be less than 10% of the amount of tax, if any, which would have been avoided if the income returned by such a person had been accepted as the correct income. The maximum amount of penalty is 50% of the aforesaid amount of tax sought to be avoided.

The Bar Council of India Rules, 1975 made in exercise of its rule-making powers under the Advocates Act, 1961 more precisely under Section 49(1)(c) deals with the Advocate's duty to keep accounts of the clients' money entrusted to him, among the other duties. Rules 25 to 32 of the Bar Council of India Rules, 1975 deal with the duties of an advocate with regard to financial dealing with his client. Rule 24 which states that an advocate shall not do anything whereby he abuses or takes advantage of the confidence reposed in him by his client, has apart from having general application in all sorts of dealings with his client, casts a special responsibility on the advocate with regard to financial dealing, with his client. On account of the special relation between an advocate and his client, the advocate occupies a position of trustee with regard to the money of his client which comes to the hand of the advocate.

When money of the client comes into the possession of the advocate, otherwise than as earmarked for fee, the advocate is to treat himself as a trustee for the client in respect of the said money. An advocate should be meticulous in maintaining an account of client's money that come to his hands. It is no excuse for him that he has no sufficient or extensive business to necessitate accounts being maintained. Nor can he seek shelter under the plea that the accounts are not maintained by him but by his clerk. His position being that of a quasi-trustee vis-a-vis his client, he is accountable to his client for all moneys handled by him on behalf of his client and he is liable for misconduct for any malfeasance or misfeasance in respect thereof. An advocate practicing law is under, triple obligations viz., (i) an obligation to his client to be faithful to them unto the last, (ii) an obligation to the profession not to impair its value and name; and (iii) an obligation to the court to be and to remain a dependable part of the machinery through which justice is administered. One of the canons of ethics adopted by the American Bar Association as a general guide is :

> "*Money of the client or other trust property coming into the possession of the lawyer should be reported promptly, and except with the client's knowledge and consent should not be commingled with his private property or be used by him.*"

An advocate should not take liberty with the money of his client. At the same time members of the profession should keep themselves as far as possible at a respectable distance from spending money out of their own pockets for the clients, because if they do not observe such restraints, complications are bound to arise, and the noble traditions and high standards which members of this privileged profession are expected to maintain, are put in jeopardy. An advocate even if he has not much work must keep accounts and failure to do so amounts to professional misconduct.

The courts in England insist that it is barrister's duty to preserve a record of his dealings with his client and any agreement between them should be in writing. In **Anande Devi v. Banchhanidhi Samantarao**, it was held to be the duty of the pleader to keep complete and accurate accounts so that there may be no dispute between him and his clients. Keeping inaccurate and irregular account amounts to a failure to maintain accounts. The relevant rules which are Rules 25 to 32 in Part VI, Chapter II, Section II are reproduced as follows :

> **Rule 25.**—An advocate should keep accounts of the client's money entrusted to him, and the accounts should show the amounts received from the client or on his behalf, the expenses incurred for him and the debits made on account of fees with respective dates and all other necessary particulars.
>
> **Rule 26.**—Where moneys are received from or on account of a client, the entries in the accounts should contain a reference as to whether the amounts have been received for fees or expenses, and during the course of the proceedings, no advocate shall, except with the consent in writing of the client concerned, be at liberty to divert any portion of the expenses towards fees.
>
> **Rule 27.**—Where any amount is received or given to him on behalf of his client the fact of such receipt be intimated to the client as early as possible.
>
> **Rule 28.**—After the termination of the proceeding the advocate shall be at liberty to appropriate towards the settled fee due to him any sum remaining unexpended out of the amount paid or sent to him for expenses or any amount that has come into his hands in that proceeding.
>
> **Rule 29.**—Where the fee has been left unsettled, the advocate shall be entitled to deduct, out of any moneys of the client remaining in his hands, at the termination of the proceeding for which he had been engaged, the fee payable under the rules of the court in force for the time being, or by then settled and the balance, if any, shall be refunded to the client.
>
> **Rule 30.**—A copy of the client's account shall be furnished to him on demand provided the necessary copying charges is paid.
>
> **Rule 31.**—An advocate shall not enter into any arrangements whereby funds in his hands are converted into loans.
>
> **Rule 32.**—An advocate shall not lend money to his client, for the purpose of any action or legal proceedings in which he is engaged by such client.
>
> *Explanation.*—An advocate shall not be held guilty of a breach of this rule, if in the course of a pending suit or proceeding, and without any arrangement with the client in respect of the same, the advocate feels compelled by reason of the rule of the court to make a payment to the court on account of the client for the progress of the suit or proceedings.

These rules of the Bar Council of India require proper accounts of the client's money, passing of receipt for money received and to appropriate the remaining amount towards fee at the termination of proceedings. No practitioner is entitled to hold his client's money in his hands and use it himself for his own private purpose without the consent of the client.

In **K.V. Umre v. Smt. Venubai D. Gage and another,**[1] an advocate misappropriated the decretal amount of Rs. 11,760.70 in an accident claim. The Disciplinary Committee directed the advocate to pay the amount in two instalments and suspended him from practice for one year indicating that failure to pay the amount on due date entitled removal of the name of the advocate from rolls. The advocate paid the money but made a default in not paying on due dates.

The Disciplinary Committee took a serious view of the matter on the ground that if the lawyers were allowed to withhold payment of compensation awarded and pay the same in instalments, it would amount to sharing of profits of litigation. When the advocate made an application for review of the punishment, condoning the delay in payment the Disciplinary Committee rejected the application but the period of suspension was reduced to one year. The Supreme Court held that the Committee should consider the application afresh and that the Committee took a lenient view in limiting the period of suspension to one year.

In **Y.V.R. v. M.K.N.,**[2] the advocate made an Electronics Engineer believe that he would settle a transaction and in pursuance of such belief the engineer had paid money to him. The money was not returned, but postdated cheques were issued by the advocate which were dishonoured. The Disciplinary Committee held that he was guilty of misconduct of a very serious nature.

The rules relating to the professional fees are contained in Part VI, Chapter II, Section II, rules 11, 12, 20 and 23 dealing with 'duty to client' and Section IV, Rule 38 dealing with 'duty to colleagues' of the Bar Council of India Rules, 1975. The said rules read as follows :—

> **Rule 11.**—An advocate is bound to accept the brief in the Courts or Tribunals or before any other authority in or before which he professes to practice at the fee consistent with his standing at the Bar and the nature of the case. Special circumstances may justify his refusal to accept a particular brief.
>
> **Rule 12.**—An advocate shall not ordinarily withdraw from engagements once accepted, without sufficient cause and unless reasonable and sufficient notice is given to the client. Upon his withdrawal from a case, he shall refund such part of the fee as has not been earned.
>
> **Rule 20.**—An advocate shall not stipulate for a fee contingent on the results of litigation or agree to share the proceeds thereof.
>
> **Rule 23.**—An advocate shall not adjust fee payable to him by his client against his own personal liability to the client, which liability does not arise in the course of his employment as an advocate."

1. A.I.R. 1983 S.C. 1154. The Supreme Court held that "In fixing of suspension, the Disciplinary Committee must keep in view that the appellant had completely betrayed the trust reposed in him by the client."
2. Indian Bar Review (1989), Vol. 16, p. 542.

Section IV, Rule 38.—An advocate shall not accept a fee less than the fee taxable under the rules when the client is able to pay the same.

In exercise of the powers conferred under Articles 225 and 227 of the Constitution of India, the different High Courts have framed the rules regarding fees payable to advocates. The scale of fee prescribed under various rules therein are to "be entered as recoverable in a decree or order." In other words, it is for the purpose of claiming costs only and not for limiting professional fees payable by clients to advocates.

Rules 37 of the said Rules provides as follows :

Rule 37.—Nothing in these rules shall be deemed to affect any agreement between the advocate and his client regarding fees.

The Supreme Court Rules, 1966 made by the Supreme Court under Article 145 of the Constitution of India with the approval for the President, in Order IV and Rule 6 also deal with the Advocate's duty to maintain books of accounts and the same are reproduced as follows :—

Rule 6(a).—An advocate-on-record shall, on his filing a memorandum of appearance on behalf of a party accompanied by a Vakalatnama duly executed by the party, be entitled :—

(i) to act as well as to plead for the party in the matter and to conduct and prosecute before the court all proceedings that may be taken in respect of the said matter or any application connected with the same or any decree or order passed therein including proceedings in taxation and application for review; and

(ii) to deposit and receive money on behalf of the said party.

(b) No advocate other than an advocate on record shall be entitled to file an appearance or act for a party in the court.

(c) Every advocate-on-record shall keep such books of accounts as may be necessary to show and distinguish in connection with his practice as an advocate-on-record.

(i) moneys received from or on account of and the moneys paid to or on account of to each of his clients; and

(ii) the moneys received and the moneys paid on his own account.

(d) Every advocate-on-record shall before taxation of the Bill of Costs, file with the Taxation Officer a certificate showing the amount of the fee paid to him or agreed to be paid to him by his client.

Hence, it is the duty of the advocate to keep complete and accurate accounts so that there may be no dispute between him and his clients. Keeping inaccurate and irregular accounts amounts to a failure to maintain accounts and the advocate concerned will be guilty of unprofessional conduct. Therefore, in order to know the advocates duty to maintain proper accounts of the amounts collected from the clients, the fresh law graduates must have at least fundamental knowledge of the relevant laws and the rates of charges for different services. They charge the fees from clients under different heads like registration charges, stamp duty, court fees, and advocate's fee. The relevant Statutes and Rules are as follows :—

(i) The Indian Stamp Act, 1899

The Indian Stamp Act, 1899 is a fiscal Act imposing stamp duty on instruments creating, limiting and extinguishing rights in immovable properties. The stamp duty generally depends on the valuation of the property as fixed by the State Government from time to time. Further, it also depends on the location of the property within the limits of municipal corporations, selection grade municipalities, special grade municipalities and other areas. The proper stamp duty is fixed by the Government for a particular instrument depending on its monetary value. This can be clearly ascertained from the Schedules annexed to the Stamp Act, 1899, i.e., Schedule 1 and 1-A. Undervaluation of any property or subject-matter of an instrument is an offence under Section 64 of the Act. Therefore, an advocate is duty bound to charge and advise the clients about the exact rates of stamp duty and is required to maintain property accounts for the same.

(ii) The Registration Act, 1908

The Registration Act, 1908 is another legislation, every legal professional must be well acquainted with the same. It is because, certain documents are made compulsorily registerable. Section 17 of this Act lays down that certain documents like the instruments of gift of immovable property, leases of immovable property, and agreement of sale of immovable property are compulsorily registerable. The registration of certain documents is optional under Section 18 of the Act, which includes wills and instruments transferring or assigning any decree or order of a court. The State Government is empowered to fix and prepare a table of fees payable for different services like registration of documents, researching the registers, making/granting copies of reasons, entries of documents, before, on or after registration, issuing of commissions, filing translations, attending at private residences and keeping the safe custody and return of documents.[1] Hence, an advocate getting or preparing any document for registration is required to inform the client about the correct rate of registration fee and also should account for the moneys received by him for the said purpose.

(iii) Court-fees and suit valuation acts

Another important legislation is the law relating to court-fees and suits valuation, which varies from one State to another. Generally, every person who approaches a civil court seeking some relief, has to pay court fee depending on the valuation of the suit, along with process and other fees. The suit is valued depending on the market value and other factors. Different court fee has to be paid depending on the kind of property which becomes the subject matter of the suit and also on the kind of relief prayed

1. See, Section 78 of the Registration Act, 1908.

for. Hence, different fee has to be paid while filing suit for declaration, adoption suits, suits for injunction, suits relating to trust property, suits relating to easements and suits relating to mortgages, etc. Similarly, a certain fee is fixed for filing an appeal, an application for probate or letter of administration.

(iv) Advocate fee rules

An advocate cannot charge any amount he likes from the clients. His fee must be in accordance with the rules framed by the concerned High Court.[1] An advocate under Rule 6(2) of the Kerala Advocates Fees Rules, is entitled to one-half of the full prescribed fees when the suit is decided on defendant's admission even though issues had been framed.[2] An advocate is entitled to settle with his client his fee for any engagement having regard to the nature of assignment, extent of professional skill required to be used in the case and also having regard to his standing in the Bar. But this always should be subject to the Advocates' Fees rules. The fee allowed by the rules is generally known as scale fee as different scales are fixed by the rules. An advocate shall not accept a brief for an amount below the scale fee. It amounts underselling which is bad. The only exception to it is serving the cause of the poor otherwise known as legal aid to poor.

For instance, in the State of Andhra Pradesh, the Advocate Fee Rules, 1990, framed by the High Court of Andhra Pradesh governs the fee payable by the adversary in the courts, subordinate to the High Court of Andhra Pradesh. For example : In small cause suits—In all suits triable by court of small causes, the fee shall be 10% of the amount claimed subject to a minimum of Rs. 100/-.

In original suits—In all money suits, the fees shall be calculated at the rate of 10% of the claim involved in such suits when it does not exceed Rs. 10,000/-. If it exceeds Rs. 10,000/- the fee shall be calculated as follows :

For first Rs. 10,000/-	10%
For next 10,000/- (above Rs. 10,000/-)	7%
When the claim exceeds Rs. 20,000/-	7%
On the next Rs. 30,000/-	5%
On the balance	2%

Similarly, the rules also provide for fee payable to the advocates appearing in the High Court of Andhra Pradesh.

Besides the above mentioned legislations, the professional people have to maintain their accounts in accurate and proper manner. There are two systems of keeping accounts, viz., the mercantile accountancy system and cash system. Book keeping and Accountancy are generally known in Indian public as *Bahikhata* and *Lekha*. It is art of keeping records in writing of all dealings in money, goods and services. In northern India, it is kept generally in *Muria* (script with headlines) or Hindi.

The system of keeping accounts strictly on the basis of cash is quite

---

1. See, Section 34(1A) of the Advocates Act, 1961.
2. *State Bank of Travancore* v. *Sreepathy Bhatt*, 1986 KLT 22.

suitable for professional men such as advocates, doctors, accountants, etc. It is suitable because of the reason that in the case of professional men, the number of credit transactions are usually small, so it is not necessary to have elaborate mercantile accountancy system. A professional man records transactions for following purposes :

(i) All items of income and expenses may be correctly recorded.

(ii) He may be able to ascertain his professional income for a given period, it is necessary that separate accounts should be maintained for private and professional income and expenditures.

To keep of the professional income and expenditure the accounts may be maintained as follows :—

(i) Vouchers

It is very important that every transaction of amount recorded in books of accounts should be properly supported by documents evidencing the transaction. Such documents are called vouchers. Vouchers may be either Receipt-Vouchers or payment vouchers.

(A) Receipt voucher

The 'Receipt Voucher' is also termed as 'Receipt'. A receipt is a document prepared for recording the transaction of having received the money whether by cash or by cheque. When an advocate receives money from the client, the advocate has to issue him a receipt. Advocates may maintain receipt books with serially numbered receipt forms in duplicate. The original receipt is to be issued to the client and the counterfoil is to be retained in the receipt book as office copy. A receipt may be prepared in the following form :

S.S. Deshta, B.A., LL.B. P.G.D.P. M & L.W.
Advocate, Lakkar Bazar, Shimla

Number 1 Date...............

RECEIPT

Received with thanks from..a sum of rupees..by cash/cheque/draft number................. date.....................on............ bank.. subject to realisation as per the following details :

Professional fees Rs............................
Expenses fro the case Rs............................
Total Rs............................

Signature Advocate Revenue Stamp

(B) Payment Voucher

Payment vouchers are used to record such payments where receipt for such payments are not obtainable from the payees, as for example, bus fare, auto-rickshaw fare, court fees stamps, refreshment expenses, etc. In such cases, the advocate's signature with certificate of having paid the amount is treated as sufficient supporting evidence for the payment. Cash bills received during purchases may serve the purpose of payment vouchers.

In the vouchers, signature of the payee may be obtained if it is practicable, as in the cases of payment of rent, salary, etc. A payment voucher may be prepared in the following form :

S.S. Deshta, B.A., LL.B. P.G.D.P. M & L.W.
Advocate, Lakkar Bazar, Shimla
VOUCHER

Number : Date...............

Particulars | Amount Rs. Ps.

Total

Paid, the sum of Rupees...as detailed above

Paid Signature..................... | Received Signature

S.S. Deshta
Advocate | Revenue Stamp

(ii) Journal

A day to day transactions recording book of accounts is known as Journal. This book is also known as the original Book of Accounts. Literally, 'journal' means a daily record. Journal is a book of first entry or original entry. In it, the transactions are recorded in the order of their occurrence. The journal entries contain the following essentials, namely, (a) date of transaction, (b) account to which the transaction relates, (c) amount to be debited, (d) amount to be credited, and (e) explanation of the transaction. In Journal, there are short-explanations given after entries therein. The transactions which are recorded in the journal are then posted to the separate heads of accounts in another book that is known as ledger.

(iii) Cash book

The principal book of accounts in case of professional persons is the cash book. The cash book makes a record of all cash receipts and cash payments concerning the profession. A Cash Book is a sub-division of the Journal or subsidiary journals. Since all cash transactions are first entered in the cash book, it is treated as a book of original entry. The cash book should be balanced just as any other ledger account is balanced. A cash book has two sides, namely, receipt side (debit side) and payment side (credit side). When cash is received, the cash account is debited. When cash is paid, cash account is credited. At the end of a year or any other period, the cash book is summarized to know the receipts and payments under various heads for the whole period. Another method of getting the total receipts and payments under various heads for a particular period can be the preparation of an analytical cash book having a number of analysis columns on both sides. In other words, a cash book may be maintained either on day to day or month to month basis and can be summarized so that net income for a particular period may be ascertained and the financial position on a particular date may be known.

(iv) Ledger

Ledger is a very important book of accounts. In the ledger different pages will be allotted to different heads of accounts. It is a bound book. At the beginning of the ledger book, the index may be given with the heads of account and their respective pages. When the journal entries are posted to the concerned heads of accounts of the ledger, the page of that ledger is the 'ledger folio'. Standards format of ledger is as follows :

....

(Name of the Account)

Dr. Cr.

Date	Particular	JF	Amount	Date	Particular	JF	Amount
			Rs. P.				Rs. P.

A ledger folio is divided into two halves. One is a Debit side marked on the left top of the other side by Dr., and the half side is divided by a vertical dark line across the folio, marked on the top of it as Cr., for credit side. In each of the sides there are four columns. These are of Date, Particulars, Journal Folio marked shortly as JF and amount sub-divided in Rupees (Rs.) and Paisa (P) columns. In a Ledger Folio a debit side entry is provided by a word "To" and a credit side entry is preceded by a word "By". In ledger, there is no need for giving explanatory notes as given in Journal because there is a very short space on a ledger folio which itself is divided in two halves as stated earlier.

Ledger classifies the transactions into different heads.

(A) Client's account.—An advocate has to conduct several cases of different clients. Hence, it is necessary that he should maintain separate ledger accounts for each client.

(B) Fee account.—Similarly, there must be a distinct head of account called 'Fee Account'. The ledger of fees account does not pertain to any particular client, but relates to the fees received from all clients for a definite period. It is concerned with the amount of fees only and not the amount entrusted with the advocate for meeting expenses. Amounts received from all the clients towards fees are recorded in the ledger under the head 'Fees Account'. At the end of the financial year, gross amount of fees received from all clients can be ascertained.

(C) Other heads of accounts.—Besides clients and fees accounts, other heads in the ledger relate to the various expenses for maintaining the office. They include, namely, rent account, salary account, library account, telephone charges account, postage and telegraph account, printing and stationary account, electricity charges account, repair and maintenance account, conveyance charges account and other office miscellaneous expenses account.

(v) Income and expenditure account

Professional people prepare receipt and expenditure account to ascertain their net professional income for a particular period. This account is like profit and loss account. In this account, all expenditure relating to the period are debited and all income relating to the same period are credited. The balance may be either excess of income, over expenditure, or excess of expenditure over income. This account is usually prepared after the accounts are closed for a definite period, more often and normally, after the end of the financial year.

(vi) Balance sheet

A balance sheet is an important document for professional people. Its purpose is to show the financial position of the profession on the last day of the period. It is a statement drawn up at the end of the financial year setting forth the various assets and liabilities. It gives the knowledge as to what one owns (assets) and what one owes (liabilities).

14

LAW OFFICE MANAGEMENT

In absolute terms India has a very large profession, second only to the United States of America. The strength of advocates on rolls in India arose from 1,82,000 in 1979 to 3,00,000 in 1988 and to 5,00,000 in 1998. There are 50 Law Universities where from about 25,000 law graduates are coming out every year.[1] Therefore, the legal profession is overcrowded and full time attention and proper office management are necessary for getting success in the profession. Hard work, devotion and good dealing with the client will enable a junior lawyer to compete with the senior lawyers having rich experience and reputation. Hence, an advocate should never be ignorant of the current law in force. He should get acquainted with the present law by systematic study. Edison has rightly said that "extraordinary talent is nothing but 2% inspiration and 98% perspiration."[2] If one ignores the law, the law is also apt to ignore him. That is why it is said that 'law is a jealous mistress.' Lord Eldon has emphasised the need of hard work for a lawyer. He stated that "a lawyer must live like a hermit and work like a horse."[3] It requires regular; constant and systematic care and attention. The changing dimensions of office management demand that the student, manager or trainee in this field be alert and responsive to the latest developments in this management area. The activity of office management, consists of specific fundamental functions which when applied constitute a process—a management process. In today's modern business operations, office work is both a vital and an integral part of the management office work is a facilitate function. It is an essential medium through which the various activities of an enterprise are fused together. In a sense, office work can be called the 'catalytic agent' of modern management.[4]

1. Bimal Crolly, "A Minuscule Profile of a Lawyer and His Profession", A.I.R. 2000 (Journal Section), p. 206; also see "Law Day", Address by Dr. L.M. Singhvi at the inaugural function of Law Day on 26th November, 1979, published in A.I.R. 1980 (Journal Section), p. 15.
2. C.C. Anajwala, Law Relating to Advocates, Advocacy and Professional Ethics, (1977), p. 140.
3. Valedictory address delivered by Justice S.B. Majumdar on 26th September, 1999 on the conclusion of the Golden Jubilee Celebration of the High Court of Rajasthan. His speech is published in Nyaya Deep, Oct.-Dec., 1999, Vol., II, Issue 4, p. 39.
4. G.B. Reddy, Practical Advocacy of Law (2002), p. 372.

I. Meaning of Law Office Management

Office is a room or rooms used as a place of business for clerical work. Law office is the Advocate's office, where he keeps his records and advocacy is available to his clients. The word 'management' stems from the Italian *Managgiare* which means 'to train horses' or literally 'to handle'.[1] The French words 'manager', meaning 'to direct a household', i.e., 'to encourage' and 'me'nage', "an act of grinding or leading", have also influenced the present day concept of the term 'management'. Thus, management means keeping, holding, checking, controlling, contriving, maintaining and making use of the office or organization properly, orderly, skillfully, scientifically and economically in a desired and designated manner. Hence, every advocate should efficiently manage his law office in a suitable and attractive way and he should deal with his clients decorously. For this he has to take the following measures in the management of his office.

II. Location and Office Accommodation

A law office presupposes a decent and sufficient accommodation and it should be within the vicinity of courts so that they are convenient to the clients. To find a chamber in busy localities is big problem. The office of the advocate should be spacious and have partitioned rooms so as to allot the rooms to the library, staff, clients and the advocate separately. Even a small room can be arranged in such a way with the partition by keeping the racks of library as partition walls. The advocate should have a confidential room to talk with his clients and to maintain secrecy and privacy of his clients. Besides this, a good waiting room should be arranged for the clients to make them feel happy. The office should contain minimum facilities of sitting arrangements and other amenities. The office should have proper ventilation and good air flow. The curtains should be fixed to doors and windows.

Rule 5(iii) of the Supreme Court Rules, 1966 lays down that every advocate appearing before the Supreme Court shall have an office in Delhi within a radius of 16 kilometers from the court house. Further, Rule 11 of the Supreme Court Rules, 1965 states that every advocate-on-record shall notify to the Registrar the address of his office in Delhi and every change in such address and any notice, writ, summons, or other document served on him or his clerk at the address so notified by him shall be deemed to have been properly served.

III. Para-legal Personnel and other Staff

The time of an advocate is precious, therefore, it should not be spent on certain activities which can be taken care of, by other semi-legal or para-legal persons. Therefore, there should be clerks (called Munshis) who can take care of filing the suits, getting process issued/served and obtaining the certified copies of the orders/judgments. It shall be no exaggeration to say that every successful lawyer should have an efficient clerk/clerks. Besides clerks, there should be sweeper-cum-water boy, watchman, typist or computer operator and junior advocates.

1. *Ibid.*

Section 11 of the Advocates Act, 1961 empower the Bar Council to appoint staff members. It provides that every Bar Council shall appoint a Secretary and may appoint an Accountant and such number of other persons on its rolls as it may deem necessary. Since most of the law offices do lot of drafting, whether of instruments or pleadings, the stenographer who takes the dictation from the advocate becomes important. According to Rule 12(1) of the Supreme Court Rules, 1966 an Advocate-on-Record or a firm of Advocates may employ one or more clerks to attend the registry for presenting or receiving any papers on behalf of the said advocate or firm of advocates and the name of the clerk has to be registered with the Registrar on an application in the prescribed proforma made to the Registrar for the purpose and the clerk has to give an undertaking that he shall attend the Registry regularly. According to Rule 12(5) of the Supreme Court Rules, 1966, every advocate-on-record shall have a registered clerk.

IV. Maintenance of Registers in Law Office

In a law office, a number of registers are to be maintained, namely, (i) attendance register for the staff, (ii) leave register for the staff, (iii) acquaintance register, (iv) Cash Book, (v) Ledger, (vi) receipt book, (vii) provided fund account, (viii) stock register of library books, (ix) stock register of furniture, (x) case diary, and (xi) despatch diary.

V. Office Automation

The development of electronic devices and their application to office machines are bringing about revolutionary changes and amazing new era of the performance of office work. Electronic devices like personal computers, organisers, and laptop systems, etc. have now become an internal part of every law office. Therefore, the whole office may be automated for effective database management and processing computers assist the law practitioner by timing, and costing interviews with clients, beside storage of the case records. Internet facility brought the whole knowledge of the world into a laptop computer. Information technology has developed a lot and e-mail facility helps the advocates in communication. Since most of the legal literature is also available in the form of floppy discs, C.D. Roms and even 'on-line', it is essential for a lawyer to have a personal computer, connected to Internet. The computers are playing a very important role in the law libraries, as the world of legal literature can be viewed on the computer screen and can be retrieved from it in the printed form and can also be stored in any electronic form, that is, in the form of floppy discs and CD Roms, etc. He can get information through website and he can also refer to national and international statutes, agreements, details of case laws relating to a particular issue with the use of (dot)com online stores of different websites. With the help of the printer, advocates can get the printed copy of the documents needed within no time. Now computers have become an inevitable part of the legal profession, be it in the courts, the judges, the lawyers and the para-legal professionals. The computers are used for various purposes including the following :

(i) Drafting of notices, deeds and pleadings, etc.;

(ii) Storing information about details of litigation;

(iii) Searching for legal literature;

(iv) Finding case law/judicial precedents;

(v) Ascertaining the latest position about a pending litigation;

(vi) Online verification of the case to be heard on a particular day;

(vii) Maintenance of office records in a law chamber and court, etc.; and

(viii) Maintenance of accounts by lawyers, etc.

The computer plays the role of a typewriter. Now it is the age of information technology and use of computer is a must to any legal practitioner as the web is universe, with thousands of cites that get added everyday, is expanding rapidly. Hence, with the installation of the computer, an advocate can work in his office room which is sufficient to keep a drawer, an almirah and a chair, meaning thereby that the computer will also save the space of the advocate's room as the CDs and VCDs can be stored in a small almirah.

VI. Use of Telephone

A telephone is quite essential in a law office as it plays a significant role in the advocacy profession. It is the primary channel of communication. It saves the time, money and physical strain of the advocates and enables him to have a direct contact with his client. The clients often ring up the office to get appointment of the advocate and to get information about their case. For quick communication telephone proves very useful. An advocate should pay his telephone bill regularly and he should be quick to repair the phone when it is dead.

VII. Use of Electricity

An advocate has to electrify his office so that there may be proper lighting. If possible, air-conditioning can be provided for efficient functioning of the office. Proper fans have to be fixed and electricity has to be used economically due to high cost of electricity. Further, the advocate should be prompt in paying the electricity bills so that disconnection may be avoided and he can work in his office late in the night.

VIII. Office Equipment

It should be equipped with office equipment like office desk, office chairs, easy chairs, stools, benches, teapots, computer desks, almirahs, iron safes, racks for keeping books and journals, ceiling fans, mats, cases, a typewriter of a computer system, water containers, mugs, towels, napkins, etc. Care should be taken to see that the clients should have a proper and comfortable place to wait. All the furniture and other equipments available in the office should be entered in the register. If the articles are torn or damaged, they should be repaired or replaced within no time. All the items should be kept neat without dust or dirt.

IX. Sanitary Provisions

The law office should have attached toilet as many people visit the law office to meet the advocate and at the same time clients have to wait for a long time to meet their advocate. Further, the office staff have to stay for a long time in the office. Thus, for the use of all these, the law office should be provided with the sanitary fittings of western type and ordinary sit-outs.

X. Stationery

The law office of an advocate should consist of stationery articles required for office use such as white papers, wrapper papers, pens, pencils, tags, pinning machine, gum, pin, envelops, cards, money order forms, postal acknowledgment form, postal stamps, telegraph forms, pads, case file documents, different printed forms, which are to be filed in courts. These should be kept in stock and one should not go elsewhere in search of these needed office articles.

XI. Means of Transport

In order to attend the work in different courts and office, one should have a vehicle, either a two-wheeler or four-wheeler, public transport cannot be relied upon, nowadays, particularly when punctuality is to be maintained.

XII. Junior Advocates

Senior Advocates, whether designated as such, or otherwise, normally recruit junior advocates, who are mostly fresh law graduates. They are appointed, depending on the necessity of the senior, and also on the capacity of the junior. These junior advocates perform many functions assisting the senior in discharging their professional obligations. They also do lot of research on a given case.

XIII. A Good Law Library

Library is the most important element in a law office. Every lawyer is required to maintain a library of his own. The books are the basis of the legal profession. The library should contain both local and national Acts, reference books, manuals, digests, law reports and books related to social sciences. These books will help the advocate to know about the law and precedents. The law reports enable him to have the knowledge of the judicial decisions and views of the court on different issues relating to different laws, i.e., cases of both civil and criminal matters. The reference books are necessary for the knowledge of statutory laws. The reference books should be alphabetically arranged and journals and law report should be arranged year-wise. General and specific dictionaries, encyclopedias, year books, directories and bibliographic dictionary are some of the reference books that are constantly useful for advocates. The advocate should also keep all important Acts of Central Government and State Governments along with relevant rules. These Acts and Rules should be up to date. Generally, all current legislative material such as Bills, Acts, Rules, Notifications, etc. are published in the Gazettes of India and the states.

These are very much required to bring the Acts up to date. Besides this, he should subscribe to periodicals and law journals. Articles in law journals are important and indispensable source of information for an advocate.

The law reports enable him to have the knowledge of judicial decisions and views of the courts on different issues relating to different laws. The journal of Indian Law Institute, Academy Law Review, Indian Journal of International Law, Cochin University Law Review, Delhi Law Review, the Administrator, Supreme Court Journal, Criminal Law Journal, Labour Law Journal, Civil and Military Law Journal are some of the journals that an advocate should subscribe.

The All India Law Reporter is one of the reputed legal periodicals. There are also A.I.R. Manuals in multiple volumes. These volumes containing Central and State legislative material should find place in the Advocate's Library. The library should have Supreme Court Reports since 1950, the Federal Courts Reports (1939-1950) and private publications like A.I.R., S.C.C. and some other publications which report the case decisions of the Supreme Court and High Courts.

The library should be arranged section-wise by keeping all the reference books at one place and the books according to the catalogue numbers. The journals and law reports should be arranged year-wise. The general procedure of maintaining the library is the same to all the libraries. The library should be maintained basing on subject classification. For this, the lawyers should have the knowledge of library science, e.g., he should know the sub-division of other subjects of law as given in Melvin Dewey decimal classification. An advocate should maintain a catalogue register of library books with call numbers. He should allot some pages for each category of books at the beginning of the register. He should prepare an index of the subjects. The register should be numbered on the right side upper corner of each page. Whenever a new book reaches his library it should be entered in the catalogue register and properly numbered and be placed among the books of same category.

It is better for an advocate to follow the Dewey Decimal classification system, which is used by most libraries. The Melvin Dewey Decimal classification has 10 main classes and each main class has 10 subject classes. Each subject has 10 classes. Altogether there are thousand classes. Each class has sub-divisions and these sub-division numbers are placed after a decimal sign.[1] They are as under :

(i) Main classes :

000 Generalities

100 Philosophy

200 Religion

300 Social Sciences

400 Natural Sciences

500 Technology

1. For details, see S.R. Myneni, Public Interest Lawyering, Legal Aid and Para-Legal Services (2002), at pp. 98-100.

700 The Arts
800 Literature and rhetoric
900 Geography and History

(ii) Subject division of Social Sciences (300)

310 Statistics
320 Political Science
330 Economics
340 Law
350 Public Administration
360 Social Services and Associations
370 Education
380 Commerce, Communications, Transport
390 Customs, Etiquette

(iii) Division of the subject 'Law' (340)

341 International Law
342 Constitutional and Administrative Law
343 Military, Tax, Trade, Industrial Law
344 Social, Labour, Welfare, Health, Safety, Education, Cultural Law
345 Criminal Law
346 Private Law
347 Civil Procedure and Courts
348 Law (Statutes), Regulations, cases
348 Law of Specific Jurisdiction, areas.

(iv) Sub-division of Criminal Law (345)

01 Criminal Courts
02 Crimes (Offences)
03 Criminals (Offenders)
04 Liability, responsibility, guilt
05 General Criminal Procedure
06 Evidence
07 Trials
08 Juvenile Procedure
09 Specific Jurisdictions and areas.

Thus, the purpose of using a classification system as the basis for arranging materials is to bring publications on one subject together at one location and near publications on related subjects.

The columns of the Register of Library books are :

Classification No.	Title of Book	Name of Author	Place of Publication	Name of Publisher	Date of Publication	Number of Pages	Cost (Rs.)	Remarks
1	2	3	4	5	6	7	8	9

XIV. Preparation, Filing of cases and Dealing With Clients

A successful lawyer leads a strenuous life. Litigation has been compared with warfare, which calls for definite plans and the marshalling of force before action begins. Planning means wise anticipation and strenuous preparation. It is an accepted principle that one must not attack a tiger without a weapon, that is, a lawyer must not proceed with a case unprepared—he must be ready with facts, law and proof. Brains, work, will and industry with constant practice are always rewarded. Hence, it is necessary for a lawyer to foresee the various aspects of the case and prepare himself thoroughly to meet those aspects.

The first duty of a lawyer is to welcome his client's presence in the Chamber. The client must not feel that his presence is unwanted. The lawyer must give patient hearing to the client and where necessary must make enquiries. Then prepare the case of the client on the footing of warfare in strategy and tactics. Strategy is needed in the preparation of the case before the commencement of trial and tactics in the conduct of the case in the court. It is often mistaken that success at the bar is always the prize of a genius. But success in litigation largely depends upon thorough preparation of the case. A lawyer owes this duty both to the court and also to his client.

The second stage is the preparation to present a case. A lawyer must conscientiously equip himself with the art of presenting a case. He must acquaint himself both with the best as well as weak points in the case under preparation. A careful anticipation of the contingencies that are likely to arise must be undertaken. Never think that your opponent is not aware of it. A lawyer must take every point in such a way as if the opponent is present and presses each and every point that may come under contemplation. He must marshal the facts and the arguments of the case. For his marshalling he must develop a selective faculty. He must sift the more important facts from the less important. He must select the facts that need emphasis from those which do not need as much. This kind of selection is possible only when he has accurate knowledge of the details of a case. He should be so prepared that even without pausing for moment the question of the presiding officer is answered. A lawyer must ascertain the complete facts from the client and must make a study of the documents and peruse relentlessly his enquiries regarding other related facts and documents. All the rules for the drafting of a pleading and the rules of the Code of Civil Procedure must be borne in mind while preparing a claim or a defence in a litigation. Only logical and connected story of a case may be stated. A needless history, argument and rhetoric should not be given place in the drafting of the pleadings.

While preparing a case one should never feel contented only after looking up a particular point in the index of the book. It is always better to study the entire cases, and if not so, at least the relevant paras with greater detail. He must carefully go through all the cases cited in the relevant judgment. While studying the case-law, he should never be contented with the reading of head-notes. The headstones may be inaccurate or imperfect or incomplete. To understand the exact scope of a decision, the lawyer should study the whole report and the lawyer should be confident about the authority cited by him. Never allow to be humiliated on the ground that the cases cited are turned against you and used as a weapon by the opponent counsel. The cases to be cited must be prepared in their chronological order. Have the inspection of documents, obtain copies thereof and prepare notes therefrom. Make a list of facts required to be proved in chronological order and make a note of witnesses by whom those facts can be proved according to law.

When the witness is brought to you to tender evidence in the court of law on your client's side, do not believe that he will say everything that the client has told him to say in the court. First of all, always examine the witness in your chamber and correct him in accordance with needs of your case. When the witness is straightway taken to the court to give evidence you cannot command and correct his erroneous statement in the open court. For the examination of witnesses a thorough study of the law of evidence is necessary. While conducting the trial of a litigation in the court an advocate should not be hasty; he must maintain calmness; interruption with the judge and the opponent counsel in an inopportune time may be avoided. It is a totally wrong notion that one who very often intrupts the judge and the opposite counsel is an efficient lawyer. Lastly, one should not lose his temper if the Judge disagrees with him on certain points. There he should only say "I respectfully disagree with your Lordship's observation". The lawyer should imagine that the judge has no prior knowledge of the particular point of law or fact. Inaccurate and loud expression should be shunned.

An advocate is bound to accept any brief in the courts or tribunals or before any authority in or before any authority which he professes to practice at a fee consistent with his standing at the Bar and the nature of the case. However, special circumstances may justify his refusal to accept a particular brief. An advocate should not accept a brief or appear in a case in which he has reason to believe that he will be a witness, and if being engaged in a case, it becomes apparent that he is a witness on a material question of fact, he should not continue to appear as an advocate if he can retire without jeopardising his client's interests. Besides, a legal practitioner should refuse to accept a brief when he had already been consulted by the opposite party; when he is physically disabled from appearing for the client; when he may not be available to present the case in court; where the client is not prepared and able to pay him his reasonable fee; where he confined his practice in some places and some courts only; when his training in a special branch limits his usefulness in other branches, etc. An advocate shall not ordinarily withdraw from engagements once accepted, without sufficient cause and unless reasonable and sufficient notice is given to the client upon his withdrawal from a case. He shall refund such part of the fee as as not been earned. He should file the case in appropriate court immediately after accepting the brief. If he fails to do so, it will be considered as misconduct.

An advocate should keep accounts of the client's money. The Bar Council Rules, 1975 made in exercise of its rule making powers under the Advocates Act, 1961 more precisely under Section 49(1)(c) thereof, deal with Advocate's duty to keep accounts of the client's money entrusted to him, among other duties. The relevant rules which are stated under Rules 25 to 32, in Part IV, Chapter II, Section II. Besides this, the Supreme Court Rules, 1966 made by the Supreme Court under Article 145 of the Constitution of India also deal with the Advocate's duty to maintain books of accounts. Rules 25 to 32 are as follows :

25. An advocate should keep accounts of the client's money entrusted to him and the accounts should show the amounts received from the client or on his behalf, the expenses incurred for him and the debits made on account of fees with respective dates and all other necessary particulars.
26. Where moneys are received from or on account of a client, the entries in the accounts should contain a reference as to whether the amounts have been received for fees or expenses, and during the course of the proceedings, no advocate shall, except with the consent in writing of the client concerned, be at liberty to divert any portion of the expenses towards fees.
27. Where any amount is received or given to him on behalf of his client the fact of such receipt must be intimated to the client as early as possible.
28. After the termination of the proceedings the advocate shall be at liberty to appropriate towards the settled fee due to him any sum remaining unexpended out of the amount paid or sent to him for expenses, or any amount that has come into his hands in that proceeding.
29. Where the fee has been left unsettled, the advocate shall be entitled to deduct, out of any moneys of the client remaining in his hands, at the termination of the proceeding for which he had been engaged, the fee payable under the rules of the court, in force for the time being, of by then settled and the balance, if any, shall be refunded to the client.
30. A copy of the client's account shall be furnished to him on demand provided the necessary copying charges are paid.
31. An advocate shall not enter into arrangements whereby funds in his hands are converted into loans.
32. An advocate shall not in any way communicate or negotiate upon the subject matter or controversy with any party represented by an advocate except through that advocate.

An advocate shall not lend money to his client for the purpose of any action or legal proceedings in which he is engaged by such client.

Advocate shall not accept a fee less than the fee taxable under the rules when the client is able to pay the same.

An advocate shall not solicit work or advertise. His signboard or name plate should be of a reasonable size. The signboard or name plate or stationery should not indicate that he is or has been President or Member of a Bar Council or of any Association. An Advocate shall not permit his professional services or his name to be used in aid, of, or to make possible the unauthorised practice of law by any agency. Every advocate shall in the practice of the profession of law bear in mind that one genuinely in need of a lawyer is entitled to legal assistance even though he cannot pay for it fully or adequately and that within the limits of an advocate's economic condition, free legal assistance to the indigent and oppressed is one of the highest obligations an advocate owes to society. Further, it is improper for an advocate to demand or accept fees or any premium from any person as a consideration for imparting training in law under the rules prescribed by a State Bar Council to enable such person to qualify for enrolment under the Advocate Act, 1961.

An advocate appearing in the Supreme Court, High Court, Subordinate Courts, Tribunals or Authority shall wear the prescribed dress. Section 49(1)(gg) of the Advocates Act, 1961 empowers the Bar Council of India to make rules prescribing the form of dresses or robes to be worn by advocates, having regard to the climate conditions, appearing before any Court or Tribunal.[1] Order IV, Rule 3 of the Supreme Court Rules, 1966 provides that every advocate appearing before the court shall wear such robes and costume as may from time to time be directed by the court.

Advocates appearing in the Supreme Court, High Courts, Subordinate Courts, Tribunals, or Authorities shall wear the following part of their dress which shall be sober and dignified :

(i) Advocates other than Lady Advocates :

(A) a black buttoned up coat, chapkan, achkan, black sherwani and white bands with Advocate's Gown, or

(B) a black open breast coat, white shirt, white collar, stiff or soft, and white bands with Advocate's Gown.

In either case long trousers (white, black or black striped or grey) or Dhoti.

(ii) Lady Advocates :

(A) Black and full or half sleeve jacket or blouse, white collar, stiff or soft, with white bands with Advocate's Gown;

(B) Sarees, or long skirts (white or black or any mellow of subdued colour without any print or design) or flare (white, black or black stripped or grey) or Punjabi dress churidar kurta or salwar kurta with or without dupatta (white or black) :

Provided that the wearing of Advocate's Gown shall be optional except when appearing in the Supreme Court or in a High Court :

Provided further that the courts other than the Supreme Court, High Court, District Court or City Civil Courts a black

1. Published in Gazette of India dated 28th October, 1978.

tie may be worn instead of bands.

In **Jose v. State of Kerala,**[1] it was held by the Court that while appearing before Tribunals and Authorities, insistence on wearing of bands only (instead of tie) and Advocates Gown, in misconceived and uncalled for.

---

1. 1990 (1) KLT 483.

15

PUBLIC INTEREST LAWYERING IN INDIA

I. Introduction

Public interest lawyering plays an important role in getting success in legal profession. It makes an advocate popular and renowned among the people. It enables the legal practitioners to have experience which is necessary for success in the legal profession. The legal profession has been created not for private gain, but also for public welfare. Hence, it is a branch of administration of justice and lawyers are the officers of the court. Rule 46 of the rules framed by the Bar Council of India, 1975 makes it crystal clear that it is the duty of an advocate to render legal aid to anyone genuinely in need thereof. Dealing with the problems associated with public interest litigation, the problem that crops up is regarding identifying this litigation and this includes the question of determining how far a particular Public Interest Litigation is genuine, how far public spirited person is honest, sincere and serious enough and how far he adequately represents a particular downtrodden class or sub-class, etc. This onerous task of scrutiny would be an important obligation on the part of the concerned Legal Aid Committee.

II. Public Interest Litigation

Public Interest Litigation is a recent institutional innovation of the Supreme Court of India. The spirit of the Public Interest Litigation has shown a revolutionary movement in the realm of judicial functioning to ameliorate the miseries of the masses. Public Interest Law popularly known as Public Interest Litigation in India, has been described by the Supreme Court as a strategic arm of the legal aid movement and which is intended to bring justice within the reach of poor masses, who constitute the low visibility area of humanity. Litigative process against maladministration and unjust laws assumed very significant strategy of legal aid. It is concerned with litigation on issues of public interest, e.g., protection of consumers, preservation of environments, observance and compliance with the provisions of labour legislations, bonded labour, social evils like dowry, untouchability, etc. Public Interest Litigation is considered as an instrument to ensure even handed justice to the poor, ignorant and downtrodden who were neglected for long. All normal procedures are bypassed for the initiation of litigation through Public Interest Litigation. A large section of the people such as Harijans, Adivasis, landless labourers and others, who have suffered from economic exploitation and all sorts of social indignities are beneficiaries to receive social assistance, concessions, privileges and special rights through the medium of Public Interest Litigation.

Public Interest Litigation is not a unique and judicially fashioned tool in India alone, it was the United States of America, which gave lot of prominence to this concept, of course, under a different name, viz., Public Interest Law.[1] Public Interest Litigation has become popular in India because of the fact that judiciary played a vital role in order to protect the rights and interests of the oppressed sections, weaker and vulnerable quarters and the unrepresented sections of the society.

In an adversarial system of justice, the judiciary is expected to render justice when the litigating parties come before the courts seeking a remedy or redressal. Generally, the right to approach a court for redressal of a legal injury is given to an 'aggrieved party' alone. The right or standing is known s *'locus standi'* in the legal parlance. Functioning of the judiciary during the course of 1950-80, however, reveals that much could not be achieved in the field of justice by the Supreme Court for the reason that the philosophy of the term *locus standi* was given a strict interpretation. The general rule was that only those persons whose legal rights were infracted directly and substantially, could move the court for the remedy. The power of the court was exercised when this initial requirement, namely, that the party who initiated the litigation had himself a grievance, was satisfied. However, exception was made only in case of petition for *'habeas corpus'* where a relative or a friend could file a petition on his behalf.

Undoubtedly, the rigorous application of this rule of *'locus standi'* resulted in denial of access to the judicial remedies to a large majority of Indian population who were poor and illiterate. In other words, this rigid principle of *'locus standi'* has caused greater injustice than the justice in India, as every aggrieved person was not in a position to move the constitutional courts for an extraordinary remedy either under Article 32 or 226 of the Constitution. As one of the famous judges credited with the emergence and birth of Public Interest Litigation in India Hon'ble Mr. Justice V.R. Krishna Iyer points out "....the people of India are illiterate, around 70% indigent, around 50% being below the poverty line, primitive more than 20% being depressed classes and tribal miserables."[2] Thus, the raw realities of Indian society today are colossal illiteracy, intractable indigency, and countless chronic injustices, blended with a militancy generated by the preambular rhetoric of the Constitution.[3]

It was, fortunately in the year 1980 that the Supreme Court of India has broken the rigid procedural barricade and endeavoured to ratify this apathy resulting into the emergence of the new contours of the doctrine of *locus standi.* Justice V.R. Krishna Iyer and Justice P.N. Bhagwati, heralded a strong movement for opening new contours in the law of standing. The Supreme Court daringly decided to depart from the aforesaid traditional

1. S.K. Agarwala, Public Interest Litigation in India—A Critique (1985), p. 2.
2. V.R. Krishna Iyer, Justice at Crossroads (1994), p. 102.
3. *Ibid.* at p. 101.

rule and allowed any member of public or social action group acting bona fide to move an application in the Supreme Court or any High Court, to seek judicial redressal for the legal wrong or injury caused to persons who were unable to approach the court for relief for reasons of poverty or disability. Today, approach to the top judicial machinery could be made just by sending a letter to it, and the court would act upon it taking and treating it as a petition. To reiterate, Public Interest Litigation or *'Pro bono Publico Litigation'* is a litigation at the instance of a public spirited citizen espousing cause of others. It is a strategic arm of the legal aid movement and which is intended to bring justice within the reach of poor masses who constitute the low visibility area of humanity.

Justice V.R. Krishna Iyer, one of the pioneering judges who legitimised and popularised the Public Interest Litigation in India considers Public Interest Litigation as the product of creative judicial engineering. According to him, "the jurisdiction of the Indian Supreme Court is the widest in the world; the challenges of India's social changes are the sharpest; the dynamics of a functional jurisprudence is the creative expression of judicial response to the crisis of hunger for justice. Public Interest Litigation is the offspring of these social forces. This burgeoning process, seminal and innovative makes the court a catalyst of social justice, a defender of the constitutional faith and the protagonist in the drama of human rights for the common man."[1] He views Public Interest Litigation as a part of the participative justice.[2]

Public Interest Litigation for eminent jurist Professor Upendra Baxi is the medium through which (a new kind of lawyering and a novel kind of judging) as happened, and is happening. However, he uses the term, Social Action Litigation in preference to the Public Interest Litigation. He considers the Social Action Litigation as a by-product of the catharsis of 1975-76 emergency, which is primarily judge-led and even judge induced, and an exercise of judicial populism.

Accordingly, now the courts are permitting 'Public Interest Litigation' or 'Social Action Litigations' or 'General Interest Litigations' or 'Social Interest Litigation' at the instance of 'public spirited citizens' by relaxing the 'Rule of Locus Standi'. Justice V.R. Krishna Iyer, in **A.B.S.K. Sangh (Rly.) v. Union of India,**[3] declared that 'access to justice' through 'class actions', 'public interest litigation' and 'representative proceedings' is the present constitutional jurisprudence." Thus, strict rule of *locus standi* applicable to private litigation was relaxed and a broad rule of public interest has been accepted. Now procedures and techniques have been evolved by the judges to facilitate this new innovation.

The first dramatic opportunity to initiate this new kind of constitutional litigation in India was probably provided by the Supreme Court advocate Ms. Kapila Hingorani, who filed a writ based on a series of articles in 'Indian Express', a national daily, espousing the plight of

1. *Ibid.*, at pp. 105-107.
2. *Fertilizer Corp. Kamgar Union* v. *Union of India*, A.I.R. 1981 S.C. 344 at p. 355.
3. A.I.R. 1981 S.C. 298.

Bihar undertrial prisoners, most of whom had served long pre-trial detentions. This culminated in Supreme Court accepting the *locus standi* of the advocate and another in a series of six interim matters, viz. **Hussainara Khatoon (I) to Hussainara Khatoon (VI) v. State of Bihar.**[1] In 1980, a letter was received by the Supreme Court from Professors of Law.[2] This letter was addressed on behalf of the inmates of a protective home run by the state of Uttar Pradesh. Another letter was written by a journalist. It was regarding the flesh trade going on in certain parts of the State of Madhya Pradesh. Besides, a social science researcher also wrote a letter to the court complaining of the detention of several industrial prisoners in jails in the State of Bihar, particularly of four tribal boys who had almost grown up in jail from the age of twelve to eighteen or nineteen, and their trials were yet to commence. In all these cases, the Supreme Court had treated the letters as petitions, and issued appropriate directions.

The history of cases decided by the Supreme Court during the last two decades reveals that entertaining public interest litigation cases have multiplied on a very large scale giving an opportunity to court to render justice to prisoners,[3] undertrials, women,[4] children[5] bonded labourers[6] and lot of other oppressed sections of the society. The judiciary has ushered in an era of social revolution through public interest litigation.

III. Socio Economic Justice—The Role of Public Interest Litigation

The Supreme Court of India by introducing Public Interest Litigation has virtually heralded a revolutionary movement in the realm of judicial functioning to ameliorate the miseries of masses. In the recent times Public Interest Litigation is considered as an instrument to ensure even handed justice to the poor, ignorant and downtrodden who were neglected for long. During the last two decades, the Supreme Court has contributed a lot to make the socio-economic political justice as enshrined in the Preamble to the Constitution, a reality. The Court exercised the power of judicial review vested in it under Article 32 of the Constitution, in a commendable manner, with an object to ameliorate the conditions of countless masses in the

1. A.I.R. 1979 S.C. 1360, 1377, 1819, (1980) 1 S.C.C. 91; 91980) 1 S.C.C. 93.
2. *Dr. Upendra Baxi* v. *State of U.P.*, (1981) 3 SCALE 1136.
3. *Hussainara Khatoon* v. *State of Bihar*, A.I.R. 1979 S.C. 1360; *Sunil Batra (i)* v. *Delhi Administration*, A.I.R. 1978 S.C. 1775; *Sunil Batra (ii)* v. *Delhi Administration*, A.I.R. 1980 S.C. 1579 and *Prem Shankar Shukla* v. *Delhi Administration*, A.I.R. 1986 S.C. 1773.
4. *Veena Sethi* v. *State of Bihar*, A.I.R. 1983 S.C. 339; *Kamla Devi* v. *State of Punjab*, A.I.R. 1984 S.C. 1895; *Sheela Barse* v. *Union of India*, A.I.R. 1986 S.C. 1773 and *Visakha* v. *State of Rajasthan*, A.I.R. 1997 S.C. 3011.
5. *Sushila Gothala* v. *State of Rajasthan*, A.I.R. 1995 Raj. 90; *Gaurav Jain* v. *Union of India*, A.I.R. 1990 S.C. 292; *M.C. Mehta* v. *State of Tamil Nadu*, A.I.R. 1991 S.C. 417; *Labourers Working in Salal Hydro-Project* v. *State of J & K*, A.I.R. 1984 S.C. 177; *Vishal Jeet* v. *Union of India*, A.I.R. 1990 S.C. 1412 and *Kishen* v. *Orissa*, A.I.R. 1989 S.C. 677.
6. *People's Union for Democratic Rights* v. *Union of India*, A.I.R. 1982 S.C. 1973; *Sanjit Ray* v. *State of Rajasthan*, A.I.R. 1983 S.C. 328.

country, hitherto unrepresented before the court due to poverty, illiteracy or ignorance, and due to various social and economic barriers. The Judicial Activism of the court has come to the rescue of many helpless sections of the society. The Public Interest Litigation has proved to be a strong and potent weapon in the hands of the court to give directions in public interest and enforce the public duties relating to environment, child and women welfare, labour welfare, prisoners' welfare, etc. Some of the areas, where the public interest litigation has played a constructive role in emancipating the cause of helpless sections of the society are discussed as follows :

(i) Public interest litigation and prisoners' right

Prior to the advent of the Public Interest Litigation in India, the prisoners as a class, were really in a helpless position. There was no means and forum to complain against the inhuman conditions prevailing in the jails, protective homes and reformatories. The Public Interest Litigation has opened a wide avenue of remedies for the prisoner victims. The Supreme Court launched its crusade to protect the fundamental rights of the undertrial prisoners. Public Interest Litigation has provided a base to the court to secure the release of the undertrials languishing behind the bars for years together for no fault of theirs.

In **Hussainara Khatoon v. Home Secretary, Bihar**,[1] the apex court declared that keeping undertrials in prison without any trial for long durations, violates their right to speedy trial implicit in Article 21 of the Constitution. The Court ordered that all such prisoners whose names were submitted in the court should be released forthwith. In another case, **Khatri v. State of Bihar**,[2] which is popularly known as **Bhagalpur Blindings case**, the Supreme Court headed by Justice P.N. Bhagwati, explained the concept of the right to free-legal services and issued a series of directions to get the 18 blinded prisoners treated by expert doctors. The court directed the Government of Bihar to punish the policemen who committed the cruel act of blinding the undertrials in Bhagalpur jail. In **Anil Yadav v. State of Bihar**,[3] the Supreme Court admitted a writ petition filed by one of prisoners on others behalf and dealt with a *habeas corpus* petition filed by the blinded prisoners.

In **Veena Sethi v. State of Bihar**,[4] the Free Legal Aid Committee, Hazaribagh brought to the notice of the court through a letter about the illegal detention of certain prisoners in Hazaribagh jail for two or three decades without any justification. It was observed that the prisoners who were declared insane at the time of their detention were not released after they became sane. It was due to the inaction of the authorities to take steps to release them though they were in jails for 20 to 37 years. The court held that the prisoners remained in jail for no fault of theirs are entitled to be released forthwith.

1. A.I.R. 1979 1360; Also see *Sunil Batra (i) and (ii)* v. *Delhi Administration*, A.I.R. 1978 S.C. 1675 and A.I.R. 1980 S.C. 1579.
2. A.I.R. 1981 S.C. 928.
3. A.I.R. 1982 S.C. 1008.
4. A.I.R. 1983 S.C. 339.

In another case, **Sheela Barse v. State of Maharashtra**,[1] the Supreme Court entertained a writ petition based on a letter addressed by Sheela Barse, a journalist complaining of custodial violence to women prisoners while continued in the police lock-up in the city of Bombay. The question of custodial violence, i.e., assault, torture or ill-treatment was duly investigated and appropriate guidelines were recommended for improving the conditions of women prisoners.

In **Khedat Mazdoor Chetna Sangh v. Madhya Pradesh**,[2] the apex court declared and reiterated that handcuffing of undertrial prisoners by police in unfair and unconstitutional.[3] In **D.K. Basu v. State of West Bengal**,[4] the Supreme Court acting on a Public Interest Litigation filed by a non-political organisation 'Legal Aid Services of West bengal' issued a number of directions against torture, cruel and inhuman treatment during investigation and interrogation of the accused. The court issued more directions in a subsequent order, in the same case.[5]

(ii) Public Interest Litigation and Right to Health and Medical Treatment

The right to health of the citizen is not an enumerated fundamental right in Part III of the Constitution of India. We find a reference of this right in the Directive Principles of State Policy, which are not justiciable *per se*. Similarly, the right to medical treatment in case of emergency is not a fundamental right or for that matter not even a legal right. The Public Interest Litigation and the Supreme Court have succeeded in making the people aware of these rights and also reminding the State its obligation to protect and enforce the same. Some of the leading cases in this point are discussed as under :

In **Vincent v. Union of India**,[6] a public interest litigation was filed by the petitioner under Article 32 of the Constitution asking for directions for maintenance of approved standards of drugs and banning of injurious and harmful drugs. The apex court held that the right to maintenance and improvement of public health is included in the right to live with human dignity enshrined in Article 21. A healthy body is the very foundation of all human activities. In a welfare State this is the obligation of the State to ensure the creation of and sustaining of conditions congenial to good health. The court directed the Central Government to compensate and reimburse him for his expenses in recognition of his service for bringing the matter before the court.

In **Permanand Katra v. Union of India**[7] a public interest litigation was brought to the notice of the Supreme Court by a petitioner, a human rights activist fighting for general public interest. He filed the writ on the

1. A.I.R. 1983 S.C. 378.
2. A.I.R. 1995 S.C. 31.
3. *Citizens for Democracy* v. *Assam*, (1995) 3 S.C.C. 743.
4. A.I.R. 1997 S.C. 610.
5. A.I.R. 1997 S.C. 3017.
6. A.I.R. 1987 S.C. 990.
7. A.I.R. 1989 S.C. 2039.

basis of a news item entitled 'law helps the injured to die' published in the Hindustan Times. In that report it was alleged that a scooterist was knocked down by a speeding car. Seeing him profusely bleeding; a person who was on the road picked up the injured and took him to nearest hospital. The doctors refused to attend to him and asked him to take him to another hospital located some 30 kms. away authorised to handle medico-legal cases. The man carried the victim to the hospital and before he could reach there the victim succumbed to injuries. The court, in this case extensively dealt with the professional ethics of the medical profession and issued a number of directions to ensure that an injured person instantaneously given medical aid without waiting for legal formalities to be complied with by the police under Code of Criminal Procedure. Similarly, the Supreme Court issued further guidelines in this regard in **Pashchim Banga Khet Mazdoor Samiti v. West Bengal**,[1] and held that the Government is duty bound to provide timely medical assistance to the person is serious and moribund conditions.

Further, in **Common Cause v. Union of India**,[2] a public interest litigation filed by common cause, a voluntary organization, a Division Bench of the Supreme Court took the cognizance of serious deficiencies and shortcomings in the matter of collection, storage and supply of blood through the various blood-centres operating in the country. The court issued number of directions which included the direction to : (i) establish a National Council of Blood Transfusion; (ii) train the technical personnel; (iii) conduct research; (iv) start special post-graduate courses in blood collection, processing and storage; and (v) discourage the prevailing system of professional donors. The court also directed the government to make separate legislation for regulating collection, storage, distribution and transportation of blood and operation of blood banks. The court in another case, that is, **Consumer Education and Research Centre v. Union of India**,[3] dealt with a public interest litigation, complaining about the spreading of an occupational disease called 'asbestosis' afflicted to the workers engaged in asbestos mining. The court emphatically declared that the right to health and medical care of the workmen, both during and after their service is a fundamental right under Article 21 of the Constitution, because without health, no citizen can live with basic human dignity.

(iii) Public interest litigation and child welfare

The Constitution of India provides many provisions for the welfare of children.[4] Besides this, there are around 300 legislations which directly or indirectly deal with the protection of children. In spite of all these provisions children are forced to work and put to many hardships. Public Interest Litigations have been filed in the interest of child welfare. In **People's Union for Democratic Rights v. Union of India**,[5] it was

1. (1996) 4 S.C.C. 37.
2. (1996) 1 S.C.C. 753.
3. A.I.R. 1995 S.C. 922.
4. For details, see Articles 24, 39(f) and 45 of the Constitution of India.
5. A.I.R. 1983 S.C. 1473.

contended that the Employment of Children Act, 1938 was not applicable in case of employment of children in the construction work of Asiad Projects in Delhi since construction industry was not in the Schedule of the Act. The court held that the construction work is hazardous employment and therefore under Article 24 no child below the age of 14 years can be employed in construction work, even if construction industry is not specified in the Schedule of Employment of Children Act, 1938. Similarly, the court held in **Labourers Working on Salal Hydro Project v. State of Jammu and Kashmir**,[1] that the construction work is a hazardous employment and children below 14 years cannot be employed in this work. The court further observed that the scope for proper education to such working children in their work place be observed.

The court also played an activist role in **Lakshmi Kant Pandey v. Union of India**,[2] which related to inter-country adoptions. On the basis of a public interest litigation, the Supreme Court laid down the principles and norms which must be followed in inter-country adoptions in order to prevent the noble cause for degenerating into trafficking in children and the constitutional obligation under Articles 15(3) and 39(c) and (f) to ensure the welfare of the child be fulfilled.

In **Gaurav Jain v. Union of India**,[3] the Supreme Court took cognizance of the problems of the children born to prostitutes and constituted a committee with lawyers and social activists to look into the matter. In the instant case the court delivered a landmark judgment and observed that 'segregating children of prostitutes by locating separate schools and providing separate hostels' would not be in the interest of the children and the society at large. The apex court directed that they 'should be segregated from their mothers and be allowed to mingle with others and become a part of the society." The court had ordered that "Children of prostitutes should, however, not be permitted to live in inferno and the undesirable surroundings of prostitute homes." This was felt particularly so in the case of young girls whose body and mind are likely to be abused with growing age for being admitted into the profession of their mothers. While the court did not accept the plea for separate hostels for children of prostitutes, it felt that accommodation in hostels and other reformatory homes should be adequately available to help segregation of these children from their mothers living in prostitute homes as soon as they are identified." The court issued directions for rescue and rehabilitation of child prostitutes, and the children of fallen women, and further directed the establishment of Juvenile Homes for them. In another case,[4] the court acted on a petition filed by an advocate under Article 32, alleging the sexual exploitation of children in the flesh trade. The court issued directions to the State Governments to eradicate the child prostitution.

1. A.I.R. 1984 S.C. 177.
2. (1984) 2 S.C.C. 244.
3. A.I.R. 1990 S.C. 292.
4. *Vishal Jeet* v. *Union of India*, A.I.R. 1990 S.C. 1412.

In **Sheela Barse v. Union of India,**[1] the court held that the State should enforce the provisions of Children's Act enacted by States effectively. The court issued directions to the Government that the Parliament should pass a Central legislation on this subject. The court also directed the Central Government to pay the petitioner Rs. 10,000/- for the expenses and to extend all necessary assistance by personally visiting the jails in different States regarding this matter.

(iv) Public interest litigation and pollution free environment

The environment has been another major area of public interest litigation concern. The case regarding vehicular pollution in Delhi,[2] pollution of the Ganga,[3] treatment of industrial effluents,[4] limestone quarrying in the Doon Valley,[5] mining in the Sariska Tiger Sanctuary,[6] the Tehri Dam issue,[7] setting up of thermal power plant in Dehanu Maharashtra[8] and so on stand as testimony to reveal the encouraging attitudes of the higher courts in India.

The judicial activism in respect of protection of environment is notable. Great leap has been taken in environmental jurisprudence due to Public Interest Litigation. The Supreme Court has established the following principles in the Public Interest Litigation :[9]

(A) There should be sustainable development.—Development that meets the needs of the present without compromising the ability of the future to meet their own needs.

(B) Precautionary principles should be adopted.—Environment measures must anticipate, prevent, and attack the cause of environmental degradation. Where there are threats of serious and irreversible damage, lack of scientific certainty should not be used as a reason for postponing measures to prevent environmental degradation. The onus of proof is on the actor or the developer/industrialist to show that his action is environmentally benign.

(C) Polluter pays.—The financial cost of preventing or remedying damage lies with the undertaking causing the pollution. It cannot be saddled with the Government, as it would shift to the tax payers.

---

1. (1986) 3 S.C.C. 596.
2. *Madras Road Resident Association and another* v. *Lt. Governor of Delhi and others*, A.I.R. 1995 Delhi 195.
3. *M.C. Mehta* v. *Union of India*, 1991 Supp. (1) S.C.C. 181.
4. *Satish Chandra Shukla* v. *State of U.P.*, 1992 Sup. (2) S.C.C. 94.
5. *Rural Litigation and Entitlement Kendra* v. *State of U.P.*, 1991(3) S.C.C. 347.
6. *Tarun Bharat Singh* v. *Union of India*, 1992 Sup. (2) S.C.C. 448.
7. *Tehri Bandh Virodhi Sangharsa Samiti* v. *State of U.P.*, 1992 Supp. (1) S.C.C. 44.
8. *Dehanu Taluka Environment Protection Group* v. *Bombay Suburban Electric Supply Company Ltd.*, 1991 (2) S.C.C. 539.
9. *M.C. Mehta* v. *Union of India (Oleum Gas Leakage Case)*, A.I.R. 1987 S.C. 1086; *India Council For Enviro-Legal Action* v. *Union of India*, A.I.R. 1996 S.C. 1446; *Vellore Citizens Welfare Forum* v. *Union of India*, A.I.R. 1996 S.C. 2715; *M.C. Mehta* v. *Kamalnath*, (1997) 1 S.C.C. 388 and see also *T.N. Godavarman Thirumulkad* v. *Union of India*, A.I.R. 1997 S.C. 1228.

(D) The rule of absolute liability.—If any damage is caused due to hazardous or dangerous activity then the sufferer is liable to be compensated irrespective of the fact that reasonable cause was taken in carrying out the activity. The liability is absolute. Now it is partly covered by the National Environment Tribunal Act and the Public Liability Insurance Act.

(E) Public trust doctrine.—The State is a trustee of all natural resources for the benefit of the public and is under legal duty to protect the natural resources.

(F) Deforestation causes ecological imbalance.—Trees are to be protected. Forest Conservation Act, 1980 was enacted to check deforestation. It applies to all forests irrespective of nature of their ownership or classification. It includes forests designated as reserved, private or otherwise. Prior approval of Central Government is required for any non-forest activity within the area of any forest.

However, in spite of such a large volume of legislations,[1] the right of citizens to pollution free environment remained elusive for the reason that the State by and large remained indifferent in this area. The Pollution Control Boards, established under these Act, even though designed to play a pertinent role in the area of pollution prevention, by and large, failed to discharge their statutory obligations. It is in this backdrop, that Public Interest Litigation has come to play the role of a catalyst in providing a pollution free environment to the common man. The noted lawyer, M.C. Mehta, the activist judges like P.N. Bhagwati, Rangnath Mishra and Kuldip Singh and organizations like the Rural Litigation and Entitlement Kendra, Common Cause, Indian Council for Enviro-Legal Action, etc. made immense contribution in realising the right to pollution free environment. Hence, the Public Interest Litigation has played a dynamic role in protecting the environment and ensuring a pollution free environment. Thus, the evolution of Public Interest Litigation in India created justiciable environmental rights and environmental jurisprudence. It is now quite clear that there has been an increasing use of law as a device of organized social action for bringing about socio-economic change. More and more categories of rights in favour of large section of people are being created. A series of new categories of duties are being imposed on the State as well as the executive authorities to cherish the Constitutional dream of rendering justice to all.

(v) Public interest litigation and women welfare

The Public Interest Litigation, which has been judge-induced the judge-led in India, has helped in protecting the rights of women, which have been guaranteed by the Constitution and other statutes. Women have some special problems, namely, sati, child marriage, system of devadasi, sexual harassment and prostitution. The Public Interest Litigation in India

1. The legislations passed by the Central Government in this regard are : Water (Prevention and Control of Pollution) Act, 1974; the Air (Prevention and Control of Pollution) Act, 1981; the Forest Conservation Act, 1980 and the Environment Protection Act, 1986.

have brought the issues relating to prostitutes, fallen women and other related issues to women welfare before the court and the court has issued several directions for the protection of women. A few leading cases are discussed as under :

In **Dr. Upendra Baxi v. State of U.P.**,[1] on a Public Interest Litigation filed by the eminent jurist and Law Professor, the Supreme Court issued a series of administrative orders to improve the conditions in Agra and Delhi Protective Homes for women; the result was that the conditions improved steadily. In another case, i.e., **Sheela Barse v. State of Maharashtra**,[2] the Supreme Court entertained a writ petition, complaining of custodial violence on women prisoners while confined in the police lock-up. On ascertaining the veracity of the complaint, by appointing a Commissioner of the court, the Supreme Court issued a number of directions to the State to protect the dignity and honour of the women prisoners, while in the custody of the police.

In **Vikram Deo Singh Tomar v. State of Bihar**,[3] the plight of the female inmates of the 'Care Home, Patna' was taken up in a public interest litigation. These inmates were compelled to live in inhuman conditions in an old ruined building. They were provided with insufficient and poor quality of food and no medical attention was provided to them. The apex court held that right to live with human dignity is the fundamental right of every citizen under Article 21 of the Constitution. It also guarantees right to live with human dignity. The court directed the State Government to repair the building with sufficient living rooms, bathrooms and toilets. It also directed that other facilities such as, water, electricity, etc. be provided to inmates living in police lock-up. Further, it should be ensured that a doctor should visit the home daily.

In another case, i.e., **Delhi Working Women's Forum v. Union of India**,[4] on a Public Interest Litigation filed by the Delhi Domestic Working Women's Forum to expose the pathetic plight of four domestic servants who were subjected to indecent sexual assault by seven army personnel in a train. The court has given directions to the National Commission for Women to frame schemes for compensation and rehabilitation to ensure justice to the rape victims. Thereafter, the Union Government was asked to take necessary steps to implement such schemes at the earliest. The court also asked the Government to set up 'Criminal Injuries Compensation Board' to pay compensation to rape victims.

In the year 1987, the Supreme Court made a very constructive use of Public Interest Litigation and judicial activism, in coming to the rescue of the working women, who are sexually harassed at their working places in **Vishaka v. State of Rajasthan**,[5] acting on an application filed under Article 32, by a voluntary organization, the Bench consisting of Chief

1. (1981) 3 SCALE 1136.
2. A.I.R. 1983 S.C. 378.
3. A.I.R. 1988 S.C. 1782.
4. (1995) 1 S.C.C. 14.
5. A.I.R. 1997 S.C. 3011.

Justice J.S. Verma, Justice Sujata Manohar and Justice B.N. Kirpal, found that there are no suitable legislations in this sphere in India. The court with a view to protect and enforce the fundamental and human rights of working women, resorted to direct judicial legislation by issuing many guidelines and norms, to protect from such harassment. The court emphatically declared :

> "In view of the...., absence of enacted law to provide for the effective enforcement of the basic human rights of gender equality and guarantee against sexual harassment at working places, we lay down the guidelines and norms specified hereunder for due observance at all work places or other institutions until a legislation is enacted for the purpose..."[1]
>
> "...these directions would be binding and enforceable in law until suitable legislation is enacted to occupy the field."

Hence, the apex court has exhibited a dynamic attitude in ensuring that gender equality is maintained in the work place, even at the cost of encroaching upon the domain of the legislature.

(vi) Public interest litigation and bonded labour

Public Interest Litigation has extended its helping hand to ameliorate the condition of bonded labour also. Some cases of bonded labourers have come before the court only through the Public Interest Litigation. It is only through this jurisdictional expansion in the form of Public Interest Litigation that the plight of bonded labour has attracted the attention of judiciary. Some of the leading cases on this point are discussed as under :

In **People's Union for Democratic Rights v. Union of India**,[2] popularly known as Asiad Project case, the Supreme Court treated a letter written by a social action group as writ petition. The letter was based on a report made by three scientists who were commissioned for the purpose of investigating and inquiring into the conditions under which the workmen engaged in various Asiad projects were working. The Committee alleged the violation of various labour laws in respect of the workmen engaged in the projects. The court held that the payment for deduction of Re. 1 per day by the Jamadars from the wages deprived the workers of getting the minimum wage of Rs. 9.25 per day and it was violation of Article 23 of the Constitution. The court further held that non-payment of minimum wages to workers employed was a denial to them of their right to live with basic human dignity and violative of Article 21 of the Constitution.

Bandhua Mukti Morcha v. Union of India,[3] is a watershed in the evolution of Public Interest Litigation movement in India. This case added new dimensions to the concept of public interest litigation in the area of identification, release and rehabilitation of bonded labour. The apex Court was informed through a letter that bonded labour was in existence in stone quarries in Faridabad district of the State of Haryana. The Supreme Court

1. *Ibid.*, at p. 3021.
2. A.I.R. 1982 S.C. 1473.
3. A.I.R. 1984 S.C. 802.

appointed a Commission to visit the said stone quarries and make inquiries. The court in order to root out exploitation and injustice and to ensure the weaker sections their rights and entitlements, directed the authorities not only to examine as to whether human beings are continuing to remain victims of deception and exploitation at the hands of strong and powerful sections of the community, but also whether social and economic justice has become a meaningful reality for them or it has remained merely a testing illusion and a promise of unreality. The investigator submitted a comprehensive report on the conditions in which women engaged in stone quarries and stone crushers live and work. It also made various recommendations for improving the living conditions of these workmen.[1] The court held that the State is bound to ensure the observance of the labour legislation enacted for securing the workmen a life of human dignity and inaction on the part of the State in implementation of such legislation would amount to denial of the right to live with human dignity enshrined in Article 21 of the Constitution. The court directed the government to set right the inhuman living condition of the bonded labourers without filing objections whenever a public interest litigation is filed regarding the bonded labour. It is, therefore, submitted that the ruling of the highest court of the land is clearly reflective of the emergence of the Supreme Court of India as the people's court which has been providing redress to the victims of bondage.

Neerja Chaudhary v. State of Madhya Pradesh,[2] is another momentous decision of the Supreme Court where the judiciary has taken a serious note of the indifferent and callous attitude of the State Administration in identifying, releasing and rehabilitating the bonded labourers in the country. The petitioner alleged that 135 bonded labourers who were working in stone quarries in Faridabad though released from chains of bondage were not rehabilitated even after a long time. The petitioner contended that non-implementation of the rehabilitative measures amount to violation of Article 21 of the Constitution as well as the Bonded Labour System (Abolition) Act, 1976. The petitioner, therefore, prayed for a direction to the State Government to take steps for the economic and social rehabilitation of the freed labourers released from the bondage. The court in this case went to the extent of giving direction to the executive in the matter of public interest litigation and the direction extended to chalking out of programmes and rehabilitation of bonded labourers and its supervision by a vigilance committee in which persons suggested by the courts were to be taken as members.

The decision of the Supreme Court in **Bandhua Muki Morcha** recognised the right of the bonded labourers to live with human dignity, which is implicit in Article 21. The Court read the directive principles into Article 21 of the Constitution to make the right to live with human dignity meaningful to the working class of the country. **Neerja Chaudhary** went a step forward. Hitherto the practice of the court was to give directions to

1. *Ibid.*, at 810.
2. A.I.R. 1984 S.C. 1099.

the appropriate governments and to keep quite without considering whether those directions were implemented in a proper way or not. But in Neerja Chaudhary case the court departed from this practice and the writ petition was placed on board for consideration of the affidavit which may be filed by the State Government pursuant to directions given by the court. The Court adopted this practice to sustain judicial awareness whether its directions are properly implemented or not. Thus, Neerja Chaudhary has forced a new constitutionalism to secure the observance of social and welfare legislation.

(vii) Public interest litigation and pensioners' rights

In **D.S. Nakara v. Union of India**,[1] the Supreme Court at the instance of a society formed to ventilate public grievances rendered a declaratory judgment directing that all pensioners governed by 1972 Rules of Army Pension Regulations shall be entitled to pension as computed under the liberalised pension scheme from the specified date irrespective of their date of retirement.

(viii) Public interest litigation and the welfare of handicapped

In **National Federation of Blind v. Union of Public Service Commission**,[2] on a Public Interest Litigation filed by the National Federation of Blind for the eligibility to write civil services examination, the apex court held that the visually handicapped constitute a significant section of our society and as such it is necessary to encourage their participation in every walk of life. The court further held that the visually handicapped (blind and partially blind) are eligible to compete and write civil services examination in the categories of Group 'A' and 'B' posts which are suitable for the handicapped in Braille Script or with the help of scribe. The court also recommended reservation to the visually handicapped persons.

(ix) Compensatory jurisprudence and public interest litigation

Generally, compensation is claimed only for 'violation of certain civil rights', by invoking the jurisdiction of the ordinary civil courts. However, seeking compensation for violation of fundamental rights and that too by invoking the extraordinary remedies under Articles 32 and 226 of the Constitution, is new to Indian scenario of administration of justice. It is in the area that the Public Interest Litigation and judicial activism have played a dynamic and constructive role. There are catena of leading decision rendered by the Supreme Court in this area, have been discussed as under.

In **Rudal Shah v. State of Bihar**,[3] a Division Bench of the Supreme Court dealt with the case, wherein the petitioner was acquitted by the Court of Session in 1968 but he was released from jail only 14 years later in 1982, for inexplicable reasons. The court as an interim measure awarded a compensation of Rs. 35,000/- for the deprivation of his liberty, without precluding the petitioner from bringing a suit to recover appropriate

1. A.I.R. 1983 S.C. 130.
2. (1993) 2 S.C.C. 411.
3. A.I.R. 1983 S.C. 1086.

damages from the State and its erring officials, in the ordinary courts. In a judgment of lyrical beauty and poignancy, the court observed that 'Article 21 which guarantees the right to life and liberty will be denuded of its significant content if the powers of this court were limited only to passing orders of release from illegal detention'. One of the telling ways in which the violation of the right can reasonably be prevented and due compliance with the mandate of Article 21 secured is to mulct its violators by the payment of monetary compensation. This remedy has been unprecedented. Even though, this was not in a Public Interest Litigation, it has been cited to explain the beginning of the compensatory jurisprudence in writ proceedings in India.

As regards the Public Interest Litigations, for the first time in **M.C. Mehta v. Union of India,**[1] which is more popularly known as **Delhi Oleum Gas case**, a Constitution Bench of the Supreme Court speaking through Justice P.N. Bhagwati, has emphatically laid down the principle that the Supreme Court can entertain applications for compensation, on behalf of the victims of Oleum Gas leakage. The apex Court awarded remedial relief of compensation in the writ petition itself and on the other hand it propounded the theory of absolute liability in place of strict liability, prevailing there before.

Saheli, A Women's Resource Centre v. Commissioner of Police, Delhi,[2] was a milestone in the evolution of compensatory jurisprudence in writ courts. The State was held liable for the death of a 9 years old child by police assault and beating. Delhi administration was ordered to pay compensation of Rs. 75000/- to the mother of the victim. In **Consumer Education and Research Centre v. Union of India,**[3] a Division Bench also reiterated the principle that the remedy of award of compensation is available under Articles 32 and 226 of the Constitution. In a catena of cases dealing with the environment protection, where the Supreme Court has ordered either closure of certain industries or their shifting, the court directed the erring industries to pay compensation to the workers, by way of retrenchment compensation, additional compensation and shifting bonus, etc.[4]

Thus, the Public Interest Litigation has given an impetus to the compensatory jurisprudence in writ proceedings, thereby establishing the principle that any person whose fundamental rights or their statutory rights are violated either by the State action or private persons, the victims can ask for monetary compensation under Article 32 and 226.

It may, therefore, be summed up that the Indian Judiciary has won a fervent prose by touching problems affecting the public at large. There is now little doubt left that the Supreme Court has been very assertive

1. A.I.R. 1987 S.C. 1086.
2. A.I.R. 1990 S.C. 513.
3. A.I.R. 1995 S.C. 922.
4. *M.C. Mehta* v. *Union of India*, A.I.R. 1987 S.C. 734; *Indian Council for Enviro-Legal Action* v. *Union of India*, (996) 3 S.C.C. 212 and *S. Jagannath* v. *Union of India*, A.I.R. 1996 S.C. 811.

and has forcefully reminded the executive of its obligation to the citizen. The functioning of the apex court has laudably shown that Public Interest Litigation is a very valuable weapon which can do a great deal of good to the people and society by way of imparting justice to all, high or low, in accordance with the cherished commitment of our Constitution. The courts have been able to give voice to the voiceless. It is, however important to add here that the strategy of Public Interest Litigation must be used sparingly and it is also equally necessary that abuse of the process of the court must be curbed. Justice A.M. Ahmadi has rightly stated that "the Public Interest Litigation is a very valuable weapon which can do a great deal of good to the people and society but which can be blunted if wrongly or carelessly used."[1]

---

1. Quoted in Hardwari Lal, "Activism or Trespass—Use and Abuse of Judicial Process", The Tribune, January 2, 1996, p. 8.

16

LEGAL AID

The equal and even handed justice has been a cherished ideal of administration of justice since the dawn of civilisation. Manu, the most authoritative and one of the earliest law givers in ancient India, stated :

"Tasmadyama Iba Swami
Swayan Hitwa Priya Priye
Bartheta Jamyaya Brutya
Jita Krodho Jitendriya"[1]

(Let the prince, therefore, like Yama, not heeding his own likings and dislikings behave exactly like Yama suppressing his anger and controlling himself).

In Upanishad it has been said, "Law is the king of kings, far more rigid and powerful than they, there is nothing higher than law; by its prowess as by that of the highest monarch, the weak shall prevail over the strong."[2]

Equal justice for all is the cardinal principle on which the entire system of administration is based. It is so deep rooted in the body and spirit of our jurisprudence that the very meaning which we ascribe to the word "justice" embraces it. We cannot conceive of justice which is not fair and equal, which is given to one, but denied to another. The ideal has always stirred the hearts of men since the dawn of civilization and so far as Anglo-Saxon legal history is concerned, we find it manifested in the earlier laws which continually directed that justice be done alike to rich and poor. It was asserted in the Charter of Liberties of Henry II and it received its classic statement, in its most glorious enunciation, in the 40th paragraph of *Magna Carta*, where it is inscribed : "To no man will we deny, to no man will we sell, or delay, justice or right." But this great principle was not instantly translated into reality, it did not inaugurate an era of absolute freedom and equality of justice. Indeed, Gurney Champion, the author of "Justice and the Poor in England" felt so strongly that the promise was not being honoured that he printed, as an appendix to his book, a Draft Bill to repeal this section of *Magna Carta* 'in so far only the

1. D. Pathak, "Legal Aid to the Poor", Souvenir of the High Court Bar Association, Orissa, 17th November, 2002, p. 14.
2. *Ibid.*

poor persons are concerned." This, he maintained, should, for the sake of honesty, be passed by Parliament unless it was willing to increase the legal assistance given to the poor.[1]

In the wake of changing social, economic and political conditions in the modern world, the social scientists, jurists and politicians gave their thoughts to the philosophy of legal aid and they made the State responsible for eliminating social and economic wrongs, as also ensuring just and decent human living to the people at large. The present day world though sharply divided into distinct blocks, some countries having socialist Governments and some others, democratic Governments—all have, however, one aim and that is to end poverty and ignorance, to bring happiness to millions of suffering people and to wipe every tear from every eye. By the end of the nineteenth century, the mere formal right to legal protection developed into a more substantial equality of parties before the courts. Prior to this development, legal assistance to the poor always had connotation of charity by the legal practitioners, other private or philanthropic organisations or by public authorities. In the following pages an endeavour is made by the authors to discuss in brief the general trend of legal aid programmes in various countries.

I. Legal Aid Programme in France

According to Vittorio Denti, the first organic French Law on Legal assistance dates back to 1851 (Solus and Perrot Droit Judiciaire Prive, 1 Paris 1961, p. 960), and subsequently adopted by other European countries, it was expected to offer services free of charge to the poor. The application of legal aid has undergone a major transformation since the 1972 legislation, before this legal assistance was provided as a charity to the poor; now it is considered a legal right. Legal aid can be requested by any French national who has a serious cause of action and lacks financial resources. Legal aid is also available even in commercial, administrative or civil actions. It is also available in appeal, contract or execution. The request for legal aid is made to the legal aid office which decides appropriateness and extent of need, and on refusal, appeal procedure has also been incorporated. The legal aid programme in France is fairly well structured in comparison to other countries.[2]

II. Profile of Legal Aid in United Kingdom

There was no organised system of providing legal aid in England in early period except some glimpses of legal aid which was available to poor population during the reign of Henry I. A poor litigant was exempted to give essential security and ecclesiastical lawyers in temporal courts also provided legal aid to poor persons.[3] *Magna Carta* also depicts the spirit of

1. Quoted in P.N. Bhagwati, "Legal Aid in India" in L.M. Singhvi (ed.) Law and the Common Wealth, (1971), p. 206.
2. Justice Dalveer Bhandari, "Legal Aid—Comparative Evaluation : Lok Adalat and Clinical Legal Education", Nyaya Deep, July, 1998, Vol. 1, Issue 1, p. 10.
3. G.O. Koppel, Legal Aid in India, JILI, 1966, Vol. 8, pp. 238-239; also see B.R. Sharma and Sunil Chhabra, Legal Aid in United States : An Overview, Civil and Military Law Journal, April-June, 1993, Vol. 29, No. 2, p. 112.

English legal system regarding help or assistance to the poor. In the 40th paragraph it is inscribed that "to no man will we deny, to no will we sell, or delay, justice or right." During the reign of Henry VII, there were changes in Chancery courts to provide speedy and cheap justice to poor people. The common law courts were empowered to issue writs and entertain cases of poor people without court fees. A special statute dealing with *forma pauperis* in 1495 was also passed. This statute was repealed in 1883 and Rules of court were enacted to deal with the procedure of *forma pauperis* in the High Court. With the passage of time, there was a mushroom growth of various parasitical groups providing legal aid. Thus, the new Rules were enacted in 1914, dealing with the procedure for grant of legal aid. Under these rules, a person would be entitled to legal aid provided that his income from all sources did not exceed 50 pound excluding the subject matter of the action.[1] In the year 1925, the Lawrence Commission examined the question of legal aid.

Though there has been a gap between the sentiment and reality with regard to legal services to the poor in England, however, the British Legal Aid Legislation has been used as a model for a number of countries. Criminal legal aid scheme began as early as 1930 under the 'Poor Prisoners' Defence Act, 1930'. Legal Aid was made available for summary trial. Until the passing of the Legal Aid and Legal Advice Act of 1949, the legal aid movement in England lagged far behind its counterpart in the United States of America. Realising that the task of acting gratuitously for poor persons imposed a heavy burden on the legal profession and that the position in regard to legal aid was unsatisfactory, in 1944 the Lord Chancellor appointed a Committee to report and make recommendations on the question. The Committee submitted its report in May, 1945, making the following recommendations :—

1. Legal aid should be available in all courts and in such manner as will enable persons in need to have the help they require.
2. The provision for legal aid should not be limited only to those who are normally classed as poor but should include a wider income group.
3. Those who cannot afford to pay anything for legal aid should receive it free of cost. For those who can pay something towards the cost, a scale of contributions should be prescribed.
4. The cost of the scheme should be borne by the State but it should not be administered either by a department of the State or by local authorities.
5. The legal profession should be responsible for the administration of the scheme except that part of it which was dealt with under the Poor Prisoners' Defence Act.
6. Barristers and solicitors should receive adequate remuneration for their services.
7. The Law Society should be requested to frame a scheme for the

1. Legal Aid Scheme (Government of Madhya Pradesh), 1973, p. 44.

establishment of legal centres in the country.

8. The Law Society should be answerable to the Lord Chancellor for the administration of the scheme.
9. The term 'poor person' should be discarded and term 'assisted the person' should be adopted.[1]

Under the English Act, provision has been made for the giving of legal aid in all courts, civil and criminal, for all types of proceedings except personal actions. Such aid includes representation by solicitors and counsel and is not given unless the applicant shows that he has reasonable grounds for instituting or defending or being a party to any proceeding. It may also be refused if it appears unreasonable that he should receive it in the particular circumstances of the case. The question whether a person's financial circumstances are such as to entitle him to legal aid under the Act and if so whether he should receive such aid free of all cost or should himself make a contribution towards the cost is determined by reference to his disposable income and his disposable capital. Legal aid is available to any person whose disposable income does not exceed $ 420 per annum. Persons with a disposable income over $ 156 or with a disposable capital exceeding $ 75 have to make contributions towards the costs. Disposable income and disposable capital are assessed after making deductions for maintenance of dependents, interests on loans, income-tax, rent and other matters for which a person may reasonably provide. Panels of solicitors and barristers willing to act for assisted persons are maintained. The Act also contains provisions for legal advice being given on payment of a small fee.[2] The lawyers representing the assisted persons are paid their fees and out of pocket costs out of the Legal Aid Fund. Counsel is paid eighty-five per cent of the amount allowed on taxation of costs in the House of Lords and the Supreme Court and his full fee in proceedings in the County Court. A solicitor is paid eighty five per cent of the amount allowed on account of profit costs and the full amount allowed on taxation of the costs on account of disbursements in the Supreme Court and the full amounts of both profit and out of pocket costs in the County Courts. The responsibility for administering the scheme is laid upon the Law Society. The functions of the Society which are performed by its council include the establishment and administration of the Legal Aid Fund. This fund is constituted by moneys provided by Parliament, the contributions made by the assisted persons, the fees recovered for legal advice and the costs awarded to the assisted persons and recovered. The Act has also liberalised the provisions relating to legal aid in criminal courts under certain statutes.

Up to the end of the year 1959 about 10,000 assisted persons had been enabled to recover by way of damages seven million pounds sterling and about 70,000 persons had, with assistance rendered under the Act, successfully petitioned for divorce or defended divorce proceedings. The

1. Lord Rushcliffe Committee Report, 1945, p. 23. Report of the Committee on Legal Aid and Advice in England and Wales.
2. The provisions relating to the grant of legal advice have not yet been brought into force.

Report of the Select Committee of the House of Commons on Estimates reviewing the working of the scheme of legal aid stated that the scheme's greatest contribution had been to enhance the dignity and prestige of the law. In the English system, the legal aid was created through series of statutes by the State. They are : (i) The Legal Aid and Advice Act, 1949; (ii) the Legal Aid Act, 1964; (iii) The Criminal Justice Act, 1967; (iv) The Legal Advice and Assistance Act, 1972; (v) The Legal Aid Act, 1974; (vi) The Legal Aid Act, 1979 (as amended by the Administration of Justice Act, 1985) and (vii) the Legal Aid Act, 1988.

To improve upon the nature of legal advice and assistance in the country, the British Parliament enacted the Legal Advice and Assistance Act, 1972 so as to renovate and restructure the entire scheme for the giving of legal advice and assistance both in civil and criminal proceedings. One of the main objectives of the scheme under this legislation was to make free legal services more easily accessible to the public. The scheme envisaged under the Act is generally known as "The 25 Pound Scheme" or the "Green Form Scheme". The scheme now finds a place in Sections 1 to 5 of the subsequently enacted Legal Aid Act of 1974 and the regulations framed thereunder.[1] The Act of 1974 was repealed in 1982 when new Legal Aid Act was passed. The law of 1982 makes some further provisions with respect to the giving of legal aid and the provisions of advice and representation in criminal cases and allied matters. This has been done by introducing consequential amendments, modification of repeal of some of the provisions of the Act of 1974. It will be interesting to note that pursuant to the report of the Legal Aid Scrutiny in 1986, a number of suggestions and proposals to help cut cost in administration of Legal Aid Scheme had been made. Thereafter, some of these proposals were incorporated and implemented in the Legal Aid Act, 1988. The Lord Chancellor in 1991 in its Legal Aid Consultation Paper introduced and identified five main proposals to change the funding of Legal Aid Schemes. Number of reasons have been recorded for high rise in the cost of legal aid, one of them is the number of record crimes which has risen from about one per hundred population in 1950's to 4 per hundred population in 1989. With the increased crime rate and resultant cost of police involvement and creation of criminal courts, the legal cost became very high and inevitable. The English Legal Aid Scheme provides legal aid in three following areas : (i) Legal Advice and Assistance; (ii) Civil Legal Aid; and (iii) Criminal Legal Aid.

Thus, the legal aid scheme in the United Kingdom is being run on a uniform basis throughout the country. The legal aid is available both in civil and criminal proceedings. Civil legal aid is administered in a much more rigorous way than criminal legal aid. The application in civil cases have to satisfy two major tests, viz., means tests and merit test, regarding his case. Theoretically, the legal aid is available in all kinds of cases but practically in most tribunals, legal aid is not made available. The Legal Aid Scheme is administered by the Legal Aid Board which came to be

1. R.J. Walker, The English Legal System (1976), p. 233.

constituted with the help of Section 3 of the Legal Aid Act, 1988. The Constitution of the Legal Aid Board is also very interesting. There must be at least 11 and not more than 17 members of the Board and that members and Chairman shall be appointed by the Lord Chancellor. At least 2 solicitors are required to be appointed to the Board after consultation with the Law Society as per the requirement of the 1988 Act and Lord Chancellor shall consult with the general Council of the Board with a view to inclusion on the Board at least two barristers. Further, the Act of 1988 which is the latest law, makes provisions for payment of solicitors or advocates out of Legal Aid Fund. The law societies are also performing a good job in this context. Hence, in the United Kingdom, legal aid has a sound statutory base.

III. Legal Aid in United States of America

Legal Aid programme has a long history in the United States. The first Legal Aid Society was established in 1876 in New York city as a part of an organization that attempted to ease the transition for German immigrants in the Unites States. During the first half of the twentieth century, the legal aid programmes spread slowly. The need for legal aid has increased enormously with the growth and industrialism and urban conditions of life. The large mass of legislation in the modern State with the inevitable technicalities of the law has occasioned a considerable increase in litigation. In the United States, the question of legal aid has, during the present century, received considerable attention. In spite of the disturbing influences of the two World Wars, the movement for legal aid has gained considerable momentum. The spread of the legal aid movement in the United States has been due largely to the intense efforts of private voluntary organizations. Government aid is looked upon with disfavour on the ground that it brings with it governmental control. Legal aid is given by various types of organisations such as the Legal Aid Societies, the Social Service Organisations, the Law School Clinics and the Bar Association Offices. In 1921, the American Bar Association took upon itself the duty of encouraging the establishment and maintenance of legal aid organizations. In course of time a partnership was formed between the legal aid organisations and the bar and this combination provided effective national leadership to the legal aid movement.

Now, the legal aid centres are available all over in the United States. The development of legal aid programme received great impetus by the various judgments of the Supreme Court. Presently in the United States the legal aid programme is run by the Legal Service Corporation Act, 1974. The Act was amended in 1977. The Legal Services Corporation with its head office established at Washington D.C. is the main agency of administering legal aid. The Corporation is run by eleven members. Board of Directors are elected by the President of United States of America with the approval of the Senate. The American Congress is responsible for its finances. The Corporation is, however, free to work without any Government partisan pressures. It is a non-profit organization which provides financial help to the poor in civil matters. There are nine regional headquarters in U.S.A. The Corporation provides grants to these headquarters. Each such quarter has its own board of Directors. It has branches in the State capitals and other places to implement the scheme. Apart from Legal Service Corporation, some of the States in U.S.A. have people's court. American Civil Liberties Union and National Lawyers' Guild also greatly helped in the development of legal aid movement in the United States of America. A large number of aggressive legal rights organisations were set up for the protection of civil liberties, civil rights, environmental and consumer protection of the citizens because of the encouragement of Kennedy Administration.[1] There are some type of methods operating to provide legal aid in United States of America. Firstly, only the private attorneys are asked to provide services. Secondly, where staff attorney provides specific type of legal services, it included the training, advice and information to private attorney. Thirdly, the private attorneys are employed to cover those areas in which the staff attorney are not able to extend their services under the staff-attorneys system. Lastly, there are Legal Aid Clinics in which law students provide assistance to the poor and appear in courts on their behalf.

Section 13 of the By-laws of the American Bar Association reads "Duty of the Committee on Legal Aid work is :

(i) to maintain a continuing study of the administration of justice as it affects to the poorer citizens and immigrants throughout the country;

(ii) to promote remedial measures to assist poor persons in the protection of their legal right;

(iii) to encourage the establishment and efficient maintenance of the Legal Aid Organisation and co-operate with the other agencies both public and private."

There is also a working system known as 'Probono Project'; under which the private attorneys provide legal services to eligible clients without fee. Further, the corporation studied the legal services delivery system and investigated every aspect and submitted an exhaustive report to American Congress in 1980. Again in 1981, a detailed report was prepared and it was concluded that the staff attorney method was the most efficient and useful. There are a large number of voluntary legal services organisations apart from the legal aid centres set up by the Federal and State Governments. Some of the agencies are Law Firms supported by lawyers, local bar associations, community legal organisations of New York, Chicago, Volunteer Legal Services, Chicago Council of Lawyers, and the Council of New York Law Associates; other such councils also exist in Washington and San Francisco. A large number of people are taking advantage of these centres. Even then it is difficult to claim that the needy indigents and the poor persons are getting legal aid in all cases. It is because of the reason that they are not able to avail this facility due to non-availability of

1. For more details, see Supra n. 64 at p. 10 and B.R. Sharma and Sunil Chhabra, "Legal Aid in United States of America : An Overview", Civil and Military Law Journal, January-March, 1993, Vol. 29, No. 1, pp. 28-29.

sufficient funds from the State. This dream is yet to be fulfilled and translated even by the most affluent nation on the planet.

IV. Legal Aid Programme in Canada

In Canada the term 'Legal Aid' embraces 'Legal Advice'. There is no unified legal aid in Canada. Each Bar Association has its own system. The Bar Association of Ontario has established a complete organization. The Canadian Bar Association passed a resolution at its annual meeting held in 1950 advocating the establishment of a Legal Aid Organization under the auspices of the Association. In 1967, when the Ontario legal aid programme obtained a substantial financial commitment from the Ontario Government, because the first provincial plan to pay lawyers to handle both civil and criminal cases, the Ontario legal aid programme became the flagship of legal aid programme in Canada. There is a much greater growing consciousness of the need of the poor for greater access to the services of legal profession. Like other countries, the access to justice is an outgrowth of the availability of legal services. This consciousness and awareness perhaps would help in building up a countrywide well structured programme in Canada.[1]

V. Legal Aid in Australia

The system of providing legal aid to the poor is relatively a recent development in Australia. Various State Governments of Australia and lawyers' professional bodies have been providing legal aid in modest scale to the poor since middle of sixties.[2] The State Government of Australia is following the Poor Persons Legal Assistance Act, 1936 in this regard. Not only this, in Australia each State runs the legal aid programme under the various legislations enacted from time to time. These legislations and rules regarding legal aid programmes are, New South Wales : Legal Practitioners (Legal Aid) Act, 1970 and Legal Aid (Miscellaneous Provisions) Act, 1974; Queensland : Legal Assistance Act, 1964-65; South Australia : Legal Practitioners (Amendment) Act, 1969; Tasmania : Legal Assistance Act, 1962 and the Law Society's Authorised Legal Assistance Scheme, 1974; Victoria : Legal Aid Act, 1969; Western Australia : Legal Contribution Trust Act, 1967 and Legal Assistance Rules, 1971. In addition to the governmental efforts, legal aid programme is run by several bodies including trade unions, social welfare agencies, citizens advice bureaux, bank migrants services, credit unions and trade associations.

In March, 1975, the Australian Legal Aid Review Committee, headed by Roy Turner submitted its second report to the Attorney General. It recommended for establishment of a Legal Service Commission for the provision of legal services on national basis. Professor R.S. Sackville also suggested such scheme to establish, administer and finance a major new

---

1. Supra note 64 at pp. 15-16.
2. John A. Heffernan, "Legal Aid in Australia" in L.M. Singhvi and S.N. Jain (edition), Law and The Commonwealth (1971), p. 224; also see B.R. Sharma and Sunil Chhabra, Legal Aid in Australia : Some Reflections", Civil and Military Law Journal, July-September, 1994, Vol. 30, No. 3, p. 228.

legal aid system of local legal centres and other schemes and services throughout the country. He further contemplated that the Legal Services Commission should become a vehicle for social change in the field of poverty and it should perform functions beyond those of traditional legal aid extending to law reform, legal education, use of non-lawyers and community involvement.[1]

Australia has legal aid programme in various cities but the programme is inadequate to meet the full range of legal needs experienced by disadvantaged people in the community and the poor. The Commonwealth government elected in 1977 has expressed a preference for each State to create its own Legal Aid Commission which would co-ordinate all forms of legal aid provided within the State and receive grants from the Commonwealth government. In response to this government initiative, the Western Australia, Queensland and Australian Capital Territory have passed legislation establishing Legal Aid Commission. In each instance, the delivery of legal services within the State is to be organized under the relevant Act replacing both the existing Law Society Schemes and the Commonwealth Salaried Service.[2]

The chief functions of the Commission are to establish a legal services office, to provide or arrange legal assistance to determine eligibility criteria to conduct research into legal needs, to promote public education on legal rights and duties and to make grants to persons or bodies engaged in or promoting legal assistance. Section 11 of the Legal Services Commission Act, 1977 specifically directs the Commission in exercising its functions, to take into account the need for legal assistance to be readily available to disadvantaged persons, the desirability of enabling all assisted persons to obtain services of legal practitioners of their choice and the importance of maintaining independence of legal profession. Commonwealth Legal Aid Commission Act was passed in 1977. It creates a legal aid commission which is to secure an overview of the activities of the proposed State and Territory legal commission to keep statistics and to recommend additional method of delivery of legal aid.[3] In places like Queensland, Western Australia and North-West Tasmania where there are no lawyers to assist the poor and downtrodden people, the Australian Legal Aid office has introduced the unique concept of service through a 'Flying lawyer' who flies by plane from the nearest legal aid office for assisting the needy poor people in solving their legal problems at their doorsteps.[4]

A National Commission of inquiry into poverty has highlighted the deficiencies of the Australian legal system and the legal profession's approach to poor people. A climate for further sympathetic and effective development of law has been created. Hence, it is axiomatic from the foregoing study that comprehensive and broad based legal aid programme so far is lacking, but the future of legal aid programme in Australia seems

1. Quoted in Bhagwati Committee Report, 1977 at p. 8.
2. Supra note 64 at p. 15.
3. *Ibid.*
4. Supra note 73 at p. 29.

to be more encouraging, because of widespread awareness and appreciation of the concept of legal aid to the poor.

VI. Legal Aid Programmes in Socialist Countries

Socialists consider the principle of equality to be the foundation of the system. Thus, the court cannot restrict its role to a certain class of people. The court must ensure that the equality of the parties is not affected by a difference in position which is a result of economic conditions, education or familiarity with the law. Principle of access to the courts is one of the basic principles of the administration of justice. The principle is clearly expressed in Article 5 of ZPO (Zivilprozessordnungen = Rules of Practice) of the Soviet Socialist Republic. According to Article 5 of Rules of Practice of the Soviet Socialist Republic (Now Russia) it is clear that every interested party is entitled to stress the equal rights of all to justice, irrespective of birth, means, occupation, race and religion. Similarly, according to Article 3 of Czechoslovakia Rules of Practice, everyone has the right to demand protection from the court if his rights are endangered. Similar provisions exist in Bulgarian, German Democratic Republic (now part of Germany after unification). But the Rules of Practice in Poland do not contain a principle similar to that of the Czechoslovakian ZPO. The 'court costs' present no obstacle to asserting a claim in the socialist status. Low costs of lawyers fees and court costs have been designed to permit greater access to justice for a large number of people.

VII. Legal Aid Programmes in various Countries

Legal aid programmes are also in existence in Italy, Japan, Mexico, Spain, South Africa, Rwanda, Kenya, Namibia, Sudan, Nigeria, Rhodesia, Angola, Burundi, East Cameroon, Ivory Coast, Malagasy, Mali, Mozambique, Zaire, Tanzania, Togo, Uganda, Indonesia, Malaysia, Singapore and Sri Lanka. A small number of indigents are getting benefits from the legal aid programmes in these countries but by no stretch of imagination these programmes can be either said to be comprehensive, broad based or well structured programmes.

VIII. Legal Aid in India

In India, after submission of Rushcliffe Committee recommendations to the British Parliament, suggestion was made by the Bombay Legal Aid Society in 1945 that a Committee be set up in India to examine the question of legal aid to the poor. In 1949, under chairmanship of Mr. Justice Natwarlal H. Bhagwati (then a Judge of the Bombay High Court), the committee on legal aid and legal advice was set up to consider the question of the grant of legal aid in civil and criminal proceedings to poor persons, persons of limited means and persons belonging to the backward classes and to make recommendations for making justice more easily accessible to these persons. This committee went exhaustively into the question of legal aid and made a detailed report in October, 1949 and suggested therein that legal aid was a governmental responsibility. The same year, the Government of West Bengal set up a committee under the Chairmanship of Sir Arthur Trevor Harries, the then Chief Justice of Calcutta High Court to examine this question and the said Committee strongly emphasized the need for rendering legal aid to poor litigants. Since then the matter was debated from time to time but it did not take any concrete shape as the State Governments expressed their inability to implement recommendations on account of financial difficulties.

The Law Commission of India, in its 14th Report on 'Reform of Judicial Administration' published in 1958, strongly advocated the need for rendering legal aid to poor litigants as not a minor problem of procedural law, but a question of fundamental character. In 1960, the Central Government drew up an outline of a scheme for legal aid and forwarded it to various existing legal aid organisations and the States for comment. In a Conference of the State Law Ministers in 1962, financial burden was again advanced as an argument to hold up the recommendations. Then came the Committee under the Chairmanship of Hon'ble Mr. Justice V.R. Krishna Iyer, then a Member of the Law Commission of India, constituted by the Government on October 27, 1972 to consider the question of making available to the weaker sections of the community and persons of limited means in general and citizens belonging to the socially and educationally backward class in particular, facilities for : (a) legal advice so as to make them aware of their constitutional and legal rights and obligations; and (b) legal aid in proceedings before Civil, Criminal and Revenue Courts so as to make justice more easily available to all sections of the community.

The Committee submitted its report on May 27, 1973; elaborately dealing therein with the various aspects of the question and recommending various projects aimed at giving legal assistance to the poor and the needy. Realising the need of providing legal aid and advice to the weaker sections of the country, for proper and effective implementation of social and economic programmes of the nation and with a view to establishing adequate and various legal services programmes throughout the country on uniform pattern, the Union Government appointed a Committee under the Chairmanship of Justice P.N. Bhagwati on the 19th May, 1976. This Committee submitted its report captioned, "Report on National Juridicare : Equal Justice—Social Justice" to the Central Government on the 31st August, 1977. The report elaborately dealt with all aspects of the subject and submitted specific recommendations particularly emphasizing on establishment of Nyaya Panchayats and Lok Nayayalayas at the grass root level for administering justice in the rural areas. In the report it is stated that 'no law, no order' is basic to the survival of civilised societies and that is why the rule of law has been deeply rooted in the judicial system. Laws of the country have to be made to fulfil the objective set out in the Constitution. It is mentioned in the report that at performance level, the laws have failed to protect the socially and economically poor. Socio-economic equality promised by the Constitution will become a living reality only if free legal services to the weaker sections of the community are guaranteed as a State responsibility. It is further stated that if the State is to secure a just social order for the welfare of the people and if legal justice is the root of orderly progress, there can hardly be any doubt that poverty jurisprudence must be developed in the manner so that social justice through laws can be promoted and faith of the common man in the laws and Constitution would be fully established.

With a view to implementing the report of Bhagwati Committee and in fulfilment of its constitutional obligations under Article 39-A,[1] a Committee known as the "Committee for Implementing Legal Aid Schemes (CILAS) was constituted by the Government of India on 26th September, 1980 under the Chairmanship of Justice P.N. Bhagwati to monitor and implement legal aid programmes on a uniform basis in all the States and Union Territories. CILAS evolved a model scheme for legal aid programme applicable throughout the country by which several Legal Aid and Advice Boards have been set up in the States and Union Territories. CILAS is funded wholly by grants from the Central Government. The legal aid has a comprehensive constitutional status in our country. Our Constitution is wedded to democracy, socialism, secularism, equality of status and equal protection of laws. Legal aid for weaker sections is a social obligation and constitutional mandate. Legal aid is not a mere constitutional obligation. In our country it is a social necessity. It should not be viewed as charity but should be conceived as an integral part of our legal system.

In pursuance of the Directive Principles of State Policy of the Constitution, the Legal Services Authorities Act, 1987 was drafted with a view to constitute Legal Services Authorities at National, State, District and Taluq levels to provide free and competent legal services to the weaker sections of the society. This Act was finally enforced on 9th November, 1995 after certain amendments introduced therein. After enactment of the Legal Services Authority Act, many States have enacted legislation or adopted schemes for organizing legal aid in civil and criminal proceedings. The Central Legal Services Authority, is funded by the Union Government comprising of members of all Sates provided adequate financial aid for the said purpose. The State Legal Services Authority is funded by the State Government and functioning under a Judge of the respective High Court, nominated by the Chief Justice. District and Taluq committees have also been set up to organise legal aid through appropriate committees and panels.

Section 3 of the Act contemplates the creation of a National Legal Services Authority. Besides the Chief Justice of India who is to be the Patron-in-Chief, and a serving or retired judge of the Supreme Court who is to be the Executive Chairman, the authority is to consist of such number of other members possessing such experience and qualification as may be prescribed by the Central Government, to be nominated by the Government in consultation with the Chief Justice of India. Under Section 3-A of the Act, the National Legal Services Authority or the Central Authority is to

1. Article 39-A of the Constitution provides that the State shall secure that the operation of the legal system promotes justice on a basis of equal opportunity and shall, in particular provide free legal aid by suitable legislation or schemes or any other way, to ensure that opportunities for securing justice are not denied to any citizen by reason of economic or other disabilities.

constitute a committee called the Supreme Court Legal Services Committee which is to perform such functions as may be determined by regulations made by the Central Authority.

Similarly, under Section 6 of the Act every State Government is to constitute a body to be called the State Legal Services Authority, consisting of the Chief Justice of the High Court, a serving or retired judge of the High Court who is to be the Executive Chairman and such number of other members, possessing such experience and qualifications as may be prescribed by the State Government, to be nominated by that Government in consultation with the Chief Justice of the High Court under Section 6(1) of the Act. Further, each State Authority is to constitute a Committee called the High Court Legal Services Committee which is to perform such functions as may be determined by regulations made by the state Authority under Section 8-A of the Legal Services Authorities Act, 1987. Similarly, under Section 9 of the Act, District Legal Services Authority is constituted. The State Government shall, in consultation with the Chief Justice of the High Court constitute the body and it shall consist of the District Judge who shall be the Chairman and such number of other members, possessing such experience and qualifications as may be prescribed by the State Government to be nominated by that Government in consultation with the Chief Justice of the High Court. Under Section 11-A of the Act Taluq Legal Services Committee may be constituted for each Taluq or mandal or for group of taluqs or mandals. The Committee consists of the senior-most judicial officer operating within the jurisdiction of the Committee who shall be the ex-officio Chairman and such other members as may be prescribed by the State Government.

The persons who are entitled to legal services under the Act, are listed under Section 12 of the Act which is reproduced hereunder.

Every person who has to file or defend a case shall be entitled to legal services under this Act if that person is :—

(a) a member of a scheduled caste or scheduled tribe; or

(b) a victim of trafficking in human beings or begar as referred to in Article 23 of the Constitution; or

(c) a woman or a child; or

(d) a person with disability as defined in clause (i) of Section 2 of the persons with disabilities (Equal Opportunities, Protection of Rights and Full Participation) Act, 1995;

(e) a person under circumstances of undeserved want such as being a victim of a mass disaster, ethnic violence, caste atrocity, flood, drought, earthquake or industrial disaster; or

(f) an industrial workman; or

(g) in custody, including custody in a protective home within the meaning of clause (g) of Section 2 of the Immoral Traffic (Prevention) Act, 1956 (104 of 1956), or in a Juvenile Justice Act, 1986 (53 of 1986), or in a psychiatric hospital or psychiatric nursing home within the meaning of clause (g) of Section 2 of the Mental Health Act, 1987 (14 of 1987; or

(h) in receipt of annual income less than rupees nine thousand or such other higher amount as may be prescribed by the State Government if the case is before a court other than the Supreme Court, and less than rupees twelve thousand or such other higher amount as may be prescribed by the Central Government, if the case is before the Supreme Court.

According to Rule 12 of the National Legal Services Authority Rules, 1995, any citizen of India whose annual income from all sources does not exceed Rs. 50,000/- (Rupees fifty thousand only) shall be entitled to legal services under cl. (h) of Sec. 12 of the Legal Services Authorities Act, 1987.

Different States fixed the upper limit of annual income of a person entitling him to legal services if the case is before a court other than the Supreme Court.

According to Rule 16 of Andhra Pradesh State Legal Services Authority Rules, 1995 any citizen of India, whose income from all sources does not exceed Rs. 25,000/- (Rupees twenty-five thousand only) or such higher amounts as may be notified by the State Government from time to time, shall be entitled to legal services under clause (h) of Section 12 of this Act.

Section 13 of the Legal Services Authority Act, 1987 provides that :—

(1) Persons who satisfy all or any of the criteria specified in Section 12 shall be entitled to receive legal services provided that the concerned authority is satisfied that such person has a prima facie case to prosecute or to defend.

(2) An affidavit made by a person as to his income may be regarded as sufficient for making him eligible to the entitlement of legal services under this Act unless the concerned authority has reason to disbelieve such affidavit.

Legal services or legal aid may be refused :—

(a) to a person in a case of contempt of court;

(b) to a person in a proceeding relating to any election;

(c) in proceedings under Immoral Traffic (Prevention) Act, 1956 except to a victim of trafficking in human beings;

(d) in proceedings under the Protection of Civil Rights Act, 1955 except to a person who is subjected to any disability under this Act;

(e) to a person accused of an offence committed under the Scheduled Tribes (Prevention of Atrocities) Act, 1989.

Legal services may also be refused in respect of a case of defamation or malicious prosecution where the secretary is satisfied that it is suitable case for such refusal in the totality of facts :

Provided that reasons for refusing legal services shall be recorded in writing and order of the Chairman shall be obtained before the legal services are refused.

Legal services may be given in any one or more of the following modes, namely,—

(a) towards payment of court-fee, process fee and other charges payable or incurred in connection with any legal proceedings;

(b) through engagement of a legal practitioner;

(c) for obtaining and supply of certified copies of judgment order and other documents in legal proceedings :

Provided that payment of court-fee, process-fee and other expenses shall be allowed to the extent as per the general order of the State Authority.

17

PARA-LEGAL SERVICES AND PARA-LEGAL PERSONNEL

I. Introduction

Lawyers play a very active role in restoring high values of the profession. They are the officers of the court and should assist the court in the enforcement of the rule of law in the country. Besides this, the law students may also contribute much to the public welfare and public good, if they are encouraged from providing legal and para-legal services. The need of the hour is to establish in every law college or law department of the University a legal services clinic. The clinic should provide the legal and para-legal services to the poor, illiterate and weak persons. The law students, teachers, advocates, judges and social organisations should be made the members of the clinic. The law students may not appear before the court on behalf of the litigant, but certainly they may assist the litigants by providing legal advice and by negotiating the disputes. They may play a pertinent role in settling the disputes. They may draft public interest petition and file in the court. They may draft plaints, prepare written statements and points of arguments. They may also collect relevant cases on the specific issues involved in the specific cases. Hence, they may assist the advocates in numerous ways. Rendering the legal and para-legal services is beneficial not only to the society but also to the students rendering such services. It will enable the students to have the professional knowledge which is necessary for success in the legal profession. It will enable them to be aware of the lawyering process and attain the skill of advocacy. Such services will definitely develop a sense of social responsibility among the students.

II. Position in United States of America

The National Federation of Para-Legal Association of United States of America has defined that a para legal or legal assistant is a person qualified through education, training or work experience to perform substantive legal work that requires knowledge of legal concepts and is customarily, but not exclusively, performed by a lawyer. The same person may be retired or employed by a lawyer, law office, governmental agency or other entity or may be authorised by administrative, statutory or court authority to perform the work. The National Federation of Para-legal Associations preferred the term 'para-legal' where few members of the

Association, use the term 'Legal Assistant'.

The history of the para-legal profession in the United States of America can be traced to the 1960's when individuals were trained to assist attorneys in making legal services available to the poor during the 'War on Poverty'. Thereafter, public agencies began hiring para-legal, private law firms, and corporations recognized the benefits of employing para-legals, to supply efficient support, reduce the expense of legal services, and increase the availability of services of the public. Individuals with distinct backgrounds are employed as para-legals. Education and training requirements differ widely but are generally related to the responsibilities of the position.

Place of Work

Para-legals are employed almost everywhere where law related work is performed, e.g., private firms, banks, corporations, insurance agencies, legal clinics, courts, government agencies, companies, accounting and engineering firms and legal aid offices. Para-legals either work with attorneys who assume professional responsibility for the final work product, or work in areas where 'lay' individuals are explicitly authorized by statute or regulation to assume certain law related responsibility. Para-legals who work in the private sector are usually employed by law firms and corporations and often specialise in areas of law such as litigation, probate, real estate, corporate taxation, domestic relations, or employee benefits. On the other hand, para-legals who work in the public sector are often employed by non-profit public law firms, State or local government agencies in areas such as welfare, family law, health care, landlord/tenants, disability benefits, unemployment compensation or social security.

Nature of Para-legals' Work

The specific tasks assigned to para-legals vary according to the area of practice and level of experience and education. The para-legals may be classified as : (i) litigation paralegals, (ii) probate paralegal; (iii) corporate paralegals; (iv) real estate paralegals; and (vi) employment law paralegals.

Litigation paralegals interview witnesses, analyze and digest legal documents, investigate facts, perform legal and factual research, draft pleadings, legal memoranda and briefs, obtain and manage information to assist in trial preparation, assist at trial and aid in preparing appeals. A probate paralegal's responsibilities could include interviewing clients, arranging for collection, valuing the transferring assets, administering estate accounts, analyzing the best treatment of assets and distribution to obtain the greatest tax benefit, and preparing tax returns. A corporate paralegal is likely to be involved in drafting agreements and employee benefits plans, fulfilling securities reporting requirements, and conducting patent and trade mark searches. A real estate paralegal could draft transaction documents, prepare for closings, and research title and administrative processes involved in land and environmental use. A government paralegal can work for the Federal Trade Commission, the Justice Department, or even the White House. Depending upon the agency or area of practice, government paralegals perform a wide range of duties, including collecting and evaluating evidence, conducting hearings, drafting proposed legislation, and answering inquiries about federal laws and regulations. An employment law paralegal can draft employee policy and procedures manuals, help facilitate positions in organized labour campaigns, prepare position papers, complaints and affidavit in the discrimination cases, and perform work similar to litigation paralegals. Paralegals in legal services programmes work as counsellors or advocates. They may obtain government benefits for clients. They often maintain their own caseloads and have total responsibilities from the initial client interview through client representation at various administrative agency proceedings. Thus, paralegals play an important role in the legal profession.

III. Paralegal Services in India

In a comprehensive and well written articles, Charles Morrison, of Michigan State University, US has traced the history of lawyers' clerks and para professionals.[1]

The average Indian lawyer's office is far simpler than that of the humblest of his Western counterparts nowadays; his need for personal clerical assistance is correspondingly modest. A lone clerk (called Munshi) and a part-time typist are the usual staff. The Munshi is frequently either a youth or an old man and typically he has had little more than a year or two of secondary education. He is a low-levels journalist whose duties include domestic errand running and message-carrying, besides the more obviously clerical tasks of record-keeping. The Munshi or clerk may be described as a para-professional who provides role-support to the lawyer. The content of his role includes a wide variety of acts ranging from persuading a litigant to engage the lawyer to whom he is attached, to manage the procedural and routine aspects of lawyer's practice and even to personal services to the lawyer.

Like domestic peons in India, Munshis tend to be transient. They move from lawyer to lawyer after a year or two's service for each master. And they drift in and out of the occupation, between it and others of equal marginal nature. The insecurity of the job is related both to the tensions that go with its ambiguous definition and to the less renounced transience or mobility of the lawyers themselves. Law training in Indian as elsewhere in Asia, is usually viewed as a step in the direction of government service. Actual private legal practice is regarded by many (younger lawyers particularly) as merely incidental and temporary, a form of disguised unemployment.

The leaders of the local bar are, by definition, men with bustling practices. They demand more clerical or even outright legal competence of the Munshis, but they offer them in turn greater prestige and security. They come in contact with far more clients, however, so what they did to

1. Charles Morrison, "Clerks and Clients : Para-Professional Roles and Cultural Identifies in Indian Litigation," Indian Bar Review, Vol. 13 (3 & 4) : 1986 at pp. 273-294.

a para-professional nature may in the long run have been of greater significance.

The Munshis contribute significantly but informally to the daily organization of a district law practice in India. For instance, enquiries about procedures which a beginner at the bar might not wish to know how to make for himself are typically handled by his Munshi. Other Munshis, minor government clerks, police constables and even unsuspecting another lawyers can all be quizzed by a younger lawyer's Munshi to the advantage of his master. Established lawyers also find valuable the Munshi's marginality and ambiguous status, somewhere between trusted confident and mistrusted domestic drudge. The very transience of Munshis between lawyers means that Munshis are often sources of information about the practice of rivals in the bar; conversely, they are forever being accused of treachery by their former masters or suspected of it by their present ones.

Much of this mistrust and suspicion emerges in disputes over the payment of Munshis. Munshiana is a clerk's fee, usually said to be ten per cent of the lawyer's fee. It is traditionally received by the Munshi in each of his master's cases that reach the hearing before a judge. Some lawyers also pay a small salary (averaging about Rs. 25 per month in 1970). The larger the practice, the smaller the salary, since the munshiana is proportionately more. A few lawyers claimed to discourage munshiana and said they paid their munshis larger wages. An additional tip, called a shukriana, is often paid to both lawyers and Munshis by elated clients after a successful outcome in a case. It is apparently not uncommon for a shukriana to be promised by the client and then reneged or evaded. At the District Court the lawyer-Munshi relationship is more than that of a business partnership in that the Munshi is paid fixed proportion of the lawyer's fee, called munshiana usually one-tenth. On the other hand, the more qualified clerk of the lawyers practicing at the higher courts may be paid a monthly salary, thus having an employer-employee relationship.

It is, however, in relationships with the clients that the Munshi can best be characterized as para-professional. He sees as such of the litigant as the lawyer does—more, perhaps for he often sits chatting with him at the lawyer's booth while the latter is in court or on other cases. In this context of informal gossip crucial information may be exchanged. When the lawyer returns, the interaction shifts (slightly perhaps by perceptibly) to a more guarded and formal mode. With the Munshi, however, the client often can, if he chooses, "be himself"—profession ignorance of the legal procedures being followed, or admitting curiosity or, if he is experienced and affluent, assuming a patronizing air and attempting to direct the Munshi's efforts. In providing the supportive role to the lawyer the Munshi undertakes three important activities : routine maintenance, tactical maneuvering and business promotion. He manages the appointments of the lawyer with clients and guests, keeps the papers in order for consultation, arranges the journals and books to be used as reference material methodically, handles the records to be handed over to the court officials. His tactical maneuvering includes 'tutoring and preparing the clients and witnesses for their appearance in the court before the judge. The Munshi also plays the role of public relations officer and information agent on behalf of his lawyer *vis-a-vis* the adversary lawyer and client and court officials. Further, the Munshi may act as a negotiator to settle cases out of courts, if from point of view of his lawyer's client the court decision is not likely to be favourable or unduly prolonged. Finally, the Munshi may have to handle graft money to be palmed off to the appropriate officials on behalf of the lawyer. Neither the professional image or the professional ethics of a lawyer permit him to take on these responsibility directly. He also serves his lawyer as a business promoter either directly canvassing the litigants or operating through touts, particularly at the district courts.

Moreover, according to local theory there is likely to be less divergence between the public style of the clerk and the client than between the latter and the lawyer. The bulk of clients at the district court are rural folk. The Munshi's occupation is an urban one, part of a bureaucratic system that perhaps more than anything else in urban provincial India, contrats with the village. Obviously no one employs a raw and illiterate villager as a Munshi.

Hence, one can note that in dealing with the bureaucracy, the Munshi and his master present a unified front. Their relationships with one another are, however, often tense and hostile. The financial basis of the lawyer-Munshi relationship provides the main focus for this tension and for the dispute that erupt between lawyer, clients, and clerks. Suspicion and mistrust pervade the relationships of those who regularly have business at the district courts. Between rival parties in a case, of course, these attitudes are openly expressed. They are common, but more covert, in relations between clients, clerks and lawyers.

(a) Clerks as "Fixers" and "Touts"

A view common among Indian litigants depicts lawyer and clerk as involved hand in glove in an unscrupulous alliance to fleece the client. It is in this view of the legal profession that the term 'tout' is most often used. In Indian usage, a 'tout' is an agent who brings in business to a specialist in return for a commission. It is sometimes said that herbalists and genealogist employ touts. These agents are frequent at bus and train stations, at major regional centres to bring gullible clients to the *pandits* and *vaids* who make a business of maintaining local family records or curing a variety of ailments. The term 'tout' is overwhelmingly associated with the legal profession, and is one of the derogatory labels used in discussing 'para-professional' activity and services.

(b) Chronic litigants as para-professionals

The *Mukadma baz* or 'chronic litigant' is another professional in legal profession in India. Like the Munshi, however, the *mukadma baz* acts as an unofficial purveyor of informal information about the legal system. To some extent, any litigant becomes an informal source of information about the legal system in his own community; yet not all litigants in rural North India are considered *mukadma baz.*

A *mukadma baz* is a litigant who has acquired the reputation of being litigious. He is depicted as being involved in the prosecution of cases as an end in itself. He is sometimes said to be 'addicted' to litigation, or is compared to a gambler who cannot resist the temptation of cards. The term *mukadma baz* (one of many phrases used for this cultural identity) denotes one who plays (from bajna, to perform) at litigation (*mukadma*). He acquires this reputation in the first place in his own local community and his place in this community is what interests us here. Later, a *mukadma baz* may become well-known to the district bar for his persistence, for the complexity of his law suits, or for his sequential retention of many lawyers. But this *mukadma baz* identity at the courts may be less pronounced than at home in the rural hinterland. He may speak of himself as "known to everyone" or as "knowing everyone" (and on the latter score he may in fact accumulate a surprising amount of information, a circumstance that can in turn contribute to an accusation of 'indulging in toutism'). But individual district lawyers may also be well acquainted with the rural hinterland and their knowledge of a *mukadma baz's* reputation may come more from their personal sources of gossip than from his professional contacts with them.

(c) Paralegal services and the present position

At present, there are many types of persons who discharge different functions. They include document writers, registration brokers, real estate brokers and even stamp vendors. But the most important of them are the advocate's clerks, who perform tasks like filing the pleadings and petitions in the court, paying the process fee, doing filing work in the office procuring the order or judgment copies from the court and other offices and obtaining information about market value of a property, stamp duty and registration duty payable, etc. One striking feature of paralegal services and personnel in India is that there is no degree course offered by any institution or University, on paralegal services. Even the Bar Council of India and the State Bar Council also have not done anything to import scientific paralegal training to the personnel serving as advocate clerks. There is no association in India like the National Federation of Paralegal Association of USA to take care of the standard and quality of paralegal services. It is high time that the managers of the legal profession in India, viz., the Bar Council do something for improving the quality of para-legal services. It may lead to elimination of touting and champerty also.

18

FUNCTIONING OF LOK ADALATS LEGAL SERVICES AUTHORITIES (AMENDMENT) ACT, 2002 AND CONCEPT OF PERMANENT LOK ADALATS IN INDIA

The institution of Lok Adalat in India, as the very name suggests means, People's Court. "Lok" stands for "people" and the vernacular meaning of the term "adalat" is the Court. Lok Adalat is not an invention but a discovery that arose out of necessity. It is not new in India and has very deep and long roots not only in recorded history but even in pre-historical era. It existed in all societies[1] and continues to exercise decisive influence in the life of village folk even today. There is a considerable unanimity on the point that people's courts in India, popularly known as Lok Adalats, as an agency for settling local disputes has remained in existence since time immemorial.[2]

Undoubtedly, Lok Adalat concept and philosophy is an innovative Indian contribution to the world of jurisprudence. The concept of Lok Adalat was in practice centuries ago in India. We find mentioning of the existence of Lok Adalat in both *Vedic* and *post-Vedic* literature. In Ancient India, the *Sabha* or village people assembly of the vedic age functioned as a popular court. Manusmriti, Naradasmriti, Yajnavalkyasmriti, commentary of Brihaspati and Buddhist literature find many references about the mode and style of its functioning in ancient India. Yajanavalkya mentions three types of popular courts, viz., (a) *Puga*, (b) *Sreni*, and (c) *Kula*. Brihaspati also agrees with the views of Yajnavalkya and points out that an appeal lay to the *Sreni* court from the decision of the *Kula* court and to the *Puga* from the decision of the *Sreni* court. P.V. Kane, Dean of Dharamasastra is of the opinion that *Kulani, Sreni* and *Puga* were the arbitration tribunals like modern panchayats or the Lok Adalats of today. The Muslim rulers in

---

1. Nomita Aggarwal, Handbook on Lok Adalat in India (1991), p. 2, see also P.L. Mehta and Sunil Deshta, "Genesis of Lok Adalat : A Study with Special Reference to India", Civil and Military Law Journal, Vol. 29, No. 2, April-June, 1993, p. 132-137; Sunil Deshta, "Lok Adalat in India : Justice at the Doorsteps", Nyaya Deep, July-September, 2002, p. 19.
2. We find mentioning of the existence of Lok Adalats in both Vedic and post-vedic literature. For more details, see Birendra Nath, Judicial Administration in Ancient India (177), p. 245.

India made substantial inroads into the existing judicial system by way of creating the courts of judicature totally at variance with the indigenous system, yet the effect of these changes did not percolate to the village level. It is true that the advent of Britishers in India gave a death blow to the functioning of Lok Adalats, yet we find that these courts survived for long and existed even at the time of the British rule in India.[1]

However, the modern version of Lok Adalat has arisen out of a deep concern expressed by three different, expert committees, viz., Committee of Processual Justice to the People (1973); Gujarat Legal Aid Committees (1977) and the Juridicare : Equal Justice Social Justice Report (1977), set up by the Central Government and the Government of Gujarat to make recommendations for improving justice delivery system and the alarm generated by the judicial circles on mounting arrears of cases pending for long at different levels in our country. Thus, the Lok Adalat has its origin not in any statutory law but is devised and developed by people themselves as a "participatory instrument of democratic judicial making."

Lok Adalat is a system of dispensation of justice by way of discussion, counselling, persuasion and conciliation without any element of coercion, threat or allurement. Element of mediation, negotiation, arbitration and participation are so inherent in the system that Lok Adalats have now been regarded as participatory justice delivery system. Not only the litigants participate in the process of dispensation of justice but also the age old myth that the Judges are silent spectators has been exploded with the advent of Lok Adalats in India. With the passage of time, awareness has permeated among the disputants that their welfare and interest can be best protected by arriving at amicable settlement of disputes through Lok Adalats. Generally speaking, Lok Adalat is a para-judicial institution being developed by the people themselves. Lok Adalat is a place of justice for common man.

Frankly speaking, the primary aim behind the experiment of holding Lok Adalat in India was that we need to prevent the institutional miscarriage of justice which had virtually surfaced the whole legal system for a mere reason what we could not switch over to our indigenous legal system which at one time was serving the entire need of justice on a wider scale because of its simplicity. Despite the fact that the Indian Constitution seeks to salvage the people from injustice and stresses justice as the first imperative and more so, the Preamble of our National Character is a historic undertaking to secure to every citizen justice in its ampler dimensions—political, social and economic justice, it is quite painful to point out the bitter truth that our judicial system has badly failed to meet the requirements of justice to which our wise founding fathers of the Constitution were strongly committed. The stark reality is that the over rising graph of arrears have aggravated the situation. More and more cases are being filed and the piles of arrears continue to mount. They seem like a tide—a tide of papers and dockets that cannot be stopped. The institution

1. For more details, see Sunil Deshta, Lok Adalats in India : Genesis and Functioning (1994), pp. 9-48.

of cases in the Supreme Court of India arose from 1,602 in 1950 to 2,131 in 1955 and to 6,441 in 1960. Further, the institution of cases arose from 5,351 in 1961 to 7,979 in 1965 to 16,106 in 1970 to 12,787 in 1975 to 14,501 in 1977 and 28,382 in March, 1978.[1] Apparently, no less than 2.5 crore cases are awaiting disposal in various courts. According to a report submitted to Parliament, as many as 64,330 cases are pending in the Supreme Court alone while 40.54 lakh cases are yet to be disposed of in the High Courts as in 2016.

It is admitted that the accumulated frustration is the biggest single reason for the people having responded with hope, excitement and zeal to experiment in holding Lok Adalats in our country.[2] The philosophy of Lok Adalat Scheme contains within its fold the objective to root out the triple vices of delay, cost and complexity from the existing courts. It has been hammered out to reduce the backlog of arrears of cases and provide justice without any delay.[3] Our justice system is terribly cumbersome, exorbitantly expensive, long time consuming, dilatory, complex, cumulatively disastrous and also stressful, on account of variety of reasons, viz., the poor cannot reach the court because of heavy court fee and other expenditure and mystique of legal procedure. P.V. Narasimha Rao, the then Prime Minister, while inaugurating a one day meet of Chief Ministers and Chief Justices from all over the country said that the highest priority should be given to resolving disputes at the grass root level by a system that is simple and inexpensive and serves the needs of the constantly changing community by giving timely justice.[4] It was in this light that he announced the Government was in the process of giving statutory status to Lok Adalats soon since they had helped in ensuring speedy, effective and economic remedies all over the country.[5] The same views were expressed by Late Rajiv Gandhi, former Prime Minister of India. While highlighting the role of Lok Adalats, he stated, "Lok Adalats are a major breakthrough in the judicial system of the country."[6] It was in the same spirit that Late Satyasaachi Mukherjee, the then Chief Justice of India expounded the need to simplify the judicial system, revive the indigenous system and devise further means to ease the pressure on courts.[7]

Article 39-A which was inserted to our National Charter by the 42nd Amendment Act, 1976 provides for free legal aid by suitable legislation or schemes or in any other way to ensure that opportunities for securing justice are not denied to any citizen by reasons of economic or other disabilities. With the introduction of Article 39-A, it led the Government of

1. Rajeev Dhawan, The Supreme Court in India : A Socio-Legal Analysis of Its Justice Technique (1977), p. 11; also see Sanjay K. Das, State of the Judiciary, Onlooker, July 15, 1990, p. 18.
2. *Virendra Singh Barhat, Judicial Courts* v. *Lok Adalats*, A.I.R. 1987, Journal Section, p. 5.
3. *Ibid.*
4. Indian Express, December 5, 1993, p. 5.
5. *Ibid.*
6. Nomita Aggarwal, *op. cit*, p. iii.
7. Sanjay K. Das, *op. cit*, pp. 8 and 18.

India to constitute a Committee of Implementing the Legal Aid Scheme (CILAS) with Justice P.N. Bhagwati as its Chairman who propounded a model scheme. The State Government too constituted Legal Aid and Advice Boards which are funded by CILAS. The State Boards organised Lok Adalats as well as took up legal aid schemes and other legal services. The Parliament, however, impressed and influenced by the positive and enthusiastic response of the public towards Lok Adalats, has endeavoured to give it a statutory status with the result that the Legal Services Authorities Act, 1987 has been passed. The Lok Adalats, which have so far been functioning on an informal basis, tried to have a statutory base with the enforcement of the Legal Services Authorities Act, 1987. The Act could so far been brought into force on account of several amendments on November 9, 1995. The Act has been passed to achieve the social objective of the Directive Principles of State Policy embodied in Article 39-A of the Constitution. The Preamble of the Act signifies that the Act has been enacted with a view, firstly, to provide free and competent legal services to the weaker sections of the society; secondly, to ensure that opportunities for securing justice are not denied to any citizen on account of economic or other disabilities and thirdly, to organize Lok Adalats so that operation of Legal System promotes justice on the basis of equal opportunities. The basic objectives of the Act is to evolve a mechanism to deal with the arrears of cases which have become really a great threat to the dignity and survival of the judiciary itself. This Act provides for the constitution of National Legal Services Authority, State Legal Services Authorities, District Legal Services Authorities, along with the High Court Legal Services Committees and Taluka Legal Services Committee with a view to provide free legal aid and competent legal services as well as to organize Lok Adalats in their respective spheres. Under Chapter VI of the Act it is enjoined upon the Legal Services Authorities and Committees to organise Lok Adalats. It has now been widely accepted and recognised as an effective machinery for conciliating and settling dispute. The alternative modes of settlement of disputes have been given impetus by the recent amendments to the Code of Civil Procedure, 1908. Under Section 89 of the Code, courts have been empowered to explore the possibilities of settlement of disputes through Lok Adalats, arbitration and conciliation. During the last few years Lok Adalat has been found to be a successful tool of alternative dispute resolution in India. It is most popular and effective because of its innovative nature and inexpensive style. It has been functioning continuously and permanently in every district and Taluk centres. Several thousands of pending cases and disputes which had not reached law courts have been settled through Lok Adalats. All such matters except the matter relating to an offence not compoundable, may be referred to Lok Adalat where both the parties agree to it or where one party applies but the court is prima facie satisfied that there are chances of settlement between the parties. The Lok Adalat is required to pass an award on the basis of compromise and the award shall be final and binding on the parties and no appeal shall lie to any court against the award.

Frankly speaking, Lok Adalat is not a court in its accepted connotation. It is a forum provided by the people themselves or by interested parties including social activists, legal aiders and public spirited people belonging to every walk of life. Here voluntary efforts are aimed at bringing about settlement of disputes between the parties through conciliatory and persuasive efforts. To reiterate, the system of Lok Adalat is an innovative concept which can provide an effective mechanism for resolving disputes in a spirit of conciliation outside the Court. However, the efficiency of the system remained low because in case of failure to reach a settlement, the parties were allowed to invoke the jurisdiction of the Courts. It is in this context the Parliament in the year 2002 amended the Legal Services Authorities Act by inserting a new Chapter VI-A to set up Permanent Lok Adalats to provide compulsory pre-litigative mechanism for conciliation and settlement of cases relating to public utility services. The idea of establishing permanent and continuous Lok Adalats in all the districts in the country was first thrown up for deliberations by the then Chief Justice Dr. A.S. Anand vide his letter dated 8.12.1997 addressed to all Chief Justices of the High Courts. The schematic concept of Permanent Lok Adalats received statutory recognition with the introduction of Section 22-B of the Act by way of amendment. Under the new scheme, the Permanent Lok Adalat will, in the first instance, try to bring about conciliation between the parties and in case the parties are not able to arrive at settlement, the Permanent Lok Adalat shall proceed to dispose of the matter on merit. There is a difference between the Lok Adalat and Permanent Lok Adalat. In Lok Adalat, if the parties fail to resolve their disputes, the cases will go back to court and in the case of pre-trial Lok Adalat the parties on failure of such conciliation may approach the court, but the Lok Adalat cannot try the cases. The novelty of the Permanent Lok Adalat is that, in the event of failure of disposal of dispute by way of conciliation, the Permanent Lok Adalat shall proceed to decide the dispute on merit provided the dispute does not relate to any offence. Hence, the Permanent Lok Adalat can act as a Court or Tribunal in case of failure of reconciliation between the parties. The award of the Permanent Lok Adalat, whether made on merit or on settlement shall be final and binding on parties and be deemed to a decree of a civil court.

The newly inserted Section 22-B provides for establishment of Permanent Lok Adalats for exercising jurisdiction in respect of public utility services and important features of the amendments to the Legal Services Authorities (Amendment) Act, 2002 are as follows :

(i) It seeks to provide compulsory pre-litigative mechanism for conciliation and settlement of cases relating to public utility services.

(ii) The public utility services like transport of passengers or goods by air, road or water, postal, telegraph or telephonic service, supply of power and water to the public, public conservancy or sanitation, hospitals and insurance have been brought within the purview of the Permanent Lok Adalats under Section 22-A(b) of the Act.

(iii) After an application is filed by any party before the Permanent Lok Adalat for settlement the opposite party is summoned. Both the parties thereafter are requested to file statement, reply and documents and Permanent Lok Adalat assists the parties in their attempt to reach an amicable settlement of the dispute in an independent and impartial manner. If settlement is arrived at, an award is passed. Where the parties fail to reach at an agreement, the Permanent Lok Adalat decides the dispute on merit. In deciding the dispute on merit, the Permanent Lok Adalat is guided by the principles of natural justice, objectivity, fair play, equity and other principles of justice but is not bound by the Code of Civil Procedure, 1908 and the Indian Evidence Act, 1872.

(iv) After application is made to Permanent Lok Adalat, no party to that application is entitled to invoke jurisdiction of any court in the same dispute.

(v) The Permanent Lok Adalat shall not have jurisdiction in respect of any matter relating to an offence not compoundable under any law or where the property in dispute exceeds ten lakh rupees.

(vi) Every award of the Permanent Lok Adalat shall be deemed to be a decree of a Civil Court. It shall be final, binding and shall not be called in question in "original suit, application or execution proceedings."

(vii) Permanent Lok Adalat envisaged under the Act shall consist of a person who is or has been, a District Judge or Additional District Judge or has held judicial office higher in rank than that of the District Judge as Chairman and two other persons having adequate experience in public utility services as members. These Permanent Lok Adalats have to be established by the National Legal Services Authority or the State Legal Services Authorities.

The importance of the amendment in Legal Services Authorities Act lies in promoting the welfare of the society by enabling the people to approach Permanent Lok Adalats. The amendment attempts to remove the helplessness of a consumer which he faces in the field of Public Utility Services.[1] Hence, the Act is a milestone on the path of civil society in realising equal justice for all. Courts in India are over-burdened with pending cases. Lack of financial resources of the State exchequer has all along been a hindrance in the way of providing adequate infrastructure to meet the ever growing needs of the litigants. The statistical returns in many States make it evidence that the problem of docket of explosion has sufficiently been arrested by the mechanism provided under the Act resulting in qualitative as well as quantitative improvement of justice delivery system in India. The Permanent Lok Adalats, when established in all the States, prove to be effective, litigant friendly and less expensive mechanism to resolve certain serious disputes. As the Public Utility Services are rendered mainly by corporate bodies, this virtually will be a

1. Justice Shiv Kumar Sharma, "2002—An Year of Public Utility Services", Nyaya Deep, September, 2002, p. 17.

forum for ordinary men and women to ventilate their grievances against such corporate bodies. In the changing economic scenario of the country where insurance, communication and other services are thrown open to corporate giants, it is all the more necessary to provide for cost effective and delay free tools for resolution of disputes. Hence, it is structured in such a manner that it is a conciliatory mode with certain features of arbitration to arrive at decision even if sharp criticism against this machinery is there especially from advocates. The criticism or opposition against the amendment is three fold, viz.; (i) with regard to constitution of Permanent Lok Adalat; (ii) in so far as the Permanent Lok Adalat is given power to decide a dispute unlike the ordinary Lok Adalats envisaged as per Section 19 of the Act which only conciliates the dispute; and (iii) as no appeal is provided against the decision of the Permanent Lok Adalat. To be true, there is no basis of criticism. As the Government is nominating the members of the Permanent Lok Adalats, there may be political consideration in their appointment, it is said. It is a truism that the members shall be nominated by the respective Governments. But, such nomination shall be in terms of Section 22-B(2)(b) of the Legal Services Authorities (Amendment) Act, 2002, on recommendation by the Legal Services Authority concerned. After such nomination, they have to be appointed by the Legal Services Authority concerned. So anyone of Government's choice cannot be appointed.

There is a Central Authority called "National Legal Services Authority" and its patron is the Chief Justice of India. Its Executive Chairman is the senior most Judge of the Supreme Court of India. Two among the members are two Chairmen of the State Legal Services Authorities who are invariably sitting Judges of the concerned High Courts. Another member is the Secretary of the Department of Legal Affairs and there is a Member Secretary who is a District Judge. Apart from that, there are members like the Secretary, Department of Expenditure and members appointed by the Government in consultation with the Chief Justice of India. Those persons shall be eminent persons in the field of law are persons of repute in the legal services schemes or eminent social workers. Similarly, the Patron-in-Chief of the State Legal Services Authorities is the Chief Justice of the concerned High Court. A sitting or a retired Judge of the High court functions as the Executive Chairman and is nominated by the Governor. A District Judge functions as the Member Secretary. Besides this, the State Authority may appoint any such number of officers and other employees as may be prescribed by the State Government, in consultation with the Chief Justice of the High Court, for efficient discharge of its functions under the Act. To reiterate, every Lok Adalat organized for an area shall consist of such members of :—(a) serving or retired judicial officers; and (b) other persons, of the areas as may be specified by the State Authority or the District Authority or the Supreme Court Legal Services Committee or the High Court Legal Services Committee or, as the case may be, the Taluk Legal Services Committee, organizing such Lok Adalat.

Rule 13 of the National Legal Services Authority Rules, 1995 which prescribes the qualifications and experiences of other persons of the Lok Adalat organized by the Supreme Court Legal Services Committee specifies in sub-section (3) of Section 19 that a person shall not be qualified to be included in the Lok Adalat unless he is :—

(a) a member of the legal profession; or

(b) a person of repute who is specially interested in the implementation of Legal Services Scheme and programmes; or

(c) an eminent social worker who is engaged in the upliftment of the weaker sections of the people, including Scheduled Castes, Scheduled Tribes, women, children, rural and urban labour.

The qualifications and experience of other persons referred to in clause (b) of sub-section (2) of Section 19 of Lok Adalats other than those referred to in sub-section (3) shall be such as may be prescribed by the State Government in consultation with the Chief Justice of the High Court. There is a criticism that the persons so appointed will not have legal background. Presently, the specialised tribunals are appointed with the representatives of social organizations or experts. In the case of machineries set up to try disputes raised by consumers, members other than chairman are persons without legal background. There is further criticism that the decision taken by the members forming majority may prevail over the decision taken by the Chairman with judicial or legal background, of course there is some force in this criticism. The need of the hour is that there shall be some definite qualifications for other members of the Permanent Lok Adalat. Presently, what is required is that they shall have "adequate experience in public utility service". Hence, it is advisable to have definite qualifications so that the litigants will have confidence that the persons deciding their disputes are having sufficient intellectual acumen.

The second criticism is with regard to the functioning of the Permanent Lok Adalat insofar as it is given the power to decide a dispute when the parties do not agree for a settlement. While deciding the dispute, it is made clear that the provisions of the Code of Civil Procedure and the Indian Evidence Act will not have application. In other words, the determination or decisions will be in a summary manner. The Permanent Lok Adalat is given ample power in the matter of reception of evidence, examination of witnesses, etc., the power that a civil court has. A decision is possible only in those cases where in the opinion of Permanent Lok Adalat "there exists elements of settlement." In such cases, the Permanent Lok Adalat formulates the terms of a possible settlement and gives such terms to the parties concerned for their observations. These observations will be considered based on the evidence produced by the parties. If they do not come to a settlement, the Permanent Lok Adalat shall decide the dispute. Meaning thereby, the Permanent Lok Adalat is not given the power to decide every dispute coming before it. Only those disputes where there exists element of settlement alone can be decided by the Permanent Lok Adalat. Further, the decision or opinion of the Permanent Lok Adalat as to whether there exists elements of settlement is also a matter which can be subjected to judicial review under Article 226 of the Constitution of

India. Hence, there shall be a check in that respect as well.

It is further ensured in the Legal Services Authorities Act that while deciding the dispute on merit, the Permanent Lok Adalat shall be guided by the "principle of natural justice". Thus, a fair procedure is always envisaged. Therefore, there is no reason for any criticism towards the power granted to the Permanent Lok Adalat to decide the dispute, if no settlement is arrived at by the parties in the cases "where there exists an element of settlement."

It cannot be said that there is no appeal against the decision of the Permanent Lok Adalat. So far as the ordinary Lok Adalats are concerned—which is in existence even prior to the amendment and is still being continued in many States—no appeal will lie against an award of that Lok Adalat. There is express exclusion of Appeal from awards of ordinary Lok Adalats, as per Section 21(2) of the Act. The ordinary Lok Adalat adopts only a conciliatory method and does not decide a dispute. Therefore, disputes are settled on consent of the parties. So, there arises no question of an appeal. But the award of Permanent Lok Adalat envisaged in the new introduced Chapter VI-A is different. If it is an award upon consent of parties and is as a result of compromise, necessarily, nobody will think of an appeal. When there is a decision by the Permanent Lok Adalat, whether it is on consent of the parties, or compromise or upon the decision, "shall be deemed to be a decree of a civil court". Thus, the decision taken by the Permanent Lok Adalat will have all the attributes of a decree of civil court. It will be taken and considered in all respects, as a decree of a civil court. Every decree unless it is appealed against and so long as it is allowed to continue, will be final and binding on the parties. Same is the case of an award of Permanent Lok Adalat. It is admitted that there is no provision in the Legal Services Authorities Act providing for an appeal. But appeal is not expressly excluded, in the case of award of Permanent Lok Adalat. But it is made crystal clear that such award shall not be called in question in "original suit, application or execution proceedings." Nowhere it is stated that an award of Permanent Lok Adalat shall not be called in question in any appeal, as is done in the case of the award of an ordinary Lok Adalat in Section 21(2) of the Act.

The appeal will lie only if it is provided somewhere by law. In the case of the awards of ordinary Lok Adalat, statute specifically provides that it shall not be challenged in an appeal. But the very same legislature did not legislate such a provision when it is dealt with the award of Permanent Lok Adalat. The manifest difference in the provisions relating to the awards of Permanent Lok Adalat and ordinary Lok Adalat is not accidental. The difference really brings different idea to mean that an appeal is possible against an award of Permanent Lok Adalat in terms of Section 96(1) of the Code of Civil Procedure, when it is not specifically barred by the Legal Services Authorities Act, 1987, as the award has all attributes of a decree of a civil code.

The Lok Adalat may thus be called as the brain-child of necessity. The scheme is basically judge inspired, judge induced and judge aided, invented as a result of social philosophy expounded in the light of social justice in crisis. There is only a single and uniform procedure to all civil and criminal cases. The procedure is informal, flexible, pleasant, friendly, quick, and devoid of all technicalities and baffling formalities but moulded in consonance with the exigencies of the situation. Everyone will sit around a table in close proximity for efficient transaction of business. The Lok Adalats function purely on democratic lines as there is no compulsion to settle the dispute through them. The mechanism of Lok Adalat is not just a dispute resolution forum or a contrivance introduced to reduce the court arrears, but a people's movement for orderly progress through rule of law and participation in self-government in the cause of social justice.

The overall success of the functioning of Lok Adalats in India reveals that it has attained tremendous success in settling the long pending disputes amicably. On the basis of information available with NALSA office, 2,52,800 Lok Adalats have been organized throughout the country up to 31st December, 2004 in which 17,413,112 cases have amicably settled. Out of these 8,38,171 relate to MACT cases and a total sum of Rs. 54,239,596,981/- have been awarded as compensation. The figure has crossed 39 lakhs cases in 2015.

Hence, it may be summed up that the Legal Services Authorities Act is a milestone on the path of the civil society in realising equal justice for all. Courts in India are over-burdened with pending cases. Lack of financial resources of the State exchequer has all along been a hindrance on the way to providing adequate infrastructure to meet the ever growing needs of the litigants. The statistical returns in different States in India make it evident that the problem of docket explosion has sufficiently been arrested by the mechanism provided under the Act resulting in qualitative as well as quantitative improvement of justice delivery system in India. The concept of Lok Adalat is no longer an experiment in India, but it is accepted as a viable, economic, efficient, informal, expeditious form of resolution of disputes. It is a hybrid or admixture of mediation, negotiation, arbitration and participation.[1] Experience has shown that it is one of the very efficient and important alternative disputes resolution and most suited to Indian environment, culture and social interest.

---

1. Justice Jitendra N. Bhatt, "A Round Table Justice Through Lok Adalat (People's Court)—A Vibrant ADR in India", Supreme Court Cases (Journal Section), Vol. 1 (2002), Parts 5-6, p. 14.

19

MOOT COURTS, ADVOCACY AND PRE-TRIAL PREPARATIONS

I. Introduction

The profession of lawyering shares along with doctors and power to decide on the life and death of another. With such awesome responsibilities being laid on their shoulders, it seems only appropriate that the profession should be accorded commensurate education and training. A large part of the life saving and advocacy skills required by lawyers will develop with experience. However, it is strongly felt that neither our legal system nor our social system can afford the luxury of slow and expensive method of learning from mistakes. It is essential for the efficient functioning of the legal system that its primary players be well equipped in both law and lawyering skills.[1]

II. Moot Courts

Till recently most of the law graduates learnt about the practical skills of legal profession only after entering the Bar. They had either little or no exposure to the practical subjects. The clinical legal education has moot courts as the major component in its curriculum from the academic year 1998-99. The Bar Council of India, the University Grants Commission, the Universities and the judiciary, etc. have made a concerted effort to revamp the syllabus of LL.B. throughout the country. Hence, it is pertinent to know the meaning of the expressions like moot court and mooting for a better understanding of the moot courts conducted as part of their legal curriculum.

(i) Meaning of Moot Court

A moot court is an artificial court designated to debate on a specific case decided by a court of law, or an imaginary or hypothetical case prepared for the purpose of practical training of law students. The purpose of organising moot courts is to provide opportunities to the law students to equip them with the skill for participation in the proceedings of a court of law when they enter in law profession after obtaining the degree of Bachelors of Laws from a University. Generally, moot courts are arranged in law colleges or law faculties of the Universities for law students to

1. See Foreword written by Justice M.S. Liberhan in Moot Court For Interactive Legal Education edited by Amita Dhanda.

provide practical training of lawyering to them. Moots are legal problems in the form of imaginary cases, which are argued by two students 'counsel' (a leader and a junior) on each side, with a 'Bench' of three 'Judges' or (or perhaps only one) representing the Court of Appeal or sometimes the House of Lords (in England). By participating in a moot court a law student acquires the necessary equipment to become a good counsel. The moot court is a forum of providing advance information about the possible problems that a fresh law graduate may come across in the profession. When a student is asked to prepare a case for a client with a hypothetical problem, and present it before a Bench specially created in a moot court, a churning begins. This case he can take up as a sport, without any fear of failure. Following are a few tips which could assist a mooter preparing for a moot problem.

(A) Understand the problem.

(B) Locate the area of law, remedy and the forum.

(C) Interpret the facts.

(D) Apply the law to the problem.

(E) Research for the relevant case law.

(F) Prepare a written memorial or argument for both the sides.

(G) Get ready for facing the questions from the Bench and the points raised by the other side.

In the moot court, the counsel has to do research and prepare written memorials. In the written memorials the counsel must first write the facts of the case. He must write the facts by diving into paragraphs. Each paragraph should be numbered.

After writing the facts of the case the counsel should prepare the issues. The counsel should discuss each issue separately. Each issue should be discussed by citing the relevant section and enactment, if any. In order to support the argument the counsel should cite the case and citation. At the end he must prepare : (a) Bibliography; (b) Table of Statutes; (c) Table of cases including the citation; (d) List of abbreviations. At the time of arguments the counsel should address the judge as My Lord in case if the court is a High Court or Supreme Court and Your Honour in any other courts. The counsels must wear any uniform which is required for them.

Moot court is the best method of practical learning of law, its interpretation and application. A teacher might be successful in conveying the basic principles of law as it developed over a period of time and may also explain its merits and demerits. Its real practical utility can be understood only when the student puts his knowledge to test of real life. In actual practice a much more difficult task, which a mooter is not confronted with, is extracting the information and diagnosing the problem from the heap of facts given by the client. It is popularly known as client interviewing.[1] Unless the advocate takes pains to collect all facts necessary or unnecessary, he cannot make up his mind as to what the problem is and where the remedy lies. After that he may shift the necessary and

1. Tim Kaye and Lynne Townley, Blackstone's Book of Moots (2002), p. 3.

relevant facts from the rest to prepare the brief. In a moot court no client has to be interviewed. The facts, revealing the problem, are available and settled. It is enough for a mooter to understand the supplied facts. Research for evidence, tracing of witnesses and securing their presence in court, some of the most important and serious tasks of a lawyer, need not be undertaken by a student advocate in a moot court. Examination and cross-examination of a witness are other tasks to be undertaken by a lawyer in the court. In order to train law students in these aspects the method of mock trial has been evolved.

(ii) What is mooting?

Mooting in its earliest form dates from about 1485 when moots were organised by the Inns of Court in England.[1] These early moots differed from the format familiar today, where moots are generally concerned only with points of law. The early moots set by the Inns of Court were perhaps best viewed as a kind of pleading exercise. A moot is a legal debate in a court room setting. It is based on a hypothetical case. Moots are set to test the ability of the mooter to present a legal argument. The standard of the mooter is judged by paying particular attention to the mooter's ability to make use of the available legal authorities, answer questions, observe the etiquette of the court room and generally appear competent as an advocate.

A typical moot problem is solely concerned with a point (or points) of law. Normally, it will take the form of a case heard on appeal with the grounds of appeal clearly stated. Unlike the ancient moots, a modern moot speech will have a strict time limit of 15-20 minutes. The speakers are given a certain time limit in which to present their arguments. The moot is presided over by at least one judge who delivers a judgment at the end of the moot both on law and on the result of the moot itself.

The organisation of a moot requires a good deal of advance preparation on the part of both mooters and the moot organizer. It is necessary for the mooters to prepare their arguments in advance of the moot and to select the most appropriate legal authorities for the purposes of argument. The organizers of moot courts and the mooters must know that effective time management is the hallmark of a good advocate. Within the available time, the mooters are expected to put forth their arguments in a methodical, logical and precise manner without wasting the court's precious time.

(iii) Advantages of mooting

Mooting provides students with what is perhaps a unique and unparalleled experience during their time in legal education. Preparation for a moot helps develop good basic research and presentation skills. A moot speech requires the mooter to acquire the ability to identify rapidly the legal issue or issues posed by the moot question. This is not merely because mooting promotes a facility and confidence in public speaking, imparts skills of persuasion and enhances the ability to see both sides of

1. M. Sridhar Acharyulu, "Preparing for Moot Courts", in Amita Dhanda, op. cit., p. 62.

argument. Further, in conducting the research for a moot, many students will also become familiar with certain legal materials and information retrieval systems, which might otherwise have escaped them throughout their time in higher education. With some experience, skillful mooters become well able to 'argue both sides of the case', which involves identifying with ease not only the arguments in their favour, but also those less favourable to their side of the case. A mooter must be prepared to attack any opposing authorities and finer points of the case must be noted and in searching for favourable arguments, the students become familiar with perhaps previously uncharted territory such as dissenting judgments. This can only benefit the student in the course of his or her academic studies. Further, few exercises can provide the practical experience and encourage a growth in the confidence of the law student in the way that participation in mooting can. In short, the mooting goes far to bridge the gap in a system of legal education which, for the most part, places greater emphasis on the written arguments.[1] In the words of Glanville Williams : "much stress has been laid by educationists on literacy and numeracy, but we hear little about the importance of being articulate. Footballers practice passing and shooting, singers and claws practice assiduously. Why is it supposed that speaking comes naturally and needs no effort or concentration? Fluency and clear enunciation are particularly important for lawyers, when our forensic practice is largely oral."[2]

(iv) Difference between Moot courts and Mock trials

Moot courts are different from mock trials. Whereas moot court is a court held for the arguing of moot cases or questions, a mock trial is a fictitious trial organized to allow students, or sometimes lawyers to practice the techniques or trials advocacy. A mock trial also could be a fictitious trial arranged by a litigant's attorney, to assess trial strategy, to estimate the case's value or risk and to evaluate the case's strengths and weaknesses.

On the other hand, a moot court is a fictitious court held usually in law schools to argue moot or hypothetical cases especially at the appellate level. It is a practice session for an appellate argument in which a lawyer presents the arguments to other lawyers, who first act as judges by asking questions and who later provide criticism on the argument. It is also termed as 'private court'. The basic distinction between a moot court and a mock trial is that in the former only questions of law are argued and in the later there would be original trial with jury and witnesses and it is not on an argument of law.[3] In mock trials, the proceedings may be somewhat humorous, witnesses may dress themselves up, and court and counsel wear robes. The audience may consist of non-lawyers, who, of course, come simply to be entertained. Therefore, the mock trial can be compared to the mock Parliament session conducted in degree colleges.

---

1. Supra note 2 at p. 5-6; Also see Paul Dobson and Berry Fitzpatrick, The Observer Book of Moots (1986), p. vii.
2. Glanville Williams, Learning the Law (1982), p. 160.
3. *Ibid.*, at p. 169.

(v) Some important hints

(A) One should not try to controvert the judge. He should have patience to hear the judge or other side completely, without interrupting now and then even when occasions arise.

(B) Generally in the lower courts, i.e., other than High Courts and Supreme Court, one should address the judges as "Your Honour" or "May it Please Your Honour", and if it is in the higher court of judicature, it is substituted by "My Lord" or "May it Please Your Lordship". Some of the Bar associations have adopted the move to drop these words describing them as feudal expressions. Therefore, they insist that "The Honourable Court" or "My Judge" will be sufficient departure from the commonly accepted address.

(C) The counsel should present his client's case. But he should not state his opinion in the course of arguments, if he does, he may be charged with disrespect to the court.

(D) The student counsel should avoid reading extensively from the texts or from the written memorials. Glanville Williams has stated that "a frequent fault is to read out passages from textbooks as though they represented the last word on the law. Although textbooks and treatises are not taboo in court, they should be used sparingly and cautiously'.

(E) At the beginning of the presentation of the case, the counsel may seek permission of the court to present his case. But it is not necessary at every stage of the arguments to to on repeating "May I seek Your Lordship's permission". If it is necessary from the circumstances, or if the mooter feels that there is no perceptible link between what he has argued already and what he is to present before the court, then permission of the court may be obtained with the caveat that its relevance will emerge only when the whole point is placed before the court. The expression "My Lord" should not be used as a suffix or prefix to every sentence.

(F) It is the duty of the lawyer to represent his client completely without any fear or favour. The young lawyers having some histrionic talent should not try to do more from their gestures than from their arguments.

(G) Opposing counsel should be referred to as "My learned friend Mr./Mrs./Ms. (Surname)." Senior and junior counsel may refer to one another as "My learned junior" and "My learned leader" respectively.

(H) The counsel should always stand when speaking to the judge. Only one person should be standing at one time.

(vi) Judging the performance in a Moot Court

The performance of an individual mooter, and a team participating in a moot court competition is judged, by taking into consideration the following parameters as pointed by Dr. G.B. Reddy in his book, "Practical Advocacy of Law".

(A) Knowledge and use of facts;

(B) Correct articulation of factual issues, factual analysis and use of evidence;

(C) Knowledge of law and its interpretation;
(D) Use of authorities and citations;
(E) Response to questions;
(F) Skills of advocacy and persuasiveness;
(G) Language and style;
(H) Clarity, brevity and ingenuity;
(I) Court manners and general impression.

Generally, marks are awarded for the above criteria and for oral arguments, a total of 80 marks are awarded by giving weightage to the above parameters and remaining 20 marks are given usually to written memorials. Hence, law students participating in moot courts are expected to be thorough with the facts and the legal provisions pertaining to the given problem.

III. Advocacy and Pre-Trial Preparations

(i) Introduction

Advocacy is not a craft but a calling; a profession wherein devotion to duty constitutes the hallmark. Sincerity of performance and the earnestness of endeavour are the two wings that will bear aloft the advocate to the tower of success. Given these virtues other qualifications will follow of their own account. This is the reason why legal profession is regarded to be a noble one. Many a people do say that 'Advocacy' is an art. No doubt it may more depend upon the skill, but it is not always so since experience shows that at certain times in certain cases, hard work definitely proves to be having upper hand to the so-called efficiency, art or skill of a person, as an Advocate. It does not mean that efficiency has no relevance at all but hard work prevails over efficiency. Constant touch with the subject and serious concentration on different matters in courts will make an Advocate to be more efficient and practical too.

Advocacy is a special case of vicarious conduct. An Advocate devotes his life and career to acting for other people and deals with other people's troubles like a priest or a banker who handles spiritual aspiration and money of others respectively. But the lawyer's case is not like that. It is his private practice. His loyalty runs to his client. The relationship between an advocate and his client is of trust and therefore sacred. It is no doubt true that advocate is expected to ventilate the grievances of his clients. As a true professional, an advocate is no doubt expected to ventilate the grievances of the client, but equally at the same time, the advocate is an officer of the court also, having certain duties and responsibilities towards the court and a balance has to be carefully maintained by the professionals in this regard. Truth, simplicity, candour and expounding the poor man's cause are the hallmarks of brilliant and sincere lawyers. A good lawyer has to possess as wide a knowledge of subjects as he can, and wide knowledge will immensely help him in presentation of the case. But Munkman says that "knowledge of all kinds of things is useful to a lawyer but there are certain subjects which are of outstanding value." They include the following :

(a) The law of evidence and procedure;
(b) Professional ethics;
(c) Logic;
(d) Knowledge of mankind and of affairs;
(e) General principles of law.[1]

Hence, it may therefore be stated that, advocacy is the presentation of logical facts of any dispute in a right perspective, dealing with the criterion of differentiating between right and wrong, just and unjust, equitable and inequitable by applying the knowledge of law acquired by extensive and intensive training, and in doing so, it employs the noblest faculties of human mind and soul in order to discover the true motives of his actions. Advocacy analyses the facts of any given dispute by presenting them in an accurate and forceful form and penetrates into the inner-most part of the human mind and soul and thereby helps in redressal of grievances. To be brief, the object of advocacy is to settle the disputes whenever and wherever they arise and not to create and promote any strife and litigation. It is to be kept in mind by the advocates that advocacy is a profession and not a business. It is abundantly clear that the profession of law is an honourable profession since time immemorial in India. Hence, the legal profession can play a pivotal role in upholding the individual rights, promoting more efficient and widespread justice and acting as an integrating force in national life. For this, an Advocate should be jack of all trades but master of none except the case which he is pleading in a court of law. As rightly pointed out by Lord Broughman, "a lawyer must know everything about something and something about everything."

(ii) Seven lamps of advocacy

A good lawyer as Lord Brougham puts, "must know everything about something and something about everything." This indicates the elements of lawyers' equipment in the legal learning. There are eight lamps of advocacy. Seven lamps of advocacy were advocated by Judge Abbott Parry in his well-known book of the same title, that it, "The Seven Lamps of Advocacy" and eighth has been added by Justice Raj Kishore Prasad in his article published in A.I.R. Journal Section in 1956 and K.V. Krishnaswamy Aiyer in his book "Professional Conduct and Advocacy."

Advocacy is an honourable profession. Advocates are part and parcel of court. Their efforts solve the conflicts in the society. Advocates defend the rights and liabilities. They hold a unique place in the society. Advocacy is not a craft but a calling; a profession wherein devotion to duty constitutes the hallmark.

Legal profession is regarded to be a noble one. A good advocate should possess some essential qualities and equipment. Judge Abbot Parry called these important characteristics of advocacy as 'seven lamps of advocacy' and listed them as honesty, courage, industry, wit, eloquence, judgment and

1. Quoted from Gururaja Chari, Advocacy and Professional Ethics, p. 325.

fellowship.

(1) Honesty

Honesty means the quality of straightforwardness, freedom from deceit, cheating or stealing and not telling lies. The best advocates of all generations have been devotees of honesty. Example for honest character is Abraham Lincoln, who founded his fame and success on what some called 'perverse honesty'. Justice Nageshwar Prasad pointed out, "His honesty should be unquestioned and unquestionable. No temptation should move him from his path of rectitude. No favour or frowns should be able to deflect him from his duties to the client and the court. No hopes of personal benefit expected from any individual or the State should stand in the way of his honest discharge of duties." According to Judge Abbot Parry, the best advocates of all generations have been devotees of honesty. The nobleness of legal profession lies in honesty itself. An advocate should not do illegal practices. He should not do any act which will lead to professional misconduct. He should disclose the real facts and legal position to his clients frankly. Honestly, integrity and character are inseparable. These three virtues together are essential for the success of advocate. The great sages of law had sucked the law from the breasts of knowledge, honesty, gravity and integrity.

(2) Courage

Courage is the most essential quality that enables a person to control fear in the face of danger, pain, misfortune, etc. An advocate must possess courage. R. Jethamalani argues that it requires highest moral courage to prevent a Judge from falling into an error of taking a view of law which is unknown to the other side but has been clearly and finally overruled. An advocate should face the pressures from outside with courage. Sometimes he has to fight against the State. He should not fear about the executive and politicians. He must perform his duty to safeguard the interests of his client. Advocacy is a form of combat, where courage in times of danger is half won battle. Courage is as good a weapon in the forum as in the war camp. Charles Hutton's: He hath in perfection the three chief qualifications of an advocate : Boldness, Boldness and Boldness. It is the knowledge and the skill of the advocate that gives him necessary courage and confidence to present the case fearlessly and to uphold the interest of the client. The knowledge can be attained and developed by mastery of facts, attained and developed by mastery of facts, mastery of law, skill in drafting, taking evidence, timely submissions and presentation of convincing arguments.

(3) Industry

Advocacy is indeed a life of industry. An advocate must study his brief in the same way that an actor studies his part. Success in advocacy is not arrived at by intuition but through industry. Industry is the quality of being hard working; being always employed usefully.

Lord Eldon says, "An advocate must live like a hermit and work like a horse." Advocacy is an intellectual profession. Intelligence and knowledge will be hardened with hard work and strenuous efforts. Advocacy is the profession which requires 'study' and 'study' throughout the career. An advocate must know about every trade. He must acquire the knowledge of every field. He must learn about all professions. Industry brings a good fame and name to an advocate. Law changes day to day. To acquire up to date knowledge, an advocate must refer to international and national journals, reference books of his library and the bar library. He has to work hard like a spider for the benefit of his client. In the words of Edison, "Extraordinary talent is nothing but 2% inspiration and 98% perspiration". If one ignores law, the law is also apt to ignore him. That is why it is said that "law is a jealous mistress." Lord Atkin too regards capacity for hard and regular work as essential element for the success of a lawyer. It is rightly observed that industry is fortune's right hand. An advocate is the maker of his own destiny by industry, it is rightly said : "Luck generally comes to those who look after it and a notion is, it laps once in a life-time at everybody's door, and if industry does not open, away it goes."

(4) Wit

Wit means clever and humorous expression of ideas; liveliness of spirit. Wit flows from intelligence; understanding and quickness of mind. Wit lessens the work-load of an advocate. It relaxes his mental strain. Often the wit of an advocate will turn a judge from a unwise course, where judgment, or rhetoric would certainly fail. The lamp of wit is needed to lighten the darkness of advocacy. Judges and lawyers have to deal with a variety of serious and important matters affecting life, liberty, property and other human relations. Constant clash between diverse thoughts amidst the aim and anxiety for a favourable verdict on the part of the lawyers; and perpetual worry during the pursuit of truth on the part of the judge generate strain, tension and excitement in their mental faculties. Occasional, incidental and undetermined deflection of thoughts or words to irrelevance effected by wits and humour provoking a smile or laughter will help them to ease the tension, refresh and sharpen their mental faculty and restore the necessary balance for the effective discharge of their duties.

(5) Eloquence

It is the gift of speech which more than any other equips the advocate to achieve his primary purpose, that is, persuasion. The success of an advocate depends upon his eloquence. Eloquence means fluent speaking and skillful use of language to persuade or to appeal to the feelings of others. Fluent speaking impresses the listener. An advocate must be fluent, skillful in using appropriate words to impress the court. Eloquence attracts the attention of the listener. Eloquence is related to the art of oratory. Eloquence of manner is real eloquence and there is a physical as well as psychological side of advocacy. The main task of an advocate should be to impress the essential points with vigour, speed, and perfect clarity. Eloquence is the faculty of presenting a point of view, whether argumentative or emotional in such language as to impress the minds of the audience, whatever that audience may be.

(6) Judgment

Judgment is an intellectual capacity, 'the inspiration which enables a man to translate good sense into right action.' In judgment one has to estimate, consider and form an opinion about the issues with good sense and ability. An advocate could be in a position to judge the merits and demerits of the case on hearing the brief and seeing the document. He should inform his client the legal position openly after judging the issues. Here judgment is not 'giving the decision of the case by the Judge in the Court.' Judgment means the study of the case in deep by considering all shades of the consequences. In nothing does the lawyer more openly exhibit want to judgment than in prolixity.

Judge Abbot Parry has referred to judgment as one of the seven lamps; but he refers to it essentially as an intellectual capacity, 'the inspiration' which enables a man to translate good sense into right action, e.g., 'seeing the right point of his case' and the like.

(7) Fellowship

The seventh lamp according to Judge Parry is fellowship. In legal profession, a learned advocate fights with another learned advocate before a learned judge. The advocates refer to each other as 'learned friend'. Fellowship means the membership in friendly association or companionship. Fellowship is exactly like a great public school, the boys of which have grown older, and have exchanged boyish for manly objects. Though the advocates are opponent parties before the Bench, they are not enemies with each other. Their conflict ends as they come out of the doorsteps of the court. Daniel Webster says : "Lawyers on opposite sides of a case are like the two parts of shears, they cut what comes between them, but not each other." There is no discrimination of age, ability, experience and riches, etc. between the advocates. All are equal. Courts give them all equal respect. Among advocates, there is just the same rough familiarity, the general ardour of character, the same kind of unwritten code of moral and manners, the some kind of public opinion expressed in exactly the same blunt, unmistakable manner. By keeping the lamp of fellowship burning, advocates encourage each other by sharing the knowledge to walk in the light of the seven lamps of advocacy.

(8) Tact

One of the greatest assets of an advocate is tact. It is the eighth lamp which enlightens an advocate to move forward in his profession. K.V. Krishnaswamy Aiyer, in his book 'Professional Conduct and Advocacy' adds one more lamp, i.e., tact. Tact means handling people and situations skillfully and without causing offence. An advocate must be in a position to tackle and win his client opponent party, opponent advocate in a smoother way. Many people of unequal ability have failed for want of tact. An advocate should not quarrel with court or lose temper over trifle things in the court and outside. Man of unquestioned ability have suffered for quarreling with the tribunal or for standing on their dignity over trifles, forgetting their clients, or for losing their tempers; they are men of parts but without tact. Tact involves and is in reality founded on judgment but more properly refers to the human side of putting into action the result of one's judgment. A judge is after all a human being, however anxious he may be to do justice, tactlessness by a counsel often damages his client's case.

(iii) Equipments of an Advocate

Justice Raj Kishore Prasad, former Judge of Patna High Court, in his article on "What do I expect from an Advocate" published in A.I.R. Journal Section, 1956 suggests that an Advocate must be equipped with qualities of : (i) honesty, integrity and character; (ii) patience and perseverance; (iii) legal learning; (iv) general education; (v) memory; (vi) study of law reports; (vii) the use of legal phraseology; (viii) manners in court; (ix) presentation of case; (x) citation of authorities; and (xi) independence and dignity. These qualifies are elaborated as follows :—

(1) Honesty, integrity and character

An advocate should be honest, and must be a man of integrity and character. Along with these he should possess straightforwardness to be appreciated by the court and the client alike. All great people became great due to their divine knowledge, honesty, gravity and integrity. Honesty is the quality of freedom from deceit, cheating, stealing and telling lies. Honesty is not restricted to uprightness in money transactions. Suppression of the real situation of a case from the court, coaching witnesses, etc. are some of the instances of dishonest dealings. Integrity is the quality of completeness and upright in character. Character consisting of both mental and moral qualities, make one person different from others. These three virtues of honesty, integrity and character go a long way towards the success of an advocate. The noble exhortation of Lord Coke to the lawyers of England should always be borne in mind : "There is no jewel in the world comparable to learning; no learning so excellent both for princes, and subjects as knowledge of laws; ....cast thin eye upon the sages of law that have been before three, and never shall though find that hath excelled in the knowledge of these laws, but hath, sucked from the breasts of that divine knowledge, honesty, gravity and integrity."

(2) Patience and perseverance

Patience is the power of enduring trouble, suffering, inconvenience, without complaining. An advocate with patience will have ability to wait for results, to deal with problems calmly and without haste. Perseverance is constant effort to achieve something. Patience and perseverance are two hands of success. As the saying goes : 'perseverance is the right hand of success, and patience her left hand'. An advocate who is capable of labour, with maximum patience, self-confidence and faith is honoured by all. He should not be a defeatist and pessimist. Exact thinking and exact expression are needed for a successful advocate. "Accuracy and diligence are much more necessary to a lawyer than great comprehension of mind or brilliancy of truant" says Daniel Webster.

(3) Legal learning

The foremost essential thing for an advocate is to equip himself in legal learning and it should be wide and accurate. The learning of law does not stop with the acquisition of law degree from a University. To acquire professional knowledge he has to continue the learning process. To learn law an advocate should study law, and not merely read it. He should not taste and chew the law but he should digest it. The law should be studied in a spirit of enquiry. He must be thorough with the sections of Acts and case study. He must study law to reach the heights of 'running encyclopaedia of law.' A young advocate, immediately on his entry in the profession, wishes to get clients, but he should not forget that 'a little knowledge is a dangerous thing.' To wait for clients, and then to learn at the expense of the clients is bad. It mars the reputation of the advocate amongst litigants. He should not wait for the clients, but should preserve in order to equip himself with learning and then, you will see that the clients wait for you, and not you for them.

(4) General education

An advocate should not only be the master of his faculty, law but also the contemporary knowledge of all the branches of sciences. He should have the knowledge of both Social Sciences and Natural and Physical Sciences. He must touch every field of human being and he has to study all walks of life of human beings. If he is gifted with knowledge of all subjects, he can claim to be an architect in the profession.

(5) Memory

In general sense, memory means the power of keeping facts in the conscious mind and of being able to call them back at will. An advocate should possess tenacious memory. An advocate has no use of reading if he fails to store the matter in memory. Prof. Blackie says, "by memory I do not mean wholesale reproduction, but the faculty of the mind that will help an advocate at the hour of need to put his hand in the proper place, one that is cultivated and gained by system, order and classification, as a result of intensive study." An advocate may have in memory many things, but if he fails to use them skillfully when needed, they are of no use to him. An advocate must cultivate memory. He should possess a tenacious memory. To acquire such a memory, an advocate should study with precision and accuracy and should arrange them on the shelf of his mind in their appropriate places.

(6) Study of law reports

An advocate should read the current law reports to make his knowledge up to date. The Law Journal and Reports publish the case laws and articles on law issues. An advocate should not only study the law reports, he should also preserve them to refer again and again and to produce in the court in support of his argument. It will be helpful to an advocate if he draws up head notes for the reports that he studies, as that will clarify his ideas, and give him accurate knowledge.

(7) Use of legal phraseology

Every science has its own terminology. In the similar way law also has its phraseology peculiar to itself. Every phrase of law has its peculiar and special meaning it carries. No other word is suitable to be used in its place. To express some feeling an advocate should use appropriate word to convey such meaning. The elegance and dignity of arguments in court can be exposed through correct use of the language.

(8) Manners in court

An advocate should always maintain calmness. He should be respectable to the court. He should never interrupt the Judge when he speaks, but should wait for the Judge to complete his statement. He should not reply in a hurry to the question put by the Judge. He should speak politely and is required to maintain frankness, fearlessness and dignity. An advocate should not argue when he is not asked for by the Judge. He should not continue his argument when the Judge asks him not to proceed further.

An advocate should not lose balance, or temper in the Court if anything is expressed against his opinion. He can forcibly submit his opinion but with humility and modesty along with humour. He should be exemplary, calm and cool and ever smiling. He should argue logically but not confront or quarrel. Self restraint and respectful attitude towards the Court, presentation of correct facts and law with a balanced mind and without overstatement, suppression, distortion or embellishment are the requisites of good advocacy. The advocate's most valuable asset is the respect and good will he enjoys among his colleagues and the court. Presentation of argument with honesty, courtesy, character and court manners will double the strength of argument.

(9) Presentation of case

The first and foremost requirement to present a clear argument is a thorough knowledge of one's own case and also that of the opponent. Presentation of the case must be in such a way as to create the best impression and confidence possible and to incite the interest of the Judge taking into consideration, a clear perception of his sentiments and prejudices as well. An advocate should present meaningfully his case by arranging his thoughts in proper sequence and chronological order without confusion. He should present records of citation for his law points presented. He should not give scope for the lapses of inaccuracy and misstatements of facts. He should not repeat the arguments once again. An advocate should not conceal adverse points, but present the special circumstances of them. A misstatement is seriously dangerous because the Judge may not forget it and even if he may forget, the adversary will make use of every opportunity to remind him as to the same. While presenting a case, an Advocate is required to maintain frankness, fearlessness, assertion of right, humility, courtesy, politeness and dignity.

(10) Citation of authorities

An advocate should quote the applicable citations. He should always take care of citing the latest authority on the particular point. If the decision of the Supreme Court or Privy Council are there which support his case, he should present them instead of the decisions of lower courts. He should skillfully select correct and suitable one amongst several decisions. He need not go for a number of citations. It is always better to cite a few recent cases which have a close resemblance to the facts of his case. He should refer the volume, number, and page on which he wants to rely for his proposition of law.

(11) Independence and dignity

An advocate should maintain his dignity, independence and integrity. An advocate should discharge his duties fearlessly and faithfully. He should not be a headstrong and arrogant. He should not be pound of himself. He should give consideration for others. He should fulfil his duties with the eternal and immutable interests of truth and justice. Lord Cockburn, C.J. said, "The arms which a counsel wields are to be the arms of the warrior, and not of assassin. It is his duty to strive to accomplish, the interest of his client—*'per fas'*, but not *'per nefas'*. It is his duty to the utmost of his power to seek to reconcile the interests he is bound to maintain, and the duty it is incumbent upon him to discharge, with the eternal and immutable interests of truth and justice."

(iv) Elements of advocacy

Advocacy is the presentation of logical facts of any dispute in a right perspective and an advocate is a person who argues in favour of his clients in courts of justice. Advocacy is pleading in support of his case. Advocacy is not a craft but a calling. The art of advocacy consists in presentation. A mere bold recitation of dry and uninterested facts or a mere encyclopaedic citation of innumerable authorities does not constitute advocacy. The facts never change, but art consists in the manner in which they are presented, which one is emphasized and which one is gently touched; the perspective in which they are placed, the interpretation that is put upon them and the skill with which they are marshalled and arrayed. Words can cast a spell even over facts and the wizardry of language can sway even the most hard-headed judges. Language was intended not only to give expression to thoughts and ideas but also to make that expression pleasant and graceful. The first and foremost quality that an advocate should possess is the quality of presentation. The art of advocacy also consists in the handling of witness. There is a common belief that cross-examination is intended solely to destroy the case that the witness has set-up in examination-in-chief. Cross-examination has also a constructive and positive aspect. A clever advocate in his cross-examination does not merely destroy the case of his opponent, but also succeeds in building up the case of his own client. It has been said that you must never put a question in cross-examination unless you are sure of the answer you will get. Sir Patrick Hastings does not subscribe to this doctrine. He believes that a good cross-examination must take risks. But even if you take risks you must take reasonable risks and you must never forget that a damaging reply might completely destroy your client's case.[1] The following are the elements of advocacy :—

(1) Accepting brief and pre-trial preparations for conducting a case

An advocate is bound to accept any brief in the Courts or Tribunals or before any other authority in or before which he professes to practice at a fee consistent with his standing at the bar and the nature of the case. Lawyers or advocates are the officers of the Court and as such it is their duty to help the Court in the administration of justice whole-heartedly. An advocate has to be courteous and respectful to the Court to read the mind of the court and the attempt to carry the court towards himself by a skillful and masterful presentation of the facts. A reasonable and appropriate interpretation of law is a great art which a lawyer should try to learn. For this purpose the lawyer should marshal the facts of the case in which he is appearing carefully and thoroughly and also be fully appraised of the knowledge of the connected laws in connection with the appropriate case. For that purpose a counsel must equip himself with the art of presenting a case. He should receive all possible instructions from the client in all details, study the brief including the documents in original furnished by the client and scrutinisingly, thoroughly and carefully examine those documents, sort out the points both for and against his client. He must acquaint himself both with the strong points and the weak points in the case on hand. After ascertainment of facts, he must study in detail the law on the matter. While studying the case law, he should never be contended with the reading of head notes. He should study the whole case from beginning to end. While preparing the case, the counsel should look up authority and precedent for everything. Careful thought should be given as to how tactfully and efficiently to meet the points in favour of the adversary at the trial of the suit and how to disprove the documents filed by the adversary. Every advocate should remember the words of caution of Michael Hyam in his book entitled "Advocacy Skills" as follows :

> *"It is necessary to prepare your case by taking both general and special view of it; so that you have clear in your mind not only what you have to prove or disprove, but also the way in which you are going to to it."*

Therefore, a thorough study of the case and deep thinking should be developed as a habit of mind in order to reduce the case into certain formal propositions so as to place the same before the Judge in the form of argument. An advocate shall never misstate a case. Once a Judge feels that the advocate has either been careless in his statement of facts or is trying to mislead him deliberately, the advocate loses his confidence with disastrous result for his professional reputation.

1. M.C. Chagla's, Introduction to Soonawala's Advocacy—Its Principles and Practice.

(2) Thorough knowledge of law necessary

A counsel would do well to remember the observations of Justice Holmes, "Theory is the most important part of the dogma of the law as the architect is the most important man who takes part in the planning of a house." Therefore, the essential equipment of a counsel is to acquaint himself with the fundamental principles of law, the theory of law. It is highly desirable that he must equip himself not only in the analytical method but also in the comparative, historical and the ethical aspects of law. Every counsel must remember that no man can ever be truly great counsel, who is not in every sense of the word a good man. Frankly admitting that it is necessary for an advocate to acquire a thorough knowledge of the law of evidence and procedure, otherwise he will be handicapped at every turn by uncertainty as to whether a piece of evidence is admissible, whether it has to be proved by oral evidence, whether, if it is contained in a document, it is necessary to call the maker of it and so forth. Hence, it is essential for a lawyer not only to know the facts well, but also the law applicable to his case. He must never cite an authority which he has not read for himself and facts of which he has not completely mastered. A successful lawyer before citing a legal authority before the court must read it carefully and fully. A lawyer is expected to equip himself with the latest position to the best of his ability.

(3) Necessity of studying the records

Necessity of studying the records thoroughly and carefully can never to too much emphasized. This is what should be done by a lawyer in every case before proceeding with the case and specially with the cross-examination. A lawyer who has a thorough grip of the facts, has in his hands a powerful weapon to fight his adversary with. After the facts have been gathered, the next thing that most pressingly demands the lawyer's attention is the record. Therefore, it will be useful to bear in mind two questions, viz. (i) what has to be proved or disproved; and (ii) how is your case to be proved and the case of an adversary to be disproved. The advocate should ascertain all documents and prepare a chronology of events. It is useful and in fact essential to prepare chronology of events as soon as the advocate begins the preparation of facts in earnest. This will not only be useful during the preparation of the case, but also an aid to the memory to guide him when presenting the case in court.

(4) Interview with client

Most important step in the study of the case is an interview with the client. Whenever a client approaches a lawyer with a view to engaging his services in connection with a litigation, the first step is the interview of client by the lawyer. The lawyer is required to follow certain well established techniques and apply certain necessary skills. A lawyer has to be very sympathetic to what the client tells him and understanding of human psychology is required by encouraging his client to tell all the relevant facts of the case. After getting all the facts, the lawyer has to gain his client's confidence. He has to create an atmosphere of calmness when he is having an interview with his client so that a thorough understanding between the advocate and his client is built-up. It is necessary at this stage for the lawyer to note a complete chronological narrative of what his client tells him and note down separately all obscure points which still remained to be cleared. The advocate should study the whole narrative in the light of surrounding circumstances finding out where there are weaknesses of his client's case. Besides such narrative and noting down, he should prepare a chart listing the areas needing further exploration. After that, the lawyer should embark upon the study of all the obscure points or any technical points which require further research. Finally, all these processes have been gone through, an advocate should prepare a trial chart before embarking upon the study of law.

(v) Researching the law

Another aspect of general preparation is researching the law which applies to the case. While researching a point of law, the advocate should work it through to a conclusion before passing to the next point. The lawyer does not always get unlimited time for the preparation of the case and he may be engaged at a short notice. Whatever may be the period of time, the preparation has to be made with orderliness and has to be completed before a lawyer appears before the court on the first date of hearing.

(vi) Filing of the case

In civil cases a suit is required to be instituted by presenting a plaint to the court. The statement of a plaint regarding his claim is taken as a plaint. The plaintiff presents his case along with cause of action, etc. through the plaint. The plaint is also called the written statement. Every pleading is required to contain a statement in a concise form of material facts on which the party filing the plaint relies for his claim or defence.

(vii) Opening of the case

Normally if an advocate appears on behalf of the plaintiff in a civil case or for the prosecution in a criminal case, the burden of proof rests on the plaintiff or the prosecution, as the case may be. Therefore, it is the advocate for the plaintiff or for the prosecution, as the case may be, who should begin and give a brief account of his case in a clear and logical way in opening the case. However, this can only be done best if the points are previously thought of and arranged. If necessary, a genealogy and a list of material dates should be given to the court at the time of opening. At the opening stage a lengthy argument is always to be avoided. As a general rule, brevity in a speech of any sort is a great virtue. When the advocate, however, appears on behalf of the defendant, he should briefly set out before the court and convincingly the defence of his client and indicate to the court as to how he would prove his defence or lead his defence evidence.

(viii) Pleadings

The fundamental rules of pleadings are four :

(i) Every pleading must state facts and not law.

(ii) It must state all material facts and material facts only.

(iii) It must state only the facts on which the party's pleading relies and not the evidence by which they are to be proved; and

(iv) It must state facts concisely, but with precision and certainty.

The object of the pleading is to make both the parties aware of their cases and allegations made against each other. In other words, it gives a fair notice to each party of what the opponent's case is. Pleading brings forth the real matters in dispute between the parties. It is necessary for the parties to know each other's stand, what facts are admitted and what denied, so that at the trial they are prepared to meet them. Every pleading shall be signed by the party and his pleader. Order VI of the Civil Procedure Code deals with pleadings. It contains several rules relating to pleading. An advocate shall follow those rules in his pleading. Suit is commenced by presentation of the plaint.

(ix) Examination of witnesses

The parties have to adduce sufficient evidence, both documentary and oral, to establish the claim or defence, as the case may be. Ordinarily, in a civil case the initial onus is upon the plaintiff to prove his case. Therefore, he has the right to begin his case, that is, the plaintiff will examine his witness or witnesses to substantiate the allegations made in the plaint and to give a denial to points raised in defendants written statement which are not admitted by the plaintiff vide Order 18, Rule 2 Civil Procedure Code and Section 138 of the Evidence Act. This is to be done by examining his own witnesses which is known as examination-in-chief which is taken orally in open court, unless a witness is examined on commission. As the examination-in-chief of each witness is concluded, it is the duty of the lawyer for the defendant to cross-examine the witness. If there are any ambiguities in cross-examination, to clear those ambiguities, the plaintiff's advocate again examine the plaintiff and his witnesses. This is called re-examination. In the same way the court examines the defendant and his witnesses. After this the plaintiff's advocate and defendant's advocate submit their arguments. Then the court delivers the judgment.

In the criminal case also, it is the duty of the prosecution to prove his case beyond all reasonable doubt by producing evidence, both oral and documentary and when the examination-in-chief of the witness for the prosecution is completed, the counsel for the accused has to cross-examine such witness as soon as the examination-in-chief of the particular witness is completed.

(A) Examination-in-chief

Examination-in-chief is the way in which advocates present almost all the evidence through witnesses, whether as counsel for plaintiff or defendant. The witness is expected to give testimony untutored, and one would not therefore question him in a manner that will suggest the answer; in other words, one is not allowed to put leading questions. During the examination-in-chief, the advocate has to observe the following rules :

(1) Be thorough with the leading features of the case. This

knowledge supplies the basis of the style to be adopted, and enables to elicit the evidence with advantage.

(2) Arrange all the relevant questions in simple form touching the material points only in their order of events. Aimless questions should never be asked.

(3) Do not ask any leading question. Questions should be framed in short, distinct sentences. Complex and compounded sentences should be avoided.

(4) Choose only the best witness. Uncertain and faithless witnesses should be guarded against. Adverse witnesses must be dismissed soon. A good story told by one witness is better than half-hearted story told by two or more witnesses.

(5) Elicit all the necessary points, foreseeing the possible questions of cross-examination.

(6) Be careful not to elicit undesired answers.

(7) As far as possible allow the witness to answer in his own words. Answers from witnesses of poor memory should be restricted to pointed questions only. Witnesses going astray should be brought back to the original track by necessary tactics.

(8) As far as possible be friendly to the witness. A timid witness should be encouraged, a bold one repressed, and frightened witness should be put in his poise.

(9) Be self controlled and patient. Do not be ruffled by any unfavourable answer.

(10) Never call the witness whom the adversary will be compelled to call. Reserve your opportunity to cross-examine him.

(11) Objected questions must be connected to the issue in the case. Never ask a question without an object.

(12) Do not put frivolous and unenforceable objections.

(13) Modulate your voice as circumstance may direct, "inspire the fearful and repress the bold."

(14) Never begin before you are ready, and always finish when you have done. In other words, do not question for question's sake, but for an answer.

(B) Cross-examination

The examination of a witness by the adverse party is called the cross-examination. The main object of cross-examination is to discredit the veracity of the testimony of the witness during his examination-in-chief. The art of cross-examination can be learnt only by experience and constant practical training. The object of cross-examination is to discover the truth before the court of justice. It is a principle of law of evidence that omission to cross-examine a witness called by the opponent amounts to acceptance of the witness. Cross-examination needs much preparation, deep thought, sound planning and powerful memory particularly when the case abounds in facts. Cockburn, C.J. has rightly observed that "an advocate must be fearless in carrying out the interest of his client." He further stated that "the arms he wields are to be the arms of the warrior and not of the assassin." It is his duty to strive to accomplish the interests of his client *per fas*, but not *per nefas*; it is his duty to the utmost of his power to seek to reconcile the interests he is bound to maintain, and his duty it is incumbent upon him to discharge with the external and immutable interests of truth and justice. In cross-examination, the advocate has to observe the following rules :

(1) Master the facts, law and also the technical points, if any.
(2) As far as possible, arrange the question in simple form avoiding verbosity and broadness so as to elicit positive replies.
(3) Begin to cross-examine with a friendly attitude and a gentle smile.
(4) Adjust the speed so as to facilitate the judge to note down the points.
(5) Control the temper and emotions.
(6) Never take your eye from the witness except in indifferent matters.
(7) Give due regard to the voice of the witness.
(8) Be skillful and attentive during the whole cause.
(9) Apply sense of logic and common sense.
(10) Witty and refractory attitude of the witness should be checked at the beginning itself.
(11) With some suitable apology, bring out some past unfortunate incident of the witness's life.
(12) Try to show that the witness is interested and partial.
(13) Do not expect too much from the witness.
(14) Never begin the examination with your weak points.
(15) Each question should be aimed at a specific single object and purpose.
(16) Put the important questions indirectly after putting several unimportant questions directly.
(17) Do not give the witness to understand your technique.
(18) Get the important answers as early as possible.
(19) Do not give the witness time to think.
(20) Try to bring out a story favourable to you, which the witness never intended to tell.
(21) Never attempt either to distort facts or to make out unnecessary information.
(22) The witness need not be reminded often, that he is under oath.
(23) Do not make comments on the answers.
(24) Never argue with the witness.
(25) If the matter is technical, do not cross-examine much, and

reserve to make up the same in arguments.

(26) Do not interfere with the Judge when he cross-examines.

(27) Favourable answers give in chief examination must not be reopened.

(28) Favourable points already covered in cross-examination must not be repeated.

(29) Do not attack the character of the witness unless there is proof.

(30) Do not undervalue the adversary, but guard against him.

(31) Handle the whole cross-examination very carefully so as not to allow the same to recoil on you.

(32) Do not give room for an effective and damaging re-examination.

(33) Do not appeal to the emotions and sympathy of the Judge too much.

(34) Maintain your dignity.

(35) Be respectful to the opposite counsel and to the court.

(C) Re-examination

The examination of witness subsequent to the cross-examination, by the party who called and examined him first is called the re-examination. The object of re-examination is to clarify points, to remove ambiguities and to explain the inconsistencies in the answers given during the cross-examination. During the re-examination, no new matters can be introduced except with the permission of the Court. In such cases the witness may be further cross-examined on those points. Re-examination cannot be allowed for new matters except with leave of the courts. In the re-examination an attempt is to be made to restore the credit of the witness during the cross-examination. In re-examination leading questions must not be asked.

(x) Arguments

After the examination of the witnesses is over, then the next stage of advocacy is argument in support of the client's case and to demolish the opponent's case. A successful cross-examination can destroy your adversary's case, but may not help you to win your case. Successful cross-examination is only the foundation on which the vast structure of your argument must always rest. The art of advocacy is never complete without an ability to argue the case effectively. A lawyer who falters generally always fails. No one can argue a case successfully unless he knows all the facts and points of law involved in it. A successful lawyer or advocate must be a voracious reader. Lord Eldon has rightly stated that "to become a great lawyer, one should live like a hermit and work like a horse."

During the course of a case before court, a lawyer may have to argue on various occasions on different points as the circumstances require, as for example, an opening speech, argument on several interlocutory matters and the like, up to the closing speech. Argument of every claim, defence, allegation, averment or assertion with respect to any particular matter is its summation, and the highest point or a climax in the art of advocacy. By a convincing argument a cause which was thought of as seemingly lost may be rescued. Hence, an advocate must develop the ability to argue cases effectively. Since the subject-matter of litigations may be of different varieties, he must acquire sound knowledge of every branch of learning. In every particular case, his knowledge must be deep as to its entire facts, law, circumstances and evidence. From the very start itself, he must try to arrest the attention of the Judge and inspire the interest. An advocate must have a clear perception of the conviction, sentiments and prejudices of the Judge. He should follow the court procedure and conduct observing the high standards of professional etiquette with pleasing manner. Of all men, the advocate should know much of life and much of human nature. He should be novice of nothing and wide minded in all things, not a genius in everything but ripe in broad knowledge and general experience. The following facts make successful arguments :—

(i) Eloquence

It is the gift of speech which more than any other skill equips the advocate to achieve his primary purpose, that is, persuasion. It is the faculty of presenting a point of view, whether argumentative or emotional, in such language as to impress the minds of the audience, whatever that audience may be. The language must be clear, controlled and saturated with facts and ideas.

(ii) Art of spontaneous debate

It is necessary on many occasions to argue and reason offhand without previous preparation. It is rightly said that law life is not rail road with resting stations; it is a quick lien with few stops to take on baggage. Art of spontaneous debate depends upon the resources of the moment and readiness of tongue and wit. The arguments should be delivered extemporaneously. It should be with great deliberations and force. No doubt, references to the brief may be necessary, but the quotations therefrom should be as few and brief as possible. Strong points should come first, then the weak points and the arguments must be concluded with the strongest points. Weaker arguments should never precede the stronger. If the advocate finds that a point of the opponents is very strong and cannot be met, then it is better to concede it. The weak point in the opponent case should be emphasized much so as to prove that the weakness is of such a nature that in spite of everything else cannot be sustained. If the advocate is satisfied that he has convinced the Judge, better he may stop the argument, and not go on repeating it.

(iii) Honesty in arguments

All round honesty and integrity are virtues which have a very high place in legal profession. An advocate should present the law correctly and honestly and avoid any deception on the court. It should be remembered that the lawyer who tries to mislead the court by showing decisions which have long been overruled is found out quickly. He is never believed by the court and as soon as it tickles out that the Judges have no faith in him, he starts losing his clients. Suppression of the real situation of a case from the court, coaching witnesses, etc. are some of the instances of dishonest dealings. Hence, honesty in advocacy as in any other field always pays.

(iv) Preparation for arguments

Arguments require an intense preparation. It requires research, study and application. Mathew Arnold said that most of us are what we must be, not what we should be, not even what we ought to be. Only if we cultivate the habit of study from the beginning, the habit will be a second nature. Until then, success is only a cloud in the horizon. The entire argument proceeds on the line of a what has been prepared for it. Therefore, a thorough study of the case and deep thinking should be developed as a habit of mind in order to reduce the case into certain formal propositions so as to place the same before the Judge in the form of argument. Preparation of argument includes the study of all the relevant rulings on the points involved in the case. A list of all the cases and texts of authority, which the lawyer intends to cite in support of his argument must be separately prepared. Citation of authorities must be made with accurate reference to the Law Reports, books of authorities, title of the case, court by which it is decided, year, volume and page.

(v) Art of persuasion

An advocate must bear in mind that the Judge is always searching for the determining facts, law evidence and circumstances of the case to arrive at the correct decision. Therefore, the most important task of the advocate is to convince the Judge as to the determining factors and to lead his mind to the ultimately desired conclusions. This may be broadly called as the art of persuasion. To be a good lawyer one must have a personality, a command over the language, a confidence in own self, a capacity for clear and logical thinking and logical manner. Lloyd Paul Stryker, the author of "The Art of Advocacy" quotes Professor Hill, "Short explanations, vivid descriptions, happy illustrations, indirect suggestions, all may be instruments of persuasion, if they are so used as to advance the main purpose." Argument of every point must be so convincing as to persuade the Judge to accept all the propositions of facts and law presented.

Arthur T. Vanderbilt in his article "Forensic Persuasion" has pointed out six factors in the work of advocate which broadly come within the ambit of forensic persuasion of an advocate. They are as follows :—

(i) The capacity of grasping of the facts of a case in all their inner relations and implications quickly and comprehensively;

(ii) A thorough understanding of the fundamental principles and rules of law and the ability to apply them to the facts of a case;

(iii) Knowledge of human nature in all its manifestation and an ability to get along with people generally;

(iv) A comprehension of economic, political, social and intellectual environment of modern litigation for cases are never tried in a vacuum;

(v) The ability to reason concerning the facts, the law, the personalities involved in the litigation and the environment of a case in such a way as to solve the pending problem in the most satisfactory way possible;

(vi) The art of expressing oneself clearly and cogently orally and in writing.

(vi) Efficacy of words

The advocate should know what to say and how and when to say it. He should finish and embellish his reasons, drape and paint the subject to his description. His words should strike like a hammer, pierce like a stiletto or soothe like a mother's lullaby. Lord Denning observed that "To succeed in the profession of law, you must seek to cultivate command of language. Words are the lawyer's tools of trade. When you are called upon to address a judge, it is your words which count most. It is by them that you will hope to persuade the Judge of the rightness of your cause. When you have to interpret a section in a statute or a paragraph in a regulation, you have to study the very words. You have to discover the meaning by analyzing the words—one by one—to the very last syllable. When you have to draw up a will or a contract, you have to choose your words well. The reason why words are so important is because words are the vehicle of thought. Apart from writing, there is addressing the court. Speaking needs even more practice; and even more experience."

(vii) Luck

An English lady once asked the Lord Chief Justice what were the ingredients of a successful court case. The Judge replied :

First you need a good case.
Then you need good evidence.
Then you need good witnesses.
Then you need a good Judge.
Then you need a good jury.
Then you need good luck.

20

WRITING AN ARTICLE ON THE TOPIC OF LAW

Apart from attending classroom teaching and writing exams, the law students are required to write articles, monographs, project reports and seminar papers. Writing an article on any subject is an art. This art has to be cultivated based on scientific process. A student of law should be writing articles on the topics of law to enlighten the society relating to legal issues and problems. The student undertakes research generally when he investigates and uses materials beyond his personal resources. The research paper presents the findings and conclusion of such an inquiry.

Articles on the topics of law may be divided as 'expository articles' and 'persuasive articles'. The 'expository articles' seek to explain and acquaint the reader with a body of knowledge. By explaining, the article writer is demonstrating his or her own knowledge of the subject and classifying thoughts through feedback. On the other hand, a 'persuasive article' must make a case for the side chosen, consider and refute alternative arguments and provide to the reader that the view presented is the unique one. The articles should be reader friendly.[1]

Further, it may be pointed out that the research paper is based generally on primary research, or a combination of the two. It is pertinent to mention here that the primary research is the study of a subject through firsthand observation and investigation, viz., analyzing a historical text, and conducting a survey. Primary sources include statistical data and historical documents. Secondary research, on the other hand, is the examination of studies that other researchers had made of a subject. Examples of secondary sources are books and articles about legal issues, historical events, debates or literary works. Most of the academic papers depend at least partly on a secondary research. Ideas and views of other researches will play a dynamic role in development of a student. Further, the kind of activities that constitute a research paper—identifying, locating, assessing and assimilating others research and then developing and expressing one's own ideas clearly and persuasively—are at the centre of the educational experience.[2] Learning how to write a research paper, can help prepare a student for assignments in his professional career. It

1. S.R. Myneni, Public Interest Lawyering, Legal Aid and Para-Legal Services, (2002), p. 228.
2. G.B. Reddy, Practical Advocacy of Law, (2002), p. 394.

increases one's knowledge and understanding of a subject.

Writing an article itself is a learned craft, which requires practice. Frankly, the process of researching and writing an article does not follow a fixed pattern. The truth is that different paths can and do lead to successful research papers. The most widely accepted pattern of activities, that nearly all writers of research paper/article perform, viz., selecting a suitable topic, using the library, compiling a working bibliography, taking notes, outlining and writing, is given hereunder for the benefit of writers of articles/research papers on a topic of law.

(i) Selection of a topic

Law is not for law sake. It is an instrument of social control. Law and society are not divisible as water-tight compartments. They are interlinked. The researcher or an article writer on the topics of law has to select an appropriate topic of law in relation to social life. While selecting the topic, the writer/researcher should have a clear idea/picture in mind about the size, i.e., the number of pages. The writer should ensure that the topic is not too broad. One should begin with a fairly general topic and then to refine it, by thought and research, into a more specific one than can be fully explored. It is called 'from macro' to 'micro'. One must try to narrow his topic by focussing on an aspect of the subject or an approach to it. The broader/general topics may be, for example, law and poverty, tax imposition and social change, white-collar crimes and their impact on society, Prevention of Terrorism Act and public opinion, abolition of death sentence, judicial activism of Supreme Court, etc. For instance, if the general topic is 'Judicial Activism of Supreme Court', the specific topic could be with special reference to right to life.

(ii) Reading and collection of related information

When one begins focussing on the topic, he should check his library's resources to see whether enough work has been done on the subject to permit adequate research and whether the pertinent source materials are readily available. After this, he has to do a lot of reading on it from variety of sources—journals, reference books, magazines, supplementary newspapers, etc. He can utilize the information from the websites of computers. One should become thoroughly acquainted with libraries to which he has access. Consulting a librarian at key points in research may save considerable time and effort. Often librarians prepare and handout informative bulletins that describe library resources and services. Systematic note-taking and note-keeping throughout the process of study are indispensable instruments of the writer. However, there is no uniformity in the method followed in taking notes. The MLA Handbook for writers of research papers mention that generally speaking there are three methods of note-taking : (a) summary, (b) paraphrase; and (c) quotation. The writer should be careful in note-taking and acknowledge the source so that it may not amount to infringement of copyright. The writer, after selecting the topic should begin formulating his thesis by thinking about it closely, doing exploratory reading, drawing on lectures and discussions on the central issue or problems, which the topic raises.

(iii) Compiling a working bibliography

The next step in writing a legal article, is to prepare and compile a working bibliography. In this context, working bibliography means keeping a list of books, articles and other sources which appear relevant for the paper. The same can be prepared only after a preliminary reading. The best ways of compiling a working bibliography is to use index cards. Writing each source on a separate index card allows greater flexibility than does listing sources on a sheet of paper. Similarly, results can be achieved by using a personal computer, by creating files for the working bibliography. The latter method is more advantageous because, computer files can be amended by adding more information or by deleting some of the existing information, if needed.

While compiling a working bibliography, the researcher should take care to record the publication information, which will be needed for the works-cited list, to be used as either footnotès or end-notes. The standard methods of citation are :

(a) In case of a book :—

(i) Author's full name (last name first)

(ii) Full title of the book (including any subtitle)

(iii) Edition

(iv) No. of the Volume and the total No. of volumes (if the work is multi volume work)

(v) City of publication

(vi) Publisher

(vii) Year of publication.

Illustration.—Dordick, Herbert. The Information Society—A Retrospective View, 2nd Ed., London, Sage Publication, 1993.

(b) In case of an article :—

(i) Author's name

(ii) Title of the article

(iii) Title of the Journal

(iv) Volume No. (and issue No. if needed)

(v) Year of Publication

(vi) Inclusive page nos. of the article.

Illustrations.—Vartanov, Anri. "Television as Spectacle and Myth"; Journal of Communication 4 (1991) : 162-71.

(c) In case of newspaper or magazine article :—

(i) Author's name

(ii) Title of the article

(iii) Title of the periodical

(iv) Date of Publication

(v) Inclusive page Nos. of the article

Illustration.—(1) Shea, Christopher. "The Limits of Free Speech", Chronicle of Higher Education, 1 Dec., 1993 : A 37-38.

(2) Dhavan, Rajeev, "A Patent Mistake", The Hindu (Hyd), 17 May, 2002 : 10.

(iv) Writing a first draft

The writer should draw outlines from his notes after thorough readings from several sources. For writing research papers, outlining will be very useful. It denotes the conceptualization of the sequence and format of the article. The object of the first draft is comprehensiveness and fullness of facts. Arrangement of ideas and systematic presentation contain the following steps :

(A) Title of the Article

The title forms the first contact of the reader with the article. The title :—

(a) should project the scope of the problem in generalized terms,

(b) should be appropriate enough to catch the eye of the reader,

(c) should be as brief as possible, and

(d) should be as precise as possible.

Below the title, there should be the name(s) of the writer(s) of that article.

(B) Introduction

The text of the article consists of : (a) introduction; (b) presentation; and (c) conclusion. Introduction should consist of clear-cut statement as to the value, scope and aim of the presentation.

(C) Presentation

The text contains the information relating to the central theme of the subject that is dealt with. The proof or evidences, both numerical and logical must be given in support of the statement. Each of the new statements made in the discussion should contribute something fresh to the reader's understanding of the subject. The inferences that are drawn from the observation should be clearly presented. The writer should lead his reader step by step through a well organized analysis of problem. Heading should be specific, brief and represent the content. Logical relationship of various points should be brought out by appropriate headings and sub-heading. Effective writing depends mostly on clarity and readability of the contents. Therefore, right from writing the first draft, the writer should be cautious about coherence of his presentation, his command of sentence structure and grammar. Besides, there should be uniformity and consistency in the presentation of ideas.

(D) Conclusion

The whole subject-matter should be presented in brief in the conclusion or summary form at the end of the article. The suggestions for any improvement in the subject may be highlighted at the end of the conclusion.

(v) Footnotes

Footnotes are the important subject-matter of the article. It enriches the article. It is assumed that the more footnotes are there in an article, the same is termed as a good article. The source of authority of the statements or quotations contained in the text should be given in the footnotes at the foot of the page or at the end of the article according to the convenience. The foot notes should contain the author's name, title of the book, publisher's address, year of publication and page numbers. After the first reference is given in a foot note, it is not necessary to report the name of the author, publisher and so on for second or subsequent references of the author. For this, *supra* note or *op. cit.* can be used. *Ibid.* and *Id.* should be used which means in the same place and at some other place of the same book or article respectively. In order to avoid the detailed description, *op. cit.* along with page number can be mentioned with the name of the author.

(vi) Appendices

If everything is added to the text, it will be a congested one. Hence, it is not desirable to mention every detail in the text. The unimportant details but relevant be separated from the main body and be placed as appendix for the purpose of reference.

(vii) Language

The language of the article should be simple and faultless. It should be clear, precise and to the point. The writer should economize on words, should not try to use one word more than necessary. He should not use jargons. Similarly, he should use simple sentences rather than complex and compound sentences. The sentences should be short and direct without twist. The sentences should be in active voice to the maximum extent possible.

(viii) Paragraphs

Each paragraph should contain one major idea. Paragraph of the text should be short. Paragraphs can be developed by comparing and contrasting, going step by step into details and by following chronological sequence of the subject. The best writer is the one who finds the words, phrases, clauses, sentences and paragraphs that express his thought and ideas precisely and that make them interesting to others.

(ix) Punctuation marks

The punctuation marks should be used correctly to give clear idea of the meaning of a particular word or part of sentence and for the purposes of sentence construction.

(x) Style

Style is the artistic and distinctive manner of writing or speaking. It is an important means of transport of ideas. Clear presentation is required for clear thinking. There must be clarity of thought. Flaws in style obstruct the view or distract the reader.

(xi) Revision

After completing the article, the writer should leave it for a day or two. Then again he should improve both in form and the language by considerable trimming and pruning. He should add more information, delete superfluous matter and go on changing and improving upon the language to make it more effective.

(xii) Physical features of an Article

The manuscript of the article should be typed on one side of qualitative standard paper. There should be a margin of four cms. at the top and left side and a margin of 2.5 cms. to 4 cms. at the right side and bottom. Each paper should be numbered. The body of the text is normally 1.5 spaced. The quotations should be in indented form. The writer should go through the typed matter and correct the mistakes, if any. After that the writer may send the same for publication.

21

IMPORTANT JUDGMENTS RELATING TO MISCONDUCT AND CONTEMPT OF COURT

In re, Nand Lal Balwani etc.[1]

The brief facts of the case were that Mr. Nand Lal Balwani passed the law in the year 1973. He served as cashier-cum-supervisor in Bombay Telecom Communication Department. He took voluntary retirement at the age of 51 years and thereafter he enrolled himself as an Advocate with the Bombay Bar Association in 1995. On February 26, 1999, he shouted slogans and hurled shoe in the open court which was being conducted by Chief Justice Dr. A.S. Anand, Justice Shrinivasan and Justice N. Santosh Hegde. Mr. Nand Lal Balwani had apparently no case on the Board of this Bench. He interrupted the court proceedings. His action intimidated the court and caused interference with judicial proceedings. The Supreme Court started *suo motto* contempt proceeding and he was informed of the charge and asked if he had anything to say in his defence. At his request, time was given to file an affidavit in response to the charge. In his affidavit, he admitted his intemperate behaviour in the court. He did not say anything in his defence but filed a detailed affidavit giving details of how he had been prosecuted by the police agencies so far.

The Supreme Court while hearing the contempt case rejected his defence based on his grievance at the alleged sufferings at the hands of police agencies. The Court held that according to Section 14 of the Contempt of Courts Act, 1971, when it appears to the Supreme Court or the High Court upon its own view, that a person has been guilty of contempt committed in its presence or hearing, the court may cause such person to be detained in custody and, it any time before the rising of the court, inform him about the charges and afford him an opportunity to make defence. An order of punishment or discharge can thereafter be made.

The Supreme Court found the action of the contemner, both by his words and deeds, in the presence of the court, amounts to gross criminal contempt of court. His action was aimed at intimating the court and causing interference in judicial proceedings. It is unfortunate that a person belonging to the Bar had behaved in this manner. The contemner advocate has, however, tendered unqualified apology in the following words :

1. A.I.R. 1999 S.C. 1300 : (1999) 1 SCALE 645.

"I tender my unqualified apology for my intemperate behaviour in this court this morning. I have been through a harrowing time and have been disturbed in the matter of the present litigation. I have no intention of causing any disrespect to this Hon'ble Court in any manner lowering the dignity of this Hon'ble court. I once again tender my unqualified apology. I say during the period that I have practising as a lawyer, I have never caused any disrespect to the legal system."

The apex court has observed that :

"Law does not give a lawyer, unsatisfied with the result of the litigation, licence to permit himself the liberty of causing disrespect to the court or attempting, in any manner to lower the dignity of the court. A lawyer does not enjoy any special immunity under the Contempt of Courts Act, where he is found to have committed a gross contempt of court. The courts cannot be intimidated to seek favourable orders."

The conclusion reached out by the Court was that "the action of the contemner advocate is most reprehensible and has the tendency to interfere with the administration of justice and undermine the dignity of the Court and the majesty of law. From the manner in which the contemner advocate has behaved a deliberate, motivated and calculated attempt to impair the administration of justice is discernible."

Further, the apology tendered by the contemner advocate cannot be accepted as it does not appear to be at all bona fide and genuine in view of his attitude exhibited in the court during his questioning and seems to have been made only to escape punishment. He does not appear to be repentant at all. The court, therefore, does not accept the apology.

The Court, keeping in view the seriousness of the offence committed by the contemner advocate imposed a deterrent punishment on him so that it could serve as an example to others and no one indulges in repetition of such acts. The court sentenced him to suffer simple imprisonment for four months and to pay a fine of Rs. 2000/- and in default of payment of fine, to further undergo simple imprisonment for two months. As the contemner advocate was present in the court and was taken in custody forthwith to serve the sentence.

Rameshwar Prasad Goyal, Advocate, In re[1]

The facts of this case present a very sorry state of affairs. Mr. Rameshwar Prasad Goyal was an Advocate-on-Record. The controversy has arisen due to the fact that in **Mohd. Israfil v. Raufunnessa Bibi,**[2] was dismissed in default as none appeared to press the appeal. An application for restoration of the said appeal was filed by Shri Rameshwar Prasad Goyal. The said application was listed in the court on 8.7.2013. The Court was of the view that the facts contained in the application were not correct and the counsel appearing for the applicant was not able to clarify the same. The court passed over the matter and asked the counsel appearing

1. (2014) 1 S.C.C. 572.
2. Civil Appeal No. 1398 of 2005, Order dated 8.3.2013 (SC).

therein to call the Advocates-on-Record who would be able to explain the factual controversy. When the matter was taken up in second round, the court was informed that Shri Rameshwar Prasad Goyal, Advocates-on-Record refused to come to the Court. It has also been pointed out that the said Advocates-on-Record has filed extremely large number of cases in this court but never appears in the court. It is revealed from the record of the court that he has entered appearance in as many as 1678 cases in the year 2010, in 1423 cases in the year 2011, and in 1489 cases in the year 2012. Upto 19.7.2013, he has entered appearance in 922 cases.

In view of the refusal of the Advocates-on-Record to come to the court, this court had no option but to dismiss the application. However, the court issued a show-cause notice to the said Advocates-on-Record as to why his name should not be removed from the register of Advocates-on-Record, as his conduct was "unbecoming" of an Advocates-on-Record. Prima facie, his conduct would tantamount to interfering with the administration of justice.

Considering the gravity of the issue involved, the court also requested the Association of Advocates-on-Record, through its President and Secretary, to assist the court in dealing with this situation as some of Advocates-in-Record have filed large number of cases in which they have lend their signatures for consideration and took no responsibility for the matter and never appeared in the court. In response to this, Shri Rameshwar Prasad Goyal has filed his reply tendering an absolute and unconditional apology and has given an undertaking that he would not repeat such mistake again in future. He also put forward many reasons for not appearing in the court but none of them has impressed the court.

The court observed that "the facts of this case present a very sorry state of affair. A noble profession has been allowed to be converted by this Advocate-on-Record into a profession of cheating. An Advocate-on-Record, whom the litigant has never briefed or engaged, has lent his signature for a petty amount with a clear understanding that he would not take any responsibility for any act in any of the proceedings in the Registry or the Court in the matter."

The court further observed that "an Advocate-on-Record is the source of lawful recognition through whom the litigant is represented and therefore, he cannot deviate from the norms prescribed under the Rules. The Rules have been framed to authorise a legally trained person with prescribed qualification to appear, plead and act on behalf of a litigant. Thus, not only his physical presence, but effective assistance in the court is also required. He is not a guest artist nor is his job of a service provider nor is he in a professional business nor can he claim to be a law tourist agent for taking litigants for a tour of the court premises. An Advocate-on-Record is a seeker of justice for the citizens of the country. Therefore, he cannot avoid court or be casual in operating and his presence in the court is necessary. There are times when pleadings and records have to be explained and thus, he has to do a far more serious job and cannot claim that his role is merely a formal one or his responsibilities simply optional. An Advocate-on-Record is accountable and responsible for whatever is written and pleaded by putting his appearance to maintain solemnity of records of the court."

Shri Rameshwar Prasad Goyal, not only tendered absolute and unconditional apology and promised not to repeat the misconduct in future but also assured the court that he would remain present in the court in all the cases where he had entered appearance for either of the parties. Some senior Advocates and a large number of members of the Bar have also asked the Court to pardon him as he would abide by the undertaking given by him.

The court held that "though the conduct of Shri Goyal, Advocate-on-Record, has been reprehensible and not worth pardoning but considering the fact and circumstances involved herein, his conduct is censured and warn him not to behave in future in such manner and to appear in court in all the cases wherever he has entered appearance. The court shall examine his conduct for one year and if no improvement is found, the court may initiate the proceedings again."

R.D. Saxena v. Balram Prasad Sharma[1]

The main issue posed in an appeal before the Supreme Court was of sequential importance for members of the legal profession. The issue was whether the advocate has a lien for his fees on the litigation papers entrusted to him by his client? In this case, the advocate concerned was directed by the Bar Council of India to return all the case bundles which he got from his respondent client without any delay. Therefore, the appeal is filed by the advocate under Section 38 of the Advocates Act, 1961 to the Supreme Court of India.

The brief facts of the case were that the appellant was appointed as legal advisor to Madhya Pradesh State Co-operative Bank Ltd. in 1990 and the Bank continued to retain him in that capacity during the succeeding years. He was also engaged by the said Bank to conduct cases in which the Bank was a party. However, the said retainship did not last long. On July 17, 1993, the Bank terminated the retainership of the appellant and requested to return all the case files relating to the Bank. Instead of returning the files, the appellant forwarded a consolidated bill to the tune of Rs. 97100/- as the balance payable by the Bank towards the legal remuneration to which he was entitled. He informed the Bank that the files would be returned only after settling his dues.

The Bank filed a complaint before the State Bar Council of Madhya Pradesh on 3rd February, 1994. It was alleged in the complaint that the appellant is guilty of professional misconduct by not returning the files to his client. In the reply submitted by the appellant has admitted that the files were not returned but claimed that he has a right to retain such files by exercising his right of lien and offered to return the files as soon as payment is made to him.

After holding the inquiry, the Disciplinary Committee of the Bar Council of India reached the conclusion that appellant was guilty of

1. A.I.R. 2000 S.C. 2912 : (2000) 7 S.C.C. 264 : 2000 (8) SRJ 113.

professional misconduct. The Disciplinary Committee of the Bar Council of India has stated the following in the impugned order :

"On the basis of the complaint as well as the documents available on record we are of the opinion that the respondent is guilty of professional misconduct and thereby he is liable for punishment. The complainant is a public institution. It was the duty of the respondent to return the briefs to the Bank and also appear before the Committee to revert his allegations made in application dated 8.11.1995. No such attempt was made by him."

In appeal the learned counsel for the appellant contended that the failure of the Bar Council of India to consider the singular defence set up by the appellant that is, he has a lien over the files for his unpaid fees due to him, has resulted in miscarriage of justice. The Bank contended that there was no fee payable to the appellant and the amount shown by him was on account of inflating the fees. Alternatively, the respondent contended that an advocate cannot retain the files after the client terminated his engagement and that there is no lien on such files.

The court came to the conclusion that keeping in view the rules framed by the Bar Council of India, no advocate can adjust the fees payable to him by a client against his own personal liability to the client. A a rule an advocate shall not do anything whereby he abuses or take advantage of the confidence reposed in him by his client. Thus, even after providing a right for an advocate to deduct the fees out of any money of the client remaining in his hand at the termination of the proceeding for which the advocate was engaged, it is important to notice that no lien is provided on the litigation files kept with him. In the conditions prevailing in India with lots of illiterate people among the litigant public it may not be advisable also to permit the counsel to retain the case bundle for the fees claimed by him. Any such lien if permitted would become susceptible to great abuses and exploitation. The court held that the refusal to return files of the client when he demanded the same amounted to misconduct under Section 35 of the Act. Hence, the appellant in the present case was liable to punishment for such misconduct.

New India Assurance Co. Ltd. v. A.K. Saxena[1]

The facts of the case were that the respondent was an advocate on the panel of the appellants. As such a number of matters used to be assigned to him. There arose a dispute between the appellants and the respondent as a result of which the respondent was asked to return all papers. The respondent was willing to return the papers provided that all his fees were paid. The High Court has directed the appellant, New India Assurance Co. Ltd. to pay full fees of Sri. A.K. Saxena. The court further held that on payment of full fees, he will immediately return the files as required by the appellant.

On appeal, the Supreme Court has directed the respondent to return all files. The counsel for the respondent insisted that full fees for all the

1. A.I.R. 2004 S.C. 311.

matters must be paid to him. The court has referred to the case of **R.D. Saxena v. Balram Prasad Sharma**,[1] wherein the court has held that advocates have no lien over the papers of their clients. In the instant case, the court held that at the most the advocate may resort to legal remedies for unpaid remuneration.

The Supreme court did not go into the question as to whether or not fees are payable to the respondent. It will be open for the respondent to file appropriate proceedings for recovery of his fees.

Anju Mishra v. The High Court of Judicature at Patna and another[2]

In this case, the amendment incorporated in "Registration of Advocates as Advocates-on-Record of Patna High Court Rules" has been challenged. The High Court caused the amendment in exercise of the power conferred under Section 34 of the Advocates Act, 1961. Rule 4 prohibits any advocate from being engaged by parties, unless he is registered as an advocate-on-record, this runs contrary to Sections 29 and 30 of the Advocates Act, 1961. The petitioners were the advocates, registered with the State Bar Council. Their contention was that the amendment made is contrary to the Article 14 and 19(1)(g) of the Constitution of India and Section 30 of the Advocates Act and ultra vires to the power conferred upon the High Court under Section 34 of the Advocates Act.

The contention of the petitioners was that the Bar Council of India and the respective Bar Council of the State are conferred with the power to regulate the legal profession; including the conferment of right to practice in the courts of various categories in India, and the amendment has the effect of scuttling the right of an Advocate, to practice in the Patna High Court. They pleaded that : (a) their fundamental right to pursue the profession is infringed; (b) their legal right conferred under Section 30 of the Act is abrogated; (c) the High Court has encroached into the powers of the Bar Council; and (d) that the Rules are not only arbitrary and oppressive, but also are, discriminatory in nature.

The gist of the arguments on behalf the petitioners was that the activity of practicing in the courts of law is governed exclusively by the provisions of the Act, and the Rules made thereunder and the Bar Council of India at the national level and the Bar Councils at the level of the State, are constituted thereunder for this purpose.

It is pleaded that once a person, who acquired the qualification of law, is enrolled as an Advocate, he is entitled to practice in the Courts all over the country, including the Supreme Court and no other agency or authority has the right to prevent an advocate from practicing in any Court so long as the enrolment or registration with the Bar Council subsists.

The Court was of the view that stipulation of 60% minimum qualifying marks were too stringent. Such a harsh measure would only inject an element of frustration in enthusiastic youngsters. The court was of the view

1. (2000) 7 S.C.C. 264.
2. A.I.R. 2015 Patna 179.

that minimum aggregate marks can be reduced to 50% and minimum marks in each subject to 40%.

The court partly allowed the writ petitions holding that the High Court does have power to frame rules under Section 34 of the Act, but in such a manner that the right to practice is not taken away. The court further held that the right of an advocate to practice based on his enrolment with the Bar Council and Section 30 of the Act cannot be taken away in the name of Regulation. Further, Rules 4, 5, 6, 7(vi)(a) of the Rules framed by the Patna High Court do not satisfy the test of law and are in conflict with Article 19(1)(g) of the Constitution of India and Section 30 of the Advocates Act, 1960, apart from being unreasonable, oppressive and discriminatory and are accordingly set aside. Further, the court held that the minimum marks to be secured by an advocate in the examination for Advocate-on-Record shall stand modified to 50% in aggregate and 40% in each subject. Further, it has been left open to the High Court to frame the said rules, afresh.

A. Santhos Yadav v. The Bar Council of Tamil Nadu & Others[1]

The facts of the case were that the petitioner completed his degree in law from Dr. Ambedkar Law College, Chennai in June 2014 and submitted an application in November 2014 to the Bar Council for enrolment. But, the application was not processed for the reason that an F.I.R. against him was pending under Section 285 of the Indian Penal Code. In the past, the Bar Council did not have the practice of verifying the antecedents of persons, who apply for enrolment as advocates. By an order passed by this court directions were issued to the Bar Council to verify the criminal antecedents of persons, who apply for enrolment. This was done with a view to stop the entry of candidates with criminal antecedents into this noble profession. The petitioner was the District Secretary of a political party and participated in an agitation in which the effigy of Subramaniam Swamy, a political personality was allegedly burnt by him. Hence, a complaint under Section 285 of the Indian Penal Code was registered. The question for consideration was as to whether the participation of a person in an agitation to advance a political cause and the burning of an effigy as part of the agitation, could be taken to be something that will make the offender, a person with criminal background, so as to disentitle him from getting enrolled as an advocate or not.

The court held that in the absence of any specific provision relating to burning of effigies which makes the same a punishable offence, the petitioner cannot be stated to be a person with criminal background and his entry into the profession cannot be barred. Directions in this regard were issued to the Bar Council to process the application of the petitioner for enrolment as Advocate.

O.P. Sharma & Ors. v. High Court of Punjab and Haryana[2]

The brief facts of the case are that the District and Sessions Judge,

1. A.I.R. 2015 Mad. 194.
2. A.I.R. 2011 S.C. 2101.

Faridabad forwarded two letters to the Registrar, High Court of Punjab & Haryana written by one Shri Rakesh Singh, Civil Judge, Faridabad in which he demanded action against 15-20 advocates for shouting slogans, hurling abuses and derogatory remarks against him. In another letter to the District and Sessions Judge, he stated that Mr. L.N. Prasher and Mr. O.P. Sharma (both Advocates) had criminal record and these persons have indulged in pressure tactics since long. Civil Judge was dealing with the remand of accused Soran under Sections 393/452/506/34 of the Indian Penal Code. The Assistant Public Prosecutor requested him for remanding the accused to police custody. By that time, L.N. Prasher, Advocate one of the contemners/appellants herein, who represented the accused, opposed the request of police remand. After hearing the arguments, the Magistrate remanded the accused to police custody. When the order of police remand was not found favourable, L.N. Prasher became enraged and started hurling abuses and derogatory remarks against him. The accused Soran was being produced in four criminal cases on that very day and was being represented by L.N. Prasher in all the matters. When he took another remand paper of the same accused, L.N. Prasher became furious and again uttered unparliamentary words and also threatened him. Prasher called his fellow colleagues including O.P. Sharma, Rajinder Sharma, Surinder Sharma and 15-20 advocates who all belonged to the same group. O.P. Sharma sided with Prasher and shouted slogans and abused in filthy language and also threatened him.

The High Court initiated contempt proceedings against the contemners under Section 2(c) of the Contempt of Courts Act, 1971 relating to the incident which took place in the Court of Civil Judge, Faridabad. The contemners/advocates filed affidavits and highlighted the circumstances under which the unfortunate incident occurred. Another separate affidavits were filed in which they tendered unconditional apology and also regretted the same. The High Court found all of them guilty of criminal contempt within the meaning of Section 2(c) of the Act and imposed simple imprisonment six months/three months with a fine of Rs. 1000-2000/- each.

The appellants challenged the said conviction and sentence by filing appeals in the Supreme Court. Mr. Ram Jethmalani, counsel for the appellants submitted that the appellants have realized their mistake and immediately offered unconditional apology by filing affidavits before the High Court and also appeared before the Magistrate before whom the unfortunate incident had occurred, tendered apology and regret for their action, prayed for leniency and setting aside the order of the High Court sentencing the contemners to jail.

The Supreme Court has accepted the unconditional apology tendered in the form of affidavits in terms of proviso to Section 12(1) of the Act and discharged all the appellants.

M.B. Sanghi Advocate v. High Court of Punjab & Haryana[1]

The facts of the case are that the appellant, a practicing advocate has

1. A.I.R. 1991 S.C. 1834 : (1991) 3 S.C.C. 600.

filed appeal under Section 19(1)(b) of the Contempt of Courts Act, 1971 against the judgment and order of High Court of Punjab and Haryana, whereby he was convicted for committing contempt of court under Section 2(c)(i) of the Act and was sentenced to Rs. 1000/- as fine and in case of default in payment of fine, to undergo simple imprisonment for seven days. Mr. M.B. Sanghi, the appellant and a practicing lawyer, was representing the plaintiff in a civil suit on 20.9.1985, the appellant appeared for the plaintiff and orally prayed for *ex parte ad interim* stay but the same was declined by the subordinate judge, Narnaul, who ordered for issuance of notice to the defendants for 24th September, 1985. On 24th September, 1985, Shri B.L. Sharma appeared for the defendants and requested for a date for filing a reply to the said application which request was not opposed by the appellant but the appellant prayed for *ad interim* stay in favour of the plaintiff. The subordinate judge told the appellant the question of *ad interim* stay would be considered after filing of the reply by the defendants and adjourned the case for September 26, 1985. The appellant was not satisfied with this order passed by the subordinate judge and according to the subordinate judge, Shri S.R. Sharma, the appellant uttered the following words in the court :

> "You are wholly favouring the Municipal Committee. Are you sitting as Judge or as Administrator of Municipal Committee? To me it seems that you are deciding the case as Administrator of Municipal Committee. You are acting as if you are a contractor of the Municipal Committee. I do not expect any justice from you. I do not think that you will grant stay to me as you are fully siding with the Municipal Committee. You are not granting stay to me as you are in collusion with the Deputy Commissioner and under his (Deputy Commissioner) influence, you do not want to grant stay to me and that he will complain against me to the Hon'ble High Court."

The subordinate judge submitted the report to the District and Sessions Judge, Narnaul on September 25, 1985 for taking necessary action against the appellant. The District and Sessions Judge submitted the report to the High Court on October 12, 1985 and on that basis proceedings for contempt were initiated against the appellant by the High Court. The appellant submitted a reply by way of affidavit wherein he denied to have uttered the words mentioned in the report and also offered an unqualified apology. The Subordinate Judge filed his affidavit in the High Court and he was examined as a witness. In addition, the High Court examined the reader who was present in the court at the relevant time and three advocates. The appellant did not examine himself as a witness before the High Court.

High Court arrived at the conclusion that the appellant has attacked the integrity of the sub-judge by saying that he was a contractor of Municipal Committee, that he was in collusion with the Deputy Commissioner and he was under his influence and that the attack made on the sub-judge was disparaging in character and derogatory to his dignity. This would vitally shake the confidence of the public and create distrust in the people's mind and impair confidence of the people in court. The High Court was, therefore, of the view that the appellant had brought himself clearly within the ambit of contempt of the court and he was accordingly found guilty under Section 2(c)(i) of the Act. As regards the apology tendered by the appellant, the High Court observed that this was not the first occasion and earlier also the proceedings for contempt had been initiated against him. Wherein also the appellant had tendered an unqualified apology in the High Court. It was held that the appellant is addicted to using contemptuous language and making scurrilous attacks on the Judges. Hence, the High Court did not accept the apology tendered by the appellant. Hence, this appeal before the Supreme Court.

The Supreme Court has carefully perused the statements of the three advocates on which reliance has been placed by the appellant's counsel. Their evidence has been considered alongwith the statements of the sub-judge and the reader in the court at that time. In the present case, it has been found that the proceedings for contempt had been initiated against the appellant on an earlier occasion also and he was discharged on his tendering unqualified apology before the High Court. In those proceedings also the appellant had made some disparaging remarks against the judge. The Supreme Court taking into consideration the facts and circumstances of the case and the fact that the appellant, a fairly senior advocate, is prone to use disparaging and contemptuous remarks against the judges, ruled that this is not a case in which the apology tendered by the appellant, may be accepted.

The Supreme Court found no merit in the appeal and dismissed the same.

R.K. Garg v. State of Himachal Pradesh[1]

The brief facts of the case were that Mr. R.K. Garg, the appellant was a practicing advocate at Solan which is a district place in the State of Himachal Pradesh. Shri Kuldip Chand Sud, the Presiding Officer of the Court, was hearing a petition under the Rent Act in which the appellant was representing the petitioner. When the case was called out for hearing, the Presiding Officer noticed that the petitioner had not paid the process fee, as a result of which the summons could not be issued to the respondent. The judge, therefore, proceeded to dismiss the petition under Order 9, Rule 2 of the Civil Procedure Code. Taking umbrage at the dismissal of the petition, the appellant hurled his shoe at the Judge which hit him on the shoulder. The Judge asked his orderly to take the appellant in custody but the appellant slipped away. The judge evidently wanted to proceed under Section 228 of the Penal Code for which he issued a warrant of arrest against the appellant. The appellant successfully evaded the warrant and managed to prevent proceedings being taken by the judge for the contempt of his court. The judge then made a reference to the High Court of Himachal Pradesh under Section 15(2) of the Contempt of Courts Act. The High Court issued notice to the appellant enclosing therewith a

1. A.I.R. 1981 S.C. 1382.

copy of the reference made by the judge.

The appellant did not dispute in the High Court that he hurled a shoe at the judge. He explained his conduct by saying that he acted under an irresistible impulse generated by the provocative language used by the judge. The appellant had stated before the High Court that the Judge abused the appellant as "you rascal, I will set you right". He repeated the same again. The appellant, thereafter lost control over himself and under the extreme heat of moment and passion, his hand fell on his shoe" which he threw towards the dias. Many persons were there who witnessed the incident. After hurling shoe at the dias, the appellant took off his coat and tie and told the court, "An unfortunate incident has happened. Do you want to take action against me? I surrender". Upon this the judge remarked, "You scoundrel, get out of my court." The appellant thereafter left the court room.

The High Court had called for the comments of the judge on the version of the appellant, from which it was satisfied that the appellant was making a false allegation that the judge had used abusive language against him. The High Court held that the appellant had given an untrue version of the very genesis of the incident. The court sentenced him to six months imprisonment and a fine of Rs. 200/-.

The counsels for the appellant stated before the court that he did not desire to take a contentious attitude. He was prepared to tender an unconditional written apology to this court and to produce evidence of having tendered a similar apology to the trial court. Such apologies have been duly tendered. The counsel for the appellant submitted before the Supreme Court that the appellant was genuinely repentant for his conduct and he should be enlarged on a mere admonition. The Court, however, did not propose to impose a long sentence of imprisonment on the appellant, since he has tendered an unconditional apology to this court and to the learned trial judge, histrionics cannot entirely be ruled out. The court has formed an impression that the appellant is deeply regretful and genuinely contrite. He has suffered enough in mind and reputation and no greater purpose would be served by subjecting him to a long bodily suffering. Accordingly, the Supreme Court reduced the sentence of six months to a period of one month but enhanced the fine from Rs. 200/- to Rs. 1000/- and directed that the fine, if recovered should be paid over to a Legal Aid Society, if any, functioning in the State of Himachal Pradesh.

In re : Vinay Chandra Mishra[1]

The brief facts of the case were that M/s. Bansal Forging Ltd. took loan from U.P. Financial Corporation. It could not pay instalments of the loan. In view of the default of payment, the Corporation proceeded against the company under Section 29 of the U.P. Financial Corporation Act. The company filed a Civil Suit against the Corporation and it has also filed an application for grant of temporary injunction. The trial court passed an order that the corporation will not seize the factory of the company and

1. A.I.R. 1995 S.C. 2348.

the company shall pay the amount of instalments and it will furnish also security for the disputed amount on 31.1.94. Against this order, appeal was filed in the High Court and it was argued that the court had no jurisdiction to pass an order for payment of instalments of loan and further no security could have been ordered. Mr. Vinay Chandra Mishra appeared on behalf of M/s. Bansal Forging Ltd. The two judge bench consisted of Mr. Justice Anshuman Singh and Mr. Justice S.K. Keshote heard the appeal. Mr. Justice Keshote happened to be the junior judge on the bench. He put a question to Mr. Vinay Chandra Mishra under which provision that order had been passed. On putting of question, Mr. Mishra started to shout and said no question could have been put to him. He said that he would get the judge transferred and see that impeachment motion was brought against him in Parliament. He further said that he had turned many judges. He created a good scene in the court. He asked the judge to follow the practice of the court. In sum and substance, except to abuse the Judge of mother and sister and he insulted him like anything. It is not the question of insulting the judge of this institution but it is a matter of institution as a whole. On March 10, 1994 Justice Keshote addressed the letter to the acting Chief Justice of Allahabad High Court and narrated the whole incident and demanded appropriate action.

The acting Chief Justice Mr. V.K. Khanna forwarded the said letter to the then Chief Justice of India and the Chief Justice of India constituted a three Judge Bench consisting of Kuldip Singh, J.S. Verma and P.B. Sawant, JJ. to hear the matter on 15th April, 1994. On that day, the Court took the view that there was prima facie case of criminal contempt of court committed by Vinay Chandra Mishra and issued a notice against him to show cause why contempt proceedings be not initiated against him. By the same order, Shri D.P. Gupta, the then learned Solicitor General of India was requested to assist the court in the matter. The contemner filed his reply by affidavit on May 10, 1994 and also an application seeking discharge of show cause notice, and in the alternative for an inquiry to be held into the incident referred to by Justice Keshote in his letter which had given rise to contempt proceedings.

In his affidavit, the contemner, Vinay Chandra Mishra denied that he had lost temper and referred to any impeachment and did not mention that a judge got himself transferred earlier on account of his inability to command the goodwill of the Bar due to lack of mutual reverence. He also stated that he had utmost respect and regard for the courts and he never intended nor intends not to pay due respect to the court. Alongwith the aforesaid affidavit, the contemner forwarded a writ petition stating therein that he had not gone beyond the legitimate limits of fearless, honest and independent obligations of an advocate as it was Justice Keshote himself who had lost temper and extended threats to him which were such as would be punishable under Section 16 of the Contempt of Courts Act, 1971. He prayed that notice issued to him be discharged.

The contemner filed his supplementary/additional counter affidavit in which he challenged the maintainability of initiating contempt proceedings against him. His first objection was to the assumption of jurisdiction by this court to punish for an act of contempt committed in respect of another Court of Record which is invested with identical and independent power for punishing for contempt of itself. According to him, this court can take cognisance only of contempt committed in respect of itself. He has further stated that if the contempt proceedings are taken against him, the statement of Justice Anshuman Singh who was the senior judge on the Bench before which the incident took place, would also be necessary.

The court dismissed the application of the contemner praying for discharge of the notice. Thereafter, Justice Keshote by a letter forwarded his comments on the counter-affidavit and the supplementary/additional counter-affidavit filed by the contemner. Justice Keshote denied that he took charge of the court proceedings and virtually foreclosed the attempts made by the senior judge to intervene, as alleged by the contemner. He further said that the contemner created such a situation in which it was difficult to continue to court proceedings, and when it became difficult to continue proceedings, he requested the senior learned judge on the Bench to list the case before another Bench and retired to the chamber.

The contemner filed his unconditional written apology on 7th October, 1994 in which he has regretted the situation which gave rise to present proceedings. He *nolo contendre* submitted humble and unconditional apologies for the happenings in the Court of Justice Keshote. The contemner also withdrew from record all applications, petitions, counter affidavits, and prayers made to the court earlier. The court was adjourned for the day and was not inclined to accept the apology tendered by the contemner.

The Supreme Court held the contemner guilty of the offence of Criminal Contempt of Court for having "interfered with and obstructed the course of justice by trying to threaten, overawe and overbear the court by using insulting, disrespectful and threatening language." The court also took notice of the fact that "since the contemner is a senior member of the Bar and also adorns the high offices such as those of the Chairman of the Bar Council of India, the President of the U.P. High Court Bar Association, Allahabad and others, his conduct is bound to infect the members of the Bar all over the country." Therefore, the court arrived at a conclusion that an exemplary punishment has to be meted out to him and sentenced him to undergo simple imprisonment for a period of six weeks. However, in the circumstances of the case, the sentence will remain suspended for a period of four years and may be activated in case the contemner is convicted for any other offence of contempt of court within the said period; and the contemner shall stand suspended from practicing as an advocate for a period of three years with the consequence that all elective and nominated offices/posts at present held by him in the capacity as an advocate shall stand vacated by him forthwith.

APPENDIX I

THE ALL INDIA BAR COUNCIL (FIRST CONSTITUTION) RULES, 1961[1]

G.S.R. 1292, dated 20th October, 1961—In exercise of powers conferred by Section 57 of the Advocate Act, 1961 (25 of 1961), the Supreme Court hereby makes the following rules :

1. Short title.—These rules may be called the All India Bar Council (First Constitution) Rules, 1961.

2. Definitions.—In these rules, unless the context otherwise requires :

(i) "Act" means the Advocates Act, 1961;

(ii) "All-India Bar Council" means the Bar Council for India constituted under Section 4 of the Act;

(iii) "Attorney-General" means the Attorney-General for India;

(iv) "State Bar Council" means a Bar Council constituted under Section 3 of the Act.

3. Summoning of meeting of State Bar Council for election of members to All India Bar Council.—(1) As soon as may be after a State Bar Council is constituted, a meeting of the State Bar Council shall be convened for the purpose of electing a member of the Bar Council to the All India Bar Council.

(2) The Chairman of the State Bar Council shall appoint a date for such meeting and notice of the date, time and place of the meeting shall be given to all the members of the State Bar Council over the signature of the Secretary of the said Council not less than thirty clear days before the date of the meeting.

4. Candidates how to be proposed.—Every candidate for election as a member of the All India Bar Council shall be proposed by two members of the State Bar Council by letter addressed to the Secretary by the State Bar Council and signed by each member and delivered to the said Secretary not less than ten and not more than twenty-one days before the date of the election and such letter shall contain an endorsement of the candidate proposed signifying his acceptance of the proposal made therein.

---

1. Published in Gazette of India, Part II, Section 3(i), dated 28th October, 1961.

5. Withdrawal from Election.—Any person whose name has been proposed as a candidate may withdraw his name by communication in writing so as to reach the Secretary of the State Bar Council not less than seven days before the date of the election, and thereupon his name shall be omitted from the list of the candidates.

6. Publication of the candidates.—Not less than five days before the date fixed for election, the Secretary of the State Bar Council shall cause the names of all the candidates proposed to be posted on a notice board in the office of the State Bar Council.

7. Election.—(1) When only one candidate is proposed, the Secretary of the State Bar Council shall declare that candidate as having been duly elected.

(2) When more than one candidate has been proposed, an election shall be held by ballot and the candidate securing the largest number of votes shall be declared as having been duly elected.

(3) When between two or more candidates who have secured the highest number of votes an equality of votes is found to exist, the election out of such candidates shall be decided by drawing of a lot and the candidate in whose favour the lot falls shall be declared as having been duly elected.

8. Publication of list of candidates elected.—The name of the person elected to the All India Bar Council shall be published in the official Gazette and shall also be sent to the Secretary of the All India Bar Council.

9. Disputes as to validity of election.—(1) A candidate may contest the validity of the election of a candidate declared to have been elected to the All India Bar Council by letter signed by him and addressed to the Secretary of the State Bar Council.

(2) Such letter shall state the grounds on which the validity of the election is contested and shall be delivered to the Secretary of the State Bar Council within seven days from the date of publication in the official Gazette of the name of the successful candidate under Rule 8.

(3) The Secretary of the State Bar Council shall on receipt of any such letter, refer the dispute arising therefrom to the authority specified in Rule 11 for decision.

(4) Subject to the other provisions contained in this rule, after the expiry of ten days from the date of such publication, the election of such candidate shall not be contested on any ground whatsoever.

10. Finality of election.—At the expiry of ten days from the date of the publication of the result of election under Rule 8, the election shall be final and the voting papers shall be destroyed :

Provided that if the validity of the election has been challenged under Rule 9, the voting papers shall be preserved and dealt with, as the authority specified in Rule 11 may direct.

11. Determination of disputes.—(1) Any dispute arising under Rule 9 shall be decided by a committee of Advocates appointed by by the Attorney-General, and for the purpose of deciding the dispute the said committee may hold such inquiry into the matter and in such manner as it may deem fit.

(2) The decision of the said committee shall be final.

12. Invalid election.—If the Committee appointed under Rule 11 decides that a candidate has not been validly elected, the State Bar Council shall hold a fresh election in the manner hereinbefore provided.

13. Filling of casual vacancy.—Any casual vacancy among the elected members of the All India Bar Council shall be filled in such manner as the Council may determine.

14. Election of Chairman and Vice-Chairman.—The All India Bar Council shall, as soon as may be after it is constituted, elect a Chairman and Vice-Chairman from among its members.

15. Secretary and accountant.—The All India Bar Council shall appoint a Secretary and may, if it thinks fit to do so, appoint an accountant.

16. Quorum.—The quorum for any meeting of the All India Bar Council shall be seven.

17. Decisions of the All India Bar Council.—(1) The decisions of the All India Bar Council shall be by a majority of votes of the persons present at any meeting.

(2) Each member present shall have one vote and the Chairman of the meeting shall have a casting vote.

18. Transitional provision.—(1) Until a Chairman is elected to the All India Bar Council, the functions of the Chairman shall be performed by the Attorney-General.

(2) Until a Secretary is appointed by the All India Bar Council, the functions of such Secretary shall be performed by the Registrar of the Supreme Court.

APPENDIX II

THE ADVOCATES (REMOVAL OF DIFFICULTIES) ORDER 1963[1]

S.O. 2510, dated 31st August, 1963—In exercise of the powers conferred by sub-section (1) of Section 59 of the Advocates Act, 1961, the Central Government hereby makes the following order, namely :

1. Short title and commencement.—(1) This order may be called the Advocates (Removal of Difficulties) Order, 1963.

(2) It shall come into force on the 1st day of September, 1963.

2. Definitions.—In this Order :—

(a) "Act" means the Advocates Act, 1961;

(b) "Appointed day" means the date on which chapter V of the Act comes into force;

(c) "Existing advocates" means a person who was enrolled as advocate on the roll of any High Court under the Indian Bar Councils Act, 1926 (38 of 1926) and who, at the time when any proceeding in respect of any disciplinary matter is initiated against him, is not enrolled as an advocate on a State roll under the Act.

3. Removal of certain difficulties.—(1) As from the appointed day, every proceeding, in respect of any disciplinary matter in relation to an existing advocate of a High Court shall, save as provided in sub-clause (2), be disposed of by the State Bar Council in relation to that High Court, as if the existing advocate has been enrolled as an advocate on its roll.

(2) If immediately before the appointed day, there is any proceeding in respect of any disciplinary matter in relation to an existing advocate pending before any High Court under the Indian Bar Councils Act, 1926 (38 of 1926), such proceeding shall stand transferred to the State Bar Council in relation to that High Court as if it were a proceeding pending before the corresponding Bar Council under clause (c) of sub-section (1) of Section 56 of the Act :

Provided that wherein respect of any such proceeding, the High Court has received the finding of a Tribunal constituted under Section 11 of the Indian Bar Councils Act, 1926, the High Court shall dispose of the case and it shall be lawful for the High Court to exercise for the purpose of all

1. Published in Gazette of India (Extraordinary), Part II, Section 3(ii), dated 31st August, 1963.

the powers conferred on it under Section 12 of the said Act, as if that section has not been repealed by the Act :

Provided further that where the High Court has referred back any case for further inquiry under sub-section (4) of Section 12 of the said Act, the proceeding shall stand transferred to the State Bar Council in relation to that High Court, as if it were a proceeding pending before the corresponding Bar Council under clause (c) of sub-section (1) of Section 56 of the Act.

(3) If immediately before the appointed day there is any proceeding in respect of any disciplinary matter pending in relation to any pleader, vakil or attorney, who has been enrolled as an advocate on any State roll under the Act, such proceeding shall stand transferred to the State Bar Council on the roll of which he was enrolled and be dealt with under the Act as if it were a proceeding arising against him thereunder.

APPENDIX III

THE ADVOCATES (REMOVAL OF DIFFICULTIES) NO. 2 ORDER, 1963

S.O.3553, dated 21st December, 1963—In exercise of the powers conferred by Section 59 of the Advocates Act, 1961, the Central Government hereby makes the following order, namely :

1. Short title and commencement.—(1) This order may be called the Advocates (Removal of Difficulties) No. 2 Order, 1963.

(2) It shall be deemed to have come into force on 1st day of October, 1963.

2. Extension of term of office of elected members of the State Bar Council.—The elected members of a State Bar Council constituted for the first time shall continue to hold office until the State Bar Council is re-constituted in accordance with the provisions of the Advocates Act, 1961 (25 of 1961).

APPENDIX IV

THE ADVOCATES (REMOVAL OF DIFFICULTIES) ORDER, 1966

S.O. 162, dated 10th January, 1966—In exercise of powers conferred by Section 59 of the Advocates Act, 1961 (25 of 1961), the Central Government hereby makes the following order, namely :

1. Short title and commencement.—(1) This order may be called the Advocates (Removal of Difficulties) Order, 1966.

(2) it shall be deemed to have come into force on the 1st day of November, 1965.

2. Extension of term of office of elected members of the State Bar Council required to retire under Section 8 of the Advocates Act, 1961.—Every elected member of State Bar Council due to retire after the 1st day of November, 1965 under Section 8 of the said Act on the expiration of the second year from the date of such reconstitution shall, notwithstanding such expiration, continue to hold office for a further period of one year with effect from the date of such retirement.

APPENDIX V

THE ADVOCATES (REMOVAL OF DIFFICULTIES) ORDER, 1968

S.O. 740, dated the 22nd February, 1968—Whereas difficulty has arisen in giving effect to the provisions of the Advocates Act, 1961 (25 of 1961) in the Union Territory of Delhi consequent on the abolition of the office of Additional Solicitor-General of India.

Now, therefore, in exercise of the powers conferred by Section 59 of the Advocates Act, 1961 (25 of 1961), the Central Government hereby makes the following order, namely :

1. Short title and commencement.—(1) This order may be called the Advocates (Removal of Difficulties) Order, 1968.

(2) It shall come into force at once.

2. Constitution of references to Additional Solicitor-General of India.—Until other provision is made in this behalf, the references to the Additional Solicitor-General of India in clause (a) of sub-section (2) of Section 3, and Explanation to Section 35 of the Advocates Act, 9161 (25 of 1961) shall be construed as references to the Solicitor-General of India.

APPENDIX VI

THE ADVOCATES (RIGHT TO TAKE UP LAW TEACHING) RULES, 1979

G.S.R. 587 (E), dated 24th October, 1979—In exercise of the powers conferred by Section 49-A of the Advocates Act, 1961 (25 of 1961), the Central Government hereby makes the following rules, namely :

1. Short title and commencement.—(1) These rules may be called the Advocates (Right to Take Up Law Teaching) Rules, 1979.

(2) They shall come into force on the date of their publication in the official Gazette.

2. Definition.—In these rules, "Act" means the Advocates Act, 1961 (25 of 1961).

3. Right of practicing advocates to take up law teaching.—(1) Notwithstanding anything to the contrary contained in any rule made under the Act, an advocate may, while practicing, take up teaching of law in any educational institution which is affiliated to a University within the meaning of the University Grants Commission Act, 1956 (3 of 1956), so long as the hours during which he is so engaged in the teaching of law do not exceed three hours a day.

(2) When any advocate is employed in any such educational institution for the teaching of law, such employment shall, if the hours be deemed, for the purposes of the Act and the rules made thereunder, to be a part-time employment irrespective of the manner in which such employment is described or the remuneration receivable (whether by way of a fixed amount or on the basis of any time scale of pay or any other manner) by the advocate for such employment.

APPENDIX VII

THE BAR COUNCIL OF INDIA RULES

(As amended by Regulation 65/1993, dated 28.8.1993)

[Rules made by the Bar Council of India in exercise of its rule-making powers under the Advocates Act, 1961]

PART I

Definitions

Definitions.—In these rules, unless the context otherwise requires :

(a) 'Act' means the Advocates At, 1961, as amended from time to time;

(b) 'Advocate' means an advocate entered in any roll, under the provisions of the Act;

(c) 'Casual Vacancy' means a vacancy caused otherwise than by the expiry of the term;

(d) 'Chairman' means the Chairman of the Bar Council of india;

(e) 'Clear days' means that time is to be reckoned exclusive of both the first and the last days;

Illustration.—The election of members to a State Bar Council is fixed for the 15th January, 1965. Under the rules of the State Bar Council, ballot papers have to be dispatched 10 clear days before the date of election. Consequently the last date for the dispatch of ballot papers will be 4th January, 1965.

(f) 'Council' means the Bar Council of India;

(g) 'Prescribed' means prescribed by the rules;

(h) 'Rules' means the Rules made by the Council.

(i) 'Secretary' means the Secretary of the Bar Council of India, and includes any person howsoever designated and entrusted for the time being with the duties of the Secretary;

(j) 'State Council' means a Bar Council constituted under Section 3 of the Act;

(k) 'Vice-Chairman' means the Vice-Chairman of the Bar Council of India.

PART II

Matters Relating to the Bar Council of India

Chapter I

[Rules under Section 15(2), (c), (d), (f0 and (g) read with Section 4 and 10-B of the Act].

A. Election of the members of the Council

1. Notice of every meeting of the Council and committees shall ordinarily be sent by the Secretary not less than 15 days before the date of the meeting except when the Chairman requires a meeting to be called on short notice on grounds of urgency. If any five or more members of the Council require in writing meeting to be called on short notice of not less than 10 days for consideration of specified matters, the Secretary shall convene the meeting on such date as requisitioned and the agenda for such meeting shall include matters specified by such members. No proceeding shall be invalidated merely on the ground that the rule relating to notice is not strictly complied with.

2. (1) The Notice and Agenda for the first meeting of the State Council held after the election of its members on the expiry of the term of its members elected at the previous election under Section 8 of the Act may include the election of a member of the State Council to the Council under Section 4(1)(c) of the Act.

(2) Every such election shall be held not later than 30 days after the first meeting of the State Council after election under Section 8 of the Act.

3. The election of a member of the Council shall be conducted by the Secretary of the State Council who shall act as the Returning Officer.

4. A person elected as a member of the Council under Section 4(1)(c)of the Act, shall cease to be such member :

(a) from the date when he ceases to be a member of the State Council as mentioned in Section 4(3)(ii) of the Act;

(b) on the acceptance by the Council of his resignation.

5. (1) in the case of vacancy in the office of the member of the Council arising for any reason mentioned in Rule 49a) of this Chapter or on account of death, intimation of the vacancy shall be given by the Secretary of the State Council to the Secretary of the Council forthwith.

(2) The election to fill the vacancy under Rule 4(a) or (b) shall be held within 30 days from the date of the vacancy.

6. (a) If the State Council does not take steps in time for the holding of the election as referred it in these Rules, and

(b) in the case of a vacancy of the member of the Council arising under Section 10-B of the Act, the Secretary of the Council shall call upon the concerned State Council requiring it to elect its member to the Council within 30 days of such notice.

7. Every notice by the Secretary of the State Council fixing a date for the election of a member to the Council under these rules shall be sent not less than 15 clear days before the date fixed for the election. A copy

of the said notice shall be sent simultaneously to the Secretary of the Council.

8. (1) The name of each candidate for the election shall be proposed by one member and seconded by another member of the State Council at the meeting. No member shall propose or second more than one name.

(2) If only one candidate has been duly nominated, the Returning Officer shall declare him elected.

(3) Any nominated candidate can withdraw before the voting takes place.

(4) If the number of candidates duly nominated is more than one, there shall be an election by secret ballot. The Returning Officer shall provide voting papers with the names of the candidates typed. Each voting paper shall bear the signature of the Returning Officer.

(5) A voter in giving his vote shall place in his voting paper the mark 'X' against the name of the candidate of his choice.

The voting paper shall not be signed by the voter; and in the event of any erasures, obliterations or alterations in the voting papers, or of the voting paper purporting to have been signed by the voter, the voting paper shall be deemed to have been defaced and the vote purporting to have been given thereby shall not be taken into account for the purposes of the election. Subject to the provisions of Rule 10, the decision of the Returning Officer whether the voting paper has or has not been defaced shall be final.

A voting paper shall be invalid on which :—

(a) the mark 'X' is not made, or

(b) the mark 'X' is set opposite the name of more than one candidate or is so placed as to render it doubtful to which candidate is intended to apply, or

(c) the mark 'X' and any other mark or figures are set opposite the name of the same candidate, or

(d) there is any mark in writing by which the voter can be identified.

(6) The Returning Officer shall count the valid votes immediately after the close of voting in the presence of the candidates or their nominees who may choose to be present.

(7) The candidate securing the largest number of votes shall be declared elected by the Returning Officer.

(8) Immediately after the declaration of the result, the Returning Officer shall put the ballot papers used for voting in the election in a separate cover, have the cover closed and sealed with his signature and that of all the contesting candidates if they desire to do so.

(9) The result of the election shall be communicated forthwith to the Secretary of the Council, and sent to the State Gazette or Gazettes concerned for publication.

(9) (1) In case of dispute arising out of the election, any of the contesting candidates, or any other member of the State Council may

challenge the election by a petition which shall be filed with, or dispatched by registered post to the Secretary of the Council within 10 clear days of declaration by the Returning Officer of the result of the election as mentioned in Rule 8(7). The petitioner shall also send copies of the petition to all the contesting candidates and to the Secretary of the State Council.

(2) As soon as possible after the receipt of the copy of the petition under sub-rule (1), the Secretary of the State Council shall send the sealed cover containing the ballot papers referred to in Rule 8(8) above, and all other papers and records relating to the election to the Secretary of the Council.

(10) (1) The Council may reject any petition received under Rule 9, if in its opinion, there is no prima facie case.

(2) If the Council is of the opinion that there is a prima facie case, either the Council or a Committee of the Council comprising not more than 3 members of the Council constituted therefor shall, after hearing all the parties concerned, determine the said dispute.

(3) The Council, or the Committee, as the case may be, shall have all or any of the following powers :

(a) to dismiss the petition;

(b) to set aside the election;

(c) to declare any candidate as having been duly elected;

(d) to order a fresh election; and

(e) to make an order as to costs.

(4) A copy of the order of the Council or the Committee may be sent to the State Councils.

(5) The State Council concerned shall cause such fresh election to be held as may be ordered under sub-rule (3) of this rule.

(6) The parties shall be entitled to obtain copies of the order or the decision of the Council or of the Committees, as the case may be, on payment of the charges, if any, prescribed therefor under the rules of the Council. The Chairman of the Council or the President of the Committee, as the case may be, may also permit copies of any other part of the record of the enquiry to be furnished on payment of such charges as may be prescribed during the pendency of the election petition.

B. Expiry of term of Office of Chairman, Vice-Chairman and Members of Committees of the Council

11. A member of the Council elected as Chairman or Vice-Chairman or Member of any Committee of the Council, shall cease to hold office as such Chairman, Vice-Chairman or Member of Committee, on the expiry of his term as a member of the State Council for which he was elected under Section 8 of the Act, and fresh elections thereto shall be held for the residue of the term of the said office.

C. Election of Chairman and Vice-Chairman

12. (1) (a) The election of the Chairman and Vice-Chairman shall be

held at a meeting of the Council.

(b) At every such meeting for the election of the Chairman, the Vice-Chairman, if he is not a candidate shall preside. In the absence of the Vice-Chairman, a member of the Council who is not a candidate, elected by the members present, shall preside.

(c) In the case of the election of the Vice-Chairman, the Chairman, or in his absence the Vice-Chairman, if he is not a candidate shall preside.

In the absence of the Chairman and the Vice-Chairman, any member of the Council who is not a candidate, elected by the members present, shall preside.

(d) (i) The name of the candidate for the election shall be proposed by one member and seconded by another member at the meeting.

(ii) No member shall propose or second more than one name.

(iii) If only one member has been duly nominated, he shall be declared elected.

(iv) Any candidate nominated may withdraw before voting takes place.

(e) If the number of candidates duly nominated is more than one, there shall be an election by secret ballot.

(f) The Secretary shall provide voting papers with the names of the candidates. Such voting paper shall bear the signature of the Secretary.

(g) A voter in giving his vote shall place on his voting paper a mark 'X' against the name of the candidate of his choice.

The voting paper shall not be signed by the voter and in the event of any erasures, obliterations or alterations in the voting paper, or of the voting paper purporting to have been signed by the voter, the voting paper shall be deemed to have been defaced, and the voting purporting to have been given thereby shall not be taken into account for the purposes of the election. The decision of the Chairman of the meeting whether the voting paper has or has not been defaced shall be final.

A voting paper shall be invalid on which :

(i) the mark 'X' is not made, or

(ii) the mark 'X' is set opposite the name of more than one candidate or is so placed as to render it doubtful to which candidate it is intended to apply, or

(iii) the mark 'X' and any other mark or figures are set opposite the name of the same candidate, or

(iv) there is any mark in writing by which the voter can be identified,

(v) the Secretary shall count the valid votes immediately after the close of the voting.

The member securing the largest number of votes shall be declared elected. In the case of two or more members securing an equal number of votes, the Chairman of the meeting shall decide the election by drawing lots.

(2) The Chairman or the Vice-Chairman shall hold office for a period of two years, or until his term of office in the State Council in which he was elected under Section 4(1)(c) ceases, whichever is earlier.

(3) The Chairman or the Vice-Chairman may resign his office by letter addressed to the Secretary of the Council. Such resignation shall take effect from the date of the acceptance thereof by the Council or from such other date as the Council may fix :

Provided that in the eventuality of mid-term poll of the Office of the Chairman or Vice-Chairman the term shall be of the residuary term.

13. If the Chairman or the Vice-Chairman ceases to be a member of the Council for any reason, the vacancy shall be filled up by election as far as possible at the next meeting of the Council.

14. The result of the election of the Chairman or the Vice-Chairman shall be sent forthwith to the Gazette of India for publication.

D. Powers and Duties of the Chairman and Vice-Chairman

15. Save as otherwise provided in these rules, and subject to the resolutions of the Council, the Chairman shall exercise general control and supervision over the affairs of the Council.

16. He shall preside over the deliberations of the Council and of all Committees of which he is a member.

17. Save as otherwise decided at a meeting of the Council or the Committee, as the case may be, he shall cause the meetings of the Council or the Committee convened at such time as he may fix. He shall also settle the items for agenda for the meetings of the Council.

18. He shall have power to pass interim orders in revisional and other matters arising out of the supervisory jurisdiction of the Council.

19. He shall have power to punish any employee of the Council by way of censure or reprimand and may initiate proceedings for suspensions, removal or dismissal.

20. He shall be the authority to sanction the disbursement of salaries of the staff and to order payment of any bill outstanding against the Council.

21. The Vice-Chairman shall exercise all the powers and discharge all the functions of the Chairman in his absence and under his direction.

Chapter II

Meeting of Council and its Committees other than those of the Disciplinary Committee

[Rule under Section 15(2)(h) and (j) of the Act]

1. Notice of every meeting of the Council and the Committees shall ordinarily be sent by the Secretary not less than 15 days before the date of the meeting, except when the Chairman or any two members require a meeting to be called on short notice on grounds of urgency. No proceedings shall be invalidated merely on the ground that the rule relating to notice is not strictly complied with.

2. Notice of the meeting shall specify the time and place of the meeting and shall contain the agenda fixed for the meeting.

3. No member shall be entitled to bring forward for the consideration of the meeting any matter of which he has not given ten day notice to the Secretary, unless the Chairman in his discretion permits him to do so.

4. The minutes of the previous meeting shall ordinarily be read and recorded at the subsequent meeting.

5. The quorum for the meeting of the Council shall be seven and for all other Committees, except the Executive Committee and the Legal Education Committee, the quorum shall be two. The quorum for the Executive Committee and the Legal Education Committee, shall be four.

6. If urgent action by the Council or by any Committee of the Council other than a Disciplinary Committee becomes necessary, the Chairman of the Council or of such Committee as the case may be, may permit the business to be transacted by circulation of papers to the members of the Council or the Committee, as the case may be. The action proposed to be taken shall not be taken unless agreed to by a majority of the members of the Council or the Committee, as the case may be. The action so taken shall be forthwith intimated to all the members of the Council or the Committee concerned. The papers shall be placed before the next meeting of the Council or the Committee concerned for confirmation.

7. The Council, or any Committee may adjourn from day to day or any particular day, without further notice.

8. A member shall address the chair when speaking at a meeting of the Council and he shall be entitled to speak only once on each subject, unless otherwise required or permitted by the Chairman to do so.

9. Save as otherwise provided in these rules, the decision on any matter shall be by majority, and in the case of equality of votes, the Chairman of the meeting shall have a second or casting vote.

10. No matter once decided shall be reconsidered for a period of three months unless the Council by a two-thirds majority of the members present, so permits.

11. Any Committee may refer for advice any matter to the Council.

12. In the absence of the Chairman and the Vice-Chairman at any meeting, a member chosen by members present shall preside at the meeting.

Chapter III

Constitution, Functions and Procedure of Committees of the Bar Council of India

[Rules under Section 9, 9-A, 10 and 15(2)(i) and (j) of the Act]

1. The Council may appoint from amongst its members, one or more Committees as it may deem necessary, in addition to those specified in the Act and delegate such powers, duties and functions to such Committees as it deems fit.

2. Any casual vacancy in the above Committees shall be filled up by

the Council.

3. Save where the Chairman or the Vice-Chairman is a member of the Committee or Sub-committee, the Committee or Sub-committee shall choose its Chairman for the meeting, unless at the time of the constitution thereof the name of the Chairman has been specified.

4. Unless otherwise determined at the time of election, the term of the members of the Committees of the Council shall be as follows :

(a) Executive Committee—2 years

(b) Disciplinary Committee—3 years

(c) Legal Education Committee—4 years

(d) Legal Aid Committee—2 years

(e) Advocates Fund Committee—2 years

(f) Any other Committee not falling under the above clauses—2 years.

The Executive Committee :

5. (1) The procedure for the election of the Members of the Executive Committee shall be by secret ballot and in accordance with the rules, in so far as they are applicable, laid down in Rule 12, Chapter I, Part II.

(2) A casual vacancy in the Committee shall be filled up by election by the Council.

(3) The Committee shall elect its own Chairman and Vice-Chairman.

The Chairman shall preside over the deliberations of the Committee and in his absence the Vice-Chairman shall preside.

(4) The Committee shall be executive authority of the Council and shall be responsible for giving effect to the resolutions of the Council. It shall have powers :

(a) to manage the funds of the Council;

(b) to invest the funds of the Council in the manner directed by the Council from time to time;

(c) to grant leave to members of the staff, other than casual leave;

(d) to prescribe books of account, registers and files for the proper management of the affairs of the Council;

(e) to appoint and supervise the work of the members of the staff and prescribe their conditions of service;

(f) to appoint auditors and fix their remuneration;

(g) to consider the annual audit report and place it before the Council with its comments for its consideration;

(h) to maintain a library and under the directions of the Council, publish any journal, treatise or pamphlets on legal subjects;

(i) to prepare and place before the Council, the annual administration report and the statement of account.

(j) to provide the proper annual inspection of the office and its registers;

(k) to authorize the Secretary to incur expenditure within prescribed limits;

(l) to fix travelling and other allowances to members of the Committees or the Council, and to members of the staff;

(m) to delegate to the Chairman and/or the Vice-Chairman any of its aforementioned powers;

(n) to do all other things necessary for discharging the aforesaid functions.

The Legal Education Committee

6. (1) The procedure for the election of the members of the Legal Education Committee shall be by secret ballot, and in accordance with the rules in so far as they are applicable, laid down in Rule 12, Chapter I, Part II.

(2) The names of the remaining five members of the Committee to be co-opted shall be proposed and seconded by the members of the Council. In case more than five persons are proposed, they shall be chosen by a show of hands. If there is equality of votes, the Chairman of the meeting shall have a casting vote.

7. A casual vacancy in the Committee shall be filled in by the Council from amongst its members or non-members, as the case may be, in the manner specified in Rule 6 above.

8. The Committee shall have the following powers and duties :

(a) to make its recommendations to the Council for laying down the standards of legal education for the University;

(b) to visit and inspect Universities and report the results to the Council;

(c) to recommend to the Council the conditions, if any, subject to which foreign qualifications in law obtained by persons other than citizens of India may be recognized for admission as Advocates under the Act;

(d) (i) to recommend to the Council for recognition of any degree in law of any University in the territory of india under Section 2491)(c)(iii) of the Act; and

(ii) to recommend the discontinuance of any recognition already made by the Council.

The Disciplinary Committee

9. (1) The procedure for the election or co-option of the Members of the Disciplinary Committee shall be by secret ballot and in accordance with the rules in so far as they are applicable, laid down in Rule 12, Chapter I, Part II.

(2) Any casual vacancy shall be filled in by the Council by election or co-option from amongst its members or non-members, as the case may be.

(3) The Chairman or the Vice-Chairman of the Executive Committee

shall assign and allocate all matters relating to the Disciplinary Committees amongst them if more than one such Committee is constituted or is in existence.

10. For the purpose of determining the senior most member of a Disciplinary Committee under Section 9 of the Advocates Act, 1961—the seniority :

(i) of a senior Advocate; and

(ii) of an Advocate of the Supreme Court enrolled before 1st December, 1961, shall be determined in accordance with the date of his enrolment under the Bar Councils Act, 1926.

Election of Representatives

11. The procedure for electing its representative to the Press Council of India under the Press Council Act, 1965, or for electing any other representative or representatives by or from amongst its members to any other statutory body by virtue of any special power conferred under any other enactment or for any other election by the Council provided that any member so requires; shall be in accordance with the same procedure and shall, in so far as it may be applicable, be as laid down in Rule 12, Chapter I, Part II.

Chapter IV

Qualifications and Conditions of Service of the Secretary, Accountant and other Members of the Staff

[Rules under Section 15(2)(k) of the Act]

Secretary :

1. The Secretary shall :

(a) be a citizen of India;

(b) be a law graduate or barrister-at-law;

(c) have been either :—

(i) Registrar of the Supreme Court or of a High Court in India, or

(ii) an Advocate with 10 years' practice at the Bar, or

(iii) Secretary of a Bar Council for at least 10 years, or

(iv) District Judge having five years experience as a District Judge, or

(v) Principal of a recognized Law College having experience as a Principal for five years, and seven years' standing at the Bar, or

(vi) Professor or Reader of Law in a University recognized by the Council with 10 years' standing and having seven years' experience at the Bar, and

(d) be ordinarily not less than 40 years and not more than 50 years' of age at the time of appointment :

Provided that if, at any time, the Council considers that a person having the necessary qualifications is not available, it may relax any of the qualifications mentioned in sub-rules (c) and (d) of this rule.

2. The Secretary shall draw a salary in the grade of Rs. 4500-150-5,100-150-6,300-200-6,700. He shall be paid such allowances as the Council may determine from time to time.

3. The Secretary shall be the Chief Executive Officer of the Council and shall perform *inter alia* the following duties :

(i) attend all meetings of the Council or of the Committees unless otherwise directed;

(ii) keep records and minutes of the proceedings of the Council and of its Committees;

(iii) keep in his custody the property of the Council including the seal of the Council;

(iv) exercise general control and supervision over the employees of the Council;

(v) arrange for the deposit of the monies received on behalf of the Council in Bank and see to the security of the cash in hand;

(vi) act as Secretary of all Committees, and convene meetings of the Council or its Committees, unless otherwise decided by the Council;

(vii) appoint such temporary staff as may be necessary with the permission of the Chairman to transact urgent work;

(viii) issue requisite notifications as prescribed and circulars as may be required;

(ix) attend to the correspondence of the Council and of the Committee;

(x) act as Registrar of Disciplinary Committees, issue notices and subpoenas and be in charge of all works in proceedings under Chapter V of the Act including the grant of certified copies of documents and evidence or statements of witnesses;

(xi) grant certified copies of documents or other proceedings referred to in the Act or in these rules;

(xii) shall be the custodian of the records, registers, accounts, furniture, library and such other property as the Council might acquire from time to time ;

(xiii) perform such other duties as may be assigned to him by the Council or the Committees, or the Chairman.

4. The Secretary shall retire on attaining the age of 60 years provided that the Council may extend his term by a period not exceeding 2 years at a time, but not exceeding 5 years in the aggregate.

Additional, Joint, Assistance Secretaries

5. The Council may also appoint one or more Additional, Joint, or Assistant Secretaries on such scales of pay and allowances as may be fixed by it.

6. The Additional, Joint, or Assistant Secretary shall, save as

otherwise directed by the Council or the Executive Committee perform such work or discharge such functions as may be entrusted to them by the Secretary.

7. The Additional, Joint, or Assistant Secretary shall retire on attaining the age of 60 years provided that the Council may extend the term by a period not exceeding two years if it thinks fit.

Accountant

8. The qualifications of the Accountant shall be :

(a) M. Com. of any University in India or its equivalent or a Chartered Accountant,

(b) Experience as Accountant preferably in a limited company or reputed commercial concern for not less than 5 years;

(c) Ordinarily not less than 30 years of age at the time of appointment :

Provided, however, that any of the above qualifications may be waived in the case of a person who had already been in the service of the Council as Deputy or Assistant Accountant or otherwise and is considered fit for such appointment as Accountant or if a suitable candidate possessing the above qualifications is not available, and the Council considers it fit to appoint him :

Provided further the 'ACCOUNTANT' shall mean and include the Accounts Officer wherever it occurs.

9. The Accountant shall draw a salary in the grade of Rs. 650-30-740-35-880-40-1, 200 (pre-revised) with effect from 1st April, 1977.

10. The Accountant shall be responsible for the maintenance of all the accounts of the Council and he may also be required by the Council or Secretary to discharge such additional work of the Council as may be entrusted to him.

11. The accountant shall retire on attaining the age of 60 years provided that the Council may extend his term by a period not exceeding two years if it thinks fit.

12. The accountant and other permanent members of the staff shall be entitled to Dearness Allowance, House Rent Allowance and City Compensatory Allowance from 1st January, 1973 at the rate as is paid to the staff of the Supreme Court of India.

13. All the permanent employees of the Council shall be entitled to the benefit of Provident Fund and Gratuity in accordance with such rules as may be framed in that behalf by the Executive Committee.

14. All the employees of the Council shall be subject to such conditions of service as to leave and such other matters as may be resolved in this behalf by the Executive Committee of the Council.

Chapter V

Rule Relating to Finance

[Rules under Section 15(2)(I), (m) and (n) of the Act]

1. All monies received on behalf of the Council shall be acknowledged by a receipt signed by the Secretary or any other person authorized by the Executive Committee. Amounts received shall be credited into the account of the Council in the Bank on the next working day of the Bank.

2. The books of the account and registers shall be strongly bond and paged. On the 1st or title page, the number of pages of the book or the register shall be entered and the entry shall be signed by the Secretary. Corrections in the entries shall be made in red ink and attested by the Accountant. Erasures shall, on no account, be permitted.

3. Receipt forms shall be numbered consecutively and bound into books of 50 or 100 forms each. On the front page of each book shall be entered the first and the last number of the receipt in the book, be so certified by the Secretary. Receipts shall be in triplicate. The third part shall remain in the book and the second part shall be kept for the record, and the 1st part shall be given to the payee. All receipts shall be signed by the Secretary or by such person as the Council may direct.

4. Payments of Rs. 50/- and over shall ordinarily be by cheque.

5. Bill presented for payment shall be examined by the Accountant and on his being satisfied that the claim is admissible, and the payment is duly authorized by the Secretary, the Accountant shall pay the amount against a receipt. The entry in the account book shall show if the payment is made by cash or by cheque. The bill and the relevant receipt shall be pasted together and shall be numbered consecutively in the year as payment voucher and shall be pasted in the bound book.

6. Salary bills shall be in such form as the Executive Committee may direct.

7. A bill presented for payment three months after the money becomes due, shall not be paid without the sanction of the Executive Committee.

8. The Executive Committee may fix the amount of a permanent advance to be made to the Secretary and the Accountant, as the case may be.

9. The Accountant shall maintain an acquaintance register in the following form/or in such other form as the auditor may direct :

Name	Designation	Pay	Dearness Allowance etc.	Total Salary (add Col 3 and 4)	Contribution towards provident fund	Net Salary Payable (Col. 5 minus 6)
1	2	3	4	5	6	7
.....	.....	.....	.....	.....	.....	.....

Installment amount Signature Towards Provident Fund loan taken	Amount of interest payable on the principal loan amount outstanding	Total	Signature with date
8	9	10	11
.....	.....	.....	.....

10. All monies received and spent shall be immediately brought into account in the cash book and ledger. The cash book shall be balanced at the close of every month and signed by the Secretary and the Accountant.

10-A. The Bar Council of India shall have power to borrow money from any Bank or other financial institution or other for the purposes of acquiring or construction of any property or building on a specific authorization of the Bar Council of India.

10-B. That for the purposes of borrowing, the Bar Council of India may authorize any Officer or Officer-bearer to sign necessary documents.

10-C. The Bar Council of India shall have power to mortgage property belonging to the Council for the purpose of taking loans from Banks and other Financial Institutions.

Note : Rules 10-A and 10-B will come into force from 11th Feb., 1990 and Rule 10-C will come into force from 22nd April, 1990.

11. (1) (i) The Chairman; (ii) The Vice-Chairman; or (iii) any other person authorised by the Council, shall be entitled to incur expenditure sanctioned in the budget without any further authority.

(2) The Chairman and/or the Vice-Chairman or any other person authorized by the Council, shall have authority to spend or incur expenditure of an emergent nature not provided for in the budget not exceeding Rs. 2,000/- a month for purpose of the Council.

12. The Chairman and/or the Vice-Chairman shall be the authority to sanction travelling allowance and daily allowance bills of the members.

13. The accounts of the Council shall be audited once a year.

14. The annual statement of income and expenditure of the year so audited shall be laid before the Executive Committee not later than the 31st July each year.

15. The funds of the Council may be invested as follows :

(i) in the State Bank of India or such other nationalized Bank as the Council may decide;

(ii) in any of the securities specified in Section 20 of the Indian Trusts Act, 1982, as the Council may decide;

(iii) in Fixed Deposit with Government Companies as defined in the Companies Act, 1956.

16. Budget estimates of Income and Expenditure for the coming year shall be made by the Executive Committee and laid before the Council for approval before the 31st March every year.

17. (1) All cheques other than those mentioned in sub-rule (2) shall be signed or endorsed and all bills, notes or other negotiable instruments shall be drawn, accepted or made on behalf of the Council by two persons, viz., (i) by the Chairman or the Vice-Chairman of the Council and in their absence by such other members as may be authorized by the Council in that behalf, and (ii) the Secretary and in his absence the Joint or Assistant Secretary, if any, authorized by the Council.

(2) Notwithstanding anything contained in Rule 11, Chapter V, Part

II of the Council Rules, the Council may, by resolution, open a separate Saving Bank Account in any Bank specified by it or in a Post Office to be operated by the Secretary of the Council.

18. All monies and securities belonging to the Council shall stand in the name of the Council.

19. The Council shall open a Provident Fund account in a Bank authorized by the Council in accordance with the Provident Fund rules.

Chapter VI

A. Miscellaneous : Publication of Rules and other Information and date of coming into force of the Rules

[Rules under Section 7(m) and 49(j) of the Act]

1. Unless the Council otherwise directs, all rules of the Council shall come into force on the date of their publication in the Gazette of India.

2. Information, *inter alia*, on the following matters shall, unless the Council determines otherwise, be communicated to all the State Councils :

(i) Election of Chairman, Vice-Chairman,

(ii) Order of the Council under Proviso to Section 26(1) of the Act removal of name under Section 26-A of the Act and orders on matters dealt with under Section 48A and 48B of the Act as are approved by the Council for communication.

(iii) Consent expressed under Section 27 of the Act to the enrolment of a person whose application on a former occasion had been refused by a State Council.

(iv) Decision of the Council relating to recognition of degree referred to in Section 24(1)(c) (iii), (iiia) or (iv) of the Act.

(v) Decisions of the Council or its Committees on election disputes under Rule 10 of the rules in Chapter I, Part II of these rules.

3. Subject to such directions, specific or general as may be given by the Council, the Secretary shall send to all the State Bar Councils copies of all final orders of the Disciplinary Committees of the Bar Council of India made under Sections 36, 36B and 37 of the Act.

4. Subject to such directions, specific or general, as may be given by the Council, the Secretary of the Council may furnish certified copies of the orders mentioned in Rule 3 on payment of charge of Rs. 1/- after deleting the name of the advocate against whom the enquiry is made for publication in any legal journal or to any Bar Association as may apply therefore :

Provided that copies of the orders mentioned in this Rule shall not be issued : (a) where an appeal has been filed in the Supreme Court, before the disposal of the appeal; and (b) where no such appeal has been preferred to the Supreme Court, before the expiry of the period of limitation for filing the appeal.

5. Whenever any disciplinary action is taken or confirmed by the Disciplinary Committee or the Council, as the case may be, against an

advocate, information thereof shall be communicated by reference to the name and number of the roll of the advocates and the date of the enrolment to the following :

All the State Bar Councils through the State Bar Council where the advocate was practicing, the High Court, the District Courts, and such Bar Association as the said State Bar Council may deem fit.

B. Inspection of Records and Copies

6. (1) Save as otherwise directed by the Chairman or the Vice-Chairman of the Council or the Chairman of the Committee concerned, as the case may be, inspection of any of the records in any proceedings of a judicial nature of the Council or its Committees other than those of a Disciplinary Committee may be permitted to the parties or their Counsel, on any working day, except during the summer of other vacations of the Supreme Court on presentation to the Secretary of an application duly signed by the applicant or his counsel.

(2) An application for inspection shall be accompanied by the fees prescribed therefor in cash. The Secretary may permit the inspection in his presence or in the presence of any member of the staff authorized by him. The person inspecting shall not be entitled to make copies of the records of which inspection is permitted. He shall, however, be permitted to make short notes in pencil.

(3) Save as otherwise directed by the Chairman or Vice-Chairman of the Council or the Chairman of the Committee concerned, as the case may be, certified copies of the records of a proceedings of a judicial nature of the Council or of its Committees, as the case may be, may be granted to the parties or to their counsel on an application made in that behalf and on payment in cash of the prescribed fees.

Chapter VII

Proceedings for Removal of Name from Roll under Proviso to Section 26(1) of the Act

1. Whenever a State Council, or any Committee duly authorized by the State Council, has credible information from any source whatever that an advocate on the roll of the State Council has obtained his enrolment under circumstances which, if established, will render his name liable to be removed by the Council under the proviso to Section 26(1) of the Act, it shall be the duty of the State Council or the said Committee to enquire into the matter and report its findings to the Council.

In holding such enquiry, the Council or the Committee shall hear the advocate concerned and otherwise follow the principles of natural justice.

2. In disposing of any proceedings under the said proviso, whether instituted on a report under Rule 1 or otherwise, the Council may, if it considers it just and expedient cause an enquiry into disputed questions of fact to be made by any State Council or Committee thereof or any other Committee consisting of the case may be, shall follow the procedure mentioned in Rule 1.

Chapter VIII

Additional qualification for Enrolment as Advocates

Any person who has held office as a Judge of any High Court in India may, on retirement, be admitted as an advocate on the rolls of any State Council where he is eligible to practice.

Chapter IX

Revision under Section 48-A of the Act

1. (1) An application for revision shall be in the form of a petition duly signed setting out the necessary facts and shall be accompanied by the copy of the Order in respect of which the Revision is filed, giving the address of the Petitioner and the Respondent or Respondents. It shall be supported by an affidavit and shall be accompanied by the prescribed fee which is payable in cash or could be sent by M.O. The applicant shall file at least 5 more copies of the petition and affidavit, and if there is more than one Respondent as many additional copies as are necessary to serve the other Respondents.

He shall file translations in English of such of the papers as may be necessary for reference at the time of hearing.

(2) No applicant for revision shall ordinarily be entertained after 90 days from the date of the Order complained of.

2. (1) If the Revision Petition is in order, the papers shall be called for and the Council, or a Committee of the Council constituted or authorized in this behalf, may direct notice to the Respondent. The papers shall not, however, be called for unless so directed by the Council in a Revision petition against an order of the Disciplinary Committee.

(2) If the Council or the Committee considers that there are no merits in the Revision Petition, opportunity shall be given to the Petitioner to appear before the Council in support of the petition.

3. The Council may, after hearing the petitioner, direct notice to the Respondent or dismiss the petition, as it may consider fit.

4. Upon notice being issued under the above rules after giving reasonable opportunity of hearing to the parties, the Council may pass such orders on the Revision Petition as it deems proper.

5. Unless the Council otherwise specially directs, the petitioner and the Respondent may appear by advocates, who shall file a vakalatnama signed by the party.

6. A copy of the Order on the revision shall be sent to the parties.

FORM-A

Subject to Necessary Modifications

[Under Rule 3, Chapter IX, Part II of the Rules of the Bar Council of India]

For Revision under Section 48-A

THE BAR COUNCIL OF INDIA

Notice under Section 48A of the Advocates Act, 1961, read with

the rules in Chapter IX, Part II of the Rules of the Bar Council of India

BCI REVISION CASE NO................/20...........

In the mater of...

Petitioner... respondent.

WHEREAS on the application above referred to/*suo motu*/ the Bar Council of India having come to the conclusion that in exercise of the powers conferred upon it under Section 48A of the Advocates Act, 1961, it should satisfy itself as to the legality or propriety of such disposal/of the Bar Council of/of the Committee of the Bar Council of/dated..............(set out the necessary gist of the Order).

The respondent is hereby informed that the said application will be heard by the Bar Council of India on..................... at (time)..................at (place) ....and if the respondent does not appear in person or through his advocate on the said date or on such other date to which the hearing may be adjourned, the matter will be heard and disposed of in his absence.

Secretary

Date............. (The Bar Council of India)

Chapter X

Application for Review under Section 48AA of the Act

1. (1) An Application for Review made under section 48AA of the Act shall set out the necessary facts and the grounds for review and be accompanied by an affidavit and the fee prescribed under these rules.

(2) A true copy o the order shall be filed along with the application.

(3) If the application for review received is in order, the Council may direct the issue of notice to the petitioner and such other persons as it may consider necessary.

(4) A copy of the order on the review application shall be sent free of charge to the petitioner and the other party, if any.

(5) Save as otherwise directed, the parties to whom notice has been issued may appear in person or by advocate or through authorized agent and if any of the parties fail to appear pursuant to the notice issued on any date of hearing, the Council may dispose of the application in such manner as it may think fit.

2. The procedure prescribed in the above rules in this Chapter shall apply to the extent to which they are applicable when the Council acts of its own motion.

Chapter XI

Orders of the Bar Council of India

1. Every decision of the Council under the Proviso to Section 26(1) or under Section 48-A or under any other provisions of the Act shall be signed by the Chairman of the meeting at which the said decision was taken or if so authorized by any other member or the Secretary on behalf of the Council.

2. The Secretary shall send to the party or parties concerned, a copy of the order, fee of charges.

PART III

Certain Matters Relating to State Council

Chapter I

Electoral Roll, Disqualification of Membership and Vacation of Office

[Rules under Sections 3(4), 10B, 15(2)(a) and 49(1)(a) and (ab) of the Act.]

1. Every advocate whose name is on the Electoral Roll of the State Council shall be entitled to vote at an election.

2. The name of an advocate appearing in the State Roll shall not be on the Electoral roll, if on information received or obtained by the State Bar Council concerned on the basis of which it is satisfied that :

(a) His name has, at any time, been removed;

(b) He has been suspended from practice, provided that his disqualification shall operate only for a period of five years from the date of the expiry of the period of suspension.

(c) He is an undischarged insolvent;

(d) He has been found guilty of an election offence in regard to an election to the State Council by an election tribunal, provided however that such disqualification shall not operate beyond the election next following after such finding has been made;

(e) He is convicted by a competent court for an offence involving moral turpitude, provided that his disqualification shall cease to have effect after a period of two years has elapsed since his release;

(f) He is in full time service or is in such part-time business or other vocation not permitted in the case of practicing advocates by the rules either of the State Council concerned or the Council;

(g) He has intimated voluntary suspension of practice and has not given intimation of resumption of practice.

Explanation

If an advocate who has incurred any disqualification as referred to in Rule 2 and does not furnish details about it as required in the notice under Rule 4 of these Rules within time specified shall be deemed to have committed an act of other misconduct as referred to in Section 35(1) of the Act.

3. Subject to the provisions of Rule 2, the name of every advocate entered in the State Roll shall be entered in the electoral roll of the State Council.

4. (1) In preparing the Electoral Roll, unless the State Bar Council concerned is already maintaining a list of advocates who are entitled to be voters in terms of Rule 2 of these Rules, at least 150 days before the date of election, shall publish notice issued by the Secretary of the State Bar

Council concerned in prescribed form in the Official Gazette and in two or more local newspapers—one English and the other of local language, as may be decided by the State Bar Council, asking each of the advocates on the Roll of the concerned State Bar Council to intimate the State Bar Council within the time to be specified in the said notice or within such extended time as may be given/allowed by the State Bar Council for reasons to be recorded, as to whether he has incurred any disqualification mentioned in Rule 2 of these Rules in the said Notice.

(2) A preliminary electoral roll containing the names of all advocates whose names are required to be included under these rules shall be put up on the notice board of the State Council within 120 clear days before the expiry of the term of the members of the said State Council necessitating the election, (and relevant position thereof shall be sent to such Bar Association as the Secretary considers fit) :

Provided that the Bar Councils whose term of office has already expired or shall expire within 120 days from the date of commencement of these rules shall, as far as possible, publish the electoral roll forthwith and fix the elections for a date after not less than 120 clear days from the date of publication of the electoral rolls.

(3) Before final publication of the electoral Roll, a State Bar Council may, if satisfied, on an application made by any particular advocate giving sufficient reasons, allow his name to be included in the Electoral Roll in question, and on such inclusion advocate concerned shall be entitled to take part in the election.

5. The final electoral roll shall be prepared after incorporating such changes as may be necessary including the addition of the names of Advocates enrolled after the preparation of the preliminary roll and put up on the notice board of the State Council not more than 75 clear days and not less than 60 clear days, before the date of election.

(Intimation of such publication shall be given within a week after the publication to the bar Associations aforesaid).

Revision of Electoral Roll

6. If for any reason the election to the State Council is postponed beyond the date of expiry of the term of its members, the preliminary or the final electoral roll shall be revised so as to include therein the names of advocates enrolled upto 75 clear days before the date of the election.

Particulars to be maintained in the Electoral Roll

7. The electoral roll of the State Council shall *inter alia* contain the following particulars :

(i) Serial number;

(ii) Number on the State Roll;

(iii) Name of Advocates as on the Roll; and

(iv) Address of the Advocate.

Disqualification for being a Candidate in the Election

8. The nomination of any person who, at the date of scrutiny thereof, is subject to any of the disqualification referred to in Rule 2 shall be rejected.

9. Application of these Rules.—These rules shall govern the elections of all State Bar Councils to be held after those Rules are enforced, and all State Bar Councils holding the elections of their members shall prepare their Electoral Rolls in terms of these rules.

10. An elected member of the State Council shall be deemed to have vacated his office :

(a) if he is suspended from practice, or his name is removed from the rolls by an order of a competent authority, or for any reason whatsoever he ceases to be an advocate.

(b) If he is adjudicated as an insolvent, or

(c) If his name is transferred to the roll of another State Council.

11. No Elections shall be called in question for any non-compliance of the provisions of the Act or of any rules made thereunder unless the results of the Election in so far as it concerns a returned candidate or candidates have been materially affected.

Form of Notice under Rule 4

It is hereby notified that for the purpose of preparing final Electoral Roll in accordance with Rules 2 & 3 of Chapter I, Part III of the Rules framed by the Bar Council of India under Sections 3(4), 10B, 15(2)(a), 49(1)(a) and (ab) o the Advocates Act, 1961, for the next election of Members to this Council, the particulars as to any of the disqualifications as referred to in Clauses (a) to (g) of Rule 2 shall be furnished by an Advocate who has incurred them to the State Council within the time specified in the notice issued under Rule 4. (Hereinbelow to reproduce Rule 2 with Explanation).

Dated the (Secretary)

Number of the State Roll :

1. Name of the advocate as on the Roll :

(In block letters)

2. (a) Address of the Advocate :

(as on the State Roll)

(b) Present address :

3. (a) Have you incurred any of the disqualifications mentioned in Rule 2 of Chapter 1, Part III of the Rules of the Bar Council of India?

4. Are you a member of any Bar Association?

(If so, give the name)

5. Where do you intend to cast your vote?

(If you are not a voter entitled to vote by Postal Ballot)

I, hereby, declare and affirm that the foregoing statements are true to may knowledge and I have not concealed anything thereto.

Date ....

Signature in full

Note : These rules have come into effect from 1st January, 1991.

Chapter II

Rules to Secure at least a minimum number of Advocates of 10 years' standing

[Rules under Section 3(2)(b) and Proviso, Sections 3(5) and 49(1)(ac) of the Act]

1. (a) These rules shall apply to the election of members of all the State Councils in India.

(b) In the case of any repugnancy between these rules and any rule or rules of any of the State Councils, these rules shall prevail and the rules framed by the State Councils shall be void to the extent of such repugnancy.

2. The elections of members of the State Councils shall be in conformity with the proviso to Section 3(2) of the Act and these rules.

3. There shall be no limit to the number of candidates on the State roll for at least 10 years that could be declared elected under these rules.

4. In the case of an election by a State Council for electing all the members specified in Section 3(2)(b) of the Act, the following procedure shall be adopted in the counting of votes.

Election of candidates with quota :

(a) If, at the end of any count, or at the end of the transfer of any parcel or sub-parcel of an excluded candidate the value of the voting papers credited to a candidate is equal to or greater than the quota, then, he shall be declared elected :

Provided that :

(i) No candidate whose name has not been on the State Roll for at least 10 years shall be elected under Section 3(2)(b0 and the proviso thereto of the Act.

(a) if 7 candidates of less than 10 years' standing in the case of a State Council where 15 members are to be elected, have been declared elected; or

(b) if 10 candidates of less than 10 years' standing in the case of a State Council where 20 members are to be elected, have been declared elected; or

(c) if 12 candidates of less than 10 years' standing in the case of a State Council where 25 members are to be elected, have been declared elected.

(ii) if at the end of any count, there are two or more candidates, who have not been on the State Rolls for at least 10 years, getting more than the quota as aforesaid, but the number of candidates that can yet be elected from such category under the proviso to Section

3(2)(b) is less than that number, the candidate who has obtained the greater value of votes shall be declared elected in preference to the candidate whose value of votes is less.

(iii) In the case of two or more persons of the category referred to in proviso (ii) above, getting the same value of votes at the end of any count, the Secretary or other Returning Officer conducting the election shall decide by lot which of such persons shall be declared elected.

(iv) The other candidate or candidates not declared elected as aforesaid by reason of the proviso to Section 3(2)(b) of the Act and these rules shall be excluded from the poll as provided in Rule 4(b0 of these rules.

Exclusion of candidates lowest on poll or who have been on rolls for less than 10 years.

(b) (1) The Secretary or Returning Officer conducting the election shall exclude from the poll :—

(i) when there are two or more candidates who have obtained more than the quota, the candidate who cannot be declared elected under proviso (i) to Rule 4(a0 of these rules;

(ii) the candidates lowest in the poll in the following order, after all the surpluses have been transferred as provided in the rules of the State Council with regard to transfer of surplus, and the number of candidates elected is less than the required number, and after the exclusion from the poll; if any, under sub-clause (i) of this sub-rule.

First such candidates whose names are on the State Roll for less than 10 years, if the number of such candidates declared elected as provided for in these rules :

(a) 7 in the case of a State Council wherein all 15 members have to be elected; or

(b) 10 in the case of a State Council wherein all 20 members have to be elected; or

(c) 12 in the case of a State Council wherein all 25 members have to be elected;

Next the other candidates

Illustration No. 1.—At an election to a State Council where under the Act, and these rules, the total number of elected members is 20,300 is arrived at as the quota. At the end of a count, when there is no further surplus to be distributed, *M* and *N* are the contesting candidates.

M whose name has not been on the State Roll for at least 10 years gets 150, and

N who has been on the State Rolls for more than 10 years, gets 100.

Only 9 candidates whose names have been on State Roll for at least 10 years have already been declared elected. Hence, M has to be excluded and the voting papers of *M* will be thereafter transferred as provided for in these rules.

If in the same case, 10 candidates whose names have been on a State Roll for not less than 10 years had already been declared elected, *N* will be excluded. The voting papers of *N* will be transferred as provided in these rules.

Illustration No. 2.—At an election to State Council where under the Act and these rules, the total number of elected members is 15,300 is arrived at as the quota. At the end of a count, when there is no further surplus to be distributed, *M* and *N* are the contesting candidates.

M whose name has not been on the State Rolls for at least 10 years gets 150; and

N whose name has been on the state Rolls for more than 10 years gets 100.

Only 7 candidates whose names have been on a State Roll for at least 10 years have already been declared elected. Hence, *M* has to be excluded and the voting papers of *M* will be thereafter transferred as provided in these rules.

If in the same case, 8 candidates whose names have been on a State Roll for not less than 10 years had already been declared elected, *N* will be excluded. The voting papers of *N* will be transferred as provided for in these rules.

Illustration No. 3.—At an election to a State Council where under the Act and these rules the total number of elected members is 25,300 is arrived at as the quota. At the end of a count, when there is no further surplus to be distributed, *M* and *N* are the contesting candidates.

M whose name has not been on the State Rolls for at least 10 years gets 150, and

N whose name has been on the State Rolls for more than 10 years gets 100.

Only 12 candidates whose names have been on a State Roll for at least 10 years have already been declared elected. Hence, *M* has to be excluded and the voting papers of *M* will be thereafter transferred as provided in these rules.

If in the same case, 13 candidates whose names have been on a State Roll for not less than 10 years had already been declared elected, N will be excluded. The voting papers of *N* will be transferred as provided for in these rules.

(2) (i) The Secretary or other Returning Officer shall distribute the unexhausted paper of the candidates excluded under these rules among the continuing candidates according to the next preference recorded therein and all exhausted papers shall be set apart as finally dealt with.

(ii) The papers containing original votes of an excluded candidate shall first be transferred, the transfer value of each paper being one hundred.

(iii) The papers containing votes of an excluded candidate shall then be transferred in the order of the transfers in which and at the value at which he obtained them.

(iv) Each of such transfers shall be deemed to be a separate transfer, but not a separate count.

(v) If, as a result of the transfer of papers, the value of the votes obtained by a candidate is equal to or greater than the quota, the counting then proceeding shall be completed, but no further papers shall be transferred to him.

(vi) The process directed by this rule shall be repeated on the successive exclusion one after another of the candidates lowest on the poll until such seat is filled either by the election of a candidate with the quota or as otherwise provided in these rules.

(vii) If at any time it becomes necessary to exclude a candidate and two or more candidates have the same value of votes and are the lowest on the poll, regard shall be had to the original votes of each candidate and the candidate for whom fewest original votes are recorded, and if the values of their original votes are equal, the candidate with the smallest value at the earlier count at which these candidates had unequal votes shall be excluded.

(viii) If two or more candidates are lowest on the poll and each has the same value of votes at all counts, the Returning Officer shall decide by lot which candidate shall be excluded.

(ix) If during as count, any candidate getting the quota or more has to be excluded by reason of rule 4(a) above, the transfer of his votes shall be deferred and made immediately after the other candidate having got the above quota in that count are declared, and their votes transferred as provided for in these rules.

Filling last vacancies :

(c) (1) When at the end of any count the number of counting candidates is reduced to the number of seats remaining unfilled, the counting candidate shall be declared elected subject to the following :

If the total number of candidates so far declared elected from amongst the advocates whose names have been on the State Roll for at lest 10 years at the relevant date is less than :

(i) 8 in the case of State Council where 15 members are to be elected; or

(ii) 10 in the case of a State Council where 20 members are to be elected; or

(iii) 13 in the case of the State Council where 25 members are to be elected.

Then, the requisite number of candidates of such standing shall first be declared elected and only the balance from amongst other candidates shall be declared elected.

(2) When at the end of any count only one seat remains unfilled and the value of the papers of someone candidate exceeds the total value of the papers of all the other continuing candidates together with any surplus

not transferred; that candidate shall be declared elected. Such candidate shall not, however, be declared elected if he had been on the State Roll for less than 10 years and if the total number of candidates so far declared from amongst advocates on the State Roll for at least 10 years as provided in these rules in less than 8 or 10 or as aforesaid, as the case may be.

(3) When at the end of any count only one seat remains unfilled and there are only 2 continuing candidates, and each of them has the same value of votes and no surplus papers can be transferred, the Returning Officer shall decide by lot which of them shall be excluded, and, after excluding him in the manner aforesaid, declare the other candidate to be elected :

Provided that if the total number of candidates who have been on the State Roll for at least 10 years on the relevant date so far elected is less than the required number, then that candidate who will be on the State Roll for at least 10 years shall be declared elected and the other candidate shall be excluded.

Filling up vacancies or co-option :

(4) In the case of any election to fill vacancy amongst the members of the State Council, or while co-opting a member, the State Council shall conform to the requirement of Section 3(2)(b) of the Act, and the principles laid down in these rules.

Particulars regarding seat to be filled :

(5) In the case of every election of members of a State Council, the State Council shall :

(a) notify the minimum number of seats would be filled up from amongst advocates who, on the relevant date, will be advocates on a State Roll for at least 10 years.

(b) require every candidate to specify in his nomination paper the date of his enrolment and the period for which his name had been on the roll of one or more High Courts under the Indian Bar Councils Act, 1926, and the roll or rolls of State Councils under the Advocates Act, 1961 with full particulars thereof.

(c) indicate on the voting paper which of the candidates have been on a State Roll for at least 10 years as required :

Provided that this rule shall not be applicable to any election held by any State Council before these rules have come into force.

Computation of Period :

(6) For the purpose of computing the minimum period of 10 years provided for in the proviso to Section 3(2)(b) of the Act, and these rules :

(i) the period during which an advocate may have been on the roll of any other State Council or Councils on the roll of any High Court or High Courts under the Indian Bar Councils Act, 1926, shall be taken into account, and

(ii) The period shall be computed as on the last date notified for receiving the nominations for the election.

PART IV

Standards of Legal Education and Recognition of Degrees in Law or Admission as Advocates

[Rules under Sections 7(h) & 9I) 24(1)(c)(iii) and (iiia), 49 (1)(af), (ag) and (d) of the Advocates Acts, 1961]

There shall be two streams of law courses leading to LL.B. degree, viz., a 5 years course and a 3 years course for the purpose of enrolment as advocates as prescribed under the Rules contained in Section A and Section B respectively given hereunder :

Section-A

1. The five years' course of law after 10+2 or 11+2 shall comprise of two parts, viz., Part I which will be a two-years' course programme of pre-law study and Part II which will be a three years' course programme for professional training in law.

2. (1) Save as provided in Rule 5 and Section B, Part IV of the rules hereunder, a degree in law obtained from any University in the territory of India shall not be recognized for purposes of enrolment as Advocate under the Advocates Act, 1961 from June 1, 1982 unless the following conditions are fulfilled :

(a) That at the time of joining the course of instruction in law for a degree in law, the person concerned has passed an examination in 12+2 or 11+1 course of schooling recognized by the educational authority of Central or State Government or possesses such academic qualifications which are considered equivalent to 10+2 or 11+1 courses by the Bar Council of India.

(b) The law degree has been obtained after undergoing a regular course of study in a duly recognized law college under these rules for a minimum period of five years, out of which the first two years shall be devoted to study of pre-law courses as necessary qualifications for admission to three years course of study in law to be commenced thereafter. The last six months of the three years of the law course shall include a regular course of practical training.

(c) That the course of study in law has been by regular attendance for the requisite number of lectures, tutorials moot courts and practical training given by a college affiliated to a University recognized by the Bar Council of India.

3. (1) The the law education as prescribed in Section A shall be through whole time law colleges or University Department.

(2) A college will be deemed to be a whole time college for the purpose of sub-rule 3(1), if the working time of the College or University Department extends to at least thirty hours per week including contact and correspondence programme, tutorials, home assignments, library, clinical work, etc., with the further provision that the actual time for class-room lecturers is not less than 20 hours per week.

4. The students shall be required to put in a minimum attendance

of 66% of the lectures on each of the subjects as also at the moot courts and practical training course :

Provided that in exceptional cases for reasons to be recorded and communicated to the Bar Council of India, the Dean of Faculty of Law or Principal of the law college may condone attendance short of those required by this rule, if the student had attended 66% of the lectures in the aggregate for the semester or annual examination, as the case may be.

5. Lateral entry will be permitted to Part II of the five year law course to a candidate who is a graduate of a University, or possesses such academic qualifications which are considered equivalent to a graduate's degree of a University by the Bar Council of India.

6. (1) The Part I examination should be so conducted as to be called a University Examination. A student who has passed Part I of the law course shall be eligible for enrolment in the final year of the three year degree course in arts, social science, etc., to supplicate for the B.A. degree. A student who has completed three years of the 5 year course in law is eligible to get a degree from the University on passing such examination conducted by the same University which is equivalent to B.A. (Law) but such degree shall not entitle student to enroll as an advocate.

(2) Papers listed in Rule 9(1) of the Bar Council of India rules in Part IV, section-A for the two year pre-law study under the scheme of 5 year course may be adopted by the Universities with such modification to make it possible for students to enter the B.A. programme after passing Part I with a view to supplicating for B.A. degree in one year. Modification of the listed papers may be made keeping in view of the requirements of legal education for those who enter Part II of course from other faculties.

7. Individual Universities may frame their own rules of admission to Part II in such manner that post-graduates as well as graduates may be able to get admission.

8. (1) A law college shall be located at a place where there is a District Court or a Circuit District Court or within such distance thereof as the Bar Council of India permits.

(2) The Principal of the College shall ordinarily be a full time teacher in the college.

(3) The library of the college or University Department shall remain open for at least 8 hours on every working day.

9. (1) The courses of instruction for the Part I for law degree course shall include the following 6 compulsory subjects :

1. General English (Graduate Standard) (Part I and Part II)	2 Papers
2. Political Science (Part I, Part II and Part III)	2 Papers
3. Economics	1 Paper
4. Sociology	1 Paper
5. History	1 Paper

6. History of Courts, Legislature and Legal Profession in India	1 Paper

NOTE.—The Bar Council of India in consultation with experts formulated tentative outline of the courses in the preparatory stage and recommends them to the Universities imparting professional education in law. The suggested course outlines are attached to these rules as appendices A to F.

(2) The courses of instruction for Part II of the study in law shall include the following 13 compulsory subjects :

1. (a) General Principles of Contracts	1 Paper
(b) Special Contracts	1 Paper
2. Torts	1 Paper
3. Family Law—	
(a) Hindu Law	1 Paper
(b) Mohammedan Law, Indian Succession Act and Indian Divorce Act	1 Paper
4. Law of Crimes and Procedure	2 Papers
5. Constitutional Law of India	1 Paper
6. Property Law and Easements	1 Paper
7. Evidence	1 Paper
8. Legal Theory (Jurisprudence)	1 Paper
9. Civil Procedure, Limitation and Arbitration	1 Paper
10. Administrative Law	1 Paper
11. Public International Law	1 Paper
12. Legal Language including legal writing	1 Paper

13. Practical Training—Six months instruction which shall include court-visits, documents, rules of courts, exercises in drafting, pleading, work at Lawyer's Chamber and attendance at Professional Ethics Lectures. The student shall be required to pass an examination in this Course to be conducted by the University concerned.

(3) Not less than 6 more subjects which may be chosen from the list hereunder and from amongst such other law subjects locally relevant as may be prescribed by the Universities at their option :

(1) Equity
(2) Company Law
(3) Labour Law
(4) Taxation
(5) International Organization
(6) Bankruptcy
(7) Law of Co-operation and Public Control of Business
(8) Legislative Drafting
(9) Military law
(10) Insurance

(11) Trusts and Other Judiciary Obligations
(12) Trade Marks, Copy Rights and Patents
(13) Criminology and Criminal Administration
(14) International Economic Law
(15) Interpretation of Statute and Principles of Legislation
(16) Legal Remedies
(17) Private International Law
(18) Comparative Law
(19) Law and Social Change
(20) Law and Poverty
(21) Law Relating to Land Revenue, Land Reforms and Rural Development
(22) Law and Planning
(23) Law Relating to Local Self-Government
(24) Socialistic Concept of Law
(25) Maritime Law
(26) Law of Environment

10. For each paper there shall be lecture classes for at least 3 hours and one hour of tutorial work per week.

11. The examination shall ordinarily be held at the end of every year.

The University shall, however, be at liberty to hold examinations at the end of every 6 months. Suitable allocation of subjects for the period of one year or six months, as the case may be, shall be made by the University and the same be intimated to the Bar Council of India.

12. Full time teachers of law including the Principal of the college shall ordinarily be holders of Master's degree in law and where the holders of Master's degree in law are not available, persons with teaching experience for a minimum period of 5 years in law may be considered. Part-time teachers other than one with LL.M. Degree shall have a minimum practice of 5 years at the Bar.

13. The teaching load of full time and part-time teachers shall be according to the norms prescribed by the UGC from time to time.

14. The salaries paid to the Principal, full-time and part-time teachers shall be according to the scales recommended by the UGC from time to time.

15. Other benefits like D.A., C.L.A. (Compensatory Local Allowance), House Rent Allowance, Provident Fund, etc. shall be according to the norms prescribed by the University concerned from time to time.

16. A law college affiliated to a University shall, by June 1, 1987, be an independent law college and shall cease to be a department attached to a college.

17. (1) No college after coming into force of these rules shall impart instruction in a course of study in law for enrolment as an advocate unless its affiliation has been approved by the Bar Council of India.

(2) An existing law college shall not be competent to impart instruction in a course of study in law for enrolment as an advocate if the continuance of its affiliation is disapproved by the Bar Council of India.

18. The Bar Council of India shall cause a law college affiliated or sought to be affiliated to a University to be inspected by a Committee to be appointed by it for the purpose, when :

(a) An application for approval of affiliation of new college is received by it, or

It *suo motu* decides in order to ensure that the standards of legal education laid down by it are being complied with.

(b) The application for approval of affiliation of a new college shall be addressed to the Secretary, Bar Council of India and shall be sent only through the Registrar of the University concerned with his recommendation and the application be accompanied by an inspection fee of Rs. 15,000/-.

(c) The college and/or the University concerned shall furnish all information to the Committee of inspection and the Bar Council of India as and when required and shall co-operate with them in every possible manner in the conduct of inspection.

(d) The Committee of inspection shall submit a detailed report to the Bar Council of India with a clear recommendation as to whether the affiliation of the new law college be approved/disapproved or that of an existing college be withdrawn/continued or that certain directions be given for improvements to be carried out within the period to be specified. The report shall incorporate the reasons for the recommendations.

(e) If an unfavourable report is received, the Secretary of the Bar Council of India shall cause a copy of the same to be sent to the Registrar of the University concerned for his comments and explanations, if any. Such comments and explanations on the report shall be sent by the Registrar of the University within a period of six weeks from the date of the receipt of the communication.

(f) The Secretary of the Bar Council of India shall cause the report and comments/explanation of Registrar of the University concerned to be placed before the next meeting of the Legal Education Committee of the Bar Council of India.

(g) If the Legal Education Committee is satisfied that the standards of legal education and/or the rules for affiliation or continuance of affiliation provided for these rules by the Bar Council of India are not complied with and/or that the courses of study, teaching and/or examination are not such as to secure to persons undergoing legal education, the knowledge and training requisite for the competence practice of law, the legal education committee shall recommend to the Bar Council of India, the approval/disapproval of affiliation or continuance of affiliation, as the case may be.

The Legal Education Committee may also recommend that

certain directions be given for improvements to be carried out within the period to be specified.

(h) This recommendation of the Legal Education Committee along with the accompanying papers shall be placed before the Bar Council of India for its decision. In case the Bar Council of India disagrees with or modifies the recommendation of the Legal Education Committee, it shall communicate its views to the Legal Education Committee, for its consideration before arriving at a final decision in the matter.

(i) If the Council is of the opinion that affiliation of a college be disapproved, it shall give notice of the proposed action to the Principal of the college and Registrar of the University to show cause within 30 days of the receipt of the notice and the Council shall take into consideration the reply received before making final orders.

(j) The decision of the Bar Council of India shall be communicated to the Registrar of the University.

It shall be effective from the commencement of the next academic year following the date on which it is received by the Registrar of the University.

19. (1) The Council shall publish by notification in the Gazette of India and in prominent newspapers in India, the names of the Universities whose degrees in law are recognized under these rules with a list of law colleges under the Universities which are eligible to impart professional legal education as provided for under these rules and send a copy of the notification above referred to, to all the Universities imparting legal education and State Bar Councils :

Provided that for the purpose of sub-rule (1) above, the existing University Law Department and Law Colleges affiliated to Universities shall be deemed to be professional Law Colleges under these rules unless otherwise decided by the Council.

(2) Information about non-recognition or derecognition of the degree in law of a University shall be sent to all the Universities in India imparting legal education and to all State Bar Councils.

20. If the Universities located in State where the 10+2 or 11+1 school system is not yet in vogue, propose to start the 5 years LL.B. course under these rules, they will be free to do so.

21. The Bar Council of India may issue directives from time to time for maintenance of the standards of legal education. The College/University is expected to follow them as compulsory.

Schedule I

(To Rules in Part-A)

(Directives issued under Rule 21)

1. The teaching of the course programme in Part I of the law course may be done with the help of teachers in the disciplines concerned from the respective University/College departments.

2. The maximum strength of students in any class (LL.B. 1, II, III,

IV or V) shall not exceed 320 in any given College or University, Departments of Law and the number of students in any section of each such class shall not exceed 80. In other words, no college or University Department of Law shall have on its rolls a total student strength of over 1600 students in all its 1st, 2nd, 3rd, 4th and 5th years put together.

3. Law College and University Law Departments shall ensure that :

(a) Multiple copies of prescribed and recommended readings are available to the students.

(b) Seating arrangement is provided for at least 15 of the students at a time in the reading hall.

(c) The teacher student ratio is at least 1 : 40.

4. Building :

(1) (a) The building of a College shall be available for its exclusive use, during the working hours of the college.

(b) The accommodation provided for classes, hostel, if any, and the residential quarters for the Principal and the teacher to be in charge of the hostel, if any will be separate.

(2) The college buildings shall consist of the following :

(a) Classrooms;

(b) A common room for men students;

(c) A common room for women students;

(d) A library hall with book shelves and reading tables; sufficient to seat 20% of the students on the roll;

(e) Office rooms for the Principal and his office staff;

(f) A teachers' common room.

(3) (a) All buildings shall be well lighted and ventilated and shall have adequate sanitary arrangements and water supply;

(b) All buildings shall be duly furnished.

(4) (a) If the college has no buildings of its own and it is proposed to be housed temporarily in a hired building, the College authorities shall create the building fund which shall be set apart and deposited in a Scheduled Bank or a District Central Co-operative Bank.

(b) Deposits so made in the name of the College shall not be withdrawn except when required for meeting the cost of the portion of the building already construed.

(c) The building shall be completed within a period of 5 years from the date of the approval of affiliation is communicated to the Registrar of the University concerned.

5. Library

(a) The library shall be adequately equipped with law reports, books, periodical and reference books to meet the requirements of the course of instruction taught in the college.

(b) The library shall be in the charge of a qualified and trained librarian.

(c) The minimum initial and recurring annual expenditure on the library shall be as below :

Initial	Rs. 50,000.00
First Year	Rs. 15,000.00
Second Year	Rs. 15,000.00
Third Year	Rs. 15,000.00
Subsequent Years	Rs. 10,000.00 per year

6. The building fund, as provided in Directive 4(4) shall be created at least for Rs. 9 lakhs through instalments as under :

Initial	Rs. 5,00,000.00
First Year	Rs. 1,00,000.00
Second Year	Rs. 1,00,000.00
Third Year	Rs. 1,00,000.00
Fourth Year	Rs. 1,00,000.00

7. The accommodation provided for classes, hostel, if any, and the residential quarters for the Principal and the teacher to be in charge of the hostel, if any, will be separate.

8. Quarters for the Principals

Quarters for the teacher-in-charge of the hostel, if any, located near the hostel.

Quarters for other permanent teachers as and if required by the University.

9. Provision may also be made if possible for a playground and adequate facilities for games and sports.

10. Every University shall endeavour to supplement the lecture method with the case method, tutorials and other modern technique of imparting legal education.